AMERICAN LION

AMERICAN ★LION★

Andrew Jackson in the White House

JON MEACHAM

RANDOM HOUSE
LARGE PRINT

To Mary, Maggie, and Sam

The darker the night the bolder the lion.
—THEODORE ROOSEVELT,
Life-Histories of African Game Animals

I was born for a storm and a calm
does not suit me.
—ANDREW JACKSON

CONTENTS

I: THE LOVE OF COUNTRY, FAME AND HONOR
Beginnings to Late 1830

II: I WILL DIE WITH THE UNION
Late 1830 to 1834

III: THE EVENING OF HIS DAYS
1834 to the End

A NOTE ON THE TEXT

In the interest of clarity, I have often taken the liberty of modernizing the (distractingly erratic) spelling, punctuation, and sentence structure in primary sources from Jackson's era. On some occasions I have let the Ur-formulation stand to give readers a sense of the texture and style of correspondence in those years. In any event, the source for every quotation in this book is cited in the Notes. In no case has an edit altered the writer's intention or meaning.

PRINCIPAL CHARACTERS

John Quincy Adams (1767–1848)   sixth president of the United States, he served as a congressman from Massachusetts from 1831 until his death

Louisa Catherine Adams (1775–1852)   wife of John Quincy Adams and a shrewd observer of Washington politics

Thomas Hart Benton (1782–1858)   onetime aide-de-camp to General Jackson, he later brawled with Jackson; in 1821 he was elected senator from Missouri, and was a Jackson ally on Capitol Hill during the White House years

Nicholas Biddle (1786–1844)   president of the Second Bank of the United States

Francis Preston Blair (1791–1876)   founding editor of the pro-Jackson **Washington Globe** and Jackson adviser

John C. Calhoun (1782–1850)   vice president of the United States under Adams and Jackson, senator from South Carolina during Jackson's second term

Henry Clay (1777–1852)   Kentucky congressman and senator, secretary of state under John Quincy Adams, Jackson's 1832 National Republican opponent for president

John Coffee (1772–1833)   Tennessee planter, military officer, and Jackson confidant

Andrew Jackson Donelson (1799–1871)   nephew of Rachel and Andrew Jackson, private secretary to President Jackson, husband of Emily Tennessee Donelson

Emily Tennessee Donelson (1807–1836)   niece of Rachel and Andrew Jackson, official White House hostess, wife of Andrew Jackson Donelson

Mary Eastin (1810–1847)   friend and cousin of Emily Donelson's and member of Jackson's White House circle; married Lucius Polk in the White House in 1832

John Henry Eaton (1790–1856)   Tennessee senator, Jackson adviser, secretary of war

Margaret O'Neale Timberlake Eaton (1799–1879) widow of John Timberlake of the U.S. Navy and wife of John Henry Eaton

Jeremiah Evarts (1781–1831)   corresponding secretary of the American Board of Commissioners for Foreign Missions, author of the "William Penn" essays opposing Indian removal

Theodore Frelinghuysen (1787–1862)   New Jersey senator, defender of the rights of the Indians

Andrew Jackson (1767–1845)   seventh president of the United States

Rachel Donelson Robards Jackson (1767–1828) wife of Andrew Jackson

Amos Kendall (1789–1869) Kentucky editor, Jackson adviser, Democratic strategist, postmaster general

William B. Lewis (1784–1866) second auditor of the Treasury, Jackson adviser

Edward Livingston (1764–1836) lawyer, Louisiana congressman, senator, secretary of state, minister to France, and Jackson friend

John Marshall (1755–1835) chief justice of the U.S. Supreme Court from 1801 until his death thirty-four years later

Joel R. Poinsett (1779–1851) world traveler, congressman, physician, botanist, and crucial Jackson ally in the nullification crisis with South Carolina in 1832–33

Roger B. Taney (1777–1864) attorney general, secretary of the Treasury, chief justice of the U.S. after John Marshall

Martin Van Buren (1782–1862) governor of New York, secretary of state, vice president after Calhoun, and eighth president of the United States

Daniel Webster (1782–1852) lawyer, congressman, and senator from Massachusetts; a supporter of Jackson's on the question of the Union, Webster opposed the president on almost everything else

PROLOGUE: WITH THE FEELINGS OF A FATHER
The White House, Washington, Winter 1832–33

I T LOOKED LIKE war. In his rooms on the second floor of the White House, in the flickering light of candles and oil lamps, President Andrew Jackson was furious and full of fight. He had just been reelected to a second term as America's seventh president, and South Carolina was defying him. He hated it, for he believed to his core that the state was about to destroy the nation. For Jackson, the crisis was not only political. It was personal. Four hundred and fifty miles down the Atlantic seaboard from Washington, in Charleston, radicals were raising an army to defend South Carolina's right to nullify federal laws it chose not to accept—the first step, Jackson believed, toward secession, and the destruction of the Union. "I expect soon to hear that a civil war of extermination has commenced," Jackson said, musing about arresting the Southern leaders and then hanging them.

Gaunt but striking, with a formidable head of white hair, a nearly constant cough, a bullet lodged in his

chest, Jackson, sixty-five years old that winter, stood six
foot one and weighed 140 pounds. Over a midday glass
of whiskey in the White House with an old friend, Jackson pounded a table as he pondered the crisis: "By the
God of Heaven, I will uphold the laws." Week after
week, he threatened to field a formidable force, and he
knew who should lead them. "When everything is
ready, I shall join them myself," Jackson said.

At Boston's Faneuil Hall, Daniel Webster, the great
Massachusetts senator, rallied to the president's defense,
denouncing South Carolina's defiance in epic terms: "It
is nothing more nor less than resistance by **force**—it is
disunion by **force**—it is secession by **force**—it is Civil
War!" The danger was real, for there was nothing foreordained about the future of American democracy in
the Jackson years. The nation itself, dating from the
Declaration of Independence, was barely half a century
old. Now, as Jackson began his fifth year in the White
House, the United States might collapse into fratricidal
conflict, and foreign powers—always a threat watched
with anticipation. In a private letter in the winter of
1833, Richard Wellesley, the Marquis Wellesley and
elder brother of the Duke of Wellington, hoped for "the
dissolution of the American confederacy, which I think
would be a great benefit to the civilized world."

Dispatching troops and a warship, the **Natchez,** to
Charleston, Jackson, the general whose steadfastness in
adversity and against the British in the War of 1812 had
earned him the nicknames "Old Hickory" and "the Old
Hero," was determined to keep America together. He
loved the Union with a consuming devotion. In the

radicals' camp, Robert Woodward Barnwell, a South Carolina congressman, passed along reports that Jackson was set on war if the state defied him. "Nothing but blood will satisfy the old scoundrel," Barnwell said. Jackson's own vice president, John C. Calhoun, had resigned and taken up South Carolina's cause. Though the immediate issue was money—South Carolina felt oppressed by federal tariffs, which it wanted to lower—the real question, everyone knew, was about power, and ultimately about slavery. If Jackson won the showdown, then Washington would be stronger and the South weaker, and a stronger Washington meant a greater threat to the future of what Calhoun called "the peculiar domestic institution of the Southern states."

Watching the crisis grow, Webster said, "I am prepared any day to hear that matters have come to blows in Charleston." It was rumored that excited radicals in South Carolina were buying medals emblazoned "John C. Calhoun, First President of the Southern Confederacy," and readers of the Columbia **Telescope** in the state capital considered this fiery plea: "The present is not a time for cold temporizing policy. . . . THIS UNION MUST BE DISSOLVED."

To save the country required strength, subtlety, and a sure sense of what the broader American public wanted. "I will meet all things with deliberate firmness and forbearance," Jackson said, "but woe to those nullifiers who shed the first blood." He would be patient, but he would do what it took. His blend of solicitude and sanction reflected his view that politics was at once clinical and human, driven by both principles and passions that he had to master and harness for the good of the whole. As president, Jackson believed he bore the duties of a father who alone carried the responsibility for protecting the nation.

Jackson valued two things in life above all others: his country and his family. He saw little distinction between the two, and his instinct to fight and to defend both—to be a father twice over—drove him from his obscure birth in the Carolinas to the pinnacle of power.

Orphaned at fourteen, Jackson never knew his own father, who died the year he was born. "I have been Tossed upon the waves of fortune," Jackson once said, and he spent his life seeking order amid chaos and authority among men. The Revolutionary War had claimed the lives of his mother and his brothers. Suffering those losses at such a young age, Jackson saw his life and the life of the country as one. America, he once said, was "one great family." In a draft of his second inaugural address in 1833, he wrote, "I feel in the depths of my soul, that it is the highest, most sacred and most irreversible part of my obligation, to **preserve the union of these states, although it may cost me my life.**"

The nation, then, played a decisive role in his emotional universe. Jackson carried an image of the Union around in his head, a vision of the United States and its people as an extension of his own clan in which he was alternately father and son. From childhood, Jackson was in search of a structure into which he could fit, find reassurance and stability, and come to control. In the midst of the crisis with South Carolina in the winter of 1832–33, in a draft of his proclamation on nullification to the people of that state, Jackson wrote, "I call upon you in the language of truth, and with the feelings of a Father to retrace your steps."

With the feelings of a father. Jackson's familial vision had intriguing implications for the life of the nation. For General Jackson, it meant that in battle he was fighting not for a distant cause but for the survival of his own kin. For President Jackson, it meant that there was little difference between the personal and the political. His was a White House roiled by intrigue, war, and sexual scandal, and it left a permanent mark on the nation. This book is not a history of the Age of Jackson but a portrait of the man and of his complex relationships with the intimate circle that surrounded him as he transformed the presidency. The story of Jackson's life and of his White House years is of his long, unrelenting war to keep his family and his country safe—a long, unrelenting war that helped shape the way we live now.

ONE OF AMERICA'S most important and most controversial presidents, Andrew Jackson is also one of our least understood. Recalled mainly as the scourge of the Indians or as the hero of the 1815 Battle of New Orleans, he is only dimly remembered in the popular imagination, too far out of mind to be instructive or intriguing.

Yet of the great early presidents and Founders, Andrew Jackson is in many ways the most like us. In the saga of the Jackson presidency, one marked by both democratic triumphs and racist tragedies, we can see the American character in formation and in action. To understand him and his time helps us to understand America's perennially competing impulses. Jackson's life and work—and the nation he protected and pre-served—were shaped by the struggle between grace and rage, generosity and violence, justice and cruelty.

A source of inspiration to Lincoln on the eve of the Civil War, revered by Theodore and Franklin Roosevelt, and hailed by Harry Truman as one of the four greatest presidents—along with Washington, Jefferson, and Lincoln—Jackson expanded the powers of the presidency in ways that none of his six predecessors had. He was the first president to come from the common people, not from an educated elite, and he never ceased to see himself as their champion. He was the first to build what we would recognize as a political party. He was the first to maintain a large circle of private advisers—what was called his Kitchen Cabinet—to help make policy. And he was the first to insist on the deference he thought due the chief executive as the only official elected by all the people. It was a distinction he believed made the White House, not Capitol Hill, the center of national power and national action.

The country that Jackson presided over from 1829 to 1837 was smaller than one might think, surrounded by once and possibly future foreign foes. There were twenty-four states in 1828. Arkansas and Michigan would be admitted late in Jackson's presidency, with Florida coming in just before his death in 1845 and Texas not long after. The British had the nation hemmed in to the north, in Canada; Britain and Russia had claims to the Pacific Northwest. The Gulf of Mexico worried Jackson as an invasion route for a foreign power.

Beyond the physical threats, Jackson saw more oblique but no less dangerous perils. Before Jackson, power tended toward the elites, whether political or financial. After Jackson, power was more diffuse, and government, for better and for worse, was more attuned to the popular will. He may not have consciously set out to leave such a legacy, but he made the case for democratic innovation and popular engagement in politics at a time when many in Washington would have preferred that the people play the role they were assigned at Philadelphia in the summer of 1787: as voters who cast their ballots and then allowed intermediary institutions—from the state legislatures that elected U.S. senators to the Electoral College, which chose presidents—to make the real decisions. Jackson wanted to give the people a more dramatic part to play, and he rewrote the script of public life to give them one.

It would be both glib and wrong to say that the Age of Jackson is a mirror of our own time. The cultural, political, moral, and intellectual universe Jackson inhabited has to be viewed on its own terms. Still, there is much about him and about his America that readers in the early twenty-first century may recognize. His was an age of fascination with politics, patriotism, gossip, and religion; both "My Country, 'Tis of Thee" and "Amazing Grace" took root in the popular culture during Jackson's presidency. The America of Andrew Jackson was a country that professed a love of democracy but was willing to live with inequality, that aimed for social justice but was prone to racism and intolerance, that believed itself one nation but was narrowly divided and fought close elections, and that occasionally acted arrogantly toward other countries while craving respect from them at the same time.

He was the most contradictory of men. A champion of extending freedom and democracy to even the poorest of whites, Jackson was an unrepentant slaveholder. A sentimental man who rescued an Indian orphan on a battlefield to raise in his home, Jackson was responsible for the removal of Indian tribes from their ancestral lands. An enemy of Eastern financial elites and a relentless opponent of the Bank of the United States, which he believed to be a bastion of corruption, Jackson also promised to die, if necessary, to preserve the power and prestige of the central government. Like us and our America, Jackson and his America achieved great things while committing grievous sins.

Jackson was the only American president to take a bullet in a frontier gunfight, and the only one who tried to assault his own would-be assassin. An uneducated boy from the Carolina backwoods, the son of Scots-Irish immigrants, he became a practicing lawyer, a public prosecutor, a U.S. attorney, a delegate to the founding Tennessee Constitutional Convention, a U.S. congressman, a U.S. senator, a judge of the state Superior Court, and a major general, first of the state militia and then of the U.S. Army. The glow of his victory over the British at New Orleans in 1815—as mythic a battle as Lexington and Concord—transformed him into a fabled figure. Popular songs were written about him; the anniversary of the victory, January 8, was a national occasion for Jackson banquets and Jackson parades. There were darker moments, too. He had massacred Indians in combat, fought duels, and imposed martial law on New Orleans, imprisoning those who defied him. He had married the love of his life, Rachel Donelson Robards, before she was divorced from her first husband. The scandal of his marriage stayed with him through the decades, and he believed that the stress of the charges of adultery and bigamy ultimately killed her.

Commanding, shrewd, intuitive yet not especially articulate, alternately bad-tempered and well-mannered, Jackson embodied the nation's birth and youth. He came from virtually nothing, yet had married into, and helped define, Tennessee aristocracy. He could seem savage, yet he moved in sophisticated circles with skill and grace. In December 1814, with the Battle of New Orleans at hand, a leading hostess was disturbed to learn that her husband had invited Jackson to dinner. After warning her other guests about this "wild man of the woods," the lady was stunned to find Jackson both elegant and charming. "Is this your backwoodsman?" her friends asked after Jackson left. "He is a prince!"

JACKSON WAS FOND of well-cut clothes, racehorses, dueling, newspapers, gambling, whiskey, coffee, a pipe, pretty women, children, and good company. One of his secretaries observed that "there was more of the woman in his nature than in that of any man I ever knew—more of a woman's tenderness toward children, and sympathy with them." Depending on the moment, he could succumb to the impulses of a warlike temperament or draw on his reserves of unaffected warmth. Jackson spoke with the accent of a provincial in the capital—yet was discriminating in his choice of wines and favored Greek Revival architecture.

He was a skilled operator, the consummate self-made man. As an orphan, Jackson adapted to shifting circumstances and cultivated the powerful. Dependent on others in his first years—largely his mother's extended family, cousins and uncles and aunts—he spent much of his life seeking both affection and deference. The roles Jackson chose to pursue and play—frontier lawyer, state judge, military commander, foster father, attentive uncle, American president—reflected this urge to be at once admired and in charge. He was gloomy when people left him, even for a short time, and he could be the most demanding of men, insisting that others bend their lives to his. His was an interesting kind of neediness, often intertwined with sincere professions of love and regard. But in the end, when a choice came down to what Jackson wanted or what anyone else wanted, Jackson's will, and no one else's, prevailed. And like his country, Jackson's family circle was riven with rivalries and veered between harmony and strife.

IN THE LONG winter of 1832–33, staring down South Carolina, the president relied, as he always did, on his wife's circle for affection and company. Rachel Jackson was dead; her family filled the vacuum around the man they called "Uncle Jackson." "He lived always in a crowd," wrote James Parton, his earliest scholarly biographer. Martin Van Buren, who served Jackson as secretary of state and as vice president, said: "I have scarcely ever known a man who placed a higher value upon the enjoyments of the family circle."

As he sat and stewed over South Carolina, the president relied on his nephew Andrew Jackson Donelson, whom Jackson had raised and hoped might one day succeed him to the presidency, to handle correspondence and visitors. It was the most intimate of arrangements. Donelson lived with his wife, Emily, and their children in rooms across the hall from the president in the White House, and the Donelsons were at Uncle's call.

Attractive, young, and headstrong, fond of parties but prone to bouts of piety, an ambitious figure in Washington society, Emily Donelson was Jackson's official hostess. "She was a beautiful, accomplished and charming woman," said her friend Cora Livingston, "with wonderful tact and delightfully magnetic manner. . . . Everyone was in love with her."

Andrew and Emily Donelson were joined by Major William B. Lewis, a key Jackson aide and a rival of Andrew Donelson's for the president's ear. Young people brightened the president's universe, too. There was the pretty Mary Eastin, a cousin and intimate of Emily's. The entourage included the portrait painter Ralph Earl, a favorite of the late Rachel Jackson's, who was called "the King's Painter" and had his own room in the White House.

In Washington, this inner circle was augmented by the president's Kitchen Cabinet, a shifting cast of characters that, depending on who was doing the counting, included Andrew Donelson, William Lewis, Martin Van Buren, journalists Amos Kendall and Francis Preston Blair, and Roger B. Taney, who served Jackson as attorney general and secretary of the Treasury before going on to become chief justice of the Supreme Court. A shrewd New York politician, Van Buren—he was known as "the Little Magician"—was a widower whose lack of domestic obligations enabled him to be with the president as often as the president wished it. Taken all in all, it was an eclectic circle, linked by bonds of affection and roiled by jealousies and rivalries both large and small. It was, in other words, like most families—only this one lived in the White House and shaped the private world of the president of the United States.

FEROCIOUS IN DEFENSE of the people and things he loved, Jackson was equally fierce, and often ruthless, in the pursuit of anyone or anything he believed to be a threat to the world as he saw it. He dominated the times, and the evidence of his strength and the aura of his authority led some to think of him as the "Old Lion"; to others he was "the lion of Tennessee." In 1830 Oliver Wendell Holmes published a poem, "To a Caged Lion," which captures the awe with which the creatures were regarded. Holmes's lion is "the terror of the trembling wild" before whom "all nature shrunk."

For all his vices—and he had many—Jackson refused to accept defeat, either in his own life or in the life of the country. Surrender was unthinkable, for surrender meant an end to the story, and he believed America's story and his own were still unfolding. Jackson's saga would end only when he was buried in the corner of his wife's garden in Tennessee. America's, he insisted, would never end.

"I for one do not despair of the Republic," he would often say, adding: "The Republic is safe." Another aging former president took a dimmer view. "My hopes of a long continuance of this Union are extinct," John Quincy Adams, the sixth president—who was the son of the second—told his diary.

Steadiness of faith was, in the long run, as illuminating and essential as sophistication of thought. The art of leadership required both, as did the nation. Life in the arena was rough and tiring, yet Jackson savored the fight and found solace in the unending work democracy demanded of its champions. "I was born for a storm," Jackson once said, "and a calm does not suit me." It was a good thing he felt this way, for defending and shaping America was not easy. But for Andrew Jackson, nothing ever had been.

PART I

★

THE LOVE OF COUNTRY, FAME AND HONOR

Beginnings to Late 1830

CHAPTER 1

ANDY WILL FIGHT
HIS WAY IN THE WORLD

CHRISTMAS 1828 SHOULD have been the
happiest of seasons at the Hermitage, Jackson's
plantation twelve miles outside Nashville. It
was a week before the holiday, and Jackson had won
the presidency of the United States in November. "How
triumphant!" Andrew Donelson said of the victory.
"How flattering to the cause of the people!" Now the
president-elect's family and friends were to be on hand
for a holiday of good food, liquor, and wine—Jackson
was known to serve guests whiskey, champagne, claret,
Madeira, port, and gin—and, in this special year, a pag-
eant of horses, guns, and martial glory.

On Wednesday, December 17, 1828, Jackson was
sitting inside the house, answering congratulatory
messages. As he worked, friends in town were planning a ball to honor their favorite son before he left
for Washington. Led by a marshal, there would be a
guard of soldiers on horseback to take Jackson into
Nashville, fire a twenty-four-gun artillery salute, and
escort him to a dinner followed by dancing. Rachel
would be by his side.

In the last moments before the celebrations, and his duties, began, Jackson drafted a letter. Writing in his hurried hand across the foolscap, he accepted an old friend's good wishes: "To the people, for the confidence reposed in me, my gratitude and best services are due; and are pledged to their service." Before he finished the note, Jackson went outside to his Tennessee fields.

He knew his election was inspiring both reverence and loathing. The 1828 presidential campaign between Jackson and Adams had been vicious. Jackson's forces had charged that Adams, as minister to Russia, had procured a woman for Czar Alexander I. As president, Adams was alleged to have spent too much public money decorating the White House, buying fancy china and a billiard table. The anti-Jackson assaults were more colorful. Jackson's foes called his wife a bigamist and his mother a whore, attacking him for a history of dueling, for alleged atrocities in battles against the British, the Spanish, and the Indians— and for being a wife stealer who had married Rachel before she was divorced from her first husband. "Even Mrs. J. is not spared, and my pious Mother, nearly fifty years in the tomb, and who, from her cradle to her death had not a speck upon her character, has been dragged forth . . . and held to public scorn as a prostitute who intermarried with a Negro, and my eldest brother sold as a slave in Carolina," Jackson said to a friend.

Jackson's advisers marveled at the ferocity of the Adams attacks. "The floodgates of falsehood, slander, and abuse have been hoisted and the most nauseating filth is poured, in torrents, on the head, of not only Genl Jackson but all his prominent supporters," William B. Lewis told John Coffee, an old friend of Jackson's from Tennessee.

Some Americans thought of the president-elect as a second Father of His Country. Others wanted him dead. One Revolutionary War veteran, David Coons of Harpers Ferry, Virginia, was hearing rumors of ambush and assassination plots against Jackson. To Coons, Jackson was coming to rule as a tribune of the people, but to others Jackson seemed dangerous—so dangerous, in fact, that he was worth killing. "There are a portion of malicious and unprincipled men who have made hard threats with regard to you, men whose baseness would (in my opinion) prompt them to do anything," Coons wrote Jackson.

That was the turbulent world awaiting beyond the Hermitage. In the draft of a speech he was to deliver to the celebration in town, Jackson was torn between anxiety and nostalgia. "The consciousness of a steady adherence to my duty has not been disturbed by the unsparing attacks of which I have been the subject during the election," the speech read. Still, Jackson admitted he felt "apprehension" about the years ahead. His chief fear? That, in Jackson's words, "I shall fail" to secure "the future prosperity of our beloved country." Perhaps the procession to Nashville and the ball at the hotel would lift his spirits; perhaps Christmas with his family would.

While Jackson was outside, word came that his wife

had collapsed in her sitting room, screaming in pain. It had been a wretched time for Rachel. She was, Jackson's political foes cried, "a black wench," a "profligate woman," unfit to be the wife of the president of the United States. Shaken by the attacks, Rachel—also sixty-one and, in contrast to her husband, short and somewhat heavy—had been melancholy and anxious. "The enemies of the General have dipped their arrows in wormwood and gall and sped them at me," Rachel lamented during the campaign. "Almighty God, was there ever any thing equal to it?" On the way home from a trip to Nashville after the balloting, Rachel was devastated to overhear a conversation about the lurid charges against her. Her niece, the twenty-one-year-old Emily Donelson, tried to reassure her aunt but failed. "No, Emily," Mrs. Jackson replied, "I'll never forget it!"

When news of her husband's election arrived, she said: "Well, for Mr. Jackson's sake I am glad; for my own part I never wished it." Now the cumulative toll of the campaign and the coming administration exacted its price as Rachel was put to bed, the sound of her cries still echoing in her slave Hannah's ears.

Jackson rushed to his wife, sent for doctors, did what he could. Later, as she lay resting, her husband added an emotional postscript to the letter he had begun: "P.S. Whilst writing, Mrs. J. from good health, has been taken suddenly ill, with excruciating pain in the left shoulder, arm, and breast. What may be the result of this violent attack god only knows, I hope for her recovery, and in haste close this letter, you will pardon any inaccuracies A. J." Yet his hopes would not bring her back.

Rachel lingered for five days. Jackson hovered by her side, praying for her survival. He had loved her for nearly four decades. His solace through war, politics, Indian fighting, financial chaos, and the vicissitudes of life in what was then frontier America, Rachel gave him what no one else ever had. In her arms and in their home he found a steady sense of family, a sustaining universe, a place of peace in a world of war. Her love for him was unconditional. She cared for him not because he was a general or a president. She cared for him because he was Andrew Jackson. "Do not, My beloved Husband, let the love of Country, fame and honor make you forget you have me," she wrote to him during the War of 1812. "Without you I would think them all empty shadows." When they were apart, Jackson would sit up late writing to her, his candle burning low through the night. "My heart is with you," he told her.

Shortly after nine on the evening of Monday, December 22, three days before Christmas, Rachel suffered an apparent heart attack. It was over. Still, Jackson kept vigil, her flesh turning cold to his touch as he stroked her forehead. With his most awesome responsibilities and burdens at hand, she had left him. "My mind is so disturbed . . . that I can scarcely write, in short my dear friend my heart is nearly broke," Jackson told his confidant John Coffee after Rachel's death.

At one o'clock on Christmas Eve afternoon, by order of the mayor, Nashville's church bells began ringing in tribute to Rachel, who was to be buried in her garden in the shadow of the Hermitage. The weather had been wet, and the dirt in the garden was soft; the rain made the gravediggers' task a touch easier as they worked. After a Presbyterian funeral service led by Rachel's minister, Jackson walked the one hundred fifty paces back to the house. Devastated but determined, he then spoke to the mourners. "I am now the President elect of the United States, and in a short time must take my way to the metropolis of my country; and, if it had been God's will, I would have been grateful for the privilege of taking her to my post of honor and seating her by my side; but Providence knew what was best for her." God's was the only will Jackson ever bowed to, and he did not do even that without a fight.

IN HIS GRIEF, Jackson turned to Rachel's family. He would not—could not—go to Washington by himself. Around him at the Hermitage on this bleak Christmas Eve was the nucleus of the intimate circle he would maintain for the rest of his life. At the center of the group, destined both to provide great comfort and to provoke deep personal anger in the White House, stood Andrew and Emily Donelson. They had an ancient claim on Jackson's affections and attention, and they were ready to serve.

While Andrew—who was also Emily's first cousin—was to work through the president-elect's correspondence, guard access to Jackson, and serve as an adviser, Emily, not yet twenty-two, would be the president's hostess. Attracted by the bright things of the fashionable world and yet committed to family and faith, Emily was at once selfless and sharp-tongued. Born on Monday, June 1, 1807, the thirteenth and last child of Mary and John Donelson, Emily was raised in the heart of frontier aristocracy and inherited a steely courage—perhaps from her grandfather, a Tennessee pioneer and a founder of Nashville—that could verge on obstinacy. It was a trait she shared with the other women in her family, including her aunt Rachel. "All Donelsons in the female line," wrote a family biographer, "were tyrants." Charming, generous, and hospitable tyrants, to be sure, but still a formidable lot—women who knew their own minds, women who had helped their husbands conquer the wilderness or were the daughters of those who had. Now one of them, Emily, would step into Rachel's place in the White House.

ON SUNDAY, January 18, 1829, Jackson left the Hermitage for the capital. With the Donelsons, William Lewis, and Mary Eastin, Emily's friend and cousin, Jackson rode the two miles from the Hermitage to a wharf on a neighboring estate and boarded the steamboat **Pennsylvania** to travel the Cumberland River north, toward their new home. He was, as he had said to the mourners on the day of Rachel's burial, the president-elect of the United States.

Before he left Tennessee, he wrote a letter to John

Coffee that mixed faith and resignation. His thoughts were with Rachel, and on his own mortality. "Whether I am ever to return or not is for time to reveal, as none but that providence, who rules the destiny of all, now knows," Jackson said.

His friends hoped that service to the nation would comfort him. "The active discharge of those duties to which he will shortly be called, more than anything else, will tend to soothe the poignancy of his grief," said the Nashville **Republican and State Gazette** in an edition bordered in black in mourning for Rachel. In a moving letter, Edward Livingston, a friend of Jackson's and a future secretary of state, saw that the cause of country would have to replace Rachel as Jackson's central concern. Referring to America, Livingston told the president-elect: "She requires you for her welfare to abandon your just grief, to tear yourself from the indulgence of regrets which would be a virtue in a private individual, but to which you are not permitted to yield while so much of her happiness depends upon your efforts in her service." Jackson understood. To rule, one had to survive, and to survive one had to fight.

The travelers wound their way through the country to the capital, passing through Louisville, Cincinnati, and Pittsburgh, where it snowed. The president-elect was complaining of sore limbs, a bad cough, and a hand worn out from greeting so many well-wishers. "He was very much wearied by the crowds of people that attended him everywhere, anxious to see the People's President," Mary Eastin wrote her father.

Ten days into the voyage, Emily Donelson finally found a moment to sit down. For her the trip had been a blur of cannons, cheers, and tending to colds—she had one, as did her little son Jackson. "I scarcely need tell you that we have been in one continual crowd since we started," Emily wrote her mother. Their quarters were overrun by guests, and there were ovations and shouts of joy from people along the banks of the river. The social demands of the presidency had begun, really, the moment Jackson and his party left the Hermitage. But Emily was not the kind to complain, at least not in her uncle's hearing. She loved the life that Jackson had opened to her and her husband.

"You must not make yourself unhappy about us, my dear Mother," Emily added, sending warm wishes to her father. The handwriting was shaky as the letter ended; the water was rough, the pace of the craft fast. "I hope you will excuse this scrawl," Emily said, "as it is written while the boat is running."

The speed of the boat did not seem to bother Andrew Jackson, but then he was accustomed to pressing ahead. He was constantly on the run, and had been all his life. For him the journey to the White House had begun six decades before, in a tiny place tucked away in the Carolinas—a place he never visited, and spoke of only sparingly, called Waxhaw.

JACKSON GREW UP an outsider, living on the margins and at the mercy of others. Traveling to America from Ireland in 1765, his father, the senior Andrew

Jackson, and his mother, Elizabeth Hutchinson Jackson, moved into a tiny community a few hundred miles northwest of Charleston, in a spot straddling the border between North and South Carolina. "Waxhaw" came from the name of the tribe of native Indians in the region, and from a creek that flowed into the Catawba River. Though the Revolutionary War was eleven years away, the relationship between King George III and his American colonies was already strained. The year the Jacksons crossed the Atlantic, Parliament passed the Quartering Act (which forced colonists to shelter British troops) and the Stamp Act (which levied a tax on virtually every piece of paper on the continent). The result: the Massachusetts legislature called for a colonial congress in New York, which issued a "Declaration of Rights and Grievances" against King George III. Striking, too, was a remark made by a delegate from South Carolina, the Jacksons' new home. **"There ought to be no more New England men, no New Yorkers,"** said Christopher Gadsden of Charleston, **"but all of us Americans!"**

Jackson's father, meanwhile, was trying to establish himself and his family in the New World. Though a man, his son recalled, of "independent" means, he was, it seems, poorer than his in-laws, who might have made him feel the disparity. While the other members of the extended family began prospering, Jackson moved his wife and two sons, Hugh and Robert, to Twelve Mile Creek, seven miles from the heart of Waxhaw. His wife was pregnant when the first Andrew Jackson died unexpectedly. It was a confusing, unsettling time. The baby was almost due, a snowstorm—rare in the South—had struck, and Jackson's pallbearers drank so much as they carried his corpse from Twelve Mile Creek to the church for the funeral that they briefly lost the body along the way.

Soon thereafter, on Sunday, March 15, 1767, Mrs. Jackson gave birth to her third son, naming him Andrew after her late husband. He was a dependent from delivery forward. Whether the birth took place in North or South Carolina has occupied historians for generations (Jackson himself thought it was South Carolina), but the more important fact is that Andrew Jackson came into the world under the roof of relatives, not of his own parents. Growing up, he would be a guest of the houses in which he lived, not a son, except of a loving mother who was never the mistress of her own household. One of Mrs. Jackson's sisters had married a Crawford, and the Crawfords were more affluent than the Jacksons. The loss of Mrs. Jackson's husband only made the gulf wider. When the Crawfords asked Mrs. Jackson and her sons to live with them, it was not wholly out of a sense of familial devotion and duty. The Jacksons needed a home, the Crawfords needed help, and a bargain was struck. "Mrs. Crawford was an invalid," wrote James Parton, the early Jackson biographer who interviewed people familiar with the Jacksons' days in Waxhaw, "and Mrs. Jackson was permanently established in the family as housekeeper and poor relation." Even in his mother's lifetime, Jackson felt a certain inferiority to and distance from others. "His childish recollections were of humiliating dependence and galling discomfort, his poor mother performing household drudgery in return for the niggardly maintenance of herself and her children," said Mary Donelson Wilcox, Emily and Andrew's oldest daughter. He was not quite part of the core of the world around him. He did not fully belong, and he knew it.

God and war dominated his childhood. His mother took him and his brothers to the Waxhaw Presbyterian meetinghouse for services every week, and the signal intellectual feat of his early years was the memorization of the Westminster Shorter Catechism. Most stories about the young Jackson also paint a portrait of a child and young man full of energy, fun, and not a little fury. Like many other children of the frontier, he was engaged in a kind of constant brawl from birth—and in Jackson's case, it was a brawl in which he could not stand to lose ground or points, even for a moment.

Wrestling was a common pastime, and a contemporary who squared off against Jackson recalled, "I could throw him three times out of four, but he would never **stay throwed**." As a practical joke his friends packed extra powder into a gun Jackson was about to fire, hoping the recoil would knock him down. It did. A furious Jackson rose up and cried, "By God, if one of you laughs, I'll kill him!"

Perhaps partly because he was fatherless, he may have felt he had to do more than usual to prove his strength and thus secure, or try to secure, his place in the community. "Mother, Andy will fight his way in the world," a neighborhood boy recalled saying in their childhood. Clearly Jackson seethed beneath the surface, for when flummoxed or crossed or frustrated, he would work himself into fits of rage so paralyzing that contemporaries recalled he would begin "slobbering." His prospects were not auspicious: here was an apparently unbalanced, excitable, insecure, and defensive boy coming of age in a culture of confrontation and violence. It was not, to say the least, the best of combinations.

His mother was his hope. His uncles and aunts apparently did not take a great deal of interest. They had their own children, their own problems, their own lives. Elizabeth Jackson was, however, a resourceful woman, and appears to have made a good bit out of little. There was some money, perhaps income from her late husband's farm, and gifts from relatives in Ireland—enough, anyway, to send Jackson to schools where he studied, for a time, under Presbyterian clergy, learning at least the basics of "the dead languages." He learned his most lasting lessons, however, not in a classroom but in the chaos of the Revolutionary War.

THE BIRTH OF the Republic was, for Jackson, a time of unrelenting death. A week after Jackson's eighth birthday, in March 1775, Edmund Burke took note of the American hunger for independence. "The temper and character which prevail in our Colonies are, I am afraid, unalterable by any human art," he said. Within sixteen months Burke was proved right when the Continental Congress declared independence on July 4, 1776, a midsummer Thursday. By 1778, the South was the focus of the war, and the British fought brutally in Georgia and the Carolinas. In 1779, Andrew's brother Hugh, just sixteen, was fighting at the front and died, it was said, "of heat and fatigue" after a clash between American and British troops at the Battle of Stono Ferry, southwest of Charleston. It was the first in a series of calamities that would strike Jackson, who was twelve.

The British took Charleston on Friday, May 12, 1780, then moved west. The few things Jackson knew and cherished were soon under siege. On Monday, May 29, at about three o'clock in the afternoon, roughly three hundred British troops under the command of Lieutenant Colonel Banastre Tarleton killed 113 men near Waxhaw and wounded another 150. It was a vicious massacre: though the rebels tried to surrender, Tarleton ordered his men forward, and they charged the Americans, a rebel surgeon recalled, "with the horrid yells of infuriated demons." Even after the survivors fell to the ground, asking for quarter, the British "went over the ground, plunging their bayonets into everyone that exhibited any signs of life."

The following Sunday was no ordinary Sabbath at Waxhaw. The meetinghouse was filled with casualties from the skirmish, and the Jacksons were there to help the wounded. "None of the men had less than three or four, and some as many as thirteen gashes on them," Jackson recalled.

He was so young, and so much was unfolding around him: the loss of a brother, the coming of the

British, the threat of death, the sight of the bleeding and the dying in the most sacred place he knew, the meetinghouse. The enemy was everywhere, and the people of Waxhaw, like people throughout the colonies, were divided by the war, with Loyalists supporting George III and Britain, and others, usually called Whigs, throwing in their lot with the Congress. As Jackson recalled it, his mother had long inculcated him and his brothers with anti-British rhetoric, a stand she took because of her own father, back in Ireland. The way Mrs. Jackson told the story, he had fought the troops of the British king in action at Carrickfergus. "Often she would spend the winter's night, in recounting to them the sufferings of their grandfather, at the siege of Carrickfergus, and the oppressions exercised by the nobility of Ireland, over the labouring poor," wrote John Reid and John Eaton in a biography Jackson approved, "impressing it upon them, as their first duty, to expend their lives, if it should become necessary, in defending and supporting the natural rights of man." These words were written for a book published in 1817, after Jackson defeated the British at New Orleans and preparatory to his entering national politics, which may account for the unlikely image of Mrs. Jackson tutoring her sons in Enlightenment political thought on cold Carolina evenings. But there is no doubt that Jackson chose to remember his upbringing this way, which means he linked his mother with the origins of his love of country and of the common man.

In the split between the revolutionaries and the

Loyalists Jackson saw firsthand the brutality and bloodshed that could result when Americans turned on Americans. "Men hunted each other like beasts of prey," wrote Amos Kendall, the Jackson intimate who spent hours listening to Jackson reminisce, "and the savages were outdone in cruelties to the living and indignities on the dead."

Lieutenant Colonel Tarleton—known as "Bloody Tarleton" for his butchery—once rode so close to the young Jackson that, Jackson recalled, "I could have shot him." The boy soaked up the talk of war and its rituals from the local militia officers and men. Months passed, and there were more battles, more killing. "Boys big enough to carry muskets incurred the dangers of men," wrote Kendall—and Jackson was big enough to carry a musket.

In April 1781, after a night spent on the run from a British party, he and his brother Robert were trapped in one of their Crawford relatives' houses. A neighboring Tory alerted the redcoats, and soon Andrew and Robert were surrounded. The soldiers ransacked the house, and an imperious officer ordered Jackson to polish his boots.

Jackson refused. "Sir," he said, with a striking formality and coolness under the circumstances for a fourteen-year-old, "I am a prisoner of war, and claim to be treated as such." The officer then swung his sword at the young man. Jackson blocked the blade with his left hand, but he could not fend it off completely. "The sword point reached my head and has left a mark there . . . on the skull, as well as on the fingers," Jackson recalled. His brother was next, and when he too refused the order to clean the boots, the officer smashed the sword over Robert's head, knocking him to the floor.

In some ways, Andrew was strengthened by the blows, for he would spend the rest of his life standing up to enemies, enduring pain, and holding fast until, after much trial, victory came. Robert was not so fortunate. The two boys were taken from the house to a British prison camp in Camden, about forty miles away. The journey was difficult in the April heat: "The prisoners were all dismounted and marched on foot to Camden, pushed through the swollen streams and prevented from drinking," Jackson recalled. The mistreatment continued at the camp. "No attention whatever was paid to the wounds or to the comfort of the prisoners, and the small pox having broken out among them, many fell victims to it," Jackson said. Robert was sick, very sick. Their mother managed to win her sons' release, and, with a desperately ill Robert on one horse and Mrs. Jackson on another, a barefoot Andrew—the British had taken his shoes and his coat—had to, as he recalled, "trudge" forty-five miles back to Waxhaw.

They made a ragged, lonely little group. En route, even the weather turned against them. "The fury of a violent storm of rain to which we were exposed for several hours before we reached the end of our journey caused the small pox to strike in and consequently the next day I was dangerously ill," Jackson recalled. Two days later Robert died. "During his confinement in prison," Jackson's earliest biography said, Robert "had suffered greatly; the wound on his head, all this time, having never been dressed, was followed by an inflammation of the brain, which in a few days after his liberation, brought him to his grave."

Two Jackson boys were now dead at the hands of the British. Elizabeth nursed Andrew, now her only living child, back from the precipice—and then left, to care for two of her Crawford nephews who were sick in Charleston.

JACKSON NEVER SAW her again. In the fall of 1781 she died in the coastal city tending to other boys, and was buried in obscurity. Her clothes were all that came back to him. Even by the rough standards of the frontier in late-eighteenth-century America, where disease and death were common, this was an extraordinary run of terrible luck.

For Jackson, the circumstances of Elizabeth's last mission of mercy and burial would be perennial reminders of the tenuous position she had been forced into by her own husband's death. First was the occasion of her visit to Charleston: to care for the extended family, leaving her own son behind. However selfless her motives—she had nursed the war's wounded from that first Waxhaw massacre in the late spring of 1780—Elizabeth had still gone to the coast for the sake of Jackson's cousins, not her own children. The uncertainty over the fate of her remains was a matter of concern to Jackson even in his White House years. He long sought the whereabouts of his mother's grave, but to no avail. Perhaps partly in reaction to what he may have viewed as the lack of respect or care others had taken with his mother's burial, he became a careful steward of such things—a devotee of souvenirs, a keeper of tombs, and an observer of anniversaries. The first woman he ever loved, his mother, rested in oblivion. The second woman who won his heart, Rachel, would be memorialized in stateliness and grandeur at the Hermitage after her death, and in his last years he would spend hours in the garden, contemplating her tomb. Bringing his mother home had been beyond his power. The story of Jackson's life was how he strove to see that little else ever would be.

Rachel Jackson believed her husband drew inspiration from his mother's trials. It was from her courage in facing what Rachel called "many hardships while on this earth" that Jackson "obtained the fortitude which has enabled him to triumph with so much success over the many obstacles which have diversified his life."

Jackson often recounted what he claimed were his mother's last words to him. In 1815, after his triumph at New Orleans, he spoke of his mother to friends: "Gentlemen, I wish she could have lived to see this day. There never was a woman like her. She was gentle as a dove and as brave as a lioness. Her last words have been the law of my life."

Andrew, if I should not see you again, I wish you to remember and treasure up some things I have already said to you: in this world you will have to make your own way. To do that you must have friends. You can make friends by being honest, and you can keep them by being steadfast. You must keep in mind that friends worth having will in the long run expect as much from you as they give to you. To forget an obligation or be ungrateful for a kindness is a base crime—not merely a fault or a sin, but an actual crime. Men guilty of it sooner or later must suffer the penalty. In personal conduct be always polite but never obsequious. None will respect you more than you respect yourself. Avoid quarrels as long as you can without yielding to imposition. But sustain your manhood always. Never bring a suit in law for assault and battery or for defamation. The law affords no remedy for such outrages that can satisfy the feelings of a true man. Never wound the feelings of others. Never brook wanton outrage upon your own feelings. If you ever have to vindicate your feelings or defend your honor, do it calmly. If angry at first, wait till your wrath cools before you proceed.

No matter how many of these words were hers, and how many were created by Jackson and ascribed to her memory, Elizabeth Jackson cast a long shadow in the life of her only surviving son.

JACKSON SPIRALED DOWNWARD and lashed out in the aftermath of his mother's death. Before now, living in other people's houses, Jackson had learned to manage complicated situations, maneuvering to maintain a passably cheerful (and grateful) face among people who gave him shelter but apparently little else. "He once said he never remembered receiving a gift as a child, and that, after his mother's death, no kind, encouraging words ever greeted his ear," recalled Mary Donelson Wilcox.

The Revolutionary War drew to a close with the American victory at Yorktown, Virginia, on the afternoon of Friday, October 19, 1781. Two years later, on Wednesday, September 3, 1783, came the Treaty of Paris, and the United States was now an independent nation. For Jackson, though, the end of war brought little peace. Living for a time with some Crawford relatives, Jackson got into a fight with one of their guests, a Captain Galbraith. Jackson thought him "of a very proud and haughty disposition," and the two found themselves in an argument, and "for some reason," Jackson recalled, "I forget now what, he threatened to chastise me." Jackson replied with a flash of fire. "I immediately answered, 'that I had arrived at the age to know my rights, and although weak and feeble from disease, I had the courage to defend them, and if he attempted anything of that kind I would most assuredly send him to the other world.'" That was enough for Jackson's current Crawford host to shuffle him off to another relative. Having the unstable orphan around presented too many problems, not least the possibility of his attacking other guests.

Then came a crucial interlude in Jackson's life: a sojourn in the cultivated precincts of Charleston. He had come into some money—either from his grandfather or perhaps from the sale of his mother's property—and used it to finance a trip to the coast where he fell in with a fast, sophisticated circle. Some Charlestonians had retreated to the Waxhaw region during the worst of the fighting on the coast, so Jackson had something of an entrée when he arrived. Here he found the pleasures of the turf, of good tailors, and of the gaming tables. "There can be little doubt that at this period he imbibed that high sense of honour, and unstudied elegance of air for which he has since been distinguished," wrote the early Jackson biographer Henry Lee—as well as little doubt that his love of racehorses and fine clothes had its beginnings in Charleston, too.

After Jackson returned to Waxhaw, he grew restless. From 1781 to 1784, he tried his hand at saddle making and school teaching—neither seems to have gone very well—and then left South Carolina for good. For the rest of his life, for a man who adored talk of family, friends, and old times, Jackson mentioned Waxhaw very little, the only exceptions being conversation about his mother and about Revolutionary War action in the region—both things that he could claim as his own.

Decade after decade, he never chose to find the time to go to Waxhaw. Acknowledging the gift of a map of the region the year before he was elected president, Jackson wrote a well-wisher: "A view of this map pointing to the spot that gave me birth, brings fresh to my memory many associations dear to my heart, many days of pleasure with my juvenile companions"—words that might, taken alone, suggest warm memories of his frontier youth.

Referring to his "juvenile companions," Jackson said, "but alas, most of them are gone to that bourne where I am hastening and from whence no one returns"—in other words, they were dead. "I have not visited that country since the year 1784," he added—which, since he was writing in midsummer 1827, means that forty-three years had passed since he bothered to return. Turning as close to home as he could, Jackson concluded: "The crossing of the Waxhaw creek, within one mile of which I was born, is still, however, I see, possessed by Mr John Crawford, son of the owner (Robert) who lived there when I was growing up and at school. I lived there for many years, and from the accuracy which this spot is marked in the map, I conclude the whole must be correct." With that, Jackson signs off. The subject is closed.

STILL, THE ROOTS of Jackson's intellectual and rhetorical imagination lie in Waxhaw. Down the years Jackson could quote Shakespeare, Plutarch, and Alexander Pope, and almost certainly read more books than his harshest critics believed, but the foundations of his worldview most likely came from his childhood Sundays in South Carolina, where he spent hours soaking in eighteenth-century Presbyterianism.

Elizabeth Jackson wanted her Andrew to be a minister, an ambition for him that may have been among the reasons he was able to envision himself rising to a place of authority. Even more so than in succeeding American generations, clergymen played a central and special role in the life of the eighteenth and early nineteenth centuries. They were often the most educated men in a given place, conversant not only with scripture but with ancient tongues and the touchstones of English literature. They held center stage, with a standing claim on the time and attention (at least feigned) of their flocks, and they presided at the most important public moments of a Christian's life—baptism, communion, marriage, death. Jackson's sense of himself as someone set apart—the word "ordain" shares derivation with the word "order," and an ordained figure is one who puts things in order, arranges them, controls and even commands them—may have come in part from hearing his mother speak of him in such terms.

Jackson found other, larger spheres over which to preside than Carolina churches, but it would be a mistake to pass too quickly over the lasting influence his churchgoing had on the way he thought, spoke, wrote, and saw the world. He attended services at the Waxhaw meetinghouse throughout his early years, and these childhood Sabbaths are worth considering in trying to solve the mystery of how a man with so little formal education and such a sporadic—if occasionally intense—interest in books developed his sense of history and of humanity.

The service the Jacksons attended most likely started in midmorning. A psalm was sung—but without organ music, for Presbyterians were austere not only in their theology but in their liturgy—and a prayer said. Church historians suspect such prayers could stretch beyond twenty minutes in length. Then came a lesson from scripture—the selection could range from an entire chapter of a book of the Bible to a shorter reading followed by an explication— followed by the centerpiece of the morning: the minister's sermon, an address that could range in length from thirty minutes to an hour. Another psalm or hymn closed the morning, which had by now consumed two hours of the day. There was a break for lunch, then an afternoon version of the same service, which everyone attended as well.

From his babyhood, then, Andrew Jackson probably spent between three and four hours nearly every Sunday for about fourteen years hearing prayers, psalms, scripture, sermons, and hymns: highly formalized, intense language evoking the most epic of battles with the greatest of stakes. In the words flowing from the minister on all those Sundays, Jackson would have been transported to imaginative realms where good and evil were at war, where kings and prophets on the side of the Lord struggled against the darker powers of the earth, where man's path through a confusing world was lit by a peculiar intermingling of Christian mercy and might. God may well plan on exalting the humble and meek, but Jackson also heard the call of Gideon's trumpet—the call to, as Saint Paul put it, fight the good fight.

Throughout his life, when he was under pressure, Jackson returned to the verses and tales of the Bible he had first heard in his childhood. He referred to political enemies as "Judases," and at one horrible moment during the attacks on Rachel's virtue in the 1828 campaign, Jackson's mind raced to the language and force of the Bible in a crowded collection of allusions. "Should the uncircumcised philistines send forth their Goliath to destroy the liberty of the people and compel them to worship Mammon, they may find a David who trusts in the God of Abraham, Isaac, and of Jacob, for when I fight, it is the battles of my country," Jackson wrote a friend.

That the image of King David—ancient Israel's greatest monarch—came to Jackson's mind is telling, for the connection he himself was drawing between David's struggles and his own suggests the breadth of Jackson's heroic vision of himself. David was a ruler who, chosen by the prophet Samuel, rose from obscurity to secure his nation and protect his people. A formidable soldier, he was a man of greatness and of God who was not without sin or sadness: that he stole Bathsheba, another man's wife, stretches the analogy further than Jackson would ever have gone, but the story of lost fathers and sons in the tale of the death of David's son Absalom echoed in Jackson's own life. The Lord's promise to David in II Samuel—"And thine house and thine kingdom shall be established for ever before thee; thy throne shall be established for ever"—would have resonated in Jackson's imagination, for his life was dedicated to building not only his own family but his nation, and perhaps even founding a dynasty in which Andrew Donelson, as his protégé, might, as Jackson put it, "preside over the destinies of America."

JACKSON SAID HE read three chapters of the Bible every day. His letters and speeches echo both scripture and the question-and-answer style of the Shorter Westminster Catechism. If the Bible, psalms, and hymns formed a substantial core of Jackson's habits of mind, books about valor, duty, and warfare also found their way into his imagination. Jackson had only a handful of years of formal education—he was the least intellectually polished president in the short history of the office—and his opponents made much of his lack of schooling. When Harvard University bestowed an honorary degree on President Jackson in 1833, the man he had beaten for the White House, John Quincy Adams, a Harvard graduate, refused to come, telling the university's president that "as myself an affectionate child of our Alma Mater, I would not be present to witness her disgrace in conferring her highest literary honors upon a barbarian who could not write a sentence of grammar and hardly could spell his own name." Adams's view was common in Jackson's lifetime.

Jackson was not, however, as unlettered as the caricatures suggest. He was no scholar, but he issued elegant Caesar-like proclamations to his troops, understood men and their motives, and read rather more than he is given credit for. "I know human nature," he once remarked, and he had learned the ways of the world not only on the frontier but also in snatches of literature. There was Oliver Goldsmith's 1766 novel

The Vicar of Wakefield, a story of redemption (the vicar faces much misfortune, yet perseveres through faith to a happy ending). It is not difficult to see why Jackson was drawn to the tale. "The hero of this piece," Goldsmith wrote in an "Advertisement" for the book, "unites in himself the three greatest characters upon earth: he is a priest, an husbandman, and the father of a family."

Jackson's surviving library at the Hermitage is full of books of theology, history, and biography. There are numerous volumes of sermons (most, if not all, of them Rachel's), and a fair collection of the works of Isaac Watts. His secular shelves are heavy on Napoleon, George Washington, and the American Revolution.

A favorite book was Jane Porter's **The Scottish Chiefs.** The story of Sir William Wallace—a reluctant, noble warrior brought into combat against the domineering and cruel English when the king's soldiers murder his wife—affected Jackson perhaps more than any other piece of writing outside scripture. "I have always thought that Sir William Wallace, as a virtuous patriot and warrior, was the best model for a young man," Jackson once wrote. "In him we find a stubborn virtue . . . the truly undaunted courage, always ready to brave any dangers, for the relief of his country or his friend."

The story, published in 1809, is something of a potboiler. More colorful than subtle, it is nonetheless a powerful book, and Jackson thrilled to it. "God is with me," Wallace says as he realizes his wife is dead.

"I am his avenger . . . God armeth the patriot's hand!" The cause of Scotland became one with Wallace's personal crusade for justice.

Jackson, too, had lost those he loved to the English. Orphaned in Waxhaw, he would struggle to build and keep a family everywhere else. In those distant forests, makeshift battlefields, and richer relatives' houses he had seen the centrality of strength and of self-confidence. Both elements, so essential to his character and his career, can be traced to his mother's influence, which was brief but lasting. In his mind she remained vivid and her example did, too—the example of strength amid adversity and of persevering no matter what. It is also likely that her dreams remained with him: chiefly her ambitious hope that he would become a clergyman, thus exercising authority and earning respect, all in the service of a larger cause. In the end Jackson chose to serve God and country not in a church but on battlefields and at the highest levels—but he did choose, as his mother had wished, to serve.

★

CHAPTER 2

FOLLOW ME AND
I'LL SAVE YOU YET

IN 1787, AFTER a brief period of study in Salisbury, North Carolina, Jackson received his license to practice law in that state. A wild man, he worked hard and played even harder for the next four years. He challenged the first lawyer he ever tried a case against to a duel (the challenge fizzled) and arranged for the town's prostitutes to arrive in the midst of a society Christmas ball. "He was the most roaring, rollicking, game-cocking, card-playing, mischievous fellow that ever lived in Salisbury," a contemporary recalled. When James Parton was researching his 1860 biography of Jackson, the author traveled to Salisbury in search of stories about his subject. There he learned one local woman's reaction to hearing that Jackson might be a candidate for the White House. "What! Jackson up for President? **Jackson? Andrew** Jackson? The Jackson that used to live in Salisbury? Why, when he was here, he was such a rake that my husband would not bring him into the house!" Reflecting for a moment more, she allowed, "It is true, he **might** have taken him out to the stable to weigh horses for a race, and might drink a glass of whiskey with him **there**. Well, if Andrew Jackson can be President, anybody can!"

There is no doubt that in these years Jackson was a rake, and a gambler, and a carouser. Note, however, that the "rake" had made something of a friend of the husband of this Salisbury matron, forming a connection based on sporting interests—a connection strong enough to survive the disapproval of the lady of the house.

That Jackson was on intimate terms with such established families is telling. He was not born in a station that granted him automatic access to the upper reaches of the nascent American gentry. He had to work his way into those circles with whatever he had at hand—and what he had was a charm that made other men like him and want to join him in exploits that crossed the line of respectability, but never so dramatically that they could not stumble back into the good graces of their wives and neighbors by morning. One day Jackson would draw on his capacity to make others love and follow him in the service of larger causes. But his raw ability to lead—and his sense of adventure and his infectious fearlessness—was already evident in North Carolina.

TENNESSEE WAS NOT yet a state when Jackson, then twenty-one, moved to Nashville in October 1788 and took up residence as a boarder in the house of Mrs. John Donelson, the widow of a founder of the settlement. The Donelsons were among the territory's great families. The patriarch, Colonel John Donelson, was a surveyor who had been a member of the Virginia House of Burgesses before striking out to the west. His 1779–80 voyage on the Cumberland River aboard the flatboat **Adventure** was one of the prevailing stories of the age, and his mysterious death—he was shot to death in the wilderness, perhaps by Indians, perhaps by robbers—only added to his legend.

The colonel, though, survives in history mostly as the father of the wife of Andrew Jackson. Born about 1767—the year Jackson was born—Rachel Donelson came from a clan as distinguished in early American life as Jackson's was anonymous. Rachel was a beautiful young woman with a strong sense of fun—and when Rachel met Jackson in the autumn of 1788 on the Cumberland, she was another man's wife. Rachel Donelson and Lewis Robards of Mercer County, Kentucky, had been married since 1785; they had met and courted during a Donelson family sojourn in Kentucky. At twenty-seven, Robards was a decade older than the seventeen-year-old Rachel, and the marriage was difficult from the start. John Overton, a Tennessee judge and later Jackson ally who came to board with Lewis Robards's mother in the fall of 1787—roughly two years after Rachel married Robards—recalled that "Robards and his wife lived very unhappily, on account of his being jealous. . . . My brother, who was a boarder, informed me that great uneasiness had existed in the family for some time before my arrival." Things got so bad that one of her brothers went to Kentucky to bring Rachel home—in the fall of 1788, the same season Jackson arrived in Nashville.

Mrs. Robards was, James Parton wrote, "gay and lively . . . the best story-teller, the best dancer, the sprightliest companion, the most dashing horsewoman in the western country"—the kind of woman who would hold enormous appeal for Jackson. But she was, indisputably, **Mrs. Robards**. Having driven her off, her husband decided he wanted a reconciliation, and moved to Nashville, where they again lived together for a time. Robards soon grew jealous of Jackson's attentions to Rachel and indulged his anger, reducing both Rachel and her mother to tears. Robards and Jackson exchanged words. "If I had such a wife, I would not willingly bring a tear to her beautiful eyes," Jackson was said to have remarked to Robards, who replied: "Well, perhaps . . . but she is not **your** wife."

Both threatened violence, but Jackson soon moved to another establishment—a smart tactical maneuver, as it turned out—and Robards, furious with his allegedly flirtatious wife, returned to Kentucky alone. Then came word that the unhappy husband was going to come to Tennessee yet again "to take his wife" back to his own home. He planned, it was reported, to "**haunt** her." Friends arranged for Rachel to travel to Natchez, Mississippi, then controlled by the Spanish. Jackson, who knew the route, went along, and returned to Nashville. According to the Jackson version of events, it was at this point—with Rachel in Natchez, and Jackson in Tennessee, in the winter of

1790–91—that Jackson learned Robards had obtained a divorce. Jackson rushed back to Natchez and married Rachel there. Only two years later, in December 1793, did it become clear that Robards had only **petitioned** for a divorce in December 1790. It was not granted until September 1793, which meant that Jackson had been "married" to another man's wife for several years. By January 1794, all was put right, and Jackson and Rachel were legally married in a ceremony in Tennessee.

Or so Jackson, as a presidential candidate, would later have the world—and history—believe. The weight of the evidence, however, suggests the two lived together as husband and wife and even referred to themselves as married—there are two surviving references to Rachel as "Mrs. Jackson" from late 1790 and early 1791—**before** Robards took the initial step of filing for a divorce. Their passion for each other was apparently deep enough to lead them, despite their later claims to the contrary, to choose to live in adultery in order to provoke a divorce from Robards. By the looser standards of the frontier in the last years of the eighteenth century, such a course would not have damaged their reputations, particularly if—as was the case here—the woman's family approved.

The bond Rachel and Jackson formed from their first meeting in 1788 was strong enough, and their private visions of a life together vivid enough, for them to seek the pleasure and comfort of each other's arms as rapidly as they could. But by the time Jackson was running for president more than thirty years later, the moral climate had moved in a stricter direction. So it is likely that the Jacksons' sensitivity to charges of impropriety in later years was rooted in the fact that the essential charge—that Mrs. Jackson was still Mrs. Robards when she and Jackson began their life together—was true.

What had brought them together in the first place? The drama of the abusive husband, the wronged woman, and himself as the knight defending her virtue would have appealed to Jackson's imagination: it was a role he liked to think of himself as playing. Even more fundamentally, though, from about 1788 onward, Jackson was a man in the grip of an almost feverish love, a love it seems reasonable to assume he longed to consummate as soon as he decently could. In Rachel's big eyes he found the suggestion of a lasting love. In Jackson's slender but strong frame she found the promise of protection and a tenderness her first husband had never given her. In capturing Rachel as his own Jackson got what he wanted, and he got it with a combination of subtlety (courting her in her mother's house, and staying on the right side of the family) and bravery (risking his standing, and the possibility of a duel, to have her as his wife before it was legally allowed). The road to marriage with Rachel had all the elements of life Jackson found compelling: it was a cause of the heart charged by complication and danger, but with the greatest possible rewards awaiting him if he could win through—the love of a good woman and, so important to the orphan from Waxhaw, a connection to a secure, leading family of the world in which he found himself.

THEY WERE DEVOTED to each other. When Jackson was away, Rachel was given to crying and worrying. From the road or the front, he summoned all his rhetorical power to assure her of his love. Rachel once wrote Jackson a fretful note about his safety while he was on a trip to Philadelphia. He rushed to assuage her anxieties. "I have this moment recd. your letter," he told her, "and what sincere regret it gives me on the one hand to view your distress of mind, and what real pleasure it would afford me on the other to return to your arms, dispel those clouds that hover around you and retire to some peaceful grove to spend our days in solitude and domestic quiet." But business mattered—Jackson was on a dual judicial and commercial journey—and he confessed a dark fear to her: an early return, he said, could "involve us in all the calamity of poverty—an event which brings every horror to my mind." He had been without resources once, and, hating the idea of once again finding himself in a dependent position, he pressed on, struggling to warm the chill of his wife's worries with letters. Because "you are full of apprehension and doubt with respect to my safety," Jackson told Rachel, "I have wrote you every post since I left you— and will continue to do so . . . may the all ruling power give you health and Peace of Mind until I am restored to your arms."

They shared a passionate emotional attachment,

but Jackson—like many husbands before and since— may have loved his wife rather more than he listened to her. He did what he wanted to do, and if his course upset his wife, sending her into gloomy moods and fits of tears, he was sorry, but Rachel's anguish rarely affected his decisions to leave her when duty called. A public man, he savored public adulation, though he knew his wife had a point as she tried to keep him grounded amid the cheering crowds. He respected her views, for they were informed by decades of close observation of Jackson's political life, and they were offered out of love. Rachel also knew he struggled to keep his emotions in check and warned him when she thought he was in danger of letting his passions get the better of him. "I thank you for your admonition," Jackson wrote Rachel after one such exhortation. "I hope in all my acts and conduct through life they will measure with propriety and dignity, or at least with what I believe true dignity consists, that is to say, honesty, propriety of conduct, and honest independence."

HE RELISHED THE roles of protector and savior. Just after dusk on a cold March day in 1791, when Jackson was practicing law on the circuit around Jonesborough, Tennessee, he and his friend John Overton were traveling with a small group through dangerous territory. Reaching the banks of the Emory River in the mountains, the lawyers spotted a potentially hostile Indian party. "The light of their fires showed that they were numerous," Overton recalled to Henry Lee, and "that they were painted and equipped for war." Under Jackson's leadership (Overton credited him with a "saving spirit and elastic mind"), the travelers scrambled into the hills on horseback, riding roughly parallel to the river—which they had to cross to make it home. Pursued by the Indians, Jackson, Overton, and two others pressed on through the night, coming to a place where the water looked smooth enough to allow a hastily constructed raft and the horses to make it to the other side. Jackson took charge of the raft piled high with saddles and clothes. Overton would follow with the horses.

There was immediate trouble. The waters were not as smooth as they had appeared: a powerful undercurrent swept the boat—and Jackson—downstream, toward a steep waterfall. "Overton and his companion instantly cried out and implored Jackson to pull back," Lee wrote. "But he either not being so sensible of the danger, or being unwilling to yield to it, continued to push vigorously forward." Jackson struggled with his oars: disaster was at hand. He and the saddles could be lost, and the Indians were still on their trail. "Finding himself just on the brink of the awful precipice," Lee recounted, Jackson extended his oar to Overton, who "laid hold of it and pulled the raft ashore, just as it was entering the suck of the torrent." Catching their breath on the bank of the river, Overton and Jackson looked at each other.

"You were within an ace, Sir, of being dashed to pieces," Overton told him. Jackson waved him off, replying, "A miss is as good as a mile; it only shows how close I can graze danger. But we have no time to lose—follow me and I'll save you yet." They eluded the Indians, arriving home exhausted but safe.

Here was the daring Jackson, the courageous Jackson, the cool Jackson—and the erratic, blithe, boastful Jackson, a man who saw what needed to be done in a crisis but also needed his friends to carry the day. "Follow me and I'll save you yet" are confident, inspiring, warming words, yet it was Overton who had just rescued Jackson, not the other way around. It was partly this boldness and resilience that attracted men and women to Jackson's side in the first place, for in doubtful moments people need someone who can reassure them amid danger. Jackson was such a man—and he always had wise friends nearby who loved him enough to overlook or chuckle at his professions of pride, and then mount up to ride with him again.

STILL, JACKSON'S PRIDE led him into peril more than once. In Knoxville in the autumn of 1803, in the midst of a quarrel with Tennessee governor John Sevier over which man would become major general of the state militia, Jackson alluded to his own past "services" to the state. "Services?" Sevier replied. "I know of no great service you have rendered the country, except taking a trip to Natchez with another man's wife."

"Great God!" Jackson roared. "Do you mention **her** sacred name?"

Then, according to a contemporary's recollection, "several shots were fired in a crowded street. One man was grazed by a bullet; many were scared; but, luckily, no one was hurt." The story is chiefly interesting for the light it sheds on Jackson's sensitivities about Rachel's honor. "Sevier had touched on a subject that was, with Jackson, like sinning against the Holy Ghost: unpardonable," recalled the source.

No one died in the Sevier shootout, but Jackson could, and did, kill in cold blood. In 1806, an argument over a horse race—the dispute also apparently included a slur against Rachel—degenerated into a duel between Jackson and a man in Nashville named Charles Dickinson. Jackson was determined to have satisfaction, waving off reports that Dickinson might leave the city before the showdown. "It will be in vain, for I'll follow him over land and sea," Jackson said.

At seven o'clock on the morning of Friday, May 30, 1806, on the Red River in Logan County, Kentucky, Jackson and Dickinson faced each other at twenty-four feet. Jackson let Dickinson shoot first, and he hit Jackson in the chest with a bullet. Though wounded, Jackson coolly leveled his own pistol at his opponent, and fired. The trigger caught halfway; Jackson cocked the gun again and fired, killing Dickinson. Only later, as his boot filled with blood after he had left the dueling ground, did the extent of Jackson's wound become clear. He carried Dickinson's bullet in his body until he died. Even in pain—the wound complicated his health for decades—Jackson never let his mask drop. "If he had shot me through the brain, sir," Jackson told a friend, "I should still have killed him."

In fact, Jackson made more friends than he fought duels, and in the practice of law, the pursuit of politics, and his mastery of the military—his three overlapping professions—he inspired great loyalty. Jackson's willingness to risk his own life to protect others won him the respect and thanks of his contemporaries and made them amenable to forgiving him his (many) trespasses. It was he who escorted parties of settlers through forests filled with Indians; it was he who enforced justice in a region that could have turned lawless; it was he who rallied volunteer troops and rode to the enemy. As an Indian fighter, Henry Lee wrote, Jackson's "gallantry and enterprise were always conspicuous, attracted the confidence of the whites, and inspired honour and respect among the savages, who gave him the epithets of **the sharp knife** and **the pointed arrow**." By projecting personal strength, Jackson created a persona of power, and it was this aura, perhaps more than any particular gift of insight, judgment, or rhetoric, that propelled him forward throughout his life.

As a judge of the Tennessee Superior Court—a post he held from December 1798 until July 1804—Jackson was riding circuit when he encountered the case of a man, Russell Bean, who had been indicted for "cutting off the ears of his infant child in a drunken frolic." The local sheriff was afraid of Bean, who refused to appear in court. "Russell Bean would not be taken," the sheriff told Jackson, who later related the incident to Henry Lee. "At this Judge Jackson expressed much astonishment, and peremptorily informed the officer 'that such a return was an absurdity and could not be received, that the culprit must be arrested, and that he [the sheriff] had a right to summon the **posse comitatus,** to aid in the execution of the law.'" The sheriff asked Jackson to join the posse, and after arming himself, Jackson agreed. "Sir, I will attend you and see that you do your duty," he said to the sheriff, who led Jackson to the place in town where Bean, "armed with a dirk and a brace of pistols," was "boasting of his superiority to the law and entertaining the populace with taunts and reflections upon the cowardice of the sheriff and the pusillanimity of the court." Then the court—in the person of Jackson—appeared. "Now, surrender, you infernal villain, this very instant," Jackson said, "or I'll blow you through."

Wilting under Jackson's "firm advance and formidable look," Bean was "unnerved entirely." He dropped his guns. "I will surrender to you, sir, but to no one else," Bean said to Jackson.

Jackson could be touchy and unreasonable, but here, in a corner of Tennessee, we can see the faith others put in Jackson at times of peril and the respect his bravery inspired in his foes. "When danger rears its head, I can never shrink from it," Jackson once told Rachel. He did what others would not—or could not—do. In a world of threats, that willingness made him a hero, a central figure, someone who could be counted on.

HE WAS BECOMING a man of standing in Nashville, and in that role he and Rachel were Aaron Burr's hosts in Nashville in 1805. A former vice president and the man who had killed Alexander Hamilton in a duel, Burr was an adventurer at the center of a murky ongoing conspiracy in these years to lead a military expedition of some kind in the Southwest, possibly to marry U.S. land with Spanish holdings to create a stand-alone republic or empire. It was an elusive scheme, and with Jackson, Burr seems to have spoken only of preparing a force in the event of war with Spain in Florida, a subject of perennial interest in the Southwest at the time. At Burr's request, Jackson agreed to build five boats and supply them with provisions.

That Jackson was not privy to a treasonous conspiracy seems evident; his call for the militia to make itself ready noted that they would move "when the government and constituted authorities of our country require it." Burr had other ideas, including the possibility of seizing New Orleans. Beginning to suspect trouble, Jackson wrote several officials, including President Jefferson and Louisiana governor William C. C. Claiborne. "I fear there is something rotten in the State of Denmark," Jackson told Claiborne. Ultimately Jefferson had Burr arrested and tried for treason; Burr was acquitted in 1807. The episode illuminates two elements of Jackson's character: his ambition to secure the nation from foreign threats, an ambition so abiding that he very nearly allowed himself to become entangled in a terrible conspiracy; and, second, his equally abiding love of the nation as a family that could not be broken up.

. . .

JACKSON WAS forty-five years old when America and Britain went to war in 1812, and he was viewed as a formidable leader of men. By this time he had served as attorney general for Tennessee in its territorial days, in 1791; been elected to the U.S. House of Representatives in 1796; moved to the U.S. Senate in 1797; served as a judge from 1798 to 1804; and, in 1802, had also become major general of the state militia. All the while he struggled to build his planting and commercial interests, from buying huge tracts of land to running a frontier store. "He loves his country and his countrymen have full confidence in him," Tennessee governor Willie Blount wrote to the secretary of war at the outbreak of hostilities in 1812. "He delights in peace; but does not fear war. He has a peculiar pleasure in treating his enemies as such; with them his first pleasure is to meet them on the field. At the present crisis he feels a holy zeal for the welfare of the United States, and at no period of his life has he been known to feel otherwise." Since his mother and his brothers had died for the Union, he would defend the nation to the death.

It was not only courage and conviction that turned Jackson into a great general and a transformative president. He cared about his followers, thought of them as his family, and communicated this warmth in word and deed. Speaking of his men at a low moment in the War of 1812, Jackson promised to "act the part of a father to them." Many leaders say such things and do not mean them, and many followers dismiss such sentiments as words without substance. Jackson was different. He proved his love in times of crisis, earning capital with his troops that both gave him a nickname and formed a bond of affection and respect between himself and his followers that lasted for the rest of his life.

In the cold winter of 1812–13, just months after the United States declared war on Great Britain, Jackson assembled his volunteers—2,071 in all—to march south, toward New Orleans. Jackson's army set off in January 1813, and, five hundred miles later, at Natchez, federal military authorities told Jackson to hold up, and soon the secretary of war ordered him to disband and return to Nashville. By now 150 of Jackson's men were sick, 56 could not sit up, and Jackson had a total of eleven wagons for the trip. "They abandon us in a strange country," he angrily wrote to Governor Blount, adding: **"And I will make every sacrifice to add to their comfort."** Lee captured Jackson's bleak view: "They had sacrificed domestic comforts, abandoned civilian pursuits, cherished heroic visions; and voyaged a thousand miles—all as it seemed for nothing—and were suddenly left without motives for action, subjects for hope, the power of progression, or the means of return—between them and their homes frowned a vast wilderness where the ambushed savage lurked intent on theft and murder. . . ." As they prepared to move out, the doctor, Samuel Hogg, asked Jackson what he was to do.

Jackson did not hesitate. "To do, sir? You are to leave not a man on the ground."

"But the wagons are full," Hogg said, "and they will convey not more than half."

"Then let some of the troops dismount, and the officers must give up their horses to the sick," Jackson replied. "Not a man, sir, must be left behind."

Hogg took Jackson at his word, and asked for the general's own horses, which Jackson handed over. In wonder and with admiration his men watched this tall, determined figure press on. "I led them into the field," Jackson wrote Rachel, and "I will at all hazard and risk lead them out. I will bring on the sick, or be with them—it shall never be said . . . they have been abandoned by their general." To the Tennessee politician Felix Grundy, he said: "And as long as I have friends or credit, I will stick by them. I shall march them to Nashville or bury them with the honors of war. Should I die I know they would bury me." On foot, he saw them home, and by the time they arrived in Nashville they were calling him "Old Hickory." Jackson had done what his own parents never had. He had stayed the course with those in his charge, and delivered them from danger. He had done a father's work.

BACK IN NASHVILLE for a time, Jackson slipped from the role of the protective commander and let his temper get the best of him during a foray into frontier violence. In 1813, a friend of Jackson's in Nashville quarreled with Jesse Benton, the brother of Thomas Hart Benton, a future United States senator from Missouri. Jackson became entangled in the affair and before long—such were the complexities and short fuses in frontier Tennessee—he had let it be known that he would whip Thomas Benton when their paths crossed.

They crossed on Saturday, September 4, 1813, at about nine o'clock in the morning. Jackson and General John Coffee were in Nashville, walking from the post office, when Jackson, who happened to have his riding whip in his hand, saw Tom and Jesse Benton standing by the City Hotel. Jackson, brandishing his whip, could not resist the opportunity. "Now, you damned rascal, I am going to punish you," Jackson told Tom Benton. "Defend yourself."

Jackson pulled a gun and moved toward Tom, backing him around the hotel. Chaos ensued: an armed Jesse fired at Jackson, who fell with a serious wound in his upper left arm. Coffee rushed toward the sound and, finding Jackson in a spreading pool of blood, proceeded to shoot at Tom Benton. The shot went wide, but Coffee scrambled to beat Benton with the gun when Benton crashed down a flight of stairs. A nephew of Rachel's then arrived on the scene, wrestled Jesse Benton to the floor, and tried to kill him with a dirk knife.

Everyone survived, but Jackson sustained the worst injuries in the melee. While being tended to by doctors, he bled through two mattresses. The physicians wanted to amputate Jackson's left arm, but Jackson refused, and with enough force from his bloody bed to carry the point.

"I'll keep my arm," he said simply.

A month later, while Rachel was still nursing Jackson back to health, news arrived that Creek Indians under the leadership of Red Eagle had massacred white settlers at Fort Mims, a fortification about forty miles north of Mobile. Red Eagle (his father was Scottish, his mother Creek) had been influenced by Tecumseh, the Shawnee chief who hoped to unite the Indians into a force that, armed and supplied by the British and the Spanish, would crush the white Americans who were usurping their land. "Let the white race perish!" Tecumseh said. "War now! War always! War on the living! War on the dead!"

Men like Jackson had long been troubled by visions of Indians colluding with London and Madrid to check American expansion, threaten the Union, and possibly undo the Revolution. To Jackson it was a given that the Indians—in this case the Creeks—were in league with America's European rivals.

The Creek attack on Fort Mims had taken place on Monday, August 30, 1813. It was brutal; as a historian of Alabama described it, 250 whites, including women and children, "were butchered in the quickest manner, and blood and brains bespattered the whole earth. The children were seized by the legs, and killed by batting their heads against the stockading. The women were scalped, and those who were pregnant were opened, while they were alive, and the embryo infants let out of the womb." Until then, the Creeks had been fighting a factional war; by assaulting Fort Mims, the tribe irrevocably widened the conflict. That the fort had provided protection for settlers who had themselves attacked Red Sticks—named for their red war clubs—made no difference to the whites in the region who panicked at reports of the massacre.

They sent for Jackson. "Those distressed citizens of that frontier [have] . . . implored the brave Tennesseans for aid," he said. "They must not ask in vain." Forcing himself into battle—he was in terrible shape from the Benton brawl—Jackson won a bloody victory at Tallushatchee, a village filled with Red Sticks. "We shot them like dogs," said David Crockett. Richard Keith Call, then a lieutenant under Jackson, was troubled by the toll Jackson's men had exacted. "We found as many as eight or ten dead bodies in a single cabin," Call said. "Some of the cabins had taken fire, and half consumed human bodies were seen amidst the smoking ruins." The bloodshed was repulsive. "In other instances dogs had torn and feasted on the mangled bodies of their masters," Call said. "Heart-sick I turned from the revolting scene."

Jackson, however, believed justice had been done. "We have retaliated for the destruction of Fort Mims," he told the governor of Tennessee. Difficult months followed. Supplies were few, and the troops' discontent tested Jackson's hold over his men. (Matters turned so grim that Jackson ordered the executions of six militiamen.) Still, he triumphed, winning victories from Talladega to Horseshoe Bend. The Creek War ended in August 1814—nearly a year after Fort Mims—with Jackson's winning the cession of twenty-three million acres of land to the United States (three fifths of modern-day Alabama and one fifth of Georgia).

Jackson never rested. Though he had crushed the Creeks, he still believed the Indians a live threat, a willing tool in the hands of the British and the Spanish. To the south, he defended Mobile against a British attack and then struck to the east, at Spanish Florida, where he was convinced that Madrid (and London) was "arming the hostile Indians to butcher our women and children." He threatened Pensacola, which prompted the Spanish authorities there to seek British protection; soon Jackson took the city's major fort, and then turned back to the west, toward New Orleans. It was late November 1814.

AT NEW ORLEANS, Jackson continued the work of a conqueror. On Wednesday, December 16, with the British close by, he imposed martial law on the city, defying a writ of habeas corpus and jailing the federal district judge who issued it. (Lincoln would cite Jackson when suspending habeas corpus during the Civil War.) For this he was fined, and one of the last efforts of his life was to press Congress to refund the penalty.

However ruthless his rule, Jackson impressed the city. In the second week of December 1814, he was at a party when word came of the beginning of an engagement with the British. "The dancing was over, and in the greatest alarm everyone was for hastening to their homes; when the General in his elegant, persuading, convincing manner assured the company that only himself and staff need leave, that there was no danger, and he would feel greatly obliged if the dancing was resumed," Mrs. Eliza Williams Chotard

Gould, who was there, recalled in a private memoir. "Such were his powers of persuasion that the affrighted company became calm, and cheerfully took partners again." It was a brief respite—the crowd did soon go home—but Jackson had proved himself a reassuring commander.

On the eve of the battle, from a balcony overlooking Bourbon Street, Mrs. Gould and her family watched Jackson approach on horseback. Seeing the women in tears, Jackson "expressed his regret at our alarm, insisted that we were in no danger, that the American arms would be victorious and the British whipped back to their vessels," Mrs. Gould recalled. "His confident manner and expressions . . . dissipated for a time our distress." Jackson's men, she said, "were the most splendid horsemen I ever saw."

Jackson engaged the enemy in a climactic battle on Sunday, January 8, 1815, winning a victory reminiscent of Shakespeare's Henry V at Agincourt. Though the battle came after the war had ended—news of the treaty signed in Ghent on Christmas Eve would not reach New Orleans for several weeks—the victory was stunning. The British lost nearly three hundred men, with another twelve hundred wounded and hundreds more taken prisoner or missing. Only thirteen Americans died, with thirty-nine more suffering wounds. "It appears that the unerring hand of providence shielded my men from the powers of balls, bombs, and rockets, when every ball and bomb from our guns carried with them the mission of death," Jackson said. Gazing across the battlefield as the cannon smoke lifted, John Coffee thought "the slaughter was shocking," and soon living British soldiers who had hidden beneath their fallen comrades' red coats rose from the heaps of corpses. "I never had so grand and awful an idea of the resurrection as on that day," Jackson recalled.

He was now a national, in fact international, figure of renown. In the city on Monday, January 23, 1815, the city's ranking Roman Catholic priest thanked God for Jackson: "It is Him we intend to praise, when considering you, general, as the **man of His right hand. . . .** Immortal thanks be to His Supreme Majesty, for sending us such an instrument of His bountiful designs!"

New Orleans made him, and he was becoming a player on a larger stage—a prospect that provoked anxieties on Rachel's part and insecurities on Jackson's. Worried that her husband's head would be turned by his popularity—among American figures to that date, only Washington enjoyed a reputation of comparable scope—Rachel cautioned him against valuing glory above family. "The attention and honors paid to the General far excel a recital by my pen," Rachel wrote a friend after ceremonies celebrating Jackson in New Orleans in 1821. "They conducted him to the Grand Theater; his box was decorated with elegant hangings. At his appearance the theater rang with loud acclamations, Vive Jackson. Songs of praise were sung by ladies, and in the midst they crowned him with a crown of laurel." But Rachel was thinking of things greater than earthly grandeur. "The Lord has promised his humble followers a crown that fadeth not away; the present one is already withered, the leaves are falling off. . . . Oh, for Zion! I wept when I saw this idolatry."

Her husband, however, loved it. "I wish your carriage well repaired or exchanged for a new one," Jackson wrote Rachel after New Orleans. "You must recollect that you are now a Major General's lady, in the service of the U.S., and as such you must appear elegant and plain, not extravagant, but in such style as strangers expect to see you." Louise Livingston, the wife of Jackson's friend Edward Livingston, arranged Rachel's wardrobe. Jackson wanted to look his part, too. "Bring with you my sash," he told Rachel as she set out to come to New Orleans.

She was uncomfortable with splendor; he enjoyed the great life. She hated traveling; he spent much of his time on the road. She disliked the cut-and-thrust of politics; he adored maneuvering and governing. She was drawn to the pew, the plantation, and the fireside; he was, despite many protestations to the contrary, a thoroughly social creature, delighted by crowds and parties and the risks and rewards of the public stage.

During the turmoil of the 1824 presidential campaign, she complained that Jackson had failed to heed her counsel to avoid the political arena. "I knew from the first how wrong it was, but my advice was nothing," Rachel confided to a friend. "His health is not good, and a continual uneasy mind keeps him unwell. I saw from the first it was wrong for him to fatigue himself with such an important office." Yet within eight months of his losing the White House to John Quincy Adams in the election of 1824, the campaign of 1828 was under way. Rachel was Jackson's shelter from the storm, and he loved her for that. Sadly for her, he also loved the storm, and so she had less of him than she would have liked.

CHILDREN MIGHT HAVE made the rough edges smoother, but the Jacksons did not have any of their own. Watching her husband playing with a relative's baby—"This little pig went to market; this little pig stayed home; this little pig went squeak, squeak!" said the Hero of New Orleans—Rachel, according to a family story, cried: "Oh, husband! How I wish we had a child!" With grace, Jackson said, "Darling, God knows what to give, what to withhold; let's not murmur against Him."

Rachel would recount this scene, adding: "He would have given his life for a child; but knowing how disappointed I was at never being a mother, he, pitying me, tried to console me by saying: God denies us offspring that we may help those who have large families and no means to support them." She recalled, too, that "once, returning from a child's funeral, the bereaved mother's frantic grief almost unmanning us, he said, 'Your heart, my love, will never be pierced by that cruel knife.'"

There were consolations. Andrew Donelson, who grew up to serve as his private secretary, was one. A nephew of Rachel's, born in 1799, Andrew Jackson

User name: BALCH,
DOUGLAS C.
Pickup library:
NRTHSD
Title: American lion :
Andrew Jackson in the
White House
Item ID:
R0111916744
Current time:
04/23/2018,12:30
Pickup By: 5/1/2018

Donelson could not remember a time when he was not part of the Jackson world; the Jacksons had taken charge of his care and education after his father died in 1804. Jackson, it seemed, was the only one who could fill his father's role: when a well-off planter courted his mother, Andrew Donelson cut the man's saddle stirrups. In 1808 Rachel's brother Severn Donelson's wife had twin boys and offered to allow the Jacksons to adopt one of the infants. They accepted, christening the child Andrew Jackson, Jr. "The sensibility of our beloved son has charmed me, I have no doubt, from the sweetness of his disposition," Rachel wrote Jackson in 1813.

At war with the Creek Indian Nation in November 1813, Jackson's interpreter found a small boy, Lyncoya, on the battlefield. The boy's family was dead— "destroyed," as Jackson put it to Rachel, at the hands of Jackson and his men—and Jackson saw himself and his own plight during the Revolution in the child's eyes. With a combination of charity and condescension, he adopted Lyncoya on the spot and sent him to the Hermitage "for" Andrew junior as a playmate. "Keep Lyncoya in the house," Jackson wrote Rachel. "He is a savage but one that fortune has thrown in my hands. . . . I therefore want him well taken care of, he may have been given to me for some valuable purpose. In fact, when I reflect that he as to his relations is so much like myself I feel an unusual sympathy for him." Lyncoya lived at the Hermitage for the next fifteen years, dying of illness in 1828.

Andrew junior and the numerous Donelson

cousins filled the Jacksons' lives and house; taken together, the Donelson-Jackson clan was one of the most important in the state. General Daniel Smith, Andrew Donelson's mother's father (Jackson had helped her elope with Samuel Donelson, so in a way Andrew Donelson even owed Jackson his very life), served in the U.S. Senate, and the interlocking families owned large tracts of land around Nashville and beyond. Jackson and the Donelsons moved with the mightiest men in Tennessee—generals, governors, and planters. They may have been cash-poor but they were property-rich (in acres and slaves), and they were absolutely certain of their place in the universe, which is one definition of aristocracy. General Smith built a house named Rock Castle, which was, a relative recalled, "reputed to be the handsomest south of the Ohio or west of the Alleghenies."

AFTER NEW ORLEANS Jackson continued his battles against the Indian tribes in the South and West, and between 1816 and 1820 signed treaties giving the United States tens of millions of acres (this was in addition to his vast Creek acquisition). In the spring of 1816 his obsession with securing the nation's borders— and thus ensuring the safety of the country—led him to write Mauricio de Zuniga, the commandant of Pensacola. Florida remained in Spanish hands, and Jackson's incursion before the Battle of New Orleans had only provisionally taken care of the problem of having a foreign foe in such proximity. The occasion for the letter to Zuniga: fugitive American slaves were escaping to a fort occupied by blacks along the Apalachicola River. Allowing slaves to seek shelter at what he called the "negro fort," Jackson told Zuniga that the situation "will not be tolerated by our government, and if not put down by Spanish Authority will compel us in self-defense to destroy them." Within months, another American general, Edmund Pendleton Gaines, did exactly that, destroying the fort (and the 270 people inside it).

But the Spanish remained, and by 1817 Jackson was able to direct his fire toward two of his great nemeses—Spain and the Indians—at once. The Seminoles declined to leave their lands north of the Florida border—they were supposed to under the terms of Jackson's agreement with the Creeks—and instead fought back, trading bloodbath for bloodbath with the Americans, with the Seminoles escaping to Spanish-held Florida for safety.

President Monroe, in a letter dated Sunday, December 28, 1817, authorized Jackson to quell the Seminole threat—and suggested that a broader victory would not be unwelcome. "This is not a time for you to think of repose," Monroe wrote Jackson. "Great interests are at issue, and until our course is carried through triumphantly . . . you ought not to withdraw your active support from it." Was Monroe only interested in subduing the Seminoles? Or was he hinting, and perhaps hoping, that Jackson might go further, seizing Florida and driving out the Spanish?

Whatever Monroe meant—and the letter is diplomatically oblique—Jackson moved against both the

Seminoles and the Spanish and conquered Florida. In the course of the invasion he ordered the executions of two British subjects, provoking a crisis with England. Jackson claimed he had authorization from Monroe for the seizure of Florida, but no evidence of such permission (beyond the December 28 letter) ever came to light. Jackson's adventure roiled Washington. In Monroe's Cabinet, Secretary of War John C. Calhoun and Treasury Secretary William Crawford denounced the seizure; Secretary of State John Quincy Adams, who believed in the virtues of American control of the continent, defended Jackson. In the House of Representatives, Speaker Henry Clay—like Calhoun and Crawford, a man with presidential ambitions—denounced Jackson, arguing that to allow Jackson's actions to stand uncensored would mark "a triumph of the military over the civil authority . . . a triumph over the constitution of the land."

While a congressional probe failed to produce a resolution of censure against Jackson for overstepping his authority, the questions about Florida—like those about his marriage, his duels, and martial law in New Orleans—provided Jackson's political foes with much ammunition. There would be more than a few fights over these issues in the 1820s, a decade in which Andrew Jackson moved from the front lines of the South and West to the trenches of national politics.

THE DIARY OF a young woman from South Carolina who spent two days at the Hermitage with Jackson and Rachel in September 1827, a year before his election as president and her death, offers an intimate account of the Jacksons' married life, of Rachel's kindness, and of Jackson's force of personality. The traveler, Julia Ann Conner, was from a well-connected family, and she and her party arrived at the Hermitage at dusk on Monday, September 3, 1827. As the visitors entered the front hall, they looked up to see General and Mrs. Jackson coming down the main stairs. Jackson struck Conner as a "**venerable, dignified, fine-looking man,** perfectly easy in manner. . . . Mrs. Jackson received us with equal politeness." Rachel led her guests into the drawing room for refreshments, then took Conner out into the garden for a walk. At supper Jackson "pronounced with much solemnity of manner a short grace and then performed the honors of the table with an attentive politeness which usually characterizes a gentleman— everything was neat and elegant—a complete service of French china, rich cut glass—damask napkins."

The house was filled with history, and with tokens of tribute. The brace of pistols Lafayette had given to Washington were on the mantelpiece, a gift to Jackson from the Washington family. "They are preserved with almost sacred veneration," Conner said, as was a small pocket spy glass of Washington's. There was a silver urn from South Carolina, a gold snuffbox from New York—all signs of respect to the Hero of New Orleans.

The Hero himself cast a kind of spell over Conner. "The manners of the General are so perfectly easy and polished and those of his wife so replete with kindness and benevolence that you are placed at **once at ease,**" she said.

Conner owed Jackson a small debt: he helped her at chess. She was playing another houseguest, and Conner recalled that Jackson "stood at my side, and being an excellent player he frequently directed my moves—apparently much interested in the fate of the game . . . there were no traces of the **'military chieftain' as he is called!**"

This sketch of Jackson the tactician—a player of chess, a game that rewards strategy and foresight—explains much about Jackson's character. He could sometimes seem reckless, but more often he was playing the games of politics and war with the kind of skill and patience chess requires. And Conner was surely right when she observed that he was "much interested in the fate of the game"—he was always interested in the fate of the game, or of the battle, or of the vote.

CONNER DETECTED SOMETHING in her few days under his roof that many of Jackson's foes never did: that he was far more than a frontier soldier. His enemies never quite saw that the largest fact about Jackson was not a problem with his "passions"—the contemporary sense of the word was "temper"—but his ability, more often than not, to govern them and harness the energies that would have driven other, less sophisticated men to political ruin. "Sophisticated" is not a word often used to describe Andrew Jackson, but it should be. The number of scandals that threatened to consume him between his admission to the bar and his election to the White House—martial law in New Orleans, the execution of mutineers in the field, invading Florida arguably without proper authority, killing British subjects, his murky marriage, his slaying of Charles Dickinson, the gunfight with the Bentons—would have ended most political careers.

Yet Jackson endured and conquered. He knew how to make amends when he had to and possessed enough charm to turn longtime enemies into new friends. Jackson could, of course, lapse into alarming violence, but he also had a capacity for political grace and conciliation when the spirit moved him. In Washington in 1823–24, Jackson spent a few months as a senator from Tennessee. Jackson needed to put as many hatreds and grudges as he could to rest in preparation for the 1824 presidential campaign. Thomas Hart Benton—of the brawl with the Benton brothers—was by then a senator from Missouri. He and Jackson served together on a committee. Writing to Rachel, Jackson's friend and Senate colleague John Henry Eaton reported: "The General is at peace and in friendship with . . . Col. Benton: he is in harmony and good understanding with every body, a thing I know you will be happy to hear." Eaton was not exaggerating. "His temper was placable as well as irascible, and his reconciliations were cordial and sincere," Benton said after Jackson's death. "Of that, my own case was a signal instance. After a deadly feud, I became his confidential adviser; was offered the highest marks of his favor; and received from his dying bed a message of friendship, dictated when life was departing, and when he would have to pause for breath."

Jackson could absorb the essence of a situation at a

glance. "The character of his mind was that of judgment, with a rapid and almost intuitive perception, followed by an instant and decisive action," said Benton. Was his "instant and decisive action" always right? No—far from it. But behind his bluster lay a skill for controlling, containing, and even erasing the damage his rashness could cause. **"No man,"** a longtime Jackson intimate told James Parton, **"knew better than Andrew Jackson when to get into a passion and when not."** To manage conflicting forces of emotion and pragmatism is the rarest of political gifts. For all the indictments to the contrary, Jackson had that gift—and used it to further his own fortunes, and to secure the future of the nation. Faith in his ability to maneuver out of any corner—to face down a man at twenty-four feet while blood leaked into his own boot, to save a wounded arm after taking another bullet, to elude enemies in the forest, to arrest an outlaw, to manipulate, usually from afar, congressional investigations—sustained him. "He was a firm believer in the goodness of a superintending Providence, and in the eventual right judgment and justice of the people," said Benton. "I have seen him at the most desperate part of his fortunes, and never saw him waver in the belief that all would come right in the end."

But how did he transform himself from a "slobbering" young man lashing out at an unfair and largely uncaring world to become what Henry Wise, the Virginia governor and an astute Jackson observer, called a cool calculator? Part of the answer lies in the fact that his ambition to succeed was matched by his intellectual capacity to realize that his anger would tend to block, not fuel, his rise. It is the unusual human being who can identify and control particular impulses, but Jackson turned himself into such a man in order to get what he wanted, which was a place among those at the top, not the bottom, of life.

He referred to his ability to manage his temper as his "Philosophy." When Rachel was under attack in the 1828 campaign, Jackson struggled to hold his anger in check. "How hard it is to keep the cowhide from some of these villains," he confided to John Coffee. "I have made many sacrifices for the good of my country—but the present, being placed in a situation that I cannot act, and punish those slanderers, not only of me, but Mrs. J. is a sacrifice too great to be well endure[d] yet . . . I must bear with it." Jackson strained to remain calm. "My Philosophy is almost worn out," he said as the campaign continued, "but all my enemies expect is, to urge me to some rash action, this they cannot do until the election is over." Even then, Jackson would not give his foes the satisfaction of playing into the caricature of a wild-eyed backwoodsman brandishing a whip and a pistol. He would turn a serene—and sad, after Rachel's death, but still serene—face to the country.

In doing so Jackson mirrored a national phenomenon. Control over how one appeared to the rest of the world was a subject of popular concern in the America of Jackson's time, and he was in many ways an example of a recognizable type: a man from the bottom rungs of society on the rise and in search of a code of manners. "What makes the gentleman?" had once been a topic of debate between Andrew and an uncle of his on a rainy day in Waxhaw. "The boy said, Education; the uncle, Good Principles," a son of the uncle recalled to James Parton.

They were both right: principles presumably flowed from education, whether or not the education came in a classroom. For all of the Founders' talk about equality and natural rights and the evils of monarchy and aristocracy, Americans were obsessed with marks of class distinction from colonial days. It began, in a way, with the greatest Founder of all: as a schoolboy, George Washington filled part of an exercise book with one hundred and ten **Rules of Civility and Decent Behavior in Company and Conversation**. General Daniel Smith, Andrew Donelson's maternal grandfather, advised young men in his family to consult **Lord Chesterfield's Letters,** a kind of manners manual written by Philip Stanhope, the Earl of Chesterfield. The essence of Chesterfield was to make oneself pleasant and genial but to be forever wary of others. Jackson, who believed in self-mastery, certainly spoke in such terms. "You cannot have forgotten the advice I give to all my young friends," Jackson wrote an acquaintance in 1826, "that is to say, as they pass through life have **apparent confidence in all, real confidence** in none, until from actual experience it is found that the individual is worthy of it—from this rule I have never departed. . . . When I have found men mere politicians, bending to the popular breeze and changing with it, for the self-popularity, I have ever shunned them, believing that they were unworthy of my confidence—but **still** treat them with hospitality and politeness."

This is deft Machiavellian—and Chesterfieldian—counsel. Trust no one except those who have proved themselves, yet never let those who have failed the test know that when they look at you, they are looking at a mask, not at your true self. Life, Jackson was saying, particularly political life, can be theatrical—an exercise in assessing other people's minds and motives and then designing your own response with an awareness of the gulf between appearance and reality. It was Chesterfield's creed, and Jackson subscribed to it.

CHAPTER 3

A MARRIAGE, A DEFEAT,
AND A VICTORY

THE YEAR 1824 was pivotal for Jackson and his family. It was the year Jackson first ran for president, and the year Emily and Andrew Donelson married. Raised in comfort but far from spoiled, Emily and Andrew, well-educated and well-mannered, began their married lives with high expectations. Jackson thought Donelson a likely president; Emily impressed those around her. "Emily, it is hoped, will make a fine woman and I know her to be more than ordinarily smart," her sister remarked. Their lives were already interwoven with politics. Educated at West Point, Transylvania University, and Nashville's Cumberland College, Andrew Donelson delivered a July Fourth oration at Nashville in the summer of 1824, and he spoke like an aspiring statesman—a bit floridly and overlong, perhaps, but he was young, and there was time to learn. In his uncle he had the best of teachers.

According to family tradition, Donelson was eighteen, on his way to West Point, when he found his heart stirring for the redheaded Emily, then just ten. She was leaving her log schoolhouse on Lebanon

Road, heading for home, which was known as "the Mansion" in the family. Donelson happened across the schoolchildren. "On the way, a stream had to be waded or crossed on a narrow log," a family chronicler wrote. "Other children got over as best they could, but not so Princess Emily, for her Fairy Prince took her in his arms, restoring her to earth on the other side. In later years Donelson related that he realized then that he loved her." By 1823, the love affair was evident, and Jackson began singling Emily out for his regards in letters to Donelson. "Present me affectionately to Miss E.," he wrote in January 1824.

Jackson trusted Donelson. "I sincerely thank you for your attention to my business," Jackson wrote his nephew from Washington in April 1824. "I assure you it gives me pleasure to find that my private concerns are kept so snug and all my debts paid, and accounts so nearly closed."

Flattering Donelson, Jackson told him: "I hold no correspondence with any one but yourself. . . . I will have to bring you on with me; I have been this winter at a great Loss for some confidential friend to aid me." To be with Jackson probably meant a move to Washington, for his presidential prospects looked strong. According to family tradition, it was this letter, in the spring of 1824, that prompted Donelson to propose to Emily.

He did not want to go to the capital without her as his bride. After reading his uncle's summons to duty, Donelson went to Emily and, in a conversation at the Mansion, the two realized they had reached a turning point. Rachel and Andrew Jackson helped things along. "Romance was not a stranger to Rachel's heart, and she had watched with the greatest interest the growing fondness between Andrew and Emily and had encouraged its development," noted the family chronicler. "She would send the young lovers out to walk under the tall poplars, or to sit together under the vine-covered bower in her garden." Andrew and Emily became engaged in Rachel's Hermitage garden. A September date was set.

Jackson was delighted with the match. The Donelsons were the kind of young people he loved to have with him: smart, attractive, loyal. As a wedding gift Jackson gave them a large tract of land within a mile of the Hermitage. Weeks after the wedding, performed at the Mansion by the Reverend William Hume, they would be on the road with Aunt and Uncle Jackson, heading to Washington. From their experiences on the journey, it is clear that their married life began as it would go on: marked by politics, drama, and risk.

Just a few days from Nashville, outside Harrodsburg, Kentucky, they all nearly died in a serious carriage accident. "The tongue snapped at the top of a very steep and rocky hill, and it was by the interposition of divine Providence that our lives were spared," Emily wrote home. By the next day, though, "a splendid ball" at Lexington had lifted their spirits, and it was on to Washington, where an amazed Emily watched Lafayette and Jackson greet each other at their lodgings.

Between scenes of great men saluting each other, evenings "crowded with company," and "boarding at an excellent house," Emily was finding life with Uncle congenial. "We are very comfortably situated here. We live very well [and] have everything in abundance," she wrote to her mother in December 1824. "Everything," she added, "was new and interesting to me."

Emily and Andrew spent their Sundays at the more fashionable Episcopal church rather than the Presbyterian and Methodist ones Rachel frequented; for Rachel it was another sign of the capital's dissipated ways. "Much visiting in the grandest Circles in the City," Emily's father wrote of the young couple's initial journey to the capital. "I am afraid it will spoil Emily and Andrew." The Donelsons enjoyed themselves, going to plays such as **Virginius; or, The Liberation of Rome** and **The Village Lawyer**. "The extravagance is in dressing and running to parties," Rachel wrote home. He kept quiet about it, but Jackson's own view of life in the city had more in common with the young people's than it did with his wife's. In 1824–25, however, politics was more consuming than parties, and Jackson was losing.

JACKSON'S MOST SIGNIFICANT rivals in national politics in the 1820s and 1830s were formidable men. There was John C. Calhoun, the tall, thin, Yale-educated South Carolinian with a brilliant mind and a weakness for the cause of states' rights and for the preservation of slavery. There was Henry Clay of Kentucky, a man not unlike Jackson—a frontier lawyer with a taste for gambling and strong drink who rose in the world through government service, became master of a great house in Lexington, Ashland, and was driven by presidential ambitions. A career politician, Clay saw the emerging power of the West and longed to be its voice—and its first son to live in the White House. There was John Quincy Adams, the son of the first President Adams, a scholarly diplomat and legislator whose social shyness masked a bold vision of national destiny: he championed, among other things, a proposed American university and great internal construction projects. And there was Andrew Jackson.

There were, at the same time, more and more ordinary people to think of, as more and more ordinary people—all male, to be sure, and all white—shared in the extension of the right to vote. By 1828, nearly all states had essentially universal male suffrage. The result: a surge in eligible voters, many with an economic stake in the future of the country. In 1828 and 1832, the years of Jackson's White House victories, record numbers of such Americans cast ballots. Turnout rose from 27 percent in 1824 to 57 percent in 1828.

The men who gathered in Philadelphia in 1787 had not been interested in establishing the rule of the majority. Quite the opposite: **The Federalist** and the debates on the floor of the Constitutional Convention largely concerned how the new nation might most effectively check the popular will. Hence the Electoral College, the election of senators by state legislatures, and limited suffrage. The prevailing term for America's governing philosophy was republicanism—an elegant Enlightenment-era system of balances and counterweights that tended to put decisive power in the hands of elites elected, at least in theory, by a country of landowning yeomen. The people, broadly defined, were not to be trusted with too much power.

This creed, best articulated by James Madison and Alexander Hamilton, lay at the heart of presidential politics in the first decades of the nineteenth century, years in which a small establishment in the capital essentially decided on its own who would have the chance to live in the White House. Nominees were chosen by congressional caucuses on Capitol Hill (called "King Caucus"), and the men who were nominated to run tended to be secretaries of state from Virginia or Massachusetts. It was a tidy, insular way to choose a president, and it lasted for more than a quarter of a century.

Then came 1824. In a four-way race between Jackson, Secretary of State John Quincy Adams, Speaker of the House Henry Clay, and Secretary of the Treasury William Crawford, Jackson led in the popular vote for president, but no candidate had the necessary Electoral College majority, so the contest went to the House of Representatives. There Jackson lost.

The reason: Henry Clay. In one of the defining rivalries of the age, Clay hated Jackson and Jackson hated Clay. Clay feared that a man of Jackson's temperament might turn the Republic into a dictatorship and said that he, for one, could not see how "killing two thousand five hundred Englishmen at New Orleans qualifies for the difficult and complicated business of the chief magistracy." After the resolution of the 1824 election, Jackson believed Clay, as he put it to Sam Houston, "certainly the basest, meanest scoundrel that ever disgraced the image of his God."

Amid the maneuvering in the House, Clay, not surprisingly, decided to support Adams. The Jacksonian argument that Clay's duty lay with backing the people's choice—Jackson, of course—carried no weight with Clay. Writing from the Senate floor on Monday, January 24, 1825, Jackson said, with some bitterness: "It shows the want of principle in all concerned. . . . It will give the people a full view of our political weathercocks here, and how little confidence ought to be reposed in the professions of some great political characters." The election took place on Wednesday, February 9, 1825.

Five days later Clay accepted Adams's offer to become secretary of state, the office from which presidents seemed to spring, further infuriating Jackson. Briefing William Lewis, Jackson called Clay "the **Judas** of the West" and added, "his end will be the same." He became convinced that Clay had sold his votes to Adams in exchange for the Cabinet appointment, and Jackson's fury at this alleged "corrupt bargain" never abated. "If at this early period of the experiment of our Republic, men are found base and corrupt enough to barter the rights of the people for proffered office, what may we not expect from the spread of this corruption hereafter," Jackson told Lewis. Washington, Rachel said, was a "terrible place."

That the election unfolded according to the letter of the Constitution did not matter to Jackson. The way he saw it, the son of a president, Adams, had struck a deal with the Speaker of the House, Clay, to elevate Adams, then the secretary of state, to the presidency. Though much may have been implied between them, the likely truth is that Clay and Adams did not reach an explicit deal. Clay's antipathy for Jackson was already consuming, and so the Kentuckian's decision to support Adams made the most political logic; for Adams, Clay, as a prominent and skillful lawmaker from an important state, was an obvious choice for secretary of state. No explanation would satisfy Jackson, however: he thought the country was watching the founding of a dynastic line that could perpetuate itself despite the wishes of the people.

BUT THERE WAS nothing he could do. The campaign was over. On the evening of the day on which he had lost the presidency, Jackson appeared at a party given by President Monroe at the White House. President-elect Adams, an observer noted, was "by himself; General Jackson had a large, handsome lady on his arm." Coming upon each other, neither man immediately moved. Adams and Jackson held each other's stare. Here, feet apart, on a Washington winter's evening, with the capital's elite swirling around them, stood two of the most powerful men in the nation. Adams had been born with everything, Jackson with nothing. Yet it was Jackson, not Adams, who met the moment with skill.

"How do you do, Mr. Adams?" Jackson said cheerily, extending his free hand. "I give you my left hand, for the right, as you see, is devoted to the fair: I hope you are very well, sir."

"Very well, sir; I hope General Jackson is well," Adams replied, an eyewitness said, "with chilling coldness." "It was curious to see the western planter, the Indian fighter, the stern soldier, who had written his country's glory in the blood of the enemy at New Orleans," recalled an observer, "genial and gracious in the midst of a court, while the old courtier and diplomat was stiff, rigid, cold as a statue!"

Jackson moved through the party and back to his hotel as Washington hummed with reports of his grace in the face of his foe. "You have, by your dignity and forbearance under all these outrages, won the people to your love," a friend wrote Jackson. Still, it was an unhappy conclusion to the campaign and, in the family circle, to Andrew and Emily's honeymoon. Jackson paid the boarding bill at the hotel—between the dinners and the wine, brandy, whiskey, and champagne, the total came to $86.25—and he and his family left for Tennessee.

He would be back. "Genl. Jackson's friends have made, and are still making, very great efforts to place him in the Chair," said Daniel Webster in 1827. "He is a good soldier and I believe a very honest man, but some of us think him wholly unfit for the place to which he aspires. Military achievement however, is very visible and [has] palpable merit, and on this account the Genl. is exceedingly popular, in some of the States."

The force driving Jackson after 1824: a belief in the primacy of the will of the people over the whim of the powerful, with himself as the chief interpreter and enactor of that will. The idea and image of a strong president claiming a mandate from the voters to unite the nation and direct the affairs of the country from the White House took permanent root in the Age of Jackson. "I have great confidence in the virtue of a great majority of the people, and I cannot fear the result," Jackson wrote in 1828. As long as the government heeds the popular will, Jackson said, "the republic is safe, and its main pillars—virtue, religion and morality—will be fostered by a majority of the people."

IN JACKSON'S ERA America was moving from a way of life based on farms to one fundamentally linked to a larger industrialized economy. Railroads, canals, and roads were tying the country together. Factories were growing, manufacturing burgeoning. When Jackson became president, the railroad was hardly more than a dream; by the end of the 1830s, there were 3,200 miles of track. The cotton textile workforce more than tripled from 1820 to 1840, and the number of iron wage earners increased fivefold. Immigration, much of it from Great Britain and Ireland, rose steadily in Jackson's White House years, from twenty-seven thousand in 1828 to eighty thousand in 1837. Regular transatlantic steamship travel began in 1838.

The Jackson years were also roiled by conversations and controversies about race, religion, immigrants, and the role of women. In 1829, the year Jackson took office, David Walker, the son of a slave, published his **Appeal to the Coloured Citizens of the World,** a popular pamphlet that worried Southern slaveowners and inspired abolitionists. The blacks of the United States, wrote Walker, were "the most degraded, wretched, and abject set of beings that ever lived since the world began, and I pray God that none like us ever may live again until time shall be no more." If an **"attempt"** was made by blacks for liberty, Walker said, the slaves should feel justified to take up arms. "Now, I ask you, had you not rather be killed than to be a slave to a tyrant, who takes the life of your mother, wife and dear little children? . . . Believe this, that it is no more harm for you to kill a man, who is trying to kill you, than it is for you to take a drink of water when thirsty." From 1829 to 1837, there were slave disturbances, revolts, or conspiracies in Kentucky, Virginia, Mississippi, Missouri, and Louisiana. From 1830 to 1835, Louisiana, Georgia, Virginia, Alabama, South Carolina, and North Carolina passed laws prohibiting teaching slaves to read. In 1831, William Lloyd Garrison began publishing the **Liberator.**

It was a time of reform and new thinking. In 1830, the first tract on birth control in North America, **Moral Physiology,** was published, and in 1833 Oberlin College, in Ohio, was founded—the first American college to be open to blacks and whites, men and women. In these decades the **American Journal of Science and Arts** explored chemistry, geology, zoology, botany, and mineralogy, and by the middle of the nineteenth century "scientists" were distinct from "philosophers." During Jackson's years in power liberal arts colleges were founded at more than twice the rate of the previous decade.

It was also an age of great faith and of militant atheism. Evangelical fervor was a constant force, with revivals making converts to Christianity by the thousands. In upstate New York the young Joseph Smith believed he was told by an angel to restore the Church of Jesus Christ, and so the Mormon faith was born. "There is no country in the world where the Christian religion remains a greater influence over the souls of men than in America," Alexis de Tocqueville wrote. Taking advantage of the nation's liberty of conscience, skeptics and doubters spoke out against the pious temper of the time. For eight days in Cincinnati in April 1829, two men—the evangelical Alexander Campbell and the atheist Robert Owen—faced off in a public debate pitting Christianity against atheism. Frances Trollope, a writer and mother of the novelist Anthony Trollope, was there. "All this I think could only have happened in America," she said.

In domestic politics, the familiar divisions since the Founding between Federalists and Democratic-Republicans—or, to put it in personal terms, between adherents of Alexander Hamilton and adherents of Thomas Jefferson—had broken down, with the Federalists largely extinct and the Jeffersonians turning into the Republicans, a hodgepodge of competing political and regional interests gathered under one broad label. By 1820, the year President James Monroe, a Jeffersonian, was seeking a second term, the party of Hamilton failed to field a candidate. Monroe ran unopposed.

LIKE MOST SIGNIFICANT historical shifts, the rise of democracy is a complex phenomenon, and its causes and effects extend far beyond a single man. But it was Jackson who gave voice and force at the highest levels to America's ever-widening hopes and aspirations. Democracy was making its stand.

In his own mind, Jackson was a figure of Jeffersonian restoration—an Old Republican, in the vernacular of the time, as opposed to a Federalist. To people like Jackson, "Republican" connoted Jefferson, states' rights, and the citizenry; "Federalist" evoked images of Hamilton, a central government, and an aristocracy. In the battles of George Washington's two administrations, the task of opposing the Federalist vision of a country governed more by the elites than by the people had fallen to Jefferson, who liked to think he represented an understanding of liberty that put as much power as possible closer to the states and to the people—really, the yeomanry—than to large, distant, and more easily corrupted national institutions. Yet to recall the conflict between the Federalist Alexander Hamilton and the Democratic-Republican Thomas Jefferson as a clear-cut matter of big versus small government, or federal power versus states' rights, or a strong presidency versus a dominant Congress, is overly simplistic and misses critical nuances. Yes, Jefferson philosophically believed in a smaller federal establishment, in the rights of the states, and in congressional supremacy. In practice, however, he cheerfully extended the role of the executive to, among other things, acquiring the Louisiana territory. He was an energetic president—more so than his immediate predecessor, Adams, or the men who, until 1829, followed him in the office.

Jackson took the Jeffersonian vision of the centrality of the people further, and he took Jefferson's view of the role of the president further still. To Jackson, the idea of the sovereignty of the many was compatible with a powerful executive. He saw that liberty required security, that freedom required order, that the well-being of the parts of the Union required that the whole remain intact. If he felt a temporary resort to autocracy was necessary to preserve democracy, Jackson would not hesitate. He would do what had to be done. In this he set an example on which other presidents would draw in times of national struggle. There were moments, Abraham Lincoln argued during the Civil War, when "measures otherwise unconstitutional might become lawful by becoming indispensable to the preservation of the Constitution through the preservation of the nation." It was a Jacksonian way of looking at the world.

IN NOVEMBER 1828, Jackson won 56 percent of the popular vote, defeating Adams in the Electoral College by a margin of 178 to 83. Jackson's partisans thrilled to the news; their devotion was deep. "The Hickory is a tall, graceful tree, indigenous to America," wrote the **Argus of Western America**, the paper edited by Amos Kendall, who would hand it over to Francis Preston Blair to come to Washington. "It yields gracefully to the gale of spring, and bows in whispers to the breath of autumn, but when the storms of winter invade the forest, it presents its recoiling strength to the blast, and saves its frailer neighbors from the fury of the storm."

Clay watched in horror from the State Department. That the election would even be close, Clay remarked to Webster, was "mortifying and sickening to the hearts of the real lovers of free Government." When Jackson's victory became clear, Clay thought "no greater calamity" had struck the United States "since we were a free people."

In the first weeks of 1829, Clay began thinking about his own campaign to defeat Jackson in four years' time—and, for a moment, Jackson's opponents thought providence might save them from "the People's President" altogether. There were reports that Jackson was sick, too sick, possibly, to live long. There were even suggestions that he, not Rachel, had died. "On Wednesday morning, we were waked with the rumour of the death of the Hero, which put the City generally into a state of great consternation," Louisa Catherine Adams, the wife of John Quincy Adams, wrote to their son Charles Francis on Sunday, February 1. Mrs. Adams's intelligence was wrong, but the establishment held out some hope. "The rumour of

Genl. J's death has subsided," Webster wrote a friend. "My own private opinion, however, still is, that he is very ill, and I have my doubts whether he will ever reach this place."

Jackson, however, arrived safely in Washington on Wednesday, February 11, 1829. He was not entirely well—he never was—and, Emily said, had "a very bad cough and has been a good deal troubled with headache and fever."

Cannon fire and a marching band were supposed to greet his arrival, but instead Jackson slipped into town quietly. Alfred Mordecai, a West Point contemporary of Andrew Donelson's, was in Washington and happened to see Jackson through his window that morning. It was a humble train, Mordecai said, "a plain carriage drawn by two horses followed by a single black servant." Mordecai was struck by the gulf between the emotions Jackson aroused and the reality of the president-elect's little party. A man alternately hailed as a "demigod and Hero" and denounced as a "tyrant," Mordecai recalled, arrived without ceremony: "What a spectacle must this present to those who have had opportunities of seeing the entrance of European potentates into their capitals to take possession of their thrones."

Once in the capital, Jackson was the center of a swirl of office seekers in a suite at John Gadsby's National Hotel, at Sixth Street and Pennsylvania Avenue. From across the city, Clay called them a "motley host of greedy expectants." Nearer at hand, Emily veered between her sickbed and society. "My health was so bad," she told her sister in a letter home, "I was scarcely able to keep out of bed one half of my time." But she discharged her social duties. "Owing to the death of our dear aunt and our being in mourning," Emily reported, she avoided most parties but stayed "very busy" with "so many visits to return."

Andrew Donelson and William Lewis were busy sorting out real friends from opportunists. Major William Polk, who had fought in South Carolina during the Revolution, was an old friend and genuine caller, and Donelson noted how Jackson, on shaking hands with Polk, was transported back to a skirmish against Tarleton. "'My dear old friend, how glad I am to see you!'" Donelson recalled Jackson saying. "'I fancy I can see your red face during Tarleton's raid upon the Waxhaw settlement, when you and I were running down the lane, closely pursued by the British cavalry!'"

JACKSON'S CABINET CHOICES (Martin Van Buren for state, John Eaton for war, Samuel Ingham for Treasury, John Branch for the navy, John Berrien for attorney general, and William Barry for postmaster general) struck many as underwhelming, and the private circle of advisers (Donelson, Lewis, and Amos Kendall of Kentucky among them) produced similar worries.

Kendall personified much of what the Washington establishment feared about Jackson and his men. Born in Massachusetts in 1789, Kendall grew up poor, went to Dartmouth, and eventually moved to Kentucky, where he practiced law, served as a postmaster, tutored Henry Clay's children, began to edit a newspaper (the **Argus**), and became a fervent advocate for Jackson. Moving to Washington with the new administration, Kendall officially became fourth auditor of the Treasury; unofficially he was a thoroughly political animal who advised the president and promoted the White House's causes in the capital and beyond. He was what later generations would call a networker. At a wedding party shortly after his arrival in Washington, Kendall met Major General Alexander Macomb, the head of the army. "He is very sociable, and I was surprised to find him a Jackson man," Kendall wrote to his wife. "He promised to call and see me, and I hope to find him a valuable acquaintance." Like many of Jackson's other allies, Kendall was an unknown quantity in Washington. They formed, Webster said, "a numerous **Council** about the President elect; and if report be true, it is a Council which only 'makes that darker, which was dark enough before.'"

Accustomed to wearing the mask of command, Jackson appeared serene, dignified, even regal. Emily wrote that he "always goes through everything 'like a hero.'" In interviews between the president-elect and visitors seeking a job, wrote the anti-Jackson **Daily National Intelligencer**, "a courteous and dignified decorum is observed," which prompted the paper to say archly, "Citizens who visit the President must not fall into the egregious error of supposing that they may treat him as the Farmer of Tennessee, or the unpretending republican."

While her husband worked with Jackson on the preparations for the new administration, Emily rallied from her sickbed and went shopping with Mary Eastin. The two women splurged on expensive cologne, soap, jewelry, good black veils, and yards of black satin at Abbott's, a chic Washington store. The inauguration was scheduled for the East Front of the Capitol at noon on Wednesday, March 4, 1829.

WASHINGTON WAS UNSEASONABLY frigid the week before Jackson took office. "There has not been a warm day since I came here, although I have often seen the peach trees in blossom in February," Webster wrote his sister on Monday, March 2, 1829. "The ground is still covered with snow, the river hard frozen, and the weather steadily cold." But the chilly spell broke and the capital thawed on the morning of the fourth. Winter, for the moment, gave way to spring.

Recording some "small gossiping anecdotes" in his diary, John Quincy Adams reported how "indignant" a Jackson caller had been when introduced to the president-elect "as an Aristocrat." Democracy was in; elitism was out. New forces were being unleashed and new paths taken. "When he comes, he will bring a breeze with him," Webster said of Jackson. "Which way it will blow, I cannot tell." He was not the only one.

CHAPTER 4

★

YOU KNOW BEST, MY DEAR

A T THE WHITE House, President Adams was dour in defeat. "He seems to have been in bad health," Leonidas Polk, an Episcopal seminarian in Alexandria, Virginia, wrote home after a visit with Adams. Henry Clay, meanwhile, was ill, lying on a sofa in his drawing room at Decatur House, the three-story brick town house across from the White House. When Margaret Bayard Smith, a chronicler of Washington life who had lived in the capital since 1800, called on Clay, he was "scarcely able to sit up . . . very pale, his eyes sunk in his head and his countenance sad and melancholy." At the Clays' and elsewhere, belongings were being boxed and set in straw to make way for the Jacksonians. To many in established Washington— a city and a culture of nearly three decades' standing, with roots stretching to the first Adams and to Jefferson—Jackson's arrival signaled the destruction of the rule of the nation in an atmosphere of geniality and gentility.

Taking up his presidential duties, Jackson thought the country was suffering from a crisis of corruption.

If virtue was central to the well-being of the nation, then corruption and selfishness were corrosive, and could be fatal. By corruption, Jackson did not mean only scandal and mismanagement. He meant it in a broader sense: in the marshaling of power and influence by a few institutions and interests that sought to profit at the expense of the whole. He was not against competition in the marketplace of goods and ideas. Like the Founders, he believed in vigorous debate, and like Adam Smith, he put his faith in the capacity of free individuals to work out their destinies. But he was very much against the special deal or the selfish purpose, and he was very much in favor of his own role as defender of the many and protector of the nation. In Washington, he was intent on dismantling the kind of permanent federal establishment that created a climate in which, in his view, insiders such as John Quincy Adams and Henry Clay could thrive no matter what the people beyond Washington wanted.

Jackson worried about the power of the Second Bank of the United States, an institution that held the public's money but was not subject to the public's control, or to the president's. Presided over by Nicholas Biddle—brilliant, arrogant, and as willful in his way as Andrew Jackson was in his—the Bank, headquartered in a Greek Revival building on Chestnut Street in Philadelphia, was a rival interest that, Jackson believed, made loans to influence elections, paid retainers to pro-Bank lawmakers, and could control much of the nation's economy on a whim.

. . . .

IN SOUTH CAROLINA, Jackson knew, the state's cotton and rice planters had been driven nearly mad by fears of slave rebellions. The previous decade had suggested one avenue: nullification. An early test of federal authority by South Carolina occurred after a slave conspiracy, perhaps led by Denmark Vesey, in 1822. International treaties allowed black seamen who docked in Charleston to come ashore and visit other blacks, but when it emerged that visiting sailors had possibly played a role in the plot, South Carolina ordered that black seamen had to be jailed while their ships were in port. Supreme Court Justice William Johnson, who had circuit authority over the state, ruled the law unconstitutional, but South Carolina continued to jail the sailors. The state was motivated by a fundamental fear: slave violence. According to the state senate, the "duty to guard against insubordination or insurrection" was "paramount to all **laws**, all **treaties**, all **constitutions**." Washington decided not to force matters—and South Carolina thus overrode federal authority.

The state had remained unsettled throughout the decade. South Carolina was in economic trouble, its whites were wary of slave rebellion, and protective national tariffs agitated the state even more. (Cotton prices were falling for a variety of reasons, but the tariffs, which protected American manufacturing, were a handy target, for the duties drove up prices agrarian states had to pay for things produced in manufacturing states and lowered demand abroad for Southern cotton.) Their fury had led to talk of more nullification—they recalled their de facto victory in the case of the black seamen—and perhaps secession. Thomas Cooper, the president of South Carolina College, stated the matter succinctly in 1827: the time may be at hand, he said, when the state would have "to calculate the value of the Union, and ask of what use to us is this most unequal alliance." For the hotheads things grew even less equal in 1828, when Congress passed, and President Adams signed, what became known as the Tariff of Abominations. The measure raised duties from 33 percent to 50 percent. The tariffs hurt, but should be seen as only one of several forces that led the state to consider shattering a union that seemed at best indifferent and at worst hostile to South Carolina's way of life. The chief issue was the core of that way of life: slavery.

The sense of powerlessness in South Carolina was wide and deep. In a pair of letters written to Calhoun in April and May, Francis W. Pickens of Edgefield, South Carolina—a lawyer-planter and future legislator and governor—expressed a kind of romantic regional pride as he worried about the South's ability to protect its interests. It was, Pickens said, "with the most melancholy feelings that I look on a great and gallant people, sacrificed by a government over which they have practically at present no restrictive power"— a state of things that left open possibilities of further taxation and even the abolition of slavery. "I believe after a series of years that no government that has the power to collect taxes and declare war, can be restrained but by a display of sufficient power to break it up," Pickens said. Such harsh words seem to have made Calhoun—still very much hoping to preside over the Union from the White House—uncomfortable, for he lectured Pickens about the dangers of "revolutionary" talk. Pickens denied that he was thinking of the government's immediate destruction but did not waver from asserting that force, or the threat of force, should always be an option. He was a pragmatic man, telling Calhoun "that there can be but very little practical effect produced by any thing short of a display of real power."

IN THE VAST stretches of Indian land, particularly in the Southwest, Jackson saw a monumental task: the removal of Native Americans to lands west of the Mississippi. It was, said Congressman Edward Everett of Massachusetts, "the greatest question which ever came before Congress, short of the question of peace and war." Jackson believed in removal with all his heart, and by refusing to entertain any other scenario, he was as ferocious in inflicting harm on a people as he often was in defending the rights of those he thought of as the people. To Jackson the interests of whites were paramount in the removal question. To those who argued for Indian rights, he justified his course by arguing that removal would guarantee the survival of the tribes, which would otherwise be wiped out, and by asserting that coexistence was impossible. In an 1833 book entitled **Indian Wars of the West**, Timothy Flint summed up the arguments of those in favor of removal: "Collisions, murders, escapes of fugitive slaves, and the operations of laws and usages so essentially different, as those of the white and red people, will forever keep alive between the contiguous parties feuds, quarrels, and retaliations, which can never cease until one of the parties becomes extinct." Flint concluded that advocates of removal "see the race perpetuated in opulence and peace in the fair prairies of the west. Here they are to grow up distinct red nations, with schools and churches, the anvil, the loom, and the plough—a sort of Arcadian race between our borders and the Rocky Mountains, standing memorials of the kindness and good faith of our government." But they would instead become reminders of the government's bloodthirstiness and of the American people's greed. Removal was, however, of a piece with Jackson's broader vision of securing the country—even if he was securing it primarily for the advancement of the interests of whites.

IN THE CHURCHES and meeting rooms of organizations such as the American Sunday School Union, in pulpits and pews, the leaders of evangelical Christianity's newly energetic campaign to bring religious precepts to public life were eager to enlist Jackson in their ranks. Church and state, these Christians believed, should be intertwined, arguing, in the words of a movement pamphlet entitled **An Inquiry into the Moral and Religious Character of the American Government,** that "Without religion, law ceases to be law, for it has no bond, and cannot hold society together."

In 1827 the Reverend Ezra Stiles Ely of Philadelphia, a prominent Presbyterian minister and leader of the national church, called for the formation of "a Christian Party in Politics." While many religious believers pursued large moral causes such as the abolition of slavery and justice for the Indians—causes that also attracted secular supporters—many others sought to impose a narrower religious agenda on the rest of the nation. Such Christians opposed travel and the transport and delivery of mail on the Sabbath, as well as the testimony of nonbelievers in courts of law. In early 1829, Ely wrote Jackson to pass along a letter from the Reverend Lyman Beecher of Boston, one of the great ecclesiastical figures of the age, asking that Jackson not ride on Sundays en route to Washington. Ely and Beecher hoped, they said, that "no Christian ruler of a Christian people should do violence to his own professed, personal principles," and Jackson, shrewdly, did not travel on Sundays on the way to the capital unless he was on a steamboat. He would accede that far but no further. He fought corruption in the public sphere, with political means, and left the church free to do what it could by persuasion, not by fiat.

Jackson was more anticlerical than antireligious. Like bankers or entrenched incumbents, ministers created a layer between Jackson and the people at large, and he hated such elite intermediaries. Believers were part of the public; clergy were an interest with specific demands. Broadly put, the organized church was beyond Jackson's control, and that made him suspicious of its ministers and their motives.

· · ·

IN KENTUCKY AND elsewhere, Jackson fretted about what were drily known as internal improvements—projected roads and canals that were to be funded by the federal government. The issue was at the heart of a philosophical argument. Was Washington's role to be a limited one, leaving such matters to the states except in truly national cases, or was the federal government to be a catalyst in what was known as "the American System," in which tariffs and the sales of public lands funded federally sponsored internal improvements? As president, Jackson favored the former, John Quincy Adams and Henry Clay the latter. Related, in Jackson's mind, was the issue of the national debt (the money owed by the federal government). To him debt was dangerous, for debt put power in the hands of creditors—and if power was in the hands of creditors, it could not be in the hands of the people, where Jackson believed it belonged.

IN THE WATERS off Cuba, on Sunday, February 22, 1829, well-armed pirates stormed the **Attentive**, an American merchant vessel bound for New York from the Cuban port of Matanzas. Murdering the captain and crew, the pirates captured the vessel and scoured it for money. The **New Priscilla** was also attacked in February in these waters, provoking anxiety on the busy seas between Cuba and the American ports and raising fears among American businessmen that pirates were singling out U.S. ships. Told of the **Attentive** incident on his thirteenth day in office, Jackson exerted American power: an attack on anything American was an attack on America, and on him. "These atrocities will require prompt and energetic measures on the part of the Government [in] order to put them down," Jackson told Navy Secretary John Branch, who dispatched the USS **Natchez,** an eighteen-gun sloop of war, to the coast of Cuba. "The dictates of humanity and the honor of our flag require that the piracies in those seas should be suppressed," Jackson said. The world was on notice: Jackson would strike when struck.

PATRONAGE, THE BANK, nullification, Indian removal, clerical influence in politics, internal improvements, respect abroad—these were the questions that would define Jackson's White House years. They were questions about power, money, and God, and Jackson's answers were linked to his expansive view of the office of the president. He would die for the Union; his foes were fighting to keep the possibility of secession alive. Jackson believed that the president should use his powers with a firm hand; his foes thought of the Congress as the government's center of gravity. And so Jackson began his presidency prepared for anything, in much the way he used to travel through the Tennessee wilderness forty years before, looking out for danger, guarding those in his care, and promising to save them all yet.

AS A COLD spell broke on the morning of the inauguration, sunlight poured down on the city and twenty thousand people converged on the Capitol grounds. It was, Emily reported home, "by far the greatest crowd that ever was seen in Washington." Jackson left Gadsby's Hotel, met an escort of Revolutionary War and Battle of New Orleans veterans, and walked up Capitol Hill.

He wore no hat—"the Servant in presence of his Sovereign, the People," Mrs. Smith remarked—and moved with grace and simplicity.

"There, there, that is he," called out some on the hill.

"Which?" said others.

"He with the white head."

Then they saw. "Ah, there is the old man . . . there is the old veteran, there is Jackson." The people, Mrs. Smith said, were "not a ragged mob, but well dressed and well behaved, respectable and worthy citizens." The emotion of the day was intense. "It is beautiful!" said Francis Scott Key, who was with Mrs. Smith. "It is sublime!"

From the procession, Jackson went inside to the Senate chamber, where the president pro tempore swore John C. Calhoun in as vice president. Articulate and intellectual, more at home with ideas than action, Calhoun had balanced the Jackson ticket, but the two men were not close, and never would be. To Jackson, Calhoun brought a certain polish to the administration; to Calhoun, Jackson was, God willing, a one-term president whom he would soon succeed.

As they walked from the chamber to the East Portico on this March day, they were already on different ideological and political paths. Calhoun began his career as a fervent nationalist, a celebrated "War Hawk" who enthusiastically supported the War of 1812 in order to establish the nation's credentials with the rest of the world. Moving ever nearer a pure states' rights position, however, Calhoun sensed that the protective tariff—which many of Calhoun's constituents believed helped Northern states at the expense of the South—was a sign of things to come. If the national government could tax the South against its will, the national government could, in the future, take the region's slaves away against its will.

In the late autumn of 1828, at his Fort Hill estate near Pendleton, South Carolina, he had drafted what would become the **South Carolina Exposition and Protest** to make the case for nullification. The nullification doctrine would enable a state to void a federal law within its borders. The federal government then had two choices: either leave the state alone or amend the Constitution (which required the approval of two thirds of each house of Congress or a constitutional convention called by two thirds of the states, and then ratification by three fourths of the states) to make the objectionable law explicitly constitutional. And what if the amendment passed? The nullifying state must then capitulate or secede from the Union.

For about a decade, from roughly 1828 to 1838—a period that included the crisis with Jackson—Calhoun, who nursed presidential ambitions, was unwilling to state clearly whether he believed his theory logically led to secession. Many of those around him in South Carolina did think so, and, perhaps most important, so did Jackson, who always thought of what he called "the absurd and wicked doctrines of nullification and secession" as parts of a whole. They were of a piece in his mind, and he acted accordingly. By 1838, Calhoun more openly acknowledged the possibility of disunion. "We cannot and ought not to live together as we are at present, exposed to the continual attacks and assaults of the other portion of the Union," he wrote his daughter, "but we must act throughout on the defensive, resort to every probable means of arresting the evil, and only act, when all has been done, that can be, and when we shall stand justified before God and man in taking the final step." Calhoun was a careful man, but in the end his theory threatened the existence of the Union Jackson loved.

Calhoun kept his authorship of the 1828 document secret, and the vehemence of his views quiet. He believed that the white-haired general about to take the presidential oath would heed his counsel to slash the tariff, relieve the South, and calm fears of future interference with the region's way of life. Then, Calhoun hoped, his own hour would strike, and carry him to the White House.

Emily, who had watched Calhoun's swearing-in from the Senate gallery, walked to the East Portico. Looking out, she saw only "one dense mass of living beings." Even Mrs. Smith, whose heart belonged to the capital of Madison, Monroe, and Adams, was nevertheless impressed by the scenes of democracy in action. "Thousands and thousands of people, without distinction of rank, collected in an immense mass round the Capitol," she said, "silent, orderly and tranquil, with their eyes fixed on the front of that edifice, waiting [for] the appearance of the President in the portico." When Jackson emerged, he bowed to the people, and "the shout that rent the air still resounds in my ears," said Mrs. Smith. Cannons boomed. As the sounds of the salute died off, Jackson began to read his address.

When he put his mind and hand to it, Jackson could produce stirring rhetoric—but he did so usually in moments of clarity and purpose. His addresses to his troops in the field, his letters about the Union, and his calls for the triumph of the virtue of the people over the vices of the elite were occasions on which he knew what he wanted to say because he knew what he believed and what he wanted to accomplish.

His first inaugural, however, was purposely vague. Gazing out on the admirers gathered at the foot of the Capitol steps, Jackson saw that he was the object of wide affection—but he was not yet certain of the depth of that affection. The people hailed him today but might not tomorrow. Better, then, to proceed with care, to be general rather than specific, universal rather than particular—for specificity and particularity would give his foes weapons to use against him. Many leaders would have been seduced by the roar of that crowd, lulled into thinking themselves infallible, or omnipotent, or secure in the love of their followers. But Jackson knew that politics, like emotion, is not static. There would be times when he would have to tell people what they did not want to hear, press a case they did not want to accept, point them in a direction they would prefer not to go. Best, then, to preserve capital to spend on those speeches and those battles.

The rise of a nation with a large number of voters, living at great distances from one another, dependent for information and opinion on partisan newspapers, meant that a president had to project an image at once strong and simple. His ideas should be expressed clearly for the ordinary voter, who, consumed with the tasks and troubles of his own life, had only so much time and energy to devote to divining the details of a leader's political creed. In a democracy like the one taking shape in America, the people considered both the content of a politician's message and their impression of his character in deciding whether to support him. George Washington was the first and greatest such example, a man called to power not only because of his views but also for his reassuring bearing. He was a man with whom the people felt comfortable. Jackson's political appeal came out of the same tradition—a tradition in which a leader creates a covenant of mutual confidence between himself and the broader public. If the people believe in the man, then the more likely they are to give him the benefit of the doubt on the details of governance. A Scottish visitor to Albany in the late 1820s noted an American love of what he called "the spirit of electioneering, which seems to enter as an essential ingredient into the composition of everything." But it was a highly personal kind of electioneering: "The Americans, as it appears to me, are infinitely more occupied about bringing in a given candidate, than they are about the advancement of those measures of which he is conceived to be the supporter."

The transaction between a potential president and the people is often as much about the heart as it is about the mind. "The large masses act in politics pretty much as they do in religion," a Democratic senator said in the Jackson years. "Every doctrine is with them, more or less, a matter of **faith**; received, principally, on account of their trust in the apostle." And they trusted Jackson. They might not always agree with him, they might cringe at his excesses and his shortcomings, but at bottom they believed he was a man of strength who would set a course and follow it, who would fight their battles and crush their enemies. They believed, in short, in the Jackson who, on that journey home from Natchez in the War of 1812, had said that he would not leave a man behind—not a single one. It was a pledge he had kept then, and the people believed it was one he would keep in the White House.

MORE STILTED THAN sonorous, the inaugural speech could be interpreted in almost any way a hearer chose to interpret it. Of the tariff, he said, "It would seem to me that the spirit of equity, caution, and compromise in which the Constitution was formed requires that the great interests of agriculture, commerce, and manufactures should be equally favored"—but he did not say he would lower the duties that had so enraged the South. Of the building of roads and canals—so crucial and yet so controversial, for there were disputes about whether Washington should help pay for them or leave the matter to the states—he said, "Internal improvement and the diffusion of knowledge, so far as they can be promoted by the constitutional acts of the Federal Government, are of high importance," but did not specify what "acts" might be "constitutional." Of all the points in the address, the sentence that resonated most in official Washington was a promise of "**reform**, which will require particularly the correction of . . . abuses" in the federal system.

The significance of this pledge can be understood only when we remember that Jackson represented the first major transition in the White House in more than a generation—the first since Jefferson's inauguration in 1801, twenty-eight years before. Madison, Monroe, and Adams had been their own men, but had essentially left the federal government more or less in the same hands. Now Jackson was, from the start, calling those hands "unfaithful" and "incompetent"—particularly the ones who had served the second Adams.

Jackson closed with a prayer—for order and for guidance, for himself and for the Union. As president, he said, he would depend "on the goodness of that Power whose providence mercifully protected our national infancy and has since upheld our liberties in various vicissitudes," and hoped "that He will continue to make our beloved country the object of His divine care and gracious benediction." His mother would have been pleased. He was playing the role of national pastor—a minister at last, leading the largest possible flock.

He bowed once more to the people, and the cheers rose again. Jackson then took the oath from Chief Justice John Marshall, kissed a Bible, and mounted a white horse to ride down Pennsylvania Avenue to the White House. "Country men, farmers, gentlemen, mounted and dismounted, boys, women and children, black and white" followed him, Mrs. Smith said, "carriages, wagons and carts all pursuing him to the President's house."

WHEN THE PROCESSION arrived, the mansion was all his—and theirs. Angry with Adams for the attacks on Rachel during the campaign, Jackson had refused to call on his predecessor, and so President Adams had moved out the night before and made no public appearances on Inauguration Day. (He learned of the moment of the transfer of power when, riding his horse, he heard the Capitol cannon fire in the distance.) It is possible that Jackson's failure to communicate directly with Adams helped lead to the disaster that followed, a legendary scene in American history that has forever linked Jackson with the image of a crowd trashing the White House. "No arrangements had been made," Mrs. Smith noted, and "no police officers placed on duty and the whole house [was] inundated by the rabble mob."

The reception Jackson had planned turned chaotic, with his enthusiastic followers filling the house past capacity. "The **Majesty of the People** had disappeared, and a rabble, a mob, of boys, negroes, women, children, scrambling, fighting, romping" replaced it, said Mrs. Smith. "Here was the corpulent epicure grunting and sweating for breath," reported the **New York Spectator,** "the dandy wishing he had no toes— the tight-laced Miss, fearing her person might receive some permanently deforming impulse—the miser hunting for his pocket-book—the courtier looking for his watch—and the office-seeker in an agony to reach the President." The household staff's attempts to serve the guests only made things worse. "Orange punch by barrels full was made, but as the waiters opened the door to bring it out, a rush would be made," said a congressman from Pennsylvania, "the glasses broken, the pails of liquor upset, and the most painful confusion prevailed."

Standing in the mansion, Jackson was nearly crushed by the visitors. His aides formed a protective ring around the president and spirited him back to Gadsby's. Mrs. Smith thought of the sacking of Versailles—an excessive allusion, for the worst damage she could detect, she admitted, was that "the carpets and the furniture are ruined." The cost of the destruction was limited to a few thousand dollars, but the scene was further proof, if any were needed, that the armies of democracy were pitching their tents in Andrew Jackson's White House.

THE MISTRESS OF the house, Emily Donelson, was apparently horrified. The melee was the kind of thing that embarrassed Emily, who, as a newcomer to the highest levels, was, like her uncle, sensitive to making a good appearance and leaving the rougher elements of

frontier life—even life in the frontier aristocracy—
where she believed they belonged: back on the frontier,
not in Washington.

In a long letter to her sister about the inaugural,
Emily not only failed to mention the mob scene but
cast the afternoon in a favorable, more genteel light—
rearranging reality in order to make the family's first
moments at the pinnacle appear more polished than
they had actually been.

"After the inauguration Uncle and the rest of us repaired to the White House," Emily said, "where every
one visited him that wished to treat him with respect." The only allusion—a heavily veiled one—to
the chaos of the reception came in this fragment of a
sentence: "The crowd," Emily added, "was about as
great here as it was at the Capitol." Then she moved
rapidly on, saying, "Uncle has scarcely had a moment
to himself since he arrived and has been surrounded
by visitors. . . . I hope [he] will now have time to rest
himself and attend to his health, which has been very
delicate." In her mind, then, the early days of the administration were days of presidential affairs, callers
who wished to salute Jackson "with respect," and her
warm concern about his well-being—not of what
Supreme Court Justice Joseph Story, who was at the
White House on Inauguration Day, called "the reign
of King Mob."

Emily knew that the sight of a crowd climbing
through the windows of the White House for cups of
spiked punch was the last thing her family needed.
The girl who had taken a maid with her to school in

Nashville and who had relished her first days in capital society on her 1824–25 visit was self-conscious about the Jackson clan's image. The public swirl of rumors about the Jacksons' murky marriage probably made Emily even more sensitive than she would have been if all the world had not been reading of confused wedding dates, adultery, and bigamy.

Emily began her life in national society in a curiously contradictory position. She owed her access to the grandeur of the White House to her family's connection to Andrew Jackson, but it was precisely that connection that somewhat embarrassed her. Emily may have felt that she had to transcend, or at least obscure, some uncomfortable truths about Jackson and the world they all came from: the looser late-eighteenth-century morals that the Jacksons took advantage of in order to marry; the memories of crude violence, duels, and brawling that Jackson's foes kept alive; even Jackson's lack of formal education and intellectual polish.

As she dressed in her room at Gadsby's in the early evening hours of Wednesday, March 4, 1829, Emily already knew the circles in which she wanted to move. Adjusting her gown of amber satin—Jackson had bought new dresses for her and for Mary Eastin—she hoped to transcend her provincial origins.

Emily was confident about her own capacity to build the life she wanted in Washington. Like many women on the frontier—women who ran plantations and complex households while their husbands or fathers were away at war or on business—she was ac-

customed to being independent. James A. Hamilton,
a son of Alexander Hamilton, recalled being struck
by Emily's strength and self-reliance when, one day at
the Hermitage, he watched her ride up to the house
on horseback with one of her babies in her arms. "I
was astonished to see a young and delicate lady and
mother making a visit in this manner," Hamilton
said. As many others, including her uncle, soon
learned, Emily was not afraid to ride alone.

Which was one of the reasons Jackson adored her.
He admired women—as well as men—of courage,
and he was loyal to those he loved. He liked Emily's
spirit. It may have reminded him of the young
Rachel's, back in Nashville and in Natchez. Though
Emily and Andrew sometimes resented and bridled at
Jackson's authority, as children do with fathers, they
wanted, as children also do with fathers, his affection
and his blessing.

The day of the inaugural was no different. "Tired as
he was that night," wrote a family chronicler, "Jackson viewed with interest and pride Emily Donelson
and Mary Eastin, who came into his room, seeking
his approval of their appearance in the new gowns he
had given them, as they started for the Inaugural
Ball." Still in mourning, Jackson was not going. He
limited his celebrations to a small dinner. Calhoun
was one of his companions at the table; afterward, the
vice president went from Gadsby's to the ball.

There he and Mrs. Calhoun joined Emily and
Andrew to form the most brilliant circle of the
evening. Mrs. Donelson and Mrs. Calhoun were

the ranking women at Carusi's, the assembly hall at C and Eleventh streets. In the absence of President Jackson, Vice President Calhoun was the central figure of the night. For Emily and Andrew, the mix of power, excitement, and glamor was intoxicating, and they loved the company they were in.

As the Donelsons danced and dined at Carusi's, Emily was thinking beyond this single night out, beyond this season in Washington, beyond, even, the Jackson presidency. She was ambitious for her husband. Both Donelsons had reason to expect that Uncle Jackson's wishes for Andrew to lead his own national political career might come to pass. Andrew Donelson was twenty-nine years old and, as secretary to the president, was in a unique position to master the mechanics of national and international politics. Emily kept watch over her husband's prospects, protecting his interests in the great game of who was to be close to Jackson. At the same time, however, she was attached to Jackson himself, loved him, and took seriously her duty to make him comfortable amid the tumult of the presidency.

SHE DID IT well. Family life was crucial to Jackson, who had known so little of it growing up, and Emily ensured that the White House was a sanctuary for him. The Jackson circle soon moved from Gadsby's to the mansion on Pennsylvania Avenue, and Emily, who was about three months pregnant with her second child, quickly settled in. When she brought him a question about social life in the White House—and there was really no such thing as a small question about social life in the president's home, for society and politics were linked in etiquette, precedence, and seating—Jackson would say: "You know best, my dear. Do as you please."

He trusted her and her husband as he trusted few people. An intimate of the Hermitage for so long, Emily knew what Jackson wanted and needed. He found comfort in the intimacy of a family gathered around a fireside. Looking back, Jessie Benton Frémont, the daughter of Thomas Hart Benton, remembered Emily Donelson's White House as a place where Jackson sat in a rocking chair near the hearth as light poured in through the big windows. Jessie's senator father would confer with the president, who liked to "keep me by him, his hand on my head—forgetting me of course in the interest of discussion—so that sometimes, his long, bony fingers took an unconscious grip" and Jackson "twisted his fingers a little too tightly in my curls." Little Jessie would endure the inadvertently inflicted presidential pain, then hope to be excused to the Donelson nursery down the hall.

A contemporary recalled that when Emily's children and, later, those of Sarah Jackson, Andrew Jackson, Jr.'s wife, were infants and became "restless and fretful at night, the President, hearing the mother moving about with her little one, would often rise, dress himself, and insist upon having the child, with whom he would walk the floor by the hour, soothing it in his strong, tender arms, while he urged the tired mother to get some rest." At White House meals, Jackson wanted the family's youngsters to dine at the table with him: they were not to be kept in the kitchen or nursery, but at the center of the household.

Jackson also liked his family to shine socially, and Emily was happy to accommodate him. "Madam, you dance with the grace of a Parisian," a foreign minister once told her at a party in Washington. "I can hardly realize you were educated in Tennessee."

"Count, you forget that grace is a cosmopolite," Emily said, "and like a wild flower is much oftener found in the woods than in the streets of a city." It was a perfect reply: tough but charming, pointed but gracious—like Emily herself, or, for that matter, Jackson himself. On close inspection, they had much in common, perhaps most significantly a tendency to be stubborn yet mask willfulness with charm and geniality. In just one person, that was a formidable combination of characteristics; to have two people in the same house with that capacity made for a complex and quietly charged emotional universe—one that, given the psychological arsenals at both Jackson's and Emily's disposal, was at perpetual risk of becoming a battlefield instead of a home.

THERE WERE THINGS to fight about from the start. Though the Donelsons, with one child and another on the way, formed the core of the president's world, his old quartermaster and political aide, Major William B. Lewis, was a constant factor. Lewis had made something of a show of wanting to leave Washington after the inauguration. A trusted operative, Lewis was useful to Jackson, but, like many who live and work in the orbit of the great, he was needy, and wanted reassurance about his role and relevance to Jackson. By announcing his planned departure to Tennessee, Lewis drew forth the words he longed to hear:

"Why, Major," Jackson said, "you are not going to leave me here **alone,** after doing more than any other man to bring me here?" Watching, Emily scoffed at Lewis's maneuver. Emily's hostility suggests that she worried about her Andrew's place within the government. Lewis was a rival for Jackson's attention, positioned in equal proximity to the president, with a daughter, Mary Lewis, there to be one of the women around Jackson providing him with company and comfort.

There was another likely reason for Emily's coolness toward Lewis. He was allied with a wing of Jackson's universe that could mean trouble for her and for Andrew: that of John Henry Eaton, the new secretary of war.

Handsome, energetic, and devoted to Jackson, Eaton was as close to the president as anyone, and closer than most. "Eaton was altogether a personal appointment," Amos Kendall wrote Francis Preston Blair, reporting that Jackson "said to a friend who told me that left alone as he was in the world, he desired to have near him a personal and confidential friend to whom he could unbosom himself on all subjects."

Eaton, a longtime senator from Tennessee and a Jackson strategist, was the friend Jackson chose. Born in Halifax County, North Carolina, in 1790, Eaton attended the University of North Carolina and trained as a lawyer. He moved to Franklin, Tennessee, near Nashville, in 1808, served in the War of 1812 under General Jackson, and married Myra Lewis, a ward of Jackson's. (William Lewis married a sister of the first Mrs. Eaton; both sisters were dead by the time Jackson became president.) When John Reid, one of Jackson's military aides, died before completing a biography of the general, Eaton stepped in to complete the work, which was published in 1817. He served as a U.S. senator from Tennessee from 1818 to 1829, and in that decade played a key role in the construction of Jackson's national political career. Eaton defended Jackson in the Washington debate over the general's invasion of Florida, and he wrote **The Letters of Wyoming**, a widely published case for Jackson's election in 1824. Jackson trusted him implicitly.

In coming to the Cabinet, Eaton brought Jackson a measure of comfort, the reassurance of years of loyalty, a usually sharp political sense—and a new wife, Margaret, the daughter of a Washington innkeeper named William O'Neale. The O'Neale boardinghouse was popular with visiting legislators like Eaton, and Andrew Jackson himself, who lived at the O'Neales' during his brief return to Congress from 1823 to 1825.

Married on New Year's Day 1829, the Eatons immediately created chaos in the capital. The source of the controversy: the new Mrs. Eaton's sexual virtue. In the years before their wedding, Kendall wrote Blair, "Eaton boarded at her father's, and scandal says they slept together." One of Emily's first letters home from

Washington reported that "there has been a good deal of discontent manifested here about the cabinet and particularly the appointment of Major Eaton." The crux of the matter: "His wife is held in too much abhorrence here ever to be noticed or taken into society."

HER FULL NAME was Margaret O'Neale Timberlake Eaton. Beautiful and brash, aggressive and ambitious, Margaret Eaton seems to have had few impulses on which she did not act, few opinions that she did not offer, few women whom she did not offend—and few men, it appears, whom she could not charm if she had the chance to work on them away from their wives. A contemporary described her almost breathlessly: "Her form, of medium height, straight and delicate, was of perfect proportions. . . . Her skin . . . of delicate white, tinged with red. . . . Her dark hair, very abundant, clustered in curls about her broad, expressive forehead. Her perfect nose, of almost Grecian proportions, and finely curved mouth, with a firm, round chin, completed a profile of faultless outlines."

Adept at the barroom art of creating a sense of intimacy with paying customers, Margaret was outspoken and outrageous in an age that tended to value tact. In the months after her marriage to Eaton, Margaret became the subject of rumors about alleged sexual exploits. Her first husband, John Timberlake, a navy purser, died in 1828. It was said that, despondent over her unfaithfulness, he had slit his own throat. She was alleged to have become pregnant while her husband was away at sea. She reportedly passed a man in a hallway with no flicker of recognition—forgetting that she had slept with him. She was supposed to be pregnant by Eaton, who had done the gentlemanly thing and married her; the two were also said to have registered in a New York hotel as man and wife while Timberlake was alive. By her own account, Margaret had been trouble from the beginning, an out-going flirt from childhood forward. "I suppose I must have been very vivacious," she said in her old age. "I was a lively girl and had many things about me to increase my vanity and help to spoil me. While I was still in pantalets and rolling hoops with other girls I had the attentions of men, young and old, enough to turn a girl's head."

At various points in her youth she was courted by an adjutant general, a major, and a captain—which delighted her. "The fact is, I never had a lover who was not a gentleman and was not in a good position in society," she said.

Her passions came and went—urgent one moment, gone the next. Her tongue was ungoverned, and ungovernable. "It must be remembered that I had been raised in the gayest society and was naturally of a mercurial temperament," Margaret said. "I must have said a great many foolish things. I am sure I did very few wise ones. I was foolish, hasty, but not vicious." After she married Timberlake she lived in her father's house when her husband was at sea.

It is impossible at this distance (as it was even then) to assess the truth of the charges against her. Margaret herself offered an interesting defense: "Just let a little common sense be exercised," she said. "While I do not pretend to be a saint, and do not think I ever was very much stocked with sense, and lay no claim to be a model woman in any way, I put it to the candor of the world whether the slanders which have been uttered against me are to be believed." What is certain is that the stories were in circulation—and that Margaret's demeanor made things worse.

Jackson did not care. A hopelessly romantic matchmaker, he had advised Eaton to marry Margaret after Timberlake's death. "Why, yes, Major," Jackson said, "if you love the woman, and she will have you, marry her by all means." When Eaton said there were rumors that he and Margaret had cuckolded Timberlake, Jackson replied, "Well, your marrying her will disprove these charges." Loyal to Eaton, unable to keep himself from seeing parallels between the attacks on Rachel and the rumors about Margaret, the president drew on one of his oldest instincts: defend friends against all comers. Of Eaton, Jackson said, "I will sink or swim with him, by God," and he meant it.

Down the hall, in the Donelsons' small suite, Emily took a different view. "The ladies here with one voice have determined not to visit her," she wrote home. It was a determination that would help change the course of American politics.

Had the conflict simply been about who was asked to dine at whose tables, or to visit, then the Eaton saga would be interesting but not especially important, an early Washington scandal about sexual mores. As improbable as it sounds, though, the future of the presidency was at stake.

"The whole will be traced to what I always suspected," Jackson once told Emily. He believed the campaign against the Eatons to be "a political maneuver by disappointed ambition to coerce Major Eaton out of the Cabinet and lessen my standing with the people so that they would not again urge my reelection." There was another, equally important possibility: even if Jackson decided not to seek another term himself, he would still have a strong hand in choosing a political heir from within his party. And loyalty to the Eatons was now a test of loyalty to Jackson. "It is odd enough, that the consequences of this dispute in the social and fashionable world are producing great political effects, and may very probably determine who shall be successor to the present chief magistrate," said Daniel Webster.

That the race for the White House in a large republic should have been affected by the sexual history of the wife of the secretary of war seems bizarre; yet politics is often driven not only by large ideas about policy and destiny but by affections and animosities. From Helen of Troy to Henry VIII, what Alexander Pope called "trivial Things" in **The Rape of the Lock** have led to wars, revolutions, and reformations, and so it was to be in the administration of the seventh president of the United States.

CHAPTER 5

★

LADIES' WARS ARE
ALWAYS FIERCE AND HOT

THE EATON CRISIS began, in a way, in the vice president's boardinghouse, an exclusive enclave run by Mrs. Eliza Peyton on the northwest corner of Pennsylvania Avenue and Fourth Street. Frightened by a spate of sickness among their children the year before—sickness they believed was exacerbated by Washington's humidity—the Calhouns had given up their Georgetown mansion, Oakly (later known as Dumbarton Oaks), and were planning to move the family back to South Carolina. With the big house above Rock Creek gone, the Calhouns took lodgings at Mrs. Peyton's.

The boardinghouse was well known and high toned, home at different times to men such as Webster and Clay. It was here, a dozen blocks from the White House, that the Eatons, in the weeks after their New Year's 1829 marriage, came to pay a call on the Calhouns. Even if Margaret had been diffidently charming or subtly ingratiating—and she was neither—she stood little chance of winning Floride over. Mrs. Calhoun was a complex woman, demanding in private one moment, attentive and caring among others the next. "You could not fail to love and appreciate, as I do," one of her Washington friends wrote of her, "her charming qualities; a devoted mother, tender wife, industrious, cheerful, intelligent, with the most perfectly equable temper."

Calhoun himself might have dissented on this last point. Diminutive but powerful, Mrs. Calhoun had what her husband called a "suspicious and fault-finding temper." She came from South Carolina aristocracy. Each summer her family had climbed into a beautiful coach to be driven from their mansion on the Cooper River to spend the season in Newport, Rhode Island. Calhoun would neither confront nor contradict her. Once, after a quarrel between Floride and the couple's eldest son, Calhoun wrote the son: "As to the suspicion and unfounded blame of your Mother, you must not only bear them, but forget them." Floride's stormy temperament, Calhoun added, had long been "the cause of much vexation in the family," and "I have borne with her with patience, because it was my duty to do so, and you must do the same, for the same reason. It has been the only cross of my life."

As Floride went, so went the Calhoun clan. She had brought the money to the marriage and was the kind of established Southern woman whose embrace and acceptance Emily Donelson, as a daughter of the Southwest, felt she needed to thrive in Washington. Tennesseans could be socially insecure around old South Carolina families. The frontier was newer and rougher, the silver not quite as old, the oil portraits not quite as ubiquitous. Calhoun had married up when Floride accepted him, and felt a disparity in the social calculus of their household. She was not a tyrant, not exactly. The toll she exacted on her husband appears to have been more insidious, more gradual, a sure and certain drain on his emotional reserves.

Now, sitting alone—the vice president was out—as Floride looked up to find that she had callers, she was about to become a sure and certain drain on his political ones.

AS THE EATONS entered the room, Floride did not know who Margaret was; the servant had failed to announce the guests by name. It was only when she recognized Eaton, who had served in the Senate over which her husband presided, that she realized who had come to call. The visit does not appear to have lasted long, though it passed decorously enough. "She of course treated them with civility," Calhoun said of his wife and the Eatons. "She could not with propriety do otherwise."

The Eatons left, and when Calhoun returned, as he later drily wrote, "The relation which Mrs. Eaton bore to the society of Washington became the subject of some general remarks"—general remarks, one suspects, that most likely touched on charges of adultery. The conversation was more than idle gossip: Floride had to decide whether to pay a visit to the Eatons—a sign, in the etiquette of the day, that Mrs. Calhoun recognized Mrs. Eaton as a respectable member of the

Washington society in which the wives of the great lived.

She made her decision overnight: she would not return the call. To Floride, who was about to leave town in any event, the rumors about Margaret's sexual transgressions were credible enough to keep the wife of the vice president of the United States from being on social terms with the wife of the secretary of war. Calhoun acquiesced, a choice that put the vice president in conflict with the president, for the political consequences of one's decision about whether to accept the Eatons as social equals were already clear. To acknowledge the Eatons was to side with Jackson; to snub the Eatons was to oppose Jackson.

JOHN QUINCY ADAMS liked to think of himself as a man removed from the strife of party and the scramble for power. Yet for all his scholarly interests—his readings in the classics, his writing of poetry, his meditations on scripture—Adams could never fully control his addiction to politics and public intrigue. His diaries and correspondence are replete with rumors and reports about the White House and the Capitol, the departments and the drawing rooms. In his diary in early 1829, Adams noted that a friend of his was "much scandalized by the ascendancy of Mrs. Eaton; lately Mrs. Timberlake." Writing his son about the Calhouns and the Eatons, Adams said that the vice president "forsooth was a Man of Morals, and his wife had been the first to exclaim . . . 'I so hate a whore.'" (Adams marked through the word "whore," but not so much that it could not be read.) At the time of the inauguration in 1829, in the aftermath of the Eaton call, Adams added, Floride gave "public notice . . . that sooner than submit to the contamination of [Margaret's] society, she would not show her face at Washington."

Louisa Adams, the former president's wife, was even more explicit. "War is declared between some of the ladies in the city, and . . . ladies' wars are always fierce and hot," she wrote their son.

SUCH WAS THE atmosphere when Martin Van Buren arrived at the White House on his first evening in Washington on Sunday, March 22, 1829. Greeting Jackson in the shadows of the president's office—there was just one candle burning—Van Buren, in town to begin his work as secretary of state, thought Jackson's health "poor, and his spirits depressed as well by his recent bereavement of his wife." He was right on both counts. Intuitive about the intricacies of power, Van Buren assessed the reality of life in the White House. "The cast of the Cabinet carried a suspicion to the minds of many . . . that Eaton and Lewis had exerted a preponderating influence in its construction," Van Buren recalled. The result: "Jealousies and enmities accordingly sprang up . . . many of which were never healed." Andrew Donelson, Van Buren added, "partook largely of this feeling."

Small in stature—he was about five feet six inches tall—Van Buren was the son of a tavern keeper and farmer in Kinderhook, New York, near Albany. Born in 1782, he grew up around the politicians who gathered in his father's establishment—guests included Alexander Hamilton and Aaron Burr—and, after training as a lawyer, he entered politics himself, serving as a state senator and New York attorney general before becoming a U.S. senator in 1821. A careful dresser, Van Buren was also careful about revealing too much of his own thinking or convictions; it was as though the son of the tavern keeper always wanted to keep his doors open and please as many people as he could. With his gift for building alliances, Van Buren engineered the Jackson-Calhoun victory in 1828 by, as he put it, uniting "the planters of the South and the plain republicans of the North."

VAN BUREN WAS a practical man, and his pragmatism faced an immediate test when he arrived in the capital. "You might as well turn the current of the Niagara with a ladies' fan as to prevent scheming and intrigue at Washington," he once said, and many intriguers were thinking about life after Jackson.

The president himself was the architect of the constant campaign: he had begun running for 1828 on his way home from Washington in 1825. In politics, as in so many other spheres of life, success breeds imitation. As 1829 began, many expected Jackson to be a one-term president, if that. He was an old, wounded warrior, scarred, bullet-ridden, susceptible to all sorts of sickness. He suffered intermittent hemorrhages, which he would relieve by cutting his arm with a penknife to bleed himself. It was entirely possible he would not live to see 1833. The rumors of his death before the inauguration had been plausible enough, and he often referred to his own poor health, calling on Providence to see him through.

Calhoun, Van Buren, and Clay were three of the men who longed for the presidency, obsessed over it, and judged what they did in the light of whether a given issue or question would advance or hinder their path to ultimate power. For them, succession was all. Clay would use any weapon that came to hand, including gossip, in hopes of winning the presidency four years hence. The current administration, Clay believed, was dangerous and usurping; Clay thought Jackson's election "a calamitous event," he wrote privately, and Jackson himself to be "feeble in body and mind, and irresolute." If he was to lead a restoration campaign, Clay knew he had to keep himself before the people. "We must never forget that we cannot make them lose sight of me," Clay wrote an ally. "I cannot withdraw from the gaze of the public eye."

Inside the administration, the Van Buren–Calhoun contest was obvious to the political world even before Jackson's inauguration. "Disguise it as we may, the friends of Van Buren and those of Calhoun are becoming very jealous of each other," Pennsylvania congressman James Buchanan said on Thursday, January 22, 1829. Van Buren, meanwhile, was hearing from sympathetic South Carolinians that Calhoun might be vulnerable on the home front if attacked in Washington. "A display there [in Washington], adverse to him, will enable us to triumph over him and his friends there," a foe of Calhoun's, David R. Williams, wrote Van Buren in 1829. It was interesting intelligence for Van Buren, a rival of Calhoun's.

But Van Buren fought his wars with subtlety. He would begin his campaign for supremacy indirectly. Seeing the side the Calhouns had chosen, Van Buren—a widower—made the politically rational decision to take up the Eatons' cause. James Parton looked back from the vantage point of the 1860s and, seeing that Van Buren had made it to the White House while Calhoun, and the South, were ruined, wrote that "the political history of the United States, for the last thirty years, dates from the moment when the soft hand of Mr. Van Buren touched Mrs. Eaton's knocker."

As Jackson saw things, Margaret was a convenient target for enemies who resented the president and the secretary of war. "If I had a **tit** for every one of these **pigs** to suck at, they would still be my friends," Jackson said of Eaton's foes. "They view the appointment of Eaton as a bar to them from office, and have tried here, with all the tools of Clay helping them on, to alarm and prevent me from appointing him." Jackson's interpretation of the Eaton affair was that he was acting for the common democratic good while aristocratic elites, jealous of his power in Washington, did everything they could to stop him. To Jackson, it was a matter of honor (he would not have his friend's wife assaulted as his own wife had been) and of power, and he would not be moved.

It was a political affair, but its sexual elements also

raised important questions for the women of the age. Cultural interpretations of the Eaton affair emphasize the significance of sexual purity to women in the early nineteenth century. Margaret Eaton was, fairly or not, a symbol of promiscuity. She was a threat to the domestic realm—the realm in which the women of Washington held power.

For Jackson's foes, the intersection of Jackson's loyalty to a friend with his vision of himself as the people's tribune was a colossal misfortune, since the connection of these issues in Jackson's mind meant that he would, as he put it, "sink with honor to my grave" before he would give in to those who opposed him over the Eatons.

JACKSON SAW HIS adversaries as threats to the common good—and he saw few larger threats than the Bank of the United States. In the 1828 campaign, Jackson heard allegations that Clay was manipulating the Bank to help Adams's reelection. In January 1829, then-postmaster general John McLean, a Jacksonian who later joined the Supreme Court, wrote Nicholas Biddle about the "impression that during the late elections in [Kentucky], great facilities by the state branches were given to those persons who were favorable to the re-election of Mr. Adams." McLean offered sensible counsel. Even if, he said, "the impression of unfairness" were "without any substantial foundation," the wisest course for the Bank was "to guard against every appearance of wrong." Biddle was a brilliant man, and even someone far duller than he should have understood

McLean's full meaning: Biddle had a political problem on his hands and needed to take care of it.

The president of the Bank ignored McLean's advice. Biddle's way was the right way, and he would not change course for anyone. In naming directors, Biddle told McLean, "their personal independence and their fitness for that particular duty must be the primary inquiry—their political preferences only a secondary concern. The great hazard of any **system** of equal division of parties at a board is that it almost inevitably forces upon you incompetent or inferior persons in order to adjust the numerical balance of directors."

And that was how Biddle replied to his **supporters**. "Being friendly to the Bank myself," McLean had added in his note to Biddle, "I should regret to see a political crusade got up against it. Some, I know, are ready to engage in this course, but I wish their number may be small." McLean, Biddle, and the rest of the country were about to learn that when it came to President Jackson, a party of one was more than enough for a crusade.

JEREMIAH EVARTS ALREADY understood that about Jackson. Though he is largely forgotten, Evarts was one of the great American moral figures of the first decades of the nineteenth century. In speaking out against the forced removal of the Indians from their homes to lands west of the Mississippi, he was to Indian removal roughly what William Lloyd Garrison was to slavery: a force calling on the country to respect the rights and dignity of a persecuted people.

Born in Vermont in 1781, the son of a farmer, Evarts entered Yale in 1798. Under its president, Timothy Dwight, a grandson of Jonathan Edwards, the college was suffused with the idea of Christian service. "In whatever sphere of life you are placed, employ all your powers and all your means of doing good, as diligently and vigorously as you can," Dwight preached in a sermon entitled "On Personal Happiness." For Dwight and, ultimately, for Evarts, faith was about not only personal conversion but social transformation and the health of the nation. In their minds, and in the minds of thousands of American believers, there was a direct connection between the godliness of the people and the fate of the country.

Jackson believed, too, that virtue was essential to the maintenance of a republic, but he thought religious and philanthropic organizations were as corruptible and susceptible to manipulation by the powerful as any other human institution. Evangelical leaders he referred to as "religious enthusiasts" were standing in the way of Indian removal, one of his most cherished projects.

While religion was important in his private life ("Gentlemen, do what you please in my house," Jackson would tell guests, but "I am going to church"), he believed in keeping religion and politics, as well as church and state, as separate as one reasonably could. Despite his lifelong commitment to Presbyterianism,

Jackson had never taken the public step of what was known as "joining the church"—that is, making a public confession of faith in a particular congregation, which in turn enabled one to receive Holy Communion. Around 1826, according to an early biographer, he explained to Rachel the reasons for his reluctance: he did not want to appear to be making a show of his faith for public consumption—a show that might provoke attacks. "My dear, if I were to do it **now**, it would be said all over the country that I had done it for political effect," Jackson said. "My enemies would all say so. I can not do it **now**, but I promise you that when once more I am clear of politics I will join the church."

Jackson liked to think of himself as first and foremost a republican—a man who believed the best government was the one that meddled least in the affairs of the governed. For Jackson, the primary duty of federal power, once invoked, was to protect the many from the few. Like the Bank, like the radicals of South Carolina, like the Washington elite, the Christian movement for justice for the Indians and for public purity posed a threat to Jackson's vision, which held that the people (or at least white male people) were sovereign and that intermediary forces were too apt to serve their own interests rather than the public's. Jackson's solution? Jackson. On the Indian question, he was determined to have his way, and few doubted that he would prevail. "I have not seen a single man, of any party, who thinks that anything effectual can be done to protect our weak red men of the forest," Evarts wrote to the American Board of Commissioners.

THE SOUTH CAROLINIANS were coming to the same conclusion: when Jackson did not want to be moved, he did not move. Jackson had watched the stirrings of nullification the previous year and sensed trouble. "There is nothing that I shudder at more than the idea of a separation of the Union," Jackson wrote James Hamilton, Jr., of South Carolina in June 1828. "Should such an event ever happen, which I fervently pray God to avert, from that date I view our liberty gone—It is the durability of the confederation upon which the general government is built that must prolong our liberty. The moment it separates, it is gone." He believed the nullifiers were a mortal threat to the Union. "The South Carolinians get nothing," Kendall wrote Blair on Saturday, March 7, 1829. "The General told me he should have taken a member of his cabinet from that state but for their movements last summer. They are fine fellows, but their zeal got the better of their discretion."

As time went on, Jackson thought he detected something even more sinister than straightforward partisanship in what he viewed as the persecution of the Eatons: that Calhoun and some Southern radicals were using the affair to weaken Jackson and strengthen themselves. "Some foundation there must be to give rise to so much talk," Louisa Adams wrote to her husband of Margaret's reputation, "but my own belief is that it is a trick of the Carolina party to sow discord among the Administration and to get the W[ar] D[epartment] into their own hands."

Mrs. Adams was on to something. Though it is true that Jackson initially blamed "Clay and his minions" and "these satellites of Clay" for the battle against the Eatons, he had long been suspicious of Calhoun. The vice president's snubbing of Margaret only exacerbated existing tensions. The Calhouns had left Washington for their plantation at Pendleton, South Carolina, shortly after the inauguration. (In the custom of the age, vice presidents were largely legislative figures, presiding over the Senate, and thus tended to leave Washington when Congress was not in session, from, roughly, March to December each year.) Virgil Maxcy, a Maryland lawyer who had been an enthusiastic Jackson supporter, wrote Calhoun in April 1829, saying that "we must submit to the melancholy conviction, that the U.S. are governed by the President—the President by the Secretary of War—and the latter by his Wife." Maxcy also confirmed that Calhoun's hunch was right: according to rumor, Eaton was said to be "not friendly" to Calhoun.

That should not have been surprising to the vice president, for Calhoun was himself wary of Eaton. The states' rights elements in South Carolina believed Eaton unreliable on the tariff and, by extension, an almost certain enemy of nullification, and because of these fears they were concerned about his influence over Jackson. When the so-called Tariff of Abominations was being debated in 1828, Senator

Robert Hayne said, "**Eaton** and others . . . disregarded the South." Eaton's failure to follow the South Carolina line on the evils of the tariff as a senator from Tennessee, the scholar Richard Latner noted, troubled Calhoun, who said that Eaton had shaken "our confidence in General Jackson . . . at the critical moment when the passage of the bill cast so deep a gloom over the South, and menaced with so much danger the liberty and institutions of our country." Serious words.

EMILY DONELSON HAD hated Margaret from the start. "To please Uncle, when we first came here we returned her call," Emily wrote home in late March, but Margaret appears to have assumed an uncomfortable degree of familiarity. "She then talked of intimacy with our family and I have been so much disgusted with what I have seen of her that I shall not visit her again," Emily said. "I am afraid it is to be a great source of mortification to our dear old Uncle."

Emily grasped the politics of the problem. "I think if Eaton felt any disinterested friendship he never would have accepted the appointment," Emily told her sister in a letter that was critical of both Eaton and William Lewis. "I believe there is very little of that article to be found here. . . . That sycophant Lewis that pretended to come along out of friendship to the Genl has got himself into a fat office and to save himself all expense has taken his quarters here for the next 4 years." Arch words from a young woman who sometimes affected to be unmoved and uninterested in the vicissitudes of life in Washington. These lines were written twenty-three days after the inauguration—a sign that the White House stage was set for struggles for influence and pride of place in Jackson's affections.

Andrew Donelson and John Eaton were uncomfortable with each other. To Eaton, Donelson was young, not particularly experienced, and in perhaps too much of a hurry. It had not been that long ago, Eaton knew, that he had been Donelson's chaperone on a trip from Tennessee to West Point. To Donelson, Eaton seemed to be at once ascendant and condescending, wielding more power with Jackson than any other adviser.

Jackson's household was therefore in more or less open warfare even before his first month in office had elapsed. The Donelsons formed one party, while down the hall, Lewis was allied with the Eatons. A bit farther along the passageway, Jackson himself longed for peace at home and victory in the city.

Part of the conflict stemmed from Andrew Donelson's political ambitions, part from Emily's social designs, and the two were inevitably linked. When it came to Lewis and Eaton—threats to her Andrew's position—Emily fought with spirit. "I think as Uncle wanted to give offices to his immediate friends there were others that had done more for him and deserved more at his hands than either Eaton or Lewis," Emily said.

There should be no friendship—or even the faint appearance of friendship—between the White House family and the Eatons. Visits had been paid and returned, and as far as Emily was concerned, that was that. She already knew, most likely from women such as Floride (before the Calhouns left) and the other Cabinet wives—particularly Mrs. John Branch, wife of the secretary of the navy, and Mrs. Samuel Ingham, wife of the Treasury chief—that proximity to the Eatons would mean social distance from the best families of Washington. "I am prepared to defend our course—and will not yield one inch of ground," Mrs. Ingham wrote to Emily, who had no intention of living her life in exile from the upper reaches of capital society on account of Margaret Eaton.

As usual, Margaret was her own worst enemy. Her brashness in claiming connection to Jackson's family made Emily's revulsion all the stronger. Realizing that she would find no friend in Emily, Margaret, rather than keeping a decorous silence, began to speak of Emily as "a poor, silly thing," and escalated her rhetoric from there. "I was quite as independent as they and had more powerful friends," Margaret said of the Emily faction. "None of them had beauty, accomplishments or graces in society of any kind, and for these reasons—I say it without egotism—they were very jealous of me."

Jackson's political allies were puzzled by the unfolding drama. After Jackson gave Margaret's father a federal position as an inspector of the District of Columbia prisons, James Hamilton, Jr., then a pro-Jackson South Carolinian, wrote Van Buren: "For God knows we did not make him president . . . to work the miracle of making Mrs. E. an honest woman, by making her husband **Secy of War,** or by conferring some crumbs of comfort on every creature that bears the name O'Neale."

AT GADSBY'S HOTEL one morning after a big party hosted by Sir Charles Vaughan, the British minister, Margaret was the talk of the dining room. "Mrs. Eaton brushed by me last night and pretended not to know me," one man said in front of four others at Gadsby's table. "She has forgotten the time when I slept with her."

Old Washington was at once horrified and thrilled by the scandal. After a visit to the Clays' house on Lafayette Square, Edward Bates, a congressman from Missouri who lost his 1828 reelection bid, wrote his wife an inflated account of the Eatons' history. Eaton, Bates said, "has just married Mrs. Timberlake, a lady with whom it is said he has been on very familiar terms for several years past. She was the wife of a purser in the Navy, whose duties called him to foreign parts; but the lady, notwithstanding her lonely condition, increased and multiplied surprisingly."

Bates was reflecting the prevailing gossip. "I've just returned from Mr. Clay's," he said. The "hard-featured" Lucretia Clay was there, as was a sister of Dolley Madison's. "Of course, there is no getting along in such a party without a little scandal," Bates said. "Mrs. Eaton the bride above mentioned was of course talked of and I gathered that she had not received the accustomed visits of congratulation from the ladies of the city."

On Sunday, March 8, 1829, four days after the inauguration, Lucretia and Henry Clay went to dine at
the home of Margaret Bayard Smith and her husband,
Samuel Harrison Smith, the president of the Washington branch of the Bank of the United States. The
Smiths had come to Washington immediately after
their wedding twenty-nine years before, in the autumn of 1800. Shortly thereafter John Adams became
the first president to spend a night in the White
House. Six years later Henry Clay came to Washington as a U.S. senator from Kentucky. He served in the
Ninth Congress alongside his hostess's brother, James
A. Bayard of Delaware.

Dining on this Sunday—the Smiths lived on the
square between Pennsylvania Avenue, Fifteenth Street,
and H Street, near the White House—Samuel Harrison Smith and Clay talked, Mrs. Smith said, as "the
patriot to the patriot," men whose lives were intertwined with the history of the city and its more or less
permanent powers. Smith had served as an interim
secretary of the Treasury under Madison; Clay had
risen through the Congress, becoming Speaker of the
House, and now stood as the opposition's heir apparent to reclaim the White House. Washington was
home, the public's business their business, the nation's
memories bound up with their own families'.

The weather outside was forbidding—cold and
cloudy—but inside at the table Mr. Smith and Clay
found a refuge in memories and stories from the days
when, in their view, giants, not pygmies, lived in the
White House. They did not mention Jackson. They

did not have to. The "falling-off"—as the ghost of Hamlet's murdered father put it when he spoke of how low his wife had come in marrying the usurping Claudius—was obvious to all in the dining room. "The characters and administrations of Jefferson and Madison were analyzed, and many private anecdotes were drawn," said Mrs. Smith. "Mr. Clay preferred Madison, and pronounced him after Washington our greatest statesman, and first political writer—He thought Jefferson had the most genius—Madison most judgment and common sense—Jefferson a visionary and theorist, often betrayed by his enthusiasm into rash and imprudent and impracticable measures, Madison cool, dispassionate, practical, safe."

Mr. Smith listened, then begged to differ—politely and among equals, of course. The conversation was riveting; the dishes were being cleared away, yet everyone at the table, well fed and with full glasses of wine, listened intently.

"Your father," Mrs. Smith wrote their son, "would not yield Jefferson's superiority and said he possessed a power and energy, which carried our country through difficulties and dangers; far beyond the power of Madison's less energetic character. 'Prudence and caution would have produced the same results,' insisted Mr. Clay. After drawing a parallel between these great men, and taking an historic survey of their political lives, they both met on the same point, viz. that both were **great** and **good,** and tho' **different**— yet **equal.**"

Reasonable men of affairs, reaching reasonable conclusions about matters of history and statecraft—the scene is cozy, intimate, full of talk of great men with insight and familiarity and connections between the public and the personal. These were people who believed themselves noble members of a ruling class—an aristocracy in all but name.

At ten—late for Lucretia, who tended to retire earlier—the Clays said good night, concluding a kind of tribal ritual of a band of warriors, facing enemies in the darkness beyond, warming themselves with fire and story.

THE CHIEF ENEMY—at least as the old guard saw him—was not far away, at the White House, reviewing the capital establishment, deciding who would retain office and who would not. There was, Clay said, "the greatest . . . apprehension" among the Washington elite. "No one knows who is next to encounter the stroke of death; or, which with many of them is the same thing, to be dismissed from office."

Jackson was not alone in drawing hostile fire. At a big Washington wedding uniting two important capital families—Dr. Henry Huntt, a physician who would later treat Jackson, was marrying the daughter of Tench Ringgold, a friend of President Monroe's and marshal of the District—Van Buren was moving among the guests when Judge Buckner Thruston confronted him. The judge's son had been fired as a State Department clerk. Now an "exceedingly indignant" Judge Thruston looked Van Buren in the eye and "very energetically" called him a "Scoundrel" loudly enough, Adams wrote in his diary, for a dozen other guests to hear.

People like the angry judge and the Clays and the Smiths saw the replacement of federal officials as the ruin of the country. Jackson saw it as the nation's salvation. That a president would have wide power to reward loyalists with offices, both to thank them for their steadfastness and to ensure that he had a cadre of people at hand who would presumably execute his policies with energy and enthusiasm, is now a given, but Jackson was the first president to remake the federal establishment on such a large scale.

The old officeholders could be forgiven for imagining themselves immune to the vagaries of politics. By James Parton's count, Washington and Adams had removed 9 people each; Jefferson, 39 (illustrating the victory of the Democrat-Republicans over the Federalists); Madison, 5; Monroe, 9; and John Quincy Adams, 2. By the time Jackson was done, he had turned out fewer than one might suppose, but still a historic number: about 919, just under 10 percent of the government. And he had made a particularly high number of changes among those civil servants directly appointed by the president himself.

Jackson's vision was elementary yet expansive in the context of the early Republic. He wanted a political culture in which a majority of the voters chose a president, and a president chose his administration, and his administration governed by its lights in full view of the people, and the people decided four years hence whether to reward the president with another term or retire him—and them—from public life.

The human reaction to Jackson's reform among the officeholders and their families was swift and fierce. "At that period, it must be remembered, to be removed from office in the city of Washington was like being driven from the solitary spring in a wide expanse of desert," Parton wrote three decades after the purge. John Quincy Adams monitored the terror: "A large portion of the population of Washington are dependent for bread upon these offices. . . . Every one is in breathless expectation, trembling at heart, afraid to speak."

Jackson's decisions about federal appointments involved much more than the lingering historical image of the "spoils system," a principle summed up by New York senator William Marcy in a speech he delivered about the new class of politicians: "They see nothing wrong in the rule, that to the victor belong the spoils of the enemy." Jackson was far from the last American president to arrive in Washington with the cry that the preceding administration had made a grand mess of things. Yet he firmly believed he was coming to power after a long period of sustained official corruption—he called the government "the Augean Stable," seeing himself as Hercules—and viewed what he broadly referred to as "reform" as a moral as well as a political task. In Jackson's mind, sins in the public sphere represented, as he said, a "struggle between the virtue of the people and executive patronage."

There was always graft, which was regrettable, but what truly worried Jackson was what he saw as a pattern by Washington officials to deploy public money and means to perpetuate and promote themselves and their allies in office. Such corruption, as Jackson saw it, was possibly fatal to the American experiment, a fear grounded in the old notion that society was organic, and that an affliction in one part of the state could infect and even kill the whole.

STILL, JACKSON WAS susceptible to emotional appeals from officeholders facing dismissal. He was moved by stories of courage, admiring in others what he saw in himself. In the fever of the firings, the postmaster of Albany, New York, the War of 1812 veteran General Solomon Van Rensselaer, was slated for termination. According to the logic of the removals—to reward friends and eliminate foes—the Van Rensselaer maneuver made perfect sense. He was a Federalist who had supported John Quincy Adams, and Van Buren wanted him out, as did Silas Wright, Jr., a key New York politician, so the case seemed closed. To save his job, Van Rensselaer went to the White House and waited for Jackson to finish with his guests at a reception.

"General Jackson, I have come here to talk to you about my office," Van Rensselaer said once he had the president alone. "The politicians want to take it away from me, and they know I have nothing else to live upon."

Accustomed to such pleas and committed to his

course, Jackson said nothing. Desperate, Van Rensselaer moved to strip off his own clothes.

"What in Heaven's name are you going to do?" Jackson said. "Why do you take off your coat here?"

"Well, sir, I am going to show you my wounds, which I received in fighting for my country against the English!"

"Put it on at once, sir!" Jackson said. "I am surprised that a man of your age should make such an exhibition of himself." Still, recalled Benjamin Poore, a journalist who recorded the story, "the eyes of the iron President were suffused with tears." Van Rensselaer took his leave.

The image of the scarred old man stayed in Jackson's mind overnight. As Poore told it, "The next day Messrs. Van Buren and Wright called at the White House and were shown into the President's room, where they found him smoking a clay pipe." Apparently unaware of Van Rensselaer's preemptive strike the previous evening, Wright began to make the case for sacking him. Jackson "sprang to his feet, flung his pipe into the fire," and virtually roared at his two friends.

"I take the consequences, sir; I take the consequences," Jackson said. "By the Eternal! I will not remove the old man—I cannot remove him. Why, Mr. Wright, do you not know that he carries more than a pound of British lead in his body?" The postmaster was safe.

John Quincy Adams tracked everything. "The proscriptions from office continue, and, independent of the direct misery that they produce, have indirectly tragic effects," Adams wrote on Saturday, April 25, 1829. "A clerk in the War Office named Henshaw, who was a strong partisan for Jackson's election, three days since cut his throat from ear to ear from the mere terror of being dismissed. Linneus Smith, of the Department of State, one of the best clerks under the Government, has gone raving distracted, and others are said to be threatened with the same calamity." Suicide and madness: it was the most unstable of seasons.

BUT JACKSON WAS getting his way, and Clay, returning to Kentucky as a private citizen, could not hold his tongue. "During the reign of Bonaparte, upon one of those occasions in which he affected to take the sense of the French people as to his being made Consul for life, or Emperor, an order was sent to the French armies to collect their suffrages," Clay said in a Lexington speech on Saturday, May 16, 1829. "They were told, in a public proclamation, that they were authorized and requested to vote freely, according to the dictates of their best judgments and their honest convictions. But a mandate was privately circulated among them importing that if any soldier voted against Bonaparte he should be instantly shot."

Not subtle—but then, Clay's hatred of Jackson was running ever deeper as Clay tried to grow accustomed to exile after so many years of power and the anticipation of greater office. "Is there any difference, except in the mode of punishment," Clay continued, bringing his listeners from Napoleonic France to Jacksonian America, "between that case and the arbitrary removal of men from their public stations for no other reason than that of an honest and conscientious preference of one Presidential candidate to another?"

Clay had learned a lesson from Jackson's sojourn in the wilderness after the 1824 election: that the political future belonged to men who constantly made the case for themselves in the most accessible way possible for a mass audience. By relentless repetition, Jackson had turned the phrase "corrupt bargain" into a weapon that brought Adams down and forced Clay out of office. Jackson's success suggested that the ambitions of the men who would be president were best served by total immersion in the mechanics and the substance of political life.

IN WASHINGTON, WHEN the Senate summoned up the gumption to strike back at the president over patronage, voting down several nominees, Jackson sent for Duff Green, the editor of the administration's then-favored newspaper, the **Telegraph**. "Let Congress go home, and the people will teach them the consequence of neglecting my measures and opposing my nominations," Jackson said. "The people, sir, the people will put these things to rights!" He depended on a single force against all the florid attacks in the world: his mystical link to the country.

Andrew Jackson was rapidly turning the presidency into what John F. Kennedy later called "the vital center of action." Little wonder, then, that the Washington establishment believed the end of their reign had come. It had.

CHAPTER 6

★

A BUSYBODY
PRESBYTERIAN CLERGYMAN

Writing a friend in Tennessee, Jackson linked his intransigence on the Eaton question to his most enduring conviction: that as president he was acting selflessly in the interest of the nation and of its mass of citizens, who looked to him for clarity in a chaotic world. "I was elected by the free voice of the people," Jackson told his friend John C. McLemore, a Nashville businessman. "I was making a Cabinet to aid me in the administration of the Government, agreeable to their will." In a remark that indicates how he viewed his own will and that of the country as one, he said: "I was making a Cabinet for myself." Then, returning bitterly to the immediate social dimension of the problem, he added: "I did not come here to make a Cabinet for the ladies of this place, but for the nation."

Jackson was beset—by Clay, by Calhoun, and by powerful Protestant clergymen, including his own Washington minister. On Wednesday, March 18, the same day the Calhouns started their journey south, the Reverend Ezra Stiles Ely sat down at his desk in Philadelphia to write to Jackson on the subject of the Eatons.

The pastor of the city's Third Presbyterian Church, Ely was among the best-known clerics of the day. Christian voters, Ely had said in his celebrated 1827 sermon on a "Christian Party in Politics," should join forces to keep "Pagans" and "Mohammedans" (Muslims) from office as well as deists like George Washington or Thomas Jefferson or Unitarians like John Quincy Adams. The essence of the sermon: "Every ruler **should be** an avowed and a sincere friend of Christianity. . . . Our civil rulers ought to act a religious part in all the relations which they sustain."

Ely had old connections to Jackson, dating back to Jackson's days when he had business interests in Philadelphia, and Ely was not shy about pushing Jackson on the evangelical community and evangelical causes on Jackson. When Ely published his "Christian Party" sermon before the 1828 presidential election, he added his own warm exchange of letters with Jackson and his call for voters to send Jackson to the White House—the implication being that Old Hickory was a man evangelicals could count on.

Yet Jackson handled Ely's sermon, and his problematic support, deftly. Realizing that sectarian rhetoric like Ely's struck many Americans as dangerous, Jackson articulated a middle position, arguing that one of the country's greatest strengths was freedom of religion, a freedom that also gave the skeptical the right to live unmolested and unevangelized.

Jackson acknowledged the centrality of the separation of church and state. "Amongst the greatest blessings secured to us under our Constitution," Jackson said, "is the liberty of worshipping God as our conscience dictates"—or not. But he also gave faith its due—in moderate terms: "All true Christians love each other, and while here below ought to harmonize; for all must unite in the realms above," Jackson wrote Ely after the sermon. "I have thought one evidence of true religion is when all who believe in the atonement of our crucified Savior are found in harmony and friendship together."

In his vision of Christian voters marching as to war, Ely was attempting to undo the work of decades by ensuring that only avowed Protestants would hold public office. He even had a specific timetable in mind. In preparing his sermon for publication, Ely included a quotation from the American Sunday School Union. "In ten years, or certainly in twenty, the political power of our country would be in the hands of men whose characters have been formed under the influence of Sabbath schools," resulting in "an **organized system of mutual co-operation** between ministers and private Christians, so that every church shall be a disciplined army."

Ely's crusade—for crusade it was—foundered when a specific mission, the battle to end the federal delivery of mail on Sundays, collided with Jacksonians. Jeremiah Evarts's opinion of the Sabbath mails illustrates the scope of evangelical passion on the question: "We have always viewed it as a national evil of great magnitude, and one which calls for national repentance and reformation, that the mails are carried, and the post-offices kept open, on that holy day in every part of our country," Evarts said. To desecrate the Sabbath, these activists believed, was to invite God's wrath on the nation.

Colonel Richard M. Johnson, a Kentucky congressman, senator, and later vice president under Van Buren, was in charge of a congressional committee assigned to rule on the question.

Johnson was one of the more intriguing politicians of the time. A "War Hawk" lawmaker along with Clay and Calhoun in the War of 1812, Johnson left Congress to fight in the field. At the Battle of the Thames in 1813, Johnson claimed to have personally killed Tecumseh, the Shawnee leader who was allied with the British. Johnson was open about his common-law marriage to a mulatto slave, Julia Chinn, and their two daughters; Chinn would die in the cholera epidemic of 1833. She had two successors. On discovering that his new companion was unfaithful, Johnson, Kendall reported, "sold [her] for her infidelity," and then took up with the woman's sister.

The Johnson committee's decree crippled Ely's "Christian party" movement. "It is not the legitimate province of the Legislature to determine which religion is true, or what false," wrote Johnson in 1829. "Our government is a civil, and not a religious institution."

A second Johnson report on the subject the next year depicted the Sabbath mails movement as an obstacle to the life of the mind. "The advance of the human race in intelligence, in virtue, and religion itself depends, in part, upon the speed with which . . . knowledge . . . is disseminated," Johnson wrote, concluding: "The mail is the chief means by which intellectual light irradiates to the extremes of the republic. Stop it one day in seven, and you retard one seventh of the advancement of our country." The reports issued, Congress did not move to limit Sunday mails.

The theocratic kingdom Ely hoped for was not at hand, but the evangelicals' challenge to the mainstream, so manifest in the Jackson administration, was to be a constant force in the life of the nation.

WHEN JACKSON RECEIVED Ely's letter about the Eatons in March 1829, he already understood that the minister was a man of great ambition and spotty judgment—a "busybody Presbyterian clergyman of Philadelphia," as John Quincy Adams called him. Ely had pestered Jackson with appeals not to travel on the Sabbath, but, as a minister who liked proximity to the powerful, he had also been a faithful supporter of Rachel Jackson's during the 1828 campaign. He had come to Washington for the inauguration, paid his respects, and, according to Jackson, "recommended the appointment of Major Eaton in the warmest terms" and "expressed the most favorable opinion" of both Mr. and Mrs. Eaton on that occasion.

What was behind Ely's initial enthusiasm for the Eatons? Knowing that Jackson was close to them, Ely had most likely been attempting to please the new president. The Eaton appointment was already controversial by that point, and Ely may have been trying to store up treasure with Jackson that might be drawn on in pursuit of evangelical causes.

Then everything changed. Before he left Washington for home, Ely visited with a fellow minister, the Reverend John N. Campbell, pastor of the Second Presbyterian Church in Washington, where Jackson, John Quincy Adams, and the Calhouns occasionally worshipped.

Campbell had absorbed Washington's view of the Eatons. A social creature, he enjoyed mixing with his fancier parishioners. He walked Ely through a series of damaging stories about the Eatons—stories that Ely added to a few he had picked up in Baltimore on the way home, as he wrote to Jackson. Everyone in Washington, Ely told Jackson, said that Mrs. Eaton was "a woman of ill fame before Major Eaton knew her and had lived with him in illicit intercourse." As though he were filing a brief, Ely broke down Mrs. Eaton's sins into a "sad catalogue."

He reported a rumor that Margaret had privately said that her children were Eaton's, not Timberlake's, and that "Mr. Timberlake, when he last left Washington, told this gentleman with tears, 'that he would never return to this country' on account of Eaton's seduction of his wife." An unnamed "clergyman of Washington"— Campbell—"besought me to tell you that when Timberlake had been gone more than a year from this country, Mrs. T. had a miscarriage."

And Ely brought Rachel Jackson into the conversation. He was really writing, he said, because "the name of your dear departed and truly pious wife is stained through Mrs. Eaton. In a meeting of the directors of a bank in Baltimore it was publicly said 'it's too bad, but what could you expect better: it's only supporting Mrs. Jackson,' or words to that effect." Those who consider Margaret "to have been a licentious woman for years will consider her elevation to society through the influence of the President as a reflection upon the memory of Mrs. Jackson," Ely said. "It is uttered by a thousand malicious tongues, 'he could not make an objection to [Eaton] on account of his wife.'"

As he closed, Ely rhetorically asked, "Need I apologize for this long letter? My heart's desire and prayer to God for you is that you may have the happiest presidency, and heaven at last."

AN APOLOGY WOULD not even have begun to appease Jackson. Word by word, sentence by sentence, paragraph by paragraph, page by page, Ely was both sanctimonious and salacious, questioning the honor of one of Jackson's dearest friends, assailing his friend's wife in detail, and tying Rachel to the current scandal.

Jackson's reply—immediate, passionate, precise, disputing every specific—began drily enough, with Jackson writing that "I sincerely regret you did not personally name this subject to me before you left Washington." Jackson scribbled with rising rage, disposing, he believed, of each "slander." His fiercest language was reserved for Ely as a clergyman and for the anonymous cleric—Campbell, Jackson's own pastor—who had told the story of the allegedly illicit pregnancy. With a preacherlike vehemence of his own, Jackson thundered:

With regard to the tale of the clergyman, it seems to me to be so inconsistent with the charities of the Christian religion, and so opposed to the character of an ambassador of Christ, that it gives me pain to read it. Now, my dear friend, why did not this clergyman come himself and tell me this tale, instead of asking you to do it? His not having done so convinces me that he did not believe it, but was willing, through other sources, to spread the vile slander.

In a climactic passage, Jackson again referred to Ely as a friend—in politics, often a term that should put one on guard, for a warm salutation can be followed by a knife thrust:

Whilst on the one hand we should shun base women as a pestilence of the worst and most dangerous kind to society, we ought, on the other, to guard virtuous female character with vestal vigilance. . . . When it shall be assailed by envy and malice, the good and the pious will maintain its purity and innocence, until guilt is made manifest—not by **rumors** and **suspicions,** but by facts and proofs brought forth and sustained by respectable witnesses in the face of day. . . . The Psalmist says, "The liar's tongue we ever hate, and banish from our sight."

Your friend,
Andrew Jackson

That Jackson summoned up this particular Bible verse is telling, for the words he quoted to Ely come from the 101st Psalm, which Isaac Watts translated as "The Magistrate's Psalm." At the end of his first month as president of the United States, one question for Jackson was whether his obsession with defending his old friend—and his old friend's new wife—was in fact wise. He remembered part of the psalm; could he remember, and heed, the King James Version of it, which included a prayer for the magistrate to "behave . . . wisely in a perfect way"?

★

CHAPTER 7

MY WHITE AND RED CHILDREN

ONDAY, MARCH 23, 1829, was a long day at the White House. It was the day Jackson wrote his reply to Ely's sexual allegations, and the president's correspondence was filled with political matters, from the reinstatement of a navy captain to the complaints of a former customs collector at Pensacola to nominees for appointments in England, in Pennsylvania, and in the District of Columbia.

But the most important paper Jackson took up on this cold Monday concerned the federal government's policy toward the Indian tribes in Georgia, Alabama, and Mississippi. As Jeremiah Evarts already suspected, Jackson's treatment of the Indian issue was to be a landmark chapter in a grim two-century-old story. Jackson wanted to do for the South what previous generations had done for the North: push the Indians farther west.

The clash of interests was profound. The Southern states were anxious for more land, especially to grow cotton, and the Creek, Cherokee, Chickasaw, Choctaw, and Seminole tribes held rich acreage—great chunks of what would become modern-day Georgia, Florida, Alabama, Mississippi, and Tennessee. In late 1827 and 1828, officials in Georgia and Alabama moved to assert state authority over the Indian lands within their borders. The affected tribes appealed to Washington for help on the grounds that earlier treaties had guaranteed the Indians these remnants of their ancestral holdings.

In his first weeks in office, with John Eaton's help, Jackson was direct with the Indians: either submit to state law or leave. Despite treaties signed and assurances given, he did not believe the Indians had title to the land, and he would not tolerate competing sovereignties within the nation. The Creek case that reached Jackson on the day he was busy with so much else was, in his view, a perfect example of why the Indians had to move as far from the whites as feasible. A white man had been murdered by Creeks, and the state wanted the Indians to hand over the killers. John Eaton was privately pleased about the case. The murder, Eaton said, "altho' much to be lamented, may be turned to advantageous account, by pressing it as an inducement for the entire Creek Nation now to remove west of the Mississippi."

Writing the Creeks, Jackson explained why he thought removal was essential. "Friends and Brothers, listen: Where you now are, you and my white children are too near to each other to live in harmony and peace. . . . Beyond the great river Mississippi, where a part of your nation has gone, your father has provided a country large enough for all of you, and he advises you to remove to it," Jackson wrote. "There your white brothers will not trouble you; they will have no claim to the land, and you can live upon it, you and all your children, as long as the grass grows or the water runs, in peace and plenty. It will be yours forever." The message was unmistakable: to survive, the Indians had to surrender, and go.

Jackson was hardly the first powerful white man to threaten the Indians. The beginnings of the Native Americans' fate at the hands of whites can be traced at least to 1622, when Indians attacked settlers in Virginia who were taking tribal territory, killing a quarter to a third of the whites, and the white survivors retaliated in kind. The ideology behind the whites' views of the Indians was driven by religious fervor and land fever.

In the first year of the administration of Andrew Jackson, the governor of Georgia, George C. Gilmer, said that "treaties were expedients by which ignorant, intractable, and savage people were induced without bloodshed to yield up what civilized peoples had a right to possess by virtue of that command of the Creator delivered to man upon his formation   be fruitful, multiply, and replenish the earth, and subdue it."

Indians were viewed as savages—sometimes noble, sometimes dangerous, sometimes the children of the whites, sometimes the implacable enemy. The Indians' only hope, many Americans thought, was to take on the ways and means of white civilization. Who was to decide when that civilizing process had produced the desired result? Whites. Time and again experience would prove that Indian lives and fortunes were secondary to white appetites and white safety. If white settlers wanted their land, the Indians were to give way. How else to explain why the Cherokees, who took on every "civilizing" custom the white man asked of them—writing a constitution, developing an alphabet, publishing a newspaper, farming, and living in peace—were key targets, save for the rich land on which they lived?

Promises, treaties, and assurances of fatherly solicitude and care were, in the end, worth nothing. For public consumption and to assuage private consciences, advocates of removal used the language of religion or of paternalism. Jackson spoke of himself as the Indians' "Great Father" all the time—and he almost certainly believed what he was saying. He thought he knew best, and he had convinced himself long before that he was acting on the best interests of both the Indians and white settlers. But the raw fact remains that the American government—and, by extension, the American people of the time—wanted the land. So they took it.

SKIN COLOR HAS always shaped and suffused America. "Next to the case of the black race within our bosom, that of the red on our borders is the problem most baffling to the policy of our country," said James Madison. In 1776, Thomas Jefferson thought the Cherokees and other tribes (many of which were allied with the British) should be sent west. "This then is the season for driving them off," Jefferson wrote. George

Washington's friend Henry Knox, the first president's secretary of war, attempted to formulate a humane policy. "It is presumable that a nation solicitous of establishing its character on the broad basis of justice would not only hesitate at, but reject, every proposition to benefit itself by the injury of any neighboring community, however contemptible and weak it might be," Knox wrote in 1789.

Those intentions were good, but they were defeated by realities on the ground, especially in the South and West, where Indians were seen not only as threats in their own right but as allies of hostile powers, from Spain to Britain. Power was paramount; successive presidents found it impossible to balance moral concerns with the practicalities of the white American appetite for Indian land. (As president, Washington once went to meet with senators about Indian issues and found the experience so frustrating that he said "he would be damned if he ever went there again.") Washington's successors pursued, in varying degrees, initiatives to teach the tribes white ways (through farming, trade, and conversion to Christianity) while seeking to obtain as much Indian land as possible. There were perennial professions of love and concern. But there was also no doubt who was in control. "We presume that our strength and their weakness is now so visible, that they must see we have only to shut our hand to crush them," wrote President Jefferson in 1803.

The politics of the issue as Jackson came to power in the White House reflected the ambivalence many white Americans felt about the Indians. The whites wanted the land but knew, or strongly suspected, that it was wrong to drive the Indians out. Nevertheless, by the 1820s, confronted by white settlers' demands for land in the South and West, Presidents Monroe and Adams had drafted removal plans. They were no defenders of Indians, but neither did they see the tribes as the mortal threats to the security and inviolability of the United States that Jackson did.

Under the Jackson administration the question became more urgent, and more partisan. The states asserted their authority (Georgia, for example, said it was taking over the Cherokee land by Tuesday, June 1, 1830), setting the stage for some kind of reckoning. Meanwhile, Jackson's political opponents suddenly, in 1829 and 1830, found themselves supportive of Indian claims that had seemed less compelling before Jackson moved into the White House.

An author of a removal rationale, Adams changed his mind when Jackson became the force behind one. Noting a conversation with Edward Everett of Massachusetts, in March 1830, Adams wrote that Everett "spoke also of the debate which will soon take place on the Indian question, and of the unconstitutional Acts of the Legislatures of Georgia, Alabama, and Mississippi, assuming jurisdiction over the Indians within their limits. Upon which I said there was nothing left for the minority [in Congress] to do but to record the exposure of perfidy and tyranny of which the Indians are to be made the victims, and to leave the punishment of it to Heaven."

Henry Clay was now against removal, saying that Jackson's plan would "bring a foul and lasting stain upon the good faith, humanity and character of the Nation." Only five years before, however, Clay had expressed very different sentiments to John Quincy Adams, who recalled that Clay had told him "that it was impossible to civilize Indians; that there never was a fullblooded Indian who took to civilization. It was not in their nature. . . . They were not an improvable breed, and their disappearance from the human family will be no great loss to the world."

Jackson had no interest in debating the question. He wanted the Indians removed and believed it the right thing to do. In his mind, the time for musing and pondering was over. Removal would take an act of Congress, and Jackson planned to introduce one when the lawmakers reconvened in Washington in December 1829. Until then the pro-removal forces would not let Jeremiah Evarts go unanswered in the fight for public opinion. Thomas L. McKenney, the head of the Bureau of Indian Affairs, turned to New York City, to Episcopalians and members of the Dutch Reformed Church, to create the "Board for the Emigration, Preservation, and Improvement of the Aborigines of America." Note the first step: **emigration**.

FOR JACKSON, THE Indian question began as one of security. To him the tribes represented the threat of violence, either by their own hands or in alliance with America's foes. When Indians killed white settlers, Jackson tended to see England (or Spain) as the guiding force, believing Indian skirmishes and clashes meant the Indians had been "excited to war by the secret agents of Great Britain." As a military man he added Indian lands to the country through conquest and concession from 1812 forward, and he believed the work critical to making America safe. In January 1817, Jackson told James Monroe, then the secretary of state, that the addition of lands within a Creek cession that had been claimed by the Cherokees and the Chickasaws was a cause for celebration. "The sooner these lands are brought to market, [the sooner] a permanent security will be given to what I deem the most important, as well as the most vulnerable, part of the union," Jackson said. "This country once settled, our fortifications of defense in the lower country completed, all Europe will cease to look at it with an eye to conquest." Ten years later, in 1826, when he was pondering a complete removal in the South, he wrote: "The policy of concentrating our Southern tribes to a point west of the Mississippi, and thereby strengthening our Southern border with the white population which will occupy their lands, is one of much importance." He told John Coffee that "a dense white population would add much" to the security of the South "in a state of war, and it ought to be obtained on anything like reasonable terms."

He could be both unspeakably violent toward Indians and decidedly generous. After a white woman was kidnapped by Creeks, he said he would give no quarter. "With such arms and supplies as I can obtain I shall penetrate the Creek towns until the captive with her captors are delivered up, and think myself [justified] in laying waste their villages, burning their houses, killing their warriors and leading into captivity their wives and children until I obtain a surrender of the captive and captors." Yet if anyone harmed his occasional Indian allies (he often found elements of a tribe to join him in his Indian campaigns), he reacted with equal fury. In 1818, during the First Seminole War, Jackson denounced a "base, cowardly attack" by Georgia militiamen on a village of Jackson's allies, the Chehaw, "whilst the warriors of that **village** were with me, fighting the battles of our **country**." He was outraged, he said, that "there could exist within the United States a cowardly monster in human shape that could violate the sanctity of a flag when borne by any person, but more particularly when in the hands of a superannuated Indian chief worn down with age. Such base cowardice and murderous conduct as this transaction affords has not its parallel in history and should meet its merited punishment."

The common theme: As a people Indians were neither autonomous nor independent but were to be manipulated and managed in the context of what most benefited Jackson's America—white America. Missionaries and humanitarian reformers struggled to make the case for the innate rights of the Indians, but the white agenda—more land, fewer Indians, complete control—took precedence in the North and the South (and in the West, too, in the long run).

What are we to make of Jackson on this question, one on which he embodied the attitudes of many of his contemporaries? His was an exaggerated example of the prevailing white view, favoring removal at nearly any cost where his predecessors had spoken in softer terms of "voluntary" emigration. While he took an extreme view of Indian matters, however, he was on the extreme edge of the mainstream, not wholly outside it.

Jackson was neither a humanitarian nor a blind bigot. He thought of himself as practical. And enough Americans believed that Indian removal was necessary in the late 1820s and 1830s that Jackson was able to accomplish it politically. The moral case was not hard to make, and men like Evarts and New Jersey senator Theodore Frelinghuysen did so beautifully. In the April 1830 debates over the Indian removal bill, Frelinghuysen would say: "However mere human policy, or the law of power, or the tyrant's plea of expediency, may have found it convenient at any or in all times to recede from the unchangeable principles of eternal justice, no argument can shake the political maxim— that where the Indian always **has been,** he enjoys an absolute right still **to be,** in the free exercise of his own modes of thought, government, and conduct." And: "We have crowded the tribes upon a few miserable acres on our Southern frontier—it is all that is left to them of their once boundless forests, and still, like the horseleech, our insatiated cupidity cries, give, give." And finally: "Do the obligations of justice change with the color of the skin? Is it one of the prerogatives of the white man, that he may disregard the dictates of moral principles, when an Indian shall be concerned? No."

But the answer was, tragically, yes. Indian removal was possible because enough white Americans had a stake in it, or sympathized with it, and thus the institutions of the country allowed it to go forward. Frelinghuysen and Evarts were not outliers; there was a significant anti-removal campaign across the country. And the few groups of Indians—the Iroquois in New York and Cherokees in North Carolina—who managed to carve out small spheres east of the Mississippi after removal showed that coexistence was possible. But to many, the idea that the tribes might be left alone on enclaves within states did not appear politically feasible once Georgia moved against the Cherokees. There is nothing redemptive about Jackson's Indian policy, no moment, as with Lincoln and slavery, where the moderate on a morally urgent question did the right and brave thing. Not all great presidents were always good, and neither individuals nor nations are without evil.

In the message to the Creeks he signed on Monday, March 23, 1829, Jackson repeatedly returned to the idea that he was a father leading his children, and that they should trust him. "This is a straight and good talk," he said. But it was only straight, not good.

Tough as hickory: Andrew Jackson's raw courage in combat made him a hero to his men, and then to the nation.

Rachel Donelson Robards Jackson, the great love of his life. She died after being attacked as a bigamist and adulteress. Jackson never really recovered from losing her.

The Hermitage, Jackson's plantation twelve miles outside Nashville, Tennessee. The house was always full of company.

Andrew Donelson, Jackson's nephew and private secretary. The president had the highest of hopes for Donelson, telling him that one day he, too, would "preside over the destinies of America."

"Everyone was in love with her." Beautiful, shrewd, and headstrong, Emily Donelson was twenty-one years old when she became the president's official White House hostess.

Andrew Jackson, Jr., a ward of the president's who took care of the Hermitage in Jackson's absence, was perennially hapless, running into debt and ultimately dying in a hunting accident.

Sarah Yorke Jackson of Philadelphia married Andrew, Jr., in 1833, and quickly joined Emily as a source of comfort to the aging president.

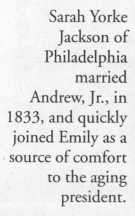

In 1780, Banastre Tarleton, a brutal British commander, led a massacre of Americans in Andrew Jackson's Waxhaw.

As a fourteen-year-old during the Revolutionary War, Andrew Jackson refused to shine a British officer's boots. The officer struck Andrew with a sword, scarring Andrew's hand and leaving a deep gash in his head, a wound he carried for the rest of his life.

After the Battle of Horseshoe Bend in 1814, where Jackson defeated the Red Sticks, a part of the Creek tribe, he adopted an orphaned infant, Lyncoya, and sent him to Rachel at the Hermitage to raise. Lyncoya died of tuberculosis in 1828, the year Jackson was elected president.

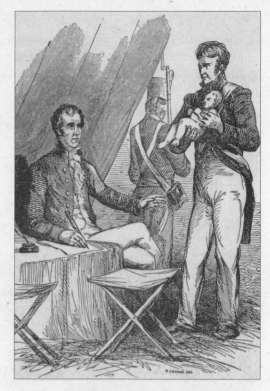

Jackson's victory over the British at New Orleans on January 8, 1815, transformed him into a figure of national renown. His military fame would ultimately propel him to the presidency.

The ninth anniversary of the Battle of New Orleans, in January 1824, brought five of the great figures of the age together in the White House: left to right, John C. Calhoun, Daniel Webster, Andrew Jackson, Henry Clay, and John Quincy Adams. Three of them—Jackson, Clay, and Adams—competed against one another for the presidency later that year.

A collector of political gossip and a translator of the
classics, John Quincy Adams was James Monroe's
secretary of state before winning the presidency in the
House in 1825. Defeated by Jackson in 1828, Adams
was elected to the House of Representatives in 1830,
where he served for nearly two decades.

Louisa Catherine Adams, wife of John Quincy Adams, presided over the White House from 1825 to 1829. Her letters are witty, perceptive accounts of life in the capital through several decades.

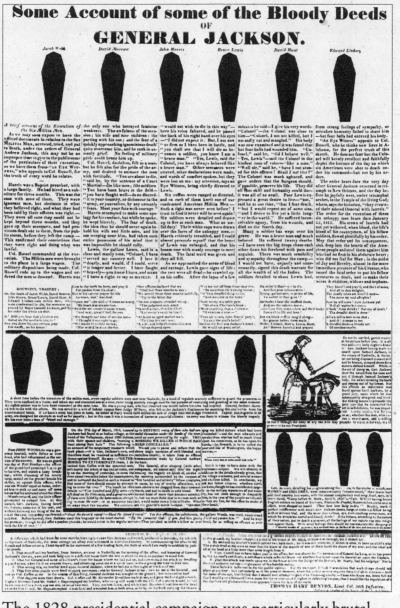

The 1828 presidential campaign was particularly brutal. Jackson was attacked for alleged military atrocities in handbills like this one, while his supporters accused John Quincy Adams of procuring women for the Russian czar and of lavishly spending public money on fancy china and billiards for the White House.

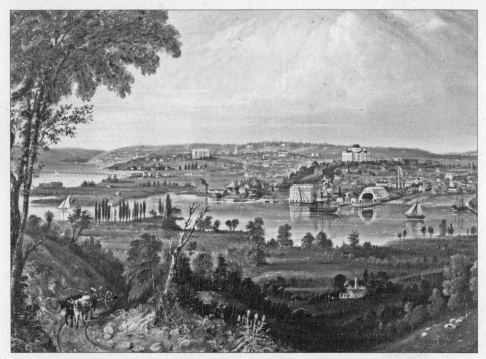

Washington in the age of Jackson was taking familiar shape, with the Capitol (the dome not yet completed) to the right and the White House to the left. This painting, entitled **The City of Washington from Beyond the Navy Yard,** was done in 1833, the midpoint of Jackson's White House years.

Jackson takes the presidential oath from Chief Justice John Marshall on Wednesday, March 4, 1829, on the East Portico of the Capitol. John Quincy Adams had not been invited to the ceremony, and learned of the transfer of power when he heard the cannon fire greeting Jackson's oath.

FIRST CAPITOL INAUGURATION · 1829

The White House as it appeared for much of Jackson's presidency.

Francis Scott Key had thought the stately scene of the huge crowds at the Capitol "sublime"; the storming of the White House later in the afternoon led Supreme Court Justice Joseph Story to lament the beginning of what he called "the reign of King Mob."

A painting captures the chaos and joy of the post-inaugural festivities at the White House in 1829. Jackson's aides had to form a protective circle around him and spirit him to safety at his hotel as the crowds cavorted.

Variously known as "the Sly Fox" and "the Little Magician," Martin Van Buren of New York served as Jackson's secretary of state, then vice president. He was a critical adviser, a cautious, calculating figure who took regular horseback rides with the president.

John C. Calhoun was Jackson's vice president from 1829 to 1832, and hoped to succeed to the presidency himself. A nationalist as a younger man, in middle age Calhoun came to believe in the theory of nullification, which Jackson considered a step toward secession. It was rumored that medals emblazoned JOHN C. CALHOUN: FIRST PRESIDENT OF THE SOUTHERN CONFEDERACY were being struck.

Shrewd, secretive, and devoted to Jackson, Amos Kendall was an invaluable adviser, quick with a pen, and a master of political organization in the early stages of the creation of what became the Democratic Party.

"Send it to **Bla-ar**" was a common order from Jackson once Francis Preston Blair arrived in the capital to edit the **Washington Globe,** the administration's newspaper. Jackson grew so close to Blair's family that he gave Rachel's wedding ring to one of Blair's daughters.

Author, social chronicler, and longtime Washingtonian, Margaret Bayard Smith kept an invaluable diary of politics and people in the capital from Jefferson forward.

The failed architect of a "Christian Party in Politics" and the man who first wrote Jackson about the alleged sexual improprieties of Margaret Eaton, Ezra Stiles Ely was a prominent Presbyterian minister from Philadelphia. John Quincy Adams thought him "a busybody clergyman." Ely's interest in fallen women, or at least supposedly fallen women, was perennial: he had written a book about his ministry among prostitutes in New York City.

Joel R. Poinsett was Jackson's man on the ground in South Carolina in the tense days of the nullification crisis in 1832–1833. "Keep me advised constantly," Jackson told Poinsett. Both men feared civil war might be imminent.

Known as "the Christian Statesman," Theodore Freling-huysen of New Jersey led the Senate fight against Jackson's Indian policy.

CHAPTER 8

★

MAJOR EATON HAS
SPOKEN OF RESIGNING

JIMMY O'NEAL, the White House doorkeeper who accepted mail and greeted visitors, lived in quarters to the right of the main entrance on the north side of the mansion. His fondness for strong drink was a frequent trial for the president and his family. Once, ringing and ringing for him, Jackson said, **"Where can Jimmy be?" "Drunk, most likely,"** Andrew Donelson replied.

In the first week of April 1829, O'Neal was in good enough shape to bring Emily Donelson a letter addressed to her from John Eaton. "You are young and uninformed of the ways and of the malice and insincerity of the world, therefore do I speak to you," Eaton wrote, advising Emily to ignore the gossip he presumed she was hearing from her new friends in Washington. "You may take it for a certain rule that those whom you hear abusing others will by and by when occasion offers, abuse you too."

Rather than approaching Emily with deference or appealing to a sense of justice or loyalty, Eaton chose to make his case on the ground that Emily herself might one day be the target of vicious gossip—hardly the way to persuade a young woman who had already bristled at Margaret's faux intimacy and who had nothing to be ashamed of. It was an odd, dissonant argument to put forward. Calling Emily's circle a "little nest of inquisitors," Eaton said that he knew "their gossiping tattle" had touched on "me and my wife." Then, making the same mistake Ely had made with Jackson, he invoked Rachel. "I should presume, that some recent events which gave pain in your own bosom would lead you to forbear attaching any importance to tales of slander."

It was the worst road to take with the self-conscious Emily, yet once embarked, Eaton could not help but go further, his words stoked by his resentments and frustrations.

> These people care nothing about you. They are eternally haunting your house, and bringing you tales and rules, only that your Uncle is in power, and they hope to give themselves consequence through the smiles they may pick up in your doors. . . . You have known me long and well, and well know that in nothing have I ever deceived you or your friends. Appreciate therefore what is written . . . for your own benefit, not mine. Let your uncle get out of office, and I greatly mistake if you do not have cause to repent that ever you nestled to your bosom such friends and such counselors.

As Emily read the letter with, as she said, "some surprise," Eaton, with a day's reflection, realized he had failed to ask a crucial question. Desperate to know the precise nature of the rumors in circulation—he and Margaret needed to hear the stories in order to mount an effective defense—Eaton scrawled Emily a second note. "On looking to the copy [of the first letter], I perceive there is omitted one of the great objects of writing it," Eaton wrote on Thursday, April 9, 1829.

The great object? " . . . to ask you, if you felt entirely at liberty, to state to me, what were the remarks" Emily had heard. He had to know: the capital was arrayed against him, speaking of his wife's easy virtue and of what Adams called Eaton's own "lewd, licentious life," and the only way to begin to possibly, just possibly, repair the damage was to determine exactly what he was facing.

HE WOULD LEARN nothing from Emily. Answering him in a polite but steely letter dated Friday, April 10, she gave no quarter. She was, she said, "totally unacquainted" with the notion that her conduct was being directed by others. She warned him off the Rachel-Margaret analogy with candor and verve: "Having drawn my attention to the slanders got up for political purposes to tarnish the reputation of my lamented Aunt, you will suffer me to say that the most conclusive proof of her innocence was the respect in which she was universally held by her neighbors, and the love and veneration entertained for her by her family." The unmistakable implication: the same could not be said of Mrs. Eaton. Yes, Emily acknowledged, "there were some unfortunate circumstances connected with her marriage growing out of the unsettled state of the country," but—and this was, to Emily, the most important point—"they never disturbed the confidence and esteem which she deserved and received at the hands of society." In two sentences, Emily thus demolished a key element in Eaton's defense of his wife: that the assault was of a piece with the campaign against Rachel, equally unfounded and equally worthy of a vigorous counterattack from all those who loved Jackson.

As for herself, Emily used restrained irony and a tone that was soft but stringent. "As to the probability of my becoming a victim to the slanders of this or any other place, I feel it due to myself to say that although I am conscious of possessing many of the faults and imperfections common to humanity, yet I hope I shall maintain my reputation as it has heretofore been unsullied, and at the close of my life that I shall have the satisfaction of knowing that my character has not only been pure but unsuspected," she wrote.

Emily then turned Eaton's condescension against him. "As you say, I am young and unacquainted with the world, and therefore will trouble myself as little as possible with things that do not concern me"—things such as rumors about Margaret Eaton.

Eaton had misjudged Emily. The young woman was getting the better of him. With subtlety and deft disingenuousness, she wrote: "I take this opportunity to assure you that I do not wish to decide upon any person's character here, nor control in any way the etiquette of this place."

As Emily knew, however, she could not act as

though she were not who she was: hostess for the president of the United States, the woman closest to him in both physical and emotional terms, the center, with her husband, her child, and the baby she was to deliver in four months' time, of what Jackson called "my family, my chosen family." Andrew Donelson sent his wife's letter to Eaton, enclosing a more conciliatory—but still lukewarm—note of his own: "No one can be more ready than myself," Donelson wrote Eaton, "to pay to yourself and to Mrs. Eaton every proper mark of respect." Andrew's insertion of "proper" left him room to maneuver, for "proper" could mean whatever Donelson wanted it to mean.

For Eaton, the exchange with Emily and Andrew was a disaster. He had set out to draft Emily into service as a defender of his cause and had failed. There seemed to be no relief at hand. With the large exception of Jackson himself, the Eatons were isolated. If they were spoken of, it was either with scorn or, at best, pity. Eaton himself bristled and seethed, hungry to challenge his wife's accusers to duels, but for now had to content himself with writing overly formal letters demanding to know whether the addressee had ever said this or that. His powerlessness to exert any kind of control drove him first to fury, then to a sense of futility.

AT SOME POINT after his exchange with Emily, Eaton weighed whether his war to survive in office was worth fighting. In a previously unknown letter of Emily's that has been in private family hands for more than a century and three quarters, there is evidence that Eaton—most likely in conversations with Jackson and Lewis that reached Andrew Donelson's ears—considered stepping down in these first months of the presidency. "Indeed the prejudice is so strong against them here, that Major Eaton has spoken of resigning and it seems the most proper course for him to pursue," Emily told her mother on Sunday, May 10.

The talk of Eaton's leaving office in the spring of 1829 came to nothing, but what if Jackson had decided to encourage his friend to leave the Cabinet, perhaps giving Eaton a diplomatic post or urging him to return to Tennessee to run for governor, thus taking the issue of his wife to the people? A quick end to the petticoat war would have brought tranquillity to Jackson's family, for what was to Emily a middle course struck her uncle as a radical one, and he hated that she and Andrew refused to bend to his will and accept the Eatons unconditionally. In politics, the battle for primacy between Calhoun and Van Buren could not have been fought in the way that it was, as Van Buren would have had to find some other means to ingratiate himself with Jackson than by becoming Margaret's courtly champion.

Without Margaret, many things might have been different. Van Buren probably would have outfoxed Calhoun in the end anyway—the Eaton affair only exacerbated and exaggerated fundamental differences of political opinion, chiefly on the question of the nature of the Union, between Calhoun and Jackson, but it would probably have been more difficult, and taken longer. Calhoun himself thought the affair crucial in Jackson's decision to turn on his first vice president. With the Margaret issue alive, Calhoun said, "the road to favor and patronage lay directly before me, could I have been base enough to tread it. The intimate relation between Gen. Jackson and Maj. Eaton was well known." That Calhoun's influence was checked by the Eatons does not necessarily mean the vice president would have thrived had Eaton left the Cabinet in the first spring of the administration. In Jackson's mind the damage was perhaps done, and in his regret at losing Eaton he might have exacted revenge on Calhoun and others. There is little question, however, that the race between Calhoun and Van Buren would have been run on a different track, and what Calhoun in 1831 called the "artful machinations" of those who "have placed Gen. Jackson and myself in our present relation"—the "present relation" at that juncture meaning, essentially, that Jackson would just as soon have shot the vice president of the United States—would have had to find a different weapon to begin dividing Jackson from Calhoun.

As it turned out, Eaton chose to soldier on, with Jackson commanding Margaret's lean but determined forces. There would be no resignation, no capitulation, no surrender.

BY JUNE 1829, after his talk of retreating from the field, Eaton hoped that the combination of Jackson's confidence and his own brave face might carry the day. "It is Sunday, the good and pious be all at Church, my-

self at home," Eaton wrote John Coffee. Eaton's gratitude to Jackson was evident; many other politicians
would have thrown Eaton over when they had the
chance. In writing to Coffee, Eaton found himself mar-
veling at the image of Jackson that came to him as he
put words to paper. "Our old friend is himself again"
after his latest illness, Eaton said. "Occasionally, when
home and the Hermitage is chanced to be named, you
may perceive something of deep emotion; but ordinarily he is lively, cheerful and agreeable—professing the
same undying industry and the same prying curiosity to
ascertain whatever is right and proper to be done, as he
ever had. . . . President Jackson and Andrew Jackson are
one and the same thing. . . . Such a man cannot fail to
win the esteem and confidence of the people."

The only exceptions, according to Eaton: "those
who have been removed from their offices" and—in
an indirect allusion to his plight—those for "whom
motive dictates a contrary feeling." It was Eaton's only
brush with self-pity. He soon returned to his rhapsody
to Jackson: "He has firmness enough, you know, to go
on with what he believes to be right, let those opposed
find fault and abuse as they may." Eaton's closing was
brief: "My wife desires to be kindly remembered to
you."

Jackson, it is true, could be wrongheaded about
things, but his defense of the Eatons should not be
seen, as it sometimes is, as simply a case of prideful defiance undertaken by a president who loved a fight for
fight's sake. That the attacks on his friend's wife came
so soon after those on his own beloved and seemed to

him—perhaps wrongly—to be as baseless surely fueled Jackson's Eaton campaign, but the echoes were not the only driving force. Jackson understood that he was expending precious political capital and untold hours battling for the Eatons' full acceptance into Washington society, but he was doing it less for Margaret than for her husband, for whom he held genuine regard and whose good sense appears to have extended to every aspect of public life except for his own marriage.

THE FIGHT OVER Biddle's Bank was progressing, too, in its way. On Saturday, June 27, 1829, Senator Levi Woodbury, a future Jackson Cabinet secretary, wrote Treasury Secretary Samuel Ingham from Portsmouth, New Hampshire, to report that parts of the business community there, and a number of Jackson supporters, were unhappy with Jeremiah Mason, the president of the Portsmouth branch. Petitions were en route to make the case that Mason, a Federalist who was close to Daniel Webster and to John Quincy Adams, had been "partial, harsh, novel, and injurious." It was the old story: the Bank was said to be under the influence of men hostile to Jackson.

As he had in the face of earlier charges against other branches, Biddle conceded nothing. In August he traveled to New Hampshire himself to look into the matter and dismissed the allegations. Jeremiah Mason would continue in charge in Portsmouth. The complaints of the Jacksonians were ignored. Biddle took the occasion, in a letter to Secretary Ingham on Tuesday, September 15, 1829, to assert his own authority in stark language. The Bank, its branches, its directors, and its president, Biddle wrote Ingham, "acknowledge not the slightest responsibility of any description whatsoever to the Secretary of the Treasury touching the political opinions and conduct of their officers, that being a subject on which they never consult and never desire to know, the views of any administration." Biddle said he and the Bank's directors were reluctant to underscore their own power, "but charged as they are by Congress with duties of great importance to the country . . . they deem it most becoming to themselves, as well as to the Executive, to state with perfect frankness their opinion of any interference in the concerns of the institution confided to their care." Biddle was essentially accurate: though the federal government named five of the Bank's twenty-five directors, there was no mechanism for Congress or a presidential administration to control the Bank once it was chartered—save two possible courses. First, the administration could remove the government's deposits from the Bank, fatally crippling it; or, second, it could kill the institution more frontally by declining to renew its charter, which was to expire in 1836.

Biddle could not really conceive of either. His view of his own power was absolute. Presidents came and went, but the Bank, Biddle believed, was eternal. Jackson's understanding of things was very different, and there was a clue to the president's thinking in a memorandum in Jackson's hand about how Ingham should reply to Biddle's assertion of autonomy. The Treasury secretary and the president, Jackson noted, could "redress all grievances complained of by the people of the interference by the branches with the local elections of the states, and all their interference with party politics, in every section of the country, where those complaints have reached the Executive." The president of the United States and no one else—certainly no banker—spoke for a free people.

DESPITE THE DISPIRITING Eaton business, Jackson was comfortable in the White House, where he was charming even old-line Washingtonians like Margaret Bayard Smith. "We visited the President and his family a few days since, in the big house," Mrs. Smith wrote shortly after the Jackson circle moved in. "Mr. Smith introduced us and asked for the General. Our names were sent in and he joined the ladies in the drawing-room. I shall like him if ever I know him, I am sure—so simple, frank, friendly. . . . His pew in church is behind ours, his manner is humble and reverent and most attentive."

Jackson knew the thrust and tenor of the conversations his foes had about him around their dinner tables and at their firesides, and he knew, too, that personal contact was one way to slow the thrust and soften the tenor. He made certain, then, not to become a distant monarch. Loyalists and skeptics alike were welcome in his house.

When Martha Jefferson Randolph, Thomas Jefferson's daughter, moved from Monticello to Washington, Emily and Jackson each paid calls on her, honoring a former mistress of the White House. Mrs. Randolph, whose mother had died in 1782, long before Jefferson's 1801–09 presidency, had served from time to time as her father's hostess when he was president. She had given birth to a son (named James after James Madison, Jefferson's secretary of state) in the White House, the first child to be born there, and Jackson instantly recognized her as a dowager figure due his respect. He asked Van Buren to write to see whether he might call on her.

The answer was yes. Jackson and Van Buren saw her together, followed by Emily and Mary—an extraordinary gesture, for it was traditional for the president and his household to receive the initial call as a mark of respect, and then return calls as they pleased. As the first provincial White House circle, however, Jackson and the Donelsons discerned the wisdom of displaying deference to a grande dame from the city's already mythical past. They knew that the highbrow dinner-table abuse of Jackson in houses such as the Smiths' and the John Quincy Adamses' presupposed a fall from the golden age of the first six presidencies. True provincial revolutionaries would not have cared what was said of them. They would more likely have reveled in their isolation, savoring the mix of disdain and fear their ascension occasioned from an elite that felt a sudden, possibly irretrievable loss of control and command.

Jackson and the Donelsons, however, were not true provincial revolutionaries. They were sophisticated about the ways and means of society and their connection to the ways and means of politics. Ralph Waldo Emerson—who, in the early years of the Jackson presidency, was a Unitarian minister at the Second Church in Boston—once wrote that "there is properly no history, only biography." Even at the pinnacle, politics is intensely personal. People who believe they are valued and set apart in the mind of a leader are less likely to be implacable foes. Jackson knew that both men and massive, impersonal forces shaped nations, and he was determined to use his own personality to, if not convert, then at least charm those who shaped the climate of opinion in which he was to govern.

Hence the sweetness to the Smiths on their first visit and the calls on Mrs. Randolph: better to keep the establishment close, or at least off guard, than to alienate it altogether. The fact of a president's power and the White House itself are the most formidable weapons on the field. It is the unusual political creature who will not be softened, at least briefly, by the gift of attention from the incumbent, especially if the gift is bestowed within the walls of the White House.

LITTLE IN WASHINGTON was as it seemed. John Campbell and Ezra Ely, clergymen who were supposed to be above the social and political fray, were instead spreading stories of sin and scandal. Emily and Andrew, the family Jackson had thought he could count on no matter what, were failing to follow his wishes with enthusiasm. He had a vice president hostile to the su-

premacy of the Union. John Eaton, far from being the
rock on which Jackson could rely in the Cabinet, was
the source of chaos.

Martin Van Buren was, for Jackson, a surprising
figure of order. They began riding on horseback most
days, and the intimacy of those hours created a strong
bond between the president and his secretary of state.
The diminutive New Yorker and gaunt Tennessean
made an unlikely match. "We are getting along extremely well. . . . The President proves to be in all respects a finer man than I anticipated," Van Buren
wrote a friend.

Van Buren knew that Jackson's political isolation
could be disastrous. Elected by a coalition of regions
and interests, Jackson could not afford to cut ties to all
who disagreed with him. In Washington, as in capitals
everywhere, this afternoon's foe may become this
evening's ally. Politics is rather like a theatrical company in which a troupe of actors are cast in different
roles depending on the moment or the issue at hand.

In this spirit, Van Buren asked Jackson about going
to pay a call on John Quincy Adams. Van Buren did
not expect Jackson to come along; he simply wanted
to clear his course with the president. Such a courtesy
toward Adams could not hurt, and might one day
help, for Van Buren's goal as he took up his duties at
the State Department was not only the success of the
Jackson years but the elimination of Calhoun as a
rival to follow Jackson. Keeping up warm—or at least
warmish—relations with the former president from
New England was good politics for a New Yorker with

national ambitions at a time when the South was inclined in another direction. Jackson heard Van Buren out and approved. Though he hated Adams for what he believed to be the former president's role in the 1828 attacks on Rachel, Jackson recognized the value of loyalty. If Van Buren wanted to see Adams, then Van Buren should see Adams.

Greeting Van Buren on the first Saturday in April, the former president was at once pleased and sour. Rejected by the voters, ignored by Jackson, struggling to find solace in literature (he was reading the eleventh Philippic of Cicero) and gossip, the former president, remembering his days of power, confided his self-pity to his diary, writing that "all the members" of Jackson's administration "have been with me upon terms of friendly acquaintance, and have repeatedly shared the hospitalities of my house." But Adams was no longer either on the rise or at the pinnacle. And so, Adams wrote, "they have all gradually withdrawn from all social intercourse with me." Receiving Van Buren, Adams was grateful for the attention. "Of the new Administration he is the only person who has shown me this mark of common civility," Adams noted. The two spoke of the weather, and of ongoing negotiations about American trade with Turkey and access to the Black Sea.

Congratulating himself that he had been "very cordially received by Mr. Adams," Van Buren believed that his mission to Meridian Hill, the Adams home in Washington, to "reestablish friendly relations" between Jackson and Adams had a "good prospect of success."

Writing in his diary that evening, Adams assessed Van Buren coldly and accurately: Van Buren was, Adams said, "by far the ablest man of them all, but wasting most of his ability upon mere personal intrigues. . . . His principles are all subordinate to his ambition, and he will always be of that doctrine upon which he shall see his way clear to rise."

VAN BUREN LIKED everyone to like him. Toward the end of a visit with Emily and Mary Eastin one day in the spring, Margaret's name came up in conversation. Though Van Buren was in the Eatons' camp, he knew Emily's views and had therefore kept his own opinions on the matter to himself when he was in her company. In the Washington of that time, though, it was impossible to go long without talking over what Van Buren called "the Eaton malaria," and Emily, anxious to know Van Buren's thinking, could not stand his diplomatic silence any longer. In a tone that Van Buren thought "conveyed, tho' gently, a complaint of my reserve," Emily "expressed her surprise that whilst almost every tongue in the city was canvassing [Margaret's] merits and demerits, she had never heard me say anything upon the subject." Van Buren had to leave, but agreed to come back another day to take up this most sensitive of subjects.

Returning, he heard Emily explain herself in terms that were consistent with her earliest letters on the subject. It was not Margaret's virtue that worried her, she said; it was, rather, Margaret's abrasive personality. Van Buren heard Emily out, then, in a failed avuncular maneuver, committed the same sin Eaton had in his letter by suggesting that Emily was "being controlled in her course by persons" whom she esteemed— the established families in Washington again—and who had "unduly influenced" her.

At this Emily's rage began to rise. Failing to detect her anger, Van Buren charged forward. This was about more than society, he lectured: it was about "the situation of her Uncle" and "the difficulties he had to contend with in the performance of his public duties"—as though Emily did not already appreciate the political stakes. Van Buren then pushed yet further. Emily's decisions, he said, were affecting "the peace and harmony" of the family circle Jackson loved, causing Jackson "misery." Mary Eastin, who had been listening to Van Buren's speech, was horrified by his candor. Grasping Emily's fury, Mary "sought to hide her emotions by gradually withdrawing herself from sight in the embrasure of the window," Van Buren recalled, and she "sobbed aloud." At this point, at the sound of Mary's crying, Van Buren realized the effect his words were having on Emily. Suddenly he saw that Emily, far from benefiting from his counsel, was "deeply agitated" and "offended."

Van Buren nearly panicked. "I rose from my seat, begging her to excuse whatever I might, under the excitement of the moment, have said to hurt her feelings," Van Buren recalled. Retreating, he "asked her permission to drop the subject"—which they did.

IT WAS A tense time. Living in close quarters, in daily if not hourly contact with Jackson, Andrew and Emily knew how important the Eaton question was to the president. They were there to comfort and to serve, not to antagonize, yet they had made their choice and they were as subject to the paralyzing force of pride as Jackson was.

On an excursion aboard the steamboat **Potomac** to Norfolk, Virginia, a few months later, in July, the Eatons joined Jackson, the Donelsons, and others for the trip. At Alexandria an artillery company fired a salute to the president; crowds of admirers awaited on the beach at Norfolk. Emily was nearly eight months pregnant, and the midsummer voyage proved too much for her. As the boat moved south, she began to feel faint. Margaret offered her fan and cologne bottle, essential tools for a fainting woman in the early nineteenth century. Even in distress, though, Emily remained consistent in her aversion to Margaret—an aversion that was by now visceral. She would not accept Margaret's help, and in her refusal made it obvious that she would rather collapse in a heap than be indebted to Margaret Eaton for anything.

As Emily fainted, the spurned Margaret grew furious. Andrew, who was elsewhere on the **Potomac**, was summoned, and once Emily was made comfortable, he saw Margaret "betray an extraordinary discomposure of temper," as he put it. Puzzled about what had happened—but sure that something had—Andrew escorted Margaret off the boat once it had docked for, he said, "the purpose of ascertaining the cause" of her latest fit of anger. "She informed me . . . that Mrs. Donelson had . . . showed a disposition not to be intimate with her," Andrew recalled.

Hot and humiliated, Margaret overplayed her hand. Rather than letting the events of the day speak for themselves—that she had acted charitably when faced with a crisis, and Emily had been cold and possibly rude—Margaret let her hatred for the couple overwhelm her. As Donelson recalled it, she announced that she felt "pity" for Andrew and Emily, for Jackson "had agreed that if we did not behave differently . . . to send us back to Tennessee."

Her presumption infuriated Andrew, but even he, as close as he was to Jackson, could not be certain whether Margaret had the power to displace Jackson's closest family. The fear of a woman's secret hand at court had ancient roots, and the worry about what Duff Green, the editor of the **Telegraph,** called Margaret's "secret influence" over not only society but politics was making a nervous capital even more so. "The interference of the lady in matters of public concern, her active interference in appointments, and the success of applicants who threw themselves on her influence, soon provoked inquiry and much speculation as to her private character, and rumor was again busy with her reputation," Green said.

It is unlikely that such charges were true. Eaton and

Lewis certainly had influence with Jackson, and observers inclined to do so could attribute the Eaton-
Lewis faction's victories in the administration to
Eaton's wife. In political terms, however, the facts
mattered little. It was said that Margaret "flatters up
the old General in great style and it runs down even to
the hem of his garment like oil." People believed Margaret to be a power, and the idea that appointments
were decided, even in part, "as the means of gratifying
the private pique of a vain and indiscreet, if not a
guilty woman," Green said, made life more complicated and difficult for Jackson.

ON THE EVENING of Wednesday, August 19—the
weather was lovely—Jackson again boarded the **Potomac** to retreat to the Rip Raps, Virginia, a seaside military enclave near Norfolk. On the trip south through
the waters of the Chesapeake Bay, his mind returned, as
it did often, to Rachel and to Tennessee. He was worried about the only thing he could do for her now: the
tending of her grave. Writing to Andrew Jackson, Jr.,
Jackson wondered "whether the weeping willows that
we planted" around the tomb were "growing, or whether
the flowers reared by her industrious and beloved hands
have been set around the grave as I had requested." It
was not an idle question. "My dear son, inform me on
this subject," Jackson wrote. "You know it is the one
dearest to my heart, and her memory will remain fresh
there as long as life lasts."

Within his circle, matters of the heart, from love to
jealousy, were bringing him only misery. Amid every-

thing else Jackson had to deal with, Andrew junior had been troubling the president with a debate about whether to marry a girl he was courting in Tennessee. Jackson was cool to the idea, hoping that the twenty-year-old Andrew would wait to wed. Writing from aboard the **Potomac,** though, Jackson had only a small hope that his son would heed him. No one else he loved seemed to be listening to him on personal matters. "I beg you, my son, enter into no more love affairs until you see me," Jackson wrote. "You have many years yet for the improvement of your mind and to make a selection of a companion."

Finishing his fatherly admonition, Jackson arrived at the Rip Raps, where the military was building a fortress named after Calhoun in recognition of the vice president's service as secretary of war under Monroe. Steaks, English cheese, turtle soup, veal, ducks, and a gallon of whiskey were ordered in over the ten-day stay. Newspapers reported Jackson's relaxing routine, telling readers that the president had been "inhaling the salubrious ocean breeze, and daily taking the salt water bath." Jackson also dealt with correspondence and, the Richmond **Enquirer** said, "is at all times accessible and affable to those who call on him merely en passant, and appears to enjoy a fine flow of spirits for an invalid." The only seaside peril he encountered: a sea-nettle jellyfish stung him, inflaming his forehead.

John Eaton kept the president company while the Donelsons remained in Washington; Emily's baby was due any day. "**My dear and sincere friend Major**

Eaton is with me," Jackson wrote Andrew junior, underscoring the words, and "**he is worthy to be called friend.**"

EATON HAD JACKSON'S ear at the moment, and Margaret's words still echoed in Donelson's memory. Were he and Emily secure, or would the rise of the Eatons eclipse them? How could Donelson be sure that his own future was not under attack in Eaton's private exchanges with Jackson?

Then, on Saturday, August 29, 1829, Andrew Donelson received an evening call from the Reverend John Campbell. It was not a social visit. Margaret had learned that Campbell was a source for Ely's charges, and Campbell decided it would be best to come forward before the Eatons—fueled by passion and armed with information—could mount their attack on him. Stiff and formal, Campbell arrived at the White House in the humid darkness and climbed the stairs to Donelson's office in the far northeast corner of the second floor.

The minister came straight to the point. At the time of the inauguration, Campbell said, he had felt bound by "feelings of the most sincere friendship" for Jackson, "as well as a sense of duty to religion and the interests of the society in which he was performing the services of a Pastor," to try to derail Eaton's nomination to the Cabinet. His reason: the story of Margaret's alleged miscarriage and implicit adultery.

Donelson immediately grasped the implications of Campbell's revelations. Here, standing only a dozen paces from the door of the president's office, was the man whose hidden hand had pushed Ely to oppose Margaret Eaton. For six months, Jackson had been raging against visible political foes (Clay and Calhoun), but, aside from Ely, had found the sources of the Eaton rumors to be maddeningly invisible. Campbell's confession, Donelson knew, opened a new front with a new enemy. Campbell must have known this, too, for he asked a favor of Donelson: Would Donelson absorb the first blows from Jackson by relating Campbell's story to the president?

It was a clever but cowardly move on Campbell's part, and Donelson refused. When it came to the Eatons, he had enough problems with Jackson without appearing to be the agent of the opposition. "I declined a conversation with the President on the subject," Donelson said. Campbell was trapped. He would have to face Jackson alone.

After Campbell left, disappearing into the night to prepare for services the next morning, Donelson walked down the hallway to bed. So much to think about, so much to balance. The pregnant Emily slept in their big room at the west end of the house. "She seems strong and ready for the trial," Donelson told Coffee, but childbirth could be harrowing. Campbell's announcement, Donelson later wrote, added "combustible qualities" to the crisis that could "be ignited in so many different ways . . . that sooner or later, we must anticipate an explosion."

Meanwhile, Donelson knew Calhoun was up to no good. A correspondent from South Carolina had told him to expect that Calhoun would "attempt much next winter at Washington and endeavor to place himself at the head of the Anti-Tariff party"—which meant the head of the nullifying party. But instead of taking the summer to gather his forces and his strength to fight Calhoun, Jackson was exhausting himself over the Eatons. Jackson's emotions "have been steamed to the highest point," Donelson told Coffee, "and have done more to paralyze his energies than years of the regular and simple operations of the Gov. ought to have done." Retiring for the night on this August Saturday, Donelson understood there were still more tumultuous months to come.

THE FOLLOWING DAY passed quietly as the household began to prepare for Jackson's homecoming on Tuesday. Then, on Monday, the thirty-first, in the Donelsons' big bedroom, Emily bore a healthy little girl, Mary Rachel. The baby, her proud father wrote Coffee, was "a fine healthy child," and Emily was "quite strong." Thanking him for the "gratifying intelligence" of the safe birth, Coffee told Donelson, "I assure you the family was greatly relieved . . . in as much as great anxiety had been felt for Emily." Arriving in Washington the next day, the first of September, Jackson declared little Mary "the Sunshine of the White House," and was reminded anew of the role Emily and Andrew played in his life.

On the evening of Tuesday, September 1, John Campbell returned to the White House and again went upstairs. Donelson greeted him and showed him to Jackson's office while Jimmy O'Neal, the door-keeper, rousted from his quarters, went to find the president, who was relaxing with William Lewis in a sitting room on the first floor. Hearing that his pastor was waiting, Jackson went upstairs, leaving a curious Lewis behind.

After Jackson arrived, Donelson left the two men alone. As he had on the previous Saturday, Campbell, having summoned up his courage to come, moved to the heart of the matter and repeated his story to the president. Jackson was stunned. "Never having suspected or even heard it lisped that the Reverend Campbell was the individual, I was truly astonished," Jackson told Ely. This was his pastor, the minister whom he had heard preach week after week through the year. Now he was being told—by the man him-self—the origins of what Jackson called "this **vile tale**": that while married to Timberlake, Margaret had miscarried a baby after Timberlake had been away at sea for at least a year. The two men disputed dates and details. The conversation was going nowhere.

"We parted," Jackson said tersely. Campbell left the mansion. The president went in search of documents that would contradict Campbell's story, and was soon confident that he found sufficient evidence in Timberlake's old papers. To Jackson, victory seemed at hand. Peace in the capital, and in his Cabinet, was imminent. It looked as though this might be the most glorious of weeks. First the birth of the new Donelson and now the vindication of Margaret: perhaps Jackson could at last dispel the shadows that had hung over him and his presidency since Rachel's death.

Jackson called for Donelson and asked him to arrange with Campbell what Jackson assumed would be one of the final interviews on the Eaton affair. Leaving Emily and the baby, Donelson did as he was asked, and the meeting was set for Thursday. It was a clear, pleasantly warm day, and Jackson awoke and dressed with every expectation that the world was about to be set right. Campbell and Donelson gathered in Jackson's office. As sunlight came in the two windows facing south toward Virginia, Jackson "stated the result of my inquiry . . . and having the proof in my hand, observed that it evidenced, beyond all contradiction, that the tale of [the miscarriage] could not be true."

His tone could not have been anything but one of satisfaction, even triumph. He awaited his foe's capitulation. He would be gracious in conquest, but he wanted the conquered to acknowledge defeat and ask how to make reparations.

BUT CAMPBELL WOULD not surrender. Jackson "must have misunderstood him as to the date," he said. Perhaps nothing Campbell might have said at that moment could have flabbergasted and infuriated Jackson more. Jackson had had enough. The appointment was over. Campbell was dismissed, but he remained central in Jackson's mind as he turned to write an urgent letter to Ely in Philadelphia summoning him to Washington:

"I think it necessary that you come on here as soon as you can." Jackson wanted to air the charges, refute them, and break Campbell.

"Man born of woman is full of trouble," Eaton had said in the midst of this maddening week. Once Ely arrived, the showdown was set for Thursday, September 10, 1829. The setting: a special meeting of the Cabinet, in the president's office, at seven in the evening.

CHAPTER 9

★

AN OPINION OF
THE PRESIDENT ALONE

ORD—GARBLED, INCOMPLETE WORD—
of the battle between the president and the
clergymen was leaking out into Washington.
Writing his wife in mid-September 1829, John Quincy
Adams said, "I have a confused story about Mr. Campbell of the Presbyterian Church and Dr. Ely . . . altogether unintelligible to me." One reason the story may
have been "confused" and even "unintelligible" to the
former president is that those who knew all were not
talking much, and those who knew only a little were
talking a great deal—a common feature of life in Washington.

The special meeting of the Cabinet took place that
Thursday, on a cloudy and rather cool evening. A
light breeze blew outside as Ely, Campbell, and the
secretaries sat at the rectangular table in front of the
fireplace. Eaton was not there; Jackson represented his
interests. Andrew left Emily and the new baby to
come down the long hall to the session. Lewis made
his way from his room, took a left, walked beneath
two arches, and came in. Jackson began with a lecture,

James Parton wrote, "upon the meanness of calumny." He and Campbell again angrily argued over the alleged miscarriage.

At a stalemate on the question—Jackson said it could not have happened; Campbell said it had, though he could not name the year—Jackson moved on. Finally came the charge of Eaton and Margaret spending the night together in a New York hotel, a tale Ely had investigated and found wanting. "The reverend gentleman told his story, and concluded by saying that there was no evidence to convict Major Eaton of improper conduct," Parton wrote.

"Nor Mrs. Eaton, either," Jackson said.

"On that point," Ely said, "I would rather not give an opinion."

Jackson could take no more. "She is as chaste as a virgin!" he said, but no one in the room appears to have seconded the president's sentiment. Campbell was unbending, gambling that the volume of rumors about Margaret outweighed any defense, even one marshaled by the president. The allegations about Margaret, Louisa Adams wrote her husband, "are so public that my servants are telling them [at the] tea table." As usual, Margaret had done herself little good by talking. Much of the to-ing and fro-ing between the president, the clergy, and the Eatons was known because of Margaret, Mrs. Adams said: "All this got abroad from the intemperate language of the Lady."

Though Jackson would not give up the fight, there is a hint that he did find the storm over Margaret's sexual history unsavory. He was standing by his friend

Eaton, but he did not want his own family to be cast in such a light.

He was relieved, therefore, to hear from Andrew Jackson, Jr., that a "little engagement" with a Tennessee girl named Flora had been broken off, following Jackson's fatherly advice. Jackson, who knew the young woman, believed she "had given herself up to coquetry," and suggested in the aftermath that his adopted son "treat her with all kindness, but I assure you I am happy at the result, as I seldom ever saw a coquette make a good wife."

He wrote these words only eleven days after declaring Margaret "as chaste as a virgin"—a defense even she herself would not have advanced. "When you marry, if ever," Jackson told Andrew junior, "I wish you to marry a lady who will make a good wife and I, a good daughter, as my happiness depends much upon the prudence of your choice." As Jackson had learned anew since the Eatons' wedding, marriage was not a private matter, and he did not want his son bringing another flirtatious woman into his circle.

JACKSON WAS FINDING executive power ever more congenial as the months went by before his first annual message, due to be delivered at the convening of Congress in December 1829. He might not be able to move the ladies of Washington, but he could put his own people in federal offices, threaten (however subtly) Biddle, make his intentions clear to the Indians, and, two days after the Eaton Cabinet meeting, he launched a secret diplomatic initiative to establish more favorable trade relations with Turkey. In a note marked "Secret and Confidential," dated Saturday, September 12, 1829, Jackson instructed Navy Secretary John Branch to put $20,000 at the disposal of the commander of the U.S. squadron in the Mediterranean to pay the costs of a mission to Sultan Mahmud II of Turkey. The sultan had lost Greece and much of his fleet in a fabled revolution in the 1820s (Lord Byron died fighting for Greek independence from the Muslim Turks). Turkey needed ships; Jackson wanted expanded commerce in that part of the world. Ignoring the Senate, which had traditionally approved the appointment of commissioners who undertook such missions, Jackson moved unilaterally: the fewer players, the stronger his control. He would deal with the Congress in due course. First he wanted action, and so the commissioners set out for Constantinople.

In the autumn of 1829, Nicholas Biddle paid a call on Andrew Jackson. It was a cordial enough session, with Jackson explaining his reservations about the Bank, and Biddle, as usual, appearing unconcerned about Jackson's skepticism. "I do not dislike your Bank any more than all banks," Jackson told Biddle, according to a memorandum Biddle kept of the conversation. "But ever since I read the history of the South Sea bubble"—referring to a failed land speculation scheme in England—"I have been afraid of banks." Jackson had also learned to fear debt and lenders in the most personal way possible: he had been nearly ruined by them. In 1795, he became involved with a speculator in Philadelphia and ended up in what he called "great difficulty" that he only narrowly escaped. From that point on, Jackson was skeptical of promissory notes, land speculation, and financial maneuvering.

He was grateful, however, that Biddle was planning to make the final payment on the national debt by the anniversary of the Battle of New Orleans in 1833, and said he would mention his thanks in his December message to Congress. "That is my own feeling to the Bank—and Mr. Ingham's also," Jackson said, according to Biddle. "[Jackson] said with the Parent Board and myself he had every reason to be perfectly satisfied," Biddle recorded, and then apparently chose not to take the president's next point seriously: "[Jackson] had heard complaints and then mentioned a case at Louisville—of which he promised to give me the particulars." Jackson was not so satisfied, then, that he was not eager to continue registering the complaints of the people.

But Biddle chose to hear what he wanted to hear. "I said, well I am very much gratified at this frank explanation," Biddle recalled himself saying. "We shall all be proud of any kind mention in the message—for we should feel like soldiers after an action commended by their General."

"Sir," said Jackson, "it would be only an act of justice to mention it."

A SERIES OF Washington parties made the Eaton matter even more unpleasant. As the December session of Congress approached, the president gave the traditional dinner in honor of his Cabinet. It was held on

Thursday, November 26, 1829, in the East Room. The evening had its glamorous elements, with elegantly dressed women and bemedaled and beribboned military officers circulating through the first-floor rooms; Barry, the postmaster general, and the only Eaton ally in the Cabinet except for Van Buren, called it "the most splendid entertainment I have ever been at in Washington." The vice president and his wife were still in South Carolina, but many of the guests—presumably led by the Inghams, the Branches, and the Berriens—were cool to the Eatons, and Van Buren noted the president's "mortification at what was passing before his eyes."

Van Buren soon gave another dinner, but not a single Cabinet wife, including Margaret, accepted. He tried again, throwing an even more ambitious evening party. This time the company was large (even Calhoun, now in town, came; his wife had remained behind in South Carolina). Margaret was there, too, and at one point during the night, Van Buren ducked downstairs to take a rest on a sofa. He was soon interrupted by word that there had been a scene on the dance floor between Margaret and the wife of Alexander Macomb, the commanding general of the U.S. Army. They had bumped into each other and quarreled; Van Buren was summoned by a friend "to prevent a fight." The evening was less than triumphant.

A later ball given by the Russian minister, Baron Paul de Krudener, nearly led to the expulsion of the Dutch envoy, Bangeman Huygens, and his wife. Because Mrs. Calhoun and Mrs. Ingham were absent,

Mrs. Eaton was the ranking Cabinet wife, and Krudener escorted her in to dinner. John Eaton offered
his arm to Madame Huygens, who was said to be furious (it was alleged that she had expected Van Buren
to escort her, but the secretary of state was detained at
the card table). Angry at being linked so overtly to the
Eatons—the Huygenses were also seated with them at
Krudener's dinner—Madame Huygens was said to
have vowed social revenge by declaring she would give
a party, snub the Eatons, and that Ingham, Branch,
and Berrien would follow suit.

Jackson heard the Huygens rumors and, after a
sleepless night worrying over the possibility that the
diplomatic world was to oppose him over the Eatons,
joining his own secretary of the Treasury, attorney general, and secretary of the navy, he called for Van Buren,
who went to see the Huygenses. If they were in fact actively conspiring against the president and the Eatons,
they would have to leave the country. In their conversation with Van Buren, the Huygenses denied that
there was any kind of plot at work. Van Buren took
their word, as did Jackson, who "received the information with unaffected pleasure." There would, at least,
be no international incident over Margaret.

AS THE AUTUMN wore on, Emily went to Jackson
to talk about Mary Rachel's baptism. She had barely
raised the subject when Jackson interrupted her. "Spare
no expense nor pains, ma'am," he said. "Let us make it
an event to be remembered; we will do all honor to the

baby." Emily was touched, and the arrangements that took shape blended the important elements in Jackson's universe—clan, faith, and country.

The service would be in the East Room, the liturgy taken from the Episcopal Book of Common Prayer. Congressmen, senators, diplomats, secretaries, judges, and military officers filled the elegant room. Emily and Andrew had chosen to have one godfather, Van Buren, and one godmother, Cora Livingston, for their daughter. Given the politics of the moment, asking Van Buren was interesting, but it also suggests that as difficult as things were, there were bonds of affection and respect among those closest to Jackson.

Was there an element of shrewdness in the choice as well? Were Emily and Andrew, even unconsciously, reaching out to Jackson's closest ally to secure their position? Perhaps, but a widowed, gentle father himself, Van Buren, like Jackson, adored children, and Emily and Andrew were at once perceptive and forgiving enough to see his essential goodness despite their differing views on the Eatons. They knew Van Buren to be a kind man who loved their uncle almost as they loved him. It is a testament to their unusual maturity of judgment and capacity to keep their political disputes free from rancor that the Donelsons so honored Van Buren.

Van Buren was to hold Mary Rachel as the minister read the office, but she burst into tears and would be calmed only when Jackson himself swept her up in his long arms. Then the officiant hushed the gathering and began with the Lord's Prayer.

Addressing Cora and Van Buren, the officiant asked, "Dost thou, in the name of this child, renounce the devil and all his works, the vain pomp and glory of the world, with all covetous desires of the same, and the sinful desires of the flesh, so that thou wilt not follow, nor be led by them?"

Cora and Van Buren did not have a chance to answer. Hearing the question, Jackson, who was not supposed to have a speaking part, could not help himself, and announced with authority, "I do, sir, I renounce them all!"—a decided, improvised, but heartfelt reply that prompted smiles in the congregation. No little girl ever had a more sincere protector speak for her at such a moment.

UPSTAIRS, AT WORK on his annual message to Congress, the sentiments from the baptism remained with the president. "In communicating with you for the first time it is to me a source of unfeigned satisfaction, calling for mutual gratulation and devout thanks to a benign Providence, that we are at peace with all mankind, and that our country exhibits the most cheering evidence of general welfare and progressive improvement," Jackson said. "Turning our eyes to other nations, our great desire is to see our brethren of the human race secured in the blessings enjoyed by ourselves, and advancing in knowledge, in freedom, and in social happiness."

The making of Jackson's speeches and messages often began with thoughts and points he would jot down and give to Donelson, who kept a running file. Cabinet secretaries and advisers were asked to sketch out what they thought the president should say about particular issues. The president then frequently produced a lengthy draft in his own hand—the documents tended to the lawyerlike, marshaling evidence—which he would hand off to Donelson, Kendall, and others for revision and refinement.

Jackson's message went to Capitol Hill on Tuesday, December 8, 1829. It was the Twenty-first Congress of the United States, with 213 representatives and 48 senators representing 24 states; the president's supporters enjoyed majorities of 136–72 in the House and 25–23 in the Senate.

The document reflected the will of a single man—Andrew Jackson—and its sweep promised a new course for the presidency and for the country. Looking abroad, he articulated the principle that had already driven him to take on piracy near Cuba and to open the secret mission to Turkey: he would protect the nation, come what may. "Blessed as our country is with everything which constitutes national strength, she is fully adequate to the maintenance of all her interests," Jackson said. "In discharging the responsible trust confided to the Executive in this respect it is my settled purpose to ask nothing that is not clearly right and to submit to nothing that is wrong."

He then turned to his vision of the White House. No institution, he argued, should stand between the people and the presidency. There should be no check on the will of the nation in the choice of a president, and that will could be ascertained only by the popular vote. No president had spoken in such a way before. Each of his predecessors, from Washington to the second Adams, had at times moved to expand the power of the office, but none had gone so far as to suggest that the office itself should be in the direct gift of the people. Only the House was so close to the populace. The Senate was controlled by the state legislatures; the presidency by the Electoral College and possibly the House; the courts by the presidency and the Senate.

The president, Jackson believed, should be an instrument of the people against the combined interests of the rich and the incumbent. "Our system of government was by its framers deemed an experiment, and they therefore consistently provided a mode of remedying its defects," Jackson wrote in the message. It was time, he said, to put the presidency on a different footing. Amend the Constitution, Jackson said, to allow the people to have their choice, but—sensitive to the possibility that a president, too, could be corrupt—limit the executive to a single four- or six-year term, thus checking the danger of a despot.

The first principle of America, Jackson believed, was that "the majority is to govern," and the context of this assertion in the message was the connection between the people and the president: "It must be very certain that a President elected by a minority cannot enjoy the confidence necessary to the successful discharge of his duties."

Partly because of his defeat at the hands of the House in 1825, partly because of his fear of the Bank, partly because of his distrust of entrenched officeholders, Jackson believed the country was being controlled by a kind of congressional-financial-bureaucratic complex in which the needs and concerns of the unconnected were secondary to those who were on the inside. It was an oversimplified view, to be sure, but he was convinced of it, as he was convinced that he was to play the hero's role.

He could do so, however, only if the office he now held—the presidency—had the means to marshal what he saw as the will of the people in order to crush the will of the few. His vision of the appointment power was a case in point. "In a country where offices are created solely for the benefit of the people, no one man has any more intrinsic right to official station than another," he said in the message. "Offices were not established to give support to particular men at the public expense. No individual wrong is, therefore, done by removal, since neither appointment to nor continuance in office is a matter of right."

Jackson believed he, as president, was the defender of the liberties of the people and of fair play; his opponents on Capitol Hill chose to see his executive exertions as prelude to dictatorship. In a speech on the Senate floor, David Barton of Missouri, an ally of John Quincy Adams, worried about the perversion of what he thought to be the Founders' will in the matter of the presidency. The Framers and the people of the time, Barton said, feared "Executive encroachment. . . . **The histories of all nations which have lost their liberties lay before them and they saw on their**

pages that arbitrary Executive discretion and will . . .
had been the destroyers of national liberty throughout the greater part of the world . . . and the fathers
did intend . . . to establish a government of law and of
checks and restraints upon Executive will, in which
no case should exist in which the fate of the humblest
citizen whether in private or in public life could depend upon the arbitrary will of a single man."

The stakes of the battle were now clear. It was Jackson and his interpretation of the will of the people
versus those congressmen, senators, Bank presidents,
nullifiers, judges, federal officials, religious activists,
and Indians who differed from him.

On the Bank, Jackson kept his word to Biddle and
mentioned the matter. Far from a salute or an offering
of thanks, though, the allusion was a signal that Jackson wanted to reconsider the Bank's very existence.
"Both the constitutionality and the expediency of the
law creating this bank are well questioned by a large
portion of our fellow-citizens," Jackson said, suggesting perhaps a simpler national bank to handle only
the government's credit and revenues, thus eliminating private profit on the government's money.

Learning of the president's remarks, Biddle tried to
make the best of things. "It is not . . . a cabinet measure, nor a party measure, but a personal measure. As
such it is far less dangerous because if the people know
that this is not an opinion which they must necessarily adopt as a portion of their party creed—but an
opinion of the President alone—a very honest opin-

ion though a very erroneous one—then the question will be decided on its own merits," Biddle wrote to a Senate ally after the message.

IT WAS A personal measure, but because it was Jackson's, it was now a public measure. His view of the presidency was that he was in the White House to fight the people's battles as best he could. Earlier presidents tended to limit their appeals to the broader public (in part because the voting population was much smaller prior to 1828). Jackson was committed to the idea that if left to their own devices, the elite would serve their own interests at the expense of the interests of the many. In 1824–25, he had been unable to stop the powers that were from taking the presidency away from him. He had promised himself and the country that nothing like that would happen on his watch, and he saw the Bank as the embodiment of unfair privilege. "I was aware that the Bank question would be disapproved by all the sordid and interested who prized self-interest more than the perpetuity of our liberty, and the blessings of a free republican government," he wrote to James A. Hamilton in mid-December. "I foresaw the powerful effect, produced by this moneyed aristocracy, upon the purity of elections, and of legislation; that it was daily gaining strength, and by its secret operations was adding to it." He had, therefore, done the most important thing he could do: "I have brought it before the people and I have confidence that they will do their duty."

There was a distinctly Old Republican tone to the annual message. Jackson was calling, in many cases and on many issues, for an approach that would limit the role of the general government. On the tariff, which so vexed South Carolina, for example, Jackson—who, as a senator, had voted in favor of the tariff in 1824—called for moderate reform, avoiding specifics (there would be time enough for those) and laid out the many virtues of retirement of the national debt. Jackson wanted the presidency to be central, but he was less interested in a centralized government, believing that such consolidation (as his contemporaries often called it) led to the rise of special interests like the ones he was now fighting.

Jackson also pressed Indian removal. In a series of twenty-four essays, signed "William Penn," published from Wednesday, August 5, to Saturday, December 19, 1829, Jeremiah Evarts had made the moral case against removal. "Most certainly an indelible stigma will be fixed upon us, if, in the plenitude of our power, and in the pride of our superiority, we shall be guilty of manifest injustice to our weak and defenseless neighbors," Evarts wrote in his first Penn essay. God, Evarts said, was watching, and would hold the country accountable.

In a self-aware passage in the annual message, Jackson admitted that government policy toward the Indians had been a failure, but he asserted that he could see no answer other than removal or submission to state laws. Emigration, he said, "should be voluntary, for it would be as cruel as unjust to compel the aborigines to abandon the graves of their fathers and seek a home in a distant land. But they should be distinctly informed that if they remain within the limits of the states they must be subject to their laws."

Signaling that he understood the moral elements of the problem, Jackson acknowledged the tragedy of it all. "Our conduct toward these people is deeply interesting to our national character. Their present condition, contrasted with what they once were, makes a most powerful appeal to our sympathies. Our ancestors found them the uncontrolled possessors of these vast regions. By persuasion and force they have been made to retire from river to river and from mountain to mountain, until some of the tribes have become extinct and others have left but remnants to preserve for awhile their once terrible names. . . . It is too late to inquire whether it was just in the United States to include them and their territory within the bounds of new states. . . . That step cannot be retraced. A state cannot be dismembered by Congress."

In the hierarchy of Jackson's concerns, the sanctity of the Union outranked any other consideration. As long as the Indians were in the heart of the nation, they were threats—and as threats they had to be removed.

CHRISTMAS 1829 WAS a dim, unremarkable affair at the White House. Sick and unhappy, Jackson was, Lewis said, "in very feeble health"—so feeble that the Jackson circle thought the end might be near. "Indeed, his whole physical system seemed to be totally deranged," Lewis recalled, "his feet and legs, particularly, had been **very much swollen** for several months and continued to get worse every day, until his extreme debility appeared to be rapidly assuming the character of a **confirmed dropsy**"—referring to a now obsolete diagnosis of swollen tissues that could be fatal. Jackson, who ordinarily thrived on offering hospitality to all comers, spent the season, as he had the last, immersed in the most solemn of thoughts. "Things are not as they ought to be here," Amos Kendall wrote Francis Preston Blair.

Lamenting that with Congress in town "my labors increase," Jackson told a friend, "I can with truth say mine is a situation of dignified slavery." Jackson was finding, as presidents do, that he could not control the crush of events.

He was faced, still, with a divided Cabinet and a vice president who was more rival than ally. Speaking of the "old differences" and the "vile tales about Mrs. Eaton," Kendall wrote Blair: "The impression is abroad, but I cannot tell whether it is true or not, that Mr. Calhoun's friends are the principal agitators and instigators of this business. Mr. Calhoun is a madman if he promotes it, and he is not a wise man if he does not put an end to it. What can he expect by separating from General Jackson? But it is useless to speculate. The old General is determined to put an end to all these intrigues as far as he can, whatever may be their object, and if those around him will not harmonize, he will scatter them like a whirlwind."

CHAPTER 10

★

LIBERTY AND UNION, NOW AND FOREVER

EVER RESILIENT, President Jackson rallied from his sickbed on Sunday, January 10, 1830, to host a White House levee. The Cabinet was there, and crowds of others, from five in the afternoon until nearly ten that night. Guests came and went, and Jackson stood with Emily and Mary, the picture of hospitality. One observer watched them approvingly. "Shaking hands with those who had just entered the room, or were about to retire from it, Mrs. Donelson and Miss Eastin of the President's family . . . were dressed in American calico and wore no ruffles and no ornaments of any sort." (Emily's descendant Pauline Wilcox Burke wrote that the calico "serves to show their loyalty to the Jackson party"; in 1828, Old Hickory's partisans had worn it as a sign of support for their candidate. Mrs. Burke added: "No doubt Emily's concession to this whim of fashion was at a personal sacrifice for her choice in dress leaned rather to velvets, brocades and rich satins.")

Emily and Mary were gracious. "They affected no superiority, showed no pride, and from their behavior no one would have supposed that they belonged to the family of the Chief Magistrate of a great nation," the observer said. "Their honor sat so easy on them that they seemed not to know it." It was, he said, "perfect good breeding . . . taught them from their earliest infancy both by precept and example by their Aunt, the good, the amiable, and ever to be lamented Mrs. Jackson."

Van Buren was working the room. His love of the swirl and his favor with Jackson were evident. "There is no scarcity of subjects for an Epistle at the Metropolis of the Union, as you know the inhabitants of Washington insist upon having their City called," John Quincy Adams wrote his daughter-in-law. "It is the prevailing opinion . . . that Mr. Van Buren is about to scale the Presidency of the United States by mounting upon the shoulders of Mrs. Eaton."

At the annual commemoration of Jackson's victory at New Orleans, the guests treated Margaret even more coolly than usual. "She is not received in any private parties, and since the 8th of January has withdrawn from public assemblies," Mrs. Smith said. "At the ball given on that occasion, she was treated with such marked and universal neglect and indignity, that she will not expose herself again to such treatment." Yet Margaret remained central in the public—and political—eye. "Our government is becoming every day more democratic, the rulers of the people are truly their servants and among those rulers women are gaining more than their share of power," Margaret Bayard Smith wrote a friend in January 1830. Referring to Margaret Eaton, Calhoun, and the members of

Jackson's Cabinet, she went on: "One woman has made sad work here; to be, or not to be, her friend is the test of Presidential favor. Mr. V. B. sided with her and is consequently the right hand man, the constant riding, walking, and visiting companion. . . . Mr. Calhoun, Ingham (his devoted friend), Branch and Berrien form one party, the President, V. B., Genl. [**sic**] E., and Mr. Barry the other. It is generally supposed that, as they cannot sit together, some change in the Cabinet must take place."

She was right: the Cabinet nearly cracked up over the matter in early 1830. There were conversations and meetings, and finally a session between the president, Ingham, Branch, and Berrien. "I will not part with Major Eaton from my Cabinet," Jackson told them, "and those of my Cabinet who cannot harmonize with him had better withdraw, for harmony I must and will have." A kind of compromise was reached: Jackson would not press the social question if his Cabinet would agree not to fuel the fires of gossip against the Eatons. There was no mistaking the president's will: he depended on John Eaton. "Any attempt to degrade him I viewed, and should continue to view, as an indignity to myself," Jackson told Ingham, Branch, and Berrien. It was a very fragile peace. William Barry, who, with Van Buren, was the Eatons' only ally in the Cabinet, said, "Society is [still] unhappily divided about her."

THERE WERE, MEANWHILE, signs of trouble in the South. In a letter from Washington to an ally in

Columbia, South Carolina, Senator Robert Hayne wrote: "Our Presses at home ought to refuse to discuss in any way the question of the next presidential election. We have questions of our own entirely above that of whether A. or B. is to be our next President. We must not . . . mix up our complaints with mere party questions." South Carolina was about to face its severest test thus far: an unexpected hearing on the floor of the Senate.

A few days after Christmas, Connecticut senator Samuel Foot put forward a resolution to limit the sale of public lands in the western part of the country, thus checking expansion and settlement—with the added benefit, Western senators noted, of keeping the manufacturers of New England well stocked with cheap labor.

Foot's resolution was the occasion for what became one of the most significant and wide-ranging interludes in American legislative history. From Tuesday, December 29, 1829, the day Foot introduced his resolution, to Friday, May 21, 1830, when Thomas Hart Benton brought the march of oratory to a close, nearly half of the nation's senators entered the fray, delivering a total of sixty-five speeches. The debate, Senator Levi Woodbury said, "seems to have metamorphosed the Senate, not only into a committee of the whole on the state of the Union, but on the state of the Union in all time past, present, and to come." Slavery, states' rights, partisanship, presidential power—very little escaped the collective attention of Jackson's Washington in the winter and spring of

1830. Ordinary citizens filled the two galleries; the overflow of ladies sat among the senators as convictions clashed beneath the gaze of John Calhoun, who presided from a dais flanked by four gray marble columns on each side and capped by a gilded eagle and shield. Lewis kept tabs on the speeches, heading out of the Capitol and down Pennsylvania Avenue to brief Jackson at the White House.

The debate began on Monday, January 18, when Thomas Hart Benton denounced Foot's resolution as an unfair attack on the West. Representing Missouri's view—the less expensive the public lands, the better, for then people, and with them power, would flow across the continent—Benton argued that a measure like Foot's was dangerous, for such legislation would benefit one region at the enormous expense of another. And if the national government was going to target the public lands today, Benton said on the floor, then every part of the country could be at risk in due time: "The whole country may be alarmed, agitated, and enraged, with mischievous inquiries; the South about its slaves and Indians; the West about its lands; the North-east on the subject of its fisheries, its navigation, its light-houses, and its manufactories."

Hearing the remark about the South and the slaves, Hayne sensed an opening to lay out a states' rights manifesto that, if triumphant, could protect slavery.

Handsome and appealing, Hayne had been shaped by the milieu of Charleston, where he had been educated, and the temper of the time in the city was sectional, even parochial. "Yankees were never in great credit here—even their consummate impudence could not gain them admission into society—but now they are in worse odor than ever," Alexander Garden, a Revolutionary War hero in South Carolina, wrote to Charlestonian Charles Manigault in 1828. Hayne shared many of these sentiments. "Viewing the United States as one country, the people of the South might almost be considered as strangers in the land of their fathers," Hayne said, and he warned that the tariff was producing "a spirit of jealousy and distrust." And the tariff, of course, was prelude to abolition in the minds of many Southerners.

Hearing Benton on the eighteenth, Hayne decided to speak on the nineteenth. That day, Daniel Webster was a floor below in the Capitol, in the Supreme Court chamber arguing a case before Chief Justice Marshall. His work there done, Webster, who had no particular business in mind, walked upstairs from the usually chilly court to the Senate with, he said, "my court papers under my arm, just to see what was passing." Amid a long address, in the context of discussing the merits of a national treasury—states' rights advocates feared that concentrated federal funds would lead to corruption—Hayne painted an emotional portrait of the South under the tariff: "The fruits of our labor are drawn from us to enrich other and more favored sections of the Union. . . . The rank grass grows in our streets; our very fields are scathed by the hand of injustice and oppression."

The answer, Hayne said, was local, not central, control. "Sir, I am one of those who believe that the very life of our system is the independence of the states, and that there is no evil more to be deprecated than the consolidation of this Government. It is only by a strict adherence to the limitations imposed by the constitution on the Federal Government that this system works well, and can answer the great ends for which it was instituted."

LISTENING, WEBSTER GREW grim. "I did not like it," he said. In the same way that South Carolina saw New England's hand behind all its troubles, New England was still absorbing Thomas Cooper's July 1827 declaration that it was time to "calculate the value of the Union."

On this windy winter Tuesday, Webster thought of Cooper's threats as he heard Hayne's words. Rising the next day, Webster took the debate to a more momentous plane: that of the nature of the Union itself. That had not been Hayne's chief point, but just as Hayne had seen an opportunity in Benton's words, so Webster saw a chance in Hayne's.

Alluding to the South Carolina hotheads, Webster said: "They significantly declare that it is time to calculate the value of the Union; and their aim seems to be to enumerate, and to magnify, all the evils, real and imaginary, which the Government under the Union produces. The tendency of all these ideas and sentiments is obviously to bring the Union into discussion as a mere question of present and temporary expediency; nothing more than a mere matter of profit and loss."

In a passage evoking the prospect of a tragic civil war, Webster said: "I am a Unionist. . . . I would strengthen the ties that hold us together. Far, indeed, in my wishes, very far distant be the day, when our associated and fraternal stripes shall be severed asunder, and when that happy constellation under which we have risen to so much renown, shall be broken up, and be seen sinking, star after star, into obscurity and night!"

Five days later, Hayne replied to Webster, whose speech had successfully baited his foe into the larger discussion. Defending slavery, laying out the argument for nullification, singing hymns to the glory of his native state, Hayne was articulating Calhoun's worldview, and there were reports that the vice president went so far as to pass notes down to his colleague from South Carolina.

The exchanges as the debate went forward were substantive and sincere, and both Hayne and Webster acquitted themselves well. An admiring nineteenth-century Webster biographer said that Hayne "was deficient in that weight and impressiveness which alone belong to men of greater **caliber**; though, while speaking, few men could exceed him in the hold with which his fluent and graceful declamation retained the attention and thrilled the feeling of an audience."

For his part, Webster projected a palpable intensity. "His dark and deeply-set eyes seemed to be kindled by the glowing ardor of thought, and glittered beneath his heavy brows like two fiery orbs gleaming at night from the darkness of a sepulcher," a biographer wrote.

Images of war were on everyone's minds. "It is a kind of moral gladiatorship in which characters are torn to pieces, and arrows, yes, poisoned arrows, which tho' not seen are deeply felt, are hurled by the combatants against each other," Mrs. Smith said. "The Senate chamber is the present arena and never were the amphitheatres of Rome more crowded by the highest ranks of both sexes."

The climax of the battle came on January 27, a cold Wednesday. With Donelson and Lewis in the Capitol, ready to take word back to Jackson down Pennsylvania Avenue, Webster, dressed in a Revolutionary blue coat with a white cravat, brought his most important speech to a close. He stood to Calhoun's left, and when his eyes wandered upward they would rest on a glorious Rembrandt Peale portrait of Washington captioned PATRIAE PATER, a visual icon of the verbal creed Webster was enunciating in the crimson-draped chamber. Addressing the presiding officer, as was customary, Webster offered words that became one of the noblest passages in the American canon:

I have not allowed myself, sir, to look beyond the Union, to see what might lie hidden in the dark recess behind. I have not coolly weighed the chances of preserving liberty, when the bonds that unite us together shall be broken asunder. I have not accustomed myself to hang over the precipice of disunion, to see whether, with my short sight, I can fathom the depth of the abyss below; nor could I regard him as a safe counselor in the affairs of this Government, whose thoughts should be mainly bent on considering, not how the Union should be best preserved, but how tolerable might be the condition of the People when it shall be broken up and destroyed. While the Union lasts, we have high, exciting, gratifying prospects spread out before us, for us and our children. Beyond that I seek not to penetrate the veil. God grant that, in my day, at least, that curtain may not rise. God grant that on my vision never may be opened what lies behind. When my eyes shall be turned to behold, for the last time, the sun in Heaven, may I not see him shining on the broken and dishonored fragments of a once glorious Union; on States dissevered, discordant, belligerent; on a land rent with civil feuds, or drenched, it may be, in fraternal blood! Let their last feeble and lingering glance, rather behold the gorgeous Ensign of the Republic, now known and honored throughout the earth, still full high advanced, its arms and trophies streaming in their original luster, not a stripe erased or polluted, nor a single star obscured—bearing for its motto, no such miserable interrogatory as, **What is all this worth?** Nor those other words of delusion and folly, **Liberty first, and Union afterwards**—but every where, spread all over in characters of living light, blazing on all its ample folds, as they float over the sea and over the land, and in every wind under the whole Heavens, that other sentiment, dear to every true American heart—Liberty **and** Union, now and forever, one and inseparable!

Webster took his seat, his words hanging in the shocked silence of the chamber. "Mr. Webster," a colleague said, "I think you had better die now, and rest your fame on that speech." Hayne disagreed. "You ought not to die," he said to his noble foe: "A man who can make such speeches as that ought never to die."

THAT NIGHT AT the White House, in the course of the usual Wednesday levee, Webster was in the East Room. The fireplaces glowed as people thronged around Webster in his hour of glory. Hayne was there, too, and wasted no time in paying his respects once more. Seeing him come into view, Webster said, "How are you this evening, Col. Hayne?" Taking Webster's hand with a smile, Hayne said, **"None the better for you, sir!"**

A gentlemanly reply—Hayne was a pleasant man—and he knew rhetorical greatness when he heard it. In a blaze of passionate imagery, Webster had led the Union forces to victory over Hayne's states' rights army. "I felt as if everything I had ever seen, or read, or heard, was floating before me in one great panorama," said Webster, "and I had little else to do than to reach up and cull a thunderbolt, and **hurl** it at him!"

Jackson had received running reports on the scene in the Senate from Donelson and Lewis. "Been to the Capitol, Major?" Jackson had asked Lewis amid the Webster-Hayne exchange.

"Yes, General."

"Well, and how is Webster getting on?"

"He is delivering a most powerful speech," Lewis said. "I am afraid he's demolishing our friend Hayne."

Jackson was not surprised. "I expected it," he said. In Jackson's view, Webster had right on his side. To the president, the answer to the overarching political question—how to resolve tensions between states and regions—seemed clear enough. Let the people, if aggrieved, decide matters peaceably and democratically. Webster had underscored the role of the judiciary; Jackson tended more, as he had said in his message to Congress, toward broad national elections on the issues. Either route, though, lay within the secure borders of the Union, and did not threaten to lead, as nullification did, into an unknown future of division and weakness.

Daniel Webster of Dartmouth, distinguished member of the Supreme Court bar, legendary writer and orator, was about as unlike Andrew Jackson as anyone could be. Webster disagreed with Jackson on virtually every other major issue, including the role of executive power. Yet these two men from opposite ends of the nation found themselves allied on the country's most fundamental question. Convinced that the Union should stand strong, with the people at its mystical center, Jackson did not believe any amount of Southern sophistry—as he saw it—could destroy America.

Webster's achievement in the last week of January 1830 was to add the elements of emotion and imagination to a debate that had been more about law and interpretation. Abstraction was now pitted against patriotism, details against ideals, particulars against the universal. It was the kind of war Andrew Jackson fought well, and he was indebted to Daniel Webster for arming the soldiers of Union with the weapons of light and memory and hope. On the other hand, Calhoun's forces believed that they, not Jackson and his followers, were battling for the true spirit of the Founders against the usurpations of a power-hungry president.

Webster had redefined—in some ways invented—an idea of perpetual union that appealed to a growing continental power seeking strength at home and respect abroad. For many, allegiance to the Union was now no longer a debatable point. It was a given, or ought to be—and if some failed to salute, then they had to be brought back into line.

Some were beginning to think—and speak, in the heat of the South and in the clubbiness of the Senate—in drastic terms. Calhoun and Hayne's colleague William Smith, of South Carolina, offered to die for a nation dedicated to states' rights and darkly suggested that as other nations had risen and fallen, so might America: "Sir . . . should the cupidity or the madness of the majority in Congress push them on to impose one unconstitutional burden after another, until it can no longer [be] borne, and no other alternative remains, I will then take upon myself the last responsibility of an oppressed People, and adopt the exclamation of the poet, **dulce et decorum est pro patria mori;** and if the exigencies of my country should ever demand it, I will be ready to shed my blood upon the altars of that country. I am attached to the Union; I wish to see it perpetuated; I wish it may endure through all time. But if the same causes exist in our Government which have overturned other Governments, what right have we to expect an exemption from the fatality of other nations?"

For his own purposes—the protection of slavery and economic relief—Smith was thinking like a European, not an American. Smith's threat, while cast in gentlemanly terms, had an unmistakable and disturbing meaning. He hoped, he said, that the grievances of the South would be alleviated peaceably—but that if not, "it will then be time for the states to determine what are their rights, and whether they have constitutional powers to secede from the Union."

There were no half measures left for Calhoun and South Carolina. Something serious—something outside the ordinary course of politics—would have to happen, and seemed ever more likely to happen. On Sunday, March 28, 1830, John W. Taylor, a congressman from New York, paid a call on Adams and told him, "Mr. Calhoun will be the Nullification candidate" in 1832.

THOUGH THE SENATE struggle has come down to us as the Webster-Hayne debate, it was another, now obscure figure, Edward Livingston, who was in some ways even more prophetic about American politics than either of the protagonists. Americans who are uncom-

fortable with reflexive partisanship and unreflective ide-
ologies can find the intellectual and rhetorical roots of
the search for a sensible center in the long-ago words of
the gentleman from Louisiana who rose to speak on
Tuesday, March 9, 1830. Though a lawyer and a member of a notable family—he was a brother of Robert
Livingston, a member of the Continental Congress and
Revolutionary War figure who had administered the
first oath of office to President Washington before becoming Jefferson's minister to France—Edward Livingston had known misfortune. Educated at Princeton,
he served in the House of Representatives and was
mayor of New York before he was forty. He took the fall
for a New York financial scandal that bankrupted him
and drove him from New York to Louisiana, where he
met Jackson and began his climb back to power. In
many ways a shy man, Livingston was pressed into the
arena by his wife, Louise. Close to Jackson in the way
his wife and daughter, Cora, were close to Emily, Livingston had been among the first (in the summer of
1815) to raise the prospect of a Jackson presidency. Livingston's legal training and his ambivalent view of
power and position—he liked them, but hated angling
for them—gave him a nuanced understanding of politics and statecraft.

Entering the debate at a late hour—Webster and
Hayne were done, Smith had done his worst, really
only Benton of the major figures had more to say—
Livingston had the advantage of having heard and
studied more than two months of arguments and
counterarguments.

Livingston's Senate speech in March 1830 consumed hour after hour. He opened by taking a satiric poke at the multiplicity of issues that had been aired. What had begun as an argument about public lands had long since set virtually everything of importance to the nation loose in the chamber. "Sir," Livingston said, addressing the chair, "might not a hearer of our debates for some days past have concluded that . . . you had said to each of the speakers, 'Sir, please to rise and speak on the disposition of the public lands; after that, you may talk to the tariff; let us know all you think on the subject of internal improvement; and, before you sit down, discuss the powers of the Senate in relation to appointments, and the right of a State to recede from the Union; and finish by letting us know whether you approve or oppose the measures of the present, or the six preceding administrations.'"

But Livingston saw virtue in the discursive debate. "For my own part, I think the discussion may be turned to useful purposes," he said. "It may, by the interchange of opinion, increase our own information on all the important points which have been examined, while, not being called on for a vote, we may weigh them at leisure, and come to a conclusion, without being influenced by the warmth of debate." But he also knew that, too often, these points were made with exaggerated invective. Superlative followed superlative. Competitive by nature, the politicians of the Senate each wanted to make their own words live longer than the previous orator's, their own images linger a greater while.

The cost of partisanship for partisanship's sake—of seeing politics as blood sport, where the kill is the only object of the exercise—was, Livingston said, too high for a free society to pay. Differences of opinion and doctrine and personality were one thing, and such distinctions formed the natural bases of what Livingston called "the necessary and . . . the legitimate parties existing in all free Governments."

Parties were one thing; partisanship another. "The spirit of which I speak," Livingston said as he argued against zealotry, " . . . creates imaginary and magnifies real causes of complaint; arrogates to itself every virtue—denies every merit to its opponents; secretly entertains the worst designs . . . mounts the pulpit, and, in the name of a God of mercy and peace, preaches discord and vengeance; invokes the worst scourges of Heaven, war, pestilence, and famine, as preferable alternatives to party defeat; blind, vindictive, cruel, remorseless, unprincipled, and at last frantic, it communicates its madness to friends as well as foes; respects nothing, fears nothing."

Even allowing for Livingston's hyperbolic imagery, his point stands. What he called an "excess of party rage," coming on like a fever, was always a threat when men of passion and ambition gathered to settle questions of power, wealth, and faith—the questions the president and the Congress, in close proximity to each other in the capital, confronted and attempted to answer. In such an intrinsically explosive atmosphere, Livingston argued for calm and common sense.

Acknowledging his own weaknesses—a good debating tactic—he said: "I am no censor of the conduct of others: it is sufficient for me to watch over my own. The wisdom of gentlemen must be their guide in the sentiments they entertain, and their discretion in the language in which they utter them. No doubt they think the occasion calls for the warmth they have shown; but of this the people must judge."

THEREIN LAY A key element of the Jacksonian creed, and the context of Livingston's remarks sheds light on the complexities of Jackson's vision of public life. For generations, Americans have thought of Jackson as the quintessential man of the people, a president who might not have been too uncomfortable with mob rule. Such a view, however, does a disservice to Jackson, and Livingston's point illuminates his friend Jackson's larger hopes for the country. "The majority is to govern"— yes, Jackson believed that, but he also believed in order, in virtue, in forbearance, and in securing the nation and its people not only from foreign foes but from the disruptive winds of their own passions. He called upon the people to reason—and he believed they would. "There is too much at stake to allow pride or passion to influence your decision," he later said. "Never for a moment believe that the great body of the citizens of any State or States can deliberately intend to do wrong. They may, under the influence of temporary excitement or misguided opinions, commit mistakes; they may be misled for a time by the suggestions of self-interest; but in a community so enlightened and patriotic as the people of the United States argument will soon make them sensible of their errors, and when convinced they will be ready to repair them."

Partisan ferocity could be just that—ferocious—but in the end, the better part of wisdom would lead the country to the place Livingston sketched in the Senate: "We undoubtedly think differently of particular measures, and have our preferences for particular men: these, surely, cannot arrange us into any but temporary divisions, lasting no longer than while the election of the man is pending, or the debate on the measure continues." The sin might be great—slavery, persecution of the Indians, neglect of the sick and the needy—the road to reform long, the battles bloody and heartbreaking, but in Livingston's view violence and disunion were no answer.

"There are legitimate and effectual means to correct any palpable infraction of our Constitution," he said. "Let the cry of constitutional oppression be justly raised within these walls, and it will be heard abroad—it will be examined; the people are intelligent, the people are just, and in time these characteristics must have an effect on their Representatives."

The words were Livingston's, the sentiments Jackson's.

CHAPTER 11

GENERAL JACKSON RULES BY HIS PERSONAL POPULARITY

O N MONDAY, April 12, 1830, Duff Green published a piece in the **Telegraph** detailing the plans for a dinner to take place the next night at the Indian Queen Hotel in commemoration of Thomas Jefferson's birthday. At the White House, Jackson decided that the program, with its toasts and speakers, would be "a **nullification affair altogether.**"

The dinner, Webster told Clay, "was to found the party on **Southern** principles." Surveying the field, Jackson rose early on the thirteenth and wrote out three different toasts. Lewis and Andrew Donelson were together in the president's office going through the newspapers when Jackson appeared. He handed Lewis the three pieces of paper and asked which he "liked best." Lewis chose one, and Jackson repeated the exercise with Donelson, who selected the same one Lewis had. Jackson was pleased. "He said he preferred that one himself for the reason that it was shorter and more expressive," Lewis recalled. "He then put that one in his pocket and threw the others into the fire."

At the Indian Queen, the room was crowded with politicians as Robert Hayne and others rhapsodized about the greatness of Jefferson's "glorious stand" against John Adams's Alien and Sedition Acts. The implications were clear: it was time to recover that anti-Federalist spirit to undo the tariff and secure slavery. At last it was Jackson's turn. Van Buren, who was seated across the room, climbed atop his chair to take in the scene. The words that had come to Jackson in the morning now produced a gasp among the Southerners and nullifiers: "Our Union—it must be preserved."

Calhoun then rose to speak. The vice president interpreted Jackson's toast as a direct threat to the Southern cause. "The Union—next to our liberty the most dear," he said, adding, "May we all remember that it can only be preserved by respecting the rights of the States and distributing equally the benefit and burden of the Union." There it was, then: a decisive rallying cry from Jackson and a legalistic, but still defiant, manifesto from Calhoun.

Van Buren tried to relieve the tension. "Mutual forbearance and reciprocal concessions: through their agency the Union was established—the patriotic spirit from which they emanated will forever sustain it." Sitting amid what Van Buren called "the bustle and excitement of the occasion," Robert Hayne reeled from this third assault on the cause of state sovereignty. First Webster, then Livingston, and now the president himself was weighing in against Hayne's beloved South Carolina. Hurrying over to Jackson,

Hayne asked whether they might add the word "Federal" to the text of his toast to be made public. "This was an ingenious suggestion," Van Buren recalled, "as it seemed to make the rebuke less pungent although it really had no such effect." Jackson agreed; he had meant to say "federal" anyway. Perhaps Hayne thought the country would interpret "Our Federal Union" differently than "Our Union"—in the event, it did not—but the editorial feint was typical of the Southern wing, which, since Webster and Livingston, was finding that the Unionists had more of a claim on the nation's passions while it struggled to argue with constitutional precision.

Nothing, however, was going to assuage the Southerners' loss on this long evening. "The veil was rent," said Van Buren, revealing that Jackson, as the **National Intelligencer** put it in its coverage of the dinner, was in effect saying: "'You may complain of the tariff and perhaps with reason, but so long as it is the law it shall as certainly be maintained as my name is Andrew Jackson.'" The paper had it right.

An old opponent understood it all—and knew that Jackson's triumph at the Jefferson dinner foreshadowed victory after victory. "That Jackson will be a candidate for reelection, if, when the time of election comes, he has a fair prospect of success, I do not doubt," said John Quincy Adams. "That his personal popularity, founded solely upon the Battle of New Orleans"—Adams's bitterness was all too evident here—"will carry him through the next election, as it did through the last, is altogether probable. The vices of his administration are not such as affect the popular feeling. He will lose none of his popularity, unless he should do something to raise a blister upon public sentiment; and of that there is no present prospect. If he lives, therefore, and nothing external should happen to rouse new parties, he may be re-elected, not only once, but twice or thrice."

Still, some Southerners seethed. "I seriously apprehend a civil war if something is not done to conciliate the discontents which prevail at this time and for aught that I can see will increase," William Crawford of Georgia wrote Van Buren the month after the Jefferson dinner.

EMILY'S WINTER AND early spring followed the now familiar but still difficult pattern. Close to Jackson, she and Andrew and the babies were able to cheer him most of the time, greeting his guests and presenting a gracious face to the outside world. Then, in April, Emily's father died, robbing her of a source of wisdom and counsel. Captain Donelson had been stoic and sensible to the end. He had been sick for three months, William Donelson wrote to John Coffee, "which he bore with great fortitude and resignation." It was, Donelson said, "only in the few last days of his existence [that] he expressed some impatience at remaining here so long. His only fear was that he would be a long time dying. . . . Yet parting with a father who had so long watched over our best interests in childhood and in riper age and who was so kind and affectionate to all his children and had grown venerable with time [will] not be a thing of light moment."

IN LATE MAY, two essential issues—the tariff and internal improvements such as federally funded roads, bridges, and canals—converged to mark a crucial moment in the evolution of presidential power. Roughly put, proceeds from the tariff filled the national treasury, and those funds helped pay for projects that were of most immediate benefit to the middle states and the West (the Deep South was a long way from seeing its own region linked with the others). However logical and appealing the idea may have seemed, skepticism about a large federal government—which was, at least in Jackson's mind, a different thing altogether from skepticism about the virtues of Union—remained the political reality of the era. Internal improvements were the pork of the age (though the term would not be coined for several more decades); Van Buren watched with bemusement as congressmen "brought forward under captivating disguises the thousand local improvements with which they designed to dazzle and seduce their constituents."

But Jackson and Van Buren believed the less government interference with the market, the better, and they worried that federally funded internal improvements in single states would lead to corruption and an unequal distribution of national resources. This was the prevailing presidential thinking when bills authorizing a number of projects, including funding for a sixty-mile Maysville Road that happened to fall within Kentucky (it was to be a leg of a north-south road like the east-west Cumberland Road), came to the White House for Jackson's signature.

Van Buren was against it and made the case to Jackson while they were on horseback. It was not a difficult sell. "The road was in Mr. Clay's own state," Van Buren said, "and Mr. Clay was, the General thought—whether rightfully or not is now immaterial—pressing the measure and the question it involved . . . rather for political effect than for public ends."

Van Buren warned Jackson that the White House's foes wanted "to draw you into the approval of a bill most emphatically local, and thus endeavor to saddle you with the latitudinarian notions upon which the late administration acted, or to compel you to take a stand against internal improvements generally, and thus draw to their aid all those who are interested in the ten thousand schemes which events and the course of the government for the past few years have engendered." The answer: approve interstate projects but veto anything that did not cross state lines.

Word about Jackson's veto intentions leaked out in Washington, and the whispers grew so persistent that Colonel Richard Johnson of Kentucky, now a member of the House, called on Jackson at the White House. There Johnson found Jackson and Van Buren alone, going over a report on the Treasury. Johnson and Jackson began to speak of the possible Maysville veto, and Johnson, fearful that Clay could turn the issue on Jackson, grew emotional and extended his hand with a flourish.

"General! If this hand were an anvil on which the sledgehammer of the smith was descending," Johnson said, "he would not crush it more effectually than you will crush your friends in Kentucky if you veto that bill!"

Jackson rose from his chair, as did Johnson, and the two faced each other.

"Sir," Jackson said, "have you looked at the condition of the Treasury—at the amount of money that it contains—at the appropriations already made by Congress—at the amount of other unavoidable claims upon it?"

"No, General, I have not!" Johnson said. "But there has always been money enough to satisfy appropriations and I do not doubt there will be now!"

Jackson was determined to pay down the debt, which he abhorred, and he watched the growing number of bills proposed in Congress with alarm—noting, in a memorandum on the veto, that they would "far exceed by many millions the amount available in the Treasury for the year 1830" if passed. "I stand committed before the country to pay off the national debt at the earliest practicable moment," he told Johnson. "This pledge I am determined to redeem, and I cannot do this if I consent to increase it without necessity. Are you willing—are my friends willing to lay taxes to pay for internal improvements?—for be assured I will not borrow a cent except in cases of absolute necessity!"

"No," Johnson said of the threat of a tax increase, "that would be worse than a **veto!**"

Jackson told Johnson that he was trying to find a way to veto the bill without bringing all internal improvements to a stop. As Van Buren recalled it, Jackson said "he was giving the matter a thorough investigation and that their friends might be assured that he would not make up his mind without looking at every side of it"—a classic piece of political tradecraft, for Jackson did not want an upset Johnson to spread the word that all was decided. Jackson never foreclosed his options until he had to, and the Maysville moment had not yet come.

When it did, on Thursday, May 27, 1830, Jackson vetoed the bill and three others but approved two land measures—a survey law that affected more than one state, and money for the Cumberland Road, which was already an interstate project—after what he described as "much, and, I may add, painful reflection to me." He truly did not believe there was enough money for Maysville, and he was more interested in paying down the debt than in spending federal resources on state enterprises. By crushing Maysville, he was distinguishing between national and local projects, though in the legislative world, such distinctions are in the eye of the beholder. One man's pork is another man's steak. "What is properly **national** in its character or otherwise is an inquiry which is often extremely difficult of solution," Jackson said in a veto message drafted by Van Buren. "The appropriations of one year for an object which is con-

sidered national may be rendered nugatory by the refusal of a succeeding Congress to continue the work
on the ground that it is local." He spoke of his grand
design to return surpluses to the states and, character-
istically, said the people should amend the Constitution if they wanted the federal government to pay for
local improvements. (Still, by the end of his second
term, Jackson spent more on internal improvements
than all previous presidents combined.)

With a flourish, Jackson also denounced taxes in
terms similar to those he had used in his exchange
with Johnson in the White House. Noting that "many
of the taxes collected from our citizens through the
medium of imposts have for a considerable period
been onerous," Jackson said that the burdens of these
taxes "have borne severely upon the laboring and less
prosperous classes of the community, being imposed
on the necessaries of life" (clothing and the like).
Americans were not complaining—not yet. But let
federal dollars begin to be spent in seemingly indiscriminate ways, and there could be trouble. The taxes,
Jackson said, "have been cheerfully borne because
they were thought to be necessary to the support of
government and the payment of the debts unavoidably incurred in the acquisition and maintenance of
our national rights and liberties. But have we a right
to calculate on the same cheerful acquiescence when
it is known that the necessity for their continuance
would cease were it not for irregular, improvident,
and unequal appropriations of the public funds?"

It was a shrewd document, one that put the presi-

ing in Jackson's time had become routine. Franklin Roosevelt, the scholar Richard Neustadt noted, occasionally asked for "something I can veto"—just to make the point that lawmakers should fall in line.

In the spring of 1830, with Maysville, Clay understood what Jackson was doing and wondered how to fight back. "We are all shocked and mortified by the rejection of the Maysville road," Clay wrote a friend. Perhaps, Clay told Webster, they could back a constitutional amendment that would allow a simple majority of Congress, rather than two thirds, to override a presidential veto. In any event, Clay knew that the veto was now yet another front in the war against Jackson's expansion of power. "We shall be contending against a principle which wears a monarchial aspect, whilst our opponents will be placed in the unpopular attitude [of] defending it," he wrote an ally in June 1830.

Jackson looked forward to such a struggle. "The veto, I find, will work well," he wrote friends. And why should he not think so? By signing a message and giving it to Andrew Donelson to take up Capitol Hill, his will had triumphed over all.

FOR JEREMIAH EVARTS, thwarting Jackson's will on Indian removal had been a consuming passion since Jackson's arrival in the capital. "The Great Arbiter of Nations never fails to take cognizance of national delinquencies," Evarts wrote in one of his "William Penn" essays. "In many forms, and with awful solemnity, he has declared his abhorrence of oppression in every shape; and especially of injustice perpetrated against the weak by the strong, **when strength is in fact made the only rule of action.**" Yes, Evarts acknowledged, white America had already significantly sinned against the Indians, but what Jackson was proposing was of a different, vaster scale. "The people of the United States are not altogether guiltless in regard to their treatment of the aborigines of this continent; but they cannot as yet be charged with any **systematic legislation** on this subject, inconsistent with the plainest principles of moral honesty."

That systematic legislation, formally entitled "The Bill for an Exchange of Lands with the Indians Residing in Any of the States or Territories, and for Their Removal West of the Mississippi," was reported out of the Indian Affairs Committee of the Senate on Monday, February 22, 1830, and out of the House committee two days later. An essential point of contention was whether the Jackson administration could simply ignore previous treaties in order to remove the Indians. Jackson believed the treaties irrelevant, but the Indians did not, and neither did the Indians' defenders in Congress. Led by Senator Theodore Frelinghuysen of New Jersey, a devout Christian who was convinced that Evarts was right and Jackson was wrong, the opposition did what it could to help, as Frelinghuysen put it, "the poor Indians." On the Senate floor, over the course of several days at the beginning of April 1830, Frelinghuysen, who had been in close contact with Evarts, gave a speech that concluded:

Mr. President, if we abandon these aboriginal proprietors of our soil—these early allies and adopted children of our forefathers, how shall we justify it to our
country, to all the glory of the past and the promise of
the future? . . . How shall we justify this trespass to
ourselves?

Appeals to white Americans' sense of fair play were
not completely wasted. Evarts's essays and sentiments
like the ones expressed by Frelinghuysen created a
"Quaker panic" in Pennsylvania, Martin Van Buren
said: the Indians' allies had successfully raised questions about the bill.

Rather than make only moral arguments, however,
those who opposed the administration decided to attack Jackson on the ground that he was seizing power,
turning despotic and acting more like a monarch than
the executive leader of a republic. If Jackson wanted a
stronger presidency, then he would have to pay politically with charges of autocracy and overreaching.
Jackson had, Frelinghuysen said, "without the slightest consultation with either House of Congress—
without any opportunity for counsel or concert,
discussion or deliberation, on the part of these co-
ordinate branches of the government"—decided to
end the decades of treaty making and coexistence.
Georgia, Tennessee, Alabama, and Mississippi were
breaking ratified agreements, and Jackson was not
only supporting them but was asking Congress to
make removal law.

One of the results of Jackson's coalition victory in

1828 was a rising sense of party identity. Soon to be known as "the Democracy," and eventually as the Democratic Party, Jackson's supporters in the House and the Senate found themselves the objects of White House wooing and lobbying. Those who backed Jackson stood to be rewarded by favorable coverage in administration newspapers and might be heeded on matters of local patronage. The political machine conceived by Van Buren and being built and maintained by Kendall and others would be at the disposal of lawmakers who voted with Jackson on key matters. On Tuesday, April 6, John Quincy Adams told his diary: "General Jackson rules by his personal popularity, which his partisans in the Senate dare not encounter by opposing anything that he does; and while that popularity shall last, his majorities in both houses of Congress will stand by him for good or evil. It has totally broken down in the Senate both the esprit de corps and the combination against the Executive, which, from the last session of Mr. Jefferson's administration, had presided in many of their deliberations and governed many of their decisions."

Evarts, too, complained of "the spirit of party" at work in Congress, saying that a Jacksonian congressman from Alabama had told him he believed in the Indians' cause but would not cross the White House. "Now what can we do, when men will act in this manner?" Evarts said. "The question is already as plain in the Senate as any question of human conduct can possibly be. Not one question of theft, robbery, or murder, in ten thousand, is so perfectly free from all doubt or cavil . . . yet it is expected that men will vote by platoons, in regular rank and file, according to party drilling, on this question of public faith. I have never before seen such a commentary on human depravity."

Jackson's supporters made the usual arguments for removal—the states were sovereign, the Indians were irredeemable in current conditions, and a fresh start beyond the Mississippi, under the protection of the president, was the only way to ensure the survival of the tribes. The Senate vote was not particularly close, with the bill passing 28 to 19. The House, though, was a different story.

God, justice, and presidential power dominated the debate, which began on Thursday, May 13, 1830. The Evarts-Frelinghuysen case resonated more in the House, it seemed, than it had in the Senate. The Indian issue had become an emotional one, and congressmen were more likely to be roiled by popular passions. Pro-Jackson lawmakers had begun attacking the anti-removal forces, arguing that religious fervor was trumping deliberate judgment. In the House, Congressman Wilson Lumpkin of Georgia dismissed the Evarts contingent as "canting fanatics" who were unjustly attacking his people as "atheists, deists, infidels, and Sabbath-breakers laboring under the curse of slavery."

Perhaps the most striking moment came when Congressman Henry R. Storrs of New York took the floor on Saturday, May 15, 1830. Past treaties had guaranteed the Indians' rights, acknowledged their sovereignty, and promised them the protection of the federal government against the states. Now, Storrs told the House, "the treaties of this Government, made with them from its first organization and under every administration, to which they have solemnly appealed for their security against these fatal encroachments on their rights, have been treated as subordinate to the laws of these states, and are thus virtually abrogated by the Executive Department. The President has assumed the power to dispose of the whole question, and . . . proposes to us little more than to register this executive decree." Jackson's course, he said, had "shocked the public feeling, and agitated the country."

Storrs was bluntest about Jackson's bid for wide authority. The government, Storrs told the House, "was to be a government of law, and not of prerogative, and especially not of executive prerogative; for if his will was to have the force of law, that [would be], to a certain degree, despotism." Finally, toward the conclusion of his long address, Storrs implicitly compared Jackson to Napoleon. Should Jackson succeed with Indian removal, Storrs said, sweeping away the earlier agreements, ratified by the Senate and signed by previous presidents, then America would look more like imperial France than a republic:

The eye of other nations is now fixed upon us. Our friends are looking with fearful anxiety to our conduct in this matter. Our enemies, too, are watching our steps. They have lain in wait for us for half a century, and the passage of this bill will light up joy and hope in the palace of every despot. It will do more to destroy the confidence of the world in free government than all their armies could accomplish. . . . It will weaken our institutions at home, and infect the heart of our social system. It will teach our people to hold the honor of their Government lightly, and loosen the moral feeling of the country. Republics have been charged, too, with insolence and oppression in the day of their power. History has unfortunately given us much proof of its truth, and we are about to confirm it by our own example.

Storrs was not being mindlessly anti-Jackson, he said, and took on a pleading tone toward the end. "Whether we favored his elevation to his present station or not, we may all unite in wishing that he may . . . advance the honor of his country beyond even the hopes of his friends," Storrs said. "We are all interested in his fame, for it is now identified with his country."

The words made no difference. After much back-and-forth and several procedural votes, Jackson won, narrowly, by a margin of 102 to 98. The vote was taken before the Congress knew about the Maysville veto; in the veto's wake, the arguments about Jackson's despotic tendencies seemed all the stronger. But it was too late: the Indian bill passed on Wednesday, May 26, 1830.

The last week of May 1830, then, was one of the finest of Andrew Jackson's life. He had done what he set out to do: he had overturned the decades-long Indian policy put in motion by Washington and Knox. He now had the authority to purge the South of its native inhabitants and, with Maysville, he had taught Congress that he must be heeded. Jackson had thus made himself arguably the most powerful president since the creation of the office forty years before.

SHORTLY BEFORE FOUR o'clock on the afternoon of Wednesday, June 9, 1830, John Eaton came home from the War Department bearing an invitation from the president for the Eatons to dine at the White House. It was the moment, Margaret decided, for total war. Up to this point Margaret had complained of the Donelsons to Jackson, but not so strongly that Jackson could not choose to avoid a showdown. Even the ablest of politicians, however, cannot always control the timing of a crisis, and as Jackson read a note from Margaret written that afternoon, he realized his strategy of temporizing had run its course.

"Circumstances, my dear General, are such that under your kind and hospitable roof I cannot be happy," Margaret wrote, playing to Jackson's instinct that his house should be a shelter against the world for those he loved and cared for, and Margaret was one of those people. "You are not the cause," Margaret assured him—needlessly but flatteringly—"for you have felt and manifested a desire that things should be different." But things were not, and Emily and Andrew were at fault. "I could not expect to be happy at your house for this would be to expect a different course of treatment from part of your family." Eaton had tried to talk her into going, arguing, she said, "that it may be a triumph to some if it may be said I were not invited, but what of that, it will only be another feast to those whose pleasure it is to make me the object of their censures and reproaches."

Tough words: she was basically accusing Emily and Andrew of open hostility, for which there is scant evidence. They might fall short on occasion—Emily did not acquit herself well on the boat trip to Norfolk the previous year, and was cooler than she might have been on the social circuit in Washington—but all in all the Donelsons had not been vicious, which was the impression Margaret was trying to give Jackson. "I ask to say to you that whatever may be the cause of the unkind treatment I have received from those under your roof . . . I have done all in my power to avoid it."

Unable to leave things there, Margaret went a beat further, asserting her own innocence in the whole affair. "I have spoken of your family in no other manner than a respectful one," she said, adding, "I have ever endeavored to return good for evil"—an allusion to an exhortation in Saint Paul's Epistle to the Romans, which would have resonated with Jackson.

Margaret was almost certainly stretching the truth here: in her memoirs she had tart things to say about both Donelsons, and when she spoke privately with Jackson it is virtually impossible to imagine that her bluntness would have failed her. As Jackson came to the end of the letter, however, he was in her hands. She had struck the right notes to convince Jackson that his family had gone too far when his house—his home—was unwelcoming to the wife of his friend.

Jackson gave Andrew the letter, and by the time Andrew had finished reading it both men were furious. Jackson unleashed his rage on Donelson. He had been defied long enough. Emily and Andrew owed him their place in Washington, and if they could not live by his rules then they must leave. Jackson's words were so painful that Andrew could not commit them to paper. There is no known record of the specifics of the conversation. Yet they were burned into Andrew's memory. Standing before his guardian—before, really, his father—he realized he and his family might well be cast out. It may have been the first time Andrew felt the full, terrific force of Jackson's anger. Even long afterward, the recollections of the scene were so raw that Andrew could speak of them only in the most formal of terms. In his anger and anguish Donelson distinguished what he called "my family" from what he referred to as "your house," saying: "You have not forgotten the note of Mrs. Eaton in which she refused to dine with you because my family was in your house," Andrew wrote to Jackson in October 1830. "I have not forgotten the language which you employed on that occasion, and the determination you then expressed of carrying us home and leaving us there."

Incredulous that this woman had done so much damage, Andrew wrote a passionate note for the president's files: "The only **unkind treatment** which my family can have practiced towards Mrs. Eaton is their refusal to acknowledge her right to interfere with their social relations. All else is imaginary or worse. This letter is abundant evidence of the indelicacy which distinguishes her character, and is disgraceful to her husband." Jackson had grown tired of his own balancing act, of fighting to make Washington do his bidding while keeping up a more benign and patient face in his own house. He told Andrew and Emily that the three of them would leave for Tennessee in a week. Who came back was an open question.

But could he happily live apart from Emily and Andrew? They had been together so long now. Andrew and Emily had known Jackson all their lives, and he had come to cherish them as the flesh of his flesh. If a rupture were really so simple, it would have come much earlier and much more decisively. Jackson's temporizing—angry one moment, calculating another, yet reluctant to take an irrevocable step—suggests that his emotions were churning, pressing him one way and then another, and that he did not know, finally, whether he could cut the Donelsons out of his innermost circle.

The trip would be a momentous one. Two of Jackson's dearest causes were to be advanced over the summer. One was Indian removal: he was summoning tribal leaders to meet with him personally in Tennessee. To succeed, he believed he needed the man he could most depend on to make his wishes reality on removal. And so Jackson decided to add two others to the party in Nashville.

He invited Margaret and John Eaton.

. . .

WHEN HE LEARNED the Eatons would be joining them, Andrew seemed resigned to having lost his influence with Jackson. There were, he told John Coffee, "embarrassments that yet attend us," and there would be no relief in Tennessee. "The Secretary of War and family"—Andrew could not bring himself to mention Margaret's name—"have started [for Tennessee] . . . a circumstance which I very much regret." In his own letter to Coffee, Jackson admitted that "there has been and are things that have corroded my peace and my mind and must cease or my administration will be a distracted one."

When Jackson and the Donelsons arrived in Nashville, it was the first time they had been home since the inauguration more than a year before. The last few weeks had been good for Jackson, who was heartened by the public reaction to his Maysville veto—he believed it "very popular" with "a large majority of the people."

Within the family, though, the journey ended, and the visit began, on a note of tension. Jackson had expected Andrew and Emily to stay with him at the Hermitage. Andrew and Emily, eager to avoid the Eatons and perhaps exhausted by the exacting emotional minuet with "Uncle," insisted on going to the Mansion, the Donelson family seat. Jackson was surprised and hurt, for, he told Andrew, he had "expected you and Emily to go to my house and remain with me as part of my family." A seemingly small thing, but the sudden physical separation, though only a few miles, gave more pronounced geographic form to the differences of opinion that had long divided them across the hallway in the White House.

Grumpy and wounded, sensitive and wary of conspiracy, Jackson was further surprised by developments at home. When he had last been in Nashville, he had been enveloped in grief for Rachel but certain that he was surrounded by loving friends who would rally in any storm. Now he was not so sure: he discovered that a formidable element of Nashville society was armed against the Eatons. Led by rivals—including General Edmund Pendleton Gaines, a great frontier fighter who opposed Indian removal—what Jackson called "a combination" refused to bow to his plans for the Eatons' reception in Tennessee. Seeing Emily and Andrew on the same side as some of his political enemies infuriated him.

Denouncing Emily and Andrew's "folly and pride"—he was quick to see in others what he could not acknowledge in himself—Jackson said: "My duty is that my household should bestow equal comity to all, and the nation expects me to control my household to this rule. Would to God my endeavors by counsel and persuasion had obtained this." But they had not, and Jackson readied for a permanent break with Andrew and Emily. "My connections have acted very strangely here," he told Lewis, "but I know I can live as well without them as they can without me, and I will govern my Household, or I will have **none**."

Back home in a place where they did not have to make their status and standing clear, Emily and Andrew might have felt some relief that others shared their views, but the affirmation of Nashville society only widened the gap between the Hermitage and the Mansion, where the broader Donelson circle felt more sympathy with Emily and Andrew than with Jackson, a fact that could not elude Jackson.

Far from improving in Nashville, then, the struggle was deteriorating into bitterness. Andrew wrote John Branch that "affairs [are] so bad" he would not even try to detail them. Consumed with "speculations upon the future" of his own "destiny," Andrew was stoic: "I am ready for the worst."

The day after Andrew wrote these words, Jackson attended a large barbecue in the Eatons' honor in nearby Franklin, Tennessee, and the turnout added to Jackson's sense that his family was in the wrong. At 3:30 on the afternoon of Wednesday, July 28, 1830, a crowd of five hundred fêted the secretary of war and his wife, and Jackson was delighted "to shake hands with my old acquaintances, neighbors and soldiers." Why, Jackson wondered as he took in the hospitable spectacle, could such courtesies and graces not rule the day at the Hermitage and at the Mansion? Why was Franklin doing what he wanted, but neither Nashville nor Washington would? "The ladies of the place had received Mrs. Eaton in the most friendly manner, and have extended to her that polite attention due to her," Jackson said. "This is as it should be, and is a severe comment on the combination at Nashville, and will lead to its prostration."

· · ·

ALWAYS, ALWAYS, THE language of combat, and as the days grew hotter in the depths of summer, the words of war were more and more frequently directed at Emily and Andrew. Seeing Calhoun at the root of all things evil, Jackson blamed the vice president, but hardly stopped there. "That my Nephew and Niece should permit themselves to be held up as [the] instruments, and **tools,** of such wickedness, is truly mortifying to me," Jackson said on July 28.

Most of Washington remained largely unaware of the gathering darkness in Tennessee. A letter from Rebecca Branch, the daughter of Secretary John Branch, indicates that she, and presumably the larger presidential circle, expected Emily to return with Jackson after the summer: "With the pleasing anticipation of seeing you soon . . . I close my letter."

There was a moment of hope for reconciliation when John Coffee, Emily's brother-in-law and Jackson's longtime friend, arrived on the scene and played peacemaker. It often requires a broker to bring serenity and stability to fraught familial situations—situations in which the main players have become so entrenched that the smallest incidents are magnified beyond their proper scope. Coffee, however, had credibility with all parties, and effected a compromise: Emily would be courteous to Margaret when Margaret arrived from Franklin for a visit in the neighborhood. According to family tradition, the bargain was struck on the Mansion's lawn on Tuesday, August 3, 1830. An exultant Jackson wrote Eaton: "General

Coffee has, since here, produced a visible and sensible change in my connections, and they will all be here to receive you and your Lady, who I trust will meet them with her usual courtesy and if a perfect reconciliation cannot take place, that harmony may prevail, and a link broken in the Nashville conspiracy."

After agreeing with Coffee to do her part, Emily walked into the Mansion, where she rejoined her children. Thinking things over—Margaret had been a constant concern for twenty months—Emily reconsidered her promise. To receive Margaret here, in Tennessee, under pressure and threat from Jackson, would betray the middle course she had charted and largely followed for more than a year and a half. If she caved in far from Washington, the distance would not matter: the news back to her friends and to the establishment whose approval she craved would be that the frontier Jackson circle—the people who were not even sure of their divorces before they married other men—had accepted a woman into their ranks whom they steadfastly refused to accept in the capital. Such a decision would make Emily look like a hypocrite and a provincial. And so sometime between the conversations with Coffee in the summer heat and the next morning, Emily changed her mind. She would not receive Margaret; she would not go to the Hermitage for dinner in the Eatons' honor. The deal Coffee had brokered lasted less than twenty-four hours.

The extent of Jackson's anger at his niece's reversal can be gauged by the iciness of his tone in a letter to Lewis written on Saturday, August 7, three days after

Emily declined to leave the Mansion for the events involving the Eatons. There was little of the emotional Jackson's usual thunderous prose or furious run-on sentences. He was crisp and matter-of-fact. "I shall have no female family in the City this ensuing winter," he told Lewis. "Mrs. Donelson remains with her widowed mother." Margaret would remain behind as well, in Franklin with her own mother, who had traveled south with the Eatons. Emily's mother no doubt appreciated her daughter's company, but Jackson revealed the real reason for the plan when he added that on her visit to Nashville, "Mrs. E. was met by all the ladies in the place with open arms, **but one**."

Andrew was in a terrible spot. Should he stay, or return to Washington? Make his life here, in Tennessee, or abandon his young family to serve a mercurial master? "Whether Mr. Donelson will or will not accompany me to the City has not as yet been determined on by him," Jackson said with more than a trace of malice. "Whether he will leave his wife and little ones to whom he is greatly attached, he will determine today or tomorrow."

JACKSON AND EATON had invited the Cherokees, Choctaws, Chickasaws, and Creeks to meet with them in middle Tennessee, but only the Chickasaws actually came; the others were holding out hopes that either the next meeting of Congress or the courts might spare them the fate Jackson intended for them. "Friends and Brothers: You have long dwelt on the soil you occupy, and in early times before the white man kindled his fires too near to yours . . . you were a happy people," Jackson said to the gathered Chickasaws after mingling with those who were on hand and smoking the ceremonial pipe with them. "Now your white brothers are around you. . . . Your great father . . . asks if you are prepared and ready to submit to the laws of Mississippi, and make a surrender of your ancient laws . . . you must submit—there is no alternative. . . . Old men! Lead your children to a land of promise and of peace before the Great Spirit shall call you to die. Young chiefs! Preserve your people and nation."

Helped along by bribes from Eaton and John Coffee, the chiefs agreed to Jackson's terms. Though the deal ultimately fell apart, Jackson and Eaton's mission to the South encapsulated much: Jackson's persistent personal engagement in the issue, the role of incentives (leaders of factions open to removal were often promised larger gifts of land if they would sign treaties that would exchange land in the East for land in the West), and the miserable planning for actual removal that proved so deadly for so many Indians. After the Tennessee meeting, Eaton and Coffee traveled to Mississippi to arrange for the removal of the Choctaws. According to pattern, they found congenial tribal leaders open to making a deal for the right price. Signed on Wednesday, September 27, 1830, the Treaty of Dancing Rabbit Creek ratified the exchange of five million Choctaw acres in Mississippi for thirteen million acres west of Arkansas. It was the first removal under the 1830 law. "Our doom is sealed," said one Choctaw. "There is no other course for us but to turn our faces to our new homes toward the setting sun."

By happenstance it fell to the French writer Alexis de Tocqueville, who was in Memphis in the winter of 1831, to record the terrors of the Choctaws' journey—terrors that were the rule, not the exception, as removal went forward. Watching the Choctaws cross the Mississippi, Tocqueville wrote: "It was then in the depths of winter, and that year the cold was exceptionally severe; the snow was hard on the ground, and huge masses of ice drifted on the river. The Indians brought their families with them; there were among them the wounded, the sick, newborn babies, and old men on the point of death. They had neither tents nor wagons, but only some provisions and weapons. I saw them embark to cross the great river, and the sight will never fade from my memory. Neither sob nor complaint rose from that silent assembly. Their afflictions were of long standing, and they felt them to be irremediable."

In March 1831, about the same time Tocqueville watched the Choctaws cross the river, the Supreme Court ruled on the first of two critical cases on the fate of the Cherokee tribe. Represented by William Wirt, attorney general under Monroe and Adams, the tribe argued that Georgia was acting illegally—in violation of decades of solemn and binding treaties—by trying to assert state law over the Cherokees on their own land.

In his majority opinion, Chief Justice John Marshall struck notes sympathetic to the Indians but announced that the Court would not render a verdict on the technical grounds that the Cherokees had filed suit as a "foreign nation" when, in Marshall's view, the tribes would be better described as "**domestic dependent** nations. . . . Their relation to the United States resembles that of a ward to his guardian."

It was a striking finding, for the government had long acted as though the Indians were a sovereign people, negotiating and signing numerous treaties with the tribes. With his opinion, Marshall was declining to take a stand in favor of the Indians, shying away from a confrontation with Jackson. (And with Georgia: the state had already demonstrated its contempt for the Supreme Court by hanging an Indian convicted of murder despite an order not to.) It is true that Marshall, while denying the Cherokees immediate help, wrote that the Court might make a different decision about Indian rights in what he called "a proper case, with proper parties." The Cherokee Nation would be back before Marshall and his colleagues the next year with another case, but for now the decision of the Court stood as a stark reminder, as if any were needed, of the prevailing sense of fatalism about the Indians' future. It was not just Jackson; even Marshall, often depicted as a hero in the story, harbored all too few hopes that the political reality of removal could be changed. "If it be true that the Cherokee nation have rights, this is not the tribunal in which those rights are to be asserted," Marshall wrote. "If it be true that wrongs have been inflicted, and that still greater are to be apprehended, this is not the tribunal which can redress the past or prevent the future." A sad verdict—but a true one.

ROUGHLY A WEEK after Emily ensured her own exile from Washington, her husband chose to return to the White House by himself. Whether driven by loyalty and love for Jackson, by ambition and a stubborn refusal to surrender his place to the Eatons—or, in all likelihood, by some combination of these motives—Andrew Donelson could not give up his proximity to power.

"No ladies will return with me," Jackson wrote Lewis on August 15. "Major A. J. Donelson, my son [Andrew Jackson, Jr.] and Mr. Earl"—the portrait painter who lived at the White House—"will constitute my family, and I hope Major Eaton will accompany me, and leave his Lady until the rise of the waters."

While Emily readied herself for exile, Andrew remained at the call and under the command of the man who was breaking up his family. For now, Andrew was resigned to following orders. Yet in a very short time resignation would give way to resentment, and the president he served would find his loyal secretary a conflicted and angry man.

ON WEDNESDAY, SEPTEMBER 1, 1830, Jackson rode in his carriage from the Hermitage to the Mansion to retrieve Andrew. Emily wept. The scene affected the sentimental side of Jackson, and he tried to reassure Emily in the best way he could, given the position he had staked out. "Uncle's last words to me were that before he would do anything to injure the honor of your-self, who he had raised as a son, he would cut off his right arm," Emily later wrote Andrew. Yet Jackson's cur-rent course was set, and it was time to go. The wife and babies were left behind, and Emily prepared for a lonely winter as the carriage pulled away into the late summer light, headed for Washington.

The trip was miserable, the roads rough. As Jackson and Eaton and Donelson and Earl bounced their way north, their horses went thirsty for a long while. Then the rains came down, turning the journey into a muddy slog. Andrew missed his family already, stay-ing up late one night at Knoxville to write to Emily. "We travel at the rate of about 30 miles a day, take a cup of coffee in the morning by candlelight, our breakfast at 10 or 11 after about 12 miles ride, our dinner at night, and then to sleep, but I, not without many thoughts about you and our dear little Jackson and Mary Rachel," Andrew said, asking his young wife to "be happier than I can without you, kissing Jackson and Mary."

Rather than dwell on Emily's absence or the price he had just forced Andrew to pay, Jackson turned his attention to politics and policy, noting on arrival at the White House in late September that "business has greatly accumulated in my absence." He had plenty of time—more than ever before—to devote to whatever awaited him on his desk.

IN THE FAMILY quarters as fall came to Washington, all was silent. When Jackson opened his bedroom door and looked across at the Donelsons' suite, he heard nothing. The nursery was empty and still. There were no children's voices, no rustle of Emily's skirts. A sulky but correct Andrew was there to serve, but he had less time for Jackson as he spent hours closeted, writing letters to his wife. What had been a home—of a toddling Jackson Donelson, of a cheerful baby Mary Rachel, of an attentive and charming Emily, of a genial and sweet Mary Eastin—was hushed. As the autumnal shadows lengthened and night fell, Jackson was in a place he had not been for five decades, not since the word of his mother's death had reached Waxhaw. Then he had been fourteen, a scrawny boy soldier. Now he was sixty-three, a charismatic commander in chief. But with Emily and the children gone, one thing had not changed after Andrew Jackson's odyssey from the Carolinas to the capital. He felt he was alone.

PART II

★

I WILL DIE
WITH THE UNION

Late 1830 to 1834

CHAPTER 12

★

I HAVE BEEN LEFT
TO SUP ALONE

NOTHING FELT QUITE right, either in Nashville or in Washington. By the middle of October 1830, little Mary Rachel, just over thirteen months old, took her first steps at the Mansion, but her father was not there to celebrate. The toddler's older brother, Jackson, now four, cross-examined his mother about when life was going to be turned right side up again. "Jackson begins to learn finely and the babe walks a little," Emily wrote Andrew on Friday, October 15, 1830. "Jackson talks a great deal about you, and he wants to know very much if you have sent us word to come on in the winter." She did not even try to conceal her own sadness: "I feel quite as anxious, and hope you will let me know as soon as possible."

President Jackson was unhappy, too. Sitting up late on an October Sunday evening, he wrote Mary Eastin. "Major Donelson has informed you that the house appears lonesome, and on his account"—and on Jackson's as well—"it would give me great pleasure that you and Emily and the sweet little ones were here." He knew what the Donelsons were feeling with their young family split apart; though capable of cruel remarks and seemingly irreversible ultimatums, he was equally given to tenderness and generosity. Thinking about the Donelsons' plight, his mind drifted across the years. "I have often experienced in life the privation of leaving my dear wife when contending against poverty [and] there I can feel for him." At the moment, though, sympathy did not translate into mercy.

Jackson was engaged in an exhausting two-front war to reunite his family and defeat nullification in South Carolina. He viewed both struggles in the same light: as battles in which kinsmen had to find ways to live together, under the same roof, no matter how vehement their quarrels, for the benefits of family outweighed the dangers of division, both at home and in the country at large. He fought both campaigns with vigor, driven by violent emotions that veered from the cruel to the conciliatory.

Like many mercurial fathers, Jackson was like a summer storm—all darkness and ferocity one moment, giving way to light and calm the next. Such emotions might be contradictory but they were commingled within Jackson, who led as he lived: sometimes with his heart, sometimes with his mind, sometimes with both. In this critical phase of his life and his presidency, from the lonely autumn of 1830 through the election of 1832 to the showdown with South Carolina in 1833, Jackson expended great stores of private energy on his family while expanding the powers of the White House, all the while facing virulent critics who thought him unbalanced and dictatorial. It is true that he had his regrettable moments of fury, but Jackson was always more rational and more calculating than his enemies supposed. He was also genuinely committed to the ideal of democracy and to the preservation of the American experiment.

From Jefferson forward, contemporaries and commentators have argued that Jackson was a prisoner of his passions, suggesting that there could be no method in a man as mad as Jackson. In fact, as the arduous wars of Jackson's White House years show, in the end he could rise above his own pride—and he had to do so regularly, since his pride was so often on display—to govern the nation far more wisely, and with more personal warmth for its people, than his opponents ever recognized. The journey from Jackson's early, often inflammatory words on an issue to politically sensitive and shrewd results was not easy, or clean, or pretty, but frequently chaotic and highly charged. Yet the journey was made.

The struggle between Washington and South Carolina would in many ways be shaped by the tensions between Jackson and Calhoun, both of whom saw their own positions in absolute terms. Privately Calhoun believed nullification "to be the fundamental principle of our system, resting on facts as historically certain as our Revolution itself." To Jackson, such talk was treason, and he could not imagine that South Carolina would push the matter too far. "I had supposed that every one acquainted with me knew that I was opposed to the nullifying doctrine, and my toast at the Jefferson dinner was sufficient evidence of the fact," Jackson wrote to Joel Poinsett, a former South Carolina congressman and Jackson ally, in late October. With hope in his tone, he added, "The South Carolinians, as a whole, are too patriotic to adopt such **mad projects** as the nullifiers of that state propose." The collision between Calhoun and Jackson—like the collision between Emily and Jackson—had far-reaching emotional and political consequences.

THE DOMESTIC ARRANGEMENTS within the presidential circle were of intense interest and debate far from the Donelsons' Mansion and Jackson's White House. In Tennessee, the Eaton issue was proving central in a congressional race, and the question of Andrew Donelson's place in the president's universe was a subject of open conjecture and controversy. Robert Burton was running for the House of Representatives on a pro-Eaton—and therefore pro-Jackson—ticket, and he attacked the incumbent, Robert Desha (who was not in the race himself but was supporting Burton's opponent), saying that Jackson had asked Burton to run in order to test the country's support for the president. Burton and Desha had encountered each other at the races in Tennessee and held an impromptu debate, with Burton lashing out at the Eatons' foes as foes of Jackson. Before a crowd of about six hundred people, Burton was particularly rough on the Donelsons' role in the story and, Emily told Andrew, "informed the people of the unfortunate split (as he called it) in the Donelson family." Burton singled Andrew out for attack, publicly implying that Jackson himself thought Andrew was being disloyal, even treacherous, for in Jackson's mind support of the Eatons translated into support for him, and opposition to the Eatons translated into opposition to him and to everything the administration was trying to do.

Sensible and sophisticated beyond her years—she had turned twenty-three the previous June—Emily suspected she knew how Burton had come by the hard words of Jackson's he had quoted about the Donelsons. Jackson, she wrote Andrew, "may have used some expression to Mr. B[urton] when he imagined himself ill-treated by us that he never intended to be mentioned again." The essential thing, she told Andrew, was to remain calm and steady: "My Dear husband, let me beg you not to let it ruffle in any way your feelings toward Uncle Jackson, for such a thing would be more acceptable to your enemies than any thing you could do. Mr. B shows plainly that they are all jealous of Uncle's friendship to you and are making use of every exertion in their power to separate you. . . . Burton's meaning will recoil upon his own head and there let it rest."

She was thinking of her husband, of course, but also of her broader circle of friends. "I had the great pleasure yesterday evening of receiving my dear husband your affectionate letter and need not tell you how much I was gratified at its contents, and I wish it had been twice as long," Emily told Andrew. "There are a great many things that I should like to hear about that you have not mentioned. I shall expect you

to write oftener and detail every thing that passes."
Her anguish in exile was palpable, and his letters to
her were her only means of connection to the world
she loved. "I was thinking of you all the evening and
would have given anything to have been there," she
said, evoking the image of her sitting in the Tennessee night, her mind on the imagined glitter of
Washington.

In a postscript, Emily scribbled: "Is Major L[ewis]
still at the President's house?" Behind those few words
lay a tangle of emotions. If Lewis remained in the
White House, then his daughter Mary was the only
woman there, and Emily knew Jackson's need for female company could not be suspended. Would Mary
Lewis rise to fill Emily's place, providing Jackson with
a sense of family and home? Mary was thought to be
romantically interested in Abraham Van Buren, the
secretary of state's son, and such a flirtation would
only bring her closer to Jackson, given the president's
own intimate connection to the potential beau's father. For Emily all of these prospects were horrifying,
and there is evidence that her friends in Washington
sought to allay her fears by writing of Mary in harsh
terms. "Mary Lewis is here. . . . Strange girl, she acts
in such a way as to have a good many malicious remarks made on her," Rebecca Branch told Emily in
October. "I pity her sometimes. She is very friendly
with me, I believe she has a good heart—Madame **Rumour** says she is terribly smitten with A.V.B. . . . They
met here a few evenings ago and her conduct on the
occasion was truly ridiculous."

Reassuring, but Rebecca's letter had its troubling elements, too. She did not paint a portrait of Andrew Donelson that his distant wife wanted to see. Describing a party, Rebecca recounted a chat with Andrew: "I saw your **good man**," she told Emily. "He says if you don't come on soon he will commence dancing"—which may well have been the last thing Emily wanted to hear reported, even in friendly jest, since she was so far from Washington. Emily was reduced to recounting the revealing adventures of her children, telling Andrew that young Jackson "sometimes . . . mounts his stick horse, rides off, and comes back and tells me he has been to Washington and brings me many fine messages from you."

IN SOUTH CAROLINA in these October weeks, the voters went to the polls to elect state legislators, who in turn chose the governor. The stronger states' rights elements took a majority of the legislative seats, and James Hamilton, Jr., who favored nullification, won the governorship. While there were not enough votes in the legislature to call a special state convention to consider nullification, South Carolina's course was beginning to be set. As governor, Hamilton wanted to take a stand on turning back the tariff in order to establish a precedent that would protect slavery. "I have always looked to the present contest with the government, on the part of the Southern states, as a battle at the out-posts, by which, if we succeeded in repulsing the enemy, **the citadel would be safe**," he said just before assuming office. The legislature passed six resolutions related to nullification, with three in particular giving the radicals hope for the future. One supported Hayne's understanding of the Union over Webster's, asserting that "each party" to the Constitution—that is, the states, not the people—could decide whether certain laws amounted to "infractions," and they could then decide "the mode and measure of redress."

As South Carolina debated the nature of the American family, Jackson entered into a new, pitched battle with Andrew Donelson over the nature of theirs. On Monday morning, October 25, 1830, the two clashed again over the terms on which Emily might return to the White House. The argument became so ugly that Andrew made a tactical retreat in order to rejoin the battle by note.

Writing with candor and verve, Andrew was honest with Jackson about his own fears for himself and about his love for the man who raised him. Tired, he wrote, of "intimations" from the Eaton camp "that my power to hold my place here depended upon my subserviency to the wishes of Mrs. Eaton," Andrew acknowledged that he could see why Jackson was angry with him—yet he refused to give in.

Jackson was determined to exert power over his household and beyond. But Andrew was equally determined to control—and to be seen by the wider world as controlling—his own family's affairs. To surrender now would be personally humiliating and politically debilitating for Andrew—he would be viewed not as his own man, a distinguished secretary to the president of the United States and a potential force in his own right, but as yet another casualty of Jackson's ambition and will. In a painful turn of events, Andrew's future depended on declaring his independence from the patron of his past and his present.

There was calculation in Andrew's course. He knew that as a man of strength, Jackson respected men of strength. The president admired in others what he valued in himself and was capable of epic reversals of opinion. A close student of Jackson's life would understand this, and Andrew Donelson was such a student.

WITH STEEL IN his tone, then, Andrew went to the brink, believing that Jackson, like many leaders, truly settled matters only when a crisis was at hand. Declining to have any further face-to-face exchanges on the Eaton topic, Andrew wrote: "You have decided the question as you have a right to do. The only remaining one for me to consider is also depending in some degree upon your decision: how long shall I remain separated from my family?" He would leave; he would not come back; there would be no Emily, no children in the White House, nor a familiar face across the way. "It may be best for you to look to some one to take my place at once, and in the meantime to allow me to be employed in putting in more intelligible files the papers of the office, preparatory to my retirement from it," Andrew told Jackson.

Jackson read Andrew's note with deepening gloom. He was tired; he hated that Andrew would not come talk to him; he was staying up late, plagued by headaches. Alternating between sorrow and anger, Jackson

replied on Saturday, October 30, telling "my dear Andrew" that "I have determined, like Mr. Jefferson, to
live without any female in my family." He asked Andrew to remain in Washington through the congressional session, then they would part permanently.

Andrew's bid had failed. Undeterred, however, he
wrote again in the autumn dusk. "In your house, my
dear Uncle, as your guest I acknowledge that the same
comity and politeness are due to Mrs. Eaton that are to
the ladies of the other Cabinet officers or those of
other gentlemen. . . . Out of your house I claim only
the same general discretion in behalf of my family that
is possessed by all others." Struggling to find a way to
break through to Jackson on this point, Andrew
reached back into Jackson's personal history, linking
the present question with the first great test of Jackson's honor. "You did not when a prisoner in the Revolutionary War obey the order of the enemy who had
you in his power to clean his boots," Andrew wrote.
"Yet you find fault with my determination merely to
keep out of the way of insult."

It was almost midnight when Jackson read these
words. Though tired, he could not let the matter rest.
He was wounded. "My dear Andrew, for so I must still
call you," Jackson wrote, "you are pleased to say in your
letter 'In your house my dear Uncle as your **guest** I acknowledge the same comity and politeness are to Mrs.
Eaton . . . etc.' When, my dear Andrew, were you my
guest or how and when treated only as such? The term
. . . is surely unjust. You and Emily and Mary were con-

sidered by me as my family. You were so considered by the world, so introduced, and so treated, and in that situation as the representative of my dear and ever to be lamented wife was Mrs. Donelson here considered by me, and as such received and treated by all."

Emily and Andrew, the president insisted, were not guests. "You were my family, my chosen family," Jackson wrote, "and were placed where I was delighted to see you, and where, had it not been for bad advisers . . . we would have been living in peace with all, and in my bosom forever." He could say no more. "Every time the subject is named it makes my heart bleed afresh."

The note was carried across the hall and, reading Jackson's emotionally charged reply, Andrew saw he had been imprecise in his own language. He had not meant to refer to his family as guests, but to Mrs. Eaton. Replying yet again, Andrew said, "Nothing was farther from my mind than to express such an idea as that we considered ourselves, or were considered by others, as guests in your house."

And so the president of the United States and his secretary were reduced to an epistolary battle over grammar, sniping at and professing love for each other, often in the same paragraph. Power and affection were at stake and in play, indistinguishable. To Jackson, hostility to the Eatons continued to be "evidence of hostility to me."

Andrew's only solace came from Emily, who wrote to reassure him that all would be well even if he lost his Washington skirmish and joined her in Tennessee. "Still, I think you should not come to me if you can possibly avoid it," Emily told her husband. "It would be the most gratifying thing to your enemies as well as to the General's that could happen, [and] it might become the subject of a newspaper paragraph and be the means of the General's losing some ground and then the whole of the blame will be put on your shoulders."

Torn between the personal and the political, between her sense of right and wrong and her ambition, Emily went a step further in a letter a few days later: "I would be willing, were I to return to the City, to visit Mrs. E. sometime officially; this I do not think would be inconsistent as I have done it before," she wrote. "I am willing to make this apparent change of opinion to please our dear old uncle. . . . It will convince him of your desire to please him who has always been to you a **kind father.**"

To Emily, as to Jackson, power was paramount, and she had now spent enough time in Tennessee to realize that she did not want to surrender her place in the great world. As she read accounts from friends of the things she was missing, she grew firmer in her resolve to return. She would wait as long as it took, reassure Andrew, and offer concessions on the Eaton question, but she was in her way as inflexible and shrewd as Jackson himself when it came to surviving and thriving in life and politics. Though Jackson had raised Andrew as a son, Emily was more a child of Old Hickory—strong, smart, tenacious, tough, and wily.

. . .

ON SATURDAY, NOVEMBER 6, at his home in Quincy, Massachusetts, John Quincy Adams briefly noted in his diary the news of the evening's paper: he had been elected as a member of the House in the Twenty-second Congress. In that entry, he wrote nothing more than the returns—no reactions, no emotions. Indeed, since the moment, on a cold September morning, when a loyal newspaper editor and the retiring incumbent had approached him about putting his name on the ballot, he had written little about whether he desired to win or not. He would only demur that he had "not the slightest desire to be elected," but if elected, it was possible that he would "deem it my duty to serve."

His wife and son were furious at the prospect of his return to the political arena; Louisa, who had been looking forward to a long retirement at their home in Quincy, had even threatened not to join him in Washington. But after hours of reflection the next evening, November 7, Adams admitted in an unusually emotional entry that his victory brought him relief from his trials—his loss to Jackson, the death of his son George, even his replacement as the president of the American Academy of Arts and Sciences. "It seemed as if I was deserted by all mankind," he said.

"My return to public life in a subordinate station is disagreeable to my family, and disapproved by some of my friends," he said. And yet, for all his professed desire for "an old age of quiet and leisure" and his lament about "the faithless wave of politics," his election to Congress brought the greatest joy. "My election as President of the United States was not half so gratifying to my inmost soul. No election or appointment conferred upon me ever gave me so much pleasure."

Adams could at times come across as an elitist—certainly Jackson thought so—but he, like his successor in the White House, cared for what the people thought. "This call upon me by the people of the district in which I reside, to represent them in Congress, has been spontaneous," he wrote. The people had chosen him, and he was grateful to them.

AS THE LETTERS between uncle and nephew were going back and forth across the hall, Jackson welcomed a new member of his circle, Francis Preston Blair, who had moved from Kentucky to Washington to become the founding editor of a new administration newspaper. The brainchild of the politically brilliant Amos Kendall—who had run his newspaper in Kentucky, the **Argus,** with the help of Blair—the newspaper, to be called the **Globe,** was to be of what Jackson called "the true faith," meaning it was to support the White House totally and without reservation.

Kendall was a critical figure in Jackson's universe. Harriet Martineau, a British writer touring the United States, once recorded a brief Kendall sighting. "I was fortunate enough once to catch a glimpse of the invisible Amos Kendall, one of the most remarkable men in America," Martineau said. "He is supposed to be the moving spring of the whole administration; the

thinker, planner, and doer; but it is all in the dark. . . .
Work is done, of goblin extent and with goblin speed,
which makes men look about them with a supersti-
tious wonder; and the invisible Amos Kendall has the
credit of it all."

Blair was Kendall's friend, but he would soon become a force in his own right. And the most important force of all, Jackson, was feeling triumphant, as
well he should have: Blair's coming gave Jackson absolute power over his own newspaper—which in turn
meant absolute power over how the country, or at
least the part of the country that read the administration's paper, saw the White House. Born in Virginia
in 1791, a graduate of Transylvania University in Lexington, Kentucky, Blair converted to Jacksonian politics after supporting Clay for president in 1824.

Jackson liked his new editor's verve, spirit, and
speed—qualities that matched the rapid rate of political strife in a nation of proliferating newspapers and
burgeoning party mechanics. Papers had always
been partisan, and previous presidents had favored
this publication over that one. Jackson was, however,
the first to set out to create his own from scratch. "I
wish you to stand just as I do—the friend of General
Jackson and his administration, having no future
political views other than the support of his principles," Kendall had written to Blair in October. With
Kendall doing the wooing, Blair had decided to take
up the task.

Kendall, who was facing Senate confirmation for a
Treasury post, promised his friend adventure in the

year to come, and the support of the president, for he knew that Jackson returned loyalty with loyalty. "Now, I want you to prepare your mind to come on here at the meeting of Congress and remain during the session," he wrote to Blair that August. "You shall be welcome to live with me in my lonely way, so that the expense to you here shall be no more than you choose. Much depends on next winter. We shall have to war with the giants"—Clay in the 1832 presidential race, the Bank forces, and the South Carolinians. "I **know** the President will enter with zeal into my views. Your sentiments in relation to the Bank will make him zealous for you. I think he will be for a new paper any how. He told a friend of mine that if I were rejected, he would sustain me with half his fortune if necessary. **All** this between ourselves."

THE MAN WHO came to the White House to see Jackson in late November 1830 did not look like a ferocious, history-changing operative and editor. This is how his friend and associate John C. Rives described Blair: "about five feet ten inches high. . . . He looks like a skeleton, lacks but little of being one, and weighed last spring, when dressed in thick winter clothing, one hundred and seven pounds, all told, about eighty-five of which, we suppose, was bone, and the other twenty-two pounds, made up of gristle, nerve, and brain—flesh he has none. His face is narrow, and of the hatchet kind, according with his meat-axe disposition when writing about his enemies. His complexion is fair, his hair sandy, and his eyes blue—his countenance remarkably mild."

The journey from Kentucky with his family had been dangerous and long, with carriage wrecks, near misses, and, finally, an accident in which Blair cut himself severely. Lewis took one look at him and said, "Mr. Blair, we want stout hearts and sound heads here." Appearances to the contrary, Blair had both, and something else, too: a gift for invective and rhetoric that invested Jackson's ideas with currency and force.

Blair was swept away by Jackson's charm, by his personality, and finally by his kindness. Invited that very first night to a dinner on the first floor of the White House full of formally dressed diplomats and politicians, the injured and unkempt Blair felt out of place, a rude provincial thrust among elegant cosmopolitans. He was, James Parton said, "abashed and miserable," until Jackson, who should have anticipated that Blair might feel out of place on his initial evening in the capital, appeared and, seeing his new editor's discomfort, took Blair by the arm and sat with him at the table—a gesture, Parton said, that "completed the conquest of his heart." Francis Preston Blair would now fight any battle for Andrew Jackson.

The editor wasted no time in getting to work. Andrew Donelson was to take the president's annual message to Congress on Monday, December 6, 1830, and Blair and Kendall wanted it to be in circulation immediately thereafter in order to take the case for Jackson to the people. Blair loved the fight, writing editorials after nightfall in lead pencil, often in the White House, "in a great hurry," John Rives said. As the deadline approached, "we had to keep two boys to run to him for copy. We have known him to send one of the boys after the other to overtake him and get the last word on the sheet sent off."

Though Jackson urged moderation in most things in his message, he attacked nullification. "Every State cannot expect to shape the measures of the General Government to suit its own particular interests. . . . Mutual forbearance becomes, therefore, a duty obligatory upon all. . . ." Still, Jackson was not being blindly confrontational on the tariff. He understood that politicians who were absolutists did not long endure. He was accustomed to waiting for the right moment to strike, and he believed a compromise on the tariff was possible.

In his message, Jackson argued the merits of the issue. "It is an infirmity of our nature to mingle our interests and prejudices with the operation of our reasoning powers, and attribute to the objects of our likes and dislikes qualities they do not possess and effects they cannot produce," he said. "The effects of the present tariff are doubtless overrated, both in its evils and in its advantages. By one class of reasoners the reduced price of cotton and other agricultural products is ascribed wholly to its influence, and by another the reduced price of manufactured articles. The probability is that neither opinion approaches the truth."

An insightful passage, but understanding the roots of irrational political sentiment cannot make such sentiment disappear. Politics, as Jackson pointed out, can be largely about belief, not fact, and in South Carolina it looked as though no amount of public policy debate was going to counter the trend toward nullification. And while Jackson would do what he could to avoid violence, he also unleashed Blair, who told the readers of the **Globe** that "the right of nullification" was attractive to "certain men, who, like Caesar, would rather reign in a village, than be second in Rome." His more sophisticated readers may also have heard an echo of John Milton's description of Lucifer in **Paradise Lost**—the fallen angel who decided it was better "to reign in Hell than to serve in Heaven."

CHRISTMAS CAME AND went quietly. There were no children in the White House, and at the Mansion, Emily and her little ones passed the holiday "soberly yet agreeably," entertaining themselves with candy pullings and games. The season—freighted again, on this second anniversary, with memories of Rachel's death—took a toll on Andrew and on Emily. They loved each other and they missed each other—so much that the political element in their lives was put to the side in an exchange of anguished and touching letters in the opening moments of the new year.

On New Year's Day 1831, Donelson excused himself from the busy public rooms of the first floor of the White House to write Emily a short, heartfelt note. "I detached myself for a moment from the New Year crowd to offer you the salutations of the season and to enjoy those which I know are breathed by you for me." He closed by quoting a poem: "Think not beloved time can break / The spell around us cast, / Or absence from my bosom take / The memory of the past; / My love is not that silvery mist / From summer blooms by sunbeams kissed— / Too fugitive to last."

The Emily who read this had lost a great deal of weight—she did not have much to lose in the first place—and looked, as one guest at the Mansion told her, "like a spectre." She was depressed and lonely, and scolded Andrew for failing to write her the kinds of letters she longed for. "Although your letters are 'like angels visits few and far between,' yet when they do come you hardly say how do you do, and goodbye; do let me know everything that passes, how you get along and what you employ yourself about, and if you think much about us. You are never absent from my thoughts. When I lay down it is only to think of you, and when I sleep [I] dream of you."

Having been a part of their marriage from the beginning, Jackson shared Emily and Andrew's sadness. "Although we have been visited by a vast number of ladies and gentlemen, and inundated as usual by office hunters, still we have appeared lonesome—several times I have been left to sup alone," Jackson wrote to Emily on Thursday, January 20, 1831. "The levee was numerously attended, but still, there being no lady of the house, there was something wanting, and ladies appeared without a pivot to move on."

Gustave de Beaumont, who was traveling in America with Tocqueville, met Jackson the same week and found both the president and the presidency unexpectedly unimposing. Jackson, Beaumont wrote his mother, "is an old man of 66 years, well preserved, and appears to have retained all the vigor of his body and spirit. He is not a man of genius. Formerly he was celebrated as a duelist and hot-head. . . . If he has courtiers they are not very attentive to him, for when we entered the **salon** he was alone."

The president and the White House seemed muted to Beaumont. "People in France have got an altogether false idea of the presidency of the United States," Beaumont said. "They see in it a sort of political sovereignty and compare it constantly with our constitutional monarchies. Of a certainty, the power of the King of France would be nil if it were modeled after the power of the President of the United States."

Power, and the efforts of those who sought to take it from him, was much on Jackson's mind. To him, the enormity of the sins committed against the Eatons, and his abiding belief in the plot against him, kept him from accepting Emily back to the White House.

IN EARLY 1831 the **Globe** announced that Jackson would seek another term in the White House. "The conquering Hero is again in the field, and it must now be seen who are his friends and who are his foes," the paper said. Twenty months before the election, however, Jackson was presiding over an administration riven with feuds and beset by scandal. His vice president was frozen out but still had alliances with three members of the Cabinet (Branch, Ingham, and Berrien); his secretary of state was viewed as the Iago of the White House, with Jackson cast in the role of the bewitched ruler in Van Buren's thrall; and, of course, his own family was divided over Margaret Eaton's status. In the late winter and early spring of 1831, several forces intersected to extricate Jackson from many of his tangled problems.

The first was the reemergence of an ancient quarrel. A dozen years earlier, in the Monroe administration, Adams and Calhoun had been in the Cabinet when Jackson had preemptively invaded Florida, leading to great controversy in Washington. At the time, Adams, the secretary of state, had defended Jackson's decision; others, including Calhoun, the secretary of war, had questioned it. Jackson, who had been aware that Calhoun had opposed his Florida campaign, had not pressed the matter in the late 1820s, a time when he needed Calhoun in order to bring along the South in the race against Adams. The calculating part of Jackson—a part of his character his foes tended to underestimate, much to their dismay—had tucked the Florida issue away until he needed it.

And now, amid threats of nullification and trouble in the Cabinet, he did. Over a period of months between 1830 and 1831, the president demanded to know (though he probably already knew) what Calhoun had thought and done in the Florida matter. Calhoun understood that the argument was being revived to complete his estrangement from Jackson. "I should be blind not to see that this whole affair is a political maneuver, in which the design is that you should be the instrument and myself the victim," Calhoun wrote Jackson. The Florida history was suddenly of present value for those Jacksonians who hated Calhoun. Even the smooth-tempered John Overton, so often a conciliating force in Jackson's private world, detected only danger when it came to Calhoun. "He is aspiring, we all know, and his eye has never been averted for a moment from the presidency, since he became a member of Mr. Monroe's Cabinet," Overton wrote Jackson. "This is not unnatural for talented men. Hence, no man saw with more pain (Mr. Clay not excepted) the rise and elevation of your character."

Isolated, Calhoun decided to publish the correspondence about the Seminole affair, a pamphlet that first appeared in Green's **Telegraph** on Thursday, February 17, 1831. Jackson feigned surprise and outrage that the vice president had taken the argument public and thus divided the party; Calhoun self-pityingly claimed that the entire controversy was "a conspiracy for my destruction." (It is likely that Jackson knew, or at least strongly suspected, that Calhoun was about to publish and did not try to stop him, gambling that the move would make Calhoun look disloyal to the president—which it did.) Blair opened a counteroffensive. "The Globe you will have seen is determined to make a bold push to keep up the war if possible between the P. and the V.P.," Ingham said, and, in Blair's capable hands, it was surely possible. Blair, Ingham said, "came out pell mell . . . to make a war of extermination against Calhoun under the banner of Gen. Jackson." Jackson was done with Calhoun forever. "A man who could secretly make the attempt . . . to destroy me, and that under the strongest professions of friendship," Jackson said, "is base enough to do anything."

Perhaps even to challenge Jackson in 1832. Clay was already running, and Jackson was in the field, and Calhoun was still assessing his own chances. On Wednesday, March 2, 1831, Calhoun went to Meridian Hill to see John Quincy Adams, with whom he had served in Monroe's Cabinet and under whom he had been vice president. Adams received him coolly. "This is the first time he has called upon me since the last Administration closed," Adams said. "I meet Mr. Calhoun's advances to a renewal of the intercourse of common civility because I cannot reject them. But I once had confidence in the qualities of his heart. It is not totally destroyed, but so impaired that it can never be fully restored. Mr. Calhoun's friendships and enmities are regulated exclusively by his interests. His opinions are the sport of every popular blast, and his career as a statesman has been marked by a series of the most flagrant inconsistencies. . . . Calhoun veers round in his politics, to be always before the wind, and makes his intellect the pander to his will."

The next day, another caller, a journalist named Matthew L. Davis, came to Adams, and they spent two hours talking politics. Davis reported some bold words of Calhoun's, telling Adams that Calhoun thought himself "the strong man of the South" who "expected to obtain the votes of all the Southern states except Georgia." When Davis told Calhoun he would not back him, Calhoun had "only asked for fair play in public and if the election should come to the House of Representatives."

AS CALHOUN DREAMED of the presidency and Clay planned for it, Jackson decided to bring order to his own house and dispatched Andrew on Tuesday, March 8, to bring Emily back. The reason for his relenting as Congress adjourned is unclear. It was most likely exhaustion at the battle combined with his characteristic belief that he would win in the end. There was the presidential campaign, the standoff with South Carolina, and the war with the Bank, and Jackson hated the idea of another lonely season. For Andrew, spring meant the promise of reunion. "The adjournment of Congress is to my feelings on this occasion what the melting of the ice and the spring navigation of the rivers is to the merchant—the source of my joy," Andrew wrote Emily as he left by stage for Tennessee. "Kiss Jackson and the little red bird for me." He was expected in Nashville shortly to collect his family and set back out for Washington, bound for the White House.

No sooner had Andrew Donelson arrived in Tennessee, however, than another letter arrived from Jackson. He had changed his mind. "As much as I desire you, and your dear little family with me," he wrote Andrew, "unless you and yours can harmonize with Major Eaton and his family I do not wish you here." Stunned, Emily and Andrew determined to stay in Nashville. "Recent information from the General makes it impossible for me to return to Washington without hearing from him first," Donelson wrote to Secretary Branch. "I need not tell you the cause, you can guess it too well."

VAN BUREN HAD been thinking about what Ingham called "this disgusting petticoat business" for a long time. A triumphant two-term Jackson administration would reflect well on the architect of the initial 1828 victory, and Van Buren, like many others, hoped one day to have the White House for himself. In the first months of 1831, worried about "the plots, intrigues and calumnies by which I had been for two years surrounded," Van Buren said, he settled on a plan: he would resign from the State Department, a move that, once accomplished, triggered a series of events that would ultimately free Jackson from scandal, strengthen him politically, and reunite the president's family.

Jackson and Van Buren were on their daily horseback ride, when a thunderstorm drove them inside a nearby tavern. Jackson's mood matched the weather. "His spirits were on that day much depressed and on our way he spoke feelingly of the condition to which he had been reduced in his domestic establishment, Major Donelson and the ladies and children, of whom he was exceedingly fond, having, some time before, fled to Tennessee to avoid the Eaton malaria," Van Buren said. Unable to bring himself to raise the issue of his resignation, Van Buren left the president alone with his thoughts, passing the interlude in the tavern chatting with a farmer. The storm over, Jackson and Van Buren resumed their ride. Soon Jackson's horse slipped on the wet road and "threatened to fall or to throw his rider," Van Buren recalled. "I was near enough to seize the bridle and thus to assist him in regaining his footing."

"You have possibly saved my life, sir!" Jackson said, then mumbled what Van Buren called "broken and half audible sentences which I understood to import that he was not certain whether his escape from death, if it was one, was under existing circumstances, worthy of much congratulation." Van Buren saw that this was hardly the time to bring up anything as momentous as the loss of the secretary of state. On a later ride, however, Jackson's humor was much improved, and the two were near the Potomac when Jackson, with more hope than certainty, said, "We should soon have peace in Israel."

"No!" Van Buren said. "General, there is but one thing can give you peace."

"What is that, sir?"

"My resignation!"

Three decades later, Van Buren said he could still exactly recall "the start and the earnest look" on Jackson's face. "Never, sir!" the president said.

But Van Buren laid out the case, arguing that "the course I had pointed to was perhaps the only safe one open to us." In his memoirs Van Buren is oblique about all that they discussed, but it is possible that he argued that his resignation from the Cabinet would enhance his chances of becoming Jackson's successor, since he would be insulated from the chaos of the capital and could campaign the way Jackson had—as an outsider, not an insider in the tradition of Adams, Jefferson, Madison, Monroe, and John Quincy Adams. Jackson's victory—both his popular one in 1824 and his undisputed triumph in 1828—was creating a new template for the presidential candidate, and Van Buren was thinking of how he might cast himself in such terms. They rode so far and talked so much—though Van Buren lectured much of the time—that they "did not reach home until long after our usual dinner hour."

They parted until morning. Van Buren fretted; Jackson did not sleep. Appearing the next day, Van Buren thought, "unusually formal and passionless," Jackson said: "Mr. Van Buren, I have made it a rule through life never to throw obstacles in the way of any man who, for reasons satisfactory to himself, desires to leave me, and I shall not make your case an exception." Jackson was wounded by his friend's prospective abandonment, and he had summoned up the psychological defenses of an orphan who had learned that the people one loves can disappear.

Van Buren jumped up and swore his allegiance, insisting he was only thinking of Jackson's interests, and that he would stay until the last hour if Jackson wished it.

"You must forgive me, my friend, I have been too hasty in my conclusions," Jackson said. "I know I have—say no more about it now, but come back at one o'clock—we will take another long ride and talk again in a better and calmer state of mind."

They did, and Jackson warmed to the idea, asking

whether he might bring Barry, Eaton, and Lewis into the conversation. Van Buren agreed, and the next day the three men met at the White House, came to consensus that Van Buren's plan was sound, and then went back across Lafayette Square to Van Buren's for dinner.

AFTER THEY ENTERED Decatur House, Eaton said: "Why should you resign? I am the man about whom all the trouble has been made and therefore the one who ought to resign." Such a development was, Van Buren admitted in his memoirs, "a consummation devoutly to be wished but one I would have assumed to be hopeless." When Eaton brought it up yet again at supper, Van Buren raised the obvious question: What, he asked, would Mrs. Eaton "think of such a movement as he proposed"? Eaton was certain, he said, that "she would highly approve of it." The more realistic and less certain Van Buren suggested that Eaton confer with his wife and then bring word again. The next day, Eaton claimed Margaret had said he should indeed leave the Cabinet, and, in the first week of April 1831, Van Buren said, "it was forthwith agreed that we should both resign with General Jackson's consent, which was obtained on the following day."

Van Buren would take over as the envoy to England, and Eaton was likely to return to Tennessee to stand for the Senate. "The long agony is nearly over," Ingham wrote Berrien on Tuesday, April 19, 1831. "Mr. V. B. and Major Eaton have resigned." Before Ingham could gloat for long, though, Jackson forced

him, Berrien, and Branch to resign as well, completing the purge of the Cabinet.

John Berrien, writing from Savannah on Sunday,
April 24, was puzzled by the breakup. For all to resign, he told Ingham, "does not seem to be perfectly
intelligible." Van Buren and Eaton could leave for
whatever reasons they chose, if the president agreed,
Berrien said, "but how it could be believed, that the
public would consider that circumstance as affecting
you, Branch, or myself, it is difficult to discover."

Jackson and Van Buren wanted them out of the
way. Writing shortly after his firing, with a sense of
irony, Ingham told the Pennsylvania lawmaker
Samuel McKean that "to make up" for being forced to
resign, he had had "a peculiar acknowledgement from
Old Hickory of my skill in diplomacy by an invitation
this day through the Secretary of State to go to Russia." He declined.

The drama at Washington was moving quickly and,
for the uninitiated, mysteriously. "You must read Tacitus and the Epistles of Pliny to understand this system of manoevering," John Quincy Adams told his
son Charles Francis. "That was the age of informers
and spies—of denunciations and conversions."

As Adams saw it, the rivalries in Washington represented a new iteration of an old and epic story. "You
are disgusted with the diminutive rivalries [and] the
paltry altercations . . . of our public men," Adams
wrote his son several days later. "They might indeed
quarrel with a better choice of words, and as Addison
says of Virgil's Georgics, cast about their dung with an

air of greater dignity. But you remember that in Homer Achilles tells Agamemnon to his face that he has the forehead of a dog and the heart of a deer. We think none the less for this either of Agamemnon or Achilles. Men have railed at each other in good set terms from that day to this. They will still do so as long as there are prizes to contend for which move their avarice or their ambition."

Jackson would not have appreciated most of Adams's literary allusions, but he agreed with the central point: politics is brutal because it engages the most fundamental human impulses for affection, honor, power, and fame. Great principles and grand visions are ennobling, but at its best politics is an imperfect means to an altruistic end.

What Van Buren had undertaken on horseback was now reality, and Jackson, at long last, emerged from the Eaton affair with a Cabinet he could control. It had come at a high price, but it had come. Beneath Jackson's warmth and passionate attachments lay a coldheartedness essential to any great leader. "The President parts from [Eaton] with great reluctance, for he maintains the greatest affection towards him," Blair said, "but he told me that he could always sacrifice every private feeling to what he considered a public duty."

While Jackson believed the dissolution a good thing, he still hated the loss of the familiar. He needed Andrew Donelson, who had barely reached Tennessee, back in the White House, both to handle the complexities of the Cabinet crisis and to provide a steadying presence. "My labours have been incessant," Jackson wrote Andrew on April 19. "I have great need of your aid." Thrilled to read these words, believing them a reprieve, Andrew hurried back to Washington, telling Emily that he thought "every moment's detention"—meaning delay on Andrew's part—"will be felt by Uncle." The opportunity to begin all over again was at hand, and Andrew did not want to miss it. Emily—though she, too, hated to be away from the center of action—stayed behind.

THE NEWS OF the Cabinet resignations broke in the **Globe** the next day, on Wednesday, April 20, 1831—a development startling enough to send diplomats in Washington scurrying to brief their governments. The British minister, Charles Vaughan, a neighbor of the Eatons', wrote Viscount Palmerston, the foreign secretary, that "this day a complete change of the ministers comprising the Cabinet of the President of the United States has taken place." The new secretaries—Edward Livingston at State, Louis McLane at Treasury, Lewis Cass at War, Levi Woodbury at Navy, and Roger Taney as attorney general—were, Vaughan said, strong appointments; in fact, he said to Palmerston, "the two persons who it is proposed should replace Major Eaton and Mr. Branch enjoy a higher reputation for talent than their predecessors." Yet it was a treacherous period. On the day the Cabinet was dissolved, Vaughan told London to watch the South, warning the foreign secretary that the tariff issue, because of the "determined opposition to it of the Southern States," could lead to "a dissolution of the Union."

The Cabinet news, Bangeman Huygens reported home to the Netherlands, "provides scenes of unmatched scandal." Recalling the 1830 provisional peace with Jackson over the Margaret question, Huygens wrote: "He was near the point of changing ministries for her sake, but . . . a compromise was made." It was, however, "false" and "unnatural," and now the president, Huygens said, felt it was time "to entirely remake his Cabinet."

Jackson decided that gratitude to Eaton for resigning compelled him to insist that the new Cabinet receive Margaret on the same terms that had so divided his first Cabinet. Establishment observers like Margaret Bayard Smith were at a loss to explain the curiosities of the Jackson White House, so they put his tenacity down to senility. "In truth, the only excuse his best friends can make for his violence and imbecilities is that he is in his dotage," Mrs. Smith said after the Cabinet dissolution. "The papers do not exaggerate, nay do not detail one half of his imbecilities."

John Quincy Adams was preparing for a trip when word arrived of the mass resignations. Calling it the "explosion at Washington," Adams reported to his son that "people stare—and laugh—and say, what next?"

It was a good question.

CHAPTER 13

★

A MEAN AND SCURVY
PIECE OF BUSINESS

SINCE HIS CHILDHOOD hiding in the Carolina countryside on the lookout for Tarleton's redcoats, Jackson loved being in on what he called "secretes." As president he was no different, and he maintained an informal network to gather bits and pieces of political intelligence. In the South, Joel Poinsett, the diplomat, world traveler, and firm Unionist who was Jackson's main source of information in the region, was hearing talk of conspiracy and rebellion. "I know not how things are moving over in Charleston, but with us the nullifiers are in motion, and . . . are endeavoring to rally their scattered forces for a new contest in 1832," Alexander Speer, a former comptroller general of South Carolina, wrote to Poinsett early in 1831 from Church Hill in Abbeville, near the western edge of South Carolina. "I will not be at all surprised if at the next presidential election Mr. Calhoun's name should be brought forward as a candidate."

A repeat of 1824, with Calhoun and Henry Clay in the villainous roles, was under consideration, Speer said, and he thought his information sound. "The understanding appears to be that Mr. Calhoun's name is to be run as a candidate, not because it is expected he can be elected, but to defeat the election by the people, and thus throw it into the House of Representatives, where it can be managed as to their best . . . interests. . . . This junto are at this time making open declarations of hostility to the Union, and expect roundly that . . . civil war must and shall be the consequence. As to Genl. Jackson their hostility is unequivocal. . . ."

The Cabinet breakup led to a national debate over Jackson's first three years of leadership and whether he should have another term. With the presidential campaign at hand, partisans on all sides—Jackson's, Calhoun's, Clay's, and others'—chattered about the resignations. The governor of Pennsylvania, George Wolf, wrote Ingham of allegations that "Jackson had turned you and Branch out because he detected you in conspiracy to turn him out and put Calhoun in his place."

The opposition continued to fear Jackson's mysterious power over so many people. "His administration is absolutely odious, and yet there is an adherence to the man," John Sergeant, a former congressman from Pennsylvania, wrote to Clay. "It remains to be seen whether this will not yield to the conviction that his continuance must be destructive of everything that is worthy to be cherished."

Civility in Washington—rare enough since the election of Adams by the House in 1825—disappeared. Writing to her son Charles Francis Adams,

Louisa Adams called the battles within the Jackson administration "altogether as mean and scurvy a piece of business as I ever saw." John McLean of Ohio, appointed by Jackson to the Supreme Court in 1829, believed that "the Jackson party is a good deal dispirited" in the wake of the resignations. "Gen. Jackson will not get on as successfully as many are inclined to think," McLean wrote Ingham in May. "The general's qualifications for the office begin to be questioned by many who have believed him capable of managing the government by the superior powers of his own mind." In Kentucky and Ohio, McLean said, Jacksonians "have lost the enthusiasm they once possessed in the cause." In South Carolina, the radicals thought the crisis would help them. "The administration at Washington cannot recover from the retreat **precipitate** of the late Cabinet," James Hamilton, Jr., wrote to James Henry Hammond from Charleston, "and consequently Jackson's reelection is placed in such hazard as scarcely to be a probable event."

THE CABINET PURGE did not bring peace to John Eaton, either. He was out of power, open to charges that his resignation proved what his enemies had been saying about his wife, and felt disoriented by his sudden official distance from Jackson—he had served with Jackson in three different decades, in wars hot and cold, and was now in an ambiguous position in Washington, close to the president but not in office. Not surprisingly, then, Eaton began to lose control of his temper. In the pages of the **Telegraph** on Friday, June 17, 1831, Duff

Green, firmly allied with Calhoun, told the Eaton story, and Branch, Berrien, and Ingham were (accurately) said to have snubbed the wife of the secretary of war on moral grounds. In response, Eaton issued a challenge to the three men in a note written that evening to "know of you, whether or not you sanction, or will disavow" this "vile abuse of me, and of my family." Ingham was the one most willing to answer.

Thus began three days of incendiary correspondence and confrontation. Ingham would not dignify the question of his having sanctioned the **Telegraph** piece with a reply, he wrote Eaton the next day, and then snarled: "In the meantime I take the occasion to say that you must be not a little deranged to imagine that any blustering of yours could induce me to disavow what all the inhabitants of this City know and perhaps half the people of the U.S. believe to be true." Answering later that Saturday, Eaton called Ingham's note "impudent and insolent" and raised the stakes: "I demand of you **satisfaction**, for the wrong and injury you have done me. Your answer must determine whether you are so far entitled to the name and character of a gentleman, as to be able to act like one."

So it was that the former secretary of war decided to kill the former secretary of the Treasury. When there was no immediate reply from Ingham to the challenge to duel, a brother-in-law of Eaton's, Dr. Philip G. Randolph, forced his way in to see Ingham on Sunday morning with what Ingham called "a threat of personal violence." Affecting a condescending tone— and thereby infuriating Eaton all the more—Ingham wrote: "I perfectly understand the part you are made to play in the farce now acting before the American people. I am not to be intimidated by threats or provoked by abuse to any act inconsistent with the pity and contempt which your condition and conduct inspire."

At this Eaton went nearly mad. "Your contempt I heed not, your pity I despise," he replied. "It is such contemptible fellows as yourself that have set forth rumors of their own creation, and taken them as a ground of imputation against me. . . . But no more; here our correspondence closes. Nothing more will be received short of an acceptance of my demand of Saturday, and nothing more be said to me until face-to-face we meet. It is not in my nature to brook your insults; nor will they be submitted to."

On the morning of Monday, June 20, 1831, Eaton and his friends searched the city for Ingham—Ingham's office, his boardinghouse, streets where he was likely to be. It was a formidable company: Lewis, Randolph, Colonel John Campbell (the treasurer of the United States), and Major Thomas L. Smith (the register of the Treasury). In Ingham's mind, there was no doubt about the mission: they were "lying in wait," he said, "for the purpose of assassination."

The Eaton party took up positions at the Treasury and in a grocery store near Ingham's F Street lodgings. "While prowling about . . . the movements of the band were so suspicious as to induce Ingham's son to go to his father's lodgings to put him on his guard," Duff Green told William Cabell Rives, the Virginia editor. Now "apprised of these movements," Ingham armed himself and, guarded by his son and a handful of friends, he managed to go to work and come home without being attacked. Daylight may have deterred the Eaton forces, and Ingham's own unexpected show of force probably played a part, too. Duff Green thought Ingham's display of strength in the streets— what Green called "the firmness of the old gentleman backed by his friends"—had spooked Eaton, who, Green believed, had "felt his courage oozing out at his fingers' ends and immediately left the building without noise or bloodshed."

Whatever momentary failure of nerve may have afflicted Eaton, it lasted only a moment, for by nightfall he was back on the march. "Having recruited an additional force in the evening," Ingham recalled, "they paraded until a late hour on the streets near my lodgings heavily armed, threatening an assault on the dwelling I reside in." Beseeching Jackson to intervene "as the chief magistrate of the U. States and most especially of the District of Columbia, whose duties in maintaining good order among its inhabitants . . . cannot be unknown to you," Ingham invoked Jackson's public responsibilities rather than his personal feelings. On reflection, however, Ingham decided that hoping Jackson would side with him against Eaton was a bad bet, and since the stakes were now life and death, guessing wrong could be fatal. So, unwilling to risk his luck any further, Ingham fled the city at four o'clock in the morning on Tuesday, June 21, taking a stage to Baltimore.

. . .

THE ESCAPE PROBABLY saved his life. Far from policing the District or chastising the officials of his government—including Lewis, the acting secretary of war and a resident of the White House—Jackson was taking a kind of perverse pleasure in Ingham's predicament and flight in the darkness. Replying to Ingham—who was already out of Washington, heading for safety—Jackson dismissed Ingham's story about the posse, telling him that the men Ingham had named had denied the charge.

To Andrew Donelson, Jackson was more forthcoming. "The truth is Eaton alone did look for him and remained in a grocer's store, after walking through the streets some time, until nearly the hour of three from ten in the morning," Jackson wrote Andrew. It was Ingham's guard that posed the real danger, Jackson said. Though he cited no source for the claim, Jackson believed the Ingham forces "had determined when Eaton made the attack to shoot three or seven balls through Eaton." The most revealing part of that sentence is Jackson's apparently blasé acknowledgment that Eaton did plan to assault, and most likely kill, Ingham.

Ingham was well out of it and sought security at home in Bucks County, Pennsylvania. Jackson left for the Rip Raps, and Eaton's plans were unclear. Eaton had, a correspondent of Henry Clay's said, "acted a most ridiculous and even crazy part," and reason seemed to be playing even less of a role than usual in the Eatons' private world. "Eaton still remains in the city and the rumor of the day varies as to his ultimate intention of leaving it for Tennessee," Duff Green wrote Ingham on Monday, July 4. "I believe that [Margaret] will resist an attempt to send her into banishment."

In New York City that April 1831, at Prince and Marion streets, near the Bowery, John Quincy Adams arrived at the Dutch-roofed house of Mr. and Mrs. Samuel Gouverneur. Mrs. Gouverneur was a daughter of former president James Monroe, and her father had come to live with her in his great old age. General Lafayette always called when in the country, and a boy who was in and out of the Gouverneurs' house in those years remembered President Monroe in satin knee breeches, sitting near a grate in the house's "dingy" parlor.

Receiving Adams, Monroe—now old and failing, only a few months from death—savored the chance to talk politics and foreign affairs with a fellow member of the most exclusive club in the country: that of the former presidents of the United States. Washington, the senior Adams, and Jefferson were all dead: only Madison, at Montpelier, survived. As for the incumbent— well, the subject of Jackson consumed a good bit of Adams's and Monroe's time on this afternoon. The two old men moved from speaking of violence in Europe to talking about what Adams called "the recent quasi revolution at Washington," and revolutions were serious things. The tumult within the Jackson administration offended the orderly sensibilities of two presidents who had, in their day, sought tranquillity. To another friend,

Adams said: "If other revolutions partake of the sublime, this one entirely and exclusively belongs to the next step"—the ridiculous.

WHATEVER EATON SAID to Margaret to convince her that he had to resign, and despite Jackson's enduring support, she had begun to feel the way those in Washington who have slipped from power often do—less important, the object of fewer eyes. As Van Buren recalled it, on a day "long enough after her husband's relinquishment of office to make her sensible of the change in her position," Margaret was at home when Jackson and Van Buren stopped by on a walk.

She was not the Margaret of old. "Our reception was to the last degree formal and cold, and what greatly surprised me was that the larger share of the chilling ingredient in her manner and conversation fell to the General," Van Buren said. Jackson now saw what so many others—including Emily—had long seen: that Margaret was changeable, mercurial, and immature. On leaving the house, Van Buren said, "There has been some mistake here," but Jackson did not want to talk about it.

"It is strange," Jackson said, and spoke of it no more.

It was not so strange to those who had assessed Margaret with a more clinical eye than Jackson had. She was selfish and grandiose. But what was done was done. The Eatons would be gone soon enough—by the end of the summer—and Jackson's Tennessee friends wanted to see Emily back in the White House.

· · ·

THE CLAY FORCES were already planning for the postelection phase in a close presidential contest in 1832. "Nothing now is more probable than that the Election may come to the House," Josiah Randall, a Philadelphia lawyer, said to Henry Clay. From the safety of his home in Pennsylvania, Samuel Ingham wanted vengeance. Chased from Washington by Eaton, Ingham turned his anger on Jackson, telling a friend that when the people "know but a small part they will dispose of Genl J. . . . The magic of Genl J's popularity is all a delusion. He has more unbearable points about him than I have ever seen in a public man."

John C. Calhoun's grandiose vision of himself and his own abilities was also on display in the critical early months of 1831. In Columbia, South Carolina, James Hammond rose early on the morning of Friday, March 18, to meet with Calhoun at the home of a Charleston lawyer. Hammond's long account of the ensuing conversation sheds much light on Calhoun's thinking at this juncture.

It was only seven o'clock in the morning, but Calhoun "immediately entered freely into the discussion of the affairs of the nation," Hammond recalled. "He said that great changes had taken and were taking place now in the political elements . . . as extraordinary as it had been unexpected." Calhoun believed that "three fourths of the members of Congress" were "with him," as were Pennsylvania, Virginia, and Kentucky (which would have surprised Clay to hear). Jackson had let him down and was "as jealous of his military fame as

ever was Othello of his wife and easily played upon
with it by the cunning men by whom he is surrounded." Calhoun's plan, according to Hammond:
"to throw himself entirely upon the South and if possible to be more Southern." At two subsequent encounters—a dinner and a tea—Hammond found that
"there is a listlessness about him which shows that his
mind is deeply engaged and no doubt that it is on the
subject of the Presidency. He is unquestionably quite
feverish under the present excitement, and his hopes."

Calhoun's Southern strategy was risky, for it depended on having enough Southerners and enough
voters in border states like Pennsylvania to cast their
lot with a South Carolinian who was in the nullifying
camp. His case was not helped when, in Charleston
on Thursday, May 19, 1831, South Carolina congressman George McDuffie laid out his popular (if inaccurate) forty-bale theory—the idea being that the
tariff cost each planter forty bales of cotton out of one
hundred—and acknowledged that the struggle was
less about money than power.

"I WILL READILY concede that a State cannot nullify
an act of Congress by virtue of any power derived from
the Constitution," McDuffie said. "It would be a perfect solecism to suppose any such power was conferred
by the Constitution." Thus dismissing the more intellectual and labored theories—including Calhoun's in
the **Exposition** and Hayne's debate with Webster—
McDuffie said: "The Union, such as the majority have

made it, is a foul monster, which those who worship, after seeing its deformity, are worthy of their chains."

Reading about McDuffie's remarks, Duff Green thought the South Carolinians were going too far; such hot rhetoric, he believed, put Calhoun in a vulnerable position nationally. Green's fear, James Hamilton, Jr., said, was that the Southern extremists "intended to start into open rebellion and insure the empire of the whore of Washington (Mrs. E. I suppose)," Hamilton told Hammond on Saturday, June 11, 1831.

Worried about Jackson's more precarious political position and disturbed by McDuffie's May broadside, the Unionists in South Carolina hastily arranged a daylong Fourth of July rally in Charleston. Congressman William Drayton spoke vividly. In a civil struggle, he said, "all the kindly feelings of the human heart would be eradicated, and for them would be substituted those burning and savage passions . . . which pour rancours into the bosoms of friends" and which, in the end, could lead to "the spectacle of brother armed against brother, of parent against child, and of the child against his parent."

Though he was secluded at the Rip Raps, Jackson had the last word of the day, in a letter that was read aloud to the meeting and echoed Drayton: "Every enlightened citizen must know that a separation, could it be effected, would begin with civil discord and end in colonial dependence on a foreign power and obliteration from the list of nations." Yet even before such an eventuality could come to pass, Jackson wrote, he would hurl all the strength at his command, "at all hazards," in order to "present an insurmountable barrier to the success of any plan of disorganization."

Anxiety about civil war was widespread. "I fear from my observations to the South that our Union is in danger," Stephen Van Rensselaer, a former congressman from New York, wrote Clay. "I had no idea of the violence of the planters. They are deluded by their ambitious leaders."

IN HIS STUDY in South Carolina, Calhoun, the most ambitious of those "planters," was having the most intense of summers. On Tuesday, July 26, 1831, Calhoun wrote what came to be known as his Fort Hill Address. It did not breathe fire. It did not summon the South to immediate disunion. In philosophical prose that tended to the dense, Calhoun argued, essentially, that the Union could survive only if the states, as the original parties to the Constitution, had the means to nullify a law if and until the Constitution were to be specifically amended to make the law in question part and parcel of the Constitution. It was an elegant theory, but largely impractical, for the place to fight those battles was in the Congress, where the Framers had taken care to ensure that the voices of the minority could be heard (chiefly, though not solely, through the granting of equal representation in the Senate regardless of a state's population). There were the courts, too, established and maintained by a combination of executive and legislative power as a check over both.

The nullifiers liked to argue that they were working in the tradition of the Kentucky and Virginia resolutions of 1798, which had been passed to protest the Alien and Sedition Acts in particular and the federalism embodied by John Adams in general. Authored by Thomas Jefferson and James Madison, the resolutions as adopted did not go as far then as South Carolina wanted to go now. (In a draft that came to light in 1832, Jefferson did make extreme arguments, but in the end the Kentucky legislature had passed a less strident version.) And from retirement at Montpelier, Madison denied that the resolutions were intended to do what South Carolina was proposing. The states, Madison said, had the right to appeal for reform, but only through the national government. As articulated in the Fort Hill Address, nullification would create the mechanical means for the states to assert more power over the laws of the nation than the laws of the nation could assert over them.

The objections of most Americans of the time, including Jackson, had less to do with the broader states' rights point—even when defending the cause of Union, men like Jackson spoke warmly and often of the old republican school of thought—than it did with what Calhoun's doctrine would inevitably create: a confederacy, not a nation, with the member states choosing which laws they would follow. Defenders of nullification pointed out that Calhoun's theory suspended the objectionable law only until such time as the Constitution might be amended, at which point the objection that the nullified bill was "unconstitutional" would be moot. At best, however, nullification would lead to a perpetual process of constitutional amendment, crippling the operations of the federal government. At worst, by codifying defiance, Calhoun's plan tilted power toward the individual states to such a degree that Washington would be, to use a favorite term of the era, "prostrate" before the leaders and people of the different states, all of which had their own ideas, their own interests, and their own passions—ideas, interests, and passions that, as McDuffie's speech at Charleston in May had shown, could rather easily carry nullification to secession. For once the principle of a state veto was established, who was to say that a state so outraged by an act of Congress—an act its representatives had played a role, if a losing one, in crafting—would graciously concede defeat in the event the rest of the Union chose to enshrine the objectionable legislation in the Constitution? It might do just that, as Calhoun said he hoped. Or it might not. One thing was clear: nullification was a step away from, not toward, investing a representative national government with the power it needed to expand America on the continent and establish it as a serious, substantive player on the global stage.

The question of the tension between the will of the majority and the rights of the minority raised in Calhoun's doctrine was an essential one. **"Let it never be forgotten that where the majority rules the minority is the subject,"** he wrote, italicizing the words as though in direct reply to Jackson's italicized **"The ma-**

jority is to govern" in the 1829 presidential message. Insofar as the personal can be removed from a political argument, this issue was the most profound disagreement between Jackson and Calhoun about the nature of government, and, as is often the case, neither extreme had it exactly right. Jackson's vision of direct democracy opened the way to mob rule in which an exercised majority had the power to make bad policy and persecute those who, in the spirit of the Constitution, deserved protection.

Despite Jackson's fervent and well-meaning convictions to the contrary, the "people" were not always right all the time. "The rule of the majority and the right of suffrage are good things, but they alone are not sufficient to guard liberty, as experience will teach," Calhoun told a friend a few days after the Fort Hill Address was published. True, but a single state was not always right, either. Great issues should be debated and decided by the national means constructed by the Framers, with the three federal branches each playing their role in the work of government.

Nullification was a means of power, and even the most dedicated Unionists, if they were being honest, could envision a hypothetical situation in which they might find such a weapon useful—if, say, a given president and a given Congress were to pass a law they found morally abhorrent. But the fact that Jackson, Webster, Livingston, and the other anti-nullification leaders trusted in the Framers' system of checks and balances was a tribute to their belief that the Union and the Constitution still seemed the finest—if sometimes flawed—practical way to govern a complex country. Reading Calhoun's argument, John Quincy Adams observed: "I have been deeply disappointed in him, and now expect nothing from him but evil."

As his manifesto made its way around the nation, Calhoun faced trouble at home. His wife lost a baby to miscarriage, rains destroyed large swaths of his crops for the year, and a slave named Aleck escaped, only to be captured shortly by a kinsman of Calhoun's. "I wish you to have him lodged in jail for one week, to be fed on bread and water and to employ someone for me to give him 30 lashes well laid on at the end of the time," Calhoun wrote. "I hope you will pardon the trouble. I only give it because I deem it necessary to our proper security to prevent the formation of the habit of running away."

IT WAS A time of division, but the mere fact of political and cultural division—however serious and heartfelt the issues separating American from American may be—is not itself a cause for great alarm and lamentation. Such splits in the nation do make public life meaner and less attractive and might, in some circumstances, produce cataclysmic results. But strong presidential leadership can lift the country above conflict and see it through. When Jackson reached out to Roger Taney of Maryland to become attorney general, Taney, a former Federalist who did not know the president well, was surprised by the appointment, and his recollection of his state of mind when he accepted illustrates the strength of commitment so many Americans felt toward Jackson even as so many others hoped for a Clay or a Calhoun. "He was at that time vehemently assailed, not only by his old enemies but by new ones who before had been his friends"—Duff Green, among others. "I had scarcely any personal acquaintance with him; and knew him only from his public acts and the history of his life. But yet my feelings toward him were warmer than mere political confidence. Pains had been taken to wound not only his fame, but his feelings and affections."

Taney was tall and thin with a weakness for stooping; a biographer noted that "some thought him . . . ugly." More than two decades before his 1857 decision as chief justice in **Dred Scott**, Taney was a player in the Jacksonian struggle over the Bank. His words, set down in a memoir known as the "Bank War Manuscript" that was long lost to scholars, capture the unifying and energizing effect the Jackson scandals— from the charges about Rachel to the Eaton affair— had on Jackson's followers. The controversies drove many away from Jackson's ranks as his foes undertook to persuade voters in the middle to oppose him. Yet the attacks also brought his loyalists together by investing them and their hero with a shared sense of persecution and a strong incentive to defeat those bent on Jackson's destruction.

Clay and Calhoun were in the vanguard of fighting a political version of total war against Jackson, and those who believed in Jackson and in his causes did not desert the field. Instead, as Taney's memoir shows, they answered in kind. Bloodthirsty bids for power often provoke equally bloodthirsty reactions—especially when the target is a man like Jackson, whose own appetite for control and for the elimination of enemies knew few bounds. Here is Taney's explanation of his own abstract connection to Jackson—a connection formed before there was any intimacy between the two men:

> His wife had been most wantonly and cruelly introduced into the electioneering contest. She had been defamed and traduced in the most ferocious spirit. The ungenerous and unmanly attacks upon her character had not been confined to the low and the base, but put forward again and again by every newspaper which supported the rival candidate; from the highest to the lowest; and if not instigated and encouraged, they were yet undoubtedly countenanced and encouraged by all the political leaders opposed to him. I should have grieved to see a high and noble spirit beaten down by those who had thus wantonly tortured him, and broken the heart of the excellent wife to whom he was so devotedly attached. It seemed to me that every man who by his support of him in 1824 had made him so prominent in the canvass of 1828 and by that means brought on him this vindictive rivalry, was bound to do more than give him a mere cold political support; was bound to make personal sacrifices if they were necessary to support his administration while he continued to deserve his confidence and continued to be unjustly assailed. Such sacrifices seemed to me to be necessary where new enemies were

combining with the old ones to wage war against him in the same fierce spirit of hostility.

In a way, Taney was calling for followers to play a more consistent and demanding role in politics than might be comfortable for them. If a mass representative democracy were to work well, a leader's troops could not be—to borrow a phrase from the Revolutionary War ethos so important to Jackson—sunshine patriots. They would have to be vigilant, keeping abreast of the shifting calculus of politics through the newspapers and standing ready to argue the party line with passion and conviction. A willingness to wage constant partisan combat, no matter what the issue, was an emerging requirement in the politics coming into being in the 1830s. Party organization was not new, but the machine Van Buren, Kendall, Blair, and others were building was larger and more complicated than any previous American political operation. And this early machine depended upon Andrew Jackson as its engine—a human engine that could inspire, charm, cajole, persuade, and, when necessary, coerce.

AS JACKSON PRESSED the known limits of presidential power, Edward Everett wrote Henry Clay asking his thoughts about whether the opposition should try to impeach the president. It was a radical thought, but Jackson was in many senses a radical president, conducting himself in ways that were difficult to fit into any generally accepted ideological category. On Maysville and in the Cherokee case, he respected states' rights; on nullification, he threatened war. Though there was a relatively coherent creed guiding him—a kind of Jeffersonian republicanism in which the preservation of the Union was central, since without a union presumably there would be no theater for Jeffersonian republicanism of any sort—Jackson was a politician, not a philosopher, and politicians generally value power over strict intellectual consistency, which leads a president's supporters to nod sagely at their leader's creative flexibility and drives his opponents to sputter furiously about their nemesis's hypocrisy.

As devoutly as Clay would have relished watching Jackson face impeachment, he believed Jackson too popular. "On the question of impeachment, suggested by you, I entertain no doubt of the President's liability to it," Clay said in reply to Everett on Sunday, June 12, 1831. "But, at present (what may be the state of the case hereafter we cannot say now) from the composition of the Senate, there is not the least prospect of such a prosecution being effectual. To attempt it, therefore, in the existing division of that body, would be unavailing, and, on that account, you would not be able to carry with you the judgment or the feelings of the public. Indeed there would be a danger of exciting the sympathies of the people in behalf of a person whom they have not yet altogether ceased to idolize."

But Jackson understood the political difficulties he was facing. Though he believed he had done the right thing in sacking the Cabinet, he also knew that entire Cabinets did not fall in America; that was a European sort of thing. The purge could cost him politically, and he was still working out precisely how many opponents he would face in 1832. He knew about Clay, and he was awaiting final word about Calhoun.

"Mr. Calhoun will run for president if his friends believe he can be got into the House," Jackson said. "This has been intended since 1828. The secret and precious plots are all leaking out." Thinking of the Hermitage, he told John Coffee that the tranquillity of the plantation held enormous appeal at the moment. "Could I with honor . . . I would fly to it, there to bury myself from the corruption and treachery of this wicked world, where the wicked never cease troubling, and there the weary can have no rest. But this to me is denied, and I must submit."

Suffering from headaches and loneliness, he hated the idea that Clay and Calhoun might be able to run against him as a dictator, sending the election to the House, where he could lose yet again. He could not afford to show his insecurities to a wide audience, and so Emily and Andrew found themselves, as his closest family, suffering the most from the emotional storms he unleashed when he was feeling overburdened, angry, anxious, misunderstood, and helpless. He lived for power. Take that away, or threaten to, and the mask would fall, revealing a vulnerable, often violent man torn between tenderness and wrath.

Worried by the trouble Jackson was confronting inside and outside the White House, Jackson's Tennessee friends—Overton; McLemore; Coffee; Alfred Balch, a Nashville lawyer; and John Bell, a Tennessee congressman—went to work in midsummer. They knew he needed signs of reassurance, respect, and affection—three essential elements in steeling presidents to engage hostile forces. They knew he needed Emily and Andrew. And they knew their man and spent hours with Jackson bashing Calhoun, praising Eaton, and bolstering Jackson's confidence by assuring him that he was not truly alone. "Our true policy now is to effect a union of action of all the **true** hearted throughout the country," Balch told Jackson. "Let us clear our decks for action. Prepare our friends at Headquarters to move in a solid column. And there will not be the slightest danger."

In late July 1831, the Tennesseans gambled that Jackson's need for family and comfort would outweigh all else, and they packed Emily, Andrew (who had returned to Tennessee in June), and the children off to Washington. On Friday, July 29, 1831, after "the most mature reflection," McLemore and Bell wrote Jackson, the group "urged it on Major Donelson to set out with his family for Washington without further correspondence, just as he did at the commencement of your administration, as a part of your family. We doubt not that his course and that of his family will be such as to afford no uneasiness to yourself or any just protest for the censure of your enemies. We think there is no necessity for the specification of terms on one side or the other. If on pursuing the course advised, Major Donelson shall go on to the city contrary to your wishes, we and **not him are to blame**."

· · ·

THE WISE MEN of Tennessee believed that the sight of the family and the sounds of the children—along with the disappearance of the Eatons and the joining of the battle against the radicals in the South—would open a new, more peaceful period in the White House.

As a lawyer, a soldier, and a politician, Jackson had long seen and experienced life in sequential chapters—case followed case, battle followed battle, election followed election, legislative fight followed legislative fight. Never dumb (only stubborn), Jackson was also ready to turn the page in the White House. He had so many other political concerns that he did not derail the reunion. McLemore told Coffee that there was every reason to hope for serenity, at least inside the White House. "All things will work right after a while."

Jackson, pen in hand, was writing a letter to Van Buren at the moment the Donelsons arrived at the front door of the White House. He had finished five paragraphs on politics, a diplomatic matter with France, and the tariff when the party from Tennessee began to come into the mansion; he had time to write one more section about the new Cabinet before his room flooded with his family, who immediately made the right moves, sending love to Van Buren and began busily resurrecting the world that had been dead for this long year of Jackson's life. "This moment the ladies have entered, and Miss Mary Eastin and Mrs. Donelson, with the Major, have desired me to make a tender to you of their kind salutations," Jackson said. "Uncle seems quite happy and everything is moving harmoniously and I sincerely hope it may remain so," Emily told her sister.

The cause of harmony was helped immeasurably at seven o'clock on the morning of Monday, September 19, when Margaret and John Eaton set out for Tennessee. "He ought to have left before this," Andrew Jackson, Jr., said of Eaton in early September.

But at least the Donelsons were back and things seemed to be veering toward order. As the Eatons' carriage headed south, a warmth and a peace fell over the domestic life at the White House. The restoration could not have waited much longer, for Jackson needed all his strength. Telling Van Buren of Eaton's departure, Jackson spoke of the reelection campaign, which he claimed to dread, saying, "Nothing reconciles me to my situation but the assurances of some virtuous men that it is now necessary for the preservation of the Union that I should permit my name to be continued for the next canvass for the Presidency."

The words of the virtuous and his own high motives played their part, but so did vengeance: "This, with the determination never to be driven by my enemies or to succumb to them, continues me here again." If he relinquished control, it would be on his timing and his terms. He had come too far to fall now, and the appetites and anxieties that drove him were the kinds of appetites and anxieties that even the presidency of the United States could not satisfy or quell.

GEORGE BANCROFT, THE historian and future secretary of the navy under President James K. Polk, called at the White House in late December 1831. He was, he wrote to his wife, "quite charmed" with Emily, and with Jackson. "Being determined to have a long and regular chat with the old man, the roaring lion I mean, I went in the evening," Bancroft wrote. The president's manners were perfect, the family warm, and the conversation touched on the centrality of virtue in a republic. Jackson, Bancroft said, "declares that our institutions are based upon the virtue of the community, and added that the moment 'demagogues obtain influence with the people our liberties will be destroyed.'" Learned and intellectually polished, Bancroft was arch about Jackson's lack of education. "He assured me that truth would in the **eend** (pronounce the word to rhyme with fiend) be every man's best policy." On his host's "qualifications for President," Bancroft said, "avast there—Sparta hath many a wiser son than he. . . ."

Another American man of letters, Nathaniel Hawthorne, recorded a conversation about Jackson that helps explain why Bancroft's 1831 impression of Jackson was correct but incomplete. A man who had been at a gathering with Jackson, Hawthorne wrote in a journal, "told an anecdote, illustrating the General's little acquaintance with astronomical science, and his force of will in compelling a whole dinner-party of better-instructed people to knock under to him in an argument about eclipses and the planetary systems generally." Jackson's personal force, in other words, swept away everything in its path. Hawthorne's verdict: "Surely, he was the greatest man we ever had; and his native strength, as well of intellect as character, compelled every man to be his tool that came within his reach; and the [more] cunning . . . the individual might be, it served only to make him the sharper tool."

WITH THE 1832 presidential campaign at hand, Jackson's adopted son, Andrew Jackson, Jr., wrote his kinsman William Donelson a chatty letter from the White House. "I have no very important news to communicate except to tell you of the safe arrival of Cousin Andrew and Emily and the young ladies," he said on Friday, September 9, 1831. "They are well and we were very glad to see them." Turning to politics, Andrew junior was optimistic but resigned to a long slog—a fair indication of Jackson's own thinking, since Andrew junior spent time with his adopted father in Emily and Andrew's absence. Andrew junior suspected that "the dissolution of the Cabinet will be a theme to harp upon for some time. . . . God only knows how they will settle it—I suppose [through] public opinion—**vox populi**; perhaps a little fighting will be had—etc. etc. and some thing else may come forth and too the reelection of the President is not too far distant."

High hopes, for victory could not be certain, as Andrew junior himself admitted a moment later. "It is thought that three or four may be put in nomination to run against the 'Old Man," he wrote. "They can hope to carry the election into the House of Representatives and there settle it by intrigue, bargain, etc etc etc." Though he was skeptical, he was unwilling to dismiss the scenario that "Clay, Calhoun or Mr. Adams will one of them oppose the General, perhaps two." Still, he believed "some of these men will have more sense—but I know that they have ambition sufficient." Ambition sometimes divorced from sense was something the Jackson circle knew very well indeed. The "Old Man" had taught them a great deal about it—often inadvertently, perhaps, but indelibly.

IN THE AFTERMATH of the Cabinet breakup, Van Buren had accepted Jackson's appointment as the envoy to England and moved to London to take up his duties. The Senate would have to confirm the posting, but few expected any problem there—until the nomination actually reached the floor in January 1832. In a sign of the divisiveness of the day, on Wednesday, January 25, 1832, the Senate voted 24–23—Vice President Calhoun broke a 23–23 tie—to reject Van Buren.

Calhoun was practicing the politics of vengeance, paying Van Buren in kind for Van Buren's long campaign to turn Jackson against him. The hope was to embarrass Jackson and wreck Van Buren's future; the first was more easily accomplished than the second. On hearing the news—word arrived as a White House dinner party was breaking up, with the president holding forth in the Red Room—Jackson said, "By the Eternal! I'll smash them!" Ill and furious, Jackson said Calhoun's refusal to confirm "has displayed a want of every sense of honor, justice or magnanimity" and asserted that Calhoun was "politically damned." His enemies were out in the open, working together—what Jackson called a "factious opposition in the Senate with Calhoun and Clay at its head."

For Calhoun, it was a rare—and brief—moment of triumph over Van Buren. "It will kill him, sir, kill him dead," Calhoun said after the Senate vote. "He will never kick, sir, never kick." Andrew Donelson gauged the politics more aptly than Calhoun. "The common sentiment on this subject is that Mr. Van Buren has been violently thrown overboard by the enemies of the Administration and that its friends are bound to avenge the insult," Andrew wrote John Coffee. "This sentiment . . . will no doubt spread throughout the Union. If so there can scarcely be a doubt that Mr. Van Buren will be nominated at Baltimore as the candidate of our party for Vice President."

Close to Jackson and again familiar with his thinking, Andrew saw what was coming: the New Yorker would replace the South Carolinian on the Jackson ticket, creating a Western-Northern axis against Clay and perhaps, if he were to run, Calhoun. In London, Van Buren was not feeling well when the news reached him. Still, wrote Washington Irving, the legation's secretary, Van Buren "received the tidings of his rejection with his usual equanimity." The British could not help but be impressed with the sheer scope of the Senate's vicious attack. In a conversation with Irving, a Foreign Office official said that "he had never known a more naked and palpable party maneuver" than to turn down a former secretary of state to be minister to a single nation. "Every thing is going on well," Clay wrote in February 1832. "V. Buren, Old Hickory and the whole crew will, I think, in due time be gotten rid of."

The battle in the Senate had grown even uglier. Senator John Holmes introduced a resolution that the nomination go to the Senate Foreign Relations Committee, "and that said committee be instructed to investigate the causes which produced the removal of the late Secretaries of the Treasury and Navy Departments, and of the Attorney General of the United States, and also the resignations of the Secretaries of the State and War Departments." Calling the dissolution a "novel and important political movement," Holmes also wanted to know "whether the said Martin Van Buren, then Secretary of State, participated in any practices disreputable to the national character, which were designed to operate on the mind of the President of the United States. . . ." The motion was tabled, but the point was made: the opposition was going to make as much of the purge as it could.

In Tennessee, the Eatons tried to be cheerful. "To myself, I feel like a new man in the little sphere where now I am placed . . . standing in the ambitious way of no one, and hence not an object of envy and destruction," Eaton wrote to Jackson after the return to Tennessee. Margaret wrote Jackson, too. Her anger had faded enough for her to realize that alienating Jackson was monumentally stupid. In her letter, she told him they were visiting the Hermitage: "Would to heaven you were here with us, for I believe you would be more happy; and when years shall roll round, and you shall again be the Cincinnatus of the West, you will see how devoted I have been in my attachment towards you. When the splendor of the President's home shall be done with, then you will be better able to tell who are **your real friends**; and I do and can say with truth none will you find more sincere than my dear Husband and myself."

THE TARGET OF Margaret's not very veiled attack loved being back at the White House. Emily found the season of 1831–32 "very gay." She was pregnant with her third child. Andrew Jackson, Jr., had fallen in love with and married a wonderful young woman from Pennsylvania, Sarah Yorke, who quickly became a favorite of Jackson's and was friendly enough with Emily that, remarkably, there seems to have been little if any tension between the two women. "Cousin Andrew arrived last Sunday with his bride," Emily wrote to her sister. "She is quite pretty, has black hair and eyes and is about an inch lower than myself—she is quite agreeable and we are all very much pleased with her, and Uncle seems much pleased."

To celebrate the wedding—Jackson had stayed in Washington during the actual ceremony in Philadelphia—Emily and Jackson gave Sarah and Andrew junior a huge party. "We were quite gay last week," Emily wrote home. "In the first place there was a large dining given to them of about forty persons, the cabinet and the diplomatic corps—The dinner party were invited at 5 o'clock, and at 8, three hundred were invited to spend the evening—the party was very brilliant and everything went off well—"

The dinner for Sarah and Andrew junior did not escape Margaret Bayard Smith's scrutiny. At issue was who followed whom into dinner, and the new secretary of the Treasury and his wife, the Louis McLanes, back from England, where he had served as minister, were acutely conscious of their status in the capital. Mrs. Smith thought Mrs. McLane "the same frank, gay, communicative woman she ever was," and found her "evidently very much elated with her past and present dignity." Yet the first three years of Jackson's administration had abundantly shown that being in Jackson's Cabinet—or being married to someone in Jackson's Cabinet—was no easy task. Chatting with Mrs. McLane after her husband's appointment, Mrs. Smith said, "She will have as difficult a part to play in society as her husband will in office, as she, as well as he, must be under the influence, I was going to say despotism, of the President's will." At Decatur House, which they had taken after Van Buren resigned the State Department, the Livingstons were the leading lights of the moment, and the McLanes were unhappy about being overshadowed by the Livingstons. "Neither Mr. or Mrs. McLane are people who will willingly follow," Mrs. Smith said, "and it is already rumored that much conflict and dissatisfaction exists in the Cabinet."

On the evening of the wedding party for Andrew

Jackson, Jr., it was announced that, in a break from custom, the secretary of state would precede the foreign diplomatic corps, followed by the rest of the Cabinet. The Treasury secretary disliked the innovation—it seemed to demote him—and told Andrew Donelson so before the walk in to dinner. "The argument was carried on some time," Mrs. Smith said, and McLane won the point. Then the foreign ministers weighed in, upset at being behind the Cabinet, and Donelson told Jackson of the counteroffensive from his other guests. With tact, Jackson said, "Well, I will lead the Bride, it is a family fête,—and we will waive all difficulties."

Relating the gossip in a letter, Mrs. Smith said: "Now, trifling as this affair will appear, it may have serious political consequences. The President and the foreign ministers are dissatisfied with the Secretary of the Treasury, and the poor man is not of a temper to conciliate dissatisfactions—and then too, the Secretary of State will resent the resistance made to the honor designed him by the President, and the ill will thus engendered between the two first members of the Cabinet will doubtless influence their deliberations. And the President himself never yet could bear opposition."

Signaling that she understood the political climate in which the social maneuvers were taking place, Mrs. Smith added: "The Bank question has been another point of controversy, so much so . . . a member of Congress told a friend of ours, he should not be surprised at another blow up." It had, after all, happened before. "Mrs. Eaton's affair, at the beginning, was but a spark, but what a conflagration it did cause," she said.

MRS. SMITH HAD personal reasons to look forward to a bonfire. She had hopes that Jackson would be bound for Tennessee after the election. Meanwhile, she liked the look of the new season. Chattering away in a letter, she said she and her husband had "several new neighbors. How we shall like them time must determine. An Empress, an ex-Minister's widow and Mrs. Secretary McLane are among those nearest to us. Madame Iturbide, the former Empress of Mexico, is close to us. We could, were we so inclined, almost shake hands from our back windows."

While Mrs. Smith soaked up the imperial, ex-imperial, and ministerial glamor, her friends Lucretia and Henry Clay arrived back in the city as winter set in. Clay was returning as senator from Kentucky. Despite a heavy snowstorm, a determined Mrs. Smith braved the ice to call on Lucretia, who could be mistress of the White House in a year's time. Mrs. Smith "hastened to welcome her back and sat the whole of a long morning with her," but found her a sadder woman than she remembered. That was understandable: one Clay son was currently battling drink, and another had been committed to "the Lunatic Asylum of Kentucky" in 1831. The former, Mrs. Smith remarked, was "irreclaimably dissipated, the other insane and confined in a hospital."

Still, Senator Clay was buoyed by the coming combat. He readied for his return to Capitol Hill and, as 1832 wore on, for his return to presidential politics as Jackson's chief rival in November. Washington Irving, who had come home to America from England, spent some time with Clay and found him in good form. "He tells me he has improved greatly in health since he was dismissed from office, and finds that it is good for man as well as beast to be turned out occasionally to grass. Certainly official life in Washington must be harassing and dismal in the extreme." It was, but politics was Clay's natural métier, and Mrs. Smith was confident for her returning friend. "Mr. Clay is borne up by the undying spirit of ambition—he looks well and animated, and will be this winter in his very element—in the very vortex of political warfare," she said. "With his unrivaled and surpassing talents, his winning and irresistibly attractive manners, what is it he cannot do? We shall see, but I shall think it strange if he does not succeed in all his aims."

The view from the White House, not surprisingly, was rather different. "Politics are waxing warmer every day," Andrew Donelson wrote his brother-in-law Stockley in early 1832. "Every engine is at work to batter down the reputation and popularity of Uncle, but as far as I can perceive he is gaining new strength in the affection and love of the people."

CHAPTER 14

★

NOW LET HIM ENFORCE IT

I N HIS OFFICE at the State Department on Wednesday, March 28, 1832, Edward Livingston issued a revealing directive to American diplomats around the globe. From Rio to Saint Petersburg, envoys were instructed to ask foreign governments to change long-standing protocol in the usual form of address in letters between nations. Though the order affected only six words, it represented a dramatic shift in Jackson's Washington in the opening months of 1832. "It is observed that official communications from foreign powers intended for the Executive of the United States, have been usually addressed to the President **and Congress of the United States,**" Livingston wrote. Such a convention was fine in the pre-1787 days of the Articles of Confederation, but now, Livingston said, "its inaccuracy is apparent—the whole executive power, particularly that of foreign intercourse, being vested in the President. You will, therefore, address a note to the Minister for Foreign Affairs apprising him that all communications made directly to the head of our executive government should be addressed 'To the President of the United States of America,' without any other addition."

Dropping the House and the Senate from diplomatic correspondence was ceremonial but telling. Jackson was consolidating presidential power, and the fight at hand was against the Bank, a struggle in which Jackson appealed to the people for support on the grounds that he—more than Congress, more than the courts, more than anything or anyone else—represented **them**.

Mrs. Smith had been on to something when she speculated about the possibility of Louis McLane turning into trouble for Jackson. The larger cause was the Bank; McLane believed the institution should be reformed, not abolished, and was open about his views. A former congressman who had chaired the House Ways and Means Committee, McLane was, his Cabinet colleague Roger Taney said, "an ambitious man; loved power, and aspired to the Presidency, which he confidently expected to reach." McLane's time as minister to England had confirmed his longtime support of the Bank—he had, Taney said, a "close intimacy with Mr. Biddle and with Barings in England"—and he came to the Treasury in late 1831 with a plan to save the Bank and accomplish much else besides. Linking most of the questions of the day, McLane proposed to pay off the national debt as Jackson had long planned, sell the government's stock in the Bank, sell the federal lands to the states, and modify the tariff—then, in future years, recharter a reformed Bank. The political price for the scheme:

McLane wanted Jackson to remain largely silent on the Bank issue in the annual presidential message so that McLane could use the occasion of the Treasury secretary's annual report to discuss his broad proposals—including the Bank's ultimate recharter. When Jackson agreed, McLane believed he had carried the day on all fronts and rescued the Bank.

It seemed a reasonable surmise. At a meeting convened in Jackson's office so that the Cabinet could listen as Andrew Donelson read a draft of Jackson's annual message aloud, the language about the Bank was so mild that it "startled" Roger Taney, who believed the phrasing suggested Jackson "would now defer to the representatives of the people and abide by the decision of Congress"—even though the president opposed recharter. As best Taney could recall it, the original wording about the Bank was:

> Having conscientiously discharged a constitutional duty I deem it proper without a more particular reference to the subject to leave it to the investigation of an enlightened people and their representatives.

New to the circle and nervous—he recalled that he was "comparatively a stranger to General Jackson"—Taney nevertheless felt he should speak up. He knew it would annoy McLane, and possibly anger Jackson. The natural tendency in a meeting like the one taking place in Jackson's office, especially when it is a meeting of politicians, men who make a business of the art of appearing agreeable, is to nod one's head, not shake it, to murmur affirmation, not mount counterattacks. "The duty of making this objection I felt to be an unpleasant one," Taney said. Yet he made it.

McLane rose to defend the paragraph, which he had written, as it was. No one else in the office came to Taney's side as McLane "objected strongly to any alteration." The other secretaries were either silent or backed McLane. "The discussion continued for some time," Taney said, and soon "the President was worried and desired it to end." McLane outranked Taney, and Jackson saw no reason to contradict McLane in open session. Jackson "always listened reluctantly to any criticism upon the language of a paper prepared under his directions," Taney said, "and he seemed to apprehend that the writer might feel mortified if it was determined that he had imputed to him opinions he did not entertain—or failed to execute the instructions under which the paper was written." It was clear "from the earnestness and tenacity with which Mr. McLane defended this paragraph" that "he himself had prepared it. . . . The President I am sure was the more unwilling to make alterations because he saw that Mr. McLane would be dissatisfied and perhaps a little hurt if the paper was materially changed."

After some back-and-forth at the long table in front of the fireplace, McLane, it seemed, had won. "He was an accomplished diplomatist, and exercised as much diplomacy in Washington to carry his measures as he would at a foreign court," Taney said. "He had great tact, and always knew whether he should address himself to the patriotism, the magnanimity, the pride, the vanity, the hopes or the fears of the person on whom he wished to operate. And he thus always had a clique about him wherever he was in power over whose opinions he exercised a controlling influence."

Jackson tended to elude those who tried to control him. As Taney saw it, McLane's "mistake was in underrating the strength and independence of the President's mind; and the extent of his information. He expected to manage him. . . . He evidently believed that he would be able to change [Jackson's] opinions, and induce him to assent to the continuance of the charter with some slight and unimportant modification, as a salve to the President's consistency."

Relieved by the apparent failure of Taney's bid to change the wording, McLane—and, at a distance, Biddle—believed the battle won. Yet Jackson's bureaucratic support in the Cabinet meeting did not mean he agreed with McLane's fundamental argument that the Bank should go on. It meant only that Jackson was, depending on one's point of view, either a courteous leader or a cleverly deceptive one, for Taney was soon in Andrew Donelson's office for a private chat with the president. Jackson thought Taney had made a sound case against the wording of the message. Now, quietly and without involving McLane, Jackson made changes to the text and wanted to know Taney's thoughts. The new passage read:

Having conscientiously discharged a constitutional duty I deem it proper **on this occasion** without a more particular reference to **the views of** the subject **then ex-**

pressed to leave it **for the present** to the investigation
of an enlightened people and their representatives.

It was hardly a clarion call, but by Taney and Jackson's estimation it was better, and gave Jackson room
to maneuver. Few read it that way on publication,
though, and many believed, as McLane did, that Jackson would allow the Bank to survive.

Biddle thought he saw an opening, and decided to
apply for recharter in January 1832—challenging
Jackson (never a good idea) to sign it, thus securing
the Bank, or to veto it and invite defeat at the polls.
Clay and Webster privately pressed for this course,
and, like Calhoun, Biddle became enamored of his
own logic and convinced himself that the world
would see things as he did and do things as he would.
He thought he could box Jackson in on the Bank's
terms. Using almost exactly the same words he used to
describe McLane, Taney said Biddle was "an ambitious man, full of vanity, and loved power. He believed that by bringing the weight and influence of
the Bank into the approaching election he could defeat General Jackson, and he wished political aspirants
to see that he had defeated him—He led the Bank
therefore into the political arena determined to show
its strength in political contests."

It was a terrible mistake. "If General Jackson does
not kill the bank, the bank will kill him," the ancient
John Randolph of Roanoke wrote to Edward Livingston. Jackson used the same metaphor. "The Bank,
Mr. Van Buren, is trying to kill me," Jackson said to

his friend in July, **"but I will kill it."** By 1832 the conflict over the Bank had become a struggle for power, and it was always risky to bet against Jackson in such a struggle. Still, Biddle pressed for recharter, believing he would defeat the president in Congress or, failing that, in the general election.

FOR THE PRESIDENT, the first half of 1832 was also a time of physical suffering, marital maneuvering, and financial fretting. In addition to fighting the flu, Jackson finally had the bullet he had carried in his left arm since the brawl with the Bentons removed. It was a brief, painful operation. Unflinching, Jackson had only his walking stick for solace; he gripped it as the doctor prepared to slice open the arm. "Go ahead," Jackson said. The doctor made the cut, and the old slug popped out, falling to the floor.

Around this time—it was January—Mary Eastin was planning her wedding to Captain William B. Finch of the U.S. Navy. An older man, Finch, Andrew Donelson told the Coffee family, was "very clever and highly respectable." The wedding was set for Valentine's Day. Jackson had long loved Mary quite as much as he loved Emily—sometimes finding the more easygoing Mary more approachable—and arranged to pay for a White House ceremony. They would use the East Room, as they had for Mary Rachel's baptism. All was set—and then Lucius Polk, a cousin of James K. Polk's, arrived in Washington from his home in Maury County, in middle Tennessee. He had heard of the impending marriage and had apparently been harboring an unspoken love for Mary for several years; emboldened by the imminent threat of losing her forever, young Polk made his case. Again the second floor of the White House became turbulent as Mary found herself choosing between Finch and Polk. It was evidently a difficult decision, for on Saturday, April 7, about three months after her engagement to Finch had become public, Jackson could only say that he **thought** Mary had settled on Polk. "I believe I may say that Miss Mary Eastin will be married on Tuesday evening next to Mr. Lucius Polk," Jackson wrote Coffee. "The guests are all invited and I trust that it will take place."

Money was also a concern. He had paid for Andrew junior's wedding and now Mary Eastin's, and he was short of cash. Discussing a land deal on Jackson's behalf the previous fall, Andrew junior said: "We farmers generally are greatly pressed for money, owing to the depressed state of our cotton market, upon which, you will know, we have to place our sole dependence. My Father cannot command the means conveniently. His expenses here and at home are very heavy."

Still, Mary Eastin's romantic drama gave him some passing relief from what Andrew Jackson, Jr., called the "quite warm" politics of the moment—the press of negotiations over the Cherokees, the Bank, the tariff, and, beginning the week Mary and Polk were finally married, the outbreak of the Black Hawk War.

IT WAS PERHAPS inevitable that some Indian warriors would strike back amid, and after, removal. In

April 1832, Black Hawk, a Sac whose people, along with the Foxes, had been forcibly removed from their lands near the Rock River in Illinois, came back across the Mississippi River to hunt, only to find white squatters in the way. Misled into believing that there would be British and fellow Indian support, Black Hawk and his band were essentially alone, facing hostile Illinois militia on the eastern side of the Mississippi. (Abraham Lincoln served in the Black Hawk War, but later said the only blood he shed was from mosquitoes.) On Tuesday, May 15, 1832, after a ceremonial feast of boiled dog with representatives of other Great Lakes tribes, Black Hawk sent emissaries to arrange a parley with the white soldiers. But the militiamen seem to have had a good deal to drink, and while accounts are confused, it appears clear that they, not Black Hawk's warriors, shed first blood. Forty of Black Hawk's men then crushed the Illinois militia, killing twelve (only three Sacs died, and they had been among those seeking a parley). Hearing the reports, Jackson ordered Winfield Scott into action, putting the general in command of a thousand federal troops.

Slowed by a deadly outbreak of cholera among his men, Scott did not make it to the front until after the war was over. Landing at Fort Gratiot, north of Detroit, some of Scott's soldiers, in terror from watching the sick die on board, escaped to the forests, only to die on the run; their corpses, it was said, were eaten by wolves and wild hogs. Along the Mississippi, the Black Hawk War basically ended with the Battle of Bad Axe on Thursday, August 2, 1832, where hundreds of Indians, including women and children, were killed, many of them drowning as they tried to escape across the river.

JACKSON'S SWIFT RESPONSE to the bloodshed in Illinois in May 1832 was in contrast to his reaction to a new Supreme Court decision—this one supporting the Cherokees against the incursions of the state of Georgia. The year before, in 1831, John Marshall had flinched from forcing the issue of Indian sovereignty in **Cherokee Nation v. The State of Georgia.** In March 1832, just before Jackson intervened in the Black Hawk War, Marshall and the Court ruled in a second case that had come to them from Georgia. Two Christian missionaries had been arrested on the Cherokee lands after the state had passed its anti-Cherokee laws prohibiting unlicensed whites from living on Cherokee lands. The missionaries, Samuel Worcester and Elihu Butler, were convicted by a Georgia court and jailed. Their sentence was four years at hard labor.

They appealed the state decision to the U.S. Supreme Court. Chief Justice Marshall found for the missionaries and, in a larger sense, for the Cherokees. It was a far different decision than 1831's. Release the missionaries, Marshall said, announcing that the Court believed Georgia's anti-Cherokee laws were "repugnant to the Constitution, laws, and treaties of the United States." Justice Joseph Story suspected the matter was not over: "The Court has done its duty," he said. "Let the nation now do theirs."

As word of the decision spread, Jackson remained

in the White House, largely silent. His stillness unnerved his foes. "Our public affairs are evidently tending to a crisis," Clay wrote on Thursday, March 10,
1832. "The consequences of the recent decision of the
Supreme Court must be very great. If it be resisted,
and the President refuses to enforce it, there is a vir-
tual dissolution of the Union. For it will be in vain to
consider it as existing if a single state can put aside the
laws and treaties of the U.S. and when their authority
is vindicated by a decision of the S. Court, the President will not perform his duty to enforce it."

In Washington, Susan Donelson, a daughter of
William Gaston's who had married into the Donelson
clan, heard an account of Jackson's views on the matter. "We were at the Capitol yesterday," she wrote her
father, a North Carolina legislator and judge, on Saturday, March 12. "A gentleman who dined with General Jackson heard him say **he thought** the decision of
the **Supreme Court erroneous** on the Cherokee Case
and tis doubted here whether he would see it executed—a pretty thing indeed, for **him** to give such an
opinion of the highest tribunal and to hesitate about
executing its decrees." Horace Greeley later claimed
that Jackson had said: "Well, John Marshall has made
his decision, now let him enforce it."

THE "NOW LET him enforce it" remark is like the
more colorful images from holy scripture: historically
questionable but philosophically true. What Jackson
did say, to John Coffee, was: "The decision of the
Supreme Court has fell still born, and they find that it

cannot coerce Georgia to yield to its mandate." The circumstances were rather mundane for such a momentous case: the Court had adjourned after handing down the decision. As the scholar Edwin A. Miles reconstructed the chronology of the case, according to Section 25 of the Judiciary Act of 1789, the Court could not render a final decision—a decision that would then have to be enforced, or not—until a case had already been "remanded once without effect." In this instance, the Court's opinion was sent to the Superior Court of Georgia. No one expected the Georgia court to follow the Supreme Court's directive, but because the Supreme Court was now in recess, nothing could be done until Marshall and his colleagues reconvened in January 1833. In the strictest sense of the law, then, Jackson was powerless to act until there was a final judgment in roughly ten months' time.

All true enough, but it is also true that Andrew Jackson never allowed anything, much less legal niceties, to stand in his way if he was determined to do something. Had he wanted to reverse Georgia's course toward the Cherokees, it is easy to imagine his declaring the enforcement of a decision of a branch of the national government a solemn presidential duty, and, if necessary, threatening the state with invasion by forces that he himself might lead—all things he contemplated in his battle against South Carolina. But he had no desire to reverse Georgia's course. There were at least two factors at work. First, he thought Georgia's pressure on the tribe would expe-

dite removal, and second, he did not want to antagonize another Southern state at a time when he was iso-
lating South Carolina in its drift toward nullification.
As usual, then, Jackson did what he liked. (In the end,
the administration convinced the governor of Georgia
to release the missionaries, and their counsel, William
Wirt, stood down.)

ON FRIDAY, MAY 18, 1832, Emily gave birth to her
third child, a boy, and all again went well. From a letter
to her mother four weeks after the delivery, it is clear
that the Eaton affair has receded, for Jackson is spoken
of as virtually a third parent: "I am thankful that I have
it once more in my power to write to you and inform
you of my convalescence, and of the good health and
growth of our dear little boy. He was a month old Friday last. . . . We have been undecided about his name,
that is Andrew and Uncle said he had better be called
Samuel and I wished him called John, so we have concluded to join the two names together and call him
John S. Donelson, which will distinguish him from the
other Johns."

As always, Emily was pushing herself. "I have been
very well all the time except a slight cold I took when
he was two weeks old. I was so well that I was walking
about and the weather being very changeable took
cold which threw me back a little." As the weather
grew warmer, she hoped to come home but was uncertain when they might be able to; politics was too
consuming. "I do not know yet what we shall do this

summer about going to Tennessee as Congress has not adjourned and [there is] no prospect of it soon. Uncle says we must go, if only to stay ten days. . . ."

Jackson's eagerness to escape Washington was understandable. A tariff reform bill was wending its way through Congress, and it was unclear whether the final result would calm the South or lead to nullification. The Bank recharter was also likely to pass—though not with a veto-proof two-thirds majority—and would probably reach the White House before long. "I had hoped before this to be on my way to Tennessee, but Congress continuing so long in session has made my trip now almost impossible," Andrew Donelson wrote to his brother-in-law Stockley in Nashville. "The Tariff bill will pass pretty much as you see it reported to the Senate: and so will the Bank as reported to the House. The latter bill will however not be approved by the President."

Even God became an issue of contention as the congressional session went on, with Jackson and Henry Clay squaring off over church and state amid a plague. The trouble had begun in Quebec, when a ship arrived from Europe in June 1832. Forty-two of the passengers were dead or dying from cholera, a communicable illness spread through food and water and caused by the bacterium **Vibrio cholerae**, which strikes the intestines, leading to diarrhea, vomiting, and, in the worst cases, death through dehydration. In two weeks the disease struck New York with such ferocity that the mayor canceled its Fourth of July parade; 2,565 people in the city ultimately died. From Philadelphia to Baltimore to Washington, west to Cincinnati and Chicago and south to New Orleans, the disease terrified the country. On June 27, 1832, Henry Clay proposed that Jackson declare a day of prayer and fasting to seek divine relief from the outbreak.

The proposition was good politics—people in the afflicted states might be grateful, and religious believers who were undecided in the presidential race could see Clay's initiative as evidence of a good soul who shared the essence of their faith.

Yet as he had been when Ezra Stiles Ely made the case for the election of "Christian Rulers," Jackson was reluctant to mix God and government so overtly. Reading the establishment clause in the First Amendment in its strictest sense, Jackson said he, too, believed in "the efficacy of prayer," but felt that the president of the United States should "decline the appointment of any period or mode" of religious activity. "I could not do otherwise without transcending those limits which are prescribed by the Constitution for the President, and without feeling that I might in some degree disturb the security which religion now enjoys in this country in its complete separation from the political concerns of the General Government," Jackson said.

LET THE PEOPLE, or even the states, tend to matters of faith. "It is the province of the pulpits and the state governments to recommend the mode by which the people may best attest their reliance on the protecting arm of the almighty in times of great public distress," Jackson said. "Whether the apprehension that cholera will visit our land furnishes a proper occasion for their solemn notice, I must therefore leave to their own consideration." It was yet another point on which Jackson and the evangelical movement failed to agree.

"I am no **sectarian,** though a lover of the Christian religion," he said while in the White House. "I do not believe that any who shall be so fortunate as to be received to heaven through the atonement of our blessed Savior will be asked whether they belonged to the Presbyterian, the Methodist, the Episcopalian, the Baptist, or the Roman Catholic [faiths]. All Christians are brethren, and all true Christians know they are such **because they love one another.** A true Christian loves all, immaterial to what sect or church he may belong."

Jackson was prepared to veto Clay's day of fast measure if it reached the White House. It did not: the resolution was tabled in the House, ending the episode. In a draft of a veto message written by Louis McLane, Jackson was to have said, "In the spirit and structure of our Constitution, we have carefully separated sacred from civilian concerns," and to sign a resolution for a religious observance struck Jackson as "incompatible with my sense of duty under the Constitution." He believed, he said, in the "efficacy of prayer in all times," from "the day of prosperity" to the "hour of . . . calamity." But he was the president, and his duties to the office, as he saw them, came first: "I deem it my duty to preserve this separation and to abstain from any act which may tend to an amalgamation perilous to both" church and state. There ended the lesson.

CHAPTER 15

★

THE FURY OF
A CHAINED PANTHER

IN THE FIRST week of July 1832, Jackson turned his energies from the prayer veto toward the Bank. The bill to recharter had passed both houses and reached the president's desk. Biddle thought he had Jackson where he wanted him. "He was offended with the course General Jackson had pursued towards the institution, and was strongly opposed to him, and determined to place him in what he supposed would be a dilemma," Roger Taney said of Biddle. "He persuaded himself that General Jackson would hardly dare to meet the bill with an absolute and unqualified veto. But if he did, [Biddle] felt confident that the popularity of the Bank and the influence it could exercise would defeat his reelection. And if he assented to the bill, or appeared to temporize and evade the issue presented to him, it would be regarded as proof that he feared the Bank, and destroy the high place he then held in the confidence and affections of the people." The Senate passed the bill on Monday, June 11, 1832; the vote in the House was expected to be close. One story sheds light on the Bank's machinations:

On a rainy day during the deliberations in the House, Taney shared a carriage up Capitol Hill with a Jacksonian congressman from North Carolina, Samuel Price Carson. Carson wanted Taney to look over a draft of an anti-Bank speech the congressman was to deliver in the House debate, saying he planned to publish the address and, as Taney recalled it, "was anxious therefore to put it upon grounds that would bear the closest examination."

Taney demurred, citing the press of business before the Supreme Court, but, given his own opposition to recharter, was pleased that Carson was so determined to vote with Jackson against the Bank. After the vote, Taney was surprised to hear that Carson had voted with Biddle. "Upon my return I mentioned what had passed to a friend . . . who [said] that [Carson] . . . had obtained a loan of twenty thousand dollars from the Bank, and had changed his opinion." Reflecting on the sequence of events, Taney was philosophical about what had transpired, seeing in it evidence of both perennial human weakness and the threat that an institution such as the Bank posed in a democracy:

Now I do not mean to say that he was directly bribed to give his vote. From the character he sustained and from what I knew of him I think he would have resented anything that he regarded as an attempt to corrupt him. But he wanted the money, and felt grateful for the favor, and perhaps thought that an institution which was so useful to him, and had behaved with so much kindness, could not be injurious or dangerous to the public, and that it

would be as well to continue it. Men when under the influence of interest or passion often delude themselves
thoughtlessly, and do not always acknowledge even to
themselves the motives upon which they really act. . . .
It was one of the dangers arising from this mammoth
money power, that its very duties as collecting and dis-
bursing agent brought it constantly in contact with
members of Congress and other public functionaries
and made it acquainted with their wants and enabled it
to place them under obligations and create a feeling of
dependence or even gratitude without the direct and offensive offer of a bribe.

Rumors of such transactions helped Jackson's cause
enormously. The Bank, Andrew Donelson said, "is
becoming desperate: **caught in its own net.**" After the
House voted, Jackson sent Taney, who was in An-
napolis, a note asking him to return to Washington.
Arriving at the White House after breakfast, Taney
was taken to Jackson's office. Kendall had drafted a
veto message, and Donelson was editing it, but Jackson wanted Taney to join in. Taney said of course.

Taney joined Donelson in Ralph Earl's room,
where the private secretary was at work; Levi Woodbury joined them on the second day. For three days
Jackson came in and out, listening and dictating and
debating. Earl was there, going about his painting and
paying no attention to the matters of state unfolding
before him; Taney did not think Earl was "even hearing what was said." Amid the faint smell of oil paints
and in the northern light, Jackson and his team

crafted one of the most significant veto messages in American history.

JACKSON'S DECISION WAS framed in sweeping terms, arguing that the goal of government should be to better the lives of the many, not reward the few. That the Bank was most likely not as guilty of the latter offense as Jackson believed was, politically, beside the point. Near the end of the message, he made a sophisticated point about human nature and the role of government, a point that reflected both realism and hope. "It is to be regretted that the rich and powerful too often bend the acts of government to their selfish purposes," Jackson said, continuing:

Distinctions in society will always exist under every just government. Equality of talents, of education, or of wealth cannot be produced by human institutions. In the full enjoyment of the gifts of Heaven and the fruits of superior industry, economy, and virtue, every man is equally entitled to protection by law; but when the laws undertake to add to these natural and just advantages artificial distinctions, to grant titles, gratuities, and exclusive privileges, to make the rich richer and the potent more powerful, the humble members of society—the farmers, mechanics, and laborers—who have neither the time nor the means of securing like favors to themselves, have a right to complain of the injustice of their Government. There are no necessary evils in government. Its evils exist only in its abuses. If it would confine itself to equal protection, and, as Heaven does its rains, shower its favors alike on the high and the low, the rich and the poor, it would be an unqualified blessing.

Jackson was oversimplifying—some classes of people and some enterprises require more protection, more resources, and more attention than others. In this passage, however, he was oversimplifying in the service of a philosophical point, arguing that an end to privilege would mark the beginning of a truly democratic era. That is not, of course, how supporters of the Bank saw it. But they were even more outraged by a passage in the middle of the message in which Jackson asserted that no single institution in American life or government was all-controlling, and that as president he had to do what he thought was right. "The Congress, the Executive, and the Court must each for itself be guided by its own opinion of the Constitution," Jackson wrote, saying:

Each public officer who takes an oath to support the Constitution swears that he will support it as he understands it, and not as it is understood by others. It is as much the duty of the House of Representatives, of the Senate, and of the President to decide upon the constitutionality of any bill or resolution which may be presented to them for passage or approval as it is of the supreme judges when it may be brought before them for judicial decision. The opinion of the judges has no more authority over Congress than the opinion of Congress has over the judges, and on that point the

President is independent of both. The authority of the Supreme Court must not, therefore, be permitted to control the Congress or the Executive when acting in their legislative capacities, but to have only such influence as the force of their reasoning may deserve.

Senators and congressmen who could see past the issue of the moment realized that Jackson had just expanded the influence of his office yet again. From the Maysville veto on, he had moved to shift power from the Capitol to the White House, and his assertions in the Bank message went further still. Jackson had made it clear that he interpreted the Court's ruling in **McCulloch v. Maryland,** the case that had established the constitutionality of the Bank, as inconclusive. But he also had made it clear that it hardly mattered—that he was bound to interpret the laws as he understood them regardless of what the Court said. His foes thought him power-mad. "Sir, no President and no public man ever before advanced such doctrines in the face of the nation," Daniel Webster said on the floor of the Senate. "There never before was a moment in which any President would have been tolerated in asserting such a claim to despotic power."

In practice, however, Jackson was not declaring himself emperor. He was not preaching defiance or despotism. His message concluded, in fact, with an acknowledgment that life would go on if he lost the war against the Bank. "I have now done my duty to my country," he said. "If sustained by my fellow-citizens, I shall be grateful and happy; if not, I shall find in the motives which impel me ample grounds for contentment and peace."

His larger argument was that a president should not simply defer to the will and wishes of the Congress or the judiciary. Instead, Jackson was saying, the president ought to take his own stand on important issues, giving voice as best he could to the interests of the people at large. Whose vision would prevail—the president's, the Congress's, or the judiciary's—was an open question, but such questions are perennially open in American politics. Unless there is a complete breakdown—some kind of history-changing coup—there are remedies for the people to bring the government back into balance. In the case of the Bank, Jackson and Biddle were taking the issue to the public in the presidential election.

American politics is organic, power fluid. One era's unquestioned good is another's certain evil. The president and the people of a given moment are not always right, but Jackson believed that "the intelligence and wisdom of our countrymen" would provide "relief and deliverance" from the "difficulties which surround us and the dangers which threaten our institutions"—in every era.

THE BANK WAS neither as venal as the Jacksonians argued nor as indispensable as Biddle's friends asserted. Was Jackson right to destroy the Bank? Interpretations, naturally, differ sharply. On balance, it seems most reasonable to say that the nation's interests would have been best served had the Bank been reformed rather than altogether crushed, but balance was not the order of the day once Jackson decided—as he had done early on—that the Bank was a competing power center beyond his control. The history of banking and finance and the American economy in the nineteenth century would have been different had the Bank survived. The more important point for the generations after Jackson, though, is that the president of the United States made a bold bid to place himself at the absolute center of the country's life and governance, eliminating a rival by building an emotional case, repeating his point over and over again, largely through friendly newspapers, then seeking and winning vindication at the polls.

Constitutional philosophy and economics aside, Jackson's Bank message was supremely good politics, and Jackson was fortunate that his foes were blind to the fact that with the veto he had successfully identified himself forever with the aspiring (and now voting) masses. The veto message "has all the fury of a chained panther biting the bars of his cage," Biddle wrote Clay from Philadelphia on Wednesday, August 1, 1832. "It is really a manifesto of anarchy . . . and my hope is that it will contribute to relieve the country from the dominion of these miserable people."

But Jackson was willing to take his chances come November.

JOHN QUINCY ADAMS recognized that there was much "profound calculation" in Jackson, and experience bore out the former president's observation. Had

Jackson been a truly wild man—blustery, threatening, and senselessly violent, both in his emotions and in his actions—then he would not have risen so far. Of course he had his moments of bluster, and he made threats, and he could, at times, seem senselessly violent, but on the whole Jackson gambled only when he liked his odds, and when he had taken care to protect himself from the worst that could happen.

A test of his ability to balance pride with pragmatism in foreign affairs came as he was finishing the Bank veto. American merchants had long enjoyed a lucrative pepper trade with Sumatra, in the East Indies. A year before, in February 1831, the **Friendship,** of Salem, Massachusetts, had arrived, as usual, in Quallah Battoo, a Sumatran port, to pick up a cargo of pepper. There was also a good deal of specie—hard money—on board, as well as opium. While the captain of the **Friendship** was ashore attending to the weighing of the pepper, armed Malays—some of whom, it was later reported, were opium smokers "rendered desperate by their habits"—came aboard the ship and stabbed Charles Knight, the first officer (he was struck in his side and in his back), killing him and two seamen, John Davis and George Chester. As the men died on the deck and other crew members dove overboard to swim for it, the Malays plundered the ship.

From shore, the captain, Charles Endicott, and a few of his officers and crew tried to return to the **Friendship** only to be chased, first, by a ferry with eight to ten men brandishing spears and knives, and second, by three Malay boats filled with nearly fifty natives. Endicott managed to escape the port and, traveling twenty-five miles to nearby Muckie, joined forces with three other American ships. The assault was no small thing: it was, in effect, a direct attack on the United States. A local rajah, Chute Dulah, accepted specie and opium from the plunderers and refused American demands for the return of the **Friendship**. Endicott, with help, retook his ship and soon landed at yet another Sumatran port, South Tallapow. The crowds of natives there jeered him and his men: "Who great man now, Malay or American?" "How many American dead?" "How many Malay dead?" As Endicott came to the end of his report of the incident, including the details of the crowds, he wrote: "May the mistake under which they rest, that the Americans have not the power to chastise them, be corrected with all convenient dispatch!"

Word of the episode reached Washington by summer, and on Tuesday, August 9, 1831, Jackson decided to dispatch the frigate **Potomac** to make clear, as the ship's orders said, that the president of the United States believed that "the flag of the Union is not to be insulted with impunity." Captain John Downes was in command, and his orders were specific. He was to "demand of the rajah, or other authorities at Quallah Battoo" restitution for the material losses and punishment for the murderers of Knight, Davis, and Chester. If talks failed, then Downes was authorized to arrest the murderers (if he could) and to destroy any ship or weapon used in the attack on the

Friendship as well as any fortification that might have played a role. If things took this more violent course, Downes was to leave with this promise from the president: if restitution were not forthcoming, or if there were any other acts of piracy, "other ships-of-war will soon be dispatched thither, to inflict more ample punishment." Negotiate first, but be willing to use force if necessary—and leave them worried about what might come next. From Jackson's perspective, they were sound orders, tough but practical.

ARRIVING AT Quallah Battoo on Sunday, February 5, 1832, Downes decided that negotiation, though ordered by the president, would be pointless. ("No demand of satisfaction was made previous to my attack, because I was satisfied, from what knowledge I already had of the character of the people, that no such demand would be answered, except only by refusal," Downes reported afterward.) An invading force of 250 sailors and marines effected an amphibious landing early the next morning. Thus began a day of close combat. Some of the Malays used javelins and darts; the Americans razed the town, overrunning forts and killing more than 100 natives, including, reportedly, women and children (two Americans were killed). The next day Downes bombarded what was left of Quallah Battoo. The only thing belonging to the **Friendship** that turned up was the ship's medicine chest.

Five months later, as Jackson was about to veto the recharter of the Bank, Washington learned about the assault, and the anti-Jackson **National Intelligencer** used the destruction of Quallah Battoo to attack the president, arguing that the failure to negotiate before resorting to violence had served no purpose. A bloody, preemptive assault on "a settlement filled with a mixed population, and the killing and wounding of one or two hundred of the people, was not, perhaps, the best possible mode of obtaining satisfaction, or indemnity" for the loss of the cargo of the **Friendship**.

Jackson did not disagree. The president had directed Downes to attempt to negotiate, for even if diplomacy failed, an ensuing use of force would be more easily justified. If Downes had done as Jackson had instructed, America would have won all around: it would have appeared reasonable for having tried to talk, and strong for having asserted its rights by military means. Instead Jackson looked grasping and bloody-minded and had to defend himself against high-minded attacks. The opposition was addressing the subject, the **National Intelligencer** said, "from an impulse of national pride, which cherishes the nation's honor as its most valuable property, and considers humanity and a strict regard to the rights of others as the brightest jewels which adorn its character."

It was a strong argument, but Jackson, who understood better than most that commanders in the field did not always follow orders precisely, had protected himself politically. The orders to Downes were irrefutable evidence that the president had wanted to balance force with diplomacy. When the House asked for copies of the relevant papers on Thursday, July 12, 1832, Jackson was happy to comply. The documents were sent up without delay. Reading them, Congressman Edward Everett of Massachusetts, a committed National Republican, saw that the president had successfully eluded the opposition once again. "From the papers communicated, it might be inferred that Captain Downes had transcended his instructions," Everett remarked. To avoid embarrassing Downes until he could reach Washington and defend himself, the House and the administration agreed not to publish the documents, and the episode, much to the opposition's chagrin, faded away. Jackson had won—not by chance but by calculation.

IN THE MONTHS before the 1832 election, both sides considered themselves safely ahead. Jackson got away from Washington on Monday, July 23, 1832, after jotting a note to Kendall: "The **veto works well**." The election was only four months away, and Jackson felt that he had repaired the political damage of 1831. With the Bank veto, Indian removal, moderate tariff reform— the Tariff of 1832 lowered rates from 1828 levels—and opposition to nullification, he had tried to give every region of the country something to like, and his popularity seemed strong. "I have been most kindly received by the old general, with whom I am much pleased as well as amused," Washington Irving said in the summer of 1832. With a writer's eye, Irving detected Jackson's depths. "As his admirers say, he is truly an **old Roman**—to which I would add, **with a little dash of the Greek;** for I suspect he is as **knowing** as I believe he is honest."

Believing himself smarter and sounder than Jackson, Clay suffered from a terrible case of overconfidence. "The campaign is over, and I think we have won the victory," Clay said privately on Saturday, July 21, 1832. His certitude kept him from seeing—and thus combating—the roots of Jackson's appeal. He thought Jackson a bullying despot and could not fathom, apparently, why anyone other than the most mindless Jackson partisans might see things differently.

As word of the Bank veto made its way through the country, Jackson relaxed in Tennessee, catching up on plantation business at the Hermitage and checking on Andrew and Emily's nearby farm. The Donelsons did not join him on the trip south; from the letters of the period, it appears that Andrew was invested with great authority and confidence to keep the White House running in Jackson's absence. For a short while, Emily took a trip to Baltimore and then the family spent a little over a week at a hot springs. Returning to the capital they found anxieties about cholera. The small White House circle—Emily, Andrew, the two children and the baby, Ralph Earl, and Mary McLemore, Emily's latest companion from Tennessee decided to decamp. "I regret the continuance of, and the virulence of the Cholera," Jackson wrote Andrew Donelson on Thursday, September 13. "I pray you to take care of yourself and remove Emily, Mary, and the children into the country if the disease should appear to seize all persons, those of regular as well as those of irregular habits."

Heading a letter to her mother "Mrs Somers, 5 mi. from Alexandria," Emily described their sundry health difficulties and the flight from Washington. "My health had been very delicate before I went to Baltimore," Emily wrote. "I had an attack of chills and fever." She recovered, but the threat of cholera was terrifying. "We will not return to the city until the Cholera is over," Emily said. From Tennessee, Jackson kept up cheerful communication. "We get several letters from Uncle giving us an account of everything at home and we were quite delighted to hear that our farm was in such fine order."

Much of the South was growing ever more concerned about the future of slavery. In the early hours of Monday, August 22, 1831, Nat Turner, a slave in southern Virginia's Southampton County, entered the house of his master, let in a small band of other slaves, and massacred the family in their beds, setting off a broader spree that killed about fifty-seven whites, a large majority of them women and children. Turner believed that "the Spirit that spoke to the prophets in former days" had commissioned him to "fight against the Serpent, for the time was fast approaching when the first shall be last and the last shall be first." A solar eclipse that year was a sign that the hour had come, Turner thought; the rebellion lasted about two days. It was answered in kind by whites, who decapitated blacks and broke the revolt with what one observer called "scenes . . . hardly inferior in barbarity to the atrocities of the insurgents"; many black victims had had nothing to do with the violence. Turner was captured, convicted, and hanged. Terrified that the uprising foreshadowed years of chaos and bloodshed,

Virginia legislators opened a debate over partial and gradual emancipation, but decided, in the words of the House of Delegates, to "await a more definite development of public opinion."

IN SOUTH CAROLINA, the Tariff of 1832 had failed to appease the state, and Calhoun was now fully engaged in the cause of nullification. As ambitious as he was, he had recognized early in 1832 that he had no clear path to the presidency, and in May it was announced that he would not be a candidate. "I heard one of [Calhoun's] best former friends say . . . he ought to be hung as a traitor to the liberties of his country," Jackson wrote Van Buren from Tennessee in late August.

The South Carolina legislature was to meet on Monday, October 22, 1832. The expectation was that the government in Columbia would move toward nullifying the federal tariff—a step that could mean the state would seize the federal forts and installations in Charleston harbor.

Jackson was hearing such rumors, and on Monday, September 17, 1832, from his study at the Hermitage, Jackson told Andrew Donelson of alleged plans for a possible mutiny among American military officers at Charleston. The president ordered Donelson and the secretary of war, Lewis Cass, to put men in place who could be trusted in the event things came to blows in South Carolina. Discretion was essential, Jackson said, as was speed. "I am confidentially advised that the nullifiers of the South have corrupted both the naval officers and those of the army in Charleston," Jackson said. The president's orders to Andrew were clear:

> The nullies are determined to push matters to extremities and expect to get possession of the forts etc. etc. See the secretary of war and let the officers and men at Charleston be relieved by men who cannot be corrupted and the forts and defenses on that station ordered to be guarded against being taken by surprise. They are sure of getting possession of the forts on that station, and it is this belief that makes them so bold. Say to the secretary of war to look to this. It is useless to change the officers without the men—if the sentinel and [the] soldiers are corrupted the officer cannot defend the garrison. Therefore let the officers and men be relieved by a faithful detachment, and this carried into effect as early as possible—at farthest by the 20th of October, and before their assembly meets. Let it be done without a hint of the cause until it is effected and as the common routine of the army. . . .

"The Presidential question is hardly even spoken of here," Calhoun told a friend in early October. "I think it not improbable this State will not vote at all. We think there is no principle involved in the contest worth struggling for."

Had Calhoun learned nothing during Jackson's reign? If Jackson had proved anything in his White House years, it was this: if he chose to, he would make himself a factor in deciding any question in American life. The trustworthy forces en route to Charleston were evidence enough of that.

CHAPTER 16

★

HURRA FOR THE HICKORY TREE!

A S SEPTEMBER GAVE way to October, Jackson set out from the Hermitage for Washington on what amounted to the first major personal presidential campaign tour. The 1832 contest featured much that was to become commonplace in American politics: national nominating conventions, intense tactical organization, considered use of the incumbent's time and energies in appearances before the public, and an interesting but unsuccessful third-party bid. Though not all of this began with Jackson and his men, much of it did, particularly the shaping of the candidate's image and the marshaling of his personal charisma. In Baltimore in late May 1832, a nominating convention chose Martin Van Buren for vice president. (Jackson's candidacy for another term as president was taken as a given.) Two other conventions had already met: the Anti-Masons and the National Republicans.

Anti-Masonry had grown out of the 1826 disappearance and suspected murder of William Morgan, an upstate New Yorker and disaffected member of the fraternal order who was threatening to publish a book revealing the secrets of Freemasonry. A strong political force in New York, New England, and parts of the Midwest, the Anti-Masons wanted to field a ticket to oppose Jackson and Clay, both of whom—like George Washington and many other important leaders of the early Republic—were Masons. Meeting in Baltimore in 1831, the Anti-Masons nominated William Wirt for president, who would face Jackson and Clay, the National Republican nominee.

As the campaign progressed, more and more "Hickory Clubs" were created to promote Jackson and his cause. There were barbecues—lots of barbecues—parades, songs, and cheers. The style of the Jackson campaign was linked to its substance: with the Bank veto as its central exhibit, the Jackson men insisted that a vote for Jackson was a vote for the people while a vote for Clay was a vote for the privileged. The means, then, matched the message, for both were about the aspirations of the enfranchised masses. "The Jackson cause is the cause of democracy and the people, against a corrupt and abandoned aristocracy," the president's supporters wrote. The National Republicans struck back, arguing that Jackson was power-mad. One opposition headline read: "THE KING UPON THE THRONE: **The People in the Dust!!!**"

But the king understood what the commoners wanted, and needed. They wanted a champion, and needed—or at least thrilled to—the drama of the new kind of campaigning. Michel Chevalier, one of the many foreign observers touring the country in the

Jackson years, took in a mile-long Jackson parade in New York in which people carried torches and banners. The procession, Chevalier said, "stopped before the houses of the Jackson men to fill the air with cheers, and halted at the doors of the leaders of the opposition, to give three, six, or nine groans."

Duff Green watched the rise of the new techniques with envy and gloom. "Lewis has gone on to Nashville, no doubt to be present and aid in the party deliberations," Green told Calhoun on Tuesday, October 23, 1832. "Kendall and Company have organized a Hickory Club here which is intended to give tone and character to all other clubs throughout the country; and one of the principles of faith is opposition to nullification. You may rest assured they do not intend to sleep."

Neither did Jackson, who used the convenient excuse of his autumn journey from Tennessee to Washington to be seen, shake hands, and, in Clay's Kentucky, show himself at a Democratic barbecue in Lexington, not far from Ashland. "This is certainly a new mode of electioneering," said the pro-Clay **National Intelligencer**. "We do not recollect before to have heard of a President of the United States descending in person into the political arena." Blair helpfully published the words of the campaign theme song, "The Hickory Tree," which was to be sung by torchlight in campaign parades: "Hurra for the Hickory Tree! / Hurra for the Hickory Tree! / Its branches will wave o'er tyranny's grave."

Clay was playing by the old rules, and it cost him.

He declined invitations like the ones Jackson accepted, saying he had promised that "whilst I continued before the public . . . as a candidate for its suffrage, I would not accept of any invitation to a public entertainment proposed on my own account."

The political class expected a close-run election. Many wise observers did not think Jackson could prevail. "His opponents (and they are not few or unimportant) denounce him as a person acting upon impulse, of an obstinate and irascible character, and as being surrounded by private Counsellors unworthy of his confidence or public support," Charles Bankhead, an English diplomat, wrote to Viscount Palmerston from Washington on Sunday, October 28, 1832. Bankhead believed the race would probably end up in the House, where Jackson would lose.

Beyond the capital, though, Kendall's Hickory Clubs were creating a sense of excitement around Jackson's reelection, a sense, for voters, of belonging to a larger and grander cause than the ordinary work of their days. It was, in a way, politics as entertainment, but it was also a serious, even sacred undertaking. Chevalier compared Jackson's torchlight parades to Catholic processions, saying that the images of Jacksonians surging through the streets "belong to history, they partake of the grand; they are the episodes of a wondrous epic which will bequeath a lasting memory to posterity, that of the coming of democracy."

THE FRENCHMAN WAS right. When the time came, Jackson won overwhelmingly. He carried the

Electoral College by a convincing 219–49 margin over Clay. The popular vote was closer, with Wirt's Anti-Mason ticket pulling 8 percent, leaving Jackson with close to 55 percent and Clay with about 37 percent. Jackson's popularity was "so unbounded," Charles Bankhead reported to London, that he was able to "overcome all anticipated difficulties, and to obtain . . . a great majority of the voice of the people." The closing weeks of the campaign, Bankhead added, had been especially emotional. "The excitement during the last fortnight has been very great, and no exertions have been wanting by the friends and supporters of the rival candidates."

For Clay, the campaign might be over, but he would not rest. "The dark cloud which had been so long suspended over our devoted country, instead of being dispelled as we had fondly hoped it would be, has become more dense, more menacing, more alarming," Clay said to Charles Hammond on Saturday, November 17, 1832. "Whether we shall ever see light, and law, and liberty again is very questionable. Still, we must go on to the last, with what spirit we can, to discharge our duty. It is under feelings of this kind that I expect, a week or two hence, to go to Washington."

Seven days later, in Columbia, the South Carolina convention nullified the Tariff of 1832, directly challenging the authority of the president of the United States. Should Jackson choose to use force to bring the state into line, the convention declared, South Carolina would "at every hazard" consider itself "absolved from all further obligation to maintain or preserve their political connection with the people of the other states, and will forthwith proceed to organize a separate government and do all other acts and things which sovereign and independent states may of right do."

According to a story making the rounds, Jackson had summoned Congressman Warren R. Davis to urge him "to go back home and tell the people of South Carolina to quit their foolishness and to return to their allegiance to the United States." When Davis replied that "the people at home were in . . . earnest," Jackson opened a drawer and said, "Warren, in that drawer I have offers of three hundred thousand volunteers to march to South Carolina." John Randolph of Roanoke was supposed to have said that "South Carolina would not yield, that she would fight; that General Jackson would be [eager] to get Hamilton, Calhoun, McDuffie and Hayne into his power; that [Randolph] had no doubt that if a war came, as some feared it must, General Jackson would hang those gentlemen if he could get hold of them . . . and there would be a bloody war of it."

In this tumultuous season—the presidential election, the meeting of the convention in South Carolina, the maneuvers to station loyal troops at Charleston—William Gaston of North Carolina, no fan of Jackson's, recognized the stakes of the showdown. "It is no longer to be doubted or denied that there is a party in our land—how numerous I know not—who desire a dissolution of our Union and hope to erect upon its ruins a Southern Confederacy," Gaston wrote to friends in Montgomery, Alabama.

JACKSON'S FOES WERE braced for the worst. He had spent his life confounding his enemies—turning cool when they thought he would be hot, or fierce when they expected him to be gentle. As the fires burned in the South, Jackson sat in the White House weighing his options. Which Andrew Jackson would show up for this fight? The diplomat or the despot? Or both?

A masterful orator, Daniel Webster of Massachusetts was a crucial figure in the Senate. It was his "Second Reply to Hayne" in 1830 that gave poetic force to Jackson's unwavering stand against South Carolina.

A man of ambition and skill, Henry Clay was John Quincy Adams's secretary of state, a senator from Kentucky, and Jackson's opponent in 1832. He and Jackson hated each other—Clay thought Jackson "a military chieftain," and fought him on virtually everything. Their rivalry helped define American politics for more than a generation.

A political cartoon, showing Henry
Clay sewing Jackson's mouth shut,
captures the senator's hostility toward
Jackson and the expanding powers of
the White House. "We are in the midst
of a revolution" of executive usurpation,
Clay argued, and he led the fight in the
Senate to censure Jackson for removing
the government's deposits from the
Bank of the United States—a censure
Jackson spent years struggling to erase.

A federal revenue cutter enforces the tariff in Charleston
harbor during the nullification crisis with South Carolina
in 1832–1833, when radicals in the state threatened to
defy Washington's authority with force of arms.

An image depicting Margaret Eaton in later life, after her marriage to John Henry Eaton roiled Washington. In her old age she married her grandchildren's nineteen-year-old Italian dancing master.

"The Rats Leaving a Falling House": a cartoon lampoons Jackson's 1831 dissolution of the Cabinet. A first in American history, the Cabinet breakup was caused by Jackson's insistence that the secretaries (and their wives) accept Margaret Eaton socially; in Jackson's eyes, opposition to Mrs. Eaton was opposition to him and his policies.

The Second Bank of the United States, headquarters of the institution Jackson called a "hydra of corruption," on Chestnut Street in Philadelphia.

Brilliant and determined, Nicholas Biddle served as president of the Second Bank of the United States. His great miscalculation was to take a fight directly to Jackson. "The Bank . . . is trying to kill me," Jackson once said, **"but I will kill it."** And he did.

A loyal Tennessee lieutenant, John Henry Eaton was an architect of Jackson's political career and a trusted secretary of war. But his marriage created a sexual, social, and political storm that consumed Jackson's first two years in Washington and shaped the presidential succession.

Edward Livingston gave a little-noted but illuminating speech during the Webster-Hayne debate, and later served as envoy to France during the crisis with Paris.

A rendering of Robert B. Randolph's attempted assault on Jackson in May 1833. Andrew Donelson believed "the object no doubt was assassination." It was the first such attack on a president in American history.

Roger B. Taney of Maryland, a member of Jackson's Kitchen Cabinet, recorded how the Bank spread money around Capitol Hill during the struggle over recharter.

The Whig critique of Jackson captured in a cartoon: Jackson as a power-mad dictator who used the veto and his personal popularity to put the presidency at the center of national political life.

The Battle of Quallah Battoo in Sumatra was brief but bloody—
and illustrated the willingness of Jackson's America to project force
around the globe to protect its economic and political interests.

A deranged man armed with two pistols tried to shoot Jackson after
a funeral service at the Capitol, but both of the assailant's weapons
miraculously failed to fire. The president fought back with his cane
and, back at the White House, speculated that Mississippi senator
George Poindexter, a political foe, had been behind the attempt.

Hugh Lawson White of Tennessee was nominated for president in the campaign of 1836 to oppose Martin Van Buren, Jackson's chosen successor. This led to a political civil war in Tennessee, and the passions of the contest enveloped Andrew Donelson and Francis Blair in scandal.

Thomas Hart Benton of Missouri moved from brawling against Jackson in the streets of Nashville to serving as the seventh president's chief defender in the Senate. Benton's campaign to expunge Clay's censure of Jackson ended on a night when the Senate galleries were so raucous and the atmosphere so tense that Benton's colleagues sent for guns.

One of the great moral figures of the first half of the nineteenth century, Jeremiah Evarts defended the rights of Indians against Jackson, but failed.

At the climactic Battle of Bad Axe during the Black Hawk War in 1832, Indians were massacred on the Mississippi River. Many were shot, and many others died by drowning.

OF

THE CHEROKEE NATION

against

THE STATE OF GEORGIA:

ARGUED AND DETERMINED AT

THE SUPREME COURT OF THE UNITED STATES,

JANUARY TERM 1831.

WITH

AN APPENDIX,

Containing the Opinion of Chancellor Kent on the Case; the Treaties between
the United States and the Cherokee Indians; the Act of Congress of
1802, entitled 'An Act to regulate intercourse with the Indian
tribes, &c.'; and the Laws of Georgia relative to the
country occupied by the Cherokee Indians,
within the boundary of that State.

BY RICHARD PETERS,
COUNSELLOR AT LAW.

Philadelphia:
JOHN GRIGG, 9 NORTH FOURTH STREET.
1831.

In 1831, Chief Justice John Marshall ruled that the Cherokees did not have the standing to sue in the Supreme Court—a judicial defeat for a tribe fighting for its life in the South.

The Trail of Tears was a deadly chapter in the long, grim story of white Americans' treatment of the Indians. Though Jackson had retired to the Hermitage by the time the Cherokees were physically driven from their ancestral homes, he was the prime architect of the policy that led to so many deaths.

The end of the journey: in pain so much of his life, Jackson, pictured here in an 1844–1845 daguerreotype, was constantly complaining about his health, yet lived to the age of seventy-eight.

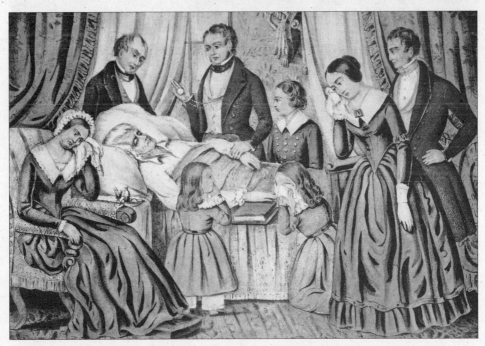

"I hope to meet you all in Heaven—yes, all in Heaven, white and black," Jackson said as he lay dying.

"Sleep sweetly, aged soldier," was among the benedictions when Jackson died and at last joined Rachel in the garden tomb in early June 1845. Three thousand people attended the funeral.

A photograph of Abraham Lincoln's first inaugural, March 4, 1861. In preparing his speech to deliver to a nation on the verge of the Civil War, Lincoln had consulted a copy of Jackson's proclamation to South Carolina. The question of secession, Lincoln said, had been "fully discussed in Jackson's time . . . and denied."

★

CHAPTER 17

A DREADFUL CRISIS OF EXCITEMENT AND VIOLENCE

A WEEK BEFORE Christmas 1832, Pierce M. Butler, a politically connected bank president in Columbia, South Carolina, sat down by his fireside to write a short note to James Henry Hammond, the Southern radical. In the nullifiers' camp, Robert W. Barnwell, a South Carolina congressman, predicted that Jackson was "bent on enforcing his mandate at the point of the bayonet." Worse, Barnwell "feared Congress or a majority [of the people] would sustain" Jackson in such a course.

Hammond was prepared to take up arms for the state's cause, and volunteered his military services to Robert Hayne, whom the South Carolina legislature had elected governor on Monday, December 10. "I shall immediately set about arranging my private affairs for taking the field at an early day, not to quit it until all is settled," Hammond told Hayne on Thursday, December 20, 1832. The next day, Hayne appointed a new military aide-de-camp, who was "charged with the duty of raising, inspecting, and granting commissions to volunteer companies" during what Hayne called "this crisis in our affairs, **when everything dear to our country is at stake.**"

The governor issued detailed secret orders to form a corps of **"Mounted Minute Men"** to be instantly summoned to the defense of the state. "My plan is this," Hayne told his aide. "Let a number of men (every one of whom **keeps a horse**), agree to repair at a moment's warning to any point which may be designated by the Governor in any emergency. Let them then come prepared with guns or rifles, or arms of any description, with a supply of powder and ball, and come in the shortest time possible." Predictably—South Carolinians being South Carolinians, to whom appearances often mattered rather more than even to other Southerners—Hayne closed his directive by advising that his staff's uniforms should have "a **short yellow crane Plume**" and advising them of the best places to purchase "Palmetto Buttons of a beautiful pattern" to wear.

In Washington, Jackson read Joel Poinsett's intelligence reports with fascination. "Keep me constantly advised," he told Poinsett, who obliged with detailed letters that reached the White House by express. "I have on every occasion told my fellow citizens that the Executive of the United States would act decidedly and vigorously," Poinsett wrote Jackson in the autumn of 1832. After the nullification vote in November, Jackson was embarking on perhaps the most delicate mission of his life—how to preserve the Union without appearing so tyrannical and power-hungry that other Southern states might join with South Carolina, precipitating an even graver crisis that could lead to the secession of several states. The Old World nations followed the trouble with great interest. Perhaps a crack-up would open the old British colonies to new exploitation, eliminating or at least weakening the United States as a global rival.

Three days after the passage of the nullification ordinance, Samuel Cram Jackson, a Presbyterian minister from New England who happened to be in South Carolina and kept a diary of events, thought Charleston more worried than exuberant. "Aspect gloomy," he wrote. "Anxiety and fear pervades many hearts. Many are looking for civil war, and scenes of bloodshed. The general government has ordered troops to the forts in the harbor." The next day the city remained in a "most anxious state; feelings excited; all uncertainty as to prospects. The nullifiers are trumpeting and carrying high-handed measures; and the Union men are determined not to submit. Things seem to be preparing for a dreadful crisis of excitement and violence."

There was danger on every side. Writing of reinforcing the federal installations in Charleston harbor, Poinsett told Jackson that "the custom house where the battle will be fought is crowded with nullifiers; ought they not be removed?" The Unionists did not trust the post office, either, and they knew they must not give the rebels cause to go to arms. "We are not disposed to make any riotous or tumultuous resistance, but we are ready to support the laws if legally called upon to do so at the hazard of our lives," Poinsett said.

Four days after Poinsett posted this letter, Samuel Cram Jackson recorded a near massacre in the streets of Charleston. A band of nullifiers staked out King Street downtown in order to challenge those Unionists who were leaving a gathering; an officer in the nullifiers' ranks sent word to Poinsett that the Union men should use Meeting Street in order to avoid a confrontation. The warning infuriated the Unionists. As the Reverend Jackson wrote, "their blood was up, to think that the nullifiers should **dictate** the street they should walk in. The cry resounded, 'King Street, King Street.' Before they left their hall, they organized into companies, chose their leaders, and promised **implicit** obedience. Both parties were armed with clubs and dirks." The nullifiers numbered about five hundred, the Unionists a thousand, and the rebels "hissed, and called opprobrious names, but chose not to assault."

Hotheads in the Union ranks wanted to strike, but those in charge restrained them. "The merest trifle, a word from a leader, would, it is confidently stated by moderate and Christian men, have led to a combat in which hundreds would have lost their lives; fathers and sons and brothers would have slain each other," Samuel Cram Jackson said. "The parties themselves were afterwards astounded at the pitch of excitement to which they were brought. . . . It was owing entirely to the firmness and wisdom of the leaders that the streets of Charleston did not run down with blood."

. . .

BUT NO ONE could know whether caution would continue to trump confrontation. In Washington, after reading Poinsett's early letters, President Jackson dispatched George Breathitt, the brother of the governor of Kentucky and a kinsman of John Eaton's, to scout the territory under the cover of a postal inspection. Breathitt's real task, according to Jackson's confidential orders: to "collect all the information . . . that you can obtain which may be serviceable to the government." As Breathitt assessed the situation, Poinsett briefed Jackson on the political divisions within the enemy camp. McDuffie, still a member of Congress, was pressing for secession; Calhoun, still vice president, argued for a more moderate course to allow his theories time to be tested. "Both parties [of the nullifiers] are anxious and indulge the hope that the general government will commit some act of violence which will enlist the sympathies of the bordering states: provided it be not their own, they care not how soon blood is shed," Poinsett told Jackson. "It will be necessary therefore to proceed with great caution in counteracting their schemes."

Poinsett was an able man, and Jackson was fortunate to have him on the ground. He was loyal, canny, and wise. When Jackson moved to send new officers, Poinsett offered good advice, asking that Jackson dispatch "a Southern man if possible. I say Southern because prejudices have been excited against Northerners, and as it is considered a Southern question exclusively, it might be politic to have it settled by Southern men."

For two agonizing months—from October through November and into the first day or two of December—Poinsett wrote long, impassioned letters to Jackson, yet Jackson merely made the right Unionist noises in reply without offering a detailed plan of support. Poinsett grew worried. On Thursday, November 29, 1832, he sent Jackson a note begging for reassurance. "We had rather die than submit to the tyranny of such an oligarchy as J. C. Calhoun, James Hamilton, Robt. Y. Hayne and McDuffie, and we implore our sister states and the federal government to rescue us from these lawless and reckless men," Poinsett told Jackson. Other Unionists, Poinsett said, believed that, in the event of nullification, "Congress will say to us, 'Let South Carolina go out of the Union if she will go,' . . . If such a course should be adopted, the Union must be dissolved in all its parts and foreign and domestic wars necessarily ensue. Whereas if these bad men are put down by the strong arm, the Union will be cemented by their conduct and by the vigor of the government, and you will earn the imperishable glory of having preserved this great confederacy from destruction."

Jackson sympathized with Poinsett, and, on Sunday, December 2, made his own opinion as clear as he could: "I fully concur with you in your views of nullification. It leads directly to civil war and bloodshed and deserves the execration of every friend of the

country." Weapons were en route to arm the Unionists, but "calmness and firmness" were essential, and
the law would be "duly executed, but by proper
means." Jackson was ready to take extraordinary steps,
but only when he was forced into it. He did not want
to exert his power until he absolutely had to.

The annual presidential message Andrew Donelson
took to Capitol Hill on Tuesday, December 4, was
drafted in something of a conciliatory spirit. "This is
all we want, peaceably to nullify the nullifiers," Jackson told Van Buren. In the wake of South Carolina's
defiance, Jackson kept his temper in check and issued
a document that opposed nullification even as it advocated tariff reform and sounded like a defense of
states' rights. High tariffs—even the ones just passed—
created, he said, "discontent and jealousy dangerous
to the stability of the Union," and as the national debt
disappeared, the theoretical need for great sources of
federal revenue would disappear, too, opening the
way to cutting tariff rates even further.

HIS TONE WAS Jeffersonian. He evoked the simpler
republican virtues of the previous generation, offering
a comforting vision of life and government: "Limited
to a general superintending power to maintain peace at
home and abroad, and to prescribe laws on a few subjects of general interest not calculated to restrict
human liberty, but to enforce human rights, this government will find its strength and its glory in the faithful discharge of these plain and simple duties."
Congressman John Quincy Adams said the message

was "in substance a complete surrender to the nullifiers of South Carolina."

At first, the message did seem difficult to reconcile with Jackson's movements behind the scenes. But that was the point: Jackson's December strategy was three-fold. With the annual message, he intended to isolate South Carolina rhetorically by appearing reasonable about the general principles at stake. With his secret military preparations, he bolstered the spirits of the Union Party in the state and put the federal government in position to fight if things came to that. Three days later, on December 7, Poinsett heard warming news from Secretary of War Lewis Cass: "The President has instructed me to inform you that the 5,000 stand of arms and 1,000 rifles, the propriety of placing which in depot at Charleston was suggested by you, have been ordered to that place, and that directions have been given to General Scott for issuing them for the use of any portion of the citizens of South Carolina for the defense of the laws of the Union."

After reassuring those sympathetic to state sovereignty and a limited federal government by sounding vaguely Calhoun-like in the annual message, Jackson revealed the third element of his year-end attack on the forces of disunion: his proclamation of Monday, December 10, 1832.

CHAPTER 18

★

THE MAD PROJECT
OF DISUNION

JACKSON WAS ALONE in his office, standing at his desk, when he began writing the document. With a steel pen in hand, he moved quickly from page to page—so quickly, in fact, that James Parton reported that Jackson had to spread the pages over his desk to let them dry: "A gentleman who came in when the President had written fifteen or twenty pages observed that three of them were glistening with wet ink at the same moment." The pages were soon sent across Lafayette Square to Decatur House, where Edward Livingston was to polish Jackson's rough draft. The final version was, then, the work of Jackson and Livingston—it drew on the ideas Livingston had outlined in the Senate in 1830—and its affirmation of the idea of Union and attack on nullification ran to roughly 8,700 words. As the document went to press, Lewis suggested a change that might mollify those Americans who believed in states rights' but not nullification. Jackson heard Lewis out and said there would be no quarter given: "Those are my views, and I will not change them nor strike them out," Jackson said.

The views were intensely nationalistic. Nullification was, Jackson said, **"incompatible with the existence of the Union, contradicted expressly by the letter of the Constitution, unauthorized by its spirit, inconsistent with every principle on which it was founded, and destructive of the great object for which it was formed."** Had a single-state veto been an option "at an earlier day, the Union would have been dissolved in its infancy," Jackson said. The War of 1812—Jackson's true trial by fire, and the theater from which he rose to power—might have been lost: "The war into [which] we were forced [in order to] support the dignity of the nation and the rights of our citizens might have ended in defeat and disgrace, instead of victory and honor, if the states who supposed it a ruinous and unconstitutional measure had thought they possessed the right of nullifying the act by which it was declared and denying supplies for its prosecution." The Constitution, he said, "forms a **government,** not a league. . . . It is a government in which all the people are represented."

The system was not perfect, and therefore there were "two appeals from an unconstitutional act passed by Congress—one to the judiciary, the other to the people and the States" through constitutional amendment. Jackson argued that "We the People" had formed the Union that produced the Constitution, as opposed to the Southern theory that the Constitution was a compact between the states in which the individual states were paramount. To Jackson, the people were paramount, and the American system of government was, he believed, equal to the task of reconciling the competing interests of modern life as well as any human institution could.

Addressing the people of South Carolina, Jackson was alternately stern and soft, painting a portrait of a rising nation whose progress to glory could only be interrupted by the attempts of a single interest to seize power from the whole:

> Contemplate the condition of that country of which you still form an important part. Consider its government, uniting in one bond of common interest and general protection so many different states, giving to all their inhabitants the proud title of **American citizen**, protecting their commerce, securing their literature and their arts, facilitating their intercommunication, defending their frontiers, and making their name respected in the remotest parts of the earth. Consider the extent of its territory, its increasing and happy population, its advance in arts which render life agreeable, and the sciences which elevate the mind! See education spreading the lights of religion, morality, and general information into every cottage in this wide extent of our Territories and States. Behold it as the asylum where the wretched and the oppressed find a refuge and support. Look on this picture of happiness and honor and say, **We too are citizens of America.**

The cost of failing to see the virtues of the Union that had brought America so far would be enormous, and Jackson did not hesitate to conjure the terrors that awaited anyone who thought they could break away, thus putting the entire experiment in liberty at risk:

Carolina is one of these proud states; her arms have defended, her best blood has cemented, this happy Union. . . . For what do you throw away these inestimable blessings? For what would you exchange your share in the advantages and honor of the Union? For the dream of a separate independence—a dream interrupted by bloody conflicts with your neighbors and a vile dependence on a foreign power. If your leaders could succeed in establishing a separation, what would be your situation? Are you united at home? Are you free from the apprehension of civil discord, with all its fearful consequences? Do our neighboring republics, every day suffering some new revolution or contending with some new insurrection, do they excite your envy?

The answers to these questions were so self-evident to Jackson that he did not care to let his audience even begin to reply. He continued:

But the dictates of a high duty oblige me solemnly to announce that you cannot succeed. The laws of the United States must be executed. I have no discretionary power on the subject; my duty is emphatically pronounced in the Constitution. . . . Disunion by armed force is **treason**. Are you really ready to incur its guilt? . . . On your unhappy state will inevitably fall all

the evils of the conflict you force upon the government of your country. It cannot accede to the mad
project of disunion, of which you would be the first
victims. Its First Magistrate cannot, if he would, avoid
the performance of his duty. . . . Declare that you will
never take the field unless the star-spangled banner of
your country shall float over you; that you will not be
stigmatized when dead, and dishonored and scorned
while you live, as the authors of the first attack on the
Constitution of your country. Its destroyers you cannot be.

Among the radicals in South Carolina, the publication of the proclamation prompted fury. To James
Henry Hammond, Jackson's words were "destined to
bring about another reign of terror." To the Unionists,
Poinsett said, the proclamation was considered "wise,
determined and firm." James A. Hamilton, a son of
Alexander Hamilton, told Jackson: "I pray God to
preserve your life . . . that you may preserve this
Union." According to Joseph Story, John Marshall became one of Jackson's "warmest supporters" after the
proclamation. Henry Clay, on the other hand, could
not get over the contrast between this and the annual
message: "One short week produced the message and
the Proclamation—the former ultra, on the side of
State rights—the latter ultra, on the side of Consolidation." To another friend, he complained: "Who can
have confidence in any man that would put forth two
such contradictory papers?"

Still unable to see the calculation behind Jackson's

confrontational style, Clay was unwilling to acknowledge what in hindsight appears clear enough: that the two messages, while different in tone—understandably, since they were written to serve different purposes in the same cause—were ideologically and philosophically compatible. The cumulative effect of the two documents was, first, to define the ideal shape and scope of the federal government, and second, to defend the existence of that government as the best means yet devised to reconcile contending forces in a peaceable and enduring way. The annual message was about the brushstrokes and colors Jackson would like to use in the art of American politics and governance. The proclamation explained the size and importance of the canvas.

DID JACKSON HAVE firm states' rights ideas? He did. They included a belief in a generally limited federal government, a debt-free nation, and a country in which the people, acting through the states more fully and frequently than through Washington, made a larger number of important decisions about public affairs. Experience had taught him, however, that there was virtue in the Union and in custom, even if he himself flouted custom when it suited him. "King Andrew the First," as his foes styled him, was the most powerful president in the forty-year history of the office, but his power was marshaled not for personal gain—he was always in financial straits—but, as Jackson saw it, for what he believed was in the best interests of the ordinary, the unconnected, the uneducated. He could be brutal in his application of power, but he was not a brute. He could be unwavering, but he was not closed-minded. He was, rather, the great politician of his time, if success in politics is measured by the affirmation of a majority of the people in real time and by the shadow one casts after leaving the stage.

Read even now, the proclamation he issued on the tenth day of December, only half a century after the Revolution, captures both what was remarkable about the nation then and which of her virtues—liberty, union, imagination, loyalty, perseverance—sustained her through decades and centuries of tumult. Henry Clay may have found Jackson inconsistent, but most of the people of the time did not. Thomas Hart Benton remarked that the "mass of the people think the Union is attacked, and that the Proclamation is to save it, and that brief view is decisive with them."

It moved even those inclined to find fault with Jackson. Philip Hone, a former mayor of New York who kept a detailed diary of the period, generally thought Jackson a rube. But the proclamation surprised him. "The whole subject is discussed in a spirit of conciliation, but with firmness and decision. . . . The language of the President is that of a father addressing his wayward children, but determined to punish with the utmost severity the first open act of insubordination," Hone wrote. "As a composition it is splendid, and will take its place in the archives of our country, and will dwell in the memory of our citizens alongside of the farewell address of the 'Father of his

Country.'" He added: "I think Jackson's election may save the Union."

ROBERT HAYNE, WHO had succeeded Hamilton as governor of South Carolina in December 1832, giving up his seat in the Senate to Calhoun, told his aide-de-camp that "measures have been taken to procure an ample supply of arms of every description" for the volunteer corps and that the cavalry should be told that "I am in hopes in a very short time to forward a supply of sabers and pistols."

Poinsett was pessimistic. "These men are reckless and desperate and I have little hope of a peaceful termination of this conflict," he told Jackson on Monday, December 17. Jackson thought his ally was reading things right. "If I can judge from the signs of the times, nullification and secession, or, in the language of truth, **disunion,** is gaining strength," Jackson wrote to Secretary of War Cass on the same day. "We must be prepared to act with promptness and crush the monster in its cradle before it matures to manhood. We must be prepared for the crisis." He then requested a report on how many muskets were on hand, as well as how much ammunition and artillery. He and Hayne were asking the same questions as they readied for the fight; a week after Jackson's note to Cass, Hayne ordered the preparation of a confidential report detailing "what supplies exist of field pieces, muskets, rifles, lead, and generally everything which it is important for me to know." A Unionist told Jackson that his supporters comforted themselves with the cry: "What have we to fear, we are right and God and Old Hickory are with us."

South Carolina was roiling. "I am lingering here to witness the 'outbreak' on the subject of the tariff," Washington Irving told his brother. The Reverend Samuel Cram Jackson took in a meeting at which Hayne and McDuffie spoke. There were more than two thousand people there, and "the vast building resounded, almost incessantly, with the thunders of applause." The Reverend Jackson "could easily see how nullification had spread. The multitude **believe** and applaud all that their leaders say, and are **blindly** led on to their destruction."

"I hope these southern Nullifiers will not break down the beautiful edifice their fathers have erected to freedom," Rebecca Gratz, a Philadelphian who was rumored to be the model for the heroine in Sir Walter Scott's **Ivanhoe,** wrote her sister-in-law on Tuesday, December 18, 1832. "Oh how I tremble lest American blood should be spilt by American hands."

As the year came to a close, Calhoun resigned the vice presidency—his brief letter to Edward Livingston was dated Friday, December 28, 1832—but he would not be moving far from the presiding officer's chair in the chamber. The state legislature at Columbia had elected him senator and now he could fight Jackson openly from the floor rather than secretly and sporadically from the shadows—for as long, in any event, as South Carolina remained in the Union.

On December 30, Calhoun was in Raleigh and

spent an entire Sunday, William Gaston said, "lecturing on nullification at the Hotel." With "zeal and animation," Calhoun made his case to a room crowded with people, many of them standing to hear him. The gist of his argument, Gaston reported, was that "our government had remained unreformed [for] upwards of forty years. No human institution could fail to require amendment after that length of time"—glossing over the existing amending process that had given the nation the Bill of Rights. For Calhoun, the wisdom of South Carolina's course was so obvious that anyone could see it. "The doctrine of nullification was perfectly understood in South Carolina, from the judge who presided on the bench to the humblest tenant of a log cabin in the piney woods," Calhoun told his listeners in Raleigh, and that "when it was more studied and better understood it could not fail to triumph."

JACKSON FEARED CALHOUN might be right, that the theory of nullification, cloaked in the garb of republican virtue, could give other unhappy Southern states the occasion and the means to cast their lot with South Carolina rather than with Washington. Nullification was, as Calhoun and others had shown, an intellectually respectable enough proposition that Virginia, North Carolina, Georgia, Alabama, and Mississippi took a long look at the doctrine. From Richmond to Raleigh to Atlanta to Montgomery to Jackson, Southern governors and lawmakers, both federal and state, hated the tariff and longed to see it reformed or killed (preferably the latter). But was nullification, with its attendant risk of civil war, worth it? Even if only a few Southerners thought so—and they did—Jackson had to worry.

He knew that elements in each of these states, some quite strong, inclined to follow South Carolina's lead. In Alabama, the influential congressman Dixon Hall Lewis—a nearly five-hundred-pound giant of a man who chaired the House Indian Affairs Committee— thought Calhoun was on to something. In Mississippi, Senator George Poindexter and John A. Quitman, the chancellor of the state courts, attempted to translate states' rights opinion into sentiment for nullification. Implacably anti-Jackson, Poindexter said that "the very existence and vital interests of the Southern states depend" on restricting presidential authority. With the settlement of its Cherokee cases in favor of the white majority, Georgia stood by Jackson. In North Carolina, officials professed simultaneous anger at the tariff and opposition to nullification—but worried that Jackson might go too far in putting down South Carolina. The use of force by federal troops could turn North Carolina's sympathies from Washington to Columbia and Charleston.

Virginia was perhaps the greatest threat. It was a divided state. On the Unionist side, figures like the aged James Madison insisted that nullification was neither constitutional nor within the spirit of the Virginia and Kentucky Resolutions. The more radical side was led by the state's governor, John Floyd, who was an intimate of Calhoun's, and he, like Calhoun, had no use for Jackson. In December, Floyd alluded to the abolitionist maneuvering in the North, warning the legislature that it was all "for the purpose no doubt of inciting our slave population to rebellion and acts of violence." But it was not until Jackson's Nullification Proclamation, with its intense language of nationalism, that Virginia began to waver in its support of the Union. The vision of Jackson sweeping into the South with the might of the army was too much for many Virginians, who fell back on the old critique of Jackson and his character: "He pursues enemies with a cruel vengeance, which knows no bounds, and is restrained by no generosity," wrote one. Floyd's confidence grew. Perhaps he and Calhoun could win after all. If Jackson "uses force," Floyd said, "I will oppose him with a military force. I nor my country will be enslaved without a struggle."

At home in Richmond, as John Marshall watched Floyd call on the state's lawmakers to weigh nullification, the chief justice's post-proclamation euphoria quickly dissipated. "I look with anxious solicitude to the proceedings of our legislature, and with much more fear than hope," Marshall told William Gaston. "Might I judge from the very little I know of its character, I should say that a considerable portion is in favor of a separate confederacy, and that this portion contains the boldest and most active of its members. Consequently it strengthens daily."

Floyd was inclined to throw in his lot with Calhoun, and there was an argument that the Union's demise could be good for Virginia, which would become the greatest power in a new Southern order.

In considering their own decisions about nullification, Virginia's neighbors worried that they might be trading the tyranny of the North for the tyranny of Virginia. "Separated from the East and united in a Southern Confederacy, would not Virginia govern with supreme control?" a correspondent asked John Branch of North Carolina. "Have you not already felt the force of her domination, when her sons were in power? And how could you protect yourself against her overwhelming population and resources? There are matters which it would seem the worthy nullifiers have not studied as they deserve. The time is approaching when it will be necessary for South Carolina to look at this side of the question—and to decide which is likely to use power most tyrannically, the General Government or the mighty and proud Dominion [of Virginia] by which she is located and before which she must tremble and crouch in the event of a contest between them."

Marshall, no alarmist, took the prospect of disunion seriously. "Insane as South Carolina unquestionably is, I do not think her so absolutely mad as to have made her declaration of war against the United States had she not counted on uniting the south—beginning with Virginia," Marshall told Gaston. Marshall knew Floyd and Calhoun were close, and he worried that the alliance might have far-reaching consequences. The whole business depressed Marshall, who expected civil war. "Were an open declaration in favor of a southern league to be made by the governments and supported by the people, I believe the terms of separation might be amicably adjusted," he told Gaston—a remarkable admission, coming from one of the architects of American nationalism. "But the course we seem inclined to take"—meaning Jackson's refusal to give in—"encourages South Carolina to persevere and the consequence of her perseverance must be civil war. In the mean time, our people will be inextricably entangled in the labyrinth of their State right theories, and the feeble attachment they still retain for the Union will be daily weakened. 'We have fallen on evil times.'" Still, the chief justice hoped he was wrong. "Old men are timid," he said, referring to himself. "Pray Heaven that my fears may proceed from the timidity of age rather than from rational calculation founded on the actual state of things."

To the north, in the White House, Jackson put on a brave face. "Virginia, except for a few nullifiers and politicians, is true to the core," he said. But a few nullifiers and politicians could cause much trouble, and at heart Jackson shared Marshall's view. In letter after letter, the more Jackson scribbled the words "the union **shall** be preserved," the more one suspects he felt things might slip out of control. He had given his word, though, and he would keep it: "I will die with the Union."

Jackson's allies responded to South Carolina's preparations for war with grim humor. Replying to a letter in which his brother, Rufus, had described Calhoun's vicious table manners, Leonidas Polk wrote: "Your account of Mr. Calhoun as a man of **grace** at least, is not very favorable. . . . I suppose, though, while he was wielding his knife and thrusting his fork in such style, he was thinking of the execution which the nullifiers would do with their bayonets and broad swords, and perhaps was practicing. Poor man, I dare say he will stand in need of all the skill he can acquire."

AT THE WHITE House, on New Year's Day 1833, the people of Washington, feeling a frisson of danger from the showdown with South Carolina, swarmed to shake Jackson's hand. For three hours Jackson and Emily stood at their posts, dutifully greeting the guests. The women of the house currently included Mary McLemore and Mary Coffee, Emily's nieces, and though Miss McLemore and Emily skirmished a bit, Emily made sure none of it reached Jackson's ears. Reporting on the comings and goings in the White House, Mary Coffee told her mother that Mary McLemore "was always of a tyrannical disposition [and] always wishes me to yield to her in everything." And while "I am willing for the sake of peace to do this," Mary Coffee added, "Aunt [Emily] is not, and always tells her of it, [and] thence ensues a dispute. . . . I do not exaggerate when I say there is seldom a day passes in perfect harmony." Emily, however, had learned the lessons of the Eaton wars and did not advertise the domestic conflicts. Mary wrote: "I am very glad that Uncle does not know [about the strife], for I am sure it would make him uneasy and I am certain that he has very few moments of perfect ease."

Nonetheless, Emily's triumph in the previous year's war was complete. Even the Eatons' brief return to the capital—he had lost a Senate bid in Tennessee—was anticlimactic. They had had their day, and it had passed, and with its sense of who has power and who does not, Washington took little note of them. Margaret slipped into a brief physical decline, as though the bill for the cumulative stress of the previous four years came due all at once. "She has been quite ill," Lewis wrote John Overton. "She looks very badly. . . . I was shocked by her pale, sickly, and emaciated appearance."

John Coffee visited Washington for a time and noted that Emily and her young connections, including his own Mary, "seem to enjoy themselves very well—there is a constant stream of visits and revisits. The ladies perform a considerable part in the drama here." His daughter reveled in the life he was describing. "You must excuse this scrawl for I have been sitting up three or four nights at parties, am very much fatigued and stayed at home tonight because I was too tired to go out," Mary Coffee wrote to her brother. A few days later, after a White House dinner with some representatives of Indian nations, Mary noted, "I suppose they were very much pleased from their looks, however we cannot always judge of an Indian's feelings by their looks or white people either, if they are all like the good people of Washington."

Like Mary Coffee, Jackson was unsure what lurked behind the masks of the politicians gathered in the capital to debate the South Carolina question. He himself, though, knew what face to show the public no matter what he might be thinking or feeling. As anxious as the early weeks of 1833 were, when Washington Irving called at the White House, Jackson, who knew Irving was in contact with some of the players in South Carolina, showed no fear, no trace of worry, no undue concern—he was placid and commanding. After his conversation with Jackson, Irving "came away with a still warmer feeling towards Old Hickory, who, I swear, is one of the truest old caballeros I have ever known." "Caballero" is an interesting choice of term, for it suggests a knightly, courtly gentleman—smooth rather than rough, calm rather than angry, calculating rather than raging.

Four days after this meeting, Jackson's campaign to resolve rather than inflame the crisis took legislative form. In the House, New York congressman Gulian C. Verplanck, the chairman of the Ways and Means Committee, introduced the administration's tariff reform bill—a key element if there was to be a peaceable settlement of the crisis. That Jackson was moving to make the most immediate cause of the trouble disappear, all while threatening to use force, suggests a cool political sense beneath his heated professions of inflexibility.

At the White House the same week, the Supreme Court justices gathered to dine with Jackson. It was a convivial evening. The power of the proclamation to South Carolina had dispelled, for the moment, the tensions produced by the Cherokee cases. Mary Coffee was unexpectedly charmed by John Marshall. "If you were to see him without knowing who it was, you would hardly notice him," she wrote her brother. "Apart from his dress, there is nothing striking in his appearance, a tall, raw-boned man, small head, all of his features very small, a remarkably low forehead for a man but a very fine eye, a small, black, restless, penetrating eye. He dresses in the old style shorts and knee buckles. He is very agreeable in conversation, very lively, will talk to the ladies upon every **light** subject but never upon any other description of subjects in mixed company, which shows his good sense, I think." Justice Story, Mary said, "appears to be of a very cheerful, jovial disposition, very much of a beau in the company of ladies."

STORY HAD REASON to be cheerful. He had been horrified by the prospect of the "reign of King Mob" at the White House four years before, but was now charmed, Story wrote his wife, when "the President specially invited me to drink a glass of wine with him." Story and Marshall had long opposed Jackson's more vehement states' rights views, but, Story told his wife, "what is more remarkable since his last proclamation and messages [is] the Chief Justice and myself have become his warmest supporters and shall continue so just as long as he maintains the principles contained in them." So the anger over the clashes of the past evaporated in the glow of the White House.

Calhoun was feeling confident, if a bit wounded. Arriving in the city fresh from his marathon day elucidating nullification in Raleigh, Calhoun checked in to Brown's Hotel. His pride was hurt: Livingston had not bothered to reply to Calhoun's vice presidential resignation letter. From his lodgings Calhoun sent a follow-up note, asking Livingston "to inform me by the bearer whether it has been received." Courtesies aside, Calhoun thought things were going his way. Between Jackson's states' rights annual message and the nationalist proclamation, the White House seemed to be pleasing neither side, and the states were still in flux. "Our cause is doing well," Calhoun wrote a friend in South Carolina on Thursday, January 10, 1833. "Let our people go on; be firm and prudent; give no pretext for force, and I feel confident of a peaceable and glorious triumph for our cause and the state."

CHAPTER 19

WE ARE THREATENED
TO HAVE OUR THROATS CUT

JACKSON WAS IN a difficult position. He needed concessions from the manufacturing states on a lower tariff and from the South (not only South Carolina but the rest of the region, too) on simply the existence of a tariff, even at reduced rates. It was evident from the nullifiers' preparations and from Poinsett's fears that passions in South Carolina could lead to violence, and once shoving or shooting began, it was impossible to predict where it might end. Jackson did not yet know, he told Van Buren, "whether some of the eastern states may not secede or nullify, if the tariff is reduced. I have to look at both ends of the union to preserve it."

One thing was clear to Jackson's foes: between the expanded veto power and his huge personal popularity, he was amassing so much power that they chose to believe the Constitution in jeopardy. "There is nothing certain but that the **will** of Andrew Jackson is to govern; and that will fluctuates with the change of every pen which gives expression to it," Clay said bitterly. Calhoun painted an even starker portrait, writing to Samuel Ingham: "The people will never again choose another Chief Magistrate. The executive power will perpetuate itself."

The delicacy of Jackson's task in this bleak winter is illuminated by a conversation he had at the White House with Silas Wright, Jr., a New York politician in town to begin a Senate term. Jackson wanted New York firmly and unmistakably in his camp, but thus far the state legislature had failed to condemn nullification. Van Buren apparently saw no advantage in rushing to his president's side, either personally (the vice president–elect remained in New York in these tense weeks) or politically (he worried that the proclamation would cost him votes in the 1836 campaign). Van Buren sent Wright to the White House on Sunday, January 13, with a letter for Jackson.

For half an hour, however, Jackson focused entirely on Wright. The news, Jackson said, was bad, and it was going to get worse. "I learned from him that instead of a diminution of the probabilities of force at Charleston those probabilities had been constantly increasing," Wright told Van Buren. Jackson warned that the rebels were "holding regular drills of the squads in the night" and fumed that Hamilton had allowed the American flag to be flown upside down—a symbol of distress—aboard a boat he rode into Augusta, Georgia. "For this indignity to the flag of the country, she ought to have been instantly sunk, no matter who owned or commanded her," Jackson told Wright. It was a dark report.

Jackson's winter campaign entered a critical new

phase on Wednesday, January 16, 1833. Already lobbying to cut the tariff and thus remove the proximate cause of the crisis, he also wanted clear authority to strike if it came to that. What the administration called the Force Bill (Southerners denounced it as the Bloody Bill) authorized the president to move the collection of federal revenue to ships off the coast of Charleston or to temporary customs houses at Fort Moultrie and Castle Pinckney—installations under federal control. The bill also specifically gave the president the power to direct the military and the state militias to carry out federal law. There was no escaping the central truth of the proposal: that a president was asking Congress to explicitly give him the power to use military strength against Americans within American borders. If he could not solve things peaceably, he would then have the option of doing so forcibly. He ruled nothing out.

IN THE SENATE, Felix Grundy of Tennessee introduced the measure, along with a copy of the Nullification Proclamation. Calhoun was not yet in the chamber when Grundy spoke. The new senator from South Carolina entered and sat down as the documents themselves were being read aloud. He instantly decided "that it ought not to pass without a blow; and I accordingly struck it." Enthralled by his own theory, guided in part by his contempt for Jackson, convinced of his own rectitude and vision, Calhoun spoke passionately. South Carolina, he said, had joined the Union "with the understanding that a state, in the last resort, has a right to judge of the expediency of resistance to oppression or secession from the Union. And for so doing it is that we are threatened to have our throats cut, and those of our wives and children."

As the words tumbled out of his mouth, Calhoun realized he should stop. "No—I go too far," he said. "I did not intend to use language so strong. The Chief Magistrate ha[s] not yet recommended so desperate a remedy." Still, he raised the prospect of an armed Jacksonian dictatorship. "Military despotism," Calhoun said—not a divided union—was "the greatest danger" facing America. Perhaps, Calhoun added, he should not speak with such "warmth," which he knew was "unbecoming." But he could not help it. In Washington, at least, the rhetorical bloodshed had begun.

CALHOUN'S FRIENDS ASSURED him that the speech had had "great effect on the Audience and the Senate." The White House's allies streamed out of the chamber and rushed to reassure Jackson that Calhoun's opening shots had fallen short. They apparently emphasized style, criticizing Calhoun for his feverish delivery. "Mr. Calhoun let off a little of his ire against me today in the Senate, but was so agitated and confused that he made quite a failure," Jackson told Poinsett after hearing accounts of the speech. On substantive grounds, though, the Calhoun argument that a Jackson presidency could lead to military despotism and curtailed civil liberties had a good deal of resonance. Jackson had been facing such charges since the controversy over martial law in

New Orleans two decades before, and he had heard Clay repeatedly make such a case.

Asking for an endorsement of executive power to exert force against the states was no small thing, and the Southern states—even the ones with no brief for nullification—were anxious. Jackson's words to Poinsett about Calhoun's alleged "failure" in the Senate, then, were more hopeful than realistic.

Late that night, on the hushed household floor of the White House, Jackson was too troubled to sleep. To save the South he had to cut the tariff, but if he cut it too much, Jackson fretted, he could alienate the North, which might begin to find new virtue in the idea of nullification. In securing the power to put down rebellion he could drive more moderate Southerners into South Carolina's camp. Yet if he did not seek the authority and things came to blows, he might stand accused of acting illegally if he did not have permission from Congress to enforce the customs laws.

In the darkness, his only solace was the memory of Rachel. He had sat up deep in the night in many battlefield tents before, his soldiers asleep, his mind racing, and now he was doing so again. Writing Poinsett, Jackson yearned for information. "Give me the earliest intelligence of the first armed force that appears in the field to sustain the ordinance [of nullification]— the first act of treason committed."

Poinsett did not think it would be long. "The Nullifiers are extremely active and do keep up the excitement in an extraordinary manner," Poinsett told Jackson. "They drill and exercise their men without intermission." On Friday, January 18, Hayne urged James Henry Hammond to prepare for "protracted warfare." Meanwhile, Poinsett said, "revolutionists in North Carolina and especially Georgia" were offering the nullifiers help. "I expect the next move will be secession," he added on Sunday, January 20. Jackson was still unwilling to strike the first blow. "The nullifiers in your state have placed themselves thus far in the wrong," Jackson said. "They must be kept there"—for as long as they were at fault and could not cast themselves as victims of armed federal force, the moral advantage remained with Jackson and with the Union.

Clay saw Jackson's political dilemma: "He has marked out two victims—South Carolina and the tariff—and the only question with him is which shall be first immolated." The manufacturing states did not want the tariff cut, the agrarian states were worried about creeping nationalism, and no one was enamored of the idea of giving the president the powers in the measure. The Calhoun newspaper, the **Telegraph,** worried that the Force Bill "arms the executive with the entire naval and military force of the country," which in turn would transform Jackson into a "military dictator." Even a senator friendly to Jackson, William R. King of Alabama, disliked putting "the whole military power of the Government at the discretion of the President. I can never consent, however great my confidence in the executive, to clothe any mortal man with such tremendous and unlimited powers."

Such reactions were more emotional than rational. Much of the Force Bill concerned details about collecting the federal tariffs in Charleston in the event of insurrection. The section of the proposed legislation involving the president's military authority was less revolutionary than many believed. Two existing laws—one from 1795, the other from 1807—gave Jackson all the technical power he needed both to call out state militias and to use federal troops to enforce federal law. (All he had to do was first issue a proclamation warning the rebels to disperse.) What Jackson was asking for—and herein lay part of his political genius—was congressional endorsement of force **in this instance**. By proposing the Force Bill, Jackson was implying that he needed it to act, which he did not—which in turn meant that he had placed himself in the best possible political position. If Congress passed the bill, then he had the might of the national government behind him; if it did not, he could do one of two things: either choose not to act, citing the will of Congress, or fall back on the older laws and strike anyway.

IT WAS GOOD politics, giving Jackson what the best politicians manage to create: options. His foes in Washington engaged the debate on the terms Jackson had set, which gave the White House an advantage in the crisis, for the arguments were taking place within boundaries it had drawn.

As January ended, it was clear that the battle would be between Washington and South Carolina. After flirting with Calhoun and the nullifiers, Georgia, Alabama, Mississippi, and North Carolina decided to let South Carolina stand alone. Mississippi's ultimate decision was representative of the rest of the South's: "We detest the tariff, but we will hold to the Union," a correspondent from Mississippi wrote to Andrew Donelson on Sunday, January 6, 1833—which was, really, the best Jackson could hope for. Under Governor Floyd, Virginia weighed its options but finally backed down.

It was probably a good thing for Floyd that the state decided to cast its lot with Jackson rather than with Calhoun. On Thursday, January 24, 1833, a weary Jackson told Poinsett: "Even if the Governor of Virginia should have the folly to attempt to prevent the militia from marching through his state to put the faction in South Carolina down and place himself at the head of an armed force for such a wicked purpose, I would arrest him at the head of his troops and hand him over to the civil authority for trial."

Strong words, and Jackson knew that if things came to such a pass it would mean civil war. "It is very late and my eyes grow dim," he told Poinsett. "Keep me well advised, and constantly." There was much to monitor. "I understand that Governor Hayne is making every preparation for warlike measure," Washington Irving wrote the next day. "I hope and trust that this will all turn out a game of brag."

On Thursday, January 31, South Carolina held a day of fasting to pray for the success of its cause. It was cloudy and cool in Columbia, where the Reverend Thomas Goulding, a Presbyterian clergyman, preached a sermon Samuel Cram Jackson thought "rather a **slim** affair," but outside the pulpit things were moving: "All went to the Methodists to see the military parade their companies of volunteers."

IN WASHINGTON, THE weather was clear as the congressional debate over nullification began. Fanny Kemble, the British actress, was in the capital to perform and left a diary of the city. "We walked up to the Capitol," Kemble wrote. "The day was most beautifully bright and sunny, and the mass of white building, with its terraces and columns, stood out in fine relief against the cloudless blue sky."

The women of the city, as was their custom, flooded into the House and Senate chambers. In the Senate, spectators climbed the narrow steps and walked through the door to the gallery, past a sign saying:

GENTLEMEN WILL BE PLEASED NOT TO PLACE
THEIR FEET ON THE BOARD IN FRONT OF THE GALLERY,
AS THE DIRT FROM THEM FALLS UPON SENATORS HEADS.

According to John Coffee, who was in Washington, gentlemen were having a difficult time getting anywhere near the action, let alone close enough to put their feet up. The women, Coffee said, "fill the legislative halls when it is understood that some lofty spirit is to speak, so that it is very difficult for the members to retain their seats or a backwoodsman to be allowed to stand near the door and look in."

No one knew what to expect. "I can give you no definitive opinion as to what will be done here," Clay wrote to his son from Washington on Thursday, January 3, 1833. "There is a general feeling of great instability in the present state of things. The Union is not believed to be free from danger whatever course may be pursued." True to his nature, though, Clay was pursuing a course of compromise, looking for a middle ground before it was too late.

Friday, February 1, 1833, was the first deadline, the date South Carolina had announced it would suspend the collection of the federal tariff, possibly leading to violence. From Washington, Calhoun urged the state to hold off for a bit. "**To take issue now** would be to play into the hands of the administration," Calhoun said. "I feel confident we want time only to ensure victory. The cause is a great one; greater than that of the Revolution." The nullifiers agreed. They would wait to see what Congress, and Jackson, would do. The first deadline thus passed quietly. "The **famous day** fixed for the operation of one 'Ordinance,' " Samuel Cram Jackson wrote in his diary on February 1, "but all is calm—no bloodshed—a beautiful day."

CLAY HAD BEEN at work on a compromise tariff since the middle of December, and spoke in the Senate to make the case for reform on Tuesday, February 12, 1833. Fix the tariff, and foil nullification. Foil nullification, and undercut the Force Bill. Undercut the Force Bill, and check Jackson.

Praising "that great principle of compromise and concession which lies at the bottom of our institutions," Clay was able to do what Jackson could not, for Jackson, though privately working for resolution, stood by his public position, which was one of implacability. South Carolina, Clay said, should be treated with respect, not contempt, so long as she gave up nullification in exchange for the lower tariff.

"If there be any who want civil war, who want to see the blood of any portion of our countrymen spilt, I am not one of them," Clay said. "I wish to see war of no kind; but, above all, I do not desire to see civil war. . . . God alone knows where such a war would end."

Subtly alluding to the impression that Jackson was intent on punishing the state in general and Calhoun in particular, Clay urged the Senate to rise above animosity. South Carolina, he said, "has been with us before, when her ancestors mingled in the throng of battle, and as I hope our posterity will mingle with hers, for ages and centuries to come, in the united defense of liberty, and for the honor and glory of the Union, I do not wish to see her degraded or defaced as a member of this confederacy."

Clay might think Jackson heavy-handed, but the president was deftly maneuvering behind the scenes. Reassuring Poinsett that the Unionists would not be abandoned, Jackson nevertheless asserted again and again that the nullifiers would have to make the first move. "Notwithstanding all their tyranny and blustering conduct, until some act of force is committed or there is an assemblage of an armed force by the orders of your Governor . . . to resist the execution of the laws of the United States, the Executive of the United

States has no legal and constitutional power to order the militia into the field to suppress it, and not then, until his proclamation commanding the insurgents to disperse has been issued," Jackson wrote on February 7. Be firm, Jackson said, but know, too, that there was hope. "The tariff will be reduced to the wants of the government, if not at this session of Congress, certainly at the next," he told Poinsett—a sign that Jackson believed a compromise was not only possible but likely.

The prospects for a peaceful resolution were rising, but Calhoun thought Jackson was another Macbeth who dreamed of "the image of a Crown." Over two days, February 15 and 16, he held the floor of the Senate, making the case for state sovereignty and against the Force Bill. The argument meant everything to him.

THE FORCE BILL, Calhoun said, was "a question of self-preservation" to South Carolina. If it passed and if Jackson used its powers, "it will be resisted, at every hazard—even that of death itself," Calhoun said. "Death is not the greatest calamity: there are others still more terrible to the free and brave, and among them may be placed the loss of liberty and honor. There are thousands of her brave sons who, if need be, are prepared cheerfully to lay down their lives in defense of the State, and the great principles of constitutional liberty for which she is contending. God forbid that this should become necessary! It never can be, unless this government is resolved to bring the question to extremity, when her gallant sons will stand prepared to perform the last duty—to die nobly."

It was a classic Calhoun performance. "Mr. Calhoun is **not** a fine looking man, so far from it he looks more like his **Satanic Majesty** when he gets into one of his violent passions (as he always does when he speaks himself or hears any one of the opposite side)," Mary Coffee wrote, "with clenched fists, teeth grinning from ear to ear, and his great white eyes. . . . Poor creature, I am sorry for him when he is not in a passion, for then he has a very melancholy expression." Clay could find Calhoun more than a little tiresome, even self-dramatic. Calhoun, Clay said, seemed "careworn, with furrowed brow, haggard and intensely gazing, looking as if he were dissecting the last abstraction which sprung from the metaphysician's brain, and muttering to himself, in half-uttered tones, 'This is indeed a real crisis.'"

When Calhoun was done, Webster, who favored the Force Bill, rose. "The people of the United States are one people," he said. "They are one in making war, and one in making peace; they are one in regulating commerce, and one in laying duties of imposts. The very end and purpose of the Constitution was to make them one people in these particulars; and it has effectually accomplished its object."

The next day, Sunday, February 17, Jackson wrote Poinsett: "The bill granting the powers asked will pass into law. Mr. Webster replied to Mr. Calhoun yesterday, and, it is said, demolished him. It is believed by more than one that Mr. C. is in a state of dementation—his speech was a perfect failure; and Mr. Webster handled him as a child."

"WELL, CLAY, THESE are fine fellows," Delaware senator John Clayton remarked, gesturing toward Calhoun and his followers. "It won't do to let old Jackson hang them. We must save them." What emerged was the Compromise of 1833, in which there was tariff reform for the South (though with higher rates over a longer period of time than many Southerners would have liked), a Force Bill for the nationalists, and distribution of public land revenues for the West (Jackson pocket vetoed this last measure). Clay's tariff bill very gradually lowered duties over the next decade. This was, in Clay's words, the olive branch to the sword of the Force Bill.

The debate had provided Calhoun, Webster, and Clay an enormous stage, and they jousted with skill and verve. In telling the story of nullification, many historians have understandably portrayed Clay as the hero of the piece—"the Great Compromiser" at work. Even his enemies saw him in this light. John Randolph of Roanoke, a Southerner who had long opposed Clay, recognized the significance of Clay's achievement in reconciling the conflicting interests. "Help me up," said the dying Randolph as Clay spoke one day. **"I have come here to hear that voice."** Webster is depicted as the thundering defender of Union, Calhoun as the tortured advocate for the states. When he makes an appearance, Jackson is sometimes painted the way his contemporary enemies (mistakenly) thought of him—

as a trigger-happy warrior raging against Calhoun in the White House, eager to march south and fight.

It takes nothing away from Clay's justified renown as a statesman to say that Jackson has not always been given his due for his own conduct in the crisis. Far from being a warmonger, Jackson was the first player in the drama to propose reforming the tariff; the Verplanck bill came from Treasury Secretary McLane, with Jackson's approval.

Had Jackson been truly unwilling to compromise, he would have found the means to use military force against South Carolina. He held back only when he chose to hold back, and struck only when he chose to strike. He had an intuitive sense of timing that served him well, and this capacity to find the right moment for action never served America better than it did in the winter of 1832–33.

Operating on two levels, Jackson projected an image of strength while looking for a way out. In the White House, Jackson summoned senators to urge this maneuver and that device as the tariff bill made its way through Congress. Even at his most hawkish, Jackson was clear that he would resort to violence only after the South Carolinians did, not before. "I beg of you not to be disturbed by any thing you hear from the alarmists at this place," he wrote Van Buren, adding: "Be assured that I have and will act with all . . . forbearance."

Jackson sought the preservation of the Union, not personal vengeance; a powerful presidency, not a military dictatorship. He achieved that on Saturday,

March 2, 1833, when he signed both the compromise tariff and the Force Bill into law. "We have beat the Nullifiers and things are quiet for a time—I verily thought we should have had a struggle and a short civil war, and was prepared once more to take the field," Joel Poinsett wrote a friend on Monday, March 25, 1833. "I was exceedingly indignant with these Radicals and rather desired to put them down with a strong arm. . . . I have fought the good fight manfully and zealously, and now I am laying out grounds and making a garden."

Poinsett was not alone in seeking ways to recover his strength. The toll of the season, and of the congressional session, had been heavy, and Henry Clay crashed with what he called "the most violent cold I ever had."

JACKSON WAS, AS ever, vigilant yet optimistic. "Keep me constantly advised of matters relating to the conduct or movements of the nullifiers," he wrote Poinsett on Wednesday, March 6, "and all will be well, and the federal union preserved." Two months afterward, on Wednesday, May 1, 1833, Jackson observed in a letter that "the tariff was only the pretext, and disunion and southern confederacy the real object. The next pretext will be the negro, or slavery question." Six days later, the president named a postmaster for New Salem, Illinois, a twenty-four-year-old lawyer who had lost a race for the state legislature. He was a Clay man, but the post was hardly major, and Abraham Lincoln was happy to accept the appointment.

CHAPTER 20

★

GREAT IS THE STAKE
PLACED IN OUR HANDS

NEITHER HENRY CLAY'S health nor his spirits could have been helped by the spectacle of Inauguration Day 1833—a ceremony Clay had hoped would be his own hour of glory. The day was wretchedly cold, so cold that the outdoor festivities were canceled and the ceremonies moved indoors to the House chamber. Flanked by Andrew Donelson and Martin Van Buren, Jackson gave a brief but important address, a much more substantive speech than the first inaugural on the nearby steps four years before. Putting an intellectual frame around the previous months of brinkmanship and negotiation, in his own way Jackson was as eloquent as Clay had been about the importance of compromise—and, unlike Calhoun, to support his conclusions he invoked not theory but his own hard-earned history, squarely placing himself, and the presidency, in the center of the national drama. "My experience in public concerns and the observation of a life somewhat advanced confirm the opinions long since imbibed by me, that the destruction of our state governments or the annihilation of their control over the local concerns of the people would lead directly to revolution and anarchy, and finally to despotism and military domination," Jackson said.

A sentence later, addressing the question of nullification, he went on: "Solemnly impressed with these considerations, my countrymen will ever find me ready to exercise my constitutional powers in arresting measures which may directly or indirectly encroach upon the rights of the states or tend to consolidate all political power in the general government. But of equal, and, indeed, of incalculable, importance is the union of these states, and the sacred duty of all to contribute to its preservation by a liberal support of the general government in the exercise of its just powers." Having reassured the states' rights elements in the country—which included his new vice president, Van Buren—his passions fully engaged, Jackson then delivered one of the great passages of oratory of his long public life, a passage little remembered and little quoted:

Without union our independence and liberty would never have been achieved; without union they can never be maintained. Divided into twenty-four, or even a smaller number, of separate communities, we shall see our internal trade burdened with numberless restraints and exactions; communication between distant points and sections obstructed or cut off; our sons made soldiers to deluge with blood the fields they now till in peace; the mass of our people borne down and impoverished by taxes to support armies and navies, and military leaders at the head of their victorious legions becoming our lawgivers and judges. The loss of liberty, of all good government, of peace, plenty, and happiness, must inevitably follow a dissolution of the Union. In supporting it, therefore, we support all that is dear to the freeman and the philanthropist.

The time at which I stand before you is full of interest. The eyes of all nations are fixed on our Republic. The event of the existing crisis will be decisive in the opinion of mankind of the practicability of our federal system of government. Great is the stake placed in our hands; great is the responsibility which must rest upon the people of the United States. Let us realize the importance of the attitude in which we stand before the world. Let us exercise forbearance and firmness. Let us extricate our country from the dangers which surround it and learn wisdom from the lessons they inculcate.

The most enduring political rhetoric both inspires and instructs, lifting an audience outside its natural selfish cares to see how a certain course will, in the end, serve a nation and its people well. This is a matter of more than soaring prose or vivid imagery, though both are crucial. It is also about arming the audience with facts or thoughts they have not yet known or contemplated. Jackson's second inaugural address met both tests. Withstand the temptations of the moment, Jackson was saying, and the nation would be all the stronger for it, all the more respected, all the more special. Jackson's words were not those of an incipient tyrant, or a shallow thinker, or a barely restrained bully. They were the words of a man who thought of himself as an American first and last—not a Carolinian, not a Tennessean, not a Westerner, not a Southerner, but an American.

A different, less emotionally nationalistic president in these middle years of the Republic might not have been able to balance the forces of respect for the essential rights of the states with a devotion to the cause of the Union. Jackson was perfectly able to do this, for he believed in both, and he knew that both would be forever in tension and sometimes in conflict. It could be no other way in a democratic republic formed from the elements that had formed America. He wanted the power to act as freely as he could because he believed his judgment would serve the country well, for he made no distinction between himself and a broad idea of "the people." Egotistical, yes; arrogant, probably. But to some degree politics and statecraft always involve the character of the leader, and the character of Andrew Jackson was, in the end, well suited for the demands of the White House. He was strong and shrewd, patriotic and manipulative, clear-eyed and determined.

Closing his inaugural address, he said he longed to "foster with our brethren in all parts of the country a spirit of liberal concession and compromise, and, by reconciling our fellow-citizens to those partial sacrifices which they must unavoidably make for the preservation of a greater good, to recommend our invaluable government and Union to the confidence and affections of the American people." Evincing a practical understanding of how a leader could make real an idealistic vision of public life, Jackson was engaged in presidential leadership of the highest order, for he was being forthright about a central truth of a democratic republic: that if each part made a sacrifice of some kind, then the whole could thrive, producing, hopefully, what Jackson called "a united and happy people."

SUCH WAS THE covenant Jackson offered the nation at a critical moment. If the different parts of the country would surrender something dear to them for the sake of a larger cause, then they would be repaid with more liberty, more prosperity, and more happiness than if each element chose to guard its selfish interests, sacrificing the whole and foreclosing the possibilities of democracy. What Jackson once called "the prudence, the wisdom, and the courage" of a good people will leave a better, freer nation to the next generation, which will in turn, it is hoped, be faithful stewards of the American experiment in liberty. That, at least, was Jackson's "most fervent prayer" for America to "that Almighty Being before whom I now stand," he said in closing, beseeching God to deliver the country "from dangers of all kinds." As a soldier of the people, Jackson would do all he could in the cause. For him it was the work of a lifetime.

The inaugural address was a brilliant but exhausting effort. With his sense of theater, Jackson, who wore his great cloak to and from the ceremonies, showed no signs of strain in the House chamber. After his speech, he took the oath again from John Marshall—it was to be the last of the chief justice's nine inaugurations—and returned to the White House through the brutal cold, where he stood with Emily to receive well-wishers. One guest, Philip Hone, glimpsed the troubling reality behind Jackson's dignified demeanor. "I would bet large odds that he does not outlive the present term of his office," Hone said—though people, including Jackson himself, had been futilely betting against his health for years. Still, by late afternoon it had already been a long day, and Emily did what Rachel would have done: she sent him to bed.

EMILY AND ANDREW led the White House circle to the inaugural party, again held at Carusi's. Jackson settled in for a quiet night in the White House as Calhoun traveled south, fast, en route to Columbia. The tariff had not been cut as much as South Carolina had asked, but it had still been cut, and Calhoun thought it wisest for the state to hold its fire. As the historian William Freehling wrote, the Clay rates were twice what the Nullification Ordinance had called for, but even James Henry Hammond "confessed that he thought that a majority of Carolinians would accept the compromise." Hammond was right.

A week after Jackson's inauguration, on Monday, March 11, 1833, the South Carolina convention met to consider what to do in light of the compromise tariff and the Force Bill. According to Samuel Cram

Jackson's diary of the convention, George McDuffie "very eloquently, **bitterly,** and **sarcastically**" attacked the compromise tariff, "condemned the administration and bragged about the South. His speech [was] calculated to influence the South against the North," and Hayne seemed "very bitter and violent."

Still, the ferocity was the exception, not the rule. The combination of the reduced duties and the fact that Congress had given the president the power to strike militarily both pacified and sobered many of the nullifiers, who rescinded the ordinance and accepted the tariff. The Force Bill was different, though. South Carolina would stand down for now, but its pride would not allow Jackson's expanded powers to go unnoticed. And so the convention nullified the Force Bill—a symbolic gesture, to be sure, but a telling one, for it signaled that though a battle over states' rights had ended, the war had not.

To underscore the point, hard-liners pressed for a test oath for officeholders to pledge, according to one proposal, "primary and paramount allegiance" to the state. Calhoun urged moderation—"We must not think of secession, but in the last extremity," he said in late January. "It would be the most fatal of all steps." While the crisis was resolved, however, its causes endured.

Frustrated by Jackson's apparent victory, the attorney general of South Carolina, Robert Barnwell Smith—who later changed his name to Robert Barnwell Rhett, after an ancestor—dispensed with politic indirection or code in remarks to the convention. "A people, owning slaves, are mad, or worse than mad, who do not hold their destinies in their own hands," he said. A powerful federal government could do slavery no good, Smith said: "Let Gentlemen not be deceived. It is not the Tariff—not Internal Improvement—nor yet the Force Bill, which constitutes the great evil against which we are contending. . . . These are but the forms in which the despotic nature of the Government is evinced—but it is the despotism which constitutes the evil: and until this Government is made a limited Government . . . there is no liberty—no security for the South."

From Jackson's vantage point, however, the tariff was cut, the powers of his office expanded, and the crisis eased. For a few days in the middle of March, calm prevailed in the White House, a well-earned respite. Jackson even indulged in philosophy, a luxury his victory had afforded him. "Reason must, when exercised, always triumph over error," he wrote Poinsett in March. Reason did not always triumph, but in this case Jackson believed it had, and he drew strength and renewed self-confidence from the struggle.

WELCOME FAMILY NEWS also cheered Jackson. In Tennessee, Mary Eastin Polk delivered a healthy girl, Sarah Rachel, and Jackson jocularly warned her of the competition in store with Sarah Yorke Jackson's Rachel, who had been born just before the presidential election the year before. "You know I have always been an advocate for the harmony of connections and families," he told Mary. "To insure this harmony between you and

Sarah I would advise you to submit the sprightliness and beauty of your Sarah Rachel and her little Rachel to the adjudication of a court of inquiry to settle this important matter, for Sarah writes me that her Rachel is one of the most sprightly and beautiful she ever saw. . . ." Closer to home, across the hall in the Donelson nursery, John Samuel Donelson, approaching his first birthday, had been sick, Jackson reported, "but his teeth have appeared through the gums, and he is better."

John Samuel's mother, meanwhile, was worried about the end of the season. "Washington will be very dull this summer," Emily wrote her mother on Monday, April 22, 1833. Cora Livingston was marrying; Louise, whom Emily called "one of my best friends," was moving to France with her husband as he took up his post as minister. But as Emily should have known by now, Andrew Jackson's Washington was never dull for long.

★

CHAPTER 21

MY MIND IS
MADE UP

JACKSON NEVER FLINCHED. On Monday, May 6, 1833, the presidential party was on a steamboat excursion to Fredericksburg, Virginia, when a disturbed former navy officer, Robert B. Randolph, came through the crowd aboard the vessel. There had been no warning sign, nothing to lead anyone to suspect a threat, but Randolph leaped at the president as though to assault him.

Andrew Donelson lunged to protect Jackson. Fueled by adrenaline and affection, the nephew was ready to kill to save his uncle. "Had I known the man or had any intimation of his presence nothing would have been easier for me than to put him to death," Donelson told Emily's brother Stockley—an assertion that must have sprung viscerally from Donelson's love for Jackson, for Donelson, who was not armed, could have used only his hands to slay the assailant. A table separated Donelson from Jackson and Randolph, and Donelson was joined by others in "hurling the villain from his position." Randolph bloodied Jackson's face, but the president's stare stopped the assailant. "The object of the attack was no doubt assassination, but the ruffian was unnerved by the countenance of Uncle and he could do no more than display his intention," Donelson said.

Still, blood had been drawn. It was the first such physical assault on an American president, and the country reacted nervously, seeing the assassination attempt as a sign of more fundamental tensions. Washington Irving happened to be in Fredericksburg and spent time with Jackson afterward. "It is a brutal transaction, which I cannot think of without indignation, mingled with a feeling of almost despair, that our national character should receive such crippling wounds from the hands of our own citizens," Irving wrote his brother. An admirer of the president's from Alexandria, Virginia, offered to avenge the attack. "Sir, if you will pardon me in case I am tried and convicted, I will kill Randolph for this insult to you, in fifteen minutes!"

Jackson demurred. "No, sir, I cannot do that," he replied. "I want no man to stand between me and my assailants, and none to take revenge on my account." He told Van Buren that if he had been standing rather than sitting behind the table, Randolph "never would have moved with life from the tracks he stood in." Jackson's frontier blood was up. He did not want, he said, "a military guard around the President," which left only this option: officials, he said, had "to be prepared . . . [to] shoot down or otherwise destroy those dastardly assassins whenever they approach us."

Randolph was a figure in the Eaton affair. John

Eaton and John Timberlake (Margaret Eaton's first husband, who had died while serving aboard the **Constitution**) had been accused of financial impropriety involving money that Timberlake had controlled as a navy purser. Kendall investigated and came to suspect Randolph, who had taken Timberlake's place as purser on the **Constitution** after Timberlake's death, of misconduct. All of this led to controversy in Washington and a naval court of inquiry; in April 1833, just before the attack, Jackson had dismissed Randolph from the navy.

The spectacle of assassination belonged more to the worlds of ancient Rome and the kingdoms of Europe, where struggles for power between monarchs, aristocrats, and the populace often led to plots and upheavals. Randolph's attack exacerbated the sense among Jackson's critics that the president had become a king, the White House a court, and Washington a conspiratorial capital.

FOR DONELSON, BLAIR, and Kendall, 1833 and 1834 were very good years—years in which they held their greatest sway. They were soldiers in an army Jackson deployed to crush foes from Philadelphia to Paris; his push for power over the Bank, over Congress, and over foreign capitals kept him engaged in constant strife. He was, as ever, confident of victory. Once, on the way to the Rip Raps, riding by steamboat down the Chesapeake, the seas were rough, and a fellow passenger, James Parton reported, "exhibited a good deal of alarm." Jackson was preternaturally calm. "You are uneasy," he said to the worried man. "You have never sailed with **me** before, I see."

In the White House, attention was once more turning to Nicholas Biddle. The recharter had been vetoed and Jackson had been reelected, but the federal government's deposits remained in the Bank, and Biddle could again try to renew the Bank in the hope that Congress would override Jackson's veto. Understanding this, Jackson looked for a way to destroy the Bank now, rather than be content with having denied it a future beyond its 1836 date of expiration. "The hydra of corruption is only **scotched, not dead**," Jackson told James K. Polk. Though the House had passed a resolution (by a margin of 109 to 46) asserting that the government's deposits were safe in the Bank and should be left there, Jackson was unconvinced. The vote came after the House decided to reject a report, crafted by Polk, alleging corruption.

"Biddle is actually using the people's money to frustrate the people's will," Blair said to Jackson early in 1833. "He is using the money of the government for the purpose of breaking down the government. If he had not the public money he could not do it." This was an obsession with Blair, who told William Lewis that "the damned bank ought to be put down, and the only effectual way of doing it was to take from it the whole of the public money."

Jackson agreed with his editor. "He shan't have the public money," Jackson said of Biddle. "I'll remove the deposits! Blair, talk with our friends about this, and let me know what they think of it."

Blair then canvassed a circle of Jacksonians—and found that none of them was for removing the deposits. Van Buren was against it; so was Silas Wright, Jr., of New York, who argued, James Parton said, "that the withdrawal of the public money from the bank would compel it to curtail its business to such a degree that half the merchants in the country would fail." Kendall and Van Buren had a tense conversation about the issue. The vice president was cool to the idea, leading Kendall to suggest that a strong Bank would probably be an able ally of the National Republicans in taking the White House away from the Democrats—that is, away from Van Buren—in three years' time. It had been an unpleasant scene. Kendall's son-in-law noted that "the parties separated, both somewhat excited."

When Blair gave Jackson the bad news that few of the White House's allies favored removing the deposits, Jackson was unimpressed. "Oh, my mind is made up on **that** matter," Jackson said. "Biddle shan't have the public money to break down the public administration with. It's settled. My mind's made up."

Even for Jackson, such resolution was more easily articulated than accomplished. Respectable opinion doubted the president had the authority to do what he wanted to do. It was Kendall who saw that breaking the Bank once and for all required taking the fight from the capital to the country. The crucial first step in democratic leadership: get the people on the president's side.

The story of Jackson's presidency thus far was about

the growth of executive power, both formally and informally. The veto on grounds of policy differences was a formal means that Jackson had put at a president's disposal. The building of public support for a president's policies, so evident in the battle over the Bank veto the previous year and in the struggle against South Carolina, was a more informal but no less potent weapon. The deposits battle would test both formal authority (who had the legal power to move the money?) and the president's ability to persuade the public of the wisdom of a particular course.

Kendall made the case to Jackson one day when the president was worrying that if he "did cause the deposits to be removed from the Bank, Congress, having resolved that they were safe there, would require them to be restored."

Kendall dismissed the anxiety. "Let the removal take place so early as to give us several months to defend the measure in the **Globe,** and we will bring up the people to sustain you with a power which Congress dare not resist," he told Jackson. His confidence was not mere bluster; he was gaining a reputation for his ability to require absolute loyalty from Jackson's men. (Hearing that Kendall was to "take charge of appointments," Samuel Ingham remarked bitterly that "the new men must harmonize"—a favorite Jackson term—"ie sign their names and register commissions decreed by the '**Argus club.**' ")

One obstacle: the new secretary of the Treasury, William J. Duane, who took office on Saturday, June 1,

1833, replacing Louis McLane, who had moved to the State Department after Edward Livingston was made minister to France.

A Philadelphian, the son of the editor of the Jeffersonian newspaper the **Aurora,** Duane was a businessman, lawyer, and legislator who was chosen, in part, to give Pennsylvania a seat in the Cabinet. At first reluctant—Jackson's Cabinet officers did not last long—Duane eventually accepted. Duane was an opponent of the Bank, but Jackson apparently never asked him what he might think of removing the deposits. By law the Treasury secretary was empowered to decide what to do with the public deposits; whether or not his decision had to reflect the will of the president would become the question of the hour.

DUANE'S TENURE BEGAN badly and never improved. On the evening of his first day as secretary, a Saturday, he was visited at his lodgings by Reuben Whitney, a merchant and former Bank official who had become an ally of Kendall's. To Duane's surprise and dismay, Whitney undertook to explain the political lay of the land—a task Jackson had chosen not to undertake himself. Whitney spoke bluntly. "He stated that the President had concluded to take upon himself the responsibility of directing the Secretary of the Treasury to remove the public deposits from [the] bank, and to transfer them to state banks," Duane recalled. Whitney added that "no doubt the President would soon speak to" Duane on the subject.

The new secretary did not take Whitney's visit well. "The communication thus made to me created surprise and mortification," he recalled. "I was surprised at the position of affairs which it revealed; and mortified at the low estimate which had been formed of the independence of my character" in the assumption that he would fall into line with the machinations of the White House. Duane complained to Louis McLane, who had recruited him. The next night Kendall himself appeared to see if he could assuage Duane's pride and make sure everything was in order.

It was not. Duane was correct and cool, saying virtually nothing to the president's adviser. "I did not invite nor check communications," Duane recalled. "Very little was said, and, perhaps, because I could not wholly conceal my mortification at an attempt, apparently made with the sanction of the President, to reduce me to a mere cipher in the administration."

The next morning, Monday, June 3, 1833, Duane went to the White House to see Jackson. "I said I feared that I should not be able to see the subject in the light in which the President viewed it," Duane recalled, "to which he remarked that he liked frankness [but] that unless the bank was broken down, it would break us down." Despite the veto, Jackson insisted, Biddle would still attempt to buy a victory for recharter in Congress before it was too late. If the last Congress had stayed a week longer, Jackson said, "two thirds would have been secured for the bank by corrupt means; and . . . the like result might be apprehended at the next Congress." Jackson wanted to withdraw the deposits, and he was the president. If Jackson thought the debate was over, it was over.

Duane disagreed, and Jackson could not even generate consensus among his official Cabinet, which made the work of Blair, Kendall, and others all the more important—and, to Duane, irritating. "I had heard rumors of the existence of an influence at Washington, unknown to the Constitution and to the country, and the conviction that they were well founded now became irresistible," Duane said. "I knew that four of the six members of the last Cabinet, and that four members of the present Cabinet, opposed a removal of the deposits, and yet their exertions were nullified by individuals whose intercourse with the President was clandestine."

Jackson was about to leave Washington for a major tour of New England, and he promised to send Duane more thoughts from the road. In the meantime, Jackson asked his new Treasury secretary to "reflect with a view to the public good." There was no doubt what Jackson believed the public good to be.

CHAPTER 22

★

HE APPEARED TO FEEL
AS A FATHER

"UNCLE'S HEALTH IS as usual," Emily wrote
her mother in the spring of 1833. He was, she
said, "often complaining. . . . He expects to
start the last of May on his tour to the North and will be
gone about two months." It took a bit longer for Jackson
to depart, but Emily's worries about his health were on
the mark, for he would have to force himself through his
trip minute by minute, hour by hour, and day by day.

Rising early on the morning of Thursday, June 6,
1833, he wrote a quick note to Van Buren before
setting out on the Northern tour. "I want relaxation
from business . . . but where can I get rest?" Jackson
asked. "I fear not on this earth. When I see you I have
much to say to you. The Bank and the change of deposits have engrossed my mind very much, is a perplexing subject, and I wish your opinion before I
finally act."

Finishing the letter, Jackson walked out of the
White House and stepped into his stagecoach for his
journey into enemy territory. Josiah Quincy, the son
of the president of Harvard University and a cousin of

John Quincy Adams, recalled that parents in the Northeast sometimes invoked the name of Andrew Jackson to frighten misbehaving children. According to Harriet Martineau, a New England Sunday school teacher once asked a child who killed Abel. The answer: "General Jackson."

Yet everything that happened to Jackson as he traveled from Baltimore to Philadelphia to New Jersey to New York to Boston filled him with confidence, convinced him of the affection of the masses, and confirmed his sense that he was at one with the people of the country. Four days into the trip, as he prepared for bed, he sat in candlelight after dinner to write to his son. The crowds and cheers of the day were still with him.

"I shall not attempt to describe the feelings of the people," Jackson said. "Suffice it to say that it surpassed anything I ever witnessed." After another four days of parades, toasts, and accolades through New Jersey and New York, Jackson returned to his lodgings after another dinner, took a warm bath, and again wrote to Andrew junior: "I have witnessed enthusiasms before, but never before have I witnessed such a scene of personal regard as I have today, and ever since I left Washington. I have bowed to upwards of two hundred thousand people today—never has there been such affection of the people before I am sure evinced. Party has not been seen here." In Boston thousands of children lined the streets, their parents behind them, and to Andrew Donelson, who was with Jackson, it seemed the only sounds were "shouts and the roar of artillery."

. . .

JACKSON LOVED THE crowds as they loved him. Knowing that they were surging into the streets to see him, he stood for hours, determined not to disappoint. The sun was so hot at Philadelphia that his face, after five hours in the open air, had blistered, but he would not stand down as long as there were people who wanted to glimpse their president. Everything was to be endured to meet the expectations and reciprocate the respect of the public. The wadding from a cannon nearly singed his hair; a low-lying bridge collapsed just behind him, sending his entourage, including Donelson and Van Buren, into the water. But Jackson persevered. "The smile—the grace—the manner of the President is very engaging," one newspaper said. "He appeared to feel as a father surrounded by a numerous band of children—happy in their affections and loving them with all a parent's love.—Such are the impressions left by the visit of Andrew Jackson."

On a steamboat trip to Staten Island aboard the **Cinderella,** Jackson was talking with the Reverend Peter Van Pelt, Jr. Suffused with the apparently unending praise of the public, Jackson turned lyrical as they crossed New York harbor. "What a country God has given us!" he said. "How thankful we ought to be that God has given us such a country to live in."

"Yes, and this harbor, General, **we** think the finest thing in it."

"We have the best country, and the best institutions in the world," Jackson said. "No people have so much to be grateful for as we." His thoughts drifted to Philadelphia, to the bank on Chestnut Street. "But ah! My reverend friend, there is one thing that I fear will yet sap the foundation of our liberty—that monster institution, the bank of the United States! Its existence is incompatible with liberty. One of the two must fall—the bank or our free institutions. Next Congress, an effort to effect a recharter will be renewed; but my consent they shall never have!"

Jackson went on about Biddle at such length, Van Pelt recalled, that the minister, who was growing tired of Jackson's indictment, brought up Rachel in order to change the subject. "I hear, General, that you were blessed with a Christian companion."

The conversational ploy worked. "Yes, my wife was a pious, Christian woman," Jackson said. "She gave me the best advice, and I have not been unmindful of it. When the people, in their sovereign pleasure, elected me President of the United States, she said to me, 'Don't let your popularity turn your mind away from the duty you owe to God. Before Him we are all alike sinners, and to Him we must all alike give account. All these things will pass away, and you and I, and all of us, must stand before God.' I have never forgotten it, Doctor, and I never shall." Jackson wept at the memory.

Reflection was restorative, but the president's contemplation of the world that might be gave way to his understanding of the world as it was. There was some confusion among the officers of the boat as it approached Manhattan, and Jackson took the opportunity to offer his views on the nature of command. "I see around me many who have seen fewer years than I have, and what I now say may be of some use to them. Always take all the time to reflect that circumstances permit, but when the time for action has come, stop thinking."

ON WEDNESDAY, JUNE 26, 1833, Jackson went to Harvard to receive an honorary degree, and later, standing on Bunker Hill, commemorated the Revolution. He was resolute, but the physical toll of the tour was rising. "It is with great difficulty we can proportion his compliance with the kind wishes of the people to see him, to what is safe on the score of comfort and health, but nothing is omitted which can be done," Andrew wrote Emily. "You can scarcely conceive of the anxiety to be introduced to him."

Jackson had been a public figure—almost always the most important person in any room he happened to be in—since the victory at New Orleans nearly twenty years before. He was accustomed to the trappings of power and celebrity, to the tedious but flattering rounds of dinners and memorials and toasts. Even by the standards of his long national career, however, the glories in June 1833 were notable, and Jackson saw what John Quincy Adams sardonically called "this magnificent tour" as vindication for what he had done and as a mandate for what he was about to do.

The trip ended grimly. Throughout the journey he had rallied, even joking about his woes. ("Now, Doctor, I can do any thing you think proper to order, and bear as much as most men," Jackson told a doctor. "There are only two things I can't give up: one is coffee, and the other is tobacco.") En route from Massachusetts to New Hampshire, though, he was feeling so sick that some feared for his life. Andrew Donelson arranged for a return to Washington, arriving on July 4.

While Jackson fought his way back to health—or to what passed for health for him—the capital's players gauged the political effects of a six-month period that began with nullification and ended with the confluence of the Northern tour and the beginning of the deposits battle. Writing to London, Sir Charles Vaughan believed the laurels of the journey "proved the increase of his personal influence and popularity from the bold and decisive line of policy which he adopted when the dissension between the State of South Carolina and the General Government threatened a separation of the Union." Word of Jackson's condition was the only troubling note. "The friends of the President have been made very uneasy by the reports of his health having suffered by the fatigue to which he has been exposed, but the alarm for his safety has subsided upon his return."

And the enemies of the president? They found the ecstasy of the tour unsettling. The cries of affection, said the Richmond **Enquirer,** "were more like the homage of subjects to their ruler, than of a free people towards their first magistrate."

. . .

ON THE ROAD, Jackson had drafted a long paper to Duane about the deposits. Completed in Boston, dated June 26, it was accompanied by a letter, more personal in tone, about Jackson's desire to strike before Congress met late in the year: "Upon a careful review of the subject in all its bearings, I have come to the conclusion that it ought to be done as soon as we can get ready." Power was more easily obtained before the enemy could prepare.

The skirmish with Duane, then, grew more critical as the days and weeks passed. The more time Jackson spent fighting his own Treasury secretary, the less he would have to remove the deposits, distribute them around the country, and thus cripple the Bank's ability to buy its way to recharter. Biddle understood the game. Referring to Jackson's men, he wrote that "the gamblers are doing everything in their power to bend Mr. Duane to their purposes. But he knows them and will not yield an inch."

Duane replied to Jackson on Wednesday, July 10, six days after Jackson's return. By custom and by his reading of the Constitution, Duane believed that Congress held the power to decide the fate of the Bank. He was still thinking in pre-Jacksonian terms about the role of the president. "Legislators alone could duly investigate such important subjects," he told Jackson. This was a principled if naïve view for a man serving under Andrew Jackson to hold, but there it was.

Jackson asked Duane to call at the White House. The conversation opened gently. Jackson was worried, Duane recalled, that "we did not understand each other." To Jackson the issue could not be clearer, and he began to explain it all again. "My object, sir, is to save the country, and it will be lost if we permit the bank to exist," he said.

The battle between the president and his secretary of the Treasury went on for nearly another week. More letters were exchanged, more meetings held. Biddle watched from Philadelphia. "I wish to wait a little while until the smoke blows off before doing anything very decisive," Biddle wrote on Tuesday, July 30, 1833. "For when once we begin, we shall have many things to do, which will crush the Kitchen Cabinet at once."

AS BLAIR JOINED Jackson, Emily, Sarah, and the children in preparing for a month at the Rip Raps, Kendall and Donelson were dispatched to see whether the state banks would be open to receiving the deposits. "They tell me the state banks, through fear of the United States Bank, which can crush them at will, cannot be induced to take the public deposits and do the business of the government," Jackson had told Kendall.

"Send me to ask them, and I will settle the argument," Kendall had said.

"You shall go," said Jackson, and finally, after a long debate with Duane, Kendall went, and Donelson soon took off for Nashville with the same task.

Duane hated the idea of Kendall's and Donelson's

missions—he sensed that once Jackson had a detailed alternative to the Bank, he would move—and in a conversation at the White House with Jackson, said that he would resign rather than do something he disagreed with. "All that I can promise, consistently with the respect due to you as well as myself, is that, when the moment for decision after inquiry and discussion shall arrive," Duane said, "**I will concur with you, or retire.**"

For Jackson, the moment of decision had come and gone. At the Rip Raps in August, he whiled away the hours with Blair. It was not an entirely cheery time. On Sunday, July 7, 1833, his old friend John Coffee died, and in crisis the grieving Jackson turned, as he tended to do, to scripture. Writing Mary Coffee from the Rip Raps on Thursday, August 15, 1833, Jackson said: "My dear Mary, his request for my prayers for his dear wife and children will be bestowed with pleasure. They will be constantly offered up at the throne of grace for you all, and our dear Savior, has spoken it—'that he will be a father to the fatherless and a husband to the widow.'" To Van Buren, Jackson said that he was struck as David had been when "his son Jonathan" had died in the Old Testament.

Both allusions are revealing about Jackson's state of mind, for both are wrong. The words about being "a father to the fatherless and a husband to the widow" are not from Jesus but from Psalm Sixty-eight, and David's dead son was Absalom, not Jonathan. Jackson's biblical confusion, rare in his correspondence, suggests that these weeks of uncertainty about the deposits—time was passing, and he still had no developed plan to move the money—were troubling.

But distance from the capital did nothing to dim Jackson's resolve. "Mr. Blair," Jackson told his editor, "Providence may change me, but it is not in the power of a man to do it."

★

CHAPTER 23

THE PEOPLE, SIR,
ARE WITH ME

THE CABINET GATHERED at the White House on Tuesday, September 10, 1833. Kendall had returned in late August with news Jackson wanted to hear: there were plenty of state banks that would take the money and appeared sound. Jackson had his alternative.

Brandishing Kendall's summary of the mission to the banks, Jackson was eager to convince his skeptical secretaries that all would now be well. Though armed with details, he spoke with wariness and uncharacteristic nervousness, as though he feared Kendall's handiwork might be found wanting. "How shall we answer to God, our country, or ourselves if we permit the public money to be thus used to corrupt the people?" he said, but then struck a more pleading tone than he usually used. "I anxiously desire . . . that we should at least do something. The report, if you put confidence in it—and I think you may—shows the readiness of the state banks to take the public money, and their ability and safety as substitutes for the present agent. Why, then, should we hesitate? Why not proceed, I say, as the country expects us to do? Here are the papers. When you have read them let us come to an understanding."

Jackson was taking no chances on what the results of the Cabinet's reading might be. In a series of articles, the **Globe** singled Duane out for attack. Confronted by Duane, Jackson—the master of the **Globe**—denied any involvement in the newspaper offensive. "It is impossible to describe the earnestness of the President's professions in reply" to Duane's complaints, Duane recalled. "He declared that no one had attempted to shake his confidence . . . that he regretted even a difference in opinion between us; and that he would put all doubts at rest by conferring on me the highest appointment then at his disposal"—the mission to Russia.

Offered a way out, Duane chose not to take it and stayed at the Treasury. (The Russian post was one of Jackson's favorite ways to try to get rid of people. He had offered the same appointment to Ingham in the Cabinet chaos of the first term. It did not work then, either.) Jackson again made clear that Duane served at the president's pleasure—not his own, and not Congress's. "It is known what my determination is, and if he cannot act with me on that determination, he ought to withdraw," Jackson told Roger Taney.

The Cabinet met again on Wednesday, September 18, 1833, a date that marks a turning point in the making of the modern presidency. In a manuscript in Andrew Donelson's hand, apparently dictated at the Rip Raps (where Donelson had joined the president after his banking mission), Jackson revealed the direction of his thinking midway through his White House years—thinking that blended an instinct for the democratic with a vision of a dynamic presidency. "The divine right of kings and the prerogative authority of rulers have fallen before the intelligence of the age," Jackson said, continuing:

Standing armies and military chieftains can no longer uphold tyranny against the resistance of public opinion. The mass of the people have more to fear from combinations of the wealthy and professional classes— from an aristocracy which through the influence of riches and talents, insidiously employed, sometimes succeeds in preventing political institutions, however well adjusted, from securing the freedom of the citizen. . . . The President has felt it his duty to exert the power with which the confidence of his countrymen has clothed him in attempting to purge the government of all sinister influences which have been incorporated with its administration.

By the time the paper was revised (by Taney) and read aloud (by Donelson) it was drier, but at its heart lay the conviction that the 1832 presidential election had settled the matter: because Jackson had won, the people wanted—and expected—the Bank to die. By asking for a new charter the previous year, Jackson said, "the object avowed by many of the advocates of the bank was to **put the President to the test**, that the country might know his final determination relative to the bank prior to the ensuing election." And so the country learned it, in the unequivocal veto message. Now, a year or so later, "whatever may be the opinions of others, the President considers his reelection as a decision of the people against the banks," Jackson said. "He was sustained by a just people, and he desires to evince his gratitude by carrying into effect their decision so far as it depends upon him."

As the session broke up, Duane walked over to Jackson and asked for a copy of the message. Duane recalled asking "whether I was to understand him as directing me to remove the deposits? He replied that it was his desire that I should remove them, but upon **his** responsibility." Duane left the White House and, the next morning, said he needed one more day to decide what to do, which would have carried matters through to Friday, September 20.

On hearing this, Jackson decided, as he might have put it, that the time for thinking was over and the time for action had come. Donelson was sent to the Treasury with a stark message: news of Jackson's decision to remove the deposits would be published in the **Globe** the next morning, the twentieth. Duane protested, but it made no difference.

On the twenty-first, Duane himself raised the stakes and decided that he would not resign—Jackson would have to fire him. He wanted it made clear to the world that he had refused to carry out Jackson's orders.

"Then I suppose you intend to come out against me," Jackson said.

"Nothing is further from my thoughts. I . . . desire to do what is now my duty; and to defend myself if assailed hereafter."

"A secretary, sir, is merely an executive agent, a subordinate, and you may say so in self-defense."

But Duane would not resign, and so Jackson fired him. In a note drafted in Taney's hand dated Monday, September 23, Jackson dismissed Duane in a short paragraph. Because Duane's "feelings and sentiments" could not be reconciled with his own, Jackson said, "I feel myself constrained to notify you that your further services as Secretary of the Treasury are no longer required."

The more Jackson thought of the episode, the angrier he became. Writing to Van Buren to inform him that Duane was out and that Roger Taney would give up the attorney generalship to become secretary of the Treasury, Jackson was brutal. He now thought Duane's "conduct has been such of late that would induce a belief that he came into the Dept. as the secret agent of the Bank [and] to disclose the Cabinet secrets for its benefit, rather than to aid the Executive in the administration of the government." The removal of the deposits was to begin in a week's time, on Tuesday, October 1, 1833.

The story, Jackson thought, was over.

IN A WAY, however, it was only beginning. Six days after the effective date for removal, on Monday, October 7, 1833, Biddle held a board meeting in Philadelphia. He would, he said, call in loans and restrict credit in order to create a popular backlash against Jackson. It was a bald, bold maneuver—and one that played into Jackson's caricature of the Bank as an aristocratic institution more interested in self-perpetuation than in the good of the country. "The ties of party allegiance can only be broken by the actual conviction of existing distress in the community," Biddle said. "Nothing but the evidence of suffering abroad will produce any effect in Congress. . . . Our only safety is in pursuing a steady course of firm restriction—and I have no doubt that such a course will ultimately lead to restoration of the currency and the recharter of the Bank." Biddle's tactics worked, to a point. By late December, James A. Hamilton noted that New York business was "really in very great distress, nay even to the point of General Bankruptcy."

The crisis had come, but what would be the end of it all? Who would prevail—Jackson, who launched his preemptive strike in late September, or Biddle, who counterattacked in October? The two agreed on this, at least: the future of the Bank was now a political question, and would be decided by public opinion as expressed in the Congress.

Jackson was betting that the people were with him. They had reelected him, and they would, he believed, stand with him, forcing Congress to capitulate if Biddle's allies on Capitol Hill attempted to impeach Jackson in the House and convict him after a Senate trial—which was, really, the only option open to them once Jackson removed the deposits. By the time Con-

gress met, the removal, as Jackson had hoped, was not
a proposal but a fact. Duane had been fired; Taney
could be rejected (and would be, in June 1834) when
his name came to the Senate for confirmation, but the
Constitution gave Jackson the power to appoint Cabinet officers during congressional recesses to serve
until the end of the next session. The difficulties of
the summer and fall—the physical pain of the Northern tour, the feeling that Duane had betrayed him—
had, it seemed, been worth the trouble, for Jackson
was in an excellent position as the test between him
and Biddle came to pass in December. The only way
Biddle could win was to convince enough of the people that Jackson was being reckless and despotic—and
further, convince enough of those people to pressure
Congress to either force Jackson to reverse himself or,
in the last extremity, to try to remove Jackson from
the White House.

Major Lewis, a practical man, raised objection after
objection to Jackson's course, to no avail. What would
Jackson do, Lewis asked, if Congress passed a resolution "directing the Secretary to restore the deposits to
the bank?"

"Why, I would veto it," Jackson said.

But, Lewis persisted, what if the House and Senate
could muster the two-thirds majority needed to override the veto? "What then would you do?" Lewis
asked. "If you refuse to permit the secretary to do it,
the next step, on the part of the House, would be to
move an impeachment, and if Congress have the

power to carry this resolution through in defiance of the veto power, they would be able to prosecute it to a successful termination."

"Under such circumstances, elevating himself to his full height and assuming a firm and dignified aspect," Lewis recalled, Jackson said: "Then, sir, I would resign the presidency and return to the Hermitage!"

Lewis was so taken aback by Jackson's reply that, he recalled, "there was a pause in our conversation for a few minutes." What struck Lewis most was that Jackson was not in a fury as they spoke. He was not indulging a passing rage. The possibility of resignation, however remote, was raised not in anger but as part of a reasonable exchange about the perils of the political course ahead.

Lewis broke the silence by asking what Jackson hoped to accomplish by withdrawing the money from the Bank.

"To prevent it from being rechartered," Jackson said.

"But can not that object be as certainly attained as well without as with the removal of them?" Lewis asked.

"No, sir," Jackson said. "If the bank is permitted to have the public money, there is no power that can prevent it from obtaining a charter—it will have it if it has to buy up all Congress, and the public funds would enable it to do so!"

"Why, General, as the bank's charter expires twelve months before you go out of office, you will at all times have it in your power to prevent it by vetoing any bill that may be sent to you for that purpose," Lewis said. "Would it not be better, then, to let it go quietly out of existence?"

"But, sir, if we leave the means of corruption in its hands, the presidential veto will avail nothing," Jackson replied.

AS LAWMAKERS TRAVELED to the capital for the 1833–34 meeting of Congress, petition after petition flowed into Washington, begging Jackson for relief from the economic woes Biddle was inflicting on the country. One day Jackson was seated at a table in his office when a delegation from New York arrived. It was led by James G. King, son of the Federalist statesman Rufus King, and they had come with a petition of six thousand signatures calling for the president to spare them from their distress. "Excuse me a moment, gentlemen," Jackson said. "Have the goodness to be seated." He said this, James Parton reported, "half rising, and bowing to the group," a sign of grace that the sophisticates from New York might not have been expecting from their frontier president. His good manners evident, Jackson returned to his work, a sign that though he might be polite, he was also the most powerful man in the room. They could wait for him.

In a moment he stood up. "Now, gentlemen, what is your pleasure with me?" The president seemed so reasonable, so deferential. King began to lay out the problems facing New York merchants.

He had barely begun when Jackson interrupted. "Mr. King, you are the son of Rufus King, I believe?"

"I am, sir."

At this point, a witness later told Parton, Jackson "broke into a harangue which astonished the grave and reverend seigniors to whom it was addressed."

"Well, sir, Rufus King was always a Federalist, and I suppose you take after him," Jackson said. "Insolvent, do you say? What do you come to me for, then? Go to Nicholas Biddle. We have no money here, gentlemen. Biddle has all the money. He has millions of specie in his vaults, at this moment, lying idle, and yet you come to **me** to save you from breaking. I tell you, gentlemen, it's all politics."

The witness and the delegation were astonished at the shift in tone from the benign man who met them to the ferocious president who now paced before them, spewing out his points. The fit seemed to last forever. "He continued to speak in a strain like this for fifteen minutes, denouncing Biddle and the bank," reported Parton. "He laid down his pipe; he gesticulated wildly; he walked up and down the room; and finished by declaring, in respectful but unmistakable language, that his purpose was unchangeable not to restore the deposits." King and his colleagues, "correctly surmising that their mission was a failure," took their leave.

Afterward, Jackson savored his performance. His madness had been all method. "Didn't I manage them well?" he said, cheerily, an old warrior thinking of a battle well fought. It was a routine that was becoming familiar in these desperate months: a delegation would arrive, he would rage and rant, and then chortle as the pleading bankers or merchants fled the

White House, convinced anew that there could be no peace until either Jackson or Biddle was vanquished.

"Go home, gentlemen, and tell the Bank of the United States to relieve the country by increasing its business," he told a group from Philadelphia. "Sooner than restore the deposits or recharter the bank I would undergo the torture of ten Spanish inquisitions. Sooner than live in a country where such a power prevails I would seek an asylum in the wilds of Arabia." Hearing of the scene, Biddle could not help virtually sneering, remarking that Jackson "may as well send at once and engage lodgings" in Arabia.

Jackson took to referring to himself in the third person, a sign that even he had come to think of himself as a force with a life of its own. "Well, what do you want?" he asked a delegation from New York. "I tell you I will never restore the deposits. I will never recharter the United States Bank. . . . Here I am receiving one or two anonymous letters every day threatening me with assassination. . . . Is Andrew Jackson to bow the knee to the golden calf? . . . I tell you if you want relief go to Nicholas Biddle."

On another day a group from Baltimore tried its luck. "General," said the chairman, "the committee has the honor to be delegated by the citizens of Baltimore, without regard to party, to come to you, sir, the fountain head, for relief. . . ."

"Relief, sir!" Jackson interrupted. "Come not to me, sir! Go to the monster! It is folly, sir, to talk to Andrew Jackson."

"Sir, the currency of the country is in a dreadful situation."

"Sir, you keep one-sided company," said Jackson. "Andrew Jackson has fifty letters from persons of all parties daily on the subject. Sir, he has more and better information than you, sir, or any of you."

"**The people, sir . . .**"

"The people! The people, sir, are with **me**."

JACKSON BELIEVED SO, and never doubted the virtue of his course. It was a wild time. The French diplomat Louis Sérurier, who had first arrived in Washington as the young representative of Napoleon in 1811, wrote of "the violent withdrawal of public funds," and told Paris that the Bank affair "had become the all-engrossing business of the executive." In the winter of 1833–34, perhaps fueled by memories of the Randolph attack, people began to say that the army was protecting Jackson from assassination. Blair took up the issue in the **Globe,** joking that a Mrs. Gadsby, supposedly an elderly admirer of Jackson's, said that "the General did not want the aid of the army. She had recruited a volunteer corps of Lady veterans that would protect him with broomsticks."

Before long a delegation of Jacksonian congressmen arrived at the White House with word that a mob from Baltimore was headed toward the capital. Taking his cue from Blair, Jackson said that he "would in person meet them at the head of Mrs. Gadsby's corps of old women armed with broomsticks at Bladensburg and drive them back." His tone turned a bit more serious when he added that "in the case Biddle's mob ever showed themselves around the Capitol to threaten the Houses, they should see the ringleaders hanging as high as Haman about the square."

Thus reassured by their chief, the congressmen left, and Jackson stretched out on a sofa. Blair was still with him. Jackson's eye fell on an old Indian headdress sitting atop a wardrobe in the room, and he put it on. "I think these fellows would not like to meet me at Bladensburg in this war equipment," Jackson said, and shook his head until the feathers rattled.

ON FRIDAY, DECEMBER 3, 1833, Andrew Donelson took Jackson's annual message to the Congress. The deposits had been removed, Jackson said, because of "the unquestionable proof that the Bank of the United States was converted into a permanent electioneering engine." The issue was "whether the people of the United States are to govern through representatives chosen by their unbiased suffrages or whether the money and power of a great corporation are to be secretly exerted to influence their judgment and control their decisions." But the Bank was not going to make it easy. On Saturday, December 4, 1833, Donelson briefed Emily's brother Stockley. "Violent opposition may be expected from the friends of the Bank and those that will combine with them for the purpose of counteracting the influence of the President."

Henry Clay, fresh from Lexington, was prepared to take up the struggle—on Biddle's behalf, and also his own. Donelson was right: Jackson's foes were anxious not only to reverse, by whatever means, the removal of the deposits, but also longed to destroy Jackson, who had become, to his enemies, a suffocatingly successful figure.

"Depend upon it, that everything for which you fought, or which you and I hold valuable in public concerns, is in imminent hazard," Clay wrote to his lifelong friend Francis Brooke on Thursday, December 16, 1833. "By means of the veto, the power **as exercised** of removal from office, the possession of the public treasury and the public patronage, the very existence of liberty and the government is, in my judgment, in peril." Jackson had won so many battles, crushed so many hopes, frustrated so many competing ambitions, that, finally, Clay believed he had to be stopped or the country was going to collapse.

A fevered view, perhaps, but a deeply felt one, and it drove Clay into a frenzied but eloquent assault on Jackson in late December. "I mean myself to open and push a vigorous campaign," Clay said as he prepared for his coming strike against Jackson on the Senate floor. Clay had failed with the people in 1832 but would not surrender completely to Jackson—not yet.

CHAPTER 24

★

WE ARE IN THE MIDST
OF A REVOLUTION

WASHINGTON READIED FOR political war. R. K. Polk, a cousin of the Speaker of the House, arrived in the city four days before Christmas. The intensity of the fight was rising; young Polk had just recovered from what he called "a burning fever and violent headache," but Jackson's foes were consumed, in a way, by their own sickness. Polk went straight to the Capitol to watch the debates over the deposits and heard George McDuffie of South Carolina denounce Jackson. McDuffie was, Polk said, "quite severe on the president of the United States in the course of his remarks and quite complimentary to the character of Biddle, observing that it had been General Jackson's whole aim . . . for the last three years to destroy that institution."

Clay was to speak on the day after Christmas, and Jackson spent the holiday so consumed by callers and business that he had time for nothing else. Thinking of home, Emily wrote a sister, "I suppose you all are at my Dear Mother's today as usual, and I can well picture to myself the happy group, and wish I was there to join it. Here everybody goes to church, but as Uncle had a great many gentlemen to visit him today we did not go, and I have been quite alone thinking of you all in Tennessee, particularly of my Dearest Mother. . . . I wish for nothing so much as to see her once more, and be quietly settled at home."

There was nothing quiet about Clay's performance the next day. "We are in the midst of a revolution, hitherto bloodless, but rapidly tending towards a total change of the pure republican character of the Government, and to the concentration of all power in the hands of one man," Clay told the Senate on Thursday, December 26, 1833. Jackson, he said, was destroying the America of the Founders, the America created by the Revolution. "In a term of eight years, a little more than equal to that which was required to establish our liberties, the government will have been transformed into an elective monarchy—the worst of all forms of government."

Clay's peroration was purple but moving. "The eyes and hopes of the American people are anxiously turned to Congress. . . . The premonitory symptoms of despotism are upon us; and if Congress [does] not apply an instantaneous remedy, the fatal collapse will soon come on, and we shall die—ignobly die—base, mean, and abject slaves; the scorn and contempt of mankind; unpitied, unwept, unmourned!" In the audience, observers said, there was "loud and repeated applause from the immense crowd"—cheers that grew so loud Van Buren was forced to "order the galleries cleared." Jackson had stymied the Washington establishment time and again. Now Clay was striking at what Jackson cherished most: his power and his honor.

JACKSON TOOK JOY in the fight. "You would be surprised to see the General," Andrew Donelson wrote to Edward Livingston on Friday, March 7, 1834. "This Bank excitement has restored his former energy, and gives to him the appearance he had ten years ago." He was thriving on the drama of the people's president standing fast against the aristocrats' banker.

His foes were flummoxed by his insistence on going straight to the nation. After Jackson's remarks to the Cabinet about removing the deposits were published in the **Globe,** an enraged Calhoun virtually sputtered in the Senate. Making the arguments to the Cabinet public, Calhoun said, "was clearly and manifestly intended as an appeal to the people of the United States, and opens a new and direct organ of communication between the President and them unknown to the Constitution and the laws."

In their understanding of the presidency, as in so much else, Calhoun and Jackson were worlds apart. Ever legalistic, Calhoun went on: "There are but two channels . . . through which the President can communicate with the people—by messages to the two Houses of Congress, as expressly provided for in the Constitution, or by proclamation, setting forth the interpretations which he places upon a law it has become his official duty to execute. Going beyond is one among the alarming signs of the times which portend the overthrow of the Constitution and the approach of despotic power."

Such was the verdict of the senator from South Carolina about the idea that a president might discuss issues directly with the nation. Calhoun's hope (and Clay's) was that a strict construction of the Constitution could hobble Jackson's campaign to make the presidency the center of action. "What, then, is the real question which now agitates the country?" Calhoun said. "I answer, it is a struggle between the Executive and Legislative departments of the Government—a struggle, not in relation to the existence of the Bank, but which, Congress or the President, should have the power to create a Bank, and the consequent control over the currency of the country. This is the real question."

Jackson and his allies were, Calhoun said, "artful, cunning, and corrupt politicians. . . . They have entered the Treasury, not sword in hand, as public plunderers, but with the false keys of sophistry, as pilferers, under the silence of midnight. . . . With money we will get partisans, with partisans votes, and with votes money, is the maxim of our public pilferers."

Calhoun was explicit about the political stakes. The removal of the deposits and the prospect of a national Democratic nominating convention filled with Jacksonians (whose loyalty and votes will have been presumably purchased) will, Calhoun said, "dictate the **succession** . . . and all the powers of our Republic [will] be consolidated in the President, and perpetuated by his dictation." The Calhoun of 1834 was terribly worried about the health of the institutions of the American Union.

"We have arrived at a fearful crisis," Calhoun said. "Things cannot long remain as they are. It behooves all who love their country—who have affection for their offspring, or who have any stake in our institutions, to pause and reflect. Confidence is daily withdrawing from the General Government. Alienation is hourly going on. These will necessarily create a state of things inimical to the existence of our institutions, and, if not arrested, convulsions must follow, and then comes dissolution or despotism, when a thick cloud will be thrown over the cause of liberty and the future prospects of our country."

At one point while Congress was in session, a Jacksonian congressman had a weak moment with Kendall. "We cannot resist this tremendous pressure; we shall be obliged to yield," the lawmaker said of the opposition's argument against removing the deposits.

"What!" Kendall said. "Are you prepared to give up the Republic? This is a struggle to maintain a government of the people against the most heartless of all aristocracies, that of money. Yield now, and the Bank of the United States will henceforth be the governing power whatever may be the form of our institutions."

THE POLITICS OF the moment seemed to be in Jackson's favor. "The distress so much complained of is disappearing," Andrew Donelson told Emily's brother, "or where it does exist illustrates only the dangerous power of the Bank; and thus instead of strengthening it justifies the ground occupied by the administration." In late February 1834, Governor George Wolf of Pennsylvania—home of the Bank, and a critical state in presidential politics—said that Biddle's curtailment policy had brought about "indiscriminate ruin." Wolf's move cheered the White House. "We are gaining strength politically," Andrew told Stockley. "Wolf's message a few days since has helped us very much. It serves to show the leaders of the Bank party that the people of that great state stand by the President."

Jackson was in control. At the end of a long session in the Senate, Thomas Hart Benton would come down to the White House. It was always at night— "for I had no time to quit my seat during the day," Benton said—and in the mansion's soft light Jackson would listen to his friend's report from the front. In all their years together, Benton said that Jackson never seemed "more truly heroic and grand than at this time. He was perfectly mild in his language, cheerful in his temper, firm in his conviction; and confident in his reliance on the power in which he put his trust."

Benton's accounts of the combat on the floor were full and detailed, and when the senator took his leave, Jackson was confiding and encouraging, drawing strength from the masses beyond the mansion. "We shall whip them yet," Jackson told Benton.

AND THEY DID. The argument against Biddle—that he had abused the Bank's power—stuck. While the more insulated Senate—whose members were still chosen by state legislatures, not the voters—thundered on about Jackson and his overreaching, the House, with its proximity to the people, gave Jackson what he wanted. On Friday, April 4, 1834, the House voted that the Bank "ought not to be rechartered" and that the state banks should keep the federal deposits. "I have obtained a glorious triumph," Jackson said. The House had at last "put to death that mammoth of corruption and power, the Bank of the United States."

In defeat, Jackson's opponents wanted to see him brought low, and they hoped a resolution of Clay's in the Senate would do it. The proposed measure would censure the president for allegedly exceeding his authority in removing the deposits and in dismissing Duane. Censure would have no legal effect. It was only a symbolic move, but symbols mattered.

The ensuing censure battle was therefore personal on both sides. A correspondent of Clay's referred to Jackson as "Caesar" and thought the president "wholly unworthy" of power like that conferred on the office by the Force Bill. "The whole community of the United States seems to be under the influence of extraordinary political excitement," Sir Charles Vaughan wrote Palmerston. Jackson's foes, Vaughan added, were attacking "what is represented to be the illegal and reckless conduct of the President."

FRIDAY, MARCH 28, 1834, was, in retrospect, one of the most consequential days of Andrew Jackson's life. In Washington, he was censured for his removal of the deposits. The tally in the Senate was 26 to 20, the language straightforward:

Resolved, That the President, in the late Executive proceedings in relation to the public revenue, has assumed upon himself authority and power not conferred by the Constitution and laws, but in derogation of both.

Half a world away, on the same Friday, the Chamber of Deputies in France opened debate on paying the United States a debt of 25 million francs (about $5 million) as an indemnity for French damage to American shipping during the Napoleonic wars. France had agreed to pay the money under an 1831 treaty, but after four days of consideration, by a margin of eight, France declined to honor its obligations.

Jackson stood convicted in the records of the Senate, and America was repudiated in the councils of a foreign government. When he pondered what the Senate had done, Jackson could not get it out of his head that a verdict had been rendered against him, and against his vision of the presidency. When he thought of France, Jackson was convinced that both he and America were being put to the test—that his honor and the honor of the nation were now in question. He would use all of his power, all of his will, all of his ebbing physical strength to strike back, at home and abroad. He would not be censured and he would not let the country be insulted. He was now sixty-seven years old, tired and often sick, but he was ready to fight any battle for the sanctity of the presidency, for the reputation of the nation, and for the glory of his name.

PART III

★

THE EVENING
OF HIS DAYS

1834 to the End

CHAPTER 25

★

SO YOU WANT WAR

ORD OF THE insult from Paris, in the form of dispatches from Edward Livingston, arrived aboard the **Liverpool** in early May 1834. As Jackson and McLane absorbed the news, Louis Sérurier, France's minister in Washington, struggled to figure out what to do. He had promised the Americans resolution, but was now the representative of a government that had chosen to ignore, at least for the moment, its obligations to the United States. Thinking of "the President's fiery character, his cruel disappointment, and his own personal political situation at the moment"—the censure vote was six weeks old—Sérurier called on McLane at the State Department.

"I was informed that the President and the Secretary of State had received the dispatches . . . that the President was incensed, and that they were talking about a message to Congress on the following Monday concerning our legislature's decision," Sérurier wrote Paris on Sunday, May 11, 1834. "It would no longer be discussed on a purely monetary basis, but would be treated as a question of national honor and injured pride."

The moment evoked uncomfortable memories. Europe and America had been here before. Jackson's reaction "is what I feared the most," Sérurier added, "as I recall that in treating the question on the same basis in 1812, Mr. Madison brought about Congress' declaration of war on England." Could it happen again?

Separately, a friend of Jackson's—unnamed in Sérurier's correspondence—came to see the Frenchman and echoed McLane's analysis. The president, the friend said, "was deeply irritated at the unexpected turn of events." But it was less the money, the friend said, than the motives behind the vote. "He told me that, for the President, the latest vote of the French legislature indicated that . . . the treaty was violated—a glaring refusal to make amends—and for him, personally, the pressing duty to protect his fellow citizens against an insulting refusal of justice" was now before him. Though Sérurier tried to explain that the decision was driven by internal French politics, not a desire to embarrass the United States, he found his caller unmoved. "But this will have serious consequences, replied my visitor, and the President, with all the calm that his astonishment allows him to muster, is now deliberating over what should be his duty to his country."

McLane made the same point to Sérurier. The French decision, McLane said, "had hit the President like a thunderbolt and . . . he was still dizzy from it."

Sérurier's day only got worse. As he arrived home, he noticed a horseman stopping at his door. It was Henry Clay, in a fury. In the space of a few hours, the worst of American political enemies, Jackson and Clay, seemed united on one thing: France had wronged the United States, and France would retreat—or else.

"Well, he said to me, so you want war," Sérurier wrote of Clay's remarks to him. "This is a case for war if anything is. You will have it if you persevere. We are a proud people, M. Sérurier. You ought to know that. We do not deserve to be insulted and scorned, and there is contempt for us in your Chamber's vote."

CLAY'S REMARKS, SÉRURIER told the Kentucky senator, were not the kind of thing one says to one's friends. Perhaps, replied Clay, but Paris had put the two nations in dangerous territory. "You are the last people on earth, replied Mr. Clay, as he shook my hand, that I would want to go to war with, but honor admits no distinctions between one's adversaries."

The two continued their conversation that evening at the Clays'. Sérurier pleaded with Clay to help him moderate the war of words before things went too far. The Americans did not have a monopoly on pride, and should Washington overreact to the French vote, Paris might have no choice but to respond harshly, and matters could escalate even further. "Above all, Mr. Clay, avoid threats," Sérurier said. "There is nothing to be gained by this kind of language, and it would cut any negotiations short."

Clay closed the exchange on a gentle but far from

conclusive note. "I promise you that, together with my friends, we will do everything we can to avoid all warlike proposals, and I hope that I may succeed."

Nine days after Sérurier's encounters with Clay, the Frenchman made his first visit to the White House since the news of the Chamber's adjournment. "It was a tricky situation," Sérurier wrote. He was prepared for any eventuality. He would be patient, and "had decided to counter any anger or threats with cold respect." But Jackson was not yet ready to strike, and Sérurier reported that "I didn't have to use any of my defensive weapons." Everything was correct—painfully so, to Sérurier, who knew the calm could not last.

"The President was very cold, but very polite, and spoke little to me, and only in generalities," Sérurier said. "He made no reference to the treaty. During the half-hour I spent in his living room, his attitude was one of great dignity . . . but the explosion is only just being delayed." A month later, on June 20, 1834, Sérurier and his wife visited the White House to, as Sérurier put it, "take the political temperature." Jackson was again kind, and "his circle of friends seemed struck by this"—a small detail suggesting that Jackson was saying and thinking quite unkind things about the French when the minister was not in the room. Speaking with subtlety, Jackson told Sérurier, "I have always loved France, and it would only be with the deepest sorrow that I would have to change my feelings." But he would, as always, do what he had to do.

CHAPTER 26

★

A DARK, LAWLESS,
AND INSATIABLE AMBITION!

FTER THE CENSURE vote in the Senate, Jackson struck back on Tuesday, April 15, 1834, with a document entitled "Protest," in which he defended himself and his presidency with a mixture of sarcasm and rage. Alluding to the censure resolution, which simply spoke of "the President," Jackson said: "Having had the honor, through the voluntary suffrages of the American people, to fill the office of President of the United States during the period which may be presumed to have been referred to in this resolution, it is sufficiently evident that the censure it inflicts was intended for myself. Without notice, unheard and untried, I thus find myself charged on the records of the Senate, and in a form hitherto unknown in our history, with the high crime of violating the laws and Constitution of my country."

The Senate's motives were not difficult to fathom, Jackson said, framing the matter in personal and familial terms: "The judgment of **guilty** by the highest tribunal in the Union, the stigma it would inflict on the offender, his family, and fame, and the perpetual

record on the Journal, handing down to future generations the story of his disgrace, were doubtless regarded by them as the bitterest portions, if not the
very essence, of that punishment." A blow against
Jackson was, to Jackson, a blow against his family,
too—and since his definition of family could include
the nation, the sting of the Senate vote was all the
more painful.

Should the precedent stand—or, worse, should
the legislature begin to deploy censure resolutions as
a routine weapon against the president—Jackson believed that the effective power of government would
shift from the presidency as Jackson envisioned it to
the legislature, which, in the case of the Senate, would
mean to those unelected by the people. "If the censures of the Senate be submitted to by the President,
the confidence of the people in his ability and virtue
and the character and usefulness of his Administration will soon be at an end, and the real power of the
Government will fall into the hands of a body holding
their offices for long terms, not elected by the people
and not to them directly responsible."

For Jackson, "responsibility" was an essential element of the debate. To whom much was given, much
was expected, and he was prepared, given the power
of his station, to, as he liked to say, "take the responsibility" on the grounds, as he told the Senate, that "the
President is the direct representative of the American
people."

In the spring of 1834, that idea was still radical. No
other president had ever made such an assertion in

such terms. The significance of the censure lay in the test it posed for Jackson's conception of the presidency. If it stood, future presidents might follow rather than lead.

The censure was at once an attack on his power and an assault on his honor. In the conclusion to his protest, he referred to the scar left on his head by that long-ago British officer and noted how much easier his life and presidency might have been had he allowed himself to be bought by the wealth of the Bank:

> In vain do I bear upon my person enduring memorials of that contest in which American liberty was purchased; in vain have I since periled property, fame, and life in defense of the rights and privileges so dearly bought; in vain am I now, without a personal aspiration or the hope of individual advantage, encountering responsibilities and dangers from which by mere inactivity in relation to a single point [the Bank] I might have been exempt. . . . In the history of conquerors and usurpers, never in the fire of youth nor in the vigor of manhood could I find an attraction to lure me from the path of duty, and now I shall scarcely find an inducement to commence their career of ambition when gray hairs and a decaying frame, instead of inviting to toil and battle, call me to the contemplation of other worlds, where conquerors cease to be honored and usurpers expiate their crimes. The only ambition I can feel is to acquit myself to Him to whom I must soon render an account of my stewardship, to serve my fellow-men, and live respected and honored in the his-

tory of my country. . . . If the Almighty Being who has hitherto sustained and protected me will but vouchsafe to make my feeble powers instrumental to such a result, I shall anticipate with pleasure the place to be assigned me in the history of my country, and die contented with the belief that I have contributed in some small degree to increase the value and prolong the duration of American liberty.

He was, he insisted, the defender of the liberties of the people. The Senate, however, was, as he put it, seeking to "concentrate in the hands of a body not directly amenable to the people a degree of influence and power dangerous to their liberties and fatal to the Constitution of their choice."

Such language was incendiary, but Congress, John Quincy Adams noted in December 1833, had itself frequently drawn on such imagery. "The domineering tone has heretofore been usually on the side of the legislative bodies to the Executive, and Clay has not been sparing in the use of it," Adams said. "He is now paid in his own coin." Still, to Webster the protest amounted to the absolutist claim of Louis XIV: "I am the state."

Calhoun was even angrier, crying: "Infatuated man! Blinded by ambition—intoxicated by flattery and vanity! Who, that is the least acquainted with the human heart; who, that is conversant with the page of history, does not see, under all this, the workings of a dark, lawless, and insatiable ambition . . . ? He claims to be, not only the representative, but the immediate

representative of the American people! What effron-
tery! What boldness of assertion! The **immediate** representative! Why, he never received a vote from the
American people. He was elected by electors."

ODDLY, PERHAPS, THE rough-hewn Jackson understood the poetry of politics better than Calhoun,
Clay, or Webster. His foes were speaking in prose, making technical arguments. Jackson was formulating a poetic narrative drama in which he was the hero defending
the interests of the people against the powerful.

Charges of kingship, common in the Jackson years,
touched core American anxieties. John C. Hamilton,
son of Alexander and brother of James, recounted an
interview with a Jefferson biographer, Professor George
Tucker, who had implied that Alexander Hamilton
harbored monarchial sympathies. Denying it, Hamilton fumed a bit, saying the "charge" meant that men
like his father "are to be handed down to posterity as
traitors to the feelings of the people and to the Constitution they had formed and sworn to maintain."
Hamilton's passion on the point illuminates how
Americans felt about the question of a king, both at
the birth of the Republic and decades on. The persistent suggestion that Jackson was overreaching in a
fashion more suited to a monarch than to a president
was a political problem for the White House.

The deposits issue was the occasion, therefore, for
a broad struggle—and the conflicts of the spring of
1834 brought a new force to life: a formal second
party in opposition to Jackson's Democrats. On Mon-

day, April 14, 1834, Clay referred to Jackson's foes as Whigs—the British term for those who opposed the monarchy. It was, Clay said on the Senate floor, "a denomination which, according to the analogy of all history, is strictly correct. It deserves to be extended throughout the whole country." Only an American Whig party can, Clay said, rescue the nation from "a Chief Magistrate who is endeavoring to concentrate in his own person the whole powers of government."

Though worn down by the strife with Jackson, Clay stayed in the arena, helping fellow anti-Jackson lawmakers carry a motion declining to enter the protest into the Senate record. At the same time Clay kept up the antimonarchial rhetoric. Claiming to have heard a rumor that Jackson "stated to the brother of Napoleon that he has made the Emperor of France his model," Clay said that the "army and the navy, thank God, are sound and patriotic to the core. They will not allow themselves to be servile instruments of treason, usurpation, and the overthrow of civil liberty, if any such designs now exist."

JACKSON DOMINATED EVERYONE'S thinking, from Clay to Sérurier. On Wednesday, July 2, 1834, when John Forsyth of Georgia replaced McLane as secretary of state—McLane left the administration—Sérurier wrote that "Mr. Forsyth is neither pro-English, nor pro-French. He will probably act according to the circumstances and impetus that the President will give him."

Jackson, always Jackson. Summer was here, and the

capital emptied, Sérurier told Paris, because of "intolerable heat and the contagious fevers of July, August and September." Even at his age, Jackson rode part of the way home to the Hermitage on horseback; Sérurier marveled at the old man's enduring vitality.

Jackson and the Donelsons were bound for Tennessee, but by different routes. Politically it was a safe time to get away. For the moment, Jackson's foes seemed either disoriented or disappointed. In Newport, Rhode Island, Sérurier came across Nicholas Biddle. "One of the first people I met here, M. le Comte, was **the Monster,** as the administration calls him," Sérurier wrote to Paris in August. "I can assure your Excellency that this could not be a worse description of the man. Mr. Biddle, President of the Bank of the U.S., is a very distinguished person, well-mannered, who has traveled in Europe and especially in France. He speaks our language with a rare fluency, knows our literature and our art. He is well-read and well-spoken."

Biddle was all these things, certainly, but he seems to have been strangely disconnected from the new realities Jackson's springtime deposits removal had created. "He believes that he will win the Bank's struggle," Sérurier reported on August 18, 1834. "He understands it to be more than just purely a question of money, but one of the country's own institutions." Biddle was in denial, the nullifiers in disarray. "The South seems to be asleep," Duff Green wrote an ally. "There is no energy—no concert among the states' rights men."

. . .

RELIEVED OF IMMEDIATE concerns, Jackson and Andrew Donelson were to go to the Hermitage directly; Emily and the four children were scheduled to pay a visit to friends in and around Charlottesville. (On April 19, 1834, a springtime Saturday in Washington, Emily had given birth to her fourth child, a daughter who was baptized Rachel Jackson Donelson. James K. Polk was godfather.)

Jackson left Francis Preston Blair and his family in the White House. Blair's wife, Eliza, and his daughter, known as Lizzie, were favorites of the president; Jackson was so fond of Lizzie that he gave her Rachel's wedding ring. Mrs. Blair was a kind of features editor for the **Globe,** and they were given the run of the White House when Jackson was away. Replying to a letter of Jackson's after a day at the races in 1834, Blair wrote that he and Lewis had drunk "Ice sangree, notwithstanding the cholera," to celebrate the news that Jackson had safely arrived and was well in Tennessee. (In late 1836, the Blairs bought the house across Pennsylvania Avenue from the White House, and would bring the president a pail of fresh milk from their cows in the morning.)

William Cabell Rives, the Virginia editor and former American envoy to France, asked Emily to visit at Castle Hill, his family estate in Albemarle County. "We are very much pleased at the prospect of a visit from Mrs. Donelson," Rives wrote Van Buren. For Emily, the stay near Monticello was a kind of social vindication. Here she was, a daughter of the frontier, moving among old Virginia families on equal terms. Her niece Elizabeth Martin, who accompanied her, was being courted by Lewis Randolph, President Jefferson's grandson. Randolph was, Emily told Andrew, "in his glory" as he showed off the fabled family estate and introduced Miss Martin to his formidable mother, Martha Jefferson Randolph, whom Emily had entertained at the White House. Still, Emily was not feeling her best. "I am well except [for] weakness and debility which is owing to my nursing," Emily wrote Andrew from Castle Hill on July 20. She did not much improve in the ensuing days, and, on the trip home to Tennessee, changed her plans in order to stop at Virginia's Warm Springs.

CHAPTER 27

★

THERE IS A RANK DUE TO THE UNITED STATES AMONG NATIONS

BY AUGUST, EMILY was in Nashville, and, a decade into their marriage, she and Andrew turned their attention to the construction of the first home of their own: a splendid brick house to be named Poplar Grove. It was to be built about a mile from the Hermitage, designed by Joseph Reiff and William Hume (John Coffee had weighed in on the design as well). The proximity to Jackson's own seat was both a sign of their mutual affection and a suggestion that after the White House, Donelson, who had now been at Jackson's side for nearly a dozen years, would remain an essential member of the circle. As the house was being built, Emily managed the details, rearranging the windows when she found they were in the wrong places and ordering that the fireplaces be widened. She kept a crate of her china close at hand, in the cellar of the Hermitage, awaiting the day it could be moved down to a finished Poplar Grove.

That china was very nearly a casualty of calamity in the second week of October, when fire broke out at the Hermitage, destroying a good deal of Jackson's beloved house. The fire began in the chimney, and a northwest wind spread the flames across the roof. It was an accident, and Sarah Yorke Jackson, who had been out riding, had returned to the house; Andrew junior was on the farm. "Oh, had I been there, it might have been prevented," he wrote. "The cursed Negroes were all so stupid and confused that nothing could be done until some white one came to their relief." In fact, the slaves who were on hand were critical in saving what they could. In Stockley Donelson's account of the episode to Jackson, Sarah "acted with firmness and gave every necessary direction to save the furniture."

Sarah and Andrew junior were distraught, but Jackson was stoic. God, he wrote to his son, had given him "the means to build it, and he has the right to destroy it, and blessed be his name. Tell Sarah [to] cease to mourn its loss. I will have it rebuilt." In Rachel's memory he would not move the house or rebuild elsewhere on the farm. "Was it not on the site selected by my dear departed wife I would build it higher up the hill, but I will have it repaired."

He gave orders about construction and moving ahead, but he was mildly depressed about the loss of furniture, papers, and other mementos. His life had been spent in pursuit of domestic order, and now fate had intervened. In the White House, writing to his son, his mind drifted to the probable loss of some of the bright things of life. "I suppose all the wines in the cellar have been destroyed, with Mrs. Donelson's box of china," he wrote with a touch of gloom. (The china was fine.) "Give me as accurate an account of the loss of furniture as you can at as early a period as possible." He would move forward. He always did.

THE FRENCH REMAINED a problem. On Wednesday, October 22, 1834, John Forsyth, the new secretary of state, met with Sérurier. "The President was deeply hurt that a treaty ratified three years ago was still not carried out," Sérurier reported Forsyth as saying. "Contrary to [Jackson's] natural tendencies, he had been patient for a long time now, counting on justice in France and my promises. However, the moment had come to speak out, and in front of everyone."

Behind the scenes, Jackson was ready for combat. The Cabinet secretaries were reluctant to endorse an unflinching stand on the French issue, but Jackson dismissed their concerns. "No, gentlemen," he said, "I know them. . . . They won't pay unless they're made to." In his annual message, sent to Congress on Monday, December 1, Jackson spent seventeen paragraphs describing foreign affairs, almost entirely cheerful and optimistic in tone. Then, in the eighteenth, he came to the French.

"It becomes my unpleasant duty to inform you that this pacific and highly gratifying picture of our foreign relations does not include those with France at this time," he wrote. The United States was "wholly disappointed" with the French approach to the treaty of 1831. Jackson believed "the whole civilized world must pronounce France to be in the wrong." Should the Chamber not authorize payment at its next session, Jackson would ask Congress for a law approving "reprisals upon French property" as a means of demonstrating the "inflexible determination on the part of the United States to insist on their rights." And should France answer in kind if reprisals became necessary, France "would but add violence to injustice, and could not fail to expose herself to the just censure of civilized nations and to the retributive judgments of Heaven."

SO THERE IT was: Jackson's vision of what the preservation of America's national honor required. "Threats are far from being avoided, and the worst possible measures are proposed," Sérurier told Paris on December 2. "General Jackson, weary of his long constraint . . . gives way to his bad disposition. His flatterers tell him that nothing can resist him." Three days later, after gauging reaction to the message, Sérurier fell back on the caricature of Jackson as a man beyond reason. "It is generally agreed . . . that this rash message, at least regarding France and its proposed measures, is entirely Jackson's work." The president, Sérurier said, could not be stopped: his "iron will subdued all resistance."

Christmas Day 1834, Emily said, was "very cold and disagreeable." The tensions with France consumed Jackson and his top men, including Forsyth. They were so busy that Emily dined alone with Mrs. Forsyth on Christmas Eve. While Emily was writing home on this dark Christmas Day, Louis Sérurier was composing a coded message to Paris, writing of war:

If we have war with the U.S., it will be very important to win the first round. This war will not be popular here: southern planters, ship-owners, northern navigators . . . will all be against it. War would bring stupendous prestige, but only for a fleeting moment—acting upon the masses as those who . . . are led by a rash and adventurous ruler with an iron will. . . .

To ensure that we win this first round—so important for American public opinion in order to halt the outburst of their juvenile vanity—I would believe it desirable that the Minister of the Navy, at the first serious indication that war is imminent with this republic, arm 4–5 of our best frigates with a crew of our most elite seamen, commanded by officers known for their boldness and their knowledge of the sea . . . [and] that they should be ordered to look for American frigates and engage them in battle. . . .

There was one spot of hope: General Lafayette had died during the summer, and the American reaction was warm and widespread. Members of Congress decided to wear black armbands for a month of mourning; John Quincy Adams was asked to give a funeral oration in the House. "Never since Washington's death has there been such an outpouring of public sympathy," Sérurier wrote. "Americans have their faults, and I have pointed them out on occasion. However, they are certainly not an ungrateful people, at least in regard to the noble and first foreign champion of their independence." On New Year's Eve, Adams rose in the House to pay tribute to Lafayette as a crucial friend of the Republic.

The sentimental warmth of the occasion did not last long. Two weeks later, on Wednesday, January 14, 1835, the king of France recalled Sérurier home to Paris—a vivid diplomatic gesture underscoring the rising hostilities. Sérurier had predicted a harsh French reaction to Jackson's words, and he was being proved right. "The impression that President Jackson's message produced here in France is as you foresaw," Count de Rigny, the French minister of foreign affairs, wrote Sérurier. "The king's government, obviously, could not counter such an injurious procedure except by an equally dazzling demonstration." De Rigny had summoned Edward Livingston, the American envoy to Paris, to inform him of the move the night before, and "passports will be at his disposal in case he feels he must leave. Such are the measures that his Majesty has deemed necessary to maintain the dignity of France."

THE AMERICAN BILL, which was finally presented to the Chamber on Thursday, January 15, 1835, was amended in light of Jackson's remarks. A new clause said that "all or part" of the 25 million francs could be used "to compensate French citizens for the losses caused by the measures adopted by the U.S." By the time the bill had made its way through the French legislature, there was an additional requirement before the money would be paid to Washington: the United

States, the Duc de Broglie, the current French minister of foreign affairs, wrote on Wednesday, June 17, 1835, must explain "the true meaning and real purport of divers passages inserted by the President in his message at the opening of the last session of Congress, and at which all France . . . was justly offended." Jackson, France said, had to offer "new testimony to the good faith of the French government."

Paris had misjudged Washington—and, for once, Jackson was not alone in his resolve. In the House, John Quincy Adams rallied to his foe's side.

> Sir, this treaty has been ratified on both sides of the ocean; it has received the sign manual of the sovereign of France, through his Imperial Majesty's principal Minister of State; it has been ratified by the Senate of this republic; it has been sanctioned by Almighty God; and still we are told . . . that the arrogance of France—nay, sir, not of France, but of her Chamber of Deputies—the insolence of the French Chambers must be submitted to, and we must come down to the **lower** degradation of reopening negotiations to attain that which has already been acknowledged to be our due! Sir, is this a specimen of your boasted chivalry? Is this an evidence of the existence of that heroic valor which has so often led our arms on to glory and immortality? Reopen negotiations, sir, with France? Do it, and soon you will find your flag insulted, dishonored, and trodden in the dust by the pygmy States of Asia and Africa—by the very banditti of the earth.

Sir Charles Vaughan told London that the French were misreading Jackson. "The President told me that he should consider any concession on his part, at this moment, as compromising the honor of his country." From the White House, Jackson said the suggestion that he would apologize in writing was absurd—"wholly inadmissible."

There was also news, Jackson said, "of naval preparations on the part of France destined for our seas." Congress should consider, then, a trade and shipping embargo against France. America would not be caught off guard. Jackson asked for "large and speedy appropriations for the increase of the Navy and the completion of our coastal defenses," for, he added, "come what may, the explanation which France demands can never be accorded, and no armament, however powerful and imposing, at a distance or on our coast, will, I trust, deter us from discharging the high duties which we owe to our constituents, our national character, and to the world."

Things seemed to be at an impasse, with the French nation and Andrew Jackson standing opposite each other, unblinking. But there had been part of a sentence in his December 1835 annual message to Congress that could serve as a face-saving measure for the French. Amid his strident rhetoric, Jackson had said: "The conception that it was my intention to menace or insult the Government of France is . . . unfounded. . . ." At this point, Britain, fearing that a war between France and the United States would be pointlessly disruptive, stepped in to play a mediating role, and both sides accepted the offer. On February 8, 1836, Jackson suspended his call for an embargo but reiterated the need for military preparations—just in case.

In these weeks Thomas P. Barton, Livingston's aide in France, returned to Washington and arrived at the White House to brief Jackson, Van Buren, and Secretary of State Forsyth. In a conversation Barton related to James Parton, Jackson was at once testy but curious. "Tell me, sir, do the French mean to repay that money?" Jackson asked.

"General Jackson, I am sorry to inform you that they do not."

"**There,** gentlemen!" Jackson said to Van Buren and Forsyth. "What have I told you all along?" He paused and, Parton reports, "strode up and down the room several times in a state of extreme excitement." He stopped and asked Barton: "What do they say about it, sir? What excuse do they give?"

"I verily believe, General, that down to a recent period, the French government was trifling with us."

Jackson jumped up. "Do you hear that, gentlemen? **Trifling with us!** My very words. I have always said so."

"I mean by trifling with us," Barton went on, "that they thought the treaty was a matter of no great importance, and one which was not pressing, and would not be pressed by the United States. It could be attended to this year, or next year—it was of small consequence which."

Parton then paraphrased the crux of Barton's explanation: "The exchargé proceeded to say that the popular opposition to the payment of the indemnity had risen to such a height in France that any ministry that should pay it before the President had apologized would not only lose their places but subject themselves to impeachment. There was no man in France who would dare encounter the odium of attempting it. The king would endanger his throne if he should give it his sanction. . . . The king, the ministry, the capitalists, and all reflecting persons sincerely desired to avoid a collision with the United States, from which France could gain nothing that she desired to gain. But the people were mad; and no one could predict how far the government might be compelled to yield to their fury."

ACCORDING TO PARTON'S account, hearing these points helped soothe "the irritation of [Jackson's] mind." But why? Though Jackson would endure no insult, as a politician himself, this firsthand account of the popular forces bearing down on Louis Philippe and his government may have helped him see the issue in more measured perspective. It was not that the king was heedlessly courting controversy with the United States, but that the French people had taken it up, and Jackson well knew that the management of public opinion was a complicated business.

The British resolved the matter quickly. France chose to take the conciliatory line of Jackson's from December as apology enough, and the matter was settled: France would pay its debt. The episode over, Jackson used the occasion to remind Americans that

while war did not come this time, it remained an inevitable element in the lives of nations, especially
great nations. On Monday, February 22, 1836, in a
message to Congress, Jackson quoted George Washington: "There is a rank due to the United States
among nations which will be withheld, if not absolutely lost, by the reputation of weakness. If we desire to avoid insult, we must be able to repel it. If we
desire to secure peace, one of the most powerful instruments of our rising prosperity, it must be known
that we are at all times, ready for war."

Andrew Jackson, at least, always was.

CHAPTER 28

THE WRETCHED VICTIM
OF A DREADFUL DELUSION

ON THURSDAY, JANUARY 8, 1835, there was a dinner in Washington to celebrate both the anniversary of the Battle of New Orleans and the payment of the national debt—a long-sought, and now achieved, goal of Jackson's. "The national debt is paid!" said Thomas Hart Benton in a toast. "This month of January, 1835, in the 58th year of the republic, Andrew Jackson being President, the national debt is paid! . . . Gentlemen, my heart is in this double celebration; and I offer you a sentiment, which, coming direct from my own bosom, will find its response in yours: PRESIDENT JACKSON: May the evening of his days be as tranquil and happy for himself as their meridian has been resplendent, glorious, and beneficent for his country."

Twenty-two days later, Jackson was walking out of the House chamber after a funeral service for Representative Warren R. Davis of South Carolina. Emerging from the Rotunda to the porch whose steps led down the East Portico, Jackson was with Levi Woodbury, the secretary of the Treasury, and Mahlon Dickerson, the secretary of the navy, when the president's eyes met those of a "handsome . . . well-dressed" young man, an unemployed house painter named Richard Lawrence.

Armed with two pistols, standing less than ten feet in front of Jackson, Lawrence raised the first gun and fired. The cap exploded but the powder did not light. Realizing the danger, Jackson charged his assailant, brandishing his walking stick. "The explosion of the cap was so loud that many persons thought the pistol had fired," said Benton. "I heard it at the foot of the steps, far from the place, and a great crowd in between." Lawrence dropped the gun and produced a second pistol, but it too failed to fire. (In both cases the cap exploded but did not light the powder necessary to discharge the bullet.)

Until that moment, Jackson had thought the assassin "firm and resolved"; now Lawrence "seemed to shrink" as the president pursued the assailant with his cane and a nearby navy lieutenant knocked Lawrence to the ground. (Jackson took no chances. "The President pressed after him until he saw he was secured," the **Globe** reported.)

The agitated Jackson was put into a carriage back to the White House. His life may have been saved, in a way, by George Washington and by the weather. In those days there was an empty tomb in the midst of the Rotunda, dug from the floor down to the damp basement, which had been readied for Washington's remains. The first president's heirs, however, resisted moving Washington from Mount Vernon to the Capitol, and so the large hole was unfilled, and it moistened the air in the Rotunda. That, added to the mistiness of the day, probably combined to dampen the powder in both guns. "The pistols were examined, and found to be well loaded; and fired afterwards without fail, carrying their bullets true, and driving them through inch boards at thirty feet," Benton said. The odds of two guns failing to fire during the attack, it was later determined, were 125,000 to one.

JACKSON SEEMED TO calm down during the ride to the White House. Later that day Van Buren found him holding one of Emily and Andrew's children on his lap and talking with Winfield Scott as though nothing exceptional had happened that morning.

Quietly, however, he was seeing enemies everywhere. Though Lawrence appeared to be insane (occasionally claiming to be the king of England, he had tried to kill his sister and had threatened others), Jackson believed Lawrence was an agent of his political foes. When Harriet Martineau visited the White House shortly after the incident, she mentioned the "insane attempt" to the president, who rebuked her. "He protested, in the presence of many strangers, that there was no insanity in the case," Martineau said. "I was silent, of course. He protested that there was a plot, and that the man was a tool. . . . It was painful to hear a chief ruler publicly trying to persuade a foreigner that any of his constituents hated him to the death; and I took the liberty of changing the subject as soon as I could."

Jackson's men blamed the president's opponents for the attack. Lawrence—"taciturn and unwilling to talk," observers recalled—was reported to have haunted the Capitol in recent years. "Whether Lawrence has caught, in his visits to the Capitol, the mania which has prevailed during the last two sessions in the Senate—whether he has become infatuated with the chimeras which have troubled the brains of the disappointed and ambitious orators who have depicted the President as a Caesar who ought to have a Brutus . . . we know not," the **Globe** said. But it was possible, the paper added, that "the infatuated man fancied he had reasons to become his country's avenger."

Jackson was even blunter and more conspiratorial. "Someone told me that you [said] on your way home that it must have been the work of a hired assassin," a friend remarked to Jackson that afternoon at the White House.

"Yes, sir," Jackson replied. "You know I always say what I think. I did say I thought it was the act of a hired assassin, and I still think so—employed by Mr. Poindexter—he would have attempted it himself long ago if he had had the courage." Others had reportedly heard Jackson say the same thing at the Capitol itself: "This man has been hired by that damned rascal Poindexter to assassinate me."

That Jackson's suspicions instantly settled on Mississippi senator George Poindexter illustrates how deeply the president felt about the things closest to him. Poindexter had supported nullification, backed the Bank, attacked the removal of the deposits, and become a rival of Van Buren's. Even in Jackson's Washington, though, for a president to accuse a senator of trying to have him murdered was remarkable. Nathaniel Niles, a diplomat who was at the White House with Jackson after the attack, thought it disturbing for the president "to name any person, especially one holding a high and honorable post in the government, as the author of this base attempt against his life. . . . The President may have private enemies like any other man but it must not be believed that mere party hostility can lead to such results—if it be so it is all over with us—our system cannot be preserved, nor, indeed, is it worth preserving."

PROFESSING INNOCENCE, SENATOR Poindexter demanded an investigation. Three weeks after the incident, Senators John Tyler and Silas Wright, Jr., two members of a five-man select committee, called on Jackson at the White House. There the president shared two affidavits alleging that Lawrence had been seen visiting Poindexter's house in Washington. One was from a blacksmith who did work for the White House, the other from a man who had loaned money to Poindexter. Their stories did not survive scrutiny. The blacksmith appeared to have some hopes of being given work on the new Treasury Department fence, and, the committee found, "has become of late years idle and intemperate, and when under the influence of liquor, which is almost continual, he is talkative and noisy, and . . . unable to discriminate objects with accuracy." The Senate dismissed the allegations against Poindexter.

Questioned afterward by two physicians seeking to determine whether he was insane, Lawrence said that he had often attended the tempestuous congressional debates of 1833–34 but denied that the vitriolic exchanges had driven him to the attack. In the end, Lawrence was found to be mad. "Hallucination of mind was evident; and the wretched victim of a dreadful delusion was afterwards treated as insane, and never brought to trial," Benton recalled. "But the circumstance made a deep impression upon the public feeling, and irresistibly carried many minds to the belief in a superintending Providence, manifested in the extraordinary case of two pistols in succession—so well loaded, so coolly handled, and which afterwards fired with such readiness, force, and precision—missing fire, each in its turn, when leveled eight feet at the President's heart."

Deprived of solid evidence of a broader plot against the president, Blair and the **Globe** settled for blaming anti-Jackson Senate speeches for the attack. Because of the assaults of men like Calhoun, the **Globe** asserted, Lawrence, a "sullen and deep-brooding fanatic" who was "violent in his expressions of hostility to the Administration of the President," took up arms. "Is it . . . a strained inference that this malignant partisan might have been fired to commit the deed by the violent denunciations fulminated against the President?" It was no strain for Jackson, or for his men.

CHAPTER 29

HOW WOULD YOU LIKE
TO BE A SLAVE?

IN THE SUMMER of 1835, Andrew Donelson, cheered by word that his cotton crop in Nashville was good, was in the market for new slaves. On the Fourth of July, Andrew told Stockley that he was "waiting for an inspection of some Negroes in Va.," which went well enough that he "bought two boys" three weeks later. Before he could get them to Tennessee, however, Andrew had vexing news to report: "One of the boys I took . . . was accidentally drowned the other day: which I regret very much as I cannot replace him."

Jackson shared his nephew's view of slavery. To them it was an accepted part of life. Andrew Jackson, Jr., wrote to a friend about exchanging slaves — Southerners euphemistically referred to them as "servants"—in gratitude for seeing that his new wife's "trunk and guitar" reached Nashville safely. The friend, Samuel Hays, apparently wrote to Andrew junior asking about the availability of a woman named Charlotte. "Late on yesterday evening your kind favor came to hand, and immediately I called up Charlotte to ascertain whether she was willing to leave

Charles and her children and I find she is half willing to leave them and Charles. I had just taken her into the house and also as a washer. She is certainly a valuable servant and I hardly know how I can well spare her—and separate her from her children and Charles—and as to the other [girl] you are welcome to take her, but she is lazy and almost worthless." Emily also spoke of slaves with an abhorrent breeziness. Writing her mother from the White House, Emily said: "Andrew has not yet bought me a girl and I am afraid will not have it in his power. Uncle's expenses are so great that they will take the whole of his salary." Jackson could be a harsh master. In an 1804 "Advertisement for Runaway Slave," he offered a fifty-dollar reward for the return of a slave—"and ten dollars extra, for every hundred lashes any person will give him, to the amount of three hundred." He owned about one hundred fifty slaves; he freed none in his will.

The direction of the nation's thinking on slavery in the Jackson years did not bode well for the South. In 1829 David Walker's **Appeal to the Coloured Citizens of the World** appeared; William Lloyd Garrison's **Liberator** newspaper, dedicated to the cause of abolition, had begun publication in January 1831. Jackson may have opposed states' rights when it came to nullification, but on slavery, as on the Indian question, he was not interested in reform. Jackson, who believed in the virtues of democracy and individual liberties so clearly and so forcefully for whites, was blinded by the prejudices of his age, and could not see—or chose not to see, for other Americans of the age did recognize the horror of the way of life Jackson upheld—that the promise of the Founding, that all men are created equal, extended to all.

A slave at the Hermitage, Alfred, once had a revealing exchange with Roeliff Brinkerhoff, a tutor Andrew Jackson, Jr., had hired for his children (Brinkerhoff was later a prison reformer and the author of a seminal text on military logistics). "Alfred was a man of powerful physique, and had the brains and executive powers of a major-general," Brinkerhoff recalled. "He was thoroughly reliable, and was fully and deservedly trusted in the management of plantation affairs." Brinkerhoff ran into Alfred one evening on the grounds but found him "unusually reticent and gloomy." Looking at Brinkerhoff, Alfred asked:

> "You white folks have easy times, don't you?"
> "Why so, Alfred?" I asked.
> "You have liberty to come and go as you will," he replied.
> I soon found that he was full of discontent with his lot, and I thought it wise to turn his attention to the brighter side. . . .
> I showed him how freedom had its burdens as well as slavery; that God had so constituted human life that every one in every station had a load to carry, and that he was the wisest and the happiest who contentedly did his duty, and looked to a world beyond, where all inequalities would be made even. Alfred did not seem disposed to argue the question with me, or to combat

my logic, but he quietly looked up into my face and popped this question at me:

"How would you like to be a slave?"

It is needless to say I backed out as gracefully as I could, but I have never yet found an answer to the argument embodied in that question.

Led by the president, the Jackson circle lived with a wrong, profited from it, and actively protected it. And so, while Andrew Donelson was in the White House, securing—or trying to secure—new slaves for Poplar Grove, Jackson, vacationing with Emily and the children at the Rip Raps, moved to curb the forces of abolition.

PREDICTABLY, THE BATTLE was joined again in South Carolina. From its headquarters on Nassau Street in Manhattan, the American Anti-Slavery Society dispatched thousands of abolitionist pamphlets to Charleston; on Wednesday, July 29, 1835, the mailings arrived aboard the steamboat **Columbia**. The question of what to do with them fell to Alfred Huger, the postmaster. Huger wanted guidance from above—specifically from Amos Kendall, now the postmaster general—and so he locked up the tracts and wrote Kendall for counsel.

Local newspapers ran stories on the contents of the cargo the next morning, and before long the streets of Charleston were once more out of control. It was nullification all over again. A mob came to the post office and burned the mailings—along with effigies of William Lloyd Garrison and other abolitionist leaders—before forty-eight hours had elapsed.

If Jackson had been a president of consistent principle, the issue would have been clear. He was the defender of the Union, the conqueror of nullification, the hero of democracy. An American organization was exercising its constitutional right to free speech and was using the public mails—mails that were to be open to all—to do so. But Jackson was not a president of consistent principle. He was a politician, subject to his own passions and predilections, and those passions and predilections pressed him to cast his lot with those with whom he agreed on the question at hand—slavery—which meant suppressing freedom of speech. He had done the same in the case of the Cherokees and the state of Georgia, allowing a particular issue to trump his more general vision of government, a vision in which people who obeyed the laws were entitled to the protection of the president.

Watching from the Rip Raps, exchanging notes with Kendall, who was in Washington, Jackson spoke as a planter, not a president, referring to the Anti-Slavery Society mailings as a "wicked plan of exciting the Negroes to insurrection and to massacre."

Modernity was working against the white order in practical ways. A Virginia congressman, John W. Jones, articulated the slaveowners' conundrum on the floor of the House in the year of the Charleston debacle. Abolition societies, Jones said, had been formed, and "had gone on to collect large sums of money, and had put into operation printing presses, which were worked by steam. . . . Yes, sir, worked by steam, with the open and avowed object of effecting the immediate abolition of slavery in the Southern states." Steam and the postal service were working in tandem, Jones said—tragic tandem, in his view, as "two great revolutionizers of the world . . . steam power and the press" were creating "large numbers of newspapers, pamphlets, tracts, and pictures, calculated, in an eminent degree, to rouse and inflame the passions of slaves against their masters, to urge them on to deeds of death, and to involve them all in the horrors of a servile war." Jones's view—and Jackson's—was not an extreme one. Northern opinion was hardly enthusiastic about abolition in the mid-1830s, either.

JACKSON REFERRED TO the kinds of tracts that had reached Charleston as "unconstitutional and wicked." In his annual message in December 1835, he asked Congress for a law to "prohibit, under severe penalties, the circulation in the southern States, through the mail, of incendiary publications, intended to instigate the slaves to insurrection."

Calhoun and Jackson agreed on slavery, but the senator from South Carolina heard Jackson's proposal as a call for more federal power, and the more federal power, Calhoun believed, the worse for the South in the long run. Calhoun moved, then, to suggest that the states, not the federal government, should have the right to determine what was incendiary, and what to do about it. The states, Calhoun said, "possessed full power to pass any laws they thought proper." To give Jackson the authority he was asking for would, Calhoun said, "virtually . . . clothe Congress with the power to abolish slavery," for the power to protect implied the power to control, and the power to control included the power to destroy.

Calhoun's proposal instructed federal postmasters to take orders from the various states about what to deliver and what to suppress. The bill was conceived in a confrontational and divisive spirit. "If you refuse cooperation with our laws [forbidding the circulation of mailings regarding slavery] and conflict should ensue between your law and our law, the Southern States will never yield to the superiority of yours," Calhoun said.

Calhoun's bill failed, though, leaving Jackson where he liked to be: in charge. The reports of the violence in Charleston had made him uncomfortable. He thought he had secured that front, and he equated South Carolina's renewed hostility to the federal government—which to Jackson meant hostility against him personally—with a slave insurrection. "This spirit of mob-law is becoming too common and must be checked," he said, "or ere long it will become as great an evil as a servile war." How to exert control over the mob, make clear his own powers, and yet not advance the abolitionist cause? Jackson and Kendall chose the simplest route: they tacitly allowed the suppression of the antislavery mailings.

THE EPISODE AFFIRMED the power of the president, and it captured the intransigence of the slaveholding class. "So the pamphlet controversy in that winter of 1835–36 first showed to the broad public of the new nation that the defenders of slavery were proposing an intellectual blockade," wrote the scholar William Lee Miller. "And it began to suggest, therefore, that that institution, even if confined to the South, was incompatible with republican government. Not only was the enslaved black person denied every freedom, but now the white person was to be denied the freedom to talk about it."

In the pages of the **Globe,** Blair could, on occasion, strike humane notes on the subject. "On principle, slavery has no advocates North or South of the Potomac," the paper once wrote. "The present generation finds the evil entailed on it [and] Providence . . . will, no doubt, in the course of time, relieve the American people of their share of this misfortune."

In the White House, however, the talk about slavery was mostly about the mundane business of acquiring slaves and transporting them back home. Andrew Donelson complained of the expense of sending the slaves he bought in Virginia down to Tennessee. "I had to employ a man, buy horses, wagon, tent, and traveling apparatus throughout for those Negroes," Andrew wrote his brother. There was hope, though, of recouping some of the money: "The wagon and horses," Andrew said, "will no doubt sell" at the conclusion of the journey.

CHAPTER 30

THE STRIFE ABOUT
THE NEXT PRESIDENCY

THE POLITICS OF 1836—the first presidential election in a dozen years in which Jackson, who was retiring in accordance with George Washington's two-term tradition, would not be a candidate—were already moving quickly. For years now, Jackson had dreamed that Van Buren would succeed him, and the Democratic convention in Baltimore in May 1835 had duly nominated the vice president. But Jackson's fellow Tennesseans, unhappy with the prospect of a Van Buren presidency, had nominated one of their own, Judge Hugh Lawson White, a former Democrat, for the White House. Jackson was furious, but he could do nothing about it—except ensure that the Democratic Party he was building was behind Van Buren, not White. The Whigs in the North ultimately settled on William Henry Harrison as their nominee (Daniel Webster was also in the field), and White was the candidate in the South.

The reaction to Van Buren's rise had been vicious. "He is not of the race of the lion or the tiger," Calhoun said of Van Buren; rather, he "belongs to a lower order—the fox." Van Buren, said fellow New Yorker William Seward, was "a crawling reptile, whose only claim was that he had inveigled the confidence of a credulous, blind, dotard old man."

Jackson could not help Van Buren too overtly. Since 1824, Jackson had argued that the selection of a president belonged to the people, not to the bankers or to the politicians. The will of the voters had been thwarted with Adams's victory in 1825, and Jackson believed Biddle and his allies had long maneuvered to manipulate elections. In his first inaugural address, the memories of Clay and Adams still fresh, Jackson had said: "The recent demonstration of public sentiment inscribes on the list of Executive duties, in characters too legible to be overlooked, the task of **reform,** which will require particularly the correction of those abuses that have brought the patronage of the Federal Government into conflict with the freedom of elections." In the Jackson years, in other words, the only kingmakers would be the people. A fine expression of principle—but politics has a way of complicating the application of such principles.

Jackson felt compelled to make his alleged neutrality explicit in an effort to convince the public that he had been steadfast in his view that the selection of a president should be in the hands of the people. "All my friends know that since I have been in the Executive Chair, I have **carefully** abstained from an interference in the elective franchise," Jackson claimed.

The president's assertions were unconvincing. Not even a full year into his administration, Jackson was promoting Van Buren for president. "Permit me here to say of Mr. Van Buren that I have found him everything that I could desire him to be, and believe him not only deserving my confidence, but the confidence of the nation," he wrote John Overton in December 1829, adding that Van Buren "is not only well qualified, but desires to fill the highest office in the gift of the people." In the autumn of 1834, when Jackson was en route from Nashville to Washington, he had a conversation about the 1836 presidential election with Orville Bradley, a prominent east Tennessean. As Jackson and Bradley rode through Hawkins County, Bradley recalled, "the subject of succession was freely discussed." Bradley explained the state's support for White, but "General Jackson entered warmly into a vindication of Van Buren; spoke of him in the highest terms, said that he was the man to whom the party, generally, out of Tennessee was looking to be his successor; that White could hardly get a vote out of Tennessee, and that Tennessee must not separate from the rest of his friends." The solution, Jackson told Bradley, was to nominate White for the vice presidency. "Judge White is yet young enough to come in after Mr. Van Buren," Bradley recalled Jackson saying, "and such an arrangement will make all right now, and secure the certain elevation of Judge White after Mr. Van Buren."

This was hardly the conversation of a disinterested incumbent. Jackson's opponents cleverly sounded more sorrowful than angry. In July 1835, the Nashville **Republican** wrote that "much as the people of Tennessee love Gen. Jackson—much as they venerate his name—they will never surrender, **even at his dictation,** the glorious prize for which he and they so bravely contended at the Battle of New Orleans— THEIR INDEPENDENCE." The paper continued, in all capital letters: "WE WILL NOT FOR AN INSTANT BELIEVE THAT HE WILL DESCEND FROM HIS HIGH ESTATE TO TAKE AN ACTIVE PART IN THE ENSUING ELECTION OR CONSENT TO LEND AN IMPROPER AND UNREPUBLICAN INFLUENCE IN THE APPOINTMENT OF HIS SUCCESSOR."

It was the kind of attack best calibrated to wound Jackson, for it undermined his image of himself as the people's champion. Unfortunately for Jackson, the administration's maneuvers at Baltimore had given the opposition papers a lot to work with. When the moment had come to select a vice presidential nominee, Francis Blair, who had been on hand at the Democratic convention to help Van Buren, successfully backed Richard M. Johnson of Kentucky against William Cabell Rives of Virginia. It was widely believed that Blair was doing Jackson's bidding.

Jackson's attempt to control the succession—he believed he was right to choose Van Buren—took a toll on Andrew Donelson and Blair. In midsummer, while Jackson and Emily were still at the Rip Raps and Donelson was working in Washington, the Nashville Donelsons, led by Stockley, were worried about a series of attacks on Andrew and on Blair in the pages of the **Republican,** an opposition newspaper that favored White over Van Buren. The charge: that the private secretary to the president and the editor of the **Globe** had conspired to use Jackson's frank—his privilege to send mail free of charge—to build up Van Buren for the presidency.

For the **Republican,** targeting Donelson and Blair was shrewd: frontal assaults on Jackson had never gotten very far. By striking at the men around the president, however, the editors of the paper were able to raise ethical questions about the White House without overtly damning Jackson—and simultaneously imply that Jackson was overly dependent on the Kitchen Cabinet.

STRIKE THEY DID, again and again in the summer weeks. The **Republican** declared itself, in the paper's words, "For President HUGH WHITE, whose claim will be submitted not to a packed jury, dignified with the name of a **National Convention**—but to the impartial decision of a free and enlightened PEOPLE." Van Buren, the paper was saying, had been anointed by Jackson and affirmed by a "packed jury" in Baltimore. The theme of Jacksonian overreach suffused the paper's crusade against Donelson and Blair. On Tuesday, July 7, 1835, the **Republican** decried an influx of editions of the **Globe** into the Nashville congressional district. Blair's newspaper, the **Republican** said, carried "the grossest calumnies against Judge White," which had been sent "to many of the prominent citizens of this Congressional District, as well as other parts of this state, **under the frank of the President.**" Jackson himself, the **Republican** said, would never "lend himself to such uses knowingly and willfully. In this conviction we are confirmed by the subscriptions of those envelopes which we have seen, and which are not in the handwriting of the President, but in the handwriting of **another individual,** whose position gives him great facilities in affording these advantages to his political friends."

Donelson had been ready for some kind of assault. "You must keep me advised of movements which will doubtless be made by the **junta** . . . intended to . . . injure me in the public estimation," Donelson wrote Stockley in mid-July. Now that those movements were under way, he tried to project confidence. "My inclinations as well as my duty enjoin upon me silence and forbearance as far as they are consistent with the preservation of my character."

His resolution was soon tested. The **Republican**'s denunciations were awaiting him on the day he returned to the White House, alone, from the Rip Raps. Away from Emily and from the president, Donelson had no one close to reassure him that all would be well, and the words were wounding. "I see that the **Republican** makes an ungenerous allusion to me as the cause of the President's frank upon copies of the **Globe** addressed to persons in Tennessee," he wrote Stockley on Tuesday, July 21. It was an outrage, Donelson thought, and the attack was not really on him but on Jackson. "It would be just as reasonable to assail the **pen** or the **paper** or the ink which the President uses as thus to charge upon those who are near him . . . with . . . responsibility for his acts," Donelson wrote.

Angrily scrawling across the page, Donelson caught himself, and seems to have realized that he was hardly appearing unmoved by the criticism. "But I have no time at present to notice this subject," he closed—after noticing it in detail, and with passion. Three days later, he took up the subject again, telling Stockley: "I have noticed the article you refer to in the **Nashville Republican**. He cannot hurt me if he would." High hopes, perhaps, but Donelson had decided how he would view the matter—that the attacks directed at him were truly intended for Jackson, and that no reasonable person (Donelson prayed) would think otherwise. "It is . . . undoubtedly aimed at the General," he wrote. Donelson was desperate to cast himself as a scapegoat because of his proximity to the president.

The **Republican** savored baiting Donelson and those in Jackson's shadow. In July, the paper kept raising the stakes. "We do not feel disposed, either from inclination or duty, to enter the lists against the **great** Jackson himself, but to all the would-be **little** Jacksons, who cloak their designs under his name, and hope to ride into office upon his back, we say—**come on—stand out like men, and fight upon your own hook,**" it said on July 14.

The opposition turned Jackson's democratic pretensions about the succession against him. If Donelson did not frank the material, then Jackson did—and if Jackson did so, he was violating his own pledges of neutrality. "It has been the professed object of the **Globe,** the **Union** and other Convention papers to show that General Jackson never did, and never wished to interfere in the approaching Presidential election," the **Republican** wrote on Saturday, July 18. Now, though, the Jackson press seemed to be saying that Jackson was behind the frank. "And yet it is now willing to admit, nay it even insists upon the fact, that the President himself is engaged in distributing these copies of a violent party paper. Does not the **Union**, by this admission, furnish at once the most abundant evidence to prove the charge which has been made against General Jackson of a wish to influence the selection of his successor?"

The **Republican**'s true agenda was becoming clear: to cast Jackson as a kingmaking hypocrite, but in language that was arch rather than bombastic, indirect rather than frontal.

It did, however, explicitly link Blair and Donelson to the scandal. "That the Editor of the **Globe** is a joint conspirator with Major Donelson in this business, is evident from the fact that all the documents thus distributed emanate from the **Globe** office. They are carefully enclosed in separate envelopes and, in that shape, no doubt, are regularly laid upon the President's table that he might frank them. To have them laid upon the table is the business, we presume, of the Major."

The next sentence underscored Jackson's assurances of neutrality. "Always supposing that the members of his own household who do not possess the franking privilege would ask the favor of him to frank nothing but what honor and public duty would sanction, he makes no inquiries," the **Republican** said of Jackson. "It would be idle to tell us that the President knows what he is about when he puts his frank upon these documents, and that their contents are well understood by him. It is impossible it should be so. He cannot read them. He would not have the time. . . ." The editorial was published on Tuesday, July 28, 1835.

THE PAPER REACHED Jackson at the Rip Raps by Saturday, August 8. In a stern letter to the editor of the **Republican,** Jackson defended Donelson and Blair absolutely, denouncing the charges as "a vile calumny, utterly destitute of truth. . . . I have never franked any letters or packages for Major Donelson without being informed of their contents."

The **Republican**'s editors could hardly contain themselves: they had now drawn the president himself into the arena. "Does he know—is he quite certain—that Major Donelson has always correctly informed him of the contents of the letters and packages which might be laid before him?"

The likely truth is that Jackson was responsible for the franked mailings, or had at least created a climate within the White House that made Donelson and Blair comfortable undertaking such a pro–Van Buren campaign in Tennessee. The significance of the episode of the **Republican**'s attacks is how it illuminates Jackson's determination to have everything arranged to suit himself, and to secure the image he so cherished.

So it was that Jackson would authorize, or tacitly allow, political work for Van Buren while insisting that he would never do such a thing.

Who paid a price? Not Jackson. Even as ferocious an opponent as the **Republican** went out of its way to depict Jackson as, at worst, a dupe of the men around him. Closest to home, it was Donelson who absorbed the most blows on Jackson's behalf. Donelson could not resist replying, and he could not suppress his anger. The letter he wrote to rebut the **Republican**'s charges, he told his brother-in-law, had been "drawn up in most haste and possibly with too much feeling." The stakes, however, demanded it. "It is painful to me to be drawn into the strife about the next Presidency," he wrote Stockley, but drawn he was, and his own political future was never far from his mind. The best way to defuse the current criticism, it seemed to him, was to argue that the questions about him and his conduct were the inevitable result of jealousy about his place in Jackson's affections.

Donelson believed his foes were hostile to him "not so much because my course was what it was in regard to Major Eaton and Mr. Calhoun, as that I did not allow it to separate me from the President," he said in mid-August. Donelson needed all the fortifications he could muster, for the **Republican** was growing ever crueler as the weeks passed. "The Major, like all weak persons, has a constant itching for intermeddling with things and subjects above his caliber, and a few soft words and fair promises from a certain 'sweet little fellow' [read: Van Buren], who knows so well how to apply them, would almost set him upon his head," the paper said in early September. The **Republican** closed the editorial contemptuously: "But we cannot afford to waste more of our time upon the Major today."

Blair tried his hand at rearranging reality to cast Jackson, and Jackson's circle, in a more flattering light. According to the **Globe**, Blair, Donelson, and Jackson were together in the president's office one day in February 1835. An editorial headlined "General Jackson's Preference" arrived in the mail, which Donelson was opening. Blair was idle; Jackson was immersed in correspondence. Holding the **Republican** in his hands, Donelson began to read aloud to Blair: "It must be apparent to the most superficial observer," the paper said, that Van Buren supporters in Tennessee were trying "to create an impression that General Jackson would decidedly prefer Mr. Van Buren to any other person as his successor, and thus to bring the influence of his powerful name to bear upon the approaching election." As Blair recalled it, "In the progress of the reading, it arrested the President's attention, and at the conclusion, he observed in substance, with some strength of manner, that he would not allow himself to be so misrepresented—that he would not sacrifice his principles to personal partialities—that he would not have the impression made, that his preference was for any man, however he might esteem him as a friend. . . ." Refusing to plead to what Blair called "a charge of **dictation**," Jackson "immediately, without waiting for a remark, glanced at the article, took up his pen and wrote a letter."

· · ·

IN TENNESSEE, THAT story sent White's supporters into an operatic rage. "The indelicacy, presumption, and insincerity of this narrative cannot fail to
strike the most hardened and credulous reader of the
Globe," the **Republican** said. The next lines illumi-
nate the scope of the opposition's fury at the Kitchen
Cabinet, a fury so reflexive in this seventh year of
Jackson's presidency that it had become an inescap-
able element of the American political culture:

> It is evident from the constrained and artificial man-
> ner in which this story is told that if . . . it should turn
> out to be true . . . it was only the execution of a pre-
> concerted plot between Major Donelson and the Edi-
> tor of the **Globe**. The industrious and vigilant Editor
> of a daily paper . . . was surely in the habit of opening
> his own packet of papers either overnight or, at all
> events, in the morning before he attended at the
> White House to assist the Private Secretary in opening
> the President's mail. We venture to say that the wily
> Editor had thus got the start of the President, that he
> had read our article in his own copy of the Republican,
> and that he henceforth repaired to Maj. Donelson and
> arranged with him to have it brought to the notice of
> the President in a way that would take him by surprise
> and be calculated to excite him.

Donelson and Blair, the **Republican** admitted, were
a "worthy pair of political jugglers or wirepullers."
Donelson knew the wars would go on; nothing less

than the presidency was at stake. He put on a brave face. "You may rest assured that I have studied my ground well and feel that I am secure against all the assaults personal or political which . . . open enemies or pretended friends can make against me," he told Stockley. He hoped that the "violence of party strife" would have a cleansing effect, and that the politicians devoted to division—any politician, in Donelson's view, who opposed Van Buren and thus Jackson— would be dispatched in due course. "It will be among the best fruits of the administration to restore to private life many such men who have not the courage to defend the truth nor virtue enough to rejoice at the blessings of republicanism." Hawkish talk aside, he remained worried that hatreds as old as the administration itself could rise up anew to roil the White House. The Donelsons longed to keep all that well in the past. "The Calhoun, the Eaton, and the ancient opposition interest have all . . . common feelings to [annoy] me," Donelson said. But, he added, "I will not be the cause of opening afresh the old wounds."

The back-and-forth was wearing on Jackson, too. One night at the shore, a messenger happened on Jackson kneeling before his miniature of Rachel, reading from her book of Watts's psalms—"the stern man," the observer reported, alone with his memories "with the meekness of a little child."

CHAPTER 31

NOT ONE WOULD HAVE EVER GOT OUT ALIVE

SUNDAY, AUGUST 16, 1835, Jackson, Emily, and the Donelson children left the Rip Raps to return home to the White House. All in all, the sun and sea had done their work, and Donelson was happy to have fresh distractions from the **Republican** attacks. Jackson would need his reserves of strength in the autumn, which was to be a season of war—and not simply political war.

First mapped by the Spanish in 1519, Texas had become a state of the Republic of Mexico in 1821 after Spain ended its three hundred years of control of Mexico. Like Florida, Texas had long tantalized Americans; it was, a visiting U.S. senator wrote in 1829, "a most delicious country." Led in part by Stephen Austin, the son of a St. Louis banker who had been granted the right to settle Anglo-Americans while Texas was still in Spanish hands, Anglo-American settlers began making their homes in Texas in the 1820s, and the region's cotton economy readily accommodated slavery. An 1826 rebellion against Mexican authority—an Anglo-American named Hayden Edwards founded the short-lived Republic of Fredonia—foreshadowed conflicts to come. Worried about the influx of settlers, Mexico began skirmishing with Texans. By Friday, October 2, 1835, the Texas Revolution had begun with a battle at Gonzales, when a hastily assembled army of Texans fought Mexican soldiers who had come to seize the town's cannon. "I cannot remember that there was any distinct understanding as to the position we were to assume toward Mexico," said a Texan who was there. "Some were for independence . . . and some for anything, just so it was a row. But we were all ready to fight."

Jackson appreciated that spirit. From his perspective in Washington, Texas was another Florida: a rich prize that could endanger American security if left in hands other than his own. He had long maneuvered to win Texas, dispatching an envoy, Anthony Butler, to Mexico City with a commission to see if $5 million could convince the Mexicans to part with it. A land speculator in Texas, Butler had been a ward of Jackson's as a child and had fought under him during the Battle of New Orleans; when Jackson became president, Butler came to Washington to see if he could turn his connections into a position with the government. For his part, Jackson regarded Butler's time in Texas and his sympathetic opinions about acquiring Texas to secure the country's borders to be strong qualifications, and appointed him as a chargé d'affaires.

Butler was even more aggressive in his pursuit of annexation than Jackson and at one point suggested bribing the Mexican government. ("A. Butler: What a scamp," Jackson wrote on one of Butler's letters.) It is possible—and perhaps probable—that Butler was simply taking the latitude that Jackson himself seemed to suggest. "This must be an honest transaction," Jackson had written Butler when describing his duties as envoy, but he went on to say: "I scarcely ever knew a Spaniard who was not the slave of avarice, and it **is not improbable** that this **weakness** may be **worth a great deal to us, in this case.**" Mexico's answer to Butler's (and Jackson's) offer was no, but Butler continued pushing for annexation.

News of the fighting in the fall of 1835 sent Mexico into "a perfect tempest of passion in consequence of the Revolt in Texas and all breathe vengeance against that devoted Country," Butler told Jackson. Antonio López de Santa Anna, the powerful leader of Mexico, was, Butler said, "perfectly furious, mad, and has behaved himself in a most undignified manner." Sounding more than a little Jacksonian, Santa Anna had told a gathering of diplomats, including the British and French ministers, that he was convinced the Americans had fomented the rebellion (the settlements led by Austin were a chief culprit in this view) and, Butler told Jackson, the Mexican leader said that he "would in due season **chastise** us. . . . Yes, sir, he said **chastise** us." Bowing to the British representative in an allusion to 1812, Santa Anna said he would "march to the capital" and "lay Washington city in ashes, as it has already been once done." By this time, Sam Houston was advertising for Americans to join the cause. He circulated posters saying: "Volunteers from the United States will . . . receive liberal bounties of land. . . . Come with a good rifle, and come soon. . . . Liberty or death! Down with the usurper!"

AS SANTA ANNA gathered his forces and American volunteers struck out for Texas in December 1835, Jackson received news of war on another front. The removal of the Seminoles from Florida had been fraught and bloody, and was about to grow more so. Osceola led the Seminole war party, and the conflict had the usual elements: white greed, internal Indian divisions (Osceola had murdered a rival Seminole who had chosen to comply with removal), and, for whites, alarming word that escaped slaves were finding sanctuary among the Seminoles.

On Friday, December 18, 1835—a week before Christmas—Osceola attacked a Florida militia wagon train at Kanapaha. Ten days later a force of 180 Seminoles routed an advance guard of Major Francis Dade's force near the Fort King road. By the time the fighting was over, Dade's soldiers—roughly a hundred—were all dead.

The conflict that ensued, the Second Seminole War, would last seven years. It was to become the nation's longest and most expensive Indian war, and while Jackson grew impatient and angry with the American commanders who lost battle after battle to the Seminoles, he never doubted that total victory was the only acceptable answer, no matter how costly. "I have been confined to my room all this day taking medicine,"

Jackson wrote during the conflict. "I have been brooding over the unfortunate mismanagement of **all the military** operations in Florida, all [of] which are so humiliating to our military character, that it fills me with pain and mortification—the sooner that a remedy can be afforded the better." Without security—from Indians, from Mexico, from Spain, from Britain, from **whomever**—Jackson believed that everything else about the American republic was at risk. He was anguished about the Seminoles' success. In a meeting with Florida's territorial delegate, the president denounced the people of Florida. "Let the damned cowards defend their country," Jackson said of Florida's militia. He fumed that if five Indians had come into a white settlement in Tennessee or Kentucky—**Jackson**'s territory—"not one would have ever got out alive." Yet the war went on.

IN NORTHERN GEORGIA in these late autumn and early winter months of 1835–36, Jackson's men were completing the work of Cherokee removal. On Tuesday, December 29, 1835, the administration signed the Treaty of New Echota, a pact purportedly with the Cherokee Nation setting terms for the final removal of the tribe west of the Mississippi.

The Cherokees who signed the treaty, however, were not representative of the tribe as a whole. They were part of what was known as the "Treaty party," a group in opposition to Chief John Ross's "National party." Ross, who represented an estimated 16,000 out of 17,000 Cherokees, was against removal and, if removal had to come, he wanted to hold out for a more advantageous deal with the government. But the Treaty party took the current offer, and the administration chose to believe that the signers had the authority to commit the entire Cherokee Nation. (The Senate ratified New Echota by one vote.) The deadline for removal was set for 1838—the year after Jackson left the White House.

The time came, but the vast majority of Cherokees had not left their lands. Thus began the Trail of Tears, the forced removal of Cherokees to the West. The military could be brutal, and an estimated 4,000 of the 16,000 Cherokees who were forced out died along the way. "I fought through the Civil War and have seen men shot to pieces and slaughtered by thousands, but the Cherokee removal was the cruelest work I ever knew," said one Georgia volunteer.

Van Buren was by then president, but the policy that led to the deaths was Jackson's. Rather than living up to the promise of his many warm words on the subject of his concern for the Indians as their "Great Father," Jackson did not ensure that removal was done humanely (if such a thing were possible). Jackson knew how to exercise power, and had he chosen to do so, he could have used his power to bring about a fairer implementation of his removal policy. In his farewell address in March 1837, Jackson said that "the philanthropist will rejoice that the remnant of that ill-fated race has been at length placed beyond the reach of injury or oppression, and that the paternal care of the General Government will hereafter watch over them and protect them." Did Jackson believe this? Probably; the human capacity to convince oneself of something one wants to think true is virtually bottomless. Given facts such as Indian removal, it has to be.

WITH VIOLENCE IN Texas, bloodshed in Florida, misery for the Cherokees, and the question of the White House succession open for another year, Jackson was buffeted from hour to hour and day to day. Emily, as always, did her best to create a kind of sanctuary for him at home. As Emily's eldest daughter recalled it decades later, Emily organized a large party for Christmas Day 1835. There were six children in the White House: four of Emily and Andrew's, ranging from eighteen months to nine years old, and two of Sarah and Andrew Jackson, Jr.'s, one eighteen months and the other three years old. On Saturday, December 19, 1835, Emily dispatched the invitations:

"The children of President Jackson's family request you to join them on Christmas Day, at four o'clock p.m., in a frolic in the East Room."

How Jackson loved both the idea and the reality of his own clan. For Jackson, home remained the center of order in a chaotic world. Surrounded by family, he tended to be more cheerful amid tribulation than if he were alone. Both Emily and Sarah had been in residence in Washington in the autumn of 1835, an interlude that brightened even Jackson's grimmest days.

This White House holiday was in many ways the pinnacle of Jackson's lifelong project to construct a comfortable and loving universe for himself. On

Christmas Eve afternoon—it was a warm, sunny winter day, Mary Donelson Wilcox (then named Mary Rachel) recalled, "more like May than December"—Jackson announced that he wanted the older children dressed to go for a ride with him in his coach: they were to meet him at the front door of the White House, next to Jimmy O'Neal's office. The household mobilized into action; as Mary Rachel recalled, those around Jackson were "always granting, often anticipating, his wishes" and the family "never dared oppose or disobey his orders." The children were marched to the front door and into the carriage, where they waited for Jackson, who soon appeared.

"To the Orphan Asylum," Jackson told George, the coachman, settling in among the children. Jackson was a strong supporter of the orphanage, a favorite charity of Washington society. (The petition to incorporate the asylum, which was founded by Marcia Van Ness, had been signed by Mrs. Van Ness, Margaret Bayard Smith, and Dolley Madison.) On the way, Mary Rachel recalled, the children quizzed "Uncle" on the absorbing question of the hour.

John: "Uncle . . . did you ever see Santa Claus?"

The President, eyeing John curiously over his spectacles: "No, my boy; I never did."

John: "Mammy thinks he'll not come tonight. Did you ever know him to behave that way?"

The President: "We can only wait and see. I once knew a little boy who not only never heard of Christmas or Santa Claus, but never had a toy in his life; and after the death of his mother, a pure, saintly woman, had neither home nor friends."

Chorus of children: "Poor little fellow! Had he come to the White House we would have shared our playthings with him."

Arriving at the asylum, Jackson said, "Here I am with some Christmas cheer for your young charges." He was a familiar figure to the orphans, and he seemed to relish his fatherly role. "The children gathered in the reception room, and it was gratifying to see their faces light up as, greeting each one, he distributed his gifts, and even more gratifying was it to note his pleasure at their grateful surprise," Mary Rachel wrote.

As the carriage rolled back to the White House through Washington, past still-green parks, Jackson delivered packages Emily and Sarah had prepared. There was, Mary Rachel said, "a hand-painted mirror for Mr. Van Buren, who was reputed to be on very good terms with his looking-glass."

The next morning the president was up early, and the children raced to his room to open their stockings. "Did Santa Claus come?" the children cried. "See for yourselves," Jackson said, and watched as they surveyed their gifts—a small gun, a bridle and saddle, a hobby horse and drum, dolls and tea sets and rattles. It was typically indulgent of Jackson. "Spare the rod and spoil the child," Emily would say in arguments about discipline with Jackson, who would reply: "I think, Emily, with all due deference to the Good

Book, that love and patience are better disciplinarians than rods."

At four that afternoon the children were dressed in their party clothes and took up their stations amid evergreens and flowering plants at the doors of the East Room, on the first floor. The guests flowed in, staying in the Red Room as the children found, Mary Rachel recalled, the East Room to be "an ideal playground, and the players, free and unrestrained as if on a Texas prairie, romping, scampering, shouting, laughing, in all the exuberance of childish merrymaking." At one point Van Buren lost a game of tag, and was forced to stand on one leg and say: "Here I stand all ragged and dirty, / If you don't come kiss me I'll run like a turkey!" No one came to kiss him, and so the vice president of the United States—and putative favorite to be president himself in fifteen months' time—"strutted like a game gobbler across the room." After two hours of games, the band in the hall connecting the East Room to the State Dining Room began to play "The President's March," and supper began.

The dining room on this Christmas Day had been transformed into a confectioner's winter wonderland. Snowballs made of starch-coated cotton towered in the center of the room; there were iced fruits, frosted trees, toy animals, and goldfish. After the meal the children seized the snowballs and raced back down to the East Room for a snowball fight.

The great room seemed, for a moment, filled with flakes of snow. It had been a spectacular, enchanting day—of family ties and affection and gifts and grace. But like the snowball skirmish, which Mary Rachel found "exhilarating and inspiring" though "provokingly brief," the day was soon over. Emily saw the guests out, and the tired children were tucked into bed upstairs.

She would be dead within the year.

CHAPTER 32

★

I FEAR EMILY
WILL NOT RECOVER

ON SATURDAY, JANUARY 2, 1836, Jackson paid a Philadelphia merchant named George W. South for a shipment of furnishings for the rebuilt Hermitage. Included in an order for crimson silk curtains, brass andirons, and marble-topped washstands were three sets of wallpaper depicting scenes from the French philosopher Fénelon's work **Telemachus**, a favorite of Jackson's. The paper was to hang in the grand entry hall of the new house.

Written in 1699, the book chronicles the political education of Odysseus's son by the tutor Mentor. "The whole world has its eyes upon him who is highly elevated above others, watching his conduct and criticizing it with the utmost severity," the book notes. "Those who judge him are unacquainted with his situation. They know nothing of his difficulties, they will not allow him to have any human weaknesses and failings, but expect he should be altogether perfect. A king, however wise and good he may be, is still only a man."

The saga of Telemachus—a child left without a father—had innate appeal to Jackson, and Fénelon's treatise, with its grasp of the subtleties of power and of the complexities of marrying monarchism with republicanism, was an engaging and resonant text for a man in the arena. At one point in the narrative, when Telemachus has complained of the burdens of office, Fénelon writes: "'True it is,' replied Mentor, 'a king is only king in order to take care of his people, as a shepherd tends his flock, or a father superintends his family. . . . The wicked he punishes, and the good he rewards, and thus represents the gods in leading the whole human race to virtue.'"

Telemachus broods on the injustices and difficulties a ruler faces. "Mentor replied to him patiently: 'You must count on the ingratitude of mankind, and yet not be discouraged by it from doing good: you must study their welfare, not so much for their own sakes, as for the sake of the gods, who have commanded it. The good that one does is never lost; if men forget it, the gods will remember and reward it. Further, if the bulk of mankind are ungrateful, there are always some good men who will have a due sense of your virtue. Even the multitude, though fickle and capricious, does not fail sooner or later to do justice, in some measure, to true virtue.'"

To some extent and to some degree, in other words, leadership is tragic. There will be disappointments and injustices and failures of imagination or of will. Jackson understood that governing was provisional—no single bill or single election would ever bring about the perfection of all things—but his experience suggested that the American people, if given world enough and time, would come to a right conclusion.

Jackson was elegiac as he began his last full year in office. He was, in Fénelon's terms, a shepherd and a father looking both forward and backward, musing on the past and the future. "You are assembled at a period of profound interest to the American patriot," Jackson had told Congress in his annual message in December 1835. "The unexampled growth and prosperity of our country having given us a rank in the scale of nations which removes all apprehension of danger to our integrity and independence from external foes, the career of freedom is before us."

It was a message, however, that alternated between hope and fear. Jackson had, in his view, triumphed over sundry sources of dissension, from South Carolina's nullification movement to the purported corrupting influence of the Bank. But there were always enemies, always forces that threatened the essential structure of the country, and Jackson remained concerned about abolitionists who were determined to be heard through the distribution of pamphlets.

He denounced abolitionists' "inflammatory appeals." Worried that antislavery forces were about to destroy the country, Jackson said: "There is doubtless no respectable portion of our countrymen who can be so far misled as to feel any other sentiment than that of indignant regret at conduct so destructive of the harmony and peace of the country, and so repugnant to the principles of our national compact and to the dictates of humanity and religion."

This was a widespread sentiment in the Jackson years. "Our happiness and prosperity essentially depend upon peace within our borders," he wrote, "and peace depends upon the maintenance in good faith of those compromises of the Constitution upon which the Union is founded." For Jackson and many others—including many Northerners—slavery was such a compromise, and abolition was seen as a threat to the Republic's precarious political balance.

Still, Southerners feared history was not on their side. "The moral power of the world is against us," Congressman Francis Pickens of South Carolina told the House in January 1836. Angelina Grimké, a native South Carolinian who had moved to the North and was, with her sister, an emerging force in the abolition movement, published an **Appeal to the Christian Women of the South** in 1836, holding up Esther and the women around Jesus as models of reform. On Friday, March 11, 1836, Calhoun acknowledged the high price of the flow of abolitionist appeals, whether by mail at home or by petition in the capital. "We must ultimately be not only degraded . . . but be exhausted and worn out on such a contest."

THE WAR OVER slavery continued to be fought by proxy. In the early years of the administration, the pretext had been the tariff. The year before, in 1835, it had been the right of states to tell postmasters to suppress abolitionist mailings. Now, in the last full year of the Jackson presidency, the question became one of the right of American citizens to petition the Congress in favor of emancipation, particularly within the District of Columbia.

To curtail the debate and avoid having to decide on the future of slavery, Congress employed what was called the gag rule, which represented the slaveholders' attempt to pretend as though—at least in the halls of Congress—there was no dispute over the question in America. In a practice devised by South Carolina congressman Henry Pinckney, the House would "table"—the parliamentary term for ignoring—abolitionist petitions, effectively denying constituents the right to be heard on arguably the most consequential issue in American life. (The Senate did the same, though it did not officially vote to "gag" abolitionists. It just did so.)

As 1836 wore on, several Jackson imperatives came into conflict with one another. There was his support, however tacit, for the Texas Revolution against Mexico; he hoped that an independent Texas would become part of the United States, frustrating any lingering British or European imperial designs. There was Indian removal, which was proving bloody and expensive and, if the Seminole case was any indication, could grow even bloodier.

John Quincy Adams saw the inherent tensions. "Mr. Chairman, are you ready for all these wars? A Mexican war? A war with Great Britain, if not with France? A general Indian war? A servile war? And, as an inevitable consequence of them all, a civil war?" Adams demanded in the House in May 1836. "From the instant that your slaveholding states become the theater of war, civil, servile, or foreign, from that instant the war powers of Congress extend to interference with the institution of slavery in every way by which it can be interfered with."

AN APPEAL FOR help from Stephen Austin came to Jackson in the middle of April 1836. It had been a dizzying few weeks for Texas. On Wednesday, March 2, Texas declared its independence at the town of Washington, on the Brazos River. Then, on Sunday, March 6, Santa Anna's Mexican troops stormed the Alamo, a fort being defended by David Crockett, James Bowie, William Barret Travis, and roughly 185 others. The Texans refused to give in, and in an hour and a half of brutal combat, Santa Anna massacred every man in the fort. Two weeks later, at Goliad, the Mexican dictator executed 330 soldiers. Then, on April 20 and 21, 1836, at the junction of Buffalo Bayou and the San Jacinto River, Sam Houston rallied his men for what became a final victory. "Victory is certain! Trust in God and fear not! And remember the Alamo! Remember the Alamo!" A Texas force of nearly one thousand defeated Santa Anna's fourteen hundred men—and the general was brought to Houston as a prisoner.

For official purposes, Jackson had maintained the appearance of neutrality in the Texas conflict. When Austin wrote asking for help in what he told Jackson was "a war of barbarism against civilization, of despotism against liberty, of Mexicans against Americans," Jackson demurred, noting on the letter: "The writer does not reflect that we have a treaty with

Mexico, and our national faith is pledged to support it. The Texans, before they took the step to declare themselves independent, which has aroused and united all Mexico against them, ought to have pondered well."

But to young Jackson Donelson, Emily and Andrew's nine-year-old son, the president expressed his true feelings on the subject in a letter about the story of the Alamo. From boarding school in Chantilly, Virginia, young Donelson had written Jackson about the Alamo, and on Friday, April 22, 1836, Jackson replied: "Your sympathies expressed on hearing of the death of those brave men who fell in defense of the Alamo displays a proper feeling of patriotism and sympathy for the gallant defenders of the rights of freemen, which I trust will grow with your growth . . . and find you always a strong votary in the cause of freedom."

ON TUESDAY, MAY 10, 1836, the spring racing season began in Washington; Andrew Donelson was to try his luck with a filly named Emily. According to Blair's **Globe**, "To give variety to the amusement of the turf a splendid ball is to be given by the members of the Jockey Club . . . at Carusi's rooms which no doubt will be graced by the beauty and the fashion of the City."

Such glamorous hours—Carusi's had been the scene of the first inaugural party, all those years ago— were growing short for Emily, who was to return to Tennessee in June. She lost a sister in April, and in May Edward Livingston died—news that shook

Emily, who was herself never in the best of health. Her letter to Louise Livingston suggests that the subject of mortality was uncomfortable, and it was only with effort that she was able to express her sympathy to the family that had been so kind to her.

"I have intended to write to you for some days past but have felt so much distressed at the loss we have all sustained [that I] have not been able to do so until today," Emily wrote on June 8; by contrast, Jackson's letter to Mrs. Livingston was dated May 26. "I expect to leave the city for our home in Tennessee in a few days and cannot bear to set off until assuring you and my dear Cora of my sincere and affectionate sympathy. . . . No one was more beloved by all who knew him and more regretted than Mr. Livingston and we may hope [he] has only exchanged this for a better world and we must all sooner or later expect to follow." Having at last rallied her energies to write, Emily forced herself to look ahead to the autumn with confidence and made a noble effort at good cheer, anticipating a journey to the Livingstons' in New York. "I hope . . . to return early in the fall and unless something should happen to prevent will see you on the North River and pay to you the long promised visit."

Yet she remained unwell as she prepared for the trip to Tennessee. She was to take three of the four children. Jackson Donelson was to stay with his father and uncle until Congress adjourned, and then come south. She was worried about her son being left in the White House. Andrew had to reassure her that he would "have nothing to do but to care for" Jackson "when I am not in my office."

EMILY'S EMOTIONAL AGITATION—a breakdown in her usual sense of orderliness and of domestic command—foreshadowed a breakdown in her physical health. She reached Nashville on Sunday, June 26, and was at work at Poplar Grove through July and much of August, awaiting her husband and her eldest son. They left Washington with the president on Sunday, July 10, but were slowed by terrible rains that turned the roads into muddy bogs. Jackson's horses' feet were "torn to the quick and left almost without hoofs." From Salem, Virginia (Jackson usually spelled it "Salum"), a week later, Andrew told Emily: "We reached here today . . . after a severe drive over the most intolerable roads that were ever travelled. It is as much as we can do to make nigh 18 miles a day and are in constant danger of breaking some part of our carriage or gear. You must not therefore be disappointed if it is the 4th or 5th of August before we reach home." He added a reassuring report about their son: "Jackson is in fine health and makes a fine traveler." For Emily, though, the spring and summer of death continued apace: the third week of July brought word that Mrs. Mary Ann McLemore, an old family friend and member of the large Donelson clan, had died. Meanwhile, her own two-year-old daughter, Rachel, was "not so well," adding to the strain.

Jackson and Andrew finally arrived at the Hermitage on Thursday, August 4. For all his talk about being tired, however, Jackson, like most politicians, could not rest for long. Three weeks later he was working a huge picnic, campaigning for Van Buren, "shaking hands," he said, "with at least 4,000 people—many from my old friends both male and female." Andrew had come along, but chose to return home to Poplar Grove rather than traveling on with Jackson to a visit with Mrs. Coffee in Florence, Alabama. It turned out to be a wise decision. He did not have much time to spend with his wife, who was now demonstrably sick. It was, it would turn out, tuberculosis.

ONCE THE BLEEDING began, it seemed to last forever. Hemorrhaging from her lungs, Emily scared those around her. The attack was of a different magnitude than anything she had suffered before. Andrew was terrified and prepared for the worst, remaining with her and the children when Jackson had to return to Washington. From a stop twelve miles south of Louisville on Saturday, September 17, 1836, Jackson wrote Andrew junior, who had also stayed in Nashville, "I will be uneasy until I hear from you—I fear Major Donelson will not be able to leave Emily—indeed I fear Emily will not recover." Six days later, from Wheeling, at nine in the evening, Jackson found himself without word from Nashville, and the silence exacerbated his fears about Emily. Was she dead already?

"My mind is sorely oppressed by not hearing from you at Louisville or this place—my fears of the situation of our dear Emily have been much heightened from not hearing from you," Jackson wrote Donelson. "Should this reach you at home I pray you to write me and let me hear how Emily and the dear little children are—I shall not rest until I hear from you."

Touching as it was, the letter ranged from personal concern for Emily to the politician's inevitable reports of how he seemed to be playing with the public as he canvassed for Van Buren. "I reached Wheeling about sunset and there was an immense crowd—such a one I have never seen there before," Jackson told Donelson. "At Cincinnati and everywhere I landed there were immense crowds so that I am nearly worn down with fatigue." He could not help wondering, too, whether Emily's illness would keep his private secretary from the White House indefinitely. "Pray write me soon how our dear Emily is and when you will be in the City—present my ardent prayers to her for her speedy recovery."

So it had always been for Emily and Andrew: their lives depended on Jackson's, and Jackson depended on them. In his old age, in the last months of a trying presidency, with an Indian war in Florida, plans for the removal of the Cherokees—a chancy business—under way, and Van Buren facing the voters, he had to have the Donelsons as he had had them from the beginning, and while he loved them without question, he also needed them to be able to serve him as they always had. Writing Van Buren, Jackson said, "I pity the Major's situation—her loss would unman him, and be a lamentable bereavement to her family." And yet there were the practical considerations, too: "I find much business has accumulated, and if Major Donelson does not come on soon I will find myself greatly oppressed with business."

In Nashville, Andrew seemed to lose hope. Emily was no longer running a fever, but there were signs, he wrote, of lung disease, and she was, her husband said, in "a kind of stupor."

Reaching the White House on Saturday, October 1, 1836, Jackson spent the evening, he wrote Andrew, "in melancholy gloom and in forebodings of unpleasant information from our dear Emily." The next morning he finally received the depressing word from Donelson that Emily was worse. It was "with painful sensations," Jackson replied to Andrew, that he "read the melancholy information of her continued ill health and forebodings of the result of her disease." Drawing on his own experience with losing Rachel, Jackson tried to reassure his nephew while preparing the young husband for the end. "I trust in the mercy of a kind superintending providence that He will restore her to health and bless her dear little children . . . and prolong her life to be a comfort to you in your declining years," Jackson said. The world, however, had a way of failing to conform to our warmest wishes.

"But my dear Andrew," Jackson went on, "should providence will it and call her hence you must summon up all your fortitude to meet the melancholy event, keeping in mind how necessary your life becomes to your dear children. . . ." In conclusion, Jackson tried to strike a more cheerful note: "Still I have a hope that as the hemorrhage has ceased and the fever checked she will soon recover, for which present to her my affectionate regards with my prayer for her speedy recovery and your safe arrival soon here, with all your dear little ones."

YET EVEN NOW, in a dark personal hour, Jackson could not stay away from politics. "I have no doubt of every republican state in the union going for Van Buren," Jackson told Andrew; Jackson so yearned for vindication through the election of his chosen successor that he willed himself into an optimistic frame of mind. To Van Buren himself, Jackson wrote, "I can say to you that the political horizon is bright and cheering." The facts were rather different. The election was close, and Jackson was simultaneously anxious for Emily and for Van Buren. He would have seen little distinction between the two concerns, for to him the country was family, too.

Andrew, who had despaired of Emily in the letter Jackson had read on October 2, nevertheless decided to leave her alone with her mother and children ten days later. The pull of Washington, and of Jackson, was too great. The president's neediness was evident to those around him. He made no effort to hide it. Mulling a farewell address, he asked Roger Taney for help: "I am so harassed with business and company, and deprived as I am of the aid of Major Donelson that I am compelled to ask the aid of friends in maturing the address I have in contemplation." As these words were written, Donelson was already on the road to Washington, and he was already trying to assuage his own guilt with assertions of good cheer.

"Words cannot express the pain which the separation from you at this time has occasioned me," Andrew wrote Emily—though the pain was not so significant that it prevented him from returning to Jackson's service. "Be assured my dear Emily that not a moment will be lost that can hasten my return. . . . From what Dr. Laurence told me I feel the strongest hopes that your strength will be gradually recovered. . . . Remember me affectionately to your Mother who is so good and kind to you and our dear children. Her remaining with you places me under obligations which I can never forget."

According to family tradition, Emily approved of Andrew's return to the White House, and perhaps she did. She had been feeling better since the terror of the long hemorrhage. She understood the claim Jackson had on her and her husband, and for her, as for Andrew, Washington remained irresistible. Still, when Andrew suggested that he might not be back at Poplar Grove until Congress met in March 1837—five months hence—Emily reacted badly. Family tradition has her "in tears" at the thought that Andrew would not return in December; in a letter to Andrew, her brother William said, "I would judge it would be best for you to be back at the time appointed."

It was about eleven o'clock on the evening of Thursday, October 20, 1836, when Andrew arrived at the White House, and as he sat down to write Emily the next day he knew what she would want to hear: "Your numerous friends in the City inquire with the greatest affection and solicitude about your health and express an earnest hope that it will be in your power to come on here in the course of the winter." Warm words, and calculated, for he had had little opportunity to field a large number of inquiries about her. To his credit, he tried to be reassuring. "I will see that all your dresses and other articles are properly attended to," he said. "You shall hear from me again in a few days. In the meantime I trust I shall receive a letter from you and that the inquietude of mind which I have [had] since I left you may be less afflicting."

Andrew had two duties at hand. Though he served as the president's private secretary, he earned a salary signing public land warrants for the General Land Office, and he had forty thousand documents awaiting him. Jackson, meanwhile, needed him to work on his annual message. Trapped between duty to his wife and his White House obligations, Andrew struck pleading notes in his letters home:

I trust, my dear Emily, that you will not allow my necessary absence from you at this time to prey on your spirits. The business which made it incumbent upon me to come here I am dispatching as fast as possible, and I shall certainly be able to join you in the course of the first week of December. . . . There is nothing, my dear, that I possess that will not be fully given to secure the recovery of your health, for without you neither life nor property can be worth anything to me.

Summoning her strength, Emily wrote to Andrew and, struggling to act as though things were normal, enclosed a list of clothes the children needed purchased in Washington.

Perhaps prodded by Donelson, Jackson wrote Emily, too, emphasizing the significance of Donelson's mission in the White House, arguing that Donelson would have been subject to attack if he had not come on to Washington—an appeal that had a good chance of resonating with the politically sensitive Emily. "The Major is working night and day to get his work in signing patents so that he may return to you—he had upwards of 40,000 when he reached here to sign all prepared for his signature. He will be with you the first moment after he can close this absolutely necessary duty, and my dear Emily you must bear his absence with patience as it is a very necessary . . . one . . . as these grants without his signature would have been entirely lost to the public and he subject to the censure of a vindictive world for the same." Andrew, meanwhile, wrote with more straightforward sympathy and love: "I am constantly filled with apprehension lest something untoward should arise to lessen your comforts and interrupt the recovery of your health," he told her. Perhaps most important, a date of departure for Andrew was fixed: he was to leave Washington for Nashville on Tuesday, November 22.

• • •

IN HER SICKROOM in Tennessee, Emily, between bouts of coughing and worries about fever, was sentimental about the flow of good wishes and prayers from Washington. Writing to Andrew on Friday, November 11, she "was so filled with gratitude for your constant attention and the solicitude and anxiety you all feel about me" that she said she "could not help crying." She had been strong all autumn, refusing to succumb to self-pity.

Now, with these tears and with the promise of Andrew's return, she indulged herself a bit. "I believe it is the first time I've been so foolish since you went away," she said, and gave herself credit for her own steeliness: "Indeed I have borne your absence like a heroine [and] have not been low-spirited unless it was a very gloomy day." She took her mind off her illness with activity, knitting stockings. The prognosis was mixed. "I have no pain, no night sweats, no flushing, but still I get my strength very slowly," she said, though on a particularly good early November day she "did not lay down all day and rode out twice."

In the White House, Donelson at last finished signing the patents, only to discover that Jackson "has made but little progress with his message"—and then, on the evening of Saturday, November 19, Jackson suffered his own hemorrhage attack. "Under the circumstances considering the near approach of Congress, and the great public responsibility resting upon him at this juncture, it would have been inexcusable for me to have left him," Donelson told Emily on November 20. "My dear Emily do not allow yourself to be disturbed by the delay.... It will only be a few days of increased pain and anxiety to me—but if my prayers can avail anything—they will be days of returning power and strength to you." Jackson came first. He always had.

From his own sickbed, Jackson reassured Emily on November 27 that all would be well: "You are young, and with care and good treatment, will outgrow your disease." He then fell back on religious imagery, linking his own illness with hers:

My dear Emily—this chastisement by our Maker we ought to receive as a rebuke from Him, and thank him for the mildness of it—which was to bring to our view ... that we are mere tenants at will here. And we ought to live daily so as to be prepared to die; for we know not when we may be called home. Then let us receive our chastisements as blessings from God, and let us so live that we can say with the sacred poet:

> What though the Father's rod
> Drop a chastising stroke,
> Yet, lest it wound their souls too deep,
> Its fury shall be broke.
>
> Deal gently, Lord, with those
> Whose faith and pious fear,
> Whose hope, and love, and every grace,
> Proclaim their hearts sincere.

I must close with my blessing to you and the children. May God bless you **all**. Emily, farewell.

Emily waited, but still Andrew did not come. There was always something to detain him. On Thursday, December 1, Jackson wrote in a note to young Jackson Donelson, "Your dear papa . . . was to have left this morning, but owing to my debility remains today and tomorrow to have my Message copied **well** and prepared for transmission to Congress next Tuesday—say to your dear Mama that I regret that he should be thus one moment detained from her." In this difficult moment another ancient dynamic was at work: the avuncular encouragement of great ambitions for a young Donelson by Andrew Jackson. While Andrew Donelson the father worked on the presidential message, while Emily Donelson the mother lay ill, possibly dying, Andrew Jackson the uncle was urging their son to think of high station. "I wish you to attend to your education . . . recollect that you never can become a great man (which I wish you, and fondly hope you will become) without a good and liberal education. . . . I hope you will become a great good and enlightened man."

In a few lines jotted to Emily, Jackson added: "Your dear husband is well—was to have left us this morning but on yesterday it was determined to abridge part of my Message and from my debilitated state he has determined to wait until Saturday [December 3]. . . . I am slowly mending—take care of yourself and I am sure you will outgrow your attacks, which may God grant is the prayer of your affectionate uncle."

Andrew left for Nashville on that Saturday, December 3, but Emily had already begun to fail. "Emily grows worse and worse, weaker and weaker daily, and to hope is almost hopeless," wrote her relative James Glasgow Martin. "Major Donelson is not at home, which is a matter of regret to us all, tho' expected by the 15th of this month, this may be in time to see his beloved once more, but is uncertain."

As Andrew drew closer to Nashville, Emily slipped ever further away. The story is told that a small bird flew into Emily's room at sunset one December day, and she stopped the children from trying to capture it. "Don't disturb it, darling," Emily said. "Maybe it comes to bid me prepare for my flight to another world. . . . Don't forget mama; love her always and try to live so that we may all meet again in heaven." On Friday, December 16, she thought the end had come, and she said good-bye to the children. She asked to be settled in bed with a view of the road.

She would wait, she said, until her husband reached home.

EMILY'S DEATH CAME to Jackson in a dream. Asleep in his bedroom in the White House on that winter Friday, he awoke from a vision of Emily in heaven, and he quickly wrote Andrew, who was still en route to Nashville. "I grow more anxious about the fate of our dear Emily—I had an extraordinary dream last night," Jackson said, "that adds to my anxiety on her account." He wrote these words on the eighth anniversary of Rachel's initial collapse inside the Hermitage in 1828— the collapse that marked the beginning of her final days.

His message to Donelson is virtually breathless with his fright at the vision of Emily's death: "If Providence has called her home I am persuaded she has a happy immortality—still I hope our . . . redeemer has spared her for the benefit of her dear children, and a comfort and consolation to you—we all join in prayers for her speedy recovery."

The sleeping Jackson, however, was closer to the truth than the waking one. On Monday, December 19, 1836, her husband still on his way to Nashville, Emily Donelson died. She was twenty-nine years old.

HER MOTHER DELAYED the burial, and finally, two days later, on the morning of Wednesday, December 21, Andrew Donelson arrived. "I thanked her from the bottom of my heart, for it was some relief to its desolation to have the privilege of beholding once more the being it had loved almost to idolatry," Donelson wrote Jackson.

At almost midnight on that evening, Donelson recommitted himself to the old man's service. Emily was gone, but his duty remained. "Let me hear from you often, for now that my dear wife is withdrawn from me, my greatest solicitude is to know that your health will last until you can reach the Hermitage once more," Donelson said.

The news did not reach the White House until New Year's Eve. "Would to God I had been there," Jackson told Donelson. "I was fearful from my dream that her God had called her hence, and . . . my forebodings increased, and are now realized." Ten days after that, he joined Andrew in taking charge of the now motherless brood: "We must summon up all that fortitude we can, to preserve our healths, and to live for their benefit." They were in this together, Jackson said: "Peace to her manes, and consolation to you and your dear children, is my prayer."

CHAPTER 33

★

THE PRESIDENT WILL
GO OUT TRIUMPHANTLY

AS EMILY LAY dying, politics in Washington ran their usual course. In November people cast their votes for the next president. It was a close race, and for a while, as the returns trickled in, Van Buren seemed likely to be defeated. If the vote was sent to the House—which was possible—he would probably lose to Harrison or White. But by the beginning of December Van Buren learned that he had won in the Electoral College. His margin of victory in the popular vote in some states measured in the hundreds.

However distracted by his own fortunes, President-elect Van Buren comforted Andrew Donelson with a report that Emily's death had touched even the most cynical in Washington. He would, he said, "never cease to admire her excellent character. . . . It will I am sure be grateful to your feelings to learn how extensively this sentiment is entertained here where such feelings are, you know, not apt to take deep root—it is much more than I have witnessed on any former occasion."

Anything connected to Emily took on significance,

particularly a portrait by Earl. Jackson had it boxed to send back to Nashville. Remembering the loss of other shipments in recent years, though, Donelson asked Jackson to put it aside until he reached Washington. "I shall write you again in a few days, in respect to the portrait of my dear wife, which you inform me is packed up with the others you design sending out," Donelson said. "I would remark that I prefer not to risk it to the chances of a consignment either by water or land to Nashville. If I can so arrange my business as to be able to leave home in the spring I can bring it with me."

In his grief, as he had with Rachel, Jackson pressed on. Eight Christmases before, he had turned to Emily and made the journey to Washington. Then he had found comfort in fighting what he saw as a war for the people. Now, in the twilight of his presidency, he wanted to win one final battle for the presidency itself, and for his personal honor, by erasing what he thought was the great blot on his record: the censure of the Senate for his removal of the Bank deposits in 1834.

The White House years of Andrew Jackson were to end as they had begun—in personal grief and political passion, with hosannas from his supporters and hatred from his foes. The era itself had been one of drama—sometimes melodrama—and danger. It would now come to a close in the Senate chamber, with speeches of praise and condemnation, with lawmakers standing implacably for him or against him. The business before the Senate in January 1837 was a motion to expunge the censure from the record—undoing, in effect, the Senate's denunciation of Jackson's unilateral decision to effectively destroy the Bank of the United States. Benton, who was leading the president's cause, wanted his troops well cared for, and ordered a supply of cold ham, turkey, wine, and hot coffee. It was, however, hardly a festive occasion. According to Isaac Bassett, a young page, "the great part of the Senate was not in a humor to eat."

Sarcastic, angry, and resigned, Clay said:

The decree has gone forth. It is one of urgency, too. The deed is to be done—that foul deed which, like the blood-stained hands of the guilty Macbeth, all ocean's waters will never wash out. Proceed, then, by the noble work which lies before you, and like other skillful executioners, do it quickly. And when you have perpetrated it, go home to the people, and tell them what glorious honors you have achieved for our common country. Tell them that you have extinguished one of the brightest and purest lights that ever burnt at the altar of civil liberty. Tell them that you have silenced one of the noblest batteries that ever thundered in defense of the constitution, and bravely spiked the cannon. Tell them that, henceforward, no matter what daring or outrageous act any President may perform, you have forever hermetically sealed the mouth of the Senate. Tell them that he may fearlessly assume what powers he pleases, snatch from its lawful custody the public purse, command a military detachment to enter the halls of the Capitol, overawe Congress, trample down the constitution, raze every bulwark of freedom; but that the Senate must stand mute, in silent submission, and not dare to raise its opposing voice. . . . And, if the people do not pour out their indignation and imprecations, I have yet to learn the character of American freemen.

Calhoun joined Clay in opposition. "No one, not blinded by party zeal, can possibly be insensible that the measure proposed is a violation of the constitution," Calhoun said. "The constitution requires the Senate to keep a journal; this resolution goes to expunge the journal. If you may expunge a part, you may expunge the whole; and if it is expunged, how is it kept?" Like Clay, however, he knew that his was a futile argument, for "this act originates in pure, unmixed, personal idolatry. It is the melancholy evidence of a broken spirit, ready to bow at the feet of power. . . . An act like this could never have been consummated by a Roman Senate until the times of Caligula and Nero."

As Benton undertook the defense of the president, the galleries filled with Jackson enemies (Benton believed them to be Bank men), prompting several pro-Benton senators to send for guns. Not surprisingly, Benton's speech making the case for Jackson was as grand in exaltation as Clay's and Calhoun's had been in denunciation.

"History has been ransacked to find examples of tyrants sufficiently odious to illustrate him by comparison," Benton said of Jackson. "Language has been tortured to find epithets sufficiently strong to paint him in description. Imagination has been exhausted in her efforts to deck him with revolting and inhuman attributes. Tyrant, despot, usurper; destroyer of the liberties of his country; rash, ignorant, imbecile; endangering the public peace with all foreign nations; destroying domestic prosperity at home. . . ." Benton dismissed all such charges.

> He came into office the first of generals; he goes out the first of statesmen. His civil competitors have shared the fate of his military opponents; and Washington city has been to the American politicians who have assailed him what New Orleans was to the British generals who attacked his lines. Repulsed! Driven back! Discomfited! Crushed! has been the fate of all assailants, foreign and domestic, civil and military. At home and abroad, the impress of his genius and of his character is felt.

Still, though, the assailants came, and came, and came again, and against any other president, Benton argued, they might have succeeded. But not against Jackson. "Great has been the opposition to President Jackson's administration; greater, perhaps, than ever has been exhibited against any government, short of actual insurrection and forcible resistance," Benton said. "The country has been alarmed, agitated, convulsed. From the Senate chamber to the village barroom, from one end of the continent to the other, denunciation, agitation, excitement, has been the order of the day. For eight years the President of this republic has stood upon a volcano, [which has been] vomiting fire and flames upon him, and threatening the country itself with ruin and desolation, if the people did not expel the usurper, despot, and tyrant, as he was called, from the high place to which the suffrages of millions of freemen had elevated him."

How had he done it? How had he survived? Benton gave a high-flown answer, but one with much merit.

> Great is the confidence which he has always reposed in the discernment and equity of the American people. I have been accustomed to see him for many years, and under many discouraging trials; but never saw him doubt, for an instant, the ultimate support of the people. . . . He always said the people would stand by those who stand by them; and nobly have they justified that confidence! That verdict, the voice of millions, which now demands the expurgation of that sentence, which the Senate and the Bank then pronounced upon him, is the magnificent response of the people's hearts to the implicit confidence which he then reposed in them.

The motion to expunge carried, and, after what Isaac Bassett called "a storm of hisses and groans" from the left wing of the Circular Gallery (the sergeant at arms rounded up the "disturbers"), the record of Jackson's censure for abuse of power was marked out of the journal by the secretary of the Senate.

THRILLED BY THE vote, Jackson invited the senators who had become known as "the expungers" to
dine at the White House with their wives. He was too
sick to sit at the table, but he greeted his guests and
seated Benton—the "head-expunger," a title that, in
these days in Jackson's world, had no rival—in his
own chair. "All going well here," Andrew Jackson, Jr.,
wrote to Stockley Donelson on the last day of January
1837, "and the President will go out triumphantly
after all." That he would. The vindication was to his
political career what New Orleans had been to his
military years: what Benton called the "crowning
mercy."

Benton sent Jackson the pen that had, in Clay's
phrase, done the deed. Jackson would treasure it, he
told Benton, as one of his "precious relics." It was,
for him, the instrument of a sacred act, for it had
vindicated his vision not only of the presidency but
of himself and his connection with the people—
a connection Jackson considered as strong as any
earthly bond could be. He loved them, or had convinced himself he loved them; how could anyone
doubt his motives, or dare criticize his means? "It has
been my fortune in the discharge of public duties,
civil and military, frequently to have found myself in
difficult and trying situations, where prompt decision and energetic action were necessary, and where
the interest of the country required that high responsibilities should be fearlessly encountered," Jackson

wrote in the farewell address he issued on March 4, 1837, "and it is with the deepest emotions of gratitude that I acknowledge the continued and unbroken confidence with which you have sustained me in every trial."

His own verdict on his decades in the arena? "My public life has been a long one, and I cannot hope that it has at all times been free from errors; but I have the consolation of knowing that if mistakes have been committed they have not seriously injured the country I so anxiously endeavored to serve," he said in the farewell address, "and at the moment when I surrender my last public trust I leave this great people prosperous and happy, in the full enjoyment of liberty and peace, and honored and respected by every nation of the world."

SATURDAY, MARCH 4, 1837, was a splendid day in Washington, cloudless and warm. Watching the transfer of power from Andrew Jackson to Martin Van Buren from a window overlooking the East Front of the Capitol, Thomas Hart Benton found the crowd "profoundly silent. . . . It was the stillness and silence of reverence and affection; and there was no room for mistake as to whom this mute and impressive homage was rendered." Van Buren appeared to sense, too, that this was as much Jackson's moment as his own, and he conceded that he was working in the shadow of a giant whose powers he could not hope to match. "In receiving from the people the sacred trust twice confided to my illustrious predecessor, and which he has discharged so faithfully and so well," Van Buren said in his inaugural address, "I know that I cannot expect to perform the arduous task with equal ability and success." It was, Benton observed from his window, an occasion on which "the rising was eclipsed by the setting sun." Leaving the Capitol for the last time, Jackson, as was his habit, bowed to the people, then returned down Pennsylvania Avenue.

It was over. "My own race is nearly run; advanced age and failing health warn me that before long I must pass beyond the reach of human events and cease to feel the vicissitudes of human affairs," Jackson said in his farewell address. "I thank God that my life has been spent in a land of liberty and that He has given me a heart to love my country with the affection of a son." A son to his country, a father to the people.

With that, he turned toward home.

★

CHAPTER 34

THE SHOCK IS GREAT, AND GRIEF UNIVERSAL

ONCE JACKSON LEFT the White House on Tuesday, March 7, 1837, there were the expected huzzas and throngs on his pilgrimage south. But the receptions were complicated—and were all the more compelling for it. In an account of Jackson's stop in Louisville written to Reuben Lewis (brother of the explorer Meriwether Lewis), a contemporary observer noted the complexities of the town's reaction to the traveling former president.

"In the heart of a city where I had heard him cursed with the most intense bitterness thousands of times—where many openly declared they would not begrudge millions to see him assassinated," the observer wrote, "all was respect and reverence, and that same feeling and deportment was evinced towards him that children show a deeply loved father."

It was a moment of unity in a world given to division. As the Louisville observer said, "I thought it was one of the most sublime moral spectacles I ever beheld or that sun perhaps ever shone upon. . . . Thank God it was so! It gives a patriot better hopes of his country."

· · ·

THE OLD NEIGHBORHOOD was a comfort. Sarah Yorke Jackson and Andrew Jackson, Jr., lived in the Hermitage with Jackson, and Donelson, though troubled in his grief, was nearby at Poplar Grove. Jackson worried about his nephew, writing to Van Buren: "The Major is so much engaged with his little family and farm, and so depressed in spirits by his late bereavement, that he does not now appear to take any lively interest in politics—this in time will change, and I hope to see him once more himself again."

Donelson did revive, as did Jackson, who, not surprisingly, was restless in retirement and never slowed down. The former president spent the next eight years advising his successors and aspiring successors, urging the annexation of Texas, and keeping up a stream of political correspondence. Letters were his lifeline. On a cold autumn Friday in 1838, Amos Kendall arrived at the outskirts of the Hermitage property about eleven o'clock in the morning. There he found his "good old chief" standing at the gate, waiting for the day's mail. Despite the raw weather, Jackson wore no coat, and Kendall admired how "his face was colored by the keen air." And Jackson always thought of his neighboring nephew, advising Donelson in 1840 to "seek out a discreet lady for a partner and marry. This can alone make you happy at home, and enable you to raise your charming little daughters and keep them under your own roof." In 1841, Donelson married Elizabeth Martin Randolph—Emily's niece, who had cared for her through her dying days, and whose own husband, Lewis Randolph, had died in 1837. (About this time the name of the Donelson house was changed from Poplar Grove to Tulip Grove; Hermitage legend has it that Van Buren made the suggestion on a visit to Nashville.) Politics remained a central part of Donelson's life: in 1844 President John Tyler appointed him chargé d'affaires to the Republic of Texas at an hour when Britain and France were both maneuvering for influence on the American continent.

AT THE HERMITAGE, Jackson grew more religious as the years passed. A vigilant sentry on what Jefferson, in a New Year's Day 1802 letter to the Danbury Baptist Association, had called the "wall of separation between church and state," he had long avoided formally joining a church. He changed that after retiring, when, sitting in his pew in the Hermitage church, he listened to the Reverend Dr. John Todd Edgar preach a sermon on "the interposition of Providence in the affairs of men."

As Edgar told the story to James Parton, the minister noticed Jackson listening intently. Moved by the moment, Edgar began to speak of "the career of a man who, in addition to the ordinary dangers of human life, had encountered those of the wilderness, of war, and of keen political conflict; who had escaped the tomahawk of the savage, the attack of his country's enemies, the privations and fatigues of border warfare, and the aim of the assassin. How is it," Edgar went on, "that a man endowed with reason and gifted with intelligence can pass through such scenes as these unharmed, and not see the hand of God in his deliverance?"

Afterward, Jackson insisted that Edgar come see him at the Hermitage. The minister had another engagement, but promised to come the next morning. Jackson was annoyed by the delay: he was unaccustomed to being put off, even for a night. Yet that evening, alone, Jackson appears to have had a kind of conversion experience. "As the day was breaking," Parton wrote after speaking with Edgar, "light seemed to dawn upon his troubled soul, and a great peace fell upon him." He told Edgar of the long night, and of the relief at sunrise.

Soon Jackson stood, leaning on a cane, in the Hermitage church, declaring his faith. It was a world away from the Waxhaw meetinghouse—so many years, so much strife, so many battles, so many struggles. Yet he had returned, in a way, to the place where he had first set out.

A FINANCIAL PANIC, followed by depression, struck the country only months after Jackson left office. There is much historical debate over whether it was Jackson's policies, crop failures, international forces, or some combination of all three that contributed to the hard times. In the middle of 1836 he had reluctantly signed a bill that increased the number of banks that received government deposits. This Deposit Bill led to the distribution of the federal surplus to banks in the states and fed speculation in the wild market for public lands. Then he issued an order called the Specie Circular, which, in an attempt to curb that speculation, directed that only gold and silver would be accepted for the purchase of public lands. (Settlers could still use paper money; the circular was aimed at speculators.) However good Jackson's intentions, the nation experienced an economic debacle in his wake. There is plenty of blame to assign to different players in the drama, from the White House to the Whigs in Congress to the bankers and the speculators—even to British demands for specie. One lesson may be that the American economy had already reached such a level of complexity, and was already sufficiently subject to global forces, that even the most attentive of presidents would find managing it a daunting and often disappointing task.

No matter what happened after he left the White House, though, Jackson's legend grew. In January 1840, Mrs. C. M. Stephens passed along a rumor to Stockley Donelson's wife, Phila Ann, from Cuba. "It was reported that Gen. Jackson was expected at Havana and it created quite a **sensation**. There are many here who would delight to see him." In June of that year, Leonidas Polk, now the Episcopal missionary bishop to the Southwest, wrote to his mother from Ashwood, his plantation in Maury County, Tennessee. "I was in Nashville the other day . . . where I met Genl. Jackson. He looks very well and is very spirited yet." George P. A. Healy, an American artist living in Paris, had been sent to the United States to paint Jackson and others—including Henry Clay, whom the painter was to meet after finishing the image of Jackson. Healy overstayed his time at the

Hermitage. When Healy at last appeared at Ashland, Clay said: "I see that you, like all who approached that man, were fascinated by him."

TRY AS HE might, however, not even Jackson could defeat mortality. In the late spring of 1845 he began his final decline. A niece wrote to Stockley Donelson of "our poor old grey headed Uncle Jackson." Sarah Jackson kept watch over him. "He is swollen all over, sometimes his face is out of all shape, and his sufferings are very great," she wrote Emma Donelson, her cousin, on Wednesday, April 30, 1845. In a postscript dictated by Jackson, he added: "My health is very low. I am compelled to employ an amanuensis, not being able today to sit up much." A few weeks later, Sarah told Emma that Jackson "still continues about the same as when I last wrote, excepting a very troublesome diarrhea, which produces at times violent pain. He is still able to sit up part of the day, but is very feeble, and very much changed."

On Sunday, May 25, 1845, he was too sick to go to the Hermitage church, and asked that the family bring the minister back to him after services. They did, and, surrounding his bed on the first floor of the house, they watched as he took Holy Communion. Jackson was stoic about his death; he felt, Andrew Jackson, Jr., wrote, "that it was not far distant" and "he had no fears of it, let it come when it might." The old warrior spoke of Jesus as he would have a comrade in arms; he was impressed by the Christian Messiah's physical courage in enduring the Crucifixion. "When

I have suffered sufficiently," Andrew junior recalled Jackson saying, "the Lord will then take me to himself, but what are all my sufferings compared to those of the blessed Savior, who died upon that crossed tree for me. Mine are nothing—not a murmur was ever heard from him—all was borne with amazing fortitude." At midnight a few days later, Sarah, at his bedside, asked how he felt, and he replied that "I cannot be long with you all," and told her to reach out to Major Lewis to arrange the funeral. "I wish to be buried in a plain, unostentatious manner without display or pomp, or any superfluous expense," he said, and fell asleep.

He died as he had lived, fighting the world's battles. In the days before his death he spoke of things close to his heart. Texas remained a question, and there were tensions between London and Washington over the Oregon territory. "He conversed generally about his farm and business and talked much of his beloved country," Andrew junior recalled. He was sure Texas would come into the Union and hoped the Oregon matter would be settled peaceably. But if not, his son recalled Jackson saying, "let war come. There would be patriots enough in the land found to repel foreign invasion come from whatsoever source."

HE SENT VALEDICTORIES to his old friends. "My dear Andrew," he wrote Andrew Donelson, who was in Texas as chargé, "you have my blessing and prayers for your welfare and happiness in this world." To Blair, Jackson wrote: "This may be the last letter I may be able to write you. But live or [die I am your] friend. . . . As far as justice is due to my fame, I know you will shield it. I ask no more. I rest upon truth, and require nothing but what truth can mete to me." To Kendall, he said: "On the subject of my papers: You are to retain them so long as you think necessary to use them. Should you die they are to pass forthwith into Mr. Blair's hands. I have full and unlimited confidence in you, both that my papers will be safe in your hands and that they never will be permitted to be used but for a proper use. . . . Here, my friend, I must for the present close, tendering you with my prayers for your health, long life and prosperity, and that we may at last meet in a blissful immortality." On Friday, June 6, he wrote President Polk, who had won the White House in 1844, a letter with advice about the Treasury Department; the next evening, Saturday, the seventh, he finished and franked his last letter, a note to Thomas F. Marshall, a congressman from Kentucky. At one point Jackson broke into what Andrew junior called "cold, clammy perspiration, an evidence of death approaching," and the attending doctor thought Jackson was gone. The sad word spread through the household, only to have the old man revive after ten minutes.

The next day, Lewis arrived. "Major, I am glad to see you," Jackson said. "You had like to have been too late."

He continued to defy expectations. Andrew Donelson's wife, Elizabeth, had hurried over from the Hermitage church, expecting to find Jackson dead. Instead, he looked up at her and asked how everyone was at home. She said all was well. "I am glad to hear it," Jackson replied.

John Samuel Donelson, who had been born in the White House in 1832, approached his uncle to say farewell. "Johnny went and kissed him," his stepmother wrote his father, and Jackson told the boy "to be a good boy and obey his parents, to remember the Sabbath and to keep it."

Unable to make out the faces of those in the bedroom in the late afternoon light, Jackson asked for his spectacles, which were on his bureau. He licked the lenses, dried them on his sheet, and put them on. Seeing the children and grandchildren in tears, he said, "God will take care of you for me." He was speaking not only to his relations and the children, but to the slaves who had gathered in the room to mark the end. Jackson said: "Do not cry; I hope to meet you all in Heaven—yes, all in Heaven, white and black."

Near death, Jackson sought comfort in the promises of the faith he had embraced in retirement. "My conversation is for you all," he said, and then renewed his talk of the world to come. "Christ has no respect to color," Jackson said. "I am in God and God is in me. He dwelleth in me and I dwell in him."

The emotion in the room grew thicker. "What is the matter with my dear children?" Jackson asked. "Have I alarmed you? Oh, do not cry. Be good children and we will all meet in Heaven."

He asked one of the slaves, George, to remove two of the three pillows beneath his head: having said all that he had to say, he was ready. The room was still. "Just then,"

Hannah said, "Master gave one breath, hunched up his shoulders and all was over. There was no struggle."

It was six o'clock in the evening, on Sunday, June 8, 1845, and Andrew Jackson, seventy-eight years old, older even than the nation, was dead.

SARAH SUFFERED WHAT Elizabeth Donelson called "spasms," fainted, and had to be carried out to be bathed in camphor while Andrew junior "seemed bewildered." Hannah, in grief, would not leave the room.

"Although it was looked for, the shock is great, and grief universal," Elizabeth Donelson wrote her husband. She told him, too, that she would hold on to a note he had written Jackson that arrived after the end—the last of so many, through so many years, through so much. "Yours to the Genl I will keep," Elizabeth wrote. "He will never see it."

With those five words—"he will never see it"—the long connection between Andrew Jackson and one of his many namesakes, Andrew Jackson Donelson, ended, coming to a close in the heat of an early summer Sunday in Tennessee. Donelson could not make the funeral in time. He remained in Texas, at work to fulfill the old dream of his uncle's, that Texas would one day join the Union. Sam Houston, who had just left Donelson, arrived at the Hermitage on the night Jackson died. He had brought his wife and son, and, after kneeling at the bed where Jackson lay, Houston turned to his boy.

"My son," he said, "try to remember that you have looked on the face of Andrew Jackson."

· · ·

JACKSON'S FUNERAL DREW a reported three thousand people to the Hermitage. The Reverend John Todd Edgar conducted the service from the front portico, looking out over the twin rows of native Tennessee Eastern red cedar trees that Jackson had planted along the carriage drive. He preached on a verse from the Revelation of Saint John the Divine, "These are they which came out of great tribulation, and have washed their robes, and made them white in the blood of the Lamb." The Ninetieth Psalm was read, and hymns were sung, including "How Firm a Foundation, Ye Saints of the Lord," a favorite of Rachel's:

> Fear not, I am with thee, O be not dismayed,
> For I am thy God and will still give thee aid;
> I'll strengthen thee, help thee, and cause thee to stand
> Upheld by My righteous, omnipotent hand.
>
> When through the deep waters I call thee to go,
> The rivers of woe shall not thee overflow;
> For I will be with thee, thy troubles to bless,
> And sanctify to thee thy deepest distress.

IN KENTUCKY, Thomas Marshall returned home from traveling in his former congressional district to find Jackson's letter to him. Marshall was moved, he wrote Andrew Jackson, Jr., to see "the last characters **his** hand ever drew," as Marshall put it. Recalling this souvenir of "the dying Hero," Marshall promised to visit the grave in the autumn. "He knew how deeply he had impressed himself upon my whole soul," Marshall wrote of Jackson.

In Washington, the historian and statesman George Bancroft painted him as an epic figure. "Before the nation, before the world, before coming ages, he stands forth the representative, for his generation, of the American mind."

In New York City, Benjamin Butler, the former attorney general, said, "Sleep sweetly, aged soldier, statesman, sage, in the grave of kindred and affection."

In Nashville, according to legend, a visitor to the Hermitage asked a slave on the place whether he thought Jackson had gone to heaven. "If the General wants to go," the slave replied, "who's going to stop him?"

FROM STATE TO state, courthouse square to courthouse square, Jackson's eulogizers loved the theme of the childless hero who rose to project paternal authority over a nation. "Washington was the father of his country, Jackson its defender and savior," said Hugh A. Garland, a lawyer, author, and legislator, in a Petersburg, Virginia, address a month after Jackson was buried. "Neither having natural children of their own, they embrace[d] the whole country in the arms of their affection." And what became of those whom Jackson embraced more intimately even than the country—the advisers and friends who saw him through?

Francis Preston Blair remained a crucial figure in the capital for decades after Jackson's death. Blair gave up the **Globe** in 1845, shortly before Jackson's death, after President Polk decided he wanted his own editor in charge of the party organ. (The paper closed in April

1845, and Polk's cause was taken up by the **Washington Union,** which Andrew Donelson edited for a time.) Always generous with the Jackson family financially, Blair had loaned Jackson $10,000 in 1842, and continued to try to help the perennially hapless Andrew Jackson, Jr., eventually playing a key role in the sale of the Hermitage to the state of Tennessee. Blair's son James brought three cedar chests full of Jackson's papers from the Hermitage for safekeeping, but Blair did not produce the Jacksonian tome he had hoped. In politics, Blair became a great Unionist, ultimately coming to believe that the slavocracy embodied by the old Jacksonian enemy Calhoun was going to destroy the nation. In 1848 Blair helped engineer the Free Soil nomination of Van Buren for president, in hopes of ending the extension of slavery as new states were added to the Union. In 1860, Blair supported Lincoln as the Republican nominee; the next year, he urged the new president to stand strong at Fort Sumter.

On Lincoln's authority, Blair invited Robert E. Lee to his family home across from the White House to offer the Virginian the Union command. "Mr. Blair," Lee said to Jackson's ancient lieutenant, "I look upon secession as anarchy. If I owned the four million of slaves at the South, I would sacrifice them all to the Union; but how can I draw my sword upon Virginia, my native state?" Blair's Silver Spring, Maryland, country house was occupied by Confederate troops. One of his sons, Montgomery Blair, served as Lincoln's postmaster general, and is depicted with Lincoln and the rest of the Cabinet in Francis Bicknell

Carpenter's painting of Lincoln reading the Emancipation Proclamation; a portrait of Jackson hangs in the background. In the last days of 1864, in part at the suggestion of the Republican newspaperman Horace Greeley, Blair asked Lincoln for permission to travel to the Confederacy on a secret peace mission. On Wednesday, December 28, Lincoln authorized the journey with a card: "Allow the bearer, F. P. Blair, Sr., to pass our lines, go South, and return." Blair reached Richmond through the good offices of General U. S. Grant and met with Jefferson Davis. Slavery, Blair told Davis, had been "the cause of all our woes," and that argument was settled. It was, Blair said, "the sin offering required to absolve us and put an end to the terrible retribution" of the war. Back in Washington, Blair reported on his meeting, and Lincoln told Blair that he would "receive any agent whom [Davis], or any other influential person now resisting the national authority, may informally send to me, with the view of securing peace to the people of our one common country." The result was a Friday, February 3, 1865, conversation between Lincoln, Confederate vice president Alexander Stephens, and others aboard a ship at Hampton Roads. Nothing came of the effort, but it was a noble one.

Blair and his daughter Lizzie were constant in their attentions to Mary Todd Lincoln in the aftermath of the assassination at Ford's Theatre, and Blair was present when Andrew Johnson was sworn in as the seventeenth president of the United States. In 1872 Blair asked to be baptized, and an Episcopal bishop performed the rite at Silver Spring—and then the baptismal party dined on ducks, oysters, and ice cream. Blair died four years later, on Wednesday, October 18, 1876. **The New York Times** noted that he had been "slashing and fierce upon occasion, and his whole political training had been aggressive and belligerent"—yet, the **Times** added, he was "in character amiable, affectionate, and grateful. The man and the editor were as dissimilar as possible."

Martin Van Buren served a single term as president of the United States. The architect of so much in the years of Jackson and beyond, he was a terrific tactician and embodied the notion that politics is the art of the possible. After leaving the White House he returned to Kinderhook, New York, retiring to Lindenwald, a richly furnished estate with large lawns and a farm. Van Buren twice sought to regain the presidency, once as the candidate for the Free Soil Party. He supported President Lincoln's fight to save the Union, and died after a long illness in the second summer of the Civil War, on Friday, July 24, 1862. "The grief of his patriotic friends will measurably be assuaged by the consciousness that while suffering with disease and seeing his end approaching," said Lincoln, "his prayers were for the restoration of the authority of the government of which he had been head, and for peace and good will among his fellow citizens."

Amos Kendall stayed on as Van Buren's postmaster general, leaving office in 1840. He remained in close contact with Jackson and published a biography of the general in 1843. In 1845 Kendall went to work for Samuel F. B. Morse, the pioneer of the electromagnetic telegraph in the United States. A Unionist, Kendall supported President Lincoln during the Civil War; he was a generous donor to Calvary Baptist Church in Washington and a founder of Gallaudet University, the school for the deaf (and, initially, for the blind) in the capital. He died on Friday, November 12, 1869, and was buried at Glenwood Cemetery in Washington.

After losing the Senate election in Tennessee in the wake of his resignation from the War Department and returning to Washington with his wife, **John Henry Eaton** was briefly president of the Chesapeake and Ohio Canal Company before accepting an appointment from Jackson to serve as governor of the Florida territory. Margaret remained Margaret. "Our friend John Eaton is harassed to death by a very sick hypochondriac wife," a friend told Martin Van Buren. In 1836 Eaton was dispatched as the minister to Spain. The man he was replacing, Cornelius Van Ness, was harsh about the Eatons in his reports home, writing that "he and she together regularly dispose of two bottles of rum of the strongest kind in the spirit every three days; this is, four glasses each and every day, besides wine; and while they are taking it and he chewing, she smokes her cigars." Eaton's years at Madrid—President Van Buren left him in the post until April 1840—were undistinguished. When Eaton returned to the United States, he committed the greatest sin in the Jacksonian universe: he betrayed an old friend, Van Buren, by campaigning for Van Buren's 1840 opponent, William Henry Harrison. The primary cause, Jackson believed, was bitterness. "My friend Maj. Eaton comes home not in good humor, he says he has been dismissed," Jackson told Kendall.

Moving to Washington, where the couple lived with Margaret's mother, Eaton practiced law before the Supreme Court and served as president of the Washington Bar Association. His old friends, though, found that he drank too much and seemed unstable. He even accepted a case against Kendall, his old ally and defender. "Never did I so much regret the ingratitude and depravity of man more than I have the course of Major Eaton in his conduct towards you. . . . **He is a lost man** . . . trying to destroy the fame of those who had risked much in the time of his need to save him and his family from **degradation and infamy**. . . . O tempora, O mores!" Jackson told Kendall. His brother-in-law from his first marriage, William Lewis, also gave up on him. "I have thought ever since he returned from Spain that he would kill himself drinking or perhaps blow his brains out," Lewis said in 1846. In the summer of 1844, in a moment of reconciliation, Jackson and the Eatons had dined together at the Hermitage, but the fervor of the friendship had long faded, a relic of distant wars. Eaton died on Monday, November 17, 1856, and was buried in Washington's Oak Hill Cemetery.

Margaret O'Neale Timberlake Eaton had yet more lives to lead after her husband's death. "We had been honored as the intimates of the grandest man who had ever sat in the chair of American President," Margaret wrote in a memoir. "I bore the name of one who as United States Senator, Cabinet officer and minister plenipotentiary to a foreign court had lived and died in honor among his fellow men. But alas! Alas! For the perversity of human nature and my own frailty." She married a third time—an Italian dancing master named Antonio Buchignani. She was fifty-nine; he was nineteen. They moved to New York City, settling in Gramercy Park, until the groom ran off with Margaret's granddaughter. Margaret divorced Buchignani, returned to Washington. She had, a Washington observer recalled, "a carriage with four horses and liveried servants. . . . There was nothing in Washington to compare with her equipage, not even the president's own. . . . I have never seen anyone so beautiful." Margaret died at age seventy-nine on Sunday, November 9, 1879. President and Mrs. Rutherford B. Hayes sent flowers to the funeral. She was buried next to John Eaton at Oak Hill Cemetery in an unmarked grave. "She belonged to the women of restless heart whose lives are always stormy, sometimes great, and rarely happy," wrote a journalist who had known her.

Politically, **John C. Calhoun** never recovered from the Jackson years. His presidential ambitions, once so strong, were to lead nowhere. Thwarted in the cause of nullification, he grew more strident in his defense of slavery. With the exception of a year as secretary of state in John Tyler's Cabinet (1844–45), Calhoun remained in the Senate, where he fought for the rights of slave owners. He died in Washington on Saturday, March 30, 1850. Floride was en route but arrived too late. Clay and Webster mourned him, as did much of the South. Clay saluted Calhoun's oratorical gifts, recalling his "torrent of mighty rhetoric, which always won our admiration even if it did not bring conviction to our understandings." Calhoun was buried in the churchyard of St. Philip's in Charleston, not far from Fort Sumter.

Henry Clay served in the Senate until 1842, seeking the presidency again in 1844 (Theodore Frelinghuysen of New Jersey was his running mate on the Whig ticket). Clay was defeated by James K. Polk, a Tennessean who was hailed as "Young Hickory." The hostility between Clay and Jackson endured. In the spring of 1842, Van Buren visited the Hermitage and Ashland. Clay asked after Jackson's health "respectfully and kindly," but that was all. Jackson never relented in the slightest. On hearing of Polk's victory over Clay in the 1844 race for the White House, Jackson wrote to Andrew Donelson: "The glorious result of the presidential election has rejoiced every democratic bosom in the United States, and as to myself I can say in the language of Simeon of old, 'Let thy servant depart in peace, as I have seen the solution of the liberty of my country and the perpetuity of our Glorious Union.'" Clay returned to the Senate, where he created the Compromise of 1850, the complex legislative achievement that attempted to balance interests among slave states, free states, and territories, delaying war for a decade. A firm Unionist, Clay reconciled with Francis Preston Blair. "Tell Clay for me," Van Buren wrote Blair, that the Compromise of 1850 was "more honorable and durable than his election to the Presidency could possibly have been." Clay died on Tuesday, June 29, 1852, in Washington, where he was the first man to lie in state in the Capitol. He was buried in Lexington.

John Quincy Adams remained in the House of Representatives for three years after Jackson's death. Adams carried on as he had set out, arguing for the rights of abolitionists to petition the Congress and becoming, through the years, what Henry Wise called "the acutest, the astutest, the archest enemy of Southern slavery that ever existed." Before the Supreme Court, he defended the African captives who had been arrested for rebellion aboard the **Amistad,** and won. Adams collapsed on the floor of the House on Monday, February 21, 1848, and died two days later. His casket was taken to Boston and then on to Quincy. Louisa survived him by four years, and ultimately they were interred beside Abigail and John Adams at the First Parish Church.

Andrew Jackson Donelson never came to "preside over the destinies" of America. After being considered for Van Buren's Cabinet, he briefly weighed a bid for Congress from Nashville, but decided against it and, in 1844, accepted President Tyler's appointment to Texas. Jackson died believing Donelson had done the job well, and that Texas would come into the Union: "All is safe and Donelson will have the honor of this important deed," Jackson wrote President Polk, Tyler's successor, as the shadows lengthened. From 1846 to 1849, Donelson served as the American envoy to Prussia, then returned to the United States and edited the **Washington Union,** the successor to Blair's **Globe,** from 1851 to 1852. By 1856 he had swerved into anti-immigrant, anti-Catholic politics, and ran for vice president on the Know Nothing ticket (so called because of the air of secrecy around its membership). As the Civil War approached, Donelson's woes compounded, both in politics and in farming.

Writing in the mid-1850s from Cleveland Hall, a Donelson family house near the Hermitage, Stockley's daughter Laura recorded the slow but steady crumbling of the world Jackson had known. "A great change" was about to come to "our old neighborhood," she wrote to a brother. "Cousin Andrew Jackson has sold the rest of the Hermitage and has purchased a large place in Mississippi, on the St. Louis Bay. . . . To hear Cousin Andrew's description of this place—the magnolia and orange groves, fertile soil and balmy breezes—you would think it some enchanted spot." One suspects Andrew junior's effusiveness was in part intended to mask his unease about breaking up his father's house, but he comforted himself, too, with the idea that the state, which bought the land, might be able to convince Washington to use it for a southern branch of West Point. But that was not to be. Always hapless in business affairs, Andrew junior killed himself in a hunting accident, shooting himself in the hand while climbing over a fence. The wound became infected, and he died of what was called lockjaw.

Meanwhile, Andrew Donelson's luck continued to deteriorate as he journeyed by river between Mississippi and Tennessee. "Uncle Andrew met with quite a loss on his way early one morning," Laura wrote. "The boat stopped for freight, Uncle Andrew left his berth for a few moments and in the meantime some daring robber stole his watch and chain which he valued at $250. . . . He is offering his place [now called Tulip Grove] for sale. If he sells, he will move to Memphis."

The decision to go west did not turn out well. In a letter from one Donelson relative to another in 1859, the family lamented Andrew Donelson's troubles: "Uncle Andrew [Donelson] was up here about three weeks since. He is in lower spirits than I ever saw him. His place in Bolivar County is all under water, so that he will make another failure this year, and a hurricane blew the roof of his house off in Memphis. He is decidedly unfortunate." During the war, like many Tennesseans, he moved from support for the Union to sympathy for the Confederacy, and was trusted by neither. He died on Monday, June 26, 1871, at the Peabody Hotel in Memphis, and was buried in that city's Elmwood Cemetery—far from Emily, and far from Jackson.

EPILOGUE: HE STILL LIVES

I N LATE JANUARY 1861, President-elect Abraham Lincoln was at home in wintry Springfield, Illinois, contemplating his course. The South was seceding, the Union in danger of dying. In search of a quiet place to work on his inaugural address, Lincoln walked through streets of mud and ice to his brother-in-law's brick general store, Yates and Smith, near the corner of Sixth and Adams. Lincoln had told his friend and law partner William Herndon that he would need some "works" to consult. "I looked for a long list, but when he went over it I was greatly surprised," Herndon recalled. In the course of drafting his inaugural, Lincoln asked for a copy of the Constitution, Henry Clay's speech on the Compromise of 1850, Webster's second reply to Hayne—and Jackson's Proclamation to the People of South Carolina.

Reading Jackson's words in the small, sparsely furnished upper room, Lincoln found what he needed: the example of Andrew Jackson, a president who had fought secession and chaos, rescuing the Union from an armed clash with a hostile South twenty-eight win-ters before. Now, three decades on, in a time of even greater trial, Lincoln looked to Jackson to arm himself against disunion and despair.

"The right of a state to secede is not an open or debatable question," Lincoln had said at the end of 1860. "It was fully discussed in Jackson's time, and denied . . . by him. . . . It is the duty of a President to execute the laws and maintain the existing government. He cannot entertain any proposition for dissolution or dismemberment. He was not elected for any such purpose." For Jackson the will of the people was majestic, even magical, and Lincoln agreed. "A majority held in restraint by constitutional checks and limitations, and always changing easily with deliberate changes of popular opinions and sentiments," Lincoln wrote, "is the only true sovereign of a free people." For Lincoln as for Jackson, a majority was neither always right nor always wrong. The right would depend on the circumstances. But the president's duty was constant: to preserve the Union, for without the Union no progress was possible.

JACKSON HAS INSPIRED some of the greatest men who have followed him in the White House—presidents who have sought to emulate his courage, to match his strength, and to wage and win the kinds of battles he waged and won. Running at the head of a national party, fighting for a mandate from the people to govern in particular ways on particular issues, depending on a circle of insiders and advisers, mastering the media of the age to transmit a consistent message at a constant

pace, and using the veto as a political, not just a constitutional, weapon, in a Washington that is at once politically and personally charged are all features of the
modern presidency that flowered in Jackson's White
House.

He also proved the principle that the character of
the president matters enormously. Politics is about
more than personality; the affairs of a great people are
shaped by complex and messy forces that transcend
the purely biographical. Those affairs, however, are
also fundamentally affected by the complex and
messy individuals who marshal and wield power in a
given era. Jackson was a transformative president in
part because he had a transcendent personality; other
presidents who followed him were not transformative,
and served unremarkably. But he gave his most imaginative successors the means to do things they thought
right.

"Jackson had many faults," said Theodore Roosevelt, "but he was devotedly attached to the Union,
and he had no thought of fear when it came to defending his country. . . . With the exception of Washington and Lincoln, no man has left a deeper mark on
American history; and though there is much in his career to condemn, yet all true lovers of America can
unite in paying hearty respect to the memory of a man
who was emphatically a true American, who served his
country valiantly on the field of battle against a foreign
foe, and who upheld with the most staunch devotion
the cause of the great Federal Union." Roosevelt approved of Jackson's "'instinct for the jugular'" and ca-

pacity to "recognize his real foe and strike savagely at the point where danger threatens."

A man of strength, TR admired Jackson's. "The course I followed, of regarding the executive as subject only to the people . . . was substantially the course followed by both Andrew Jackson and Abraham Lincoln," Roosevelt said. "Other honorable and well-meaning presidents, such as James Buchanan, took the opposite, and, as it seems to me, narrowly legalistic view that the President is the servant of Congress rather than of the people, and can do nothing, no matter how necessary it be to act, unless the Constitution explicitly commands the action." For Jackson and for TR, the presidency, in this light, was not an arm of government but its heart, beating vitally.

President Roosevelt's cousin Franklin was also fascinated by Jackson. On a visit to the Hermitage on Saturday, November 17, 1934, the paralyzed FDR was helped out of his car in front of the house, and, with locked steel braces on his legs, he forced himself forward balanced by the arm of an aide on one side and a cane on the other. Greeted at the door by the sound of "Hail to the Chief" being played on Jackson's old pianoforte, Roosevelt, one witness said, "bowed gallantly" to Mrs. Emily Walton, a descendant of Rachel's who had known Jackson in his old age—a living link from Jackson, the nineteenth-century founder of the Democratic Party, to Roosevelt, its greatest twentieth-century champion. Though ramps had been installed to smooth the way for Roosevelt's wheelchair, he chose to stay on his feet, sitting only for a grand Southern breakfast in the dining room. Walking was awkward and painful for Roosevelt, but some occasions were so important to him that he eschewed his chair. Paying tribute to Jackson was such an occasion.

IN 1941, BEFORE America entered World War II, FDR equated his coming task with Jackson's battle to save the Union. "Responsibility lay heavily upon the shoulders of Andrew Jackson," FDR told the nation that spring. "In his day the threat to the Federal Union came from within. . . . In our own day the threat to our Union and our democracy is not a sectional one. It comes from a great part of the world which surrounds us, and which draws more tightly around us, day by day." Jackson had met the challenge of the hour and rescued the Union with a "rugged, courageous spirit"— and Roosevelt found comfort in the thought that a revival of that spirit, with himself taking over Jackson's role as savior president, would see the country through.

Roosevelt's successor, Harry Truman, was so absorbed by Jackson that Eddie Jacobson, Truman's partner in a failed haberdashery, once recalled that the future president was always off in a corner reading books about Jackson rather than tending to the few customers who did come in.

Truman, who had spent his childhood soaking up heroic stories about Jackson, commissioned a statue of Old Hickory to sit outside the Kansas City Courthouse (as the presiding judge of Jackson County, he traveled to the Hermitage in 1931 to record the dimensions of Jackson's clothing in order to get the memorial exactly right), and, in 1945, put a small bronze of the Jackson statue on a table in the Oval Office. In a more substantive vein, Truman drew on Jacksonian imagery to build on the New Deal and secure America's place in a new global order—tasks not unlike the ones Jackson had faced when he broadened democracy and fought to establish the United States' place in the family of nations a century before.

"He wanted sincerely to look after the little fellow who had no pull," Truman said of Jackson, "and that's what a president is supposed to do." Looking abroad, Truman, like Jackson, spoke bluntly about America's role. It was Jackson, Truman said, who "helped once again to make it clear . . . that we were becoming a stronger and stronger country and wouldn't always be a weak, upstart little nation that had to kowtow to the big European powers."

When Truman lit the National Community Christmas Tree on a snow-covered South Lawn in 1945, the first Christmas Eve ceremony after four years of world war, the new president was facing a new and frightening age. Summoning the heroes of the Republic, Truman spoke of the Washington Monument, of the memorials on the Mall to Lincoln and to Jefferson, and of the statue of Jackson in Lafayette Square. "It is well in this solemn hour that we bow to Washington, Jefferson, Jackson, and Lincoln as we face our destiny with its hopes and fears—its burdens and its responsibilities," Truman said. "Out of the past shall we gather wisdom and inspiration to chart our future course."

· · ·

JACKSON'S REMAINS LIE next to Rachel's in the garden grave near the winding Cumberland, the river that took him so often to and from Washington. His tombstone reads only:

GENERAL
ANDREW JACKSON,
MARCH 15, 1767–
JUNE 8, 1845.

The modesty of the inscription seems fitting, for all one needs to do to see his legacy is look up from the slab and breathe in the light of a united nation, a country that has emerged from the fires of conflict both at home and abroad stronger and freer. The Hermitage's slave quarters are near Jackson's tomb, a rebuke to the generations of white Americans who limited crusades for life and liberty to their own kind, and a reminder that evil can appear perfectly normal to even the best men and women of a given time.

"The victor **in a hundred battles** has at last fallen," Levi Woodbury, whose bust the president kept in the Hermitage, said in a eulogy to Jackson. "The pilot, **who weathered the storm** in the fiercest hurricanes of political strife, looks no longer to the compass or the clouds to guide us; and the Christian as well as the sage and patriot of the Hermitage—who still prayed for his country, after the power to do aught else had ceased—has gone to his great and glorious reward, while we linger a little longer to . . . try to profit by his bright example."

We profit, too, from a leader's dim example. The great often teach by their failures and derelictions. The tragedy of Jackson's life is that a man dedicated to freedom failed to see liberty as a universal, not a particular, gift. The triumph of his life is that he held together a country whose experiment in liberty ultimately extended its protections and promises to all—belatedly, it is true, but by saving the Union, Jackson kept the possibility of progress alive, a possibility that would have died had secession and separation carried the day.

Speaking of Jackson in death, alluding to the crisis with South Carolina in 1832–33, George Bancroft said: "The moral of the great events of those days is this: that the people can discern right, and will make their way to a knowledge of right; that the whole human mind, and therefore with it the mind of the nation, has a continuous, ever improving existence; that the appeal from the unjust legislation of today must be made quietly, earnestly, perseveringly, to the more enlightened collective reason of tomorrow; that submission is due to the popular will, in the confidence that the people, when in error, will amend their doings; that in a popular government, injustice is neither to be established by force, nor to be resisted by force; in a word, that the Union which is constituted by consent, must be preserved by love."

Or, as Jackson would have said: The **people**, sir—the **people** will set things to rights.

. . .

SATURDAY, JANUARY 8, 1853, was a sparkling, unusually warm mid-winter day in Washington, and thousands gathered in and around Lafayette Square for the dedication of Clark Mills's equestrian statue of Jackson. It was a grand occasion, the anniversary of the Battle of New Orleans, and Senator Stephen A. Douglas was the keynote speaker. A vast procession—citizens and soldiers, congressmen and officers—marched from Washington's City Hall at D Street on Judiciary Square to the White House grounds. There they saluted President Fillmore and his Cabinet, then moved back across Pennsylvania Avenue to the square. A reporter for the **Washington Union** wrote that twenty thousand spectators gathered in and around the park; some watched from the tops of the houses in which the Jackson circle—Van Buren, the Donelsons, the Livingstons, the Blairs—had danced and dined. Sitting at home, not far from the new memorial, Francis Blair had drafted Douglas's remarks, eleven handwritten pages summing up the seventh president.

Douglas reminded his listeners that the man they were commemorating had begun life as an orphan, finding his family in his country. "Nobly did the widowed mother perform her duty to those fatherless children" after the death of the first Andrew Jackson, Douglas said, but then came the Revolution. "Hugh, the elder brother of Andrew Jackson, fell in his first battle at Stono. Robert became a martyr to liberty, and lost his life from wounds received while in captivity. The mother descended to the grave, a victim to grief and suffering," Douglas said. "Andrew was thus left alone in the world at a tender age, without father or mother, brother or sister, friend or fortune to assist him. All was gone save the high qualities with which God had endowed him, and the noble precepts which a pious and sainted mother had infused into his young heart."

When Jackson had died, there was a sense of completion, that the race had been finished: "He felt that his work was done—his mission fulfilled." And there was, for a moment, unanimous tribute. "All felt that a great man had fallen," Douglas said. "Yet there was consolation in the consciousness that the lustre of his name, the fame of his great deeds, and the results of his patriotic services, would be preserved through all time—a rich inheritance to the devotees of freedom."

EVEN NOW, WHEN presidents stand beneath the North Portico of the White House and look into Lafayette Square, they can see Jackson there, his sword within reach, ready to ride, ready to fight. There he is, a courageous man who could not rest, who risked everything and gave everything for his "one great family"—America.

Nearly a century and three quarters since Jackson left Washington for the last time, the sounds and sights of Lafayette Square would be familiar to him. Behind the statue of Jackson stands the bright yellow St. John's Church, where he often sat in Pew 54. In the church's steeple, beneath a gold-domed cupola topped by an arrow-tipped weathervane, hangs a bronze bell struck by Paul Revere's ancestral company. On the base of Jackson's statue, molded from molten British arms, are the seven words from that long-ago Jefferson birthday dinner toast: "**Our Federal Union: It Must Be Preserved.**"

The eyes of Jackson's statue look south, across the Potomac River and toward the pockets of rebellion he put down—keeping watch, never blinking, never tiring. "He still lives in the bright pages of history," Stephen Douglas said in dedicating the statue. **He still lives**—and we live in the country he made, children of a distant and commanding father, a father long dead yet ever with us.

AUTHOR'S NOTE
AND ACKNOWLEDGMENTS

FTER MISPLACING A traveling case of documents en route from Washington to Tennessee in the summer of 1832, a regretful Andrew Jackson told Andrew Donelson that most of the lost papers were "of a private and political nature of great use to me and the historian that may come after me." Jackson had it right: his private and political lives have kept historians and biographers on his trail for two centuries, and the complexities of his character and the consequences of his public life will always invite fresh scrutiny. A figure who could be at once so brilliant and yet so bloody-minded, so tender yet so cold, merits our attention, for the virtues and vices of this single man tell us much about the virtues and vices of our country.

This book is not an academic study of his presidency. My aim was different. There are many books for those seeking full-scale accounts and assessments of Jackson's life, or of his time, or of the politics and policies of his controversial careers in business, in the military, and in government. By drawing in part on previously unavailable documents, chiefly letters of Jackson's intimate circle that have largely been in private hands for the past 175 years—I have attempted to paint a biographical portrait of Jackson and of many of the people who lived and worked with him in his tumultuous years in power.

I was surprised—delightedly so—by the number of new sources that emerged in the course of my work on Jackson, sources that provide hitherto unknown details about a lost world that foreshadowed and shaped our own. In a private collection of letters kept by Mrs. John Lawrence Merritt, I discovered new details about Emily Donelson's role in the life of the White House, including the fact that John Henry Eaton spoke of resigning in the spring of 1829—a course that, if followed, might have preserved John C. Calhoun's viability as a presidential successor to Jackson and would certainly have changed the course of Jackson's first term. I am grateful to Mrs. Merritt and to her daughter, Caroline van den Berg, for making these papers available to me.

The correspondence owned by Mrs. Merritt and the unpublished letters in the Benjamin and Gertrude Caldwell Collection now at the Hermitage also shed fresh light on Emily and Andrew Donelson's early centrality to Rachel and Andrew Jackson and include allusions to the great issues of the White House years: the tariff, nullification, the Bank war, and the battle to succeed Jackson in 1836. In John Donelson's Cleveland Hall collection are numerous letters from Andrew Donelson and several from Andrew Jackson, Jr. They offer details about the ferocious partisan politics of the 1830s, about life in the White House and in the Jackson circle in the South, and about the extent of slave trading in the president's family during the White House years. The private collection of letters and memorabilia held by Scott Ward of Atlanta, a descendant of Andrew Jackson, Jr., was illuminating, and includes the reply of Thomas Marshall to the last letter of Jackson's life.

My debts to the owners of these papers are enormous, and not only for making their papers available to me and granting permission for me to quote from them. I am also grateful for their hospitality and grace. Janice and John Donelson, the current owners of Cleveland Hall, were welcoming, charming, witty, and gracious hosts, allowing me to spend many happy hours in their grand house near the Hermitage reading and transcribing a collection of letters, most of them between Andrew Donelson and his brother-in-law Stockley, papers that had never before been seen outside a very small family circle. This book was strengthened by their willingness to grant me access to the documents at Cleveland Hall, and by their putting me in touch with other Donelson relatives. Scott Ward and his family also kindly opened their house to me, and I spent a delightful afternoon as their guest.

The Cleveland Hall, Merritt, and Caldwell letters were critical, as were unpublished letters and diary entries from the papers of John Quincy Adams and those of his wife, Louisa, and the many collections cited in the Notes. These include letters from the British, Dutch, and French diplomatic archives; their envoys were shrewd observers of the Washington scene. From letters of Treasury Secretary Samuel Ingham detailing his near gunfight with John Eaton to a note of Richard Wellesley, the Marquis Wellesley and elder brother of the Duke of Wellington, on the possible collapse of the Union during the crisis over nullification, I found the archival sources on Jackson and his contemporaries to be rich, illuminating, and, perhaps as important, fun. I am also grateful to Maria Campbell for sharing "The Memoirs of Mrs. Eliza Williams Chotard Gould," a private, unpublished account by her great-great-great-grandmother that provides us with an eyewitness portrait of Jackson in New Orleans on the eve of, and just after, his victory over the British.

Anyone who contemplates Jackson owes a special debt to three important historians and their monumental work. James Parton's three-volume life of Jackson is indispensable. Arthur Schlesinger, Jr.'s **The Age of Jackson** is a rich and invaluable portrait of the political and intellectual milieu of the early nineteenth century and its lasting legacy to the nation. As a counselor, neighbor, and friend, Professor Schlesinger was unfailingly kind to me, and I am grateful to him and to his wife, Alexandra, for years of good company and wise guidance. The work of Robert V. Remini, the National Book Award–winning historian of Jackson, is deep and far-ranging. Dr. Remini's three-volume biography and his numerous other works offer readers intelligent and detailed accounts of Jackson's life and times. I learned much not only from Dr. Remini's books, which I read growing up in Tennessee, but from many conversations with him. He was welcoming, gracious, generous, and astute. He read the manuscript early on (some parts more than once), and I am indebted to him.

Daniel Feller, the editor of the Jackson papers and the author of two essential works (**The Public Lands in Jacksonian Politics** and **The Jacksonian Promise: America, 1815–1840**), was a welcoming adviser on all things Jacksonian. He fielded many questions with grace and read the manuscript with care. Daniel Walker Howe, the Pulitzer Prize–winning author of **What Hath God Wrought: The Transformation of America, 1815–1848**, graciously commented on the manuscript and was generous with his insights about Jacksonian America. Sean Wilentz's work is as formidable as he is approachable and kind. His **The Rise of American Democracy: From Jefferson to Lincoln** is a landmark book, and I learned much from his **Andrew Jackson**, which he wrote for a series edited by Arthur Schlesinger. Amid a hugely busy life of publishing his **The Age of Reagan** and teaching at Princeton, Professor Wilentz took the time to offer me guidance, read my manuscript, and share his insights. I am grateful for his counsel and his friendship. The historians Catherine Allgor, H. W. Brands, Andrew Burstein, Donald Cole, William Freehling, Richard Latner, and John Marszalek each took the trouble to weigh in on different sections of the manuscript, and I am grateful for their generosity and wisdom. Mark Cheathem was an invaluable reader. Matthew Warshauer, whose forthcoming **Andrew Jackson in Context** brilliantly sorts through the historiographical debate, was a wise and generous reader.

Walter Isaacson—distinguished editor and biographer of Kissinger, Franklin, and Einstein—read and commented on the manuscript with characteristic grace and insight; I am in his debt. Doris Kearns Goodwin generously read the manuscript. She is a cheerful and wise friend, as is Tina Brown, who brought her keen biographer's eye to the book.

The curator of the Hermitage, Marsha Mullin, was kind and helpful, always willing to field the oddest of questions with sure and steady grace. Tireless in her generosity, committed to the highest standards of scholarship and integrity, Marsha never failed to respond with intelligence and good cheer to my curiosity about the nooks and crannies of Andrew Jackson's life and family. I knew I was in the best of hands when she tagged along as I counted off the number of paces it would have taken Rachel Jackson's pallbearers to carry Mrs. Jackson's coffin from the house to the garden tomb.

Through the kindness of Mrs. Laura Bush and of Jean Becker, President George H. W. Bush's chief of staff, I was able to spend a delightful three hours touring the private quarters of the White House with William Allman, who was a patient and fascinating guide to the mansion and its history. I am grateful to Mrs. Bush for her courtesy and to Gary Walters, the White House chief usher, for arranging the visit, and to Melissa Naulin. It was invaluable as I tried to envision the rooms as they were in the Jackson years, and there was a quiet thrill to be able to stand in the current Lincoln Bedroom, which was Jackson's office, and listen to the ticking of the French clock on the mantel—a sound Jackson heard all those years ago.

Donald A. Ritchie, associate historian of the U.S.

Senate and a fine author, generously devoted a morning to walking me through the Capitol as it existed in Jackson's day. It was a delightful and memorable expedition, and I am grateful for his wisdom and enthusiasm. John B. Fox, Jr., of Harvard College, generously showed me the room in which Jackson received an honorary degree in 1833 (a ceremony of which John Quincy Adams decidedly disapproved). Hayden G. Bryan, the executive director for operations at St. John's Church, Lafayette Square, was helpful about the architecture and history of the parish.

In Nashville, I was fortunate to have found myself sitting next to Robin Saxon at dinner one winter night in 2003. Amid steaks and martinis with Alexandra and Arthur Schlesinger, Dolores and John Seigenthaler, and Judge Gilbert S. Merritt, talk turned to Tennessee's most formidable president. (We also spent time discussing Orestes Brownson, prompting Arthur to note that this was probably the first dinner-table conversation to do so in a very, very long time.) Judge Merritt is a Jackson cousin, and Robin was just ending a term as president of the Ladies' Hermitage Association. Later in the year, when I embarked on this project, one of my first calls was to Robin, whom I reached while she was—I love the South—shooting ducks. Robin became a friend of the book, setting up sessions with the Donelson clan and helping me collect documents from different family collections.

I am grateful to many historians who patiently answered my questions and shared their insights: James Chace, David Herbert Donald, Walter T. Durham,

David McCullough, Harold Moser, Merrill Peterson, William Seale, James Smylie, Clyde N. Wilson, and Professor the Reverend Canon J. Robert Wright. Andrea Mitchell kindly arranged for me to lunch with her husband, Alan Greenspan, when he was serving as chairman of the Federal Reserve; I was seeking guidance on Jackson's Bank war, and Dr. Greenspan was a great help.

Librarians and archivists on both sides of the Atlantic were generous guides to Jackson's vanished world. My thanks to: Charles Greene of the Princeton University Library; Nancy Shawcross of the University of Pennsylvania Rare Books and Manuscripts Library; John McDonough, now retired from the Library of Congress; Bob Duncan and Barbara Garrett of the Maury County Archives; Tom Price of the James K. Polk Home; William Bynum, Fred Hauser, Beth Bensman, and Kenneth J. Ross of the Presbyterian Historical Society in Philadelphia; Annie Armour of the University Archives of The University of the South; Jane Reed and Maureen Manning of the University Club Library; Tom Kanon of the Tennessee State Library and Archives; Deborah Pavlich of Montgomery Place, the Livingston family house in the Hudson Valley; Lydia Tedrick of the White House Curator's Office; the Office of the Director, Dumbarton Oaks, Washington, D.C.; Henry Fulmer of the South Caroliniana Library, the University of South Carolina; and the staff of the Newsweek Research Center. And a very special word of thanks to Jeffrey Flannery, head of the Library of Congress Manuscript Reading Room.

The following people and institutions kindly granted

me permission to quote from unpublished material: Mrs. John Lawrence Merritt for her collection in Winter Park, Florida. John Donelson for the Donelson Family Private Collection, Cleveland Hall, Nashville; Scott Ward for the Scott Ward Collection, Atlanta; Maria Campbell for "The Memoirs of Mrs. Eliza Williams Chotard Gould"; and The University of the South for the papers of Leonidas Polk.

For kindnesses large and small, I thank: Shaima Ally, Carl Byker, Dr. and Mrs. William T. Cocke III, Joe Contreras, Judy Cormier, Deidre Depke, E.J. Dionne, Jr., Jack Donelson, Lewis Donelson, Cynthia A. Drayton, Tammy Haddad, Hope Hartman, Lucy Howard, Robbie D. Jones, Claudia Kalb, Kate Leffingwell, the Reverend Luis Leon, Barbara Liberman, Waring McCrady, Nora Frances McRae, Susan McVea, Chris Matthews, Morgan Merrill, Deborah Millan, David Olivenbaum, Donna Pahmeyer, Rob Pearigen, Perri Peltz, Holly Peterson, William R. Polk, Anne Pope, Anna Quindlen, Julia Reed, Sam Register, Douglas Robbe, Mitchell Rosenthal, Doug Spence, Sarah Stapleton, Tom Watson, George F. Will, David Wilson, Frank Wisner, and Ted Yeatman.

Margaret Shannon once again did first-rate work, particularly in identifying and collecting the scholarly literature on Jackson and his times. Jack Bales again created a masterful bibliography and checked citations with a searching eye. Dalit Herdoon Haim was essential in searching archives in London and in Oxford, as were Alice Jouve in Paris and Celeste Walker in Massachusetts, at the Adams Papers. I am also grateful to Lennart van Oudheusden for his help with the Huygens archival material in Amsterdam, and to Jessica Rosenberg for translating documents from the French. Brian Gallagher, Matthew Price, Hanna Siegel, Molly Bennet, Christopher Swetala, and Honor Jones were terrific closing fact-checkers. And countless thanks to Barbara DiVittorio, who has long kept my life in order while playing a vital role in the culture of **Newsweek**. I owe her an enormous debt.

I am beyond fortunate to count Mike Hill as my friend. He is perennially tireless, cheerful, enthusiastic, generous, and smart.

Louisa Thomas was crucial, first in helping to search out and mine archival material and in managing the fact-checking of the manuscript, which she did from abroad before taking pains to be in New York as the book was closing. She went over every word—often more than once—and she always made sure I was on solid ground. An astute reader and perceptive critic, Louisa has been invaluable to me on two books, and I am grateful to her for her intelligence, her steadiness, her commitment, and her good humor in trying circumstances.

The subject of Jackson was first suggested to me in the summer of 2003 by Jonathan Karp, my former editor at Random House. Jon has been a friend for over a decade, and I have long been the beneficiary of his wisdom and his insightful readings. As always, I am indebted to Evan Thomas, Ann McDaniel, and Sofia and Herbert Wentz for their gifts of friendship and literary and historical counsel. They are unfailing friends.

At Random House, my editor, Kate Medina, was

her usual remarkable self—gracious, intelligent, and devoted. Anyone who thinks the art of editing has disappeared has never worked with Kate, whose exacting standards and passion for excellence are at once daunting and thrilling. Gina Centrello is the best of publishers—a champion and a friend. Millicent Bennett, who works for Kate (as we all do, really), appeared in my life one day and I soon realized that I was in the best of hands. Sally Marvin is a formidable force; I cannot imagine publishing a book without her, and thankfully she is charming more often than she is erratic (though that can be, as Wellington reportedly said of Waterloo, a close-run thing). Thanks, too, to Tom Perry, Jonathan Jao, Jennifer Smith, Frankie Jones, Abby Plesser, Robin Rolewicz, Rachel Omansky, Dennis Ambrose, Emily DeHuff, Chuck Thompson, Evan Stone, Vicki Wong, Debbie Aroff, Barbara Fillon, and Carol Poticny for their terrific work and extraordinary patience.

This is my fourth book with the remarkable Amanda Urban; I depend on her instincts and her insights and am grateful that she is my friend. Christopher Buckley once noted that Binky was the only person he would think to call if he were captured by the Taliban, and I completely concur. Thanks as well to Molly Atlas.

At **Newsweek,** I am fortunate to work both for and with the best in the business. My thanks to Donald Graham, Lally Weymouth, Rick Smith, Dan Klaidman, Mark Miller, Kathy Deveny, and Fareed Zakaria.

As always, my greatest thanks are reserved for Keith,

who endured much (not least the stream of secondhand books on subjects ranging from nullification to Nicholas Biddle that came in through the kitchen door) to give me the ways and means to disappear into Andrew Jackson's White House on and off for five years. In 2003 I knew it was time to finish a project about Franklin Roosevelt and Winston Churchill when I looked over and saw our son, Sam, then an infant, trying to teethe on a copy of **The Churchill War Papers**. Since then Sam has been joined by two sisters, Mary and Maggie, and this book is dedicated to the three of them in the small but real hope that they will do their part to see that the Republic is, as Jackson would say, always safe.

Notes

ABBREVIATIONS USED

AMVB	The Autobiography of Martin Van Buren
AAK	Autobiography of Amos Kendall
Heiskell, AJETH, I-III	S. G. Heiskell, Andrew Jackson and Early Tennessee History
Correspondence, I–VI	Correspondence of Andrew Jackson
EDT, I and II	Pauline Wilcox Burke, Emily Donelson of Tennessee
FPB	Elbert B. Smith, Francis Preston Blair
James, TLOAJ	Marquis James, The Life of Andrew Jackson
LOC	The Library of Congress
Memoirs of JQA, VIII–IX	The Memoirs of John Quincy Adams
Messages, II	Richardson, comp., Messages and Papers of the Presidents
PHC, IV–VIII	The Papers of Henry Clay
PJCC, X–XIII, XXI	The Papers of John C. Calhoun
Papers, I–VI	The Papers of Andrew Jackson
Parton, Life, I–III	James Parton, Life of Andrew Jackson
Remini, Jackson, I–III	Robert V. Remini, Andrew Jackson and the Course of American (I) Empire, (II) Freedom, (III) Democracy
TGPP	William M. Goldsmith, The Growth of Presidential Power: A Documented History, I–II
TPA	John F. Marszalek, The Petticoat Affair: Manners, Mutiny, and Sex in Andrew Jackson's White House

Epigraphs

ix "The darker the night the bolder the lion"   Theodore Roosevelt and Edmund Heller, **Life-Histories of African Game Animals** (New York, 1914), I, 173.

ix "I was born for a storm"   Heiskell, **AJETH**, III, 166. The quotation is found in a letter from James A. Hamilton to Martin Van Buren. "I have just left the General," Hamilton wrote. "He said this to me [and] this makes me well. I was born for a storm and a calm does not suit me."

Prologue: With the Feelings of a Father

xxi on the second floor   Jackson's work and living space, including his office—the Lincoln Bedroom in the current White House—his study, and his small bedroom suite were all on the second floor, as were the Donelsons' rooms and the most commonly used family sitting rooms. (William Seale, **The President's House: A History** [Washington, D.C., 1986], I, 182–84.)

xxi the White House   Emily Donelson used the term in her correspondence; see Emily Donelson to Mary Donelson Coffee, March 27, 1829, Andrew Jackson Donelson Papers, LOC. According to the Office of the Curator at the White House, "The term 'White House' was used as early as May 19, 1809, by Henry Dearborn, a member of President Jefferson's Cabinet, as a synonym for the Presidency itself. It was used by the **Baltimore Whig** on November 22, 1810, and a British Minister was using the term in the spring of 1811." In 1813, Daniel Webster, then a congressman, used the term in his letters, further suggesting the name was in circulation in official circles. (Unpublished document, "Origin of the Name 'White House,'" Office of the Curator, the White House, 1984; see also Frank Freidel and William Pencak, eds., **The White House: The First Two Hundred Years** [Boston: 1994], 23–24.) I am also grateful to the White House Curator's Office for kindly giving me a tour of the second floor.

xxi in the flickering light of candles and oil lamps   Seale, **President's House**, I, 173–74. The lamps were fueled largely by lard oil. (William Seale, **The White House: The History of An American Idea** [Washington, D.C., 1992], 85–86.)

xxi was furious and full of fight   Parton, **Life**, III, 460–63. Jackson also made his views clear to General Winfield Scott at a meeting at the White House on November 4, 1832. President Jackson, Scott recalled, "adverted to the certainty that South Carolina would very soon be out of the Union—either by nullification or secession." Jackson, Scott said, was "patriotically resolved to stand his ground—**The Union must and shall be preserved.**" (Winfield Scott, **Memoirs of Lieut.-General Scott, LL.D** [Freeport, New York, 1970], 234–35.) Jackson's passion on the question can also be found in his correspondence. See, for instance: **Papers**, VI, 476–77; **Correspondence**, V, 2–24; 28–31; 44–46; 56.

xxi Four hundred and fifty miles   This is the distance as the crow flies from Washington, D.C., to Charleston, South Carolina.

xxi radicals were raising an army   Richard E. Ellis, **The Union at Risk: Jacksonian Democracy, States' Rights, and the Nullification Crisis** (New York, 1987), and two books by William W. Freehling, **Prelude to Civil War: The Nullification Controversy in South Carolina, 1816–1836** (New York, 1966) and **Road to Disunion: Secessionists at Bay, 1776–1854** (New York, 1990), are excellent sources on the nullification crisis (in **Road to Disunion**, see especially 253–86), as is Freehling's **The Nullification Era: A Documentary Record** (New York, 1967). See also Carol Bleser, ed., **Secret and Sacred: The Diaries of James Henry Hammond, a Southern Slaveholder** (New York, 1988); Chauncey Samuel Boucher, **The Nullification Controversy in South Carolina** (Chicago, 1916); Richard J. Calhoun, ed., **Witness to Sorrow: The Antebellum Autobiography of William J. Grayson** (Columbia, S.C., 1990), 109–51; Drew Gilpin Faust, **James Henry Hammond and the Old South: A Design for Mastery** (Baton Rouge, La., 1985); Daniel Feller, **The Jacksonian Promise: America, 1815–1840** (Baltimore, 1995), 162–68; Cicero W. Harris, **The Sectional Struggle: An Account of the Troubles Between the North and the South, from the Earliest Times to the Close of the Civil War, First Part** (Philadelphia, 1902); David Franklin Houston, **A Critical Study of Nullification in South Carolina** (Gloucester, Mass.,

1968); Daniel Walker Howe, **What Hath God Wrought: The Transformation of America, 1815–1848** (New York, 2007), 395–410; Theodore D. Jervey, **Robert Y. Hayne and His Times** (New York, 1909); Edward Payson Powell, **Nullification and Secession: A History of the Six Attempts During the First Century of the Republic** (New York, 1898); Charles S. Sydnor, **The Development of Southern Sectionalism, 1819–1848** (Baton Rouge, La., 1948); Sean Wilentz, **The Rise of American Democracy: Jefferson to Lincoln** (New York, 2005); Major L. Wilson, **Space, Time and Freedom: The Quest for Nationality and the Irrepressible Conflict, 1815–1861** (Westport, Conn., 1974), 73–93. Wilson wrote: "Liberty and the Union were inseparable goods, in [Jackson's] view, and the security of the one necessarily involved the preservation of the other's." (84). The editions of **Niles' Weekly Register** from the period are instructive, too. The **Register**, founded by Hezekiah Niles, was an early nonpartisan newsweekly that was published from 1811 until 1849. In those years, wrote W. H. Earle, "it was the principal window through which many Americans looked out on their own country and the world. The scope of the work was immense, its circulation was large (the largest in the United States, by some accounts), and its influence was reflected in generous compliments from such readers of the publication as John Adams, Thomas Jefferson, and Andrew Jackson." (W. H. Earle, "Niles' Register, 1811–1849: Window on the World," **Journal of the War of 1812 and the Era 1800 to 1840** 1 [Fall 1996], http://www.nisc.com/factsheets/NR_Window.htm.)

xxi   the first step, Jackson believed, toward secession   In 1828, the South Carolina legislature had published its **Exposition and Protest** against the tariff. "Secretly authored by Vice President John C. Calhoun, the exposition argued the right of a sovereign state to declare null and void any federal law that the state deemed unconstitutional," writes Daniel Feller. "Calhoun conceived nullification as a peaceable check upon the national government's abuse of its powers. But his doctrine invited naked state defiance of federal authority, leading perhaps to secession (the withdrawal of the state from the Union) and even civil war" (Feller, **Jacksonian Promise**, 162). In the opinion of Daniel Walker Howe, "Taken as a whole, the **South Carolina Exposi-**

tion is an impressive argument on behalf of an unworkable proposition. (In an America where nullification prevailed, there might be scores of federal statutes whose operation was suspended in various states, while each awaited resolution in an endless succession of constitutional conventions.)" (Howe, **What Hath God Wrought**, 398.) In **The Rise of American Democracy**, Sean Wilentz writes: "The only cure for majority despotism, Calhoun argued, was to recognize the undivided sovereignty of the individual states that, he asserted, was anterior to the Constitution. Just as the federal government could annul any state law ruled binding, so aggrieved states could void, within their borders, any federal law they deemed unconstitutional. . . . Calhoun would always insist nullification was not secession, which was literally true. But in seizing on the theory of original state sovereignty, he offered a theoretical justification for both nullification and secession" (Wilentz, **Rise of American Democracy**, 320).

xxi "I expect soon to hear" **Correspondence**, V, 3. The quotation is from a January 13, 1833, letter to Vice President-elect Martin Van Buren.

xxi musing about arresting Freehling, **Prelude to Civil War**, 2; Parton, **Life**, III, 447, 474. As noted below, Missouri senator Thomas Hart Benton also provides evidence that such a threat was in the air, quoting an exchange between Henry Clay and Delaware senator John M. Clayton: Clay's "friend from Delaware [Mr. John M. Clayton] said to [Clay] one day—these South Carolinians act very badly, but they are good fellows, and it is a pity to let Jackson hang them" (Thomas Hart Benton, **Thirty Years' View; or, A History of the Working of the American Government for Thirty Years, from 1820 to 1850** [New York, 1871], 1, 342).

xxii stood six foot one Reda C. Goff, "A Physical Profile of Andrew Jackson," **Tennessee Historical Quarterly** 28 (Fall 1969), 303–4.

xxii Over a midday glass of whiskey Parton, **Life**, III, 462.

xvii pounded a table Ibid.

xxii "By the God of Heaven" Ibid.

xxii "When everything is ready" **AAK**, 631.

xxii "It is nothing more nor less" Ellis, **Union at Risk**, 93. Italics in quotations reflect emphasis in the original throughout unless otherwise noted.

xxii   "the dissolution of the American confederacy"   Richard Wellesley [Marquis Wellesley] to Sir Henry Halford, February 23, 1833, Halford Manuscripts, Record Office for Leicestershire.

xxii   Dispatching troops and a warship   Parton, **Life**, III, 460–61. General Winfield Scott was to lead them. (Scott, **Memoirs**, 235.)

xxii   earned him the nicknames "Old Hickory"   Parton, **Life**, I, 373–86.

xxiii   "Nothing but blood will satisfy the old scoundrel"   P. M. Butler to James H. Hammond, December 18, 1832, James H. Hammond Papers, LOC. Barnwell's report is cited in the text of Butler's letter to Hammond.

xxiii   the immediate issue was money   Ellis, **Union at Risk**, 41–46; Freehling, **Prelude to Civil War**, 47–48; Parton, **Life**, III, 433–34.

xxiii   ultimately about slavery   Ellis, **Union at Risk**, 189–98, is an intelligent and measured account of the links between nullification, states' rights, and slavery. Freehling, **Prelude to Civil War**, 134–76, is also cogent and convincing. Ellis's conclusion: "In short, in certain very important ways the nullification crisis marked the beginning of a new era. For a definite result of the crisis was the emergence of a forceful and determined pro-slavery interest in politics, better organized and more articulate than any other group that had risen to the defense of the peculiar institution. There are strong constitutional and ideological ties between the nullifiers and their supporters in 1832–33 and the fireaters of 1860–61 since both groups advocated states' rights as a device to protect the rights of minorities"—in this case, the minority was the slaveholding class. "More so than any other event that occurred in the half-century or so following the adoption of the United States Constitution, the nullification crisis created the concepts and some of the political conditions that eventually led to the Civil War" (Ellis, **Union at Risk**, 198). See also Freehling, **Prelude to Civil War**, 127–28, 256–59.

xxiii   "the peculiar domestic institution"   John C. Calhoun, **Union and Liberty: The Political Philosophy of John C. Calhoun** (Indianapolis, Ind., 1992), 525. Contemporaries recognized slavery's centrality. "The truth can no longer be disguised that the peculiar domestic institution of the Southern States . . . has placed them . . . in opposite relation to the rest of the Union," said Calhoun (**PJCC**, XI, 229).

xxiii "I am prepared any day" Ellis, **Union at Risk**, 78–79.

xxiii It was rumored that excited radicals Parton, **Life**, III, 459.; see also **AAK**, 631.

xxiii readers of the Columbia **Telescope** **Niles' Weekly Register** 43 (September 29, 1832), 78.

xxiii "I will meet" **Correspondence**, V, 3.

xxiii he would do what it took **AAK**, 635. Kendall wrote: "In his military campaigns he never submitted a decision to a vote in a council of war. He asked the opinion of each member on the case presented, dismissed them, and they knew not what was to be done until his order was issued. He never took a vote in his Cabinet. Questions were submitted and discussed; but, when it came to decision, 'he took the responsibility.' Nor was he so proud or self-conceited as to be above seeking information from any one whom he thought capable of giving it, and no President ever had a greater number or more faithful counselors; but, when it came to action, it was still, 'I take the responsibility'" (ibid.).

xxiv "I have been Tossed" **Papers**, V, 115. There are several interesting psychological studies of Jackson that explore the connections between his early years and the man (and the leader) he became. See, for instance: Hendrik Booraem, **Young Hickory: The Making of Andrew Jackson** (Dallas, 2001); Andrew Burstein, **The Passions of Andrew Jackson** (New York, 2003); James C. Curtis, **Andrew Jackson and the Search for Vindication** (Boston, 1976); and Michael Paul Rogin, **Fathers and Children: Andrew Jackson and the Subjugation of the American Indian** (New York, 1975). I by no means agree with all of these authors' conclusions, but their arguments repay consideration.

xxiv "one great family" **Papers**, VI, 476.

xxiv "I feel in the depths of my soul" **Correspondence**, V, 27.

xxv "I call upon you in the language of truth" For the conclusion of the proclamation, see Edward Livingston Papers, Manuscripts Division, Department of Rare Books and Special Collections, Princeton University Library.

xxv hailed by Harry Truman Margaret Truman, ed., **Where the**

Buck Stops: The Personal and Private Writings of Harry S. Truman (New York, 1989), 5–6.

xxvi expanded the powers of the presidency   My analysis of the significance of Jackson's presidency owes much to the following sources: Donald B. Cole, **The Presidency of Andrew Jackson** (Lawrence, Kansas, 1993); Richard B. Latner, **The Presidency of Andrew Jackson: White House Politics, 1829–1837** (Athens, Ga., 1979); and Remini, **Jackson**, II and III, among others.

There is much healthy and interesting debate about whether Jackson was the first "modern" president. Here, for instance, is Remini on Jackson as he left the White House in 1837: "More than anything else, most commentators agreed, Andrew Jackson had created a new presidential style. To be sure, not everyone liked or admired his style, but they admitted its unique character. To his friends, the Jacksonian presidential style reflected and embodied the popular will, and this identification with the Democracy meant that the President could assume a more appropriate position in a modern society, namely head of state and leader of the nation. Furthermore, to support the President in achieving his program and to help him implement his vision of the future, a party organization grounded in Jeffersonian republicanism had been established on a mass basis and committed to the doctrine that the people shall rule.

"None of the previous Presidents acted upon, much less articulated, the notion that the President was elected by the people of the entire nation. Andrew Jackson established that contention. None previously claimed that the President was 'more representative of the national will than the Congress.' Old Hickory did. None argued the superiority of a particular branch of the federal government. None tried to substitute his opinion for that of Congress, except where constitutionality was involved. Jackson did it regularly—or at least where he believed the public good required it. He is, therefore, the first modern President in American history, the first to conceive himself as the head of a democracy" (Remini, **Jackson**, III, 412). Rogin wrote: "[Jackson's] internal improvements and Bank vetoes, his nullification proclamation, and his removal of government deposits from the U.S. Bank all asserted unprecedented executive prerogatives and a new theory of political representation. The legislature represented elite interests; the executive embodied the popular will. This doctrine infused life into the nascently bureaucratic federal executive, the informal group of presidential advisers, and the specialized party apparatus. Jackson was the first modern President" (Rogin, **Fathers and Children**, 267). Cole offers a more measured view: "Many of [Jackson's] policies looked toward modern America—especially his expansion of foreign commerce, his Indian removal, his administrative reform, and the creation of a patronage system and the Democratic party. In addition, Jackson pointed the way toward the modern presidency by relying on informal advisers, using the press, dramatizing politics, and appealing to the people. He took advantage of the veto and other powers of the chief executive as no president had before.

"Yet to say that he transformed the presidency or became the first modern president is stretching the point" (Cole, **Presidency of Andrew Jackson**, 274). Dr. Cole's argument is nuanced and thought-provoking, and I am grateful to him for discussing these matters with me. I believe, however, that Jackson's was the presidency that set the pattern for all successive ones (if the president were willing and able to follow Jackson's pattern), and was the first one that we would recognize as a White House like those of our own time.

On the question of those who surrounded Jackson, the "Kitchen Cabinet" is a complicated issue in the study of Jackson's presidency. I have drawn much from Richard B. Latner's sensible and scholarly treatment of the question. The essence of his verdict. "Historians have traditionally claimed that the term [Kitchen Cabinet] originated during Jackson's presidency as a label derisively applied by the opposition to a group of aides, mostly outside the cabinet, who specialized in political manipulation, wire-pulling, and patronage. It is generally implied that these men shared similar goals and worked closely together in achieving them. There exists, however, a suspicion that the Kitchen Cabinet was largely a figment of the opposition's imagination. . . . While the Kitchen Cabinet certainly lacked the institutional self-identification, established rules of procedure, and regularized patterns of interaction associated with the cabinet, it was also something more than an organization with the limited political purpose and power of a national party committee. Rather, it most resembles the modern White House staff, a group of aides personally attached to the president and having his special trust." (See Latner, **Presidency of Andrew Jackson**, 51–57.) I share Professor Latner's conclusion and believe the Kitchen Cabinet is best understood as one of the stars, along with the family group, which moved in orbit around Jackson.

xxvii role they were assigned at Philadelphia   Wilentz, **Rise of American Democracy**, 32–33.

xxvii "My Country, 'Tis of Thee" and "Amazing Grace" took root   Marc McCutcheon, **Everyday Life in the 1800s** (Cincinnati, 1993), 300. When Arthur Schlesinger, Jr., finished **The Age of Jackson** in 1944, the penultimate year of the global war between democracy and dictatorship, he was drawn to a speech President Franklin D. Roosevelt had given at a Jackson Day dinner in Washington in January 1938. Jackson's legacy, FDR said, was "his unending contribution to the vitality of our democracy. We look back on his amazing personality, we review his battles because the struggles he went through, the enemies he encountered, the defeats he suffered and the victories he won are part and parcel of the struggles, the enmities, the defeats and the victories of those who have lived in all the generations that have followed" (Arthur M. Schlesinger, Jr., **The Age of Jackson** [Boston, 1945], x).

xxviii take a bullet in a frontier gunfight   Parton, **Life**, I, 386–98, is an engaging account of one of Jackson's peacetime skirmishes.

xxviii to assault his own would-be assassin   Parton, **Life**, III, 582–84. The episode took place on January 30, 1835, when an assailant attempted to shoot Jackson at the Capitol. "The President, the instant he comprehended the purpose of the man, rushed furiously at him with uplifted cane," Parton reported (ibid., 582). The episode is treated more fully below.

xxix imprisoning those who defied   Matthew Warshauer, **Andrew Jackson and the Politics of Martial Law: Nationalism, Civil Liberties, and Partisanship** (Knoxville, 2006), 35–39.

xxix a leading hostess was disturbed   Louise Livingston Hunt, **Memoir of Mrs. Edward Livingston, with Letters Hitherto Unpublished** (New York, 1886), 52.

xxix "wild man of the woods"   Ibid.

xxix stunned to find Jackson both elegant and charming Ibid., 53.

xxix "Is this your backwoodsman?" Ibid. This happened all the time; people accustomed to hearing stories of the frontier Jackson were constantly being surprised by his bearing in person. Even his foes granted as much. Ohio senator Thomas Ewing was a John Quincy Adams man, but he was forced to acknowledge that Jackson, while perhaps not brilliant, was sociable and engaging, which is more than President Adams could grant about Jackson. In a letter to his wife about a White House dinner in December 1831, Ewing wrote: "I told you in a former letter that I had an invitation to dine with the President. I accordingly on Tuesday evening last repaired to the palace where I was received with much courtesy by the old chief. . . . I have already told you that the manners of the President are exceedingly fine. For a how dye-do salutation, or a sitting at table chit chat, I never met his superior. He is neither wise nor learned nor witty, but he converses with freedom and ease on light and ordinary topics. . . . He is exceedingly familiar though at the same time sufficiently dignified. Now and then, however, his want of general information will disclose itself, though not often. He gave me a seat . . . at his right hand. We had an excellent dinner—fine wine—Madeira of choice and very ancient vintage and some first-rate champagne. Enough to make one a Jackson man almost—not quite" (Donald J. Ratcliffe, "My Dinner with Andrew," **Timeline** [October-November 1987], 53–54).

xxix "there was more of the woman" Parton, **Life**, III, 602. The secretary is Nicholas Trist.

xxx "He lived always in a crowd" Ibid., 596.

xxxi "I have scarcely ever known a man" **AMVB**, 403. Van Buren was impressed by Jackson's encompassing notion of family: "I have scarcely ever known a man who placed a higher value upon the enjoyments of the family circle or who suffered more from interruptions of harmony in his own; feelings which are more striking in view of the fact . . . that not a drop of his own blood flowed in the veins of a single member of it."

xxxi "She was a beautiful, accomplished" **EDT**, I, 172.

xxxii journalists Amos Kendall and Francis Preston Blair I depended on **AAK** as well as Donald B. Cole, **A Jackson Man: Amos**

Kendall and the Rise of American Democracy (Baton Rouge, La., 2004). FPB and William E. Smith, The Francis Preston Blair Family in Politics (New York, 1933), were crucial.

xxxii A shrewd New York politician   I found John Niven, Martin Van Buren: The Romantic Age of American Politics (New York, 1983), Ted Widmer, Martin Van Buren (New York, 2004), and AMVB essential to understanding the elusive eighth president.

xxxii to think of him as the "Old Lion"   Poughkeepsie Journal and Eagle, June 28, 1845; "General Jackson," Goshen Democrat and Whig, July 4, 1845. I am indebted to Matthew Warshauer for his guidance on this point.

xxxii "the lion of Tennessee"   House of Representatives, Congressman Dickinson of Tennessee on the Fine on General Jackson, 28th Cong., 1st. Sess., Congressional Globe (6 January 1844), 13, appendix: 3. Also see Matthew Warshauer, "Contested Mourning: The New York Battle over Andrew Jackson's Death," New York History 87 (Winter 2006), 29–65.

xxxii Holmes's lion is "the terror"   Oliver Wendell Holmes, The Poetical Works of Oliver Wendell Holmes (Boston, 1908), 75–76.

xxxiii "I for one do not despair of the Republic"   Papers, VI, 477.

xxxiii "My hopes of a long continuance"   Allan Nevins, ed., The Diary of John Quincy Adams, 1794–1845 (New York, 1951), 434.

xxxiii "I was born for a storm"   Heiskell, AJETH, III, 166.

Chapter 1: Andy Will Fight His Way in the World

3 "How triumphant!"   Andrew Jackson Donelson to John Coffee, November 15, 1828, Andrew Jackson Donelson Papers, LOC.

3 was known to serve guests whiskey   EDT, II, 55–56; James, TLOAJ, 609. Strong drink and good wine were hallmarks of Jackson's hospitality wherever he was, from Nashville to the White House to his summer retreats as president at the Rip Raps on Old Point Comfort. His friend General Daniel Smith was known to have one of the finer stills in the region (EDT, I, 76). The cellars at the Hermitage were a source of great pride

and interest to Jackson. As noted below, when the house burned in 1834, he gloomily wrote: "I suppose all the wines in the cellar have been destroyed" (**EDT**, II, 71). Jackson's traveling liquor case—a handsome artifact—is still in his study next to the room in which he died at the Hermitage in Nashville (Author observation).

3 was sitting inside the house **Papers**, VI, 545–46.

3 answering congratulatory messages Andrew Jackson to John Coffee, December 11, 1828, Andrew Jackson Papers, Scholarly Resources Collection, Reel 12, LOC. In this letter, Jackson laments the post-election "press of business."

3 friends in town were planning a ball **Nashville Banner**, December 16, 1828. The newspaper notice of the events tried to encourage an atmosphere of unity after the divisiveness of the campaign. "These are judicious arrangements," the paper said of the dinner and the ball, "and we hope that a liberal and magnanimous spirit will characterize all the proceedings. The object is the manifest feelings of personal attachment to Andrew Jackson, on the part of those who have been in the habit of associating with him in the various relations of private life, as well as to pay him that respect which is due to the individual selected by the people as the chief magistrate of the nation." Interestingly, the organizers were clearly worried that the Jackson or Adams forces might treat the day as yet another skirmish in the campaign—a sign of how vicious the 1828 race really was, and might still be, even though it had been decided. "In these testimonies, even those who preferred his competitor and were opposed to his election, may consistently and appropriately join," the **Banner** went on. "As a neighbor and personal acquaintance, and as the elected President of the United States, he is entitled to marks of attention, even from such as were themselves desirous of retaining in office the present incumbent. Nor can it be either necessary or proper on such occasion for the zealous supporters of the General's election, to indulge in acrimonious feelings towards the unsuccessful candidate or to recall any of the unpleasant emotions connected with the late bitter electoral contest. The battle has been fought and the triumph signal. Let us hope that the wounds unhappily inflicted will be permitted to heal. . . ."

3 Led by a marshal   **Nashville Republican and State Gazette**, December 16, 1828.

4 drafted a letter   **Papers**, VI, 545–46. The note, dated December 18 from the Hermitage, was written to Francis Preston Blair. Given the postscript reporting Rachel Jackson's collapse (see below), it seems to have been composed on December 17, the day she was stricken (**Papers**, VI, 547); Jackson apparently dated it incorrectly on the seventeenth (which is understandable, given the crisis in the house) or waited until the next day to date it.

4 "To the people, for the confidence reposed in me"   **Papers**, VI, 545.

4 went outside to his Tennessee fields   Parton, **Life**, III, 154. Hannah, one of the Jacksons' slaves, is the source for this detail.

4 The 1828 presidential campaign . . . had been vicious   Remini, **Jackson**, II, 116–42; Parton, **Life**, III, 137–50; James, **TLOAJ**, 461–72. See also Robert V. Remini, **The Election of Andrew Jackson** (New York and Philadelphia, 1963), and Arthur M. Schlesinger, Jr., ed., **The Election of 1828 and the Administration of Andrew Jackson** (Philadelphia, 2003).

4 Adams was alleged to have   Remini, **Jackson**, II, 133.

4 his wife a bigamist and his mother a whore   Paul Johnson, **The Birth of the Modern**, 930–31. Johnson offers a useful summary of the less savory aspects of the 1828 campaign, citing the pro-Adams **National Journal** ("General Jackson's mother was a **Common Prostitute**, brought to this country by British soldiers! She afterwards married a **Mulatto Man**, with whom she had several children, of which number **General Jackson is one!**") (ibid., 930), and Charles Hammond's **A View of General Jackson's Domestic Relations**, which asked: "Ought a convicted adulteress and her paramour husband to be placed in the highest offices of this land?" (ibid., 931).

4 alleged atrocities   Remini, **Jackson**, II, 122–24.

4 "Even Mrs. J. is not spared"   "Letters from Andrew Jackson to R. K. Call," **Virginia Magazine of History and Biography** 29 (April 1921), 191.

4 "The floodgates of falsehood"   William B. Lewis to John Coffee, July 27, 1828, Dyas Collection-John Coffee Papers, 1770–1917, Tennessee Historical Society War Memorial Building,

Nashville, Tennessee. Papers housed at the Tennessee State Library and Archives.

5 Some Americans thought   See, for instance, Elizabeth Parke Custis to Andrew Jackson, December 25, 1828, Andrew Jackson Donelson Papers, LOC. Among Jackson partisans there was much talk of the connection between the era of the Founding and the incoming administration. Writing to the man he saluted as "Respected Genl," Patrick G. C. Nagle of Philadelphia told Jackson: "It has been my determination and has been a long time back to make you a pair of waterproof boots (in order to keep your feet dry and warm when walking the muddy streets of Washington in the winter season)." These were no ordinary boots, but symbols tying Jackson to another, earlier savior of the nation: the Marquis de Lafayette. "I have had the honor," Nagle wrote, "of making a pair of the same kind for the nation's guest, the great and good Lafayette" (Patrick G. C. Nagle to Andrew Jackson, November 18, 1828, Andrew Jackson Papers, Reel 72, LOC).

5 One Revolutionary War veteran, David Coons   David Coons to Andrew Jackson, November 19, 1828, Andrew Jackson Papers, Reel 72, LOC. "Permit an anxious friend unknown to you but to whom you are not unknown, to introduce himself thus to your notice," Coons's letter begins. "I am an old man who in my youth stood forth at my country's call, and have always cherished that affection for my country and her defending which I consider due from every man, I could wish the same for all. The object of my introducing myself thus, plainly, to your notice is this. Through motives of the purest friendship," Coons wanted to advise Jackson of the "hard threats." Closing the letter, Coons added: "I may be unnecessarily alarmed, yet I cannot consider it a trespass in giving you this caution."

5 the draft of a speech   "Speech [undelivered] for December 23 Celebration in Nashville," Andrew Jackson Papers, Reel 36, LOC. The draft is in Andrew Jackson Donelson's handwriting.

5 While Jackson was outside   Parton, **Life**, III, 154. I have drawn on several different accounts of Rachel Jackson's death to tell the story of her collapse, final hours, and funeral: Wise, **Seven Decades**, 113–17; Parton, **Life**, III, 154–64; James, **TLOAJ**, 478–82; Remini, **Jackson**, II, 150–55; **EDT**, I, 155–59.

6   collapsed in her sitting room, screaming in pain   Parton, **Life**, III, 154.

6   "a black wench," a "profligate woman"   John William Ward, **Andrew Jackson: Symbol for an Age** (New York, 1953), 196. There is also a reference to Rachel as a "whore" in the correspondence of Henry Clay (**PHC**, IV, 553).

6   short and somewhat heavy   Vincent Nolte, **Fifty Years in Both Hemispheres** (New York, 1854), 238–39. Here is Nolte's acidic account of the Jacksons' dancing together at a ball in New Orleans in 1815: "After supper we were treated to a most delicious **pas de deux** by the conqueror and his spouse. . . . To see these two figures, the General a long, haggard man, with limbs like a skeleton, and Madame la Generale, a short, fat dumpling, bobbing opposite each other like half-drunken Indians, to the wild melody of 'Possum up de Gum Tree,' and endeavoring to make a spring into the air, was very remarkable. . . ." I am grateful to Marsha Mullin, the chief curator of the Hermitage, for bringing this quotation to my attention.

6   melancholy and anxious   "For four or five years the health of Mrs. Jackson had been precarious," wrote Parton. "She had complained, occasionally, of an uneasy feeling about the region of the heart; and, during the late excitements, she had been subject to sharper pains and palpitation. The aspersions upon her character had wounded deeply her feelings and her pride. She was frequently found in tears" (Parton, **Life**, III, 154). According to Remini, "Rachel . . . had no taste for public life, and after what had been said about her in the campaign she shivered at the thought of what lay ahead." She was, Remini added, suffering from "poor health and sagging spirits" (Remini, **Jackson**, II, 149).

6   "The enemies of the General"   **EDT**, I, 154.

6   Rachel was devastated to overhear   **EDT**, I, 157. There are different versions of the episode triggering Rachel Jackson's death. Mary Donelson Wilcox, a child of Emily and Andrew Jackson Donelson, is the source for the version I have told. Another account holds that while she was shopping in Nashville for clothes to take to Washington, Rachel Jackson found a pamphlet defending her character and was crushed. This is possible, of course, but we know that Rachel was already aware of the

charges from the letter (noted above) she wrote in July 1828: "the enemys of the Genls have dipt their arrows in wormwood and gall and sped them at me . . . to think that thirty years had passed in happy social friendship with society, knowing or thinking no ill to no one—as my judge will know . . ." (**EDT**, I, 154). See Remini, **Jackson**, II, 150, for an account of the pamphlet scene, as well as his note (tracing the story through Major Lewis down to John Spencer Bassett) on page 415 of that work.

6 "No, Emily," Mrs. Jackson replied   **EDT**, I, 157.

6 "Well, for Mr. Jackson's sake"   Parton, **Life**, III, 153.

6 Rachel was put to bed   Ibid., 154.

6 Jackson rushed to his wife   Ibid., 155.

6 sent for doctors   James, **TLOAJ**, 478.

6 "P.S. Whilst writing"   **Papers**, VI, 546.

7 "Do not, My beloved Husband"   **Papers**, II, 361.

7 his candle burning low   Ibid., 354.

7 "My heart is with you"   Ibid., 487. The letter is dated December 14, 1813.

7 Jackson kept vigil   Parton, **Life**, III, 156.

7 her flesh turning cold   Ibid.; James, **TLOAJ**, 480; Remini, **Jackson**, II, 151.

7 "My mind is so disturbed"   **Papers**, VII, 13.

7 At one o'clock on Christmas Eve afternoon   Parton, **Life**, III, 157. I drew on four detailed accounts of Rachel Jackson's funeral: Wise, **Seven Decades**, 114–16; Parton, **Life**, III, 157–64; James, **TLOAJ**, 480–82; Remini, **Jackson**, II, 153–55.

8 The weather had been wet   Parton, **Life**, III, 163.

8 led by Rachel's minister   Remini, **Jackson**, II, 153. "Every muscle of [Jackson's] face was unmoved," wrote Henry Wise, who was there, "steady as a rock, without a teardrop in his eye or a quaver in his voice. . . ." During the burial, Hannah came through the mourners and, Wise wrote, "tried to get into the grave with the coffin. . . . Her cries were agonizing: 'Mistress, my best friend, my love, my life, is gone—I will go with her!'" Jackson waved off those who were trying to help Hannah up from the ground. "'Let that faithful servant weep for her best friend and loved mistress; she has the right and cause to mourn for her loss, and her grief is sweet to me'" (Wise, **Seven Decades**, 115).

8 the one hundred fifty paces   Author observation.

8 Devastated but determined   Wise, **Seven Decades**, 116; Remini, **Jackson**, II, 154.

8 "I am now the President elect of the United States"   Wise, **Seven Decades**, 116. Of Rachel's death, Leonidas Polk wrote to his mother, Sarah Polk, on January 10, 1829: "This must have been a sad shock to him, especially as he had just been so highly honored, in defiance of the abuse heaped both on himself and her. And it must also teach him the frailty of human existence, and the necessity for being at any moment ready to resign it" (Leonidas Polk to Sarah Polk, January 10, 1829, Leonidas Polk Collection, The University of the South, University Archives and Special Collections, Sewanee).

8 to work through the president-elect's correspondence   "I receive at least one hundred letters a week," Jackson told John Coffee during the transition, adding: "Was it not for the aid of Capt. A. J. Donelson I could not reply to half of what are necessary to be answered." Andrew Jackson to John Coffee, December 11, 1828, Andrew Jackson Papers, Scholarly Resources Collection, Reel 12, LOC.

9 Emily was at once selfless and sharp-tongued   Both volumes of Burke's **EDT** are excellent on Emily.

9 Born on Monday, June 1, 1807   **EDT**, I, xi.

9 "All Donelsons in the female line"   Ibid., xv.

9 On Sunday, January 18, 1829   **Papers**, VII, 3. See also **EDT**, I, 163.

9 the steamboat **Pennsylvania**   Remini, **Jackson**, II, 157–58. See also **EDT**, I, 163.

10 "Whether I am ever to return or not"   **Papers**, VII, 12.

10 "The active discharge of those duties"   Nashville **Republican and State Gazette**, December 26, 1828.

10 bordered in black   Ibid.

10 Referring to America, Livingston told the president-elect   **Papers**, VII, 5–6.

10 passing through Louisville   Mary Eastin to William Eastin, February 15, 1829, The Dillon and Polk Papers, Southern Historical Collection, Wilson Library, The University of North Carolina at Chapel Hill.

10 "He was very much wearied"   Ibid.

11 a blur of cannons, cheers, and tending to colds   **EDT**, I, 163–64. For details of the journey, see also Nashville **Republican and State Gazette**, January 20, 1829; Frances Trollope, **Domestic Manners of the Americans** (Mineola, N.Y.; 2003), 83–85.

11 "I scarcely"   **EDT**, I, 164.

11 "You must not make yourself"   Ibid.

11 Traveling to America from Ireland in 1765   Parton, **Life**, I, 46–47. For accounts of the Jackson family background, the journey to America, and the family situation awaiting them, see ibid., 36–58; James, **TLOAJ**, 3–6; Kendall, **Life of Jackson**, 9–13; Remini, **Jackson**, I, 2–4. I found Booraem's **Young Hickory** the most detailed and measured account of Jackson's early life.

12 "Waxhaw" came from the name of the tribe   Parton, **Life**, I, 48–49; Remini, **Jackson**, I, 3. The area was also called the Waxhaw district or Waxhaw settlement, or sometimes simply "the Waxhaws."

12 Parliament passed the Quartering Act   See, for instance, Benson Bobrick, **Angel in the Whirlwind: The Triumph of the American Revolution** (New York, 1997), 69.

12 the Stamp Act   Ibid., 74–82.

12 the Massachusetts legislature called for a colonial congress   Richard M. Ketchum, ed., **The American Heritage Book of the Revolution**, 56–59.

12 **"There ought to be no more New England men"**   Ibid., 58.

12 of "independent" means   Booraem, **Young Hickory**, 2.

12 poorer than his in-laws   Ibid., 2–3; Parton, **Life**, I, 49. Parton wrote this of the extended Jackson circle: "The members of this circle were not all equally poor. There is reason to believe that some of them brought to America sums of money which were considerable for that day, and sufficient to enable them to buy negroes as well as lands in the southern wilderness. But all accounts concur in this: that Andrew Jackson [Sr.] was very poor, both in Ireland and in America" (47).

12 moved his wife and two sons   Ibid.; Booraem, **Young Hickory**, 9.

12 His wife was pregnant   Ibid., 9–10.

13 a snowstorm   James, **TLOAJ**, 9.

13 pallbearers drank so much   Booraeam, **Young Hickory**, 10.

13 naming him Andrew after her late husband   Ibid., 11.

13 under the roof of relatives   Which roof is the keystone of the great Jackson birthplace debate between North Carolina and South Carolina. See Booraem, **Young Hickory**, 11–12; James, **TLOAJ**, 791–97 (an exhaustive survey of the competing claims); Parton, **Life**, I, 52–57; Remini, **Jackson**, I, 4–5.

13 the Crawfords were more affluent   Booraem, **Young Hickory**, 16–17.

13 The Jacksons needed a home   Ibid., 58.

13 "Mrs. Crawford was an invalid"   Parton, **Life**, I, 57–58.

13 Jackson felt a certain inferiority to and distance from others Several biographers—James and Remini among them—tend to downplay the Jacksons' "poor relation" status (James, **TLOAJ**, 10; Remini, **Jackson**, I, 6). My contention that he did feel like a dependent, with resulting implications, is based on Parton, who spent time in the neighborhood among descendants of Jackson's contemporaries, and, as quoted below, on Mary Donelson Wilcox's memories of Jackson's own remarks on the question. Perhaps the most compelling evidence on this question is the fact that Jackson never returned to Waxhaw (discussed at greater length below) and observations made in a biography Jackson approved: John Reid and John Henry Eaton's 1817 book, **The Life of Andrew Jackson** (University, Ala., 1974). After the deaths of his mother and his brothers, Jackson, according to Reid and Eaton, "was thus left alone in the wide world, without a human being with whom he could claim a near relationship . . ." (13). Describing Jackson's ultimate decision to move to Tennessee after reading law in North Carolina, Reid and Eaton write that Jackson, "recollecting that he stood a solitary individual in life, without relations to aid him in the onset, when innumerable difficulties arise and retard success . . . determined to seek a new country. But for this, he might have again returned to his native state [South Carolina]; but the death of every relation he had, had wiped away all those recollections and circumstances which warp the mind to the place of its nativity" (14–15).

13 "His childish recollections"   Heiskell, **AJETH**, III, 280. Mary Donelson Wilcox was born Mary Rachel but later changed her name to Mary Emily, and she published under the name of Mary Emily Donelson Wilcox. For the sake of clarity, in the

text the child is referred to as "Mary Rachel" and the author as "Mary Donelson Wilcox."

14 His mother took him and his brothers   Booraem, **Young Hickory**, 18.

14 memorization of the Shorter Westminster Catechism   Ibid., 20–21.

14 Most stories about the young Jackson   I have drawn on Booraem, **Young Hickory**, 17–22; Parton, **Life**, I, 58–69; James, **TLOAJ**, 17–18; Remini, **Jackson**, I, 6–11.

14 Wrestling was a common pastime   Parton, **Life**, I, 64.

14 "I could throw him three times out of four"   Ibid. Drawing on his research, Parton observes this of the young Jackson: "To younger boys, who never questioned his mastery, he was a generous protector; there was nothing he would not do to defend them. His equals and superiors found him self-willed, somewhat overbearing, easily offended, **very** irascible, and, upon the whole, 'difficult to get along with.' One of them said, many years after, in the heat of controversy, that of all the boys he had ever known, Andrew Jackson was the only bully who was not also a coward."

14 his friends packed extra powder   Ibid.

14 "By God, if one of you laughs"   Ibid.

14 "Mother, Andy will fight"   Ibid., 75.

15 fits of rage so paralyzing . . ."slobbering"   Ibid., 64; Remini, **Jackson**, I, 10.

15 His uncles and aunts apparently did not take a great deal of interest   Or at least not enough interest to sustain Jackson's gratitude later in life. After the Revolution, when he was at a low ebb, Jackson became more or less completely estranged from his Waxhaw connections. As Remini wrote: "His energies found release in a series of escapades that won . . . dismay from his relatives. Drinking, cockfighting, gambling, mischief-making, he seemed determined to go as far as possible in leading an 'abandoned' life. He was almost manic. His relatives took a decidedly dim view of his activities and probably thought him a ne'er-do-well headed for an early and unfortunate end. He was never particularly close to his surviving relatives, and his irresponsible behavior only alienated them further. A complete and permanent rupture eventually resulted" (Remini, **Jackson**, I,

27). My view is that the roots of this break probably extended back into Jackson's much younger years, for it seems likely that any bonds formed between Jackson and his extended relations in peacetime and in childhood would have been strengthened, not severed, by the trauma of war and the loss of his mother. He simply appears not to have been a subject of much concern either before or after his mother's death.

15 There was some money   Parton, **Life**, I, 61–62. "It is possible," Parton wrote of Elizabeth Jackson, "that her condition was not one of absolute dependence. The farm of her deceased husband may have been held, though not owned by her; and either let to a tenant, or worked on shares, may have yielded her a small income. . . . It is possible, too, that her relations in Ireland may have contributed something to her support. General Jackson had a distinct recollection of her receiving presents of linen from the old country . . ." (ibid., 61).

15 to send Jackson to schools   Remini, **Jackson**, I, 6.

15 "the dead languages"   Reid and Eaton, **Life of Andrew Jackson**, 10.

15 Edmund Burke took note   Ketchum, ed., **American Heritage Book of the Revolution**, 9.

16 By 1778, the South was the focus of the war   George F. Scheer and Hugh F. Rankin, **Rebels and Redcoats** (New York, 1957), 389–507, is a good account of the war in the South and the Revolution's closing military phase. See also John Ferling, **Almost a Miracle: The American Victory in the War of Independence** (New York, 2007), 410–520; Kendall, **Life of Andrew Jackson**, 13–40; Bobrick, **Angel in the Whirlwind**, 392–495; Booraem, **Young Hickory**, 45–118.

16 Andrew's brother Hugh   Parton, **Life**, I, 69.

16 "of heat and fatigue"   Ibid.

16 at the Battle of Stono Ferry, south of Charleston   Ferling, **Almost a Miracle**, 387–88.

16 took Charleston on Friday, May 12, 1780   Booraem, **Young Hickory**, 48.

16 On Monday, May 29, at about three o'clock in the afternoon   Scheer and Rankin, **Rebels and Redcoats**, 402.

16 roughly three hundred British troops   Ferling, **Almost a Miracle**, 436.

16 It was a vicious massacre   Scheer and Rankin, **Rebels and Red-coats**, 402. See also Booracm, **Young Hickory**, 48–49. Ferling's description bears noting: "Whether on horseback or on foot, the [British] attackers swung their sabers, cutting men to pieces, overwhelming their stunned adversaries. Battlefields are horrid places, but this one was especially ghastly. Here were men with severed hands and limbs, crushed skulls, and breached arteries. Some men were decapitated by slashing cavalrymen. Others were trampled by maddened horses. The bellies of many were laid open by bayonets" (Ferling, **Almost a Miracle**, 436).

16 a rebel surgeon recalled   Scheer and Rankin, **Rebels and Red-coats**, 402. The doctor's name was Robert Brownfield, a surgeon with Colonel Abraham Buford.

16 Even after the survivors   Ibid. "Only fifty-three of Buford's men survived Tarleton's bayonets and swords to be taken prisoner," write Scheer and Rankin. "Tarleton's loss was five killed, fourteen wounded" (ibid).

16 The meetinghouse was filled with casualties   Parton, **Life**, I, 70.

16 "None of the men"   Booraem, **Young Hickory**, 50.

17 the people of Waxhaw, like people throughout the colonies, were divided   Booraem, **Young Hickory**, 88–91; Kendall, **Life of Jackson**, 42–45. Ferling wrote that boys such as Jackson "had been taught by their parents how the English had plundered their homeland and its inhabitants. Most backcountry rebels were Scotch-Irish who had seen America—and then American independence—as deliverance from a Great Britain they detested. Most also were Presbyterians who had always bridled at the requirement that they pay tithes to the Church of England, the established church in South Carolina. . . . Young Andy Jackson joined a partisan unit after helping his mother care for the mangled survivors of a Tory massacre, and observing that many survivors had three or four, or more, wounds" (Ferling, **Almost a Miracle**, 452–53).

17 As Jackson recalled it   Reid and Eaton, **Life of Andrew Jackson**, 10.

17 in action at Carrickfergus   Parton, **Life**, I, 37.

17 "Often she would spend"   Reid and Eaton, **Life of Andrew Jackson**, 10.

17 a biography Jackson approved   Jackson took an intense inter-

est in Reid and Eaton's book. See, for instance, **Papers**, IV, 4 and 47. Reid started it but died before it was finished; Jackson drafted Eaton to take on the task. "This has engrossed much of my time and thoughts," Jackson wrote on June 23, 1816, "and I flatter myself by the pen of Major Eaton it will be completed in a manner to meet the expectations of the publick. . . . Major Eaton will exert his best talents, his industry and research will give to the publick a Just narrative of facts" (**Papers**, IV, 47). As Frank Owsley, the editor of the edition cited here, noted: "Much of Eaton's writing was actually done at the Hermitage. It is almost certain that Jackson read and approved every line of the manuscript, probably as it was being written. Clearly this close supervision by Jackson makes the work the nearest approach to an autobiography of the General" (Reid and Eaton, **Life of Andrew Jackson**, viii).

18 Jackson saw firsthand the brutality   Kendall, **Life of Jackson**, 43–45; Remini, **Jackson**, I, 19–20.

18 "Men hunted each other like beasts of prey"   Kendall, **Life of Jackson**, 44–45. Kendall adds: "A Whig living in or near the Waxhaws, finding one of his friends murdered and mutilated, swore that he would never spare a Tory. He thenceforward made it his business to hunt and kill; and before the close of the war, sacrificed upward of twenty victims. 'But,' said General Jackson, 'he was never a happy man afterward'" (45).

18 known as "Bloody Tarleton"   Booraem, **Young Hickory**, 49.

18 once rode so close   Remini, **Jackson**, I, 15. Here is Jackson's complete recollection of the moment: "The Infantry as far as Cain creek, and Tarleton, passed thro the Waxhaw settlement to the Cotauba nation passing our dwelling but we were all **hid out**. Tarleton passed within a hundred yards of where I and a cousin Crawford, had concealed ourselves" (**Papers**, I, 5).

18 "I could have shot him"   Ibid.

18 The boy soaked up the talk of war   Kendall, **Life of Jackson**, 45; Booraem, **Young Hickory**, 52–58.

18 "Boys big enough to carry muskets"   Kendall, **Life of Jackson**, 45.

18 In April 1781   Booraem, **Young Hickory**, 96.

18 A neighboring Tory alerted the redcoats   Parton, **Life**, I, 88.

18 Andrew and Robert were surrounded   Ibid.

18 The soldiers ransacked the house   Ibid. Here is Parton's full description of the scene, which included roughing up one of Jackson's Crawford aunts and her baby: "Crockery, glass, and furniture, were dashed to pieces; beds emptied; the clothing of the family torn to rags; even the clothes of the infant that Mrs. Crawford carried in her arms were not spared."

18 an imperious officer ordered Jackson   Ibid.

18 "Sir," he said   Ibid., 89. For different renderings of this familiar Jacksonian tale, see also Bassett, **Jackson**, 10; Booraem, **Young Hickory**, 97–98; James, **TLOAJ**, 25–26; Remini, **Jackson**, I, 21.

18 "The sword point reached my head"   **Correspondence**, VI, 253.

19 a British prison camp in Camden   Booraem, **Young Hickory**, 98.

19 "The prisoners were all dismounted"   **Correspondence**, VI, 253.

19 "No attention whatever was paid"   **Papers**, I, 7.

19 Robert was sick, very sick   Ibid.

19 Robert on one horse and Mrs. Jackson on another   Ibid.

19 a barefoot Andrew   Ibid.

19 the British had taken his shoes and his coat   Ibid.

19 "trudge"   Ibid.

19 the weather turned against them   Ibid.

19 "The fury"   Ibid.

19 Two days later Robert died   Ibid.

19 "During his confinement"   Eaton and Reid, **The Life of Andrew Jackson**, 13.

20 Elizabeth nursed Andrew   Ibid.

20 to care for two of her Crawford nephews   Ibid. Jackson's recollection is powerful in its sparseness: "As soon as my recovering health would permit, my mother hastened to Charleston to administer to the comfort of two of her nephews, Wm. and Jas Crawford then prisoners at this place. On her return She died about three miles from Charleston."

20 buried in obscurity   Parton, **Life**, I, 95.

20 Her clothes were all that came back to him   Ibid.

20 He long sought the whereabouts of his mother's grave   Parton, **Life**, I, 95; **Papers**, V, 437–39; **Papers**, VI, 60–61.

21 a careful steward of such things   See, for instance, **Papers**, VII, 12, in which Jackson arranges for Rachel's tombstone. And he never forgot his mother's tragic end. "As late in his life as during his presidency, he set on foot some inquiries respecting the place of [his mother's] burial, with the design of having her sacred dust conveyed to the old church-yard at Waxhaw, where he wished to erect a monument in honor of both his parents," writes Parton. "It was too late. No exact information could then be obtained, and the project was given up. No stone marks the burial-place either of his father, mother, or brothers" (Parton, **Life**, I, 95). There are now two monuments to Mrs. Jackson in Charleston, and she is thought to have been buried "in an unmarked grave somewhere north of the line of the 1780 earthworks that bisected the peninsula" (Seabrook Wilkinson, "Revolutionary Heroines: Elizabeth Hutchinson Jackson," **Charleston Mercury**, August 4, 2005).

21 in his last years he would spend hours in the garden   Heiskell, **AJETH**, III, 686.

21 "many hardships"   **Papers**, VI, 73.

21 In 1815, after his triumph   Remini, **Jackson**, I, 11.

21 "Gentlemen, I wish she"   Ibid.

21 "Andrew, if I should not see you again"   Ibid.

22 spiraled downward and lashed out   Parton, **Life**, I, 96; Remini, **Jackson**, I, 26–27.

23 "He once said he never remembered"   Heiskell, **AJETH**, III, 280.

23 The Revolutionary War drew to a close   **American Heritage Book of the Revolution**, 372–75.

23 Jackson got into a fight   **Papers**, I, 7.

23 shuffle him off to another relative   Ibid.

23 the cultivated precincts of Charleston   Booraem, **Young Hickory**, 118–29; Parton, **Life**, I, 97–98; James, **TLOAJ**, 32–34; Remini, **Jackson**, I, 27.

24 the pleasures of the turf, of good tailors, and of the gaming tables   Booraem, **Young Hickory**, 125–26.

24 "There can be little doubt"   Lee, **Biography of Andrew Jackson**, 6.

24 he grew restless   Parton, **Life**, I, 96–101; Remini, **Jackson**, I, 28.

24 he tried his hand at saddle making   Parton, **Life**, I, 96–101.

24 Acknowledging the gift of a map   **Papers**, VI, 354.

25 "juvenile companions"   Ibid.

25 could quote Shakespeare   Arda Walker, "The Educational Training and Views of Andrew Jackson," **The East Tennessee Historical Society's Publications** 16 (1944), 23. "In his writings," Walker observes, "are numerous references to Shakespeare. Whether Jackson was cognizant of their source or not, he used such quotations as 'Ides of March,' 'There is something rotten in the state of Denmark,' 'the die is cast.' . . . These could have been acquired from the 'stump' in Tennessee."

25 Plutarch   **Papers**, V, 197–99. The full line: "a Judge ought to be like Caesar's wife, 'not only chaste, but unsuspected.'" An editor's note explaining the allusion, which is from **Lives**, Caesar, section 10, is found on page 199. And, as noted below in my discussion of the possible influence some version of **Lord Chesterfield's Letters** may have had on Jackson, I suspect Chesterfield could have been one source for the "Caesar's wife" image.

25 Alexander Pope   **Papers**, VI, 71–72. Writing of a friend, Jackson says: "I have no doubt but he is an honest man, who, in my estimation, is 'the noblest work of god.'" The quotation is from Pope's "Essay on Man," which had entered the popular vernacular since its publication in the 1730s.

25 Elizabeth Jackson wanted her Andrew to be a minister   Parton, **Life**, I, 61.

26 The service the Jacksons attended most likely started in mid-morning   William B. Bynum, "'The Genuine Presbyterian Whine': Presbyterian Worship in the Eighteenth Century," **Journal of Presbyterian History** 74 (Fall 1996), 157–69. I have depended greatly on Mr. Bynum's fine article as I have reconstructed the details of a typical Sunday for an observant Presbyterian in the time of Jackson's youth, and I am grateful to Mr. Bynum for discussing these matters with me.

27 Church historians suspect   Ibid., 157–58.

27 a break for lunch, then an afternoon version   Ibid., 159–60.

27 fight the good fight   See the Second Epistle of St. Paul to Timothy, chapter 4, verse 7: "I have fought a good fight, I have finished my course, I have kept the faith."

28　He referred to political enemies as "Judases" **Papers**, VI, 29–30. Henry Clay came in for this particular attack after accepting the appointment as secretary of state when John Quincy Adams won the presidency in the House in 1825. In a letter dated February 14, 1825, Jackson wrote William B. Lewis: "Mr Clay has been offered the office of Sec of State . . . so you see the Judas of the West has closed the contract and will receive the thirty pieces of silver—his end will be the same."

28　"Should the uncircumcised philistines send forth" **Papers**, VI, 357. The letter is dated July 9, 1827.

28　"And thine house and thine kingdom" II Samuel 4:7 (King James Version).

29　"preside over the destinies" **Papers,** V, 188.

29　Jackson said he read three chapters of the Bible every day Bassett, **Jackson**, 748.

29　the Shorter Westminster Catechism Booraem, **Young Hickory**, 20–21.

29　only a handful of years of formal education Walker, "The Educational Training and Views of Andrew Jackson," 22.

29　When Harvard University bestowed an honorary degree Ibid., 28.

29　issued elegant Caesar-like proclamations to his troops See, for instance, **Papers**, II, 290–93.

29　read rather more than he is given credit for This is not to suggest Jackson was a secret scholar, but his library at the Hermitage is eclectic, and he was known, for instance, to give copies of Fénelon's **Telemachus** as gifts, which is discussed at length in chapter 32, and he enjoyed early biographies of the Founding Fathers (**Correspondence**, III, 244). "Bibliography of Andrew Jackson's Library" (unpublished), 2000. Jackson's library is part of the collections at the Hermitage.

29　"I know human nature" **Papers**, IV, 380.

30　**The Vicar of Wakefield** Parton, **Life**, III, 604; see also Robert V. Remini, **The Life of Andrew Jackson** (New York, 1988), 6.

30　"The hero of this piece" Oliver Goldsmith, **The Vicar of Wakefield** (New York, 1982), 31.

30　A favorite book was Jane Porter's **The Scottish Chiefs** Papers, V, 163; Jane Porter, **The Scottish Chiefs** (New York, 1921). Porter's tale is based on the life of the thirteenth-century Scottish independence hero.

30 murder his wife   Porter, **Scottish Chiefs**, 25.

30 "I have always thought"   **Papers**, V, 163.

30 published in 1809   Porter, **Scottish Chiefs**, viii.

30 "God is with me"   Ibid. 35. Quoting a letter of Jackson's to Andrew Donelson about Wallace, Remini writes that "the virtues Jackson ascribed to Wallace were precisely his own"— the "undaunted courage" and willingness to "brave any dangers, for the relief of his country or his friend" (Remini, **Life of Andrew Jackson**, 6). I believe that a close reading of **The Scottish Chiefs** itself suggests that Jackson's connection to the novel went beyond seeing a heroic model in Wallace, though Jackson surely did. I think the parallels between the book and Jackson's own reaction to his losses in life drew Jackson to the story in a way that engaged Jackson's understandable anger and thirst for validation and vengeance, not just his equally understandable search for heroic literary role models.

Chapter 2: Follow Me and I'll Save You Yet

32 his license to practice law   **Papers**, I, 10.

32 "He was the most roaring"   Bassett, **Jackson**, 12.

32 When James Parton was researching his 1860 biography   Parton, **Life**, I, 108–9.

32 "What! Jackson up for President?"   Ibid., 109.

33 moved to Nashville in October 1788   Ibid., 115–24.

33 took up residence as a boarder   Ibid., 133.

34 the patriarch, Colonel John Donelson   For my account of the Donelsons' background, I have drawn on Parton, **Life**, I, 126–33; Mary French Caldwell, **General Jackson's Lady** (Kingsport, Tenn., 1936), 14–23; Heiskell, **AJETH**, I, 157–67.

34 one of the prevailing stories   Heiskell, **AJETH**, I, 159–65.

34 his mysterious death   Parton, **Life**, I, 133. "He was in the woods surveying, far from home," wrote Parton. "Two young men who had been with him came along and found him near a creek, pierced by bullets; whether the bullets of the lurking savage or of the white robber was never known. It was only known that he met a violent death from some ambushed cowardly villains, white or red; his daughter Rachel always thought

the former. She thought no Indians **could** kill her father, who knew their ways too well to be caught by them" (ibid.).

34   a beautiful young woman   Caldwell, **General Jackson's Lady**, 101.

34   when Rachel met Jackson in the autumn of 1788   Parton, **Life**, I, 133; James, **TLOAJ**, 53; Remini, **Jackson**, I, 41–42.

34   Rachel Donelson and Lewis Robards   Caldwell, **General Jackson's Lady**, 102.

34   Robards was a decade older   Ibid., 101.

34   John Overton   Parton, **Life**, I, 148.

34   one of her brothers went to Kentucky   Ibid.

35   "gay and lively"   Parton, **Life**, I, 133; Remini, **Jackson**, I, 42.

35   her husband decided he wanted a reconciliation   Parton, **Life**, I, 148–49.

35   Robards soon grew jealous . . . exchanged words   Ibid., 150.

35   "If I had such a wife"   Mary Caroline Crawford, **Romantic Days in the Early Republic** (Boston, 1912), 215.

35   Jackson soon moved to another establishment   Parton, **Life**, I, 150.

35   "take his wife"   Ibid.

35   "**haunt** her"   Ibid., 151.

36   The weight of the evidence   I drew on four accounts of the marriage controversy to reach this conclusion: Remini, **Jackson**, I, 57–69; Burstein, **Passions of Andrew Jackson**, 241–48; John Buchanan, **Jackson's Way: Andrew Jackson and the People of the Western Waters** (New York, 2001), 109–11; Matthew Warshauer, "A Review Essay on Burstein, **The Passions of Andrew Jackson**," **Tennessee Historical Quarterly** 62 (Winter 2003), 366–73. Since virtually all of the surviving sources about Rachel's divorce were produced by Jackson partisans to answer later political charges about the complex circumstances of Rachel's marriages, it is not surprising that Robards bears the overwhelming brunt of the blame for what was an unhappy situation for everyone concerned. Though Overton goes out of his way to make clear that Robards's own family took Rachel's side, Rachel did manage, from the early days of her marriage, to conduct herself in a way that fueled Robards's jealousy. They were a mismatched pair, and both had happy second marriages. One of Rachel's most admiring biographers, Mary French Cald-

well, wrote: "Lewis Robards, after his marriage to Miss Winn, lived an apparently peaceful life. He prospered in material things, reared a family of splendid children, and held a respected place in the community. If his dark moods descended upon him, he was able either to control himself more thoroughly than he had done in earlier days, or to conceal his behavior more successfully" (Caldwell, **General Jackson's Lady**, 161). Or perhaps his new wife gave him less cause for such behavior.

37 the moral climate had moved in a stricter direction Burstein, **Passions of Andrew Jackson**, 248.

38 a trip to Philadelphia **Papers**, II, 13.

38 "I have this moment recd. your letter" Ibid.

39 "I thank you for your admonition" **Papers**, IV, 62.

39 Just after dusk on a cold March day Lee, **Biography of Andrew Jackson**, 9–10. For another version of the story, see also Remini, **Jackson**, I, 45–46.

39 "The light of their fires" Lee, **Biography of Andrew Jackson**, 9.

40 "saving spirit and elastic mind" Ibid. It is unclear whether these words are Overton's or Lee's.

40 "Overton and his companion instantly cried" Ibid., 10.

41 In Knoxville in the autumn of 1803 For the Sevier story, I have drawn on Parton, **Life**, I, 163–64; James, **TLOAJ**, 92–94; Remini, **Jackson**, I, 117–24.

41 alluded to his own past "services" to the state This detail and the ensuing dialogue are drawn from the recollections of Colonel Isaac T. Avery of North Carolina, a son of Waightstill Avery, a lawyer under whom Jackson attempted to study and to whom Jackson issued his first challenge for a duel. (Parton, **Life**, I, 160–62.) The younger Colonel Avery wrote Parton a letter about the young Jackson that Parton quotes extensively, and that is the main source of details about the Sevier showdown for subsequent biographers.

41 "Services?" Parton, **Life**, I, 164.

41 "Great God!" Ibid.

41 "several shots were fired" Ibid.

42 "Sevier . . . unpardonable," recalled the source Ibid.

42 an argument over a horse race The story of the Jackson-Dickinson duel is among the most often told incidents in Jack-

son's life. I have relied on several different accounts for my brief retelling: see, for instance, Parton, **Life**, I, 267–306; James, **TLOAJ**, 113–18; Remini, **Jackson**, I, 136–43; Remini, **Life of Andrew Jackson**, 52–54. For documents relating to the argument and the duel, see **Papers**, II, 77–78; 79–82; 84–91; 96–109. (The horserace never took place. See Parton, **Life**, I, 268.)

42 also apparently included a slur against Rachel   As the editors of Jackson's **Papers** point out, there is no contemporary evidence in the Jackson-Dickinson correspondence that Rachel's name entered into the matter (**Papers**, II, 78), but Sam Houston told James Parton that Dickinson "uttered offensive words respecting Mrs. Jackson in a tavern in Nashville, which were duly conveyed by some meddling parasite to General Jackson" (Parton, **Life**, I, 269).

42 "It will be in vain"   Lee, **Biography of Andrew Jackson**, 21.

42 At seven o'clock on the morning of Friday, May 30, 1806   **Papers**, II, 99.

42 at twenty-four feet   Ibid., 100.

42 Jackson let Dickinson shoot first   Parton, **Life**, I, 296–97.

42 The trigger caught halfway   **Papers**, II, 96; Parton, **Life**, I, 299.

42 as his boot filled with blood   Parton, **Life**, I, 300.

42 the wound complicated his health for decades   Goff, "A Physical Profile of Andrew Jackson," 306–8.

42 "If he had shot me through the brain"   Lee, **Biography of Andrew Jackson**, 21.

43 Jackson's "gallantry and enterprise"   Ibid., 8.

43 As a judge of the Tennessee Superior Court   Parton, **Life**, I, 227–39.

43 Jackson was riding circuit   Lee, **Biography of Andrew Jackson**, 15. My telling is largely drawn from Lee's, but I also drew on Parton, **Life**, I, 228–29, and Remini, **Jackson**, 115–16.

44 "Now, surrender, you infernal villain"   Parton, **Life**, I, 229.

44 "firm advance and formidable look"   Lee, **Biography of Andrew Jackson**, 16.

44 He dropped his guns   Ibid.

44 "I will surrender to you"   Ibid.

44 "When danger rears its head"   **Papers**, III, 105.

44 Aaron Burr's hosts   Burstein, **Passions of Andrew Jackson**, 71–

72. Burstein closely examines the Burr conspiracy and Jackson's role (ibid., 71–85).

45 preparing a force in the event of war Remini, **Jackson**, I, 147.

45 Jackson agreed Ibid., 147–48.

45 "when the government and constituted authorities" Ibid., 148.

45 possibility of seizing New Orleans Ibid., 150.

45 wrote several officials Ibid., 151.

45 "I fear there is something rotten" Burstein, **Passions of Andrew Jackson**, 74.

45 Burr was acquitted in 1807 Remini, **Jackson**, I, 158.

46 "He loves his country" Bassett, **Jackson**, 78.

46 promised to "act the part of a father" **Papers**, II, 392.

47 In the cold winter Remini, **Jackson**, I, 171.

47 2,071 in all Ibid., 173.

47 five hundred miles later, at Natchez Ibid., 174–75.

47 150 of Jackson's men were sick, 56 could not sit up Ibid., 179.

47 "They abandon us in a strange country" **Correspondence**, I, 295. The letter was to William Blount, dated March 15, 1813.

47 "They had sacrificed domestic comforts" Lee, **Biography of Andrew Jackson**, 28. For the exchange between Hogg and Jackson, I have relied on Lee's account.

48 his men watched this tall, determined figure For accounts of the Natchez-to-Nashville journey and its significance for Jackson and his reputation, see Parton, **Life**, I, 373–86; James, **TLOAJ**, 148–50; Remini, **Jackson**, I, 178–80. Remini quotes the **Nashville Whig**'s declaration, "Long will their General live in the memory of his volunteers of West Tennessee for his benevolence, humane, and fatherly treatment to his soldiers; if gratitude and love can reward him, General Jackson has them." On the theme of fatherhood, Remini adds: "At the age of forty-six Jackson had become a father figure, protector of his men as well as guardian of the people of the frontier. Henceforth Jackson nurtured that image, speaking and acting in accordance with its recognized and required characteristics" (Remini, **Jackson**, I, 180).

48 "I led them into the field" **Papers**, II, 393.

48 "And as long as I have friends or credit" Ibid., 386.

48 they were calling him "Old Hickory" Parton, **Life**, I, 382.

48 a friend of Jackson's in Nashville quarreled with Jesse Benton
   Ibid., 386–90.

49 that he would whip Thomas Benton Ibid., 390.

49 crossed on Saturday, September 4, 1813 Ibid. 391–95, covers
   the action well, and I am indebted to his telling for the details
   that follow. For Thomas Benton's account of the skirmish, see
   Thomas Hart Benton to the Public, **Papers**, II, 425–27.

49 his riding whip in his hand Parton, **Life**, I, 391.

49 brandishing his whip Ibid., 393.

49 "Now, you damned rascal" Ibid.

49 bled through two mattresses Ibid., 394.

49 "I'll keep my arm" Ibid.

49 while Rachel was still nursing Remini, **Andrew Jackson**, I,
   187–223. I am indebted to Remini's telling for my account.

50 influenced by Tecumseh Ibid., 188.

50 as a historian of Alabama Ibid., 190. The historian to whom
   Remini refers is Albert J. Pickett.

50 settlers who had themselves attacked Ibid., 189.

50 Red Sticks Ibid., 188.

51 They sent for Jackson Ibid., 190.

51 "We shot them like dogs" Ibid., 193.

51 "We found as many" Ibid.

51 "We have retaliated" Ibid.

51 three fifths of modern-day Alabama Sean Wilentz, **Andrew
   Jackson** (New York, 2005), 26.

52 Madrid (and London) were "arming" Ibid., 27–28.

52 threatened Pensacola Remini, **Jackson**, I, 237. The Pensacola
   episode is covered on pages 239–45.

52 toward New Orleans Parton, **Life**, II, 11–343, covers the
   whole of Jackson's New Orleans experience and its aftermath.

52 imposed martial law For Jackson's defense of the action, see
   Papers, III, 312–14. Warshauer, **Andrew Jackson and the Politics of Martial Law**, is an incisive, thorough critique of Jackson's actions and the subsequent controversy.

52 defying a writ of habeas corpus Warshauer, **Andrew Jackson
   and the Politics of Martial Law**, 2.

52 Lincoln would cite Abraham Lincoln, **Abraham Lincoln:
   Speeches and Writings, 1859–1865** (New York: Library of
   America, 1989), 454–63. In addition to invoking Jackson di-

rectly, Lincoln's justification echoed Jackson's. Lincoln: "I concede that the class of arrest complained of can be constitutional only when, in cases of rebellion or invasion, the public safety may require them; and I insist that in such cases they are constitutional **wherever** the public safety does require them" (ibid., 459). Jackson: "Whenever the invaluable rights which we enjoy under our own happy constitution are threatened by invasion, privileges the most dear, and which, in ordinary times, ought to be regarded as the most sacred, may be required to be infringed for their security. At such a crisis, we have only to determine whether we will suspend, for a time, the exercise of the latter, that we may secure the permanent enjoyment of the former. Is it wise, in such a moment, to sacrifice the spirit of the laws to the letter, and by adhering too strictly to the letter, lose the **substance** forever, in order that we may, for an instant, preserve the **shadow?**" (**Papers**, III, 313).

52 he was fined   Warshauer, **Andrew Jackson and the Politics of Martial Law**, 2–3.

52 he was at a party   "Memoirs of Mrs. Eliza Williams Chotard Gould," Maria B. Campbell Private Collection.

52 "The dancing was over"   Ibid.

53 from a balcony overlooking Bourbon Street   Ibid.

53 Jackson "expressed his regret"   Ibid.

53 climactic battle on Sunday, January 8, 1815   Parton, **Life**, II, 186–222. See also **Papers**, III, 233–34.

53 after the war had ended   H. W. Brands, **Andrew Jackson: His Life and Times** (New York, 2005), 275.

53 The British lost nearly three hundred men   Ward, **Andrew Jackson**, 220. Ward's statistics come from the official American and British reports printed in Arsène Lacarrière Latour's **Historical Memoir of the War in West Florida and Louisiana in 1814–1815, with an Atlas.** Parton puts the number of British dead at 700, with 1400 wounded and 500 taken prisoner, and American dead at 8, with 13 wounded (Parton, **Life**, II, 209).

53 "It appears that the unerring hand of providence"   **Papers**, III, 258.

53 as the cannon smoke lifted   Wilentz, **Andrew Jackson**, 32.

54 "the slaughter was shocking"   Ibid.

54 hidden beneath their fallen comrades' red coats   Ibid.

54 "I never had" Ibid.

54 "It is Him we intend to praise" Reid and Eaton, **Life of Andrew Jackson**, 406–7.

54 "The attention and honors paid to the General" Parton, **Life**, II, 595. Her amazement at the glory that came to her husband was evident as early as a March 5, 1815, letter in which she described the "splendor," the "brilliant assemblage," the "magnificence of the supper," and the "ornaments of the room" of a Washington's birthday banquet at which an image of Jackson was given equal play (**Papers**, III, 297–98).

54 "The Lord has promised" Parton, **Life**, II, 595.

55 "I wish your carriage well repaired" **Papers**, III, 114.

55 arranged Rachel's wardrobe "Memoirs of Mrs. Eliza Williams Chotard Gould," Maria B. Campbell Private Collection.

55 "Bring with you my sash" **Papers**, III, 190.

55 "I knew from the first how wrong it was" **Papers**, VI, 20–21. The letter is written from Washington on January 27, 1825.

55 "His health is not good" Ibid., 21.

56 Watching her husband playing EDT, I, 30–31.

56 "He would have given his life for a child" Ibid., 30.

57 the Jacksons had taken charge Mark R. Cheathem, **Old Hickory's Nephew: The Political and Private Struggles of Andrew Jackson Donelson** (Baton Rouge, La., 2007), 10. EDT, I, 29–81, is good on Andrew and Emily's background, as is "Biographical Sketch of Andrew Jackson Donelson" by Pauline Wilcox Burke, Andrew Jackson Donelson Papers, LOC. For Andrew in particular, see also Cheathem, **Old Hickory's Nephew**; Robert Beeler Satterfield, **Andrew Jackson Donelson: Jackson's Confidant and Political Heir** (Bowling Green, Ky., 2000), 234; Charles Faulkner Bryan, Jr., "The Prodigal Nephew: Andrew Jackson Donelson and the Eaton Affair," **The East Tennessee Historical Society's Publications** 50 (1978), 92–112.

57 when a well-off planter Cheathem, **Old Hickory's Nephew**, 10.

57 Rachel's brother Severn Donelson's wife had twin boys **Papers**, II, 218.

57 "The sensibility of our beloved son" **Papers**, II, 353–54.

57 found a small boy, Lyncoya, on the battlefield **Papers**, II, 444; see also **Papers**, II, 494–95.

57 "for" Andrew junior as a playmate **Papers**, II, 444.

57 "Keep Lyncoya in the house" Ibid., 516.

57 dying of illness in 1828 Remini, **Jackson**, I, 144; see also **Papers**, II, 414.

58 General Daniel Smith Walter T. Durham, **Daniel Smith: Frontier Statesman** (Gallatin, Tenn., 1976), is an excellent account of Smith's life.

58 Jackson had helped her elope EDT, I, 25.

58 built a house named Rock Castle "Biographical Sketch of Andrew Jackson Donelson" by Pauline Wilcox Burke, Andrew Jackson Donelson Papers, LOC. Burke wrote in **Emily Donelson of Tennessee**: "It was the first stone house in this section and for a number of years the most pretentious" (**EDT**, I, 19).

58 continued his battles against the Indian tribes Remini, **Jackson**, I, 341–50.

58 between 1816 and 1820 Wilentz, **Andrew Jackson**, 36.

58 escaping to a fort occupied by blacks Remini, **Jackson**, I, 344; see also Wilentz, **Andrew Jackson**, 36–37.

59 another American general, Edmund Pendleton Gaines Remini, **Jackson**, I, 345.

59 The Seminoles declined to leave Ibid., 345–46.

59 dated Sunday, December 28, 1817 Ibid., 348–49.

60 the executions of two British subjects Ibid., 358–59.

60 claimed he had authorization Ibid., 348.

60 In Monroe's Cabinet Ibid., 366–67.

60 In the House of Representatives Ibid., 372–73.

60 a congressional probe failed Ibid., 374.

60 The diary of a young woman from South Carolina Julia Ann M. Conner Travel Journal, September 3, 1827, Conner Family Papers, South Carolina Historical Society, Charleston. In another unpublished recollection, William R. Galt of Virginia, who was ten years old at the time, recorded his memories of a stay at the Hermitage in 1828 with his father. Galt remembered being at the house when news came that a critical state had voted for Jackson (election returns came in piecemeal then), prompting the large company to cheer. "General, we must drink your health on this glorious news!" it was said, and they adjourned to a mahogany sideboard for a toast. Mrs. Jackson struck the young Galt most forcibly. Dressed plainly and, to the

boy, "rather an elderly lady, but still retaining traces of her former beauty," she appeared genuine and unaffected. "Children know good people by instinct, and I was devoted to Mrs. Jackson," Galt recalled ("Recollections of the Hermitage in 1828," William R. Galt, Virginia Historical Society, Richmond).

61 **"venerable, dignified, fine-looking man"** Julia Ann M. Conner Travel Journal, September 3, 1827, Conner Family Papers, South Carolina Historical Society, Charleston.

61 Rachel led her guests into the drawing room   Ibid.

61 "pronounced with much solemnity"   Ibid.

61 The brace of pistols Lafayette had given to Washington   Ibid.

61 "The manners of the General"   Ibid.

62 Jackson "stood at my side"   Ibid.

63 "The General is at peace"   **Papers**, III, 327.

63 "His temper was placable as well as irascible"   Benton, **Thirty Years' View**, 737.

64 "The character of his mind"   Ibid.

64 **"No man"**   Parton, **Life**, I, 113.

64 "He was a firm believer"   Benton, **Thirty Years' View**, 737.

64 called a cool calculator   Wise, **Seven Decades**, 117. "No man was cooler in his calculations than he was," Wise said of Jackson. "He would sometimes seem to fight most rashly, but no one ever knew him to fight at all unless there was a stake up worth fighting for."

65 "My Philosophy is almost worn out"   **Papers**, VI, 494.

65 Control over how one appeared   For an excellent discussion of these issues, see C. Dallett Hemphill, **Bowing to Necessities: A History of Manners in America, 1620–1860** (New York, 1999), especially 65–103.

66 "What makes the gentleman?"   Parton, **Life**, I, 66.

66 as a schoolboy, George Washington   David McCullough, **1776** (New York, 2005), 44–45.

66 one hundred and ten   Charles Moore, ed., **George Washington's Rules of Civility and Decent Behavior in Company and Conversation** (Boston and New York, 1926), ix-xv, is a thorough history of the maxims that came down to Washington.

66 General Daniel Smith . . . advised young men in his family   Durham, **Daniel Smith: Frontier Statesman**, 262. See

David Roberts, ed., **Lord Chesterfield's Letters** (New York, 1992), for Chesterfield himself.

66 Jackson, who believed in self-mastery   For a general exploration of the idea, see Hemphill, **Bowing to Necessities**, 81.

66 "You cannot have forgotten"   **Papers**, VI, 190–91. The letter was to Richard Keith Call.

Chapter 3: A Marriage, a Defeat, and a Victory

68 "Emily, it is hoped"   EDT, I, 114. The observation by Catherine Martin, Emily's sister, was written on the back of an August 1824 letter of Emily's.

68 Educated at West Point   Cheathem, **Old Hickory's Nephew**, 13–24.

68 Andrew Donelson delivered a July Fourth oration   Ibid., 112–13; Satterfield, **Andrew Jackson Donelson**, 13.

68 According to family tradition   EDT, I, 108–9.

68 her log schoolhouse on Lebanon Road   Ibid., 70–71.

68 known as "the Mansion" in the family   Ibid., 34.

69 Donelson happened across   Ibid., 71.

69 "On the way"   Ibid.

69 "Present me affectionately to Miss E."   **Papers**, V, 340. Jackson also referred to Emily as "your little girl" in correspondence (**EDT**, I, 101).

69 "I sincerely thank you"   **Papers**, V, 388.

69 "I hold no correspondence"   Ibid., 389.

69 To be with Jackson probably meant a move to Washington   EDT, I, 109. Burke's rendering of the Donelson courtship is the only surviving account of the sequence of events that led to their marriage that I have been able to locate.

70 "Romance was not a stranger"   Ibid., 110.

70 Jackson gave them a large tract   **Papers**, V, 311.

70 the Reverend William Hume   Ibid., 117.

70 outside Harrodsburg, Kentucky   Emily Donelson to her sister, December 23, 1824, Andrew Jackson Donelson Papers, LOC.

70 "The tongue snapped"   Ibid.

70 "a splendid ball"   Ibid.

70 on to Washington   **Papers**, V, 453. In a letter to Major Lewis

dated December 8, 1824, Jackson wrote: "I reached this city yesterday morning at 11 o'clock, all in good health, after a continued travel of 28 days without resting one day."

70 Emily watched Lafayette and Jackson   Emily Donelson to her sister, December 23, 1824, Andrew Jackson Donelson Papers, LOC.

71 "crowded with company"   Ibid.

71 "boarding at an excellent house"   Ibid.

71 "We are very comfortably"   Emily Donelson to Mary Donelson, December 13, 1824, Mrs. John Lawrence Merritt Collection.

71 at the more fashionable Episcopal church   **Papers**, V, 456.

71 "Much visiting in the grandest Circles"   EDT, I, 134–35.

71 plays such as **Virginius** . . . and **The Village Lawyer**   **Papers**, VI, 19.

71 "The extravagance is in dressing"   EDT, I, 128–29.

71 There was John C. Calhoun   I drew on **PJCC**; Merrill D. Peterson, **The Great Triumvirate: Webster, Clay, and Calhoun** (New York, 1987); Charles M. Wiltse, **John C. Calhoun: Nationalist, 1782–1828** (I), and **Nullifier, 1829–1839** (II) (New York, 1944, 1949); Margaret L. Coit, **John C. Calhoun: American Portrait** (Boston, 1950); Gerald M. Capers, **John C. Calhoun, Opportunist: A Reappraisal** (Gainesville, Fla., 1960).

72 Henry Clay of Kentucky   I drew on **PHC**; Peterson, **Great Triumvirate**; and Robert V. Remini, **Henry Clay: Statesman for the Union** (New York, 1991).

72 There was John Quincy Adams   I drew on Paul C. Nagel, **John Quincy Adams: A Public Life, a Private Life** (New York, 1997); Leonard L. Richards, **The Life and Times of Congressman John Quincy Adams** (New York, 1986); Samuel Flagg Bemis, **John Quincy Adams and the Union** (New York, 1956); David McCullough, **John Adams** (New York, 2001); and Jack Shepherd, **The Adams Chronicles: Four Generations of Greatness** (Boston, 1975).

72 By 1828, nearly all states   Sean Wilentz, "Property and Power: Suffrage Reform in the United States, 1787–1860," in **Voting and the Spirit of Democracy: Essays on the History of Voting and Voting Rights in America**, ed. Donald W. Rogers (Urbana and Chicago, 1992), 32–33. See also Florence Weston, **The Presidential Election of 1828** (Philadelphia, 1974), 1–3.

72　a surge in eligible voters　Weston, **The Presidential Election of 1828**, 3.

72　Turnout rose from 27 percent　Susan B. Carter, ed., **Historical Statistics of the United States, Earliest Times to the Present** (New York, 2006), V, 165.

72　The men who gathered in Philadelphia　I owe much of my discussion of the Jacksonian journey from republicanism to democratic thought to Robert V. Remini, **The Legacy of Andrew Jackson: Essays on Democracy, Indian Removal, and Slavery** (Baton Rouge, La., 1988), 7–21. I also learned much from Latner, **Presidency of Andrew Jackson**; Feller, **Jacksonian Promise**, 160–84; and Wilentz, **Rise of American Democracy**.

73　best articulated by James Madison and Alexander Hamilton　See, for instance, James Madison, **Writings** (New York, 1999), 160–365; Ralph Ketcham, **James Madison: A Biography** (Charlottesville, Va., 1990); and Garry Wills, **James Madison** (New York, 2002).

73　congressional caucuses on Capitol Hill　James Sterling Young, **The Washington Community, 1800–1828** (New York, 1966), 113–17; see also Wilentz, **Rise of American Democracy**, 246–47.

73　could not see how "killing"　Weston, **Presidential Election of 1828**, 18.

74　"certainly the basest, meanest"　**Papers**, VI, 243.

74　Clay, not surprisingly, decided to support Adams　Remini, **Henry Clay**, 251–72, covers the episode well. See also Nagel, **John Quincy Adams**, 291–98, and Wilentz, **Rise of American Democracy**, 254–57.

74　"It shows the want of principle"　**Papers**, VI, 20.

74　Five days later　Remini, **Jackson**, II, 98.

74　"the **Judas** of the West"　**Papers**, VI, 29–30. The letter to Lewis is dated February 14, 1825.

74　"If at this early period"　Ibid., 37. The letter to Lewis is dated February 20, 1825. The scene of Jackson greeting Adams (see below) predates the revelation of the precise terms of what Jackson and his supporters would call the "corrupt bargain" with Clay—that is, the evening party at the White House occurred on February 9, the day of the presidential balloting in Congress. But we know from Jackson's letters that he understood forces in Washington were working against his election. "It was stated to me yesterday," he told Lewis on January 11, "that if I was elected, it would be against the whole Cabinet influence, combined with that of the speaker" (**Papers**, VI, 15). So while Jackson's grace on the night of the ninth came without his knowing the specific detail of Clay's appointment, Jackson did well understand that he, the people's choice, had been done in by some backstage maneuvering.

74 "terrible place" Ibid., 21.

75 had struck a deal It is much more likely that Adams and Clay were politically stupid rather than politically corrupt. Here is Remini on the question: "Was there a corrupt bargain between Clay and Adams? Probably not, although absolute proof does not exist and most likely never will" (Remini, **Henry Clay**, 270). Clay had said he would support Adams in mid-December, and though the two met on January 9, 1825, it is unlikely that a quid pro quo was discussed. "During the weeks leading up to the House vote, Adams and his lieutenants had given what they discreetly called 'assurances' to various potential supporters in Congress," wrote Wilentz. "Among the least questionable of these understandings was reached with Clay. Both Adams and Clay were too sophisticated to strike any explicit bargain, either during their private meeting on January 9 or at any other time. None was needed. Clay brought with him congressional influence, charm and geographical balance, all things that the New Englander required" (Wilentz, **Rise of American Democracy**, 255).

75 Jackson appeared at a party Parton, **Life**, III, 68–69.

75 "by himself" Ibid., 69. Parton's source for the White House scene and commentary is S. G. Goodrich.

76 "How do you do, Mr. Adams?" Ibid.

76 "Very well, sir" Ibid.

76 "It was curious to see" Ibid.

76 "You have, by your dignity" **Papers**, VI, 56.

76 the boarding bill Ibid., 35.

76 "Genl. Jackson's friends" Charles M. Wiltse, ed., **The Papers of Daniel Webster. Series One: Correspondence, 1824** (Hanover, N.H., 1974), I, 235.

77 "I have great confidence" **Correspondence**, III, 412.

77 the railroad was hardly more Howe, **What Hath God Wrought**, 562–63.

77 workforce more than tripled **Historical Statistics of the United States, Earliest Times to the Present**, II, 110.

77 iron wage earners Ibid.

77 Immigration . . . rose steadily **Historical Statistics of the United States, Earliest Times to the Present**, I, 541.

77 steamship travel began Ibid., 526.

78 published his **Appeal to the Coloured Citizens of the World** James Turner, ed., **David Walker's Appeal** (Baltimore, 1993). The full title of the essay is **Appeal, In Four Articles: Together with a Preamble to the Coloured Citizens of the World, but in Particular, and Very Expressly, to Those of the United States of America.**

78 were "the most degraded" Ibid., 21.

78 If an "**attempt**" Ibid., 45–46.

78 "Now, I ask you" Ibid., 46.

78 there were slave disturbances **Historical Statistics of the United States, Earliest Times to the Present**, II, 385.

78 laws prohibiting teaching slaves to read Ibid., 390.

78 **Moral Physiology** Feller, **Jacksonian Promise**, 154. See also Richard William Leopold, **Robert Dale Owen: A Biography** (Cambridge, Mass., 1940).

78 Oberlin College . . . was founded **Historical Statistics of the United States, Earliest Times to the Present**, I, 5.

79 the **American Journal of Science and Arts** explored George H. Daniels, **American Science in the Age of Jackson** (Tuscaloosa, Ala., 1968), 38–39.

79 "scientists" were distinct Ibid., 38.

79 liberal arts colleges were founded **Historical Statistics of the United States, Earliest Times to the Present**, II, 875.

79 Evangelical fervor was a constant force Feller, **Jacksonian Promise**, 95–117, is a terrific discussion of the issue. See also Jon Butler, **Awash in a Sea of Faith: Christianizing the American People** (Cambridge, Mass., 1990); Nathan O. Hatch, **The Democratization of American Christianity** (New Haven, 1989); Mark A. Noll, ed., **Religion and American Politics, from the Colonial Period to the 1980s** (New York, 1990); Martin E. Marty, **Pilgrims in Their Own Land: 500 Years of Reli-**

gion in America (New York, 1984); Conrad Cherry, ed., **God's New Israel: Religious Interpretations of American Destiny** (Chapel Hill, N.C., 1998), 113–45; Mark A. Noll, **A History of Christianity in the United States and Canada** (Grand Rapids, Mich., 1992), 219–44; William Martin, **With God on Our Side: The Rise of the Religious Right in America** (New York, 1996), 3–6; Jon Butler, Grant Wacker, and Randall Balmer, **Religion in American Life: A Short History** (New York, 247), 182–257.

79 Joseph Smith believed he was told   Richard Lyman Bushman, **Joseph Smith: Rough Stone Rolling** (New York, 2005), 31–57.

79 "There is no country in the world"   Feller, **Jacksonian Promise,** 95.

79 For eight days in Cincinnati   Ibid., 104–6. See also J. J. Haley, **Debates That Made History: The Story of Alexander Campbell's Debates with Rev. John Walker, Rev. W. L. McCalla, Mr. Robert Owen, Bishop Purcell and Rev. Nathan L. Rice** (St. Louis, 1920), 57–115.

79 Frances Trollope, a writer and mother   Trollope, **Domestic Manners of the Americans,** 112–16.

79 "All this I think"   Ibid., 90.

79 In domestic politics   For the ensuing summary of the political surround and its personalities, I drew on: Howe, **What Hath God Wrought;** Peterson, **Great Triumvirate;** Weston, **Presidential Election of 1828;** Wilentz, **Rise of American Democracy;** Remini, **Election of Andrew Jackson; Papers,** V and VI.

79 the familiar divisions since the Founding   Woodrow Wilson, **Division and Reunion: 1829–1889** (New York, 1961), 25–35, is a crisp summary written by the future president in 1898. For details on the Jefferson-Hamilton and Republican-Federalist divide, see Dumas Malone, **Jefferson and the Rights of Man** (Boston, 1951), 420–77; Malone, **Jefferson and the Ordeal of Liberty** (Boston, 1962), 380–506. Ron Chernow, **Alexander Hamilton** (New York, 2004), is also excellent on the politics of the early Republic, as is McCullough, **John Adams,** and John Ferling, **Adams vs. Jefferson: The Tumultuous Election of 1800** (New York, 2004).

80 a hodgepodge of competing political and regional interests   Wilson, **Division and Reunion,** 30–31.

80 Monroe ran unopposed   Harry Ammon, **James Monroe: The Quest for National Identity** (Charlottesville, Va., 1990), 366–95, covers the ideal and the reality of "the Era of Good Feelings." Only one presidential elector had chosen to oppose Monroe's reelection. As Ammon wrote of American politics in 1820–21: "Every sign indicated that party warfare on the national scene had ceased—by 1819 every New England state except Massachusetts was controlled by the Republicans, and in Congress there was only a handful of Federalists, who ordinarily supported the administration with more fidelity than many Republicans. The presidential election of 1820 with its lone dissident elector seemed to be the final proof, as Monroe commented in his second inaugural address, that powerful forces had drawn the people together in a lasting unity of sentiment" (ibid., 378).

80 the rise of democracy   Wilentz, **Rise of American Democracy**, is an engaging and exhaustive examination of the course of American politics from Jefferson to Lincoln.

81 an energetic president   **TGPP**, I, 369–78; 438–50.

81 when "measures otherwise unconstitutional"   Ibid., xx.

81 Jackson won 56 percent of the popular vote   Remini, **Election of Andrew Jackson**, 187–88.

82 "The Hickory is a tall"   **FPB**, 27.

82 "mortifying and sickening"   **PHC**, VII, 515–16.

82 "no greater calamity"   Ibid., 536.

82 "since we were a free people"   Ibid.

82 There were reports that Jackson was sick   Wiltse, ed., **The Papers of Daniel Webster**, II, 394. This was something of a running theme in Webster's mind. On February 5, 1829, he wrote his brother: "Genl Jackson will be here, in a day or two. I am of the opinion his health is very feeble, and that there is not much chance of his lasting long" (ibid., 395–96).

82 "On Wednesday morning"   Louisa Catherine Adams to Charles Francis Adams, February 1, 1829, Adams Papers, Massachusetts Historical Society.

82 "The rumour of Genl. J's death"   Wiltse, ed., **The Papers of Daniel Webster**, II, 394.

83 Jackson, however, arrived safely in Washington on Wednesday, February 11   Edwin A. Miles, "The First People's Inaugural—1829," **Tennessee Historical Quarterly** 37 (Fall 1978), 296.

83 He was not entirely well   Emily Donelson to Mary Donelson Coffee, March 27, 1829, Andrew Jackson Donelson Papers, LOC.

83 "a very bad cough"   Ibid.

83 Cannon fire and a marching band   Miles, "The First People's Inaugural—1829," 296.

83 Alfred Mordecai, a West Point contemporary   Sarah Agnes Wallace, ed., "Opening Days of Jackson's Presidency as Seen in Private Letters," **Tennessee Historical Quarterly** 9 (December 1950), 367. Mordecai was class of 1823.

83 through his window   Ibid., 368.

83 "a plain carriage drawn"   Ibid.

83 "demigod and Hero"   Ibid.

83 "What a spectacle must this present"   Ibid.

83 Once in the capital   **Memoirs of JQA**, VIII, 101–3, is an interesting account of Jackson's first days in Washington from the lonely perspective of the defeated President Adams.

83 center of a swirl of office seekers . . . at John Gadsby's National Hotel   Parton, **Life**, III, 167.

83 "motley host of greedy expectants"   **PHC**, VII, 626.

83 "My health was so bad"   Emily Donelson to Mary Donelson Coffee, March 27, 1829, Andrew Jackson Donelson Papers, LOC.

84 "Owing to the death"   Ibid.

84 Andrew Donelson and William Lewis were busy   Satterfield, **Andrew Jackson Donelson**, 20.

84 Donelson noted how Jackson   W. M. Polk, **Leonidas Polk, Bishop and General** (New York, 1893), I, 69.

84 Jackson's Cabinet choices   Cole, **The Presidency of Andrew Jackson**, 27–29.

84 struck many as underwhelming   Wiltse, **John C. Calhoun**, II, 19–25.

84 Kendall personified much   For my portrait of Kendall, I am indebted to **AAK** and to Cole, **A Jackson Man.**

85 At a wedding party   **AAK**, 279.

85 They formed, Webster said, "a numerous"   Wiltse, ed., **Papers of Daniel Webster**, II, 399.

85 "always goes through everything 'like a hero'"   Emily Donelson to Mary Donelson Coffee, March 27, 1829, Andrew Jackson Donelson Papers, LOC.

85 In interviews between the president-elect and visitors seeking a job   **Daily National Intelligencer**, April 18, 1829. The writer, who signed his account "Aristides," was describing a "visit to the Hermitage" after the election, but Jackson carried his air of formality to Washington with him as well.

85 "Citizens who visit the President"   Ibid.

86 went shopping with Mary Eastin   EDT, I, 165–66.

86 splurged on expensive cologne, soap, jewelry   Ibid.

86 East Front of the Capitol   Parton, **Life**, III, 169.

86 unseasonably frigid   Wiltse, ed., **Papers of Daniel Webster**, II, 404.

86 "There has not been"   Ibid.

86 the chilly spell broke   Ibid., 406. "On the Portico, in the open air, (the day is very warm and pleasant) [Jackson] read his Inaugural, and took the oath," Webster wrote to his sister on March 4.

86 Recording some "small gossiping anecdotes"   Diary of John Quincy Adams, February 19, 1829, Adams Papers, Massachusetts Historical Society.

86 "When he comes"   Wiltse, ed., **Papers of Daniel Webster**, II, 388.

Chapter 4: You Know Best, My Dear

87 "He seems to have been"   Leonidas Polk to William Polk, November 5, 1828, Leonidas Polk Collection: The University of the South, University Archives and Special Collections, Sewanee. A future bishop of Louisiana and Confederate general, Polk was a good observer of the Washington scene, noting that his perch at the Virginia Theological Seminary in Alexandria "enables me to hear most of the things of interest that pass" (Leonidas Polk to William Polk, June 18, 1829, Leonidas Polk Collection, The University of the South, University Archives and Special Collections, Sewanee).

87 "scarcely able to sit up"   Gaillard Hunt, ed., **The First Forty Years of Washington in the Family Letters of Margaret Bayard Smith** (New York, 1965), 257.

87 belongings were being boxed   Ibid., 297.

87 a crisis of corruption   Jackson's correspondence is replete with

examples of his conviction that elites were hijacking the government from the people. "The eighteen-twenties were a decade of discontent, born in depression, streaked with suffering and panic, shaken by bursts of violence and threats of rebellion" (Schlesinger, **Age of Jackson**, 30). For Jackson's political philosophy, see Feller, **Jacksonian Promise**, 160–84; Richard Hofstadter, **The American Political Tradition and the Men Who Made It** (New York, 1948), 59–86; and Wilentz, **Rise of American Democracy**, 240–329.

88 Presided over by Nicholas Biddle   Wilentz, **Rise of American Democracy**, 364–67. Robert V. Remini, **Andrew Jackson and the Bank War** (New York, 1967), 15–48, is a good overview; see also Thomas Payne Govan, **Nicholas Biddle: Nationalist and Public Banker, 1786–1844** (Chicago, 1959), which is essentially a brief for Biddle.

89 the state's cotton and rice planters   Freehling, **Prelude to Civil War**, 7–176, brilliantly covers the background and emergence of the crisis.

89 An early test of federal authority   Freehling, **Road to Disunion**, 254–60.

89 "duty to guard against insubordination"   Ibid., 254.

90 the time may be at hand   Ibid., 257.

90 raised duties from 33 percent   Freehling, **Prelude to Civil War**, 138–39.

90 "with the most melancholy feelings"   PJCC, XI, 24.

91 "revolutionary" talk   Ibid., 47.

91 Pickens denied that he was thinking   Ibid., 46–47.

91 "the greatest question"   Lucy Maddox, **Removals: Nineteenth-Century American Literature and the Politics of Indian Affairs** (New York, 1991), 15.

91 an 1833 book entitled **Indian Wars of the West**   Ibid., 19–20.

92 advocates of removal "see the race"   Ibid., 20.

92 "Without religion"   Henry Whiting Warner and Theodore Frelinghuysen, **An Inquiry into the Moral and Religious Character of the American Government** (New York, 1838), 133.

93 called for the formation of "a Christian Party"   Joseph L. Blau, "'The Christian Party in Politics,'" **The Review of Religion** 11 (November 1946), 18–35.

93 sought to impose a narrower religious agenda   Charles I. Foster, **An Errand of Mercy: The Evangelical United Front, 1790–1837** (Chapel Hill, N.C., 1960), 54–60, 179–207, and 230–33, is good on these issues of Christian engagement in political life. See also Bertram Wyatt-Brown, "Prelude to Abolitionism: Sabbatarian Politics and the Rise of the Second Party System," **Journal of American History** 58 (June 1971), 316–41.

93 Ely wrote Jackson to pass along   **Papers**, VII, 20–22.

93 that "no Christian ruler"   Ibid., 21–22.

93 did not travel on Sundays   Ibid., 22.

93 more anticlerical than antireligious   I am indebted to Daniel Feller for this insight. See Feller, "Rediscovering Jacksonian America," in **The State of U.S. History**, edited by Melvyn Stokes (New York, 2002), 81.

94 "the American System"   Wilentz, **Rise of American Democracy**, 242.

94 the sales of public lands   Daniel Feller, **The Public Lands in Jacksonian Politics** (Madison, Wis., 1984), is an excellent examination of these issues.

94 debt was dangerous   Remini, **Andrew Jackson and the Bank War**, 20.

94 well-armed pirates stormed the **Attentive**   Washington National Journal, March 17, 1829. See also ibid., March 27, 28, and 31, 1829.

94 Told of the **Attentive** incident   **Papers**, VII, 97. The date was March 16, 1829.

95 "These atrocities"   Ibid.

95 the USS **Natchez**, an eighteen-gun sloop of war   Ibid.

95 "The dictates of humanity"   Ibid., 99.

95 sunlight poured down on the city   Wiltse, ed., **Papers of Daniel Webster**, II, 406. For detailed accounts of the inauguration, see Parton, **Life**, III, 169–70; James, **TLOAJ**, 493–95; Remini, **Jackson**, II, 173–77.

95 It was, Emily reported home, "by far"   Emily Donelson to Mary Donelson, March 27, 1829, Andrew Jackson Donelson Papers, LOC.

96 Jackson left Gadsby's Hotel   Remini, **Jackson**, II, 173–74.

96 "the Servant"   Hunt, ed., **First Forty Years of Washington Society**, 293.

96 "There, there, that is he"   Ibid. Remini, **Jackson**, II, 175, also quotes this account of Mrs. Smith's.

96 "not a ragged mob"   Hunt, ed., **First Forty Years of Washington Society**, 293.

96 "It is beautiful!"   Ibid., 294.

96 went inside to the Senate chamber   Remini, **Jackson**, II, 174.

96 where the president pro tempore   Wiltse, **John C. Calhoun**, II, 12.

97 at his Fort Hill estate   Freehling, **Prelude to Civil War**, 158–59.

97 the **South Carolina Exposition and Protest**   Calhoun, **Union and Liberty**, 313–65. Though commonly referred to as the **Exposition and Protest**, the tract is actually two documents: the **Exposition** enumerates the state's grievances against the tariff system, while the **Protest** lists the General Assembly of South Carolina's formal resolutions. Calhoun titled the draft of the **Exposition** as "Rough Draft of What Is Called the South Carolina Exposition"; no draft of the **Protest** in his writing still exists (ibid., 311–12). See also **PJCC**, X, 442–43.

98 "the absurd and wicked doctrines"   **Correspondence**, V, 75.

98 "We cannot and ought not"   Freehling, ed., **The Nullification Era**, 206.

98 kept his authorship of the 1828 document secret   Freehling, **Prelude to Civil War**, 154–59; George Dangerfield, **The Awakening of American Nationalism, 1815–1828** (New York, 1965), 284–87.

98 He believed that   Ellis, **Union at Risk**, 53–54, is a strong summary of Calhoun's political position, ambitions, and motives at this time.

98 Emily, who had watched   Remini, **Jackson**, II, 174, reports that the "invited ladies" were in the gallery with the members of the House.

98 "one dense mass of living beings"   Emily Donelson to Mary Donelson Coffee, March 27, 1829, Andrew Jackson Donelson Papers, LOC.

98 "Thousands and thousands of people"   Hunt, ed., **First Forty Years of Washington Society**, 290–91.

99 he bowed to the people   Ibid., 291.

99 "the shout that rent the air"   Ibid., 294.

99 Cannons boomed   Ibid., 291.

99 the sounds of the salute   Ibid.

100 "the spirit of electioneering"   Clement Eaton, ed., **The Leaven of Democracy: The Growth of the Democratic Spirit in the Time of Jackson** (New York, 1963), 49.

101 "The large masses act in politics"   Douglas T. Miller, ed., **The Nature of Jacksonian America** (New York, 1972), 121. The quotation is from the work of Francis J. Grund, a German who wrote **Aristocracy in America.**

101 "It would seem to me"   **Messages**, II, 1000.

102 "Internal improvement"   Ibid.

102 a promise of "**reform**"   Ibid., 1001.

102 "unfaithful" and "incompetent"   Ibid.

102 "on the goodness of that Power"   Ibid.

103 He bowed once more   Hunt, ed., **First Forty Years of Washington Society**, 294.

103 took the oath . . . kissed a Bible   Ibid., 291.

103 mounted a white horse   Remini, **Jackson**, II, 176.

103 "Country men, farmers, gentlemen"   Hunt, ed., **First Forty Years of Washington Society**, 294.

103 Jackson had refused to call on   **Memoirs of JQA**, VIII, 97, 99–102.

103 had moved out the night before   Ibid., 102–4.

103 learned of the moment of the transfer of power   Benjamin Perley Poore, **Perley's Reminiscences of Sixty Years in the National Metropolis** (Philadelphia, 1886), 94.

103 a crowd trashing the White House   This is one of the most oft-told tales in the Jackson canon. See, for instance: Parton, **Life**, III, 170–71; James, **TLOAJ**, 494–95; Remini, **Jackson**, II, 177–79; Edwin A. Miles, "The First People's Inaugural—1829," 293–307.

103 "No arrangements had been made"   Hunt, ed., **First Forty Years of Washington Society**, 295.

103 "The **Majesty of the People**"   Hunt, ed., **First Forty Years of Washington Society**, 295.

104 "Here was the corpulent epicure"   Miles, "The First People's Inaugural—1829," 305.

104 "Orange punch" Ibid., 305–6.

104 The cost of the destruction Remini, **Jackson**, II, 178.

105 In a long letter to her sister **EDT**, I, 177–79.

105 "After the inauguration" Ibid., 177.

105 "The crowd" Ibid.

105 "the reign of King Mob" Miles, "The First People's Inaugural—1829," 305.

106 gown of amber satin **EDT**, I, 171.

107 James A. Hamilton . . . recalled being struck Hamilton, **Reminiscences**, 68.

107 "Tired as he was that night" **EDT**, I, 171.

107 a small dinner Coit, **John C. Calhoun**, 198; see also Poore, **Perley's Reminiscences of Sixty Years in the National Metropolis**, 95.

107 Calhoun was one of his companions Coit, **John C. Calhoun**, 198.

107 he and Mrs. Calhoun joined Emily and Andrew Wiltse, **John C. Calhoun**, II, 13.

108 the assembly hall Hunt, ed., **First Forty Years of Washington Society**, 210, calls Carusi's a "large elegant assembly room."

108 at C and Eleventh streets Miles, "The First People's Inaugural—1829," 307. The dance floor was "tastefully and appropriately" decorated. (Miles's sources were the **United States Telegraph** of March 9, 1829, and the **New York Enquirer** of March 10, 1829.) It had been advertised in advance as a "splendid ball" (**Washington Telegraph**, February 24, 1829); tickets were five dollars each, and organizers promised that "Police officers will be stationed at every necessary point to preserve the most rigid order" (**Washington Telegraph**, March 3, 1829).

108 Calhoun was the central figure Wiltse, **John C. Calhoun**, II, 15.

108 was about three months pregnant Emily delivered her second child on August 31, 1829.

109 "You know best, my dear" Laura Carter Holloway, **The Ladies of the White House** (New York, Cincinnati and Chicago, 1870), 335.

109 a place where Jackson sat in a rocking chair Jessie Benton Frémont, **Souvenirs of My Time** (Boston, 1887), 88–90.

109 liked to "keep me by him" Ibid., 88.

109 hope to be excused   Ibid.

109 "restless and fretful"   Wharton, **Social Life in the Early Republic**, 262.

110 "Madam, you dance with the grace"   Holloway, **The Ladies of the White House**, 336.

111 "Why, Major"   Parton, **Life**, III, 180.

111 "Eaton was altogether"   Amos Kendall to Francis Preston Blair, March 7, 1829, Blair and Lee Family Papers, Manuscripts Division, Department of Rare Books and Special Collections, Princeton University Library.

111 Born in Halifax County   "Eaton, John Henry (1790–1856)," **Biographical Directory of the United States Congress,** http://bioguide.congress.gov/scripts/biodisplay.pl?index=E0000 24.

112 served in the War of 1812   Lorman A. Ratner, **Andrew Jackson and His Tennessee Lieutenants** (Westpoint, Conn., 1997), 84.

112 married Myra Lewis   Ibid.

112 Eaton stepped in   Remini, **Jackson,** I, 323–24.

112 served as a U.S. senator   "Eaton, John Henry (1790–1856)," **Biographical Directory of the United States Congress,** http://bioguide.congress.gov/scripts/biodisplay.pl?index=E0000 24.

112 defended Jackson in the Washington debate   Arda S. Walker, "John Henry Eaton, Apostate," **East Tennessee Historical Society's Publications** 24 (1952), 27.

112 and he wrote   **TPA,** 14. See also Robert P. Hay "The Case for Andrew Jackson in 1824: Eaton's 'Wyoming Letters,'" **Tennessee Historical Quarterly** 29 (Summer 1970), 139–51.

112 the daughter of a Washington innkeeper   Ibid., 22.

112 lived at the O'Neales'   **TPA,** 22–23.

112 In the years before their wedding   Amos Kendall to Francis Preston Blair, March 7, 1829, Blair and Lee Family Papers, Manuscripts Division, Department of Rare Books and Special Collections, Princeton University Library.

113 "there has been a good deal of discontent"   Emily Donelson to Mary Donelson Coffee, March 27, 1829, Andrew Jackson Donelson Papers, LOC.

113 "Her form, of medium height"   Queena Pollack, **Peggy Eaton:**

Democracy's Mistress (New York, 1931), 81. Pollack's book is an admiring portrait and spirited defense of Margaret Eaton.

113 Her first husband, John Timberlake **TPA**, 42–44. See also Parton, **Life**, III, 185.

113 despondent over her unfaithfulness Pollack, **Peggy Eaton**, 75.

113 alleged to have become pregnant **TPA**, 93–94.

114 She reportedly passed a man **Papers**, VII, 102. See also Pollack, **Peggy Eaton**, 89–90.

114 pregnant by Eaton Margaret Eaton, **The Autobiography of Peggy Eaton** (New York, 1932), 80.

114 said to have registered **TPA**, 79.

114 "I suppose I must have been" Ibid., 5.

114 "I was a lively girl" Ibid., 11.

114 "The fact is" Ibid., 14.

114 "It must be remembered" Ibid., 24.

115 "Just let a little common sense" Ibid., 34.

115 "Why, yes, Major" Parton, **Life**, III, 185.

115 When Eaton said Ibid.

115 "Well, your marrying her" Ibid.

115 "I will sink or swim" Hamilton, **Reminiscences**, 102.

115 "The ladies here" Emily Donelson to Mary Donelson Coffee, March 27, 1829, Andrew Jackson Donelson Papers, LOC.

116 "The whole will be traced" **Correspondence**, IV, 227.

116 "It is odd enough" Poore, **Perley's Reminiscences of Sixty Years in the National Metropolis**, 125.

116 "trivial Things" Alexander Pope, **The Rape of the Lock** (New York, 1902), 13.

Chapter 5: Ladies' Wars Are Always Fierce and Hot

117 Frightened by a spate of sickness Wiltse, **John C. Calhoun**, I, 340–41.

117 the year before Ibid., 343.

117 had given up their Georgetown mansion Ibid., 343.

117 Oakly (later known as Dumbarton Oaks) Ibid., 269. The Calhouns had bought the house, which sits high atop Rock Creek, in 1823.

117 the Calhouns took lodgings PJCC, XI, 435.

117 well known and high toned   **Washington Evening Star**, February 18, 1884.

117 came to pay a call   My version of the Eatons' call at the Calhouns is drawn from several sources. See Coit, **John C. Calhoun**, 198–99; Eaton, **Autobiography of Peggy Eaton**, 54–55; Wiltse, **John C. Calhoun**, II, 28–29; and **TPA**, 53–54. In a public letter published on September 15, 1831, John Eaton claimed that the Calhouns made the first social overture, calling on the Eatons while the Eatons were honeymooning. In her **Autobiography**, Margaret goes on at some length about this, asserting that her father showed a "foolish gratification" at the visit and that a nurse then attending her sister knew and recognized Floride. Calhoun explicitly denied this, and my guess is that the Calhouns' version of events is probably the truth of the matter: an early visit from the secretary of war and his wife to the vice president and his wife, which would have been customary since the vice president was the higher ranking official, makes more sense. See Eaton, **Autobiography of Peggy Eaton**, 54–55.

118 "You could not fail to love and appreciate"   Wharton, **Social Life in the Early Republic**, 192. The friend was Mrs. William Seaton.

118 Diminutive but powerful   This is a common verdict about Mrs. Calhoun's nature. See, for instance, **TPA**, 54, and Wiltse, **John C. Calhoun**, II, 28.

118 "suspicious and fault-finding temper"   Wiltse, **John C. Calhoun**, II, 164.

118 Each summer her family had climbed into a beautiful coach   Coit, **John C. Calhoun**, 32.

118 after a quarrel   Wiltse, **John C. Calhoun**, II, 164.

118 "As to the suspicion"   Ibid.

118 had long been "the cause"   Ibid.

119 felt a disparity   Coit, **John C. Calhoun**, 198. A more personal biographer than Wiltse, Coit writes of Calhoun: "He was not under the control of his wife. No one ever controlled John C. Calhoun. But neither did anyone, least of all her husband, control Floride Bonneau Calhoun."

119 the vice president was out   **PJCC**, XI, 476.

119   the servant had failed   Ibid.

119   "She of course treated them"   Ibid.

119   "The relation which Mrs. Eaton bore"   Ibid.

120   She made her decision overnight   Ibid.

120   his scholarly interests   Nevins, ed., **Diary of John Quincy Adams**, xiii.

120   "much scandalized"   Diary of John Quincy Adams, February 26, 1829, Adams Papers, Massachusetts Historical Society.

120   the vice president "forsooth was"   John Quincy Adams to Charles Francis Adams, April 28, 1830, Adams Papers, Massachusetts Historical Society.

121   Floride gave "public notice"   Ibid.

121   "War is declared"   Louisa Catherine Adams to Charles Francis Adams, January 24, 1830, Adams Papers, Massachusetts Historical Society.

121   his first evening in Washington   Remini, **Jackson**, II, 192–93.

121   just one candle burning   **AMVB**, 232.

121   thought Jackson's health "poor"   Ibid.

121   "The cast of the Cabinet"   Ibid., 340.

121   "partook largely of this feeling"   Ibid., 341.

121   Small in stature   Widmer, **Martin Van Buren**, 2.

121   son of a tavern keeper   "Life Before the Presidency," **American President: An Online Reference Resource**, Miller Center of Public Affairs at the University of Virginia, http://miller center.org/academic/americanpresident/vanburen/essays/biography/2.

122   guests included Alexander Hamilton   Ibid.

122   A careful dresser   Widmer, **Martin Van Buren**, 28.

122   "the planters of the South"   Ibid., 56.

122   "You might as well"   Martin Van Buren to C. C. Camberling, December 17, 1828, Martin Van Buren Papers, LOC.

122   cutting his arm   Parton, **Life**, III, 63–64. See also Goff, "A Physical Profile of Andrew Jackson," 307–8.

123   "a calamitous event"   Bernard Mayo, ed., "Henry Clay, Patron and Idol of White Sulphur Springs: His Letters to James Caldwell," **Virginia Magazine of History and Biography** 55 (October, 1947), 306.

123   Jackson himself to be "feeble"   Ibid.

123   "We must never forget"   **PHC**, VIII, 87–88.

123 "Disguise it as we may"   Richard B. Latner, "The Eaton Affair Reconsidered," **Tennessee Historical Quarterly** 36 (Fall 1977), 334.

123 "A display there"   David R. Williams to Martin Van Buren, November 17, 1829, Martin Van Buren Papers, LOC.

124 James Parton looked back   Parton, **Life**, III, 287.

124 "If I had a **tit** for every one of these **pigs**"   **Correspondence**, IV, 21.

124 Jackson's interpretation of the Eaton affair   The best summary of the historical debate over the political causes and effects of the Eaton affair is found in Latner, "The Eaton Affair Reconsidered," 330–51, and Professor Latner was kind enough to discuss the matter with me. Jackson believed Margaret a good woman, but he also knew that the battle was as much about the mammon of office, salary, influence, and political control as it was about the sexual morality of Margaret Eaton. When Eaton's appointment to the Cabinet had been announced, a delegation of rival Tennessee congressmen— the state was riven with feuding political factions, and Jackson and Eaton represented just one of several—tried to stop it, infuriating Jackson, who ascribed their hostility to the fact that Eaton would now control patronage in the expansive War Department. Always vigilant for any hint that Clay, his rival from the West, might be meddling, Jackson decided that the anti-Eaton party was being encouraged by the departing Clay and his allies. For the strongest pro-Calhoun, anti-Van Buren case, see Wiltse, **John C. Calhoun**, II; for the strongest anti-Calhoun, pro-Van Buren case, see, unsurprisingly, **AMVB**.

125 Cultural interpretations of the Eaton affair   Kirsten Wood, "'One Woman So Dangerous to Public Morals': Gender and Power in the Eaton Affair," **Journal of the Early Republic** 17 (Summer 1997), 237–75; Catherine Allgor, **Parlor Politics: In Which the Ladies of Washington Help Build a City and a Government** (Charlottesville, Va., 274), 198–238; and Howe, **What Hath God Wrought**, 335–42.

125 "sink with honor to my grave"   **Correspondence**, IV, 31.

125 Jackson heard allegations   Remini, **Andrew Jackson and the Bank War**, 49–50.

125 John McLean . . . wrote Nicholas Biddle Nicholas Biddle, **The Correspondence of Nicholas Biddle, Dealing with National Affairs, 1807–1844** (Boston, 1919), 63–64. The letter from McLean to Biddle was dated January 5, 1829 (ibid., 63).

125 Even if, he said, "the impression" Ibid., 64.

126 In naming directors, Biddle told McLean Ibid., 70. Biddle's reply was dated January 11, 1829.

126 "Being friendly to the Bank myself" Ibid., 64.

127 Born in Vermont in 1781 For my portrait of Evarts and his work, I drew on: John Andrew, **From Revivals to Removal** (Athens, Ga., 1992); Evarts Family Papers, Beinecke Library, Yale University; and E. C. Tracy, **Memoir of the Life of Jeremiah Evarts** (Whitefish, Mont., 2007).

127 the college was suffused Andrew, **From Revivals to Removal**, 17–19.

127 "In whatever sphere" Ibid., 14.

127 referred to as "religious enthusiasts" **Correspondence**, IV, 483.

127 "Gentlemen, do what you please" Parton, **Life**, III, 641.

128 "My dear, if I were to do it **now**" Ibid., 101.

128 "I have not seen" Andrew, **From Revivals to Removal**, 179.

129 watched the stirrings of nullification **Papers**, VI, 476.

129 "There is nothing that I shudder at more" Ibid.

129 "The South Carolinians get nothing" Amos Kendall to Francis Preston Blair, March 7, 1829, Blair and Lee Family Papers, Manuscripts Division, Department of Rare Books and Special Collections, Princeton University Library.

129 "Some foundation there must be" Louisa Catherine Adams to John Quincy Adams, September 27, 1829, Adams Papers, Massachusetts Historical Society.

130 "Clay and his minions" **Correspondence**, IV, 15.

130 "these satellites of Clay" Ibid., 31.

130 "we must submit" **PJCC**, XI, 17.

130 said to be "not friendly" Ibid., 31.

130 states' rights elements in South Carolina Latner, "The Eaton Affair Reconsidered," 347.

130 "**Eaton** and others" Ibid.

131 troubled Calhoun Ibid.

131 "To please Uncle" Emily Donelson to Mary Donelson Coffee, March 27, 1829, Andrew Jackson Donelson Papers, LOC.

131 "I think if Eaton" Ibid.

132 he had been Donelson's chaperone Cheathem, **Old Hickory's Nephew**, 15.

132 "I think as Uncle wanted" Emily Donelson to Mary Donelson Coffee, March 27, 1829, Andrew Jackson Donelson Papers, LOC.

133 women such as Floride Allgor, **Parlor Politics**, 202.

133 "I am prepared" Wood, "'One Woman So Dangerous to Public Morals': Gender and Power in the Eaton Affair," 252.

133 speak of Emily as "a poor, silly thing" Heiskell, **AJETH**, III, 330.

133 "I was quite as independent" Ibid.

133 "For God knows" James Hamilton, Jr., to Martin Van Buren, July 16, 1829, Martin Van Buren Papers, LOC.

134 At Gadsby's Hotel one morning **Papers**, VII, 102. See also Pollack, **Peggy Eaton**, 89–90.

134 "Mrs. Eaton brushed by me" Ibid. Ely's report is secondhand—as were so many of the stories told of Margaret Eaton.

134 "I've just returned from Mr. Clay's" Edward Bates to Julia Bates, December 4, 18[29], Edward Bates Papers, Virginia Historical Society.

134 "hard-featured" Ibid.

134 "Of course, there is no getting along" Ibid.

135 On Sunday, March 8, 1829 Hunt, ed., **First Forty Years of Washington Society**, 299.

135 The Smiths had come to Washington Ibid., v–vi.

135 Clay came to Washington Remini, **Henry Clay**, 59.

135 on the square between Pennsylvania Avenue Hunt, ed., **First Forty Years of Washington Society**, 238.

135 "the patriot to the patriot" Ibid., 300.

135 Smith had served as an interim secretary of the Treasury Ibid., vi.

135 Clay had risen through the Congress "Clay, Henry (1777–1852)," **Biographical Directory of the United States Congress,** http://bioguide.congress.gov/scripts/biodisplay.pl?index=C000 482.

135 The weather outside Ibid., 300. "The weather without was gloomy, cold and cloudy," wrote Mrs. Smith, "but the circle around our bright fire was not only cheerful but gay and witty."

136 "The characters and administrations"   Hunt, ed., **First Forty Years of Washington Society**, 300.

136 the dishes were being cleared away   Ibid.

136 "Your father . . . would not yield"   Ibid.

137 late for Lucretia   Ibid., 304. "Altogether," Mrs. Smith concluded, "this day and evening have been the most interesting that have occurred this winter."

137 "the greatest . . . apprehension"   PHC, VIII, 8.

137 a big Washington wedding   Diary of John Quincy Adams, February 22, 1830, Adams Papers, Massachusetts Historical Society.

138 By James Parton's count   Parton, **Life**, III, 207–8. For a breakdown of Jackson's removals, see Carl R. Fish, "Removal of Officials by the Presidents of the United States," **Annual Report of the American Historical Association for the Year 1899**, 2 vols. (Washington, 1900) 1, 84.

138 about 919, just under 10 percent   Cole, **Presidency of Andrew Jackson**, 41.

138 a particularly high number   Cole, **A Jackson Man**, 124.

139 "At that period"   Parton, **Life**, III, 213.

139 "A large portion of the population"   **Memoirs of JQA**, VIII, 149.

139 "They see nothing wrong"   **Register of Debates in Congress**, 22nd Congress, 1st session, VIII, 1833, 1325.

139 "the Augean Stable"   Wilentz, **Andrew Jackson**, 47.

139 a "struggle between the virtue"   Ellis, **Union at Risk**, 18.

140 There was always graft   In a revisionist view of what historians long called the Era of Good Feelings, Robert Remini argued that it would be more fitting to call the period after the War of 1812 "the Era of Corruption" (Remini, **Jackson**, II, 15). Quoting one visitor to Washington in the last months of President Monroe's administration, Remini captured the prevailing view: "I did, before I came to this city, entertain a most exalted opinion of the high officers of gov't; but since I have been here it has abated greatly. I find they are not, in reality, quite so good as other men" (ibid., 25). A devastating indictment, really: the Monroe and Adams administrations had more than their share of graft and contentious congressional investigations, and there was a flow of stories about how the Second Bank of the United

States, a private institution whose wealth and influence derived from its near monopoly on federal deposits, kept key lawmakers and officials on retainer.

140 the postmaster of Albany, New York Poore, **Perley's Reminiscences of Sixty Years in the National Metropolis,** 110–11.

140 "General Jackson, I have come here" Ibid.

141 "the next day Messrs. Van Buren" Ibid.

141 "I take the consequences" Ibid.

141 "The proscriptions from office continue" **Memoirs of JQA,** VIII, 144.

142 "During the reign of Bonaparte" **PHC,** VIII, 45.

142 "Is there any difference" Ibid.

143 voting down several nominees Parton, **Life,** III, 277.

143 "Let Congress go home" Ibid., 277–78.

143 "the vital center of action" Arthur M. Schlesinger, Jr., **A Thousand Days: John F. Kennedy in the White House** (New York, 2002), 120.

Chapter 6: A Busybody Presbyterian Clergyman

144 "I was elected by the free voice of the people" **Correspondence,** IV, 21.

144 "I was making a Cabinet for myself" Ibid.

144 "I did not come here" Ibid.

144 the same day the Calhouns **TPA,** 75.

144 Ely sat down at his desk in Philadelphia **Papers,** VII, 101–5.

145 "Christian Party in Politics" Ezra Stiles Ely, **The Duty of Christian Freemen to Elect Christian Rulers** (Philadelphia, 1828), 8.

145 should join forces to keep "Pagans" Ibid., 11.

145 "Every ruler **should be**" Ibid., 4.

145 dating back to Jackson's days when he had business interests **Papers,** VI, 545.

145 added his own warm exchange Ely, **Duty of Christian Freemen,** 30–32.

145 "Amongst the greatest blessings" **Papers,** VI, 358–59.

146 "All true Christians" Ibid., 358.

146 a quotation from the American Sunday School Union Ely, **Duty of Christian Freemen,** 18.

146 to end the federal delivery of mail on Sundays   Schlesinger, **Age of Jackson**, 136–40. See also Foster, **Errand of Mercy**.

146 "We have always viewed it"   Andrew, **From Revivals to Removal**, 56.

147 one of the more intriguing politicians of the time   Mark O. Hatfield, with the Senate Historical Offices, **Vice Presidents of the United States, 1789–1993** (Washington: U.S. Government Printing Office, 1997), 121–31. I am indebted to Hatfield's work for the description of Johnson's life and career.

147 "It is not the legitimate province"   Schlesinger, **Age of Jackson**, 139. In her **Freethinkers: A History of American Secularism** (New York, 2004), Susan Jacoby points out that there was ultimately a reduction in Sunday mail delivery, but "for nonreligious reasons, after the 1844 invention of the telegraph provided a more efficient form of business communication" (ibid., 80).

147 "The advance of the human race"   House Report on Sunday Mails, Report of House of Representatives, 21st Congress, 1st session, 262. The report also made this point: "Why have the petitioners confined their prayer to the mails? Why have they not requested that the government be required to suspend **all** its executive functions on that day? Why do they not require us to enact that our ships shall not sail; that our armies shall not march; that officers of justice shall not seize the suspected or guard the convicted? They seem to forget that government is as necessary on Sunday as on any other day of the week. The spirit of evil does not rest on that day. It is the government, ever active in its functions, which enables us all, even the petitioners, to worship in our churches in peace" (ibid., 261).

148 a "busybody Presbyterian clergyman"   **Memoirs of JQA**, VIII, 184.

148 a faithful supporter of Rachel Jackson's   **Papers**, VII, 101.

148 "recommended the appointment of Major Eaton"   **Correspondence**, IV, 50.

149 the Reverend John N. Campbell   TPA, 93–95. There is also an interesting, if adoring, sketch of Campbell in the history of the church he ultimately came to lead in Albany, New York. See J. McClusky Blayney, **History of the First Presbyterian Church of Albany, N.Y.** (Albany, 1877), 31–36. See also Alfred Nevin,

ed., **Encyclopedia of the Presbyterian Church in the United States of America** (Philadelphia, 1884), 123. There is some very interesting detail about Campbell to be found in another volume: "He was genial, and often jovial, in his intercourse, and was almost sure to be a commanding spirit in any social circle into which he was thrown. He had mingled much with the world, and, with his uncommon natural shrewdness, was an adept in the knowledge of human nature. He saw both clearly and quickly; and when his mind was once made up on any subject, though he could still consider and appreciate adverse evidence, he was not very likely to yield his first conviction" (**Presbyterian Reunion: A Memorial Volume, 1837–1871** [New York, 1870], 167–68).

149 Mrs. Eaton was "a woman of ill fame" **Papers**, VII, 101.

149 a "sad catalogue" Ibid., 103.

149 He reported a rumor Ibid., 102–3.

149 brought Rachel Jackson into the conversation Ibid., 101.

149 "Need I apologize" Ibid., 104.

149 began drily enough Ibid., 113.

150 disposing, he believed, of each "slander" Ibid., 113–18, is the full text of the letter.

152 from the 101st Psalm Isaac Watts, **The Psalms of David, Imitated in the Language of the New Testament** (Philadelphia, 1828), 165.

Chapter 7: My White and Red Children

153 the president's correspondence was filled **Papers**, VII, 695–96.

153 this cold Monday Diary of John Quincy Adams, March 23, 1829, Adams Family Papers, Massachusetts Historical Society.

153 the federal government's policy **Papers**, VII, 112–13.

153 a grim two-century-old story As noted below in the Bibliography, I found the following works essential to understanding both the history of the United States' treatment of the Indians and of Jackson's role in it: William L. Anderson, ed., **Cherokee Removal: Before and After** (Athens, Ga., 1991); Stuart Banner, **How the Indians Lost Their Land: Law and Power on the Frontier** (Cambridge, Mass., 2005); Grant Foreman, **Indian Removal: The Emigration of the Five Civilized Tribes of In-**

dians (Norman, Okla., 1972); William G. McLoughlin, **Cherokee Renascence in the New Republic** (Princeton, N.J., 1992); William G. McLoughlin, with Walter H. Conser, Jr., and Virginia Duffy McLoughlin, **The Cherokee Ghost Dance: Essays on the Southeastern Indians, 1789–1861** (Macon, Ga., 1984); Jill Norgren, **The Cherokee Cases: Two Landmark Federal Decisions in the Fight for Sovereignty** (Norman, Okla., 2004); Francis Paul Prucha, **The Great Father: The United States Government and the American Indians**, 2 vols. in 1 (Lincoln, Neb., 1995); Francis Paul Prucha, **The Indians in American Society: From the Revolutionary War to the Present** (Berkeley, Calif., 1985); Francis Paul Prucha, "Andrew Jackson's Indian Policy: A Reassessment," **Journal of American History** 56 (December 1969), 527–39; Ronald N. Satz, **American Indian Policy in the Jacksonian Era** (Lincoln, Neb., 1974); Anthony F. C. Wallace, **Jefferson and the Indians: The Tragic Fate of the First Americans** (Cambridge, Mass., 1999); Anthony F. C. Wallace, **The Long, Bitter Trail: Andrew Jackson and the Indians** (New York, 1993); Thurman Wilkins, **Cherokee Tragedy: The Ridge Family and the Decimation of a People**, 2d ed., rev. (Norman, Okla., 1986); Mary E. Young, "Indian Removal and Land Allotment: The Civilized Tribes and Jacksonian Justice," **American Historical Review** 64 (October 1958), 31–45.

The shifting scholarly and biographical view of Jackson and the Indians is intriguing, and says a good deal about the Indians' ambiguous place in the imaginations of many white Americans. The first major work on Jackson, James Parton's trilogy, published in the 1860s, accepted removal as a sad but necessary historical development. "The philanthropic feelings of the country were aroused. The letter of many treaties was shown to be against the measure. The peaceful Society of Friends opposed it. A volume of the leading speeches in opposition to the removal was widely circulated. The opinions of great lawyers were adverse to it. It was, indeed, one of those wise and humane measures by which great good is done and great evil prevented, but which cause much immediate misery, and much grievous individual wrong. It was painful to contemplate the sad remnant of tribes that had been the original proprietors of the soil, leaving the narrow residue of their heritage, and taking up a long and weary march for strange and distant hunting-grounds. More painful it would have been to see those unfortunate tribes hemmed in on every side by hostile settlers, preyed upon by the white man's cupidity, the white man's vices, and the white man's diseases, until they perished from the face of the earth. Doomed to perish they are. But no one, I presume, has now any doubt that General Jackson's policy of removal, which he carried out cautiously, but unrelentingly, and not always without stratagem and management, has caused the inevitable process of extinction to go on with less anguish and less demoralization to the whites than if the Indians had been suffered to remain in the States of Georgia, Alabama, and Mississippi. To this part of the policy of General Jackson, praise little qualified can be justly awarded. The 'irrevocable logic of events' first decreed and then justified the removal of the Indians. Nor need we, at this late date, revive the sad details of a measure which, hard and cruel as it was then thought, is now universally felt to have been as kind as it was necessary" (Parton, **Life**, III, 279–80). In **The Age of Jackson**, published in 1945, Arthur Schlesinger, Jr., barely addresses the topic, but other historians were already at work on recovering and reconstructing the story of removal from the perspective of the Indians and as a fundamental part of Jackson's life and legacy. See, for instance, William Graham Sumner, **Andrew Jackson** (Boston, 1899), 220–29. A good historiographical survey is Regan A. Lutz, "West of Eden: The Historiography of the Trail of Tears," Ph.D. diss., University of Toledo, 1995.

153 anxious for more land   Wallace, **The Long, Bitter Trail**, 5.

153 to grow cotton   Ibid., 6–11.

154 A white man had been murdered   **Papers**, VII, 113.

154 "Friends and Brothers, listen"   Ibid., 112.

155 Jackson was hardly the first   Norgren wrote: "A backward glance at history shows that Jackson's Indian policy recommendations did not constitute an abrupt departure from the policy direction taken by his predecessors, James Monroe (1816–1824) and John Quincy Adams (1824–1828). Monroe and the Senate had authorized the use of removal provisions in the 1817 treaty with the Cherokee and subsequent agreements, including the 1820 Treaty of Doak's Stand with the Choctaw. Adams adopted ever harsher Indian policies and increasingly ignored binding

obligations to them under international law. He ended his presidency by dispatching American soldiers to intimidate the Creek, whom he hoped to force to remove, and then by refusing to condemn Georgia's jurisdiction legislation. During the Adams presidency Congress had seriously considered a removal bill. A continentalist, as President, Adams was not uncomfortable with policies of national expansion and empire" (Norgren, **Cherokee Cases**, 80–81). See also Feller, **Jacksonian Promise**, 179–83.

155   can be traced at least to 1622   Prucha, **Great Father**, 13. The incident involved Indians led by Opechancanough: "Soon after, in New England, the Pequot War of 1637 began formal conflicts between the Indians and the English. The Pequots, moving into the Connecticut River Valley, met Puritans migrating into the same region and posed a threat to the peaceful expansion of the Massachusetts Bay Colony. Pequot harassment of the settlements brought war as the English attacked the hostile Indians in order to protect the nascent colony in Connecticut. Such conflicts set a pattern. A new surprise attack by Indians in Virginia in 1644, which killed five hundred whites, brought new reprisals, and Bacon's Rebellion of 1676 had strong anti-Indian origins. In 1675–1676 King Philip's War in New England furnished still another case of warfare instigated by the Indians in a desperate attempt to stop the advancing tide of English settlement" (ibid.). At the beginning of his book on the removal of the Southern tribes, Foreman was terse but decided in his judgment: "It is not intended here to indict the people of the South for mistreatment of the Indians. **Whatever may be charged against the white people in this regard is not sectional. The Indians have suffered at their hands throughout the country from north to south and from east to west**" (italics mine) (Foreman, **Indian Removal**, 16).

155   the white survivors retaliated   Prucha, **Great Father**, 13–14. The white response, Prucha wrote, was "immediate and vengeful; the massacre was used an excuse for a massive retaliation against the Indians, for it was looked upon as proof that Indians could not be trusted, even when professing friendship." Such cycles of violence were to become all too familiar. By 1676 the wars in New England (see above) even provided a precedent

for what came after the violence: "The terms of peace imposed on the defeated Indians were harsh and drawn up to ensure the future security of expanding white settlements," Prucha wrote. "As in the aftermath of the Virginia massacre of 1622, the Indians were killed or forced out of the areas of white settlement" (ibid., 14).

155 said that "treaties were expedients"   Ibid., 196. The remarks were made in 1830.

155 Indians were viewed as savages   Ibid., 5–11. Prucha, **Indians in American Society**, 1–54, is interesting reading, as is Wallace, **Long, Bitter Trail**, 15–29, in which Wallace details the actual worlds of the tribes as they encountered the European settlers.

156 "Next to the case of the black race"   Ronald T. Takaki, **Iron Cages: Race and Culture in 19th-Century America** (New York, 1990), 80; and James Madison, **Letters and Other Writings of James Madison** (New York, 1865), III, 516.

156 should be sent west   Sheehan, **Seeds of Extinction**, 244.

156 "This then is the season"   Ibid.

157 attempted to formulate a humane policy   Prucha, **Great Father**, 59–71.

157 "It is presumable that a nation"   Ibid., 59.

157 to meet with senators about Indian issues   Ibid., 55.

157 "We presume that our strength"   Ibid., 31.

158 Monroe and Adams had drafted removal plans   Prucha, **Cherokee Removal**, 3–4. The removal policy, Prucha noted elsewhere, had "begun long before Jackson's presidency . . ." (Prucha, "Andrew Jackson's Indian Policy: A Reassessment," 534). See also Norgren, **Cherokee Cases**, 39–40; Satz, **American Indian Policy in the Jacksonian Era**, 11–12; Wallace, **Long, Bitter Trail**, 39–41.

158 Everett "spoke also of the debate"   **Memoirs of JQA**, VIII, 206.

159 Clay was now against removal   Remini, **Henry Clay**, 362.

159 Clay had told him "that it"   **Memoirs of JQA**, VII, 89–90. Clay also told Adams, Adams said, that "he believed [the Indians] were destined to extinction, and, although he would never use or countenance inhumanity towards them, he did not think them, as a race, worth preserving. He considered them as essentially inferior to the Anglo-Saxon race which were now taking their place on this continent" (ibid.).

159 McKenney . . . turned to New York City   Herman J. Viola, **Thomas L. McKenney, Architect of America's Early Indian Policy: 1819–1830** (Chicago, 1974), 220–22; Prucha, "Thomas L. McKenney and the New York Indian Board," **The Mississippi Valley Historical Review** 48 (March 1962), 635–55. The Board existed only for a year, until August 1830, when Jackson removed McKenney from office (Prucha, **Great Father,** 200).

160 the Indians had been "excited to war"   Prucha, "Andrew Jackson's Indian Policy: A Reassessment," 528.

160 In January 1817, Jackson told James Monroe   **Papers,** IV, 80.

160 "The sooner these lands"   Ibid.

160 pondering a complete removal   **Papers,** VI, 192.

160 "a dense white population"   Ibid., 200.

160 After a white woman was kidnapped   Prucha, "Andrew Jackson's Indian Policy: A Reassessment," 529.

160 "With such arms"   Ibid.

161 denounced a "base, cowardly attack"   Ibid., 530.

161 that "there could exist"   Ibid.

162 "However mere human policy"   Frelinghuysen, **Speech of Mr. Frelinghuysen, of New Jersey, Delivered in the Senate of the United States, April 6, 1830, on the Bill for an Exchange of Lands with the Indians Residing in Any of the States or Territories, and for Their Removal West of the Mississippi,** 7–9.

163 the Iroquois in New York and Cherokees in North Carolina   Howe, **What Hath God Wrought,** 420.

163 "This is a straight and good talk"   **Papers,** VII, 113.

Chapter 8: Major Eaton Has Spoken of Resigning

164 in quarters to the right of the main entrance   Seale, **President's House,** I, 195 and 212.

164 ringing and ringing for him   Amos Kendall, "Anecdotes of General Jackson," **United States Magazine and Democratic Review** 11 (1842), 273. According to Kendall, Donelson reported that Jackson thought of firing O'Neal on several occasions but could never bring himself to go through with it (ibid.).

164 to bring Emily Donelson a letter   **EDT,** I, 184–85.

164 "You are young and uninformed"   Ibid., 184.

165 "You may take it"   Ibid.

165 a "little nest"   Ibid.

165 "their gossiping tattle"   Ibid.

165 he invoked Rachel   Ibid. "When your excellent aunt arrived here in 1815 (I have heard her tell the story)," Eaton wrote, "some of those busy folks, always and everywhere to be found, undertook to tell her of the people here; and amongst other things that a certain lady was not a proper character for her to associate with. Her answer as alike creditable to her head as to her heart was, 'I did not come here to listen to little slanderous tales, and to decide upon people's character' " (ibid.).

165 "These people"   Ibid.

165 "some surprise"   Ibid., 186.

165 realized he had failed to ask   Ibid., 185.

166 Eaton scrawled Emily a second note   Ibid.

166 " . . . to ask you"   Ibid.

166 a polite but steely letter   Ibid., 186–87.

166 "totally unacquainted"   Ibid., 186.

166 "Having drawn my attention"   Ibid.

166 Yes, Emily acknowledged, "there were some"   Ibid.

167 "As to the probability"   Ibid.

167 "As you say"   Ibid.

167 "I take this opportunity"   Ibid., 187.

168 what Jackson called "my family, my chosen family"   **Correspondence**, IV, 196.

168 Andrew Donelson sent his wife's letter   **EDT**, I, 187.

168 Eaton weighed whether his war to survive   Emily Donelson to Mary Donelson, May 10, 1829, Mrs. John Lawrence Merritt Collection.

169 "Indeed the prejudice is so strong against them"   Ibid.

169 "the road to favor and patronage"   **PJCC**, XI, 477. The occasion was Calhoun's reply to Eaton's 1831 publication of the Eatons' version of the affair (ibid., 474–82).

170 what Calhoun in 1831 called the "artful machinations"   Ibid., 481.

170 "It is Sunday"   John Eaton to John Coffee, June 21, 1829, Dyas Collection-John Coffee Papers, 1770–1917, Tennessee Historical Society War Memorial Building, Nashville, Tennessee. Papers housed at the Tennessee State Library and Archives.

171 "Our old friend is himself again"   Ibid.

171 "those who have been removed"   Ibid.

172 Woodbury . . . wrote Treasury Secretary Samuel Ingham   Remini, **Andrew Jackson and the Bank War**, 51–52. Woodbury also wrote Biddle about the matter. See Levi Woodbury to Nicholas Biddle, Nicholas Biddle Papers, LOC. Written from Portsmouth on June 27, 1829, the Woodbury letter to Biddle is marked "Confidential."

172 unhappy with Jeremiah Mason   Remini, **Andrew Jackson and the Bank War**, 52. See also Parton, **Life**, III, 260.

172 Petitions were en route   Parton, **Life**, III, 260–61. The politics of the New Hampshire episode was particularly fraught for Biddle, because Isaac Hill, a pro-Jackson newspaper editor who was now at Treasury, had instigated the move against Mason.

172 close to Daniel Webster and to John Quincy Adams   Ibid., 260.

172 "partial, harsh"   Ibid.

172 Biddle conceded nothing   Ibid., 265.

172 a letter to Secretary Ingham   Ibid., 266.

173 there was no mechanism   **Papers**, VII, 458.

173 a memorandum in Jackson's hand   Ibid., 458–60.

174 could "redress all grievances"   Ibid., 459.

174 "We visited the President"   Hunt, ed., **First Forty Years of Washington Society**, 289.

174 Martha Jefferson Randolph   EDT, I, 218–19.

175 She had given birth   "Martha Wayles Skelton Jefferson," http://www.whitehouse.gov/history/firstladies/mj3.html

175 Jackson and Van Buren saw her   Hunt, ed., **First Forty Years of Washington Society**, 308. See also **EDT**, I, 217–19.

176 "there is properly no history, only biography"   Brooks Atkinson, ed., **The Essential Writings of Ralph Waldo Emerson** (New York, 2000), 116. The line is found in Emerson's essay "History," published in his 1841 book **Essays: First Series**. Emerson believed that every reader looked to find himself in the mirror of history. "There is a relation between the hours of our life and the centuries of time," he wrote. "As the air I breathe is drawn from the great repositories of nature, as the light on my book is yielded by a star a hundred millions of miles distant, as the poise of my body depends on the equilibrium of centrifu-

gal and centripetal forces, so the hours should be instructed by the ages and the ages explained by hours. Of the universal mind each individual man is one more incarnation. . . . We, as we read, must become Greeks, Romans, Turks, priest and king, martyr and executioner; must fasten these images to some reality in our secret experience, or we shall learn nothing rightly. What befell Asdrubal or Caesar Borgia is as much an illustration of the mind's powers and depravations as what has befallen us. Each new law and political movement has a meaning for you . . . I can see my own vices without heat in the distant persons of Solomon, Alcibiades, and Catiline" (ibid., 113–14).

177 riding on horseback most days   Niven, **Martin Van Buren,** 250.

177 "We are getting along"   Ibid.

177 to pay a call on John Quincy Adams   **AMVB,** 269.

178 Jackson heard Van Buren out   Ibid.

178 at once pleased and sour   **Memoirs of JQA,** VIII, 128–29. James A. Hamilton accompanied Van Buren on the call.

178 the eleventh Philippic of Cicero   Ibid., 127.

178 "all the members"   Ibid., 128.

178 "Of the new Administration"   Ibid.

178 spoke of the weather   Ibid., 129.

178 ongoing negotiations about American trade   Ibid.

178 "very cordially received"   **AMVB,** 269.

178 "reestablish friendly relations"   Ibid., 270.

179 "by far the ablest man"   **Memoirs of JQA,** VIII, 129.

179 a visit with Emily and Mary Eastin   **AMVB,** 344–45, is a full account of the episode. See also **EDT,** I, 209–12.

179 "the Eaton malaria"   **EDT,** I, 179.

179 "conveyed, tho' gently"   **AMVB,** 344.

180 "being controlled"   Ibid.

180 "the situation of her Uncle"   Ibid.

180 "I rose from my seat"   Ibid., 345.

181 an excursion aboard the steamboat **Potomac**   **EDT,** I, 202–3.

181 At Alexandria   **National Intelligencer,** July 10, 1829.

181 crowds of admirers   **Richmond Enquirer,** July 14, 1829.

181 her fan and cologne bottle   **EDT,** I, 202.

181 he saw Margaret "betray"   Ibid., 202–3.

182 "She informed me"   Ibid., 203.

182 she announced that she felt "pity"   **Correspondence**, IV, 190.

182 "secret influence"   **PJCC**, XI, 386.

182 "The interference of the lady"   Ibid., 387.

183 Margaret "flatters up the old General" **TPA**, 114.

183 "as the means of gratifying"   Ibid., 386.

183 the weather was lovely   **Papers**, VII, 384.

183 Jackson again boarded the **Potomac**   Ibid.

183 the Rip Raps, Virginia   Ibid., 385.

183 wondered "whether the weeping willows"   Ibid., 386.

183 "My dear son"   Ibid.

184 a debate about whether to marry   Ibid.

184 a fortress named after Calhoun   Chester D. Bradley, **Fort Wool** (Fort Monroe, Va., 196[?]).

184 Steaks, English cheese, turtle soup   **Correspondence**, IV, 64–65, reprints Jackson's grocery bill from the stay.

184 "inhaling the salubrious ocean breeze"   **Richmond Enquirer**, September 1, 1829.

184 **"My dear and sincere friend"**   **Papers**, VII, 387.

185 an evening call from the Reverend John Campbell   Ibid., 411. Andrew Donelson's complete memorandum of the Campbell episode and ensuing events by Andrew can be found on 411–15. See also **TPA**, 94–95.

185 felt bound by "feelings of the most sincere friendship"   Ibid.

186 Would Donelson absorb the first blows   Ibid.

186 "I declined a conversation"   Ibid.

186 "She seems strong"   **EDT**, I, 205.

186 added "combustible qualities"   **Correspondence**, IV, 67.

187 Calhoun would "attempt much next winter"   Satterfield, **Andrew Jackson Donelson**, 24.

187 emotions "have been steamed"   **EDT**, I, 205.

187 "a fine healthy child"   Ibid., 206.

187 "quite strong"   Ibid., 205.

187 the "gratifying intelligence"   John Coffee to Andrew Jackson Donelson, September 19, 1829, Dyas Collection-John Coffee Papers, 1770–1917, Tennessee Historical Society War Memorial Building, Nashville, Tennessee. Papers housed at the Tennessee State Library and Archives.

187 "I assure you"   Ibid.

187 "the Sunshine of the White House" Alice Graham McCollin, **Ladies' Home Journal** 11 (January 1894), 7.

187 Campbell returned to the White House **Papers**, VII, 405.

188 the doorkeeper **TPA**, 95.

188 with William Lewis **Papers**, VII, 408.

188 Donelson left the two men alone Ibid., 405.

188 Jackson was stunned Ibid., 405–6.

188 "Never having suspected" Ibid., 403.

188 "this **vile tale**" Ibid., 406.

188 "We parted" **Correspondence**, IV, 67.

188 found sufficient evidence Ibid., 408–9, details Jackson and Lewis's detective work.

189 asked him to arrange Ibid., 409.

189 Thursday . . . was a clear, pleasantly warm day "Meteorological Register for September, 1829," **National Intelligencer**, October 3, 1829.

189 the two windows facing south Author's tour of the White House.

189 Jackson "stated the result of my inquiry" **Correspondence**, IV, 409.

189 Jackson "must have misunderstood" Ibid.

190 "I think it necessary" Ibid., 405.

190 "Man born of woman" Ibid., 413.

190 a special meeting Ibid., 423.

Chapter 9: An Opinion of the President Alone

191 "I have a confused story" John Quincy Adams to Louisa Catherine Adams, September 20, 1829, Adams Papers, Massachusetts Historical Society.

191 cloudy and rather cool "Meteorological Register for September, 1829," **National Intelligencer**, October 3, 1829.

191 Ely, Campbell, and the secretaries Parton, **Life**, III, 203.

191 rectangular table Seale, **The White House**, 90.

191 down the long hall Author's tour of the White House.

192 argued over the alleged miscarriage Parton, **Life**, III, 204. Parton's account is based on interviews with "sources," presumably including Lewis, who was present.

192 Jackson moved on   Ibid.

192 the charge of Eaton and Margaret spending the night together Ibid.

192 "Nor Mrs. Eaton, either"   Ibid.

192 "On that point"   Ibid.

192 "She is as chaste"   Ibid.

192 "are so public that my servants"   Louisa Catherine Adams to John Quincy Adams, September 27, 1829, Adams Papers, Massachusetts Historical Society.

192 "All this got abroad"   Ibid.

193 a "little engagement"   **Papers**, VII, 447.

193 "When you marry"   Ibid.

193 first annual message   Ibid., 776.

193 a secret diplomatic initiative   Ibid., 427.

194 a mission to Sultan Mahmud II of Turkey   John M. Belohlavek, **"Let the Eagle Soar!": The Foreign Policy of Andrew Jackson** (Lincoln, Neb., 1985), 128–50, covers Jackson's policy toward the Mediterranean world.

194 had lost Greece   Ibid., 128–29.

194 Lord Byron died   Ibid., 128.

194 Turkey needed ships   Ibid., 130.

194 had traditionally approved the appointment   Ibid., 131.

194 Biddle paid a call   **Correspondence of Nicholas Biddle**, 93–94.

194 "I do not dislike"   Ibid., 93.

194 a failed land   Remini, **Andrew Jackson and the Bank War**, 20.

194 learned to fear debt   Ibid., 18–20.

194 "great difficulty"   Ibid., 18.

195 skeptical of promissory notes   Ibid., 19.

195 He was grateful   **Correspondence of Nicholas Biddle**, 93.

195 by the anniversary   Remini, **Andrew Jackson and the Bank War**, 58.

195 "That is my own feeling"   **Correspondence of Nicholas Biddle**, 94.

195 "[Jackson] said"   Ibid.

195 "I said, well I am very much"   Ibid.

195 "Sir," said Jackson, "it would be"   Ibid. For a survey of Jackson's work on the Bank issue in the late autumn of 1829, see Remini, **Andrew Jackson and the Bank War**, 60–64. "Al-

though he toyed with several different plans at this time [late 1829], the President could not make up his mind about any one of them, acting as though he knew he had to support some form of national banking and yet could not bring himself to do it," wrote Remini. "So he vacillated. He considered one scheme, then another, and then a third, always ending where he started, not certain whether he wanted a central bank or just a government depository. Throughout the Bank War this uncertainty was repeatedly evidenced both in his letters and conversations, and it is extremely difficult at times to determine what he meant when he used the phrase 'national bank'—whether a central bank, or a multi-branched federally chartered banking operation, or simply a bank located in the District of Columbia to act as a fiscal agent of the government. Most probably he was willing to experiment with any scheme that political necessity dictated. The only alternative he totally eliminated . . . was a continuation of Biddle's Bank.

"His indecision can be seen in the variety of schemes he considered in 1829. At one point he suggested the idea of tying the BUS to the Treasury and restricting its note-issuing powers; at another, of creating a bank for deposit to serve as a government agent in the transfer of public funds; and at another, of providing a system somewhat resembling Grundy's proposal" (ibid., 60). This last is a reference to a plan of Tennessee politician Felix Grundy's that, Remini wrote, "called for the establishment of a principal bank in Philadelphia with branches in all the states. In addition, the directors of the parent bank would be elected by Congress and the directors of each branch by their Congressional delegations. The bank's capital would be established at $40 million, and the profits of each branch would be used for internal improvements within their respective states" (ibid., 59). For Grundy's letter to Jackson on the subject, see **Papers**, VII, 505–6.

195 the traditional dinner   I am indebted to **TPA**, 108–9, for the details of the evening.

196 "the most splendid"   Ibid., 109.

196 the president's "mortification"   Ibid.

196 gave another dinner   Ibid., 109–10. Van Buren asked Martha Jefferson Randolph to be the guest of honor, hoping the dowager's presence might soothe matters. It did not (ibid.).

196 an even more ambitious evening party   Ibid., 110–11. Also see Nivens, **Martin Van Buren**, 252–53.

196 A later ball given by the Russian minister   Ibid., 112–14.

197 was said to be furious   As above, for the details of this incident, see **TPA**, 112–14.

197 Jackson heard the Huygens rumors   Ibid., 113–14.

197 "Spare no expense"   EDT, I, 212.

198 The service would be in the East Room   Ibid., 212–15. I drew on Burke's account for my portrait of the occasion.

199 "Dost thou, in the name of this child"   **The Book of Common Prayer according to the Use of the Protestant Episcopal Church in the United States** (Philadelphia, 1822), 129–30.

199 "I do, sir, I renounce them all!"   EDT, I, 214.

199 "In communicating with you"   **Messages**, II, 1005.

199 thoughts and points he would jot   Parton, **Life**, III, 269.

200 136–72 in the House   "Party Divisions of the House of Representatives," http://clerk.house.gov/art_history/house_history/partyDiv.html

200 25–23 in the Senate   "Party Division in the Senate, 1789–Present," http://www.senate.gov/pagelayout/history/one_item_and_teasers/partydiv.htm

200 The document reflected   **Papers**, VII, 601–30, traces the development of the document, and includes drafts on sundry issues by Jackson and from Kendall, Van Buren, Eaton, and James A. Hamilton. The full final text can be found in **Messages**, II, 1005–25.

200 "Blessed as our country"   **Messages**, II, 1006.

201 "Our system of government"   Ibid., 1010.

201 limit the executive   Ibid., 1011.

201 **"the majority is to govern"**   Ibid., 1010.

201 the context of this assertion   Ibid., 1010–11.

202 "In a country where offices"   Ibid., 1012.

202 David Barton of Missouri   C. Perry Patterson, **Presidential Government in the United States: The Unwritten Constitution** (Chapel Hill, N.C., 1947), 73. The address was delivered on March 17, 1830.

202 feared "Executive encroachment"   Ibid.

203 a signal that Jackson wanted to reconsider   **Messages**, II, 1025.

As noted above, however, Jackson was uncertain at this point about precisely what he wanted to do about the Bank.

203 Biddle tried to make the best of things **Correspondence of Nicholas Biddle**, 94. Biddle's letter was dated January 2, 1830.

204 "I was aware that the Bank question" **Papers**, VII, 642–43.

205 the tariff, which so vexed South Carolina **Messages**, II, 1014–16.

205 as a senator, had voted in favor Feller, **Jacksonian Promise**, 67.

205 a series of twenty-four essays Prucha, ed., **Cherokee Removal**, 8.

205 "Most certainly an indelible stigma" Ibid., 49.

205 God, Evarts said Ibid., 51.

205 no answer other than removal or submission **Messages**, II, 1019–22.

205 "should be voluntary" Ibid., 1021.

206 "Our conduct toward these people" Ibid.

206 Christmas 1829 was a dim, unremarkable affair **Papers**, VII, 657–58, is a description by Lewis of the grim atmosphere of this period at the White House.

206 "in very feeble health" Ibid., 657.

207 "**confirmed dropsy**" Kenneth F. Kiple, ed., **The Cambridge Historical Dictionary of Disease** (New York, 2003), 100–5; John Walton, ed., **The Oxford Companion to Medicine** (New York, 1986), 326.

207 "Things are not as they ought to be" Amos Kendall to Francis Preston Blair, January 28, 1830, Blair and Lee Family Papers, Manuscripts Division, Department of Rare Books and Special Collections, Princeton University Library.

207 "my labors increase" **Papers**, VII, 585.

207 "I can with truth say" Ibid.

207 Speaking of the "old differences" Amos Kendall to Francis Preston Blair, January 28, 1830, Blair and Lee Family Papers, Manuscripts Division, Department of Rare Books and Special Collections, Princeton University Library.

Chapter 10: Liberty and Union, Now and Forever

208 a White House levee EDT, I, 222–24.

208 "Shaking hands" Ibid., 222–23.

208 calico "serves to show" Ibid., 223.

208 "No doubt Emily's concession" Ibid.

208 "They affected no superiority" Ibid.

209 "There is no scarcity" John Quincy Adams to Abigail Brooks Adams, January 31, 1830, Adams Papers, Massachusetts Historical Society.

209 treated Margaret even more coolly Hunt, ed., **First Forty Years of Washington Society**, 311.

209 "She is not received" Ibid.

209 "Our government is becoming" Ibid.

210 "One woman has made sad work" Ibid., 310–11.

210 a session between the president I am indebted to Marszalek's reconstruction of the meeting in **TPA**, 118. For Samuel Ingham's account, see Parton, **Life**, III, 303–7.

210 A kind of compromise **TPA**, 118–19.

210 "Any attempt" Ibid., 118.

210 "Society is [still]" Ibid., 119.

211 "Our Presses at home" Robert Y. Hayne, "Letters on the Nullification Movement in South Carolina, 1830–1834," **American Historical Review** 6 (July 1901), 738. The letter from Hayne was addressed to James Henry Hammond and was dated March 29, 1830.

211 with the added benefit Peterson, **Great Triumvirate**, 170–71, is a good summary of Benton's concerns.

211 one of the most significant Feller, **Public Lands in Jacksonian Politics**, 112–36; see also Herman Belz, ed., **Webster-Hayne Debate on the Nature of the Union: Selected Documents** (Indianapolis, 2000), ix-xv.

211 twenty-one of the nation's forty-eight senators Belz, ed., **Webster-Hayne Debate**, ix.

211 "seems to have metamorphosed" Ibid.

212 filled the two galleries Hunt, ed., **First Forty Years of Washington Society**, 309–10. See also Peterson, **Great Triumvirate**, 175.

212 a dais flanked by four gray marble columns Author's observation of Old Senate Chamber at the Capitol. See also "The Old Senate Chamber," Office of the Curator, January 1992.

212 Lewis kept tabs Parton, **Life**, III, 282.

212 Benton denounced Foot's resolution Feller, **Public Lands in Jacksonian Politics**, 112–13. See also Benton, **Thirty Years' View**, 130–33.

212 "The whole country may be"   Remini, **Daniel Webster**, 317.

212 the remark about the South   Ibid.

212 "Yankees were never in great credit"   Jervey, **Robert Y. Hayne and His Times**, 222.

213 "Viewing the United States"   Ibid., 223.

213 Webster was a floor below   Remini, **Daniel Webster**, 317–18.

213 "my court papers"   Ibid.

213 "The fruits of our labor"   Belz, ed., **Webster-Hayne Debate**, 8.

213 "Sir, I am one of those"   Ibid., 10.

214 Webster grew grim   Remini, **Daniel Webster**, 318.

214 time to "calculate the value of the Union"   Peterson, **Great Triumvirate**, 173.

214 windy winter Tuesday   Hunt, ed., **First Forty Years of Washington Society**, 309.

214 thought of Cooper's threats   Peterson, **Great Triumvirate**, 173.

214 "They significantly declare"   Belz, ed., **Webster-Hayne Debate**, 24.

215 "I am a Unionist"   Ibid.

215 Hayne replied to Webster   Ibid., 35–79. Hayne was not terse.

215 there were reports that the vice president   Wiltse, **John C. Calhoun**, II, 60. (Wiltse writes that he doubts this actually happened.)

215 Hayne "was deficient"   Samuel M. Smucker, **The Life, Speeches and Memorials of Daniel Webster** (Chicago and New York, 1859), 70.

215 "His dark and deeply-set eyes"   Ibid., 86.

216 "It is a kind of moral"   Hunt, ed., **First Forty Years of Washington Society**, 310.

216 dressed in a Revolutionary blue coat   Smucker, **Life, Speeches and Memorials of Daniel Webster**, 86. In Smucker's telling, on the morning of what was to become known as Webster's Second Reply to Hayne, "the House of Representatives was deserted. Nearly all the members hastened to the Senate-chamber. . . . The place itself was illustrious and solemn; for it was the central spot of the whole earth for high and grave discussion in reference to human freedom; and it had been hallowed by the labors and the eloquence of the fathers and heroes of the Republic" (ibid., 85).

216 He stood to Calhoun's left   The United States Senate Historical Office; I am grateful to Donald A. Ritchie, associate historian, for showing me Webster's desk.

216 a glorious Rembrandt Peale portrait   Author's observation, the Old Senate Chamber.

216 "I have not allowed myself"   Belz, ed., **Webster-Hayne Debate**, 143–44.

217 shocked silence   Remini, **Daniel Webster**, 329.

217 "Mr. Webster," a colleague said   Ibid.

218 Hayne disagreed   Ibid.

218 That night at the White House   Ibid., 332–33.

218 usual Wednesday levee   Marquis James, **Andrew Jackson: Portrait of a President** (Indianapolis, 1937), 128.

218 wasted no time   Remini, **Daniel Webster**, 332–33.

218 "I felt as if everything"   Ibid., 329.

218 "Been to the Capitol, Major?"   Parton, **Life**, III, 282.

219 Webster's achievement   Peterson, **Great Triumvirate**, 179–80, is particularly good on this. Paul C. Nagel, **One Nation Indivisible: The Union in American Thought, 1776–1861** (Westport, Conn., 1980), is also a wonderfully illuminating study of these issues.

220 in some ways invented   Peterson, **Great Triumvirate**, 179–80. See also Remini, **Daniel Webster**, 328–31.

220 offered to die for a nation   Belz, ed., **Webster-Hayne Debate**, 331.

220 "Sir . . . should the cupidity"   Ibid.

221 paid a call on Adams   **Memoirs of JQA**, VIII, 210.

222 a brother of Robert Livingston   Charles Haven Hunt, **Life of Edward Livingston** (New York, 1864).

222 Livingston had known misfortune   Belz, ed., **Webster-Hayne Debate**, 408. See also Hunt, **Life of Edward Livingston**, 20.

222 pressed into the arena by his wife   See, for instance, Louise Livingston to Edward Livingston, December 23, 1828, Edward Livingston Papers, Manuscripts Division, Department of Rare Books and Special Collections, Princeton University Library.

222 among the first . . . to raise the prospect   Hunt, **Life of Edward Livingston**, 312.

223 multiplicity of issues   Belz, ed., **Webster-Hayne Debate**, 409.

223 "Sir . . . might not a hearer"   Ibid., 410.

223 "For my own part"   Ibid.

224 "the necessary and . . . the legitimate parties"   Ibid., 431.

224 "The spirit of which I speak"   Ibid., 431–32.

224 "excess of party rage" Ibid., 433.

225 "I am no censor" Ibid.

225 "There is too much at stake" **Messages**, II, 1515.

226 "We undoubtedly think" Belz, ed., **Webster-Hayne Debate**, 433–34.

226 "There are legitimate" Hunt, **Life of Edward Livingston**, 349–50.

Chapter 11: General Jackson Rules by His Personal Popularity

227 Green published a piece in the **Telegraph** Parton, **Life**, III, 284.

227 a dinner to take place Ibid., 282–84. For accounts of the evening, its background, and its implications, see also Benton, **Thirty Years' View**, 148–49; **AMVB**, 413–17; Remini, **Jackson**, II, 233–37.

227 Indian Queen Hotel Remini, **Jackson**, II, 234.

227 "a **nullification affair altogether**" Parton, **Life**, III, 284. The traditional view of the evening as a plot of Calhoun's is challenged in Richard R. Stenberg, "The Jefferson Birthday Dinner, 1830," **Journal of Southern History** 4 (August 1938), 334–45.

227 The dinner, Webster told Clay **PHC**, VIII, 193.

227 wrote out three different toasts Parton, **Life**, III, 284.

227 going through the newspapers Ibid.

227 "He said he preferred" Ibid.

228 "glorious stand" **AMVB**, 414.

228 climbed atop Ibid., 415.

228 "Our Union—it must be preserved" Ibid.

228 "The Union—next to our liberty the most dear" Ibid., 416.

228 "Mutual forbearance" Ibid.

228 "the bustle and excitement" Ibid., 415.

229 might add the word "Federal" Ibid.

229 as the **National Intelligencer** put it Ibid., 416–17.

229 "That Jackson will be" **Memoirs of JQA**, VIII, 210.

230 "I seriously apprehend a civil war" William Crawford to Martin Van Buren, May 31, 1830, Martin Van Buren Papers, LOC. Another letter to Van Buren, written in late May 1830, further

illustrates the South's contentious views on the tariff. "Fortunately for South Carolina and for the whole South, she stands in such a situation with so much right upon her side and so much wrong to complain of, that she has no occasion to bully or bluster and has little to do but stand on her sovereignty and say to the Genl. Govt. 'thus far shalt thou go and no further . . .' " wrote James Hamilton, Jr., from Charleston (James Hamilton, Jr., to Martin Van Buren, May 1830, Martin Van Buren Papers, LOC).

230 Emily's father died   **EDT**, I, 229–30.

230 been sick for three months   Ibid.

231 congressmen "brought forward"   **AMVB**, 320.

232 funding for a sixty-mile Maysville Road   Feller, **Public Lands in Jacksonian Politics**, 136–42. See also **AMVB**, 314–38, for Van Buren's account of the administration's approach to internal improvements; and Parton, **Life**, III, 285–87.

232 while they were on horseback   **AMVB**, 321.

232 "The road was in Mr. Clay's own state"   Ibid., 320–22.

232 Johnson found Jackson and Van Buren alone   Ibid., 323–25. Van Buren's vivid recollection of the scene perhaps overemphasizes the degree to which the veto was a financial calculation—Jackson's memorandum stresses his concern for jurisdiction over projects—but it seems accurate in its passion.

233 "General! If this hand"   Ibid., 324.

233 memorandum on the veto   **Correspondence**, IV, 139.

233 "I stand committed"   **AMVB**, 324.

234 Jackson vetoed the bill and three others   Latner, **Presidency of Andrew Jackson**, 137–38, and Wilentz, **Rise of American Democracy**, 327–28. Explaining the nuances of the veto, Wilentz wrote: "In the spirit of Jeffersonian strict construction—but also displaying his propensity to placate the South, especially after the rancor over the tariff in 1828—Van Buren urged a veto. Extravagant federal spending on improvements, he reasoned, would turn elections into corrupt appeals to the voters' narrow self-interest, while opening up new opportunities for congressional logrolling at the public's expense. Jackson, who had been thinking along similar lines, decided to reject not just the Maysville project but a slew of other federal improvement bills. Yet in his Maysville veto message—written chiefly by Van Buren with the help of a young Tennessee congressman, James K.

Polk—Jackson also defended the benefits of a 'general system of improvement,' praised state road and canal projects, and supported judicious federal spending on projects of clearly national importance. Having bolstered his Old Republican southern supporters, some of whom were leaning dangerously toward Calhoun's more extreme states' rights views, the president, his political circumstances precarious, made clear that he did not oppose all government-aided economic development. He would adhere to that position fairly consistently for the rest of his presidency" (ibid., 328). See also Cole, **Presidency of Andrew Jackson**, 62–67.

234 "much, and, I may add" **Messages**, II, 1054.

234 "What is properly **national**" Ibid.

235 by the end of his second term Ellis, **Union at Risk**, 24.

235 Noting that "many of the taxes" **Messages**, II, 1052.

235 "have been cheerfully borne" Ibid.

236 "The veto message" Feller, **Public Lands in Jacksonian Politics**, 139.

236 vetoed a total of nine bills Patterson, **Presidential Government in the United States**, 50–56. Jackson, **Presidential Vetoes**, 15–27, is an excellent discussion of the internal improvement vetoes. See also Edward S. Corwin, **The President: Office and Powers, 1787–1984** (New York, 1984), 317–25; Wilson, **Division and Reunion**, 50; and Goldsmith, **Growth of Presidential Power**, 329–46; Goldsmith writes: "It would seem that Andrew Jackson's sure instinct for power dictated an early and dramatic action at the beginning of his administration in order to assert his own authority and to demonstrate that the presidency was a position of leadership as well as a vehicle for administering the will of the legislature. However, the President, under the Constitution, was given a voice in the legislative process, and Jackson (with Van Buren's approval) was anxious to assert this policymaking role and to put both the Congress and the country on warning that the age and feeble health of the old general would in no way restrict his vigorous pursuit of what he considered were the responsibilities of the President of the United States. Formal constitutional arguments were offered in the veto message, but the intent was political and the objective was the assertion of Jackson's poli-

cies—a sign which marked the beginning of a new and dynamic chapter in the growth of presidential power" (ibid., 345). See also Henry James Ford, **Rise and Growth of American Politics: A Sketch of Constitutional Development** (New York, 1898), 175–87.

236 "From motives of respect to the legislature" Patterson, **Presidential Government in the United States**, 50.

236 Watching Jackson veto Maysville **Memoirs of JQA**, VIII, 230–31.

237 "Jackson was the first President" Patterson, **Presidential Government in the United States**, 51. Patterson also quotes Levi Woodbury, the Jackson-Van Buren Cabinet secretary who became a justice of the Supreme Court, saying: "The veto power is the people's tribunative prerogative speaking again through their executive" (ibid., 52).

237 had "asserted that the veto" Ibid., 51.

238 occasionally asked for "something I can veto" Richard E. Neustadt, **Presidential Power: The Politics of Leadership** (New York, 1960), 84.

238 "We are all shocked" Remini, **Henry Clay**, 362.

238 could back a constitutional amendment Ibid.

238 "We shall be contending" Ibid.

238 "The veto, I find, will work well" **Correspondence**, IV, 156. Jackson wrote en route to Tennessee after the veto was announced.

238 "The Great Arbiter of Nations" Prucha, **Cherokee Removal**, 51.

239 "The people" Ibid.

239 formally entitled "The Bill for an Exchange of Lands" For accounts of the politics of, and the maneuvering over, the removal bill, see Cole, **Presidency of Andrew Jackson**, 67–74; Parton, **Life**, III, 279–80; Prucha, ed., **Cherokee Removal**, 5–28; Satz, **American Indian Policy in the Jacksonian Era**, 19–56; Satz, "Rhetoric Versus Reality: The Indian Policy of Andrew Jackson" in **Cherokee Removal, Before and After**, ed. William L. Anderson, 29–55; and Wallace, **Long, Bitter Trail**, 65–70.

239 reported out of the Indian Affairs Committee Cole, **Presidency of Andrew Jackson**, 71.

239 Jackson believed the treaties irrelevant   Prucha, **Great Father,** 192.

239 "the poor Indians"   Frelinghuysen, **Speech of Mr. Frelinghuysen, of New Jersey, Delivered in the Senate of the United States, April 6, 1830, on the Bill for an Exchange of Lands with the Indians Residing in Any of the States or Territories, and for Their Removal West of the Mississippi,** 27.

240 "Mr. President, if we abandon"   Ibid., 28.

240 created a "Quaker panic" in Pennsylvania   Cole, **Presidency of Andrew Jackson,** 72.

240 "without the slightest consultation"   Frelinghuysen, **Speech of Mr. Frelinghuysen, of New Jersey, Delivered in the Senate of the United States, April 6, 1830, on the Bill for an Exchange of Lands with the Indians Residing in Any of the States or Territories, and for Their Removal West of the Mississippi,** 5.

240 Georgia, Tennessee, Alabama, and Mississippi   Ibid., 17.

241 to be known as "the Democracy"   Wilentz, **Andrew Jackson,** 103.

241 "General Jackson rules by his personal popularity"   **Memoirs of JQA,** VIII, 215.

241 complained of "the spirit of party"   Prucha, ed., **Cherokee Removal,** 24–25.

241 a Jacksonian congressman from Alabama   Ibid., 25.

241 "Now what can we do"   Ibid.

242 the bill passing 28 to 19   Cole, **Presidency of Andrew Jackson,** 72.

242 Wilson Lumpkin of Georgia   Ibid.

242 attacking his people as "atheists"   Ibid.

243 "the treaties of this Government"   **Register of Debates in Congress,** 21st Congress, First Session, VI, 1830, 997.

243 had "shocked the public feeling"   Ibid., 998.

243 "was to be a government"   Ibid., 1000.

243 "The eye of other nations"   Ibid., 1015.

244 After much back-and-forth   Cole, **Presidency of Andrew Jackson,** 73–74.

245 Shortly before four o'clock   Margaret's letter to Jackson in reply to the invitation her husband brought home was written at four p.m. **EDT,** I, 231.

245 "Circumstances, my dear General" **Correspondence**, IV, 145.

246 "I ask to say to you" Ibid.

246 "I have spoken" Ibid.

247 Jackson gave Andrew the letter Ibid., 195.

247 "You have not forgotten the note" Ibid.

247 a passionate note for the president's files Ibid., 145.

248 would leave for Tennessee **EDT**, I, 233.

249 "embarrassments that yet attend us" Ibid., 234.

249 "The Secretary of War and family" Ibid.

249 Jackson admitted that "there has been" **Correspondence**, IV, 146.

249 "very popular" Ibid., 161.

249 insisted on going to the Mansion Ibid., 194–95.

249 he had "expected you and Emily" Ibid.

250 a formidable element of Nashville society **Correspondence**, IV, 173.

250 "a combination" refused **Correspondence**, IV, 164.

250 Emily and Andrew's "folly and pride" Ibid., 165.

250 "My duty is that my household" Ibid.

250 "My connections have acted very strangely" Ibid., 165.

251 "affairs [are] so bad" Ibid.

251 a large barbecue in the Eatons' honor **Correspondence**, IV, 167.

251 At 3:30 on the afternoon Ibid.

251 a crowd of five hundred Ibid.

251 Jackson was delighted "to shake hands" Ibid.

251 "The ladies of the place" Ibid.

252 "That my Nephew and Niece" Ibid.

252 A letter from Rebecca Branch **EDT**, I, 237.

252 the bargain was struck Ibid., 240–41.

252 "General Coffee has" **Correspondence**, IV, 168.

253 Emily changed her mind **EDT**, I, 241.

254 "I shall have no female family" **Correspondence**, IV, 170.

254 "Whether Mr. Donelson will or will not" Ibid.

254 only the Chickasaws actually came James, **TLOAJ**, 550–51.

255 Helped along by bribes Wallace, **Long, Bitter Trail**, 76–77.

255 the Treaty of Dancing Rabbit Creek Prucha, **Great Father**, 216–18.

255 ratified the exchange Ibid., 215.

255 "Our doom is sealed"   Ibid., 218.

256 it fell to the French writer Alexis de Tocqueville   Ibid.

256 the first of two critical cases   Norgren, **Cherokee Cases**, 98–111, is an excellent account of the litigation, its background, and its implications.

257 better described as "**domestic dependent** nations"   Ibid., 101.

257 the government had long acted   Ibid. Norgren wrote: "In spite of the dozens of international treaties agreed on by the United States and various Indian nations, Marshall concluded that the Cherokee did not constitute a foreign nation." It was, Norgren argued, a "procedural sleight of hand" (100–1).

257 declining to take a stand   Ibid. For more sympathetic accounts of Marshall's work in **Cherokee Nation v. Georgia**, see Smith, **John Marshall: Definer of a Nation**, 516–17; and R. Kent Newmyer, **John Marshall and the Heroic Age of the Supreme Court** (Baton Rouge, La., 2001), 446–51.

257 by hanging an Indian convicted of murder   Ibid., 95–98.

257 "a proper case, with proper parties"   Newmyer, **John Marshall and the Heroic Age of the Supreme Court**, 450. This helped open the way for **Worcester v. Georgia** the next year, a case treated more fully below.

257 The Cherokee Nation would be back   Norgren, **Cherokee Cases**, 112–33, details the second case.

257 "If it be true"   Ibid., 104. Politics was a factor among several in Marshall's thinking, and Jackson clearly saw the struggle over Indian removal as more of a political than a legal issue. He knew, for instance, that his enemies saw an opening to make a humanitarian case. "I have now a clue to all the maneuvers and secret plans . . . to produce opposition to my measures, and particularly to the bill for the removal of the Indians," Jackson said (**Correspondence**, IV, 269).

258 "No ladies will return with me"   **Correspondence**, IV, 173.

258 rode in his carriage from the Hermitage   **EDT**, I, 241.

258 Emily wept   Ibid., 241–42.

258 "Uncle's last words to me"   Emily Donelson to Andrew Jackson Donelson, October 15, 1830, Gertrude and Benjamin Caldwell Collection, The Hermitage.

259 their horses   **Correspondence**, IV, 181.

259 late one night at Knoxville   **EDT**, I, 242.

259 "We travel at the rate" Ibid.
259 "business has greatly accumulated" **Correspondence**, IV, 181.

Chapter 12: I Have Been Left to Sup Alone

263 took her first steps **EDT**, I, 254.
263 cross-examined his mother Ibid., 243.
263 "Jackson talks a great deal" Ibid.
263 late on an October Sunday evening **Correspondence**, IV, 186–88. The letter was dated October 24, 1830.
263 "Major Donelson has informed you" Ibid., 186.
264 "I have often experienced" Ibid., 186–87.
265 Privately Calhoun believed nullification **PJCC**, XI, 415. Wiltse, **John C. Calhoun**, II, 86–89, offers a sympathetic view of Calhoun's position, but it is difficult to reconcile Calhoun's advocacy of the doctrine and his interest in the preservation of slavery with his oft-stated desire to avoid disunion. "He realized that it was not the tariff but slavery that was at stake," Wiltse wrote of Calhoun in the 1830 period. "He saw the South as a permanent minority and knew that her only safety lay in her own ability to resist exploitation at the hands of the more populous sections of the Union. If their individual sovereignties could be preserved, the slave states could protect themselves. If the partisan majority in control of the general government were allowed to wield sovereign powers, then the South could continue to exist only on the sufferance of the stronger interest." And yet he continued to insist that he completely opposed what he called "civil discord, revolution, or disunion." The implication is that he somehow believed that if the South lost the fight for nullification, and thus lost slavery (which is Wiltse's logic), then the South would peaceably submit to living in a nation in which it would be, as Wiltse put it, at "the sufferance of the stronger interest." It seems safest to say that Calhoun's reluctance to acknowledge the full implications of his doctrine—that nullification was a step toward possible disunion—was based on his national political ambitions. At this juncture being president of the United States still held enormous appeal, much more appeal, for instance, than being president of a breakaway

Carolinian republic, or even a larger Southern confederacy (Wiltse, **John C. Calhoun**, II, 88–89).

265 "I had supposed"   **Correspondence**, IV, 191.

266 proving central in a congressional race   EDT, I, 243–44; **TPA**, 146–48; Satterfield, **Andrew Jackson Donelson**, 29. Each account reports the accusations slightly differently, with Emily Donelson's letter, unsurprisingly, dwelling on the offense to her family.

266 saying that Jackson had asked   EDT, I, 244.

266 a crowd of about six hundred people   Ibid.

266 "informed the people"   Ibid.

267 Jackson, she wrote Andrew, "may have used"   Emily Donelson to Andrew Jackson Donelson, October 15, 1830, Gertrude and Benjamin Caldwell Collection, The Hermitage.

267 "My Dear husband"   Ibid.

267 "I had the great pleasure"   Ibid.

268 "I was thinking of you"   Ibid.

268 "Is Major L[ewis] still at the President's house?"   Ibid.

268 "Mary Lewis is here"   EDT, I, 245.

269 young Jackson "sometimes"   Ibid., 243.

269 In South Carolina in these October weeks   Freehling, **Prelude to Civil War**, 212–18.

269 not enough votes in the legislature   Ibid., 218.

269 "I have always looked"   Freehling, ed., **Nullification Era**, 100.

269 passed six resolutions related to nullification   Boucher, **Nullification Controversy**, 104–7.

270 Monday morning, October 25, 1830   **Correspondence**, IV, 189.

270 of "intimations" from the Eaton camp   Ibid.

271 "You have decided the question"   Ibid., 192.

271 nor a familiar face across the way   Ibid.

271 plagued by headaches   Ibid.

271 Jackson replied on Saturday, October 30   Ibid., 193–94.

272 "my dear Andrew"   Ibid., 194.

272 asked Andrew to remain   Ibid.

272 then they would part   Ibid.

272 he wrote again in the autumn dusk   Ibid., 195–96. We can fix the hour of composition from a detail in an ensuing letter. Writ-

ing of this particular note the next day, Donelson said: "What I wrote yesterday evening was done by twilight . . ." (ibid., 197).

272 "In your house" Ibid., 195.

272 linking the present question with the first great test Ibid.

272 It was almost midnight Ibid., 196. This note of Jackson's is dated "11 o'clock p.m."

272 "My dear Andrew, for so I must still call you" Ibid.

273 "You were my family, my chosen family" Ibid.

273 Andrew saw he had been imprecise **Correspondence**, IV, 196–97.

273 Power and affection were at stake Here is just one example. This is the paragraph Jackson wrote after telling Donelson he should leave after Congress adjourned: "I have found for upwards of a year that you appeared to be estranged from me, and entirely taken up with strangers, but what I most regretted was your constant melancholy, and abstraction from me, which under my bereavements made my tears to flow often. I pray you cheer up, my tears are dried. When you leave, whatever cause I have to regret or complain, you will carry my friendship with you, and my prayers for your happiness, and that of your amiable family . . . [the] two little cherubs, Jackson and Rachel, who I can never cease to love" (ibid., 194).

273 "evidence of hostility to me" Ibid., 202.

273 who wrote to reassure him that all would be well **EDT**, I, 254.

274 "Still, I think you" Ibid.

274 Emily went a step further Ibid., 260.

274 "I would be willing" Ibid.

275 briefly noted in his diary **Memoirs of JQA**, VIII, 245.

275 on a cold September morning Nagel, **John Quincy Adams**, 335.

275 "not the slightest desire" **Memoirs of JQA**, VIII, 240.

275 Louisa . . . had even threatened Nagel, **John Quincy Adams**, 335.

275 hours of reflection **Memoirs of JQA**, VIII, 245.

275 relief from his trials Ibid., 246–47.

275 "My return to public life" Ibid., 246.

275 "the faithless wave of politics" Ibid., 243.

276 "My election as President" Ibid., 247.

276 the founding editor of a new administration newspaper   Parton, **Life**, III, 333–39, covers the founding of the **Globe**. See also **FPB**, 45–61, and Culver H. Smith, **The Press, Politics, and Patronage: The American Government's Use of Newspapers, 1789–1875** (Athens, Ga., 1977), 119–35. Jeffrey L. Pasley, **"The Tyranny of Printers": Newspaper Politics in the Early American Republic** (Charlottesville, Va., 2001), 390–99, is a good account of the Jacksonian newspaper world. As Pasley wrote: "Andrew Jackson's presidency marked a major turning point in the history of newspaper politics. Understanding exactly the role that newspaper editors played in his campaigns, Jackson amply expressed his gratitude to the network of editors that supported him, not only by doling out printing contracts but also by appointing at least seventy editors to federal offices and allowing several key editors to play crucial roles in his administration" (ibid., 390).

276 had run his newspaper   Cole, **A Jackson Man**, 59.

276 with the help of Blair   Ibid., 72.

276 what Jackson called "the true faith"   **Correspondence**, IV, 212. The context was Jackson's urging John Coffee to subscribe to the new paper in a letter dated December 6, 1830.

276 Kendall was a critical figure   Harriet Martineau, **Retrospect of Western Travel** (Armonk, N.Y., 2000), 52–54. This edition of Martineau's work was edited by Daniel Feller; I highly recommend his fine introduction.

276 "I was fortunate enough"   Ibid., 54.

277 Born in Virginia in 1791   **FPB**, 3.

277 converted to Jacksonian politics   Ibid., 25.

277 "I wish you to stand just as I do"   Amos Kendall to Francis Preston Blair, October 2, 1830, Blair and Lee Family Papers, Manuscripts Division, Department of Rare Books and Special Collections, Princeton University Library.

277 With Kendall doing the wooing   The history of the founding of the paper became a source of controversy later on when Kendall and Blair got into a dispute. See Smith, **The Press, Politics, and Patronage**, 122–26.

278 "Now, I want you to prepare"   Amos Kendall to Francis Preston Blair, August 22, 1830, Blair and Lee Family Papers, Man-

uscripts Division, Department of Rare Books and Special Collections, Princeton University Library.

278 "about five feet ten inches high" Smith, **The Francis Preston Blair Family in Politics**, I, 62.

279 The journey from Kentucky FPB, 42–43.

279 Lewis took one look at him Parton, **Life**, III, 337.

279 Blair was swept away by Jackson's charm Ibid., 337–38.

279 Invited that very first night Ibid.

279 "abashed and miserable" Ibid., 338.

279 took Blair by the arm Ibid.

279 Francis Preston Blair would now fight any battle FPB, 46, makes a similar point: "On this note began Blair's undying love for Andrew Jackson."

279 Andrew Donelson was to take the president's annual message Parton, **Life**, III, 339. Donelson was an early topic of conversation between Blair and Jackson. "There's my nephew, Donelson," Jackson told Blair. "He seems to be leaning toward the nullifiers." Such a charge was unfair to Andrew, who was dedicated to Jackson and to Jackson's philosophy, if not, obviously, to all of Jackson's appointees and social demands. If Jackson truly believed Andrew to be a nullifier, or even a serious sympathizer with the Southern cause, he would have banished Andrew long, long before, for then Andrew would have been a traitor to the country, not just a serial inconvenience. The rest of the conversation with Blair rings more true, including a warning to watch Andrew with care. "I raised him. I love him. Let him do what he will, I love him. I can't help it. Treat him kindly, but if he wants to write for your paper, you must look out for him." It is also possible that Lewis, a rival of Donelson's, was the source of the anecdote for Parton; Lewis clearly gave Parton other details about the evening (ibid., 337).

279 writing editorials after nightfall in lead pencil FPB, 63.

280 he attacked nullification **Messages**, II, 1079–80. It was subtle but unmistakable: "It is beyond the power of man to make a system of government like ours or any other operate with precise equality upon states situated like those which compose this Confederacy; nor is inequality always injustice" (ibid.). Jackson addressed extreme feelings in his discussion of conflicting interests between states and regions in which he sounded notes

similar to those struck by Edward Livingston earlier in the year and echoed Van Buren's toast at the Jefferson birthday dinner. His critics saw it differently. "There are avowals in [the message] that would drive a king of France from his throne and that would undoubtedly have cost John Quincy Adams an impeachment," Richard Rush of Pennsylvania wrote Henry Clay (**PHC**, VIII, 315).

280 "It is an infirmity of our nature"   Ibid., 1086–87.

281 told the readers of the **Globe**   FPB, 60.

281 attractive to "certain men, who, like Caesar"   Ibid.

281 passed the holiday "soberly yet agreeably"   **EDT**, I, 264.

281 Donelson excused himself   Ibid., 265.

281 quoting a poem   Ibid., 266.

282 had lost a great deal of weight   Ibid., 270.

282 "like a spectre"   Ibid.

282 scolded Andrew   Ibid.

282 "Although your letters"   Ibid.

282 "Although we have been visited"   **Correspondence**, IV, 226–27.

283 "is an old man of 66 years"   George Wilson Pierson, **Tocqueville and Beaumont in America** (New York, 1938), 663. The letter is dated January 20, 1831. Beaumont was more impressed with the secretary of state. Of an evening spent at the Livingstons', he reported: "I mingled my square dances and waltzes with most interesting conversations with Mr. Livingston on the penitentiary system and especially on capital punishment, passing thus from the serious to the pleasant. . . . It's absolutely a European salon, and the reason is simple: all the members of the diplomatic corps gathered in Washington set the tone; French is the common language, and you would believe yourself in a Paris Salon" (ibid., 665). The letter was dated January 22, 1831.

283 "People in France"   Ibid., 663.

283 In early 1831 the **Globe** announced   Remini, **Jackson**, II, 304–5.

283 "The conquering Hero"   Wiltse, **John C. Calhoun**, II, 93.

284 At the time, Adams   Remini, **The Life of Andrew Jackson**, 124.

284 Jackson, who had been aware   **Papers**, VI, 461–63.

284 "I should be blind not to see"   PJCC, XI, 173–91, is the full

text of Calhoun's reply to Jackson. The "I should be blind" quotation is on page 189.

285 "He is aspiring" **Correspondence**, IV, 151.

285 Jackson feigned surprise and outrage Remini, **Jackson**, II, 306–11, is good on the intrigue surrounding the publication of the Seminole correspondence.

285 "a conspiracy for my destruction" Wiltse, **John C. Calhoun**, II, 95.

285 "The Globe you will have seen" Samuel D. Ingham to Samuel McKean, February 25, 1831, Samuel D. Ingham Papers, Rare Books and Manuscripts Library, University of Pennsylvania.

285 "came out pell mell" Samuel D. Ingham to George Wolf, February 27, 1831, Samuel D. Ingham Papers, Rare Books and Manuscripts Library, University of Pennsylvania.

286 "A man who could secretly" **Correspondence**, IV, 216.

286 went to Meridian Hill to see John Quincy Adams **Memoirs of JQA**, VIII, 331–32.

286 spent two hours talking politics Ibid., 332–33.

287 dispatched Andrew on Tuesday, March 8 **EDT**, I, 281.

287 "The adjournment of Congress" Ibid., 280.

287 "As much as I desire you" Ibid., 282.

287 "Recent information from the General" Ibid., 283.

288 "this disgusting petticoat business" Samuel D. Ingham to Samuel McKean, February 25, 1831, Samuel D. Ingham Papers, Rare Books and Manuscripts Library, University of Pennsylvania.

288 worried about "the plots, intrigues and calumnies" **AMVB**, 402.

288 he settled on a plan My account of Van Buren's role in the Cabinet dissolution is drawn from **AMVB**, 402–8.

288 a thunderstorm drove them Ibid., 402.

289 "You have possibly saved" Ibid., 403.

289 "We should soon have peace in Israel" Ibid.

289 "the course I had pointed to" Ibid., 404–5.

290 Van Buren jumped up Ibid., 405–6.

291 "Why should you resign?" Ibid., 406.

291 "it was forthwith agreed" Ibid., 407.

291 "The long agony is nearly over" Royce McCrary, "'The Long

Agony is Nearly Over': Samuel D. Ingham Reports on the Dissolution of Andrew Jackson's First Cabinet," **Pennsylvania Magazine of History and Biography**, 100 (April 1976), 235.

291 Jackson forced him, Berrien, and Branch to resign as well   **Correspondence**, IV, 260–79, covers much of the ensuing action. See also Parton, **Life**, III, 346–59.

292 For all to resign, he told Ingham   John Berrien to Samuel D. Ingham, April 24, 1831, Samuel D. Ingham Papers, Rare Books and Manuscripts Library, University of Pennsylvania.

292 "to make up"   Samuel D. Ingham to Samuel McKean, May 27, 1831, Samuel D. Ingham Papers, Rare Books and Manuscripts Library, University of Pennsylvania.

292 "You must read Tacitus"   John Quincy Adams to Charles Francis Adams, February 26, 1831, Adams Papers, Massachusetts Historical Society.

292 "You are disgusted"   John Quincy Adams to Charles Francis Adams, March 9, 1831, Adams Papers, Massachusetts Historical Society.

293 "The President parts"   Thomas H. Clay, "Two Years with Old Hickory," **Atlantic Monthly** 60 (August 1887), 193.

294 "My labours have been incessant"   **Correspondence**, IV, 265.

294 telling Emily that he thought   **EDT**, I, 287.

294 news of the Cabinet resignations broke in the **Globe**   Remini, **Jackson**, II, 315.

294 Vaughan . . . wrote Viscount Palmerston . . . that "this day"   Charles Vaughan to Viscount Palmerston, April 20, 1831, National Archives of the United Kingdom, Kew.

294 Vaughan told London to watch the South   Ibid.

295 The Cabinet news   Bangeman Huygens to Verstolk van Soelen (minister of foreign affairs), May 13, 1831, Ministerie van Buitenlandse Zaken 1813–1896, Nationaal Archief, Den Haag.

295 "He was near"   Bangeman Huygens to Verstolk van Soelen (minister of foreign affairs), May 13, 1831, Ministerie van Buitenlandse Zaken 1813–1896, Nationaal Archief, Den Haag.

295 "false" and "unnatural"   Ibid.

295 "to entirely remake"   Ibid.

295 "In truth, the only excuse"   Hunt, ed., **First Forty Years of Washington Society**, 318–19.

295 the "explosion at Washington" John Quincy Adams to Charles Francis Adams, April 22, 1831, Adams Papers, Massachusetts Historical Society.

295 "people stare—and laugh" Ibid.

Chapter 13: A Mean and Scurvy Piece of Business

296 what he called "secretes" See, for example, **Correspondence,** V, 206.

296 "I know not how things are moving" Alexander Speer to Joel Poinsett, March 14, 1831, Joel Poinsett Papers, Historical Society of Pennsylvania.

296 "I will not be at all surprised" Ibid.

296 he thought his information sound Ibid.

297 allegations that "Jackson had turned you" George Wolf to Samuel D. Ingham, May 23, 1831, Samuel D. Ingham Papers, Rare Books and Manuscripts Library, University of Pennsylvania.

297 "His administration is absolutely odious" **PHC,** VIII, 230.

298 Louisa Adams called the battles within Louisa Catherine Adams to Charles Francis Adams, February, 21, 1831, Adams Papers, Massachusetts Historical Society.

298 "the Jackson party is a good deal" John McLean to Samuel D. Ingham, May 7, 1831, Samuel D. Ingham Papers, Rare Books and Manuscripts Library, University of Pennsylvania.

298 "The administration at Washington cannot recover" Hayne, "Letters on the Nullification Movement in South Carolina," 745.

298 Duff Green . . . told the Eaton story **TPA,** 170.

299 Eaton issued a challenge Ibid., 170–71.

299 to "know of you, whether or not you sanction" John Eaton to Samuel Ingham, June 17, 1831, Samuel D. Ingham Papers, Rare Book and Manuscript Library, University of Pennsylvania.

299 three days of incendiary correspondence and confrontation Parton, **Life,** III, 364–68; see also Remini, **Jackson,** II, 320–21, and **Memoirs of JQA,** VIII, 371–75.

299 Ingham would not dignify Samuel D. Ingham to John H. Eaton, June 18, 1831, Samuel D. Ingham Papers, Rare Books and Manuscripts Library, University of Pennsylvania.

299   "In the meantime"   Ibid.

299   called Ingham's note "impudent and insolent"   Heiskell, **AJETH**, III, 338.

299   a brother-in-law of Eaton's, Dr. Philip G. Randolph   Ibid.

299   "a threat of personal violence"   Ibid.

300   Eaton went nearly mad   Ibid.

300   searched the city for Ingham   **Correspondence**, IV, 300–1; see also Parton, **Life**, III, 366–67.

300   "lying in wait"   **Correspondence**, IV, 300.

300   took up positions at the Treasury and in a grocery store   Ibid. IV, 300.

300   "While prowling about"   Duff Green to William Cabell Rives, June 21, 1831, Duff Green Papers, LOC.

301   what Green called "the firmness of the old gentleman"   Ibid.

301   back on the march   **Correspondence**, IV, 300.

301   Beseeching Jackson to intervene   Ibid.

301   fled the city at four o'clock in the morning   Ibid., 301.

301   Jackson dismissed Ingham's story   Ibid.

302   "The truth is Eaton alone did look for him"   Ibid., 302.

302   It was Ingham's guard   Ibid.

302   the Ingham forces "had determined"   Ibid.

302   sought security at home in Bucks County   TPA, 173.

302   Jackson left for the Rip Raps   **Correspondence**, IV, 302–3.

302   "acted a most ridiculous"   PHC, VIII, 373.

302   "Eaton still remains in the city"   Duff Green to Samuel D. Ingham, July 4, 1831, Samuel D. Ingham Papers, Rare Books and Manuscripts Library, University of Pennsylvania.

303   In New York City that April 1831   Ammon, **James Monroe**, 571.

303   at Prince and Marion streets   George Morgan, **The Life of James Monroe** (Boston, 1921), 439.

303   her father had come to live   Ibid.

303   a boy who was in and out   Ibid., 440.

303   "the recent quasi revolution"   **Memoirs of JQA**, VIII, 360.

304   "If other revolutions partake of the sublime"   John Quincy Adams to Benjamin Waterhouse, May 11, 1831, Adams Papers, Massachusetts Historical Society.

304   on a day "long enough"   AMVB, 407–8.

304   "Our reception"   Ibid.

304 "It is strange"   Ibid.

305 "Nothing now is more probable"   PHC, VIII, 366.

305 the people "know but a small part"   Samuel D. Ingham to John Workman, July 8, 1831, Samuel D. Ingham Papers, Rare Book and Manuscript Library, University of Pennsylvania.

305 rose early on the morning   Hayne, "Letters on the Nullification Movement in South Carolina," 741.

305 Hammond's long account   Ibid., 741–45.

305 Calhoun "immediately entered"   Ibid., 742.

305 "as jealous of his military fame"   Ibid.

306 "to throw himself entirely upon the South"   Ibid., 744.

306 two subsequent encounters   Ibid.

306 "there is a listlessness about him"   Ibid., 745.

306 George McDuffie laid out his popular   Freehling, ed., **Nullification Era**, 104–19.

306 if inaccurate   Freehling, **Prelude to Civil War**, 192–96, analyzes the economics and politics of McDuffie's forty-bale theory.

306 "I will readily concede"   Freehling, ed., **Nullification Era**, 116.

306 "The Union, such as"   Ibid., 118.

307 Green's fear, James Hamilton, Jr., said   Hayne, "Letters on the Nullification Movement in South Carolina," 746–47.

307 a daylong Fourth of July rally   Freehling, ed., **Nullification Era,** 120–37.

307 "all the kindly feelings of the human heart"   Ibid., 127.

307 secluded at the Rip Raps   **Correspondence**, IV, 312.

307 a letter that . . . echoed Drayton   Freehling, ed., **Nullification Era,** 136–37.

308 "I fear from my observations"   PHC, VIII, 365.

308 Calhoun wrote what came to be known   PJCC, XI, 413–40. See also Wiltse, **John C. Calhoun**, II, 113–16.

309 the Kentucky and Virginia resolutions   See, for instance, Wilentz, **Rise of American Democracy**, 78–80.

309 came to light in 1832   Ellis, **Union at Risk,** 9.

309 Madison denied that the resolutions   Ibid., 10–11.

309 nullification would create the mechanical means   Wilentz, **Rise of American Democracy**, 319–21, is excellent on nullification's theoretical underpinnings. (See ibid., 376–77, for the Fort Hill Address in particular.) See also Howe, **What Hath God Wrought**, 395–410.

310 "Let it never be forgotten" PJCC, XI, 425.

311 "The rule of the majority" Ibid., 451.

312 "I have been deeply disappointed in him" **Memoirs of JQA**, VIII, 411. Adams was also hearing in these months that "the nullifiers of South Carolina are fully determined to proceed to the last extremities of civil war" (ibid., 410).

312 faced trouble at home Wiltse, **John C. Calhoun**, II, 116–17.

312 his recollection of his state of mind Carl Brent Swisher, ed., "Roger B. Taney's 'Bank War Manuscript,'" Parts 1 and 2, **Maryland Historical Magazine** 53 (June and September 1958), 103–30, 215–37.

312 "He was at that time vehemently assailed" Ibid., 117.

313 tall and thin H. H. Walker Lewis, **Without Fear or Favor: A Biography of Chief Justice Roger Brooke Taney** (Boston, 1965), 3.

313 a memoir known as the "Bank War Manuscript" Ibid., 103–6. Taney never finished it, and it was subsequently lost, Swisher wrote, until it "was rediscovered in 1929 when at a public sale in Atlanta, Georgia, a locksmith purchased an old safe. Inside he found a mass of letters and other papers. He destroyed the letters, but saved a bound manuscript, which proved to be Taney's longhand account . . ." (ibid., 105). See also John McDonough, "Notes on the Collection," Roger B. Taney Papers, LOC.

314 "His wife had been" Ibid., 117–18.

315 larger and more complicated Howe, **What Hath God Wrought**, 282–83.

315 whether the opposition should try to impeach the president **PHC**, VIII, 360.

317 "Mr. Calhoun will run for president" **Correspondence**, IV, 286.

317 Thinking of the Hermitage Ibid., 283.

317 Jackson's Tennessee friends . . . went to work EDT, I, 296–97. Jackson was newly angry over the fact that a pro-Calhoun Fourth of July gathering in Georgetown had toasted Emily as a defender of female virtue (**Correspondence**, IV, 311–12).

318 "Our true policy now" **Correspondence**, IV, 315.

318 after "the most mature reflection" Ibid., 323.

319 "All things will work" EDT, I, 296.

319 Jackson, pen in hand, was writing **Correspondence**, IV, 347; see also **EDT**, II, 1.

319   five paragraphs on politics   **Correspondence**, IV, 347–48.

319   his room flooded with his family   Ibid., 348.

319   "This moment the ladies have entered"   Ibid.

320   "Uncle seems quite happy"   **EDT**, II, 4–5.

320   when Margaret and John Eaton set out   **Correspondence**, IV, 350.

320   "He ought to have left before this"   Andrew Jackson, Jr., to William Donelson, September 9, 1831, Gertrude and Benjamin Caldwell Collection, The Hermitage.

320   "Nothing reconciles me"   **Correspondence**, IV, 351.

321   "quite charmed"   M.A. DeWolfe Howe, **The Life and Letters of George Bancroft** (New York, 1908), I, 192.

321   "He assured me"   Ibid., 193.

321   his host's "qualifications"   Ibid., 192.

321   "told an anecdote" ·   Thomas Woodson, ed., **Nathaniel Hawthorne: The French and Italian Notebooks** (Columbus, Oh., 1980), XVIII, 366.

322   "Surely, he was the greatest"   Ibid., 367.

322   "I have no very important news"   Andrew Jackson, Jr., to William Donelson, September 9, 1831, Gertrude and Benjamin Caldwell Collection, The Hermitage.

323   until the nomination actually reached   Parton, **Life**, III, 375–82.

323   the Senate voted   Remini, **Andrew Jackson**, II, 348–49, is a vivid account of the vote.

323   word arrived as a White House dinner party   Ibid., 349.

324   refusal to confirm "has displayed"   **Correspondence**, IV, 400.

324   Calhoun was "politically damned"   Ibid., 402.

324   "factious opposition"   Ibid., 401.

324   "It will kill him, sir"   Parton, **Life**, III, 380.

324   "The common sentiment"   **EDT**, II, 10–11.

324   Van Buren "received the tidings"   Washington Irving, **Letters** (Boston, 1978–82), II, 693.

325   "Every thing is going on well"   PHC, VIII, 465.

325   a resolution that the nomination   **Register of Debates in Congress**, 22nd Congress, 1st session, VIII, 1833, 1310.

325   "To myself, I feel like a new man"   **EDT**, II, 4.

325   she told him they were visiting the Hermitage   Ibid., 15.

326   "very gay"   Ibid., 5.

326   "Cousin Andrew arrived last Sunday with his bride"   Ibid., 7.

326 Jackson had stayed   Ibid., 6.

326 "We were quite gay"   Ibid., 7.

327 "the same frank, gay, communicative woman"   Hunt, ed., **First Forty Years of Washington Society**, 319.

327 "Neither Mr. or Mrs. McLane"   Ibid., 325.

328 "The argument was carried"   Ibid., 326.

328 "Well, I will lead"   Ibid.

328 "Now, trifling as this affair"   Ibid., 326–27.

328 "The Bank question"   Ibid., 327.

329 she and her husband had "several new neighbors"   Ibid., 322.

329 a heavy snowstorm   Ibid., 324.

329 one Clay son was currently battling   Remini, **Henry Clay**, 368.

329 committed to "the Lunatic Asylum"   Ibid., 375.

329 was "irreclaimably dissipated"   Hunt, ed., **First Forty Years of Washington Society**, 324.

330 Irving, who had come home   Irving, **Letters**, II, 704–5.

330 "Mr. Clay is borne up"   Hunt, ed., **First Forty Years of Washington Society**, 324–25.

330 "Politics are waxing warmer"   Andrew Donelson to Stockley Donelson, February 18, 1832, Donelson Family Private Collection, Cleveland Hall, Nashville.

Chapter 14: Now Let Him Enforce It

331 Edward Livingston issued a revealing directive   "Circular to the Ministers in Europe and at Rio de Janeiro," Department of State, Washington, D.C., March 28, 1832, Diplomatic Instructions of the Department of State—Great Britain, Reel 73, National Archives, Washington, D.C.

331 "It is observed"   Ibid. The italics are Livingston's.

332 "an ambitious man"   Swisher, ed., "Roger Taney's 'Bank War Manuscript,' " June 1958, 124.

332 confirmed his longtime support of the Bank   Ibid., 125.

332 came to the Treasury in late 1831   Remini, **Jackson**, II, 335–42, is a good account of McLane and the Bank.

332 most of the questions of the day   Ibid., 337.

332 The political price for the scheme   Ibid.

333 as Andrew Donelson read a draft   Swisher, ed., "Roger Taney's 'Bank War Manuscript,'" June 1958, 122.

333 so mild that it "startled" Roger Taney   Ibid.

333 suggested Jackson "would now defer"   Ibid., 122–23.

333 "Having conscientiously"   Ibid., 123.

334 "The duty of making this objection"   Ibid.

334 No one else in the office came to Taney's side   Ibid., 123–28.

334 "objected strongly to any alteration"   Ibid., 124.

334 Jackson "always listened reluctantly"   Ibid., 128.

334 some back-and-forth   Ibid., 127.

334 McLane, it seemed, had won   Ibid., 125.

335 soon in Andrew Donelson's office   Swisher, ed., "Roger Taney's 'Bank War Manuscript,'" September 1958, 215.

335 "Having conscientiously"   Swisher, ed., "Roger Taney's 'Bank War Manuscript,'" June 1958, 123. Italics are mine; the final version is found in **Messages**, II, 1121.

336 decided to apply for recharter   Remini, **Andrew Jackson and the Bank War**, 73–77.

336 Clay and Webster privately pressed   Henry Clay to Nicholas Biddle, December 15, 1831, Nicholas Biddle Papers, LOC; Daniel Webster to Nicholas Biddle, December 18, 1831, **Correspondence of Nicholas Biddle**, 146; Remini, **Life of Andrew Jackson**, 222.

336 Taney said Biddle was "an ambitious man"   Swisher, ed., "Roger Taney's 'Bank War Manuscript,'" June 1958, 109.

336 "If General Jackson does not kill"   Hunt, **Life of Edward Livingston**, 382.

336 "The Bank, Mr. Van Buren, is trying to kill me"   AMVB, 625.

337 In addition to fighting the flu   Remini, **Andrew Jackson**, II, 346.

337 a brief, painful operation   Parton, **Life**, III, 415–16.

337 "Go ahead"   Ibid., 415.

337 Mary Eastin was planning her wedding   EDT, II, 11.

337 Lucius Polk, a cousin of James K. Polk's   Ibid., 12.

338 "I believe I may say"   Ibid., 12–13.

338 "We farmers generally"   Andrew Jackson, Jr., to William Donelson, September 9, 1831, Gertrude and Benjamin Caldwell Collection, The Hermitage. In February 1832, Andrew junior echoed the point. "The times being hard even here in money matters," he wrote, "my father has been unable to comply with" coming up with $1,500 for a transaction (Andrew

Jackson, Jr., to William Donelson, February 6, 1832, Gertrude and Benjamin Caldwell Collection, The Hermitage).

338   the "quite warm"   Andrew Jackson, Jr., to William Donelson, February 6, 1832, Donelson Family Private Collection, Cleveland Hall, Nashville.

339   the Black Hawk War   Patrick J. Jung, **The Black Hawk War of 1832** (Norman, Okla., 2007), is a strong recent study, as is Kerry A. Trask, **Black Hawk: The Battle for the Heart of America** (New York, 2007). Frank E. Stevens, **The Black Hawk War, Including a Review of Black Hawk's Life** (Chicago, 1903), is a classic account. See also Anthony F. C. Wallace, **Prelude to Disaster: The Course of Indian-White Relations Which Led to the Black Hawk War** (Springfield, Ill., 1970); Prucha, **Great Father**, 253–57; and, for the documentary record, Ellen M. Whitney, ed., **Black Hawk War, 1831–1832**, 2 vols. in 4 parts (Springfield, Ill., 1970–78).

339   there would be British   Jung, **Black Hawk War of 1832**, 65–67; the British along the Canadian border had long been a source of anxiety for whites in the region. As in the South, Indian leaders had fought with the British in the War of 1812—and Black Hawk was among their number (Trask, **Black Hawk**, 109–10).

339   and fellow Indian support   Jung, **Black Hawk War of 1832**, 5, is very good on the internal Indian rivalries that crippled resistance to white expansion. Jung wrote: "Another factor that had a significant impact upon the course of the Black Hawk War was the escalation of intertribal warfare among the Indian communities of the upper Great Lakes and upper Mississippi Valley. In the years immediately preceding the conflict, the tribes of this region had coalesced into two loosely organized alliance systems that fought with increasing frequency and intensity. . . . The fighting gave [white] military commanders and Indian agents a tremendous opportunity . . . and both exploited these divisions during the Black Hawk War by using the enemies of the Sauks and Foxes to engage Black Hawk's band."

339   the only blood he shed   Abraham Lincoln, **The Language of Liberty: The Political Speeches and Writings of Abraham Lincoln** (Washington, D.C., 2004), 114.

339   after a ceremonial feast of boiled dog   Jung, **Black Hawk War**

of 1832, 87. It was, Jung wrote, "a common ceremonial meal among Great Lakes Indians."

339 Black Hawk sent emissaries   Ibid., 88.

339 seem to have had a good deal to drink   Ibid., 89.

339 while accounts are confused   Ibid., 88.

339 they, not Black Hawk's warriors, shed first blood   Ibid., 89.

339 Forty . . . killing twelve   Ibid.

339 Jackson ordered Winfield Scott into action   Elliott, **Winfield Scott**, 261–62.

339 deadly outbreak of cholera   Ibid., 265–66.

339 Landing at Fort Gratiot   Ibid., 266.

339 escaped to the forests   Ibid.

339 only to die on the run   Ibid.

339 wolves and wild hogs   Ibid.

339 the Battle of Bad Axe   Jung, **Black Hawk War of 1832**, 166–75.

340 a new Supreme Court decision   Norgren, **Cherokee Cases**, as noted above, is an excellent survey of the 1831 and 1832 cases, their origins, and their implications. Edwin A. Miles, "After John Marshall's Decision: **Worcester v. Georgia** and the Nullification Crisis," **The Journal of Southern History** 39 (November 1973), 519–44, is also critical to understanding the issues. See also Satz, **American Indian Policy in the Jacksonian Era**, 40–52.

340 **Cherokee Nation v. The State of Georgia**   Ibid., 98–111. "Valid treaties with the United States guaranteed their sovereignty, which represented nothing if not the power to govern themselves. Georgia's proposed assertion of jurisdiction violated those treaties—treaties that according to Article 6 of the U.S. Constitution were the supreme law of the land, superior to state law" (Norgren, **Cherokee Cases**, 48).

340 Two Christian missionaries   Smith, **John Marshall**, 517.

340 "repugnant to the Constitution, laws, and treaties"   Ibid., 518.

340 Justice Joseph Story suspected the matter   Ibid.

341 "Our public affairs"   PHC, VIII, 472.

341 "We were at the Capitol yesterday"   Susan Donelson to William Gaston, March 12, 1832, William Gaston Papers, Southern Historical Collection, Wilson Library, University of North Carolina at Chapel Hill.

341 Horace Greeley later claimed Miles, "After John Marshall's Decision: **Worcester v. Georgia** and the Nullification Crisis," 519. The remark first appeared in his 1865 **The American Conflict: A History of the Great Rebellion in the United States of America, 1860–'64**; Greeley's source was Massachusetts congressman George N. Briggs.

341 historically questionable Ibid., 528–29. Miles wrote: "If [Jackson] made the statement attributed to him about John Marshall's decision, no one recorded it until years later, but he did refer to the ruling as 'still born' when Georgia refused to honor the Court's mandate. And on one occasion, 'he sportively said in private conversation that if . . . called on to support the decree of the Court he will call on those who have brought about the decision to enforce it[;] that he will call on the Militia of Massachusetts.'"

341 "The decision of the Supreme Court" **Correspondence**, IV, 430.

342 reconstructed the chronology of the case Miles, "After John Marshall's Decision: **Worcester v. Georgia** and the Nullification Crisis," 527.

342 In the strictest sense of the law Prucha, **Great Father,** 212. As Prucha wrote: "United States marshals could not be sent to free the prisoners until the state judge had refused formally to comply with the order. But Georgia ignored the court's proceedings, and no written refusal was forthcoming. Anyway, the Supreme Court adjourned before it could report Georgia's failure to conform. Nor was there any other procedure that Jackson could adopt, even if he had wanted to."

342 at least two factors at work Ibid., 212–13.

343 the administration convinced Wilentz, **Andrew Jackson**, 141–42.

343 Emily gave birth to her third child **EDT**, II, 17.

343 "I am thankful" Emily Donelson to Mary Donelson, June 17, 1832, Mrs. John Lawrence Merritt Collection.

343 "I have been very well" Ibid. Emily added: "I am quite well now and have been all about upstairs, but have not been down yet, though I will in a day or two. I had an old nurse who stayed with me the month. She has now left me and I miss her a good deal. I have no one now but Eliza and a little girl Andrew

bought about 8 years old who does very well to rock the crib. He bought her brother who is 10. They are very bright and will make good servants in the course of time but are not much use at present. I have been very lonesome since Mary left me though I have had a great many visitors every day it is not like having some one always in the house."

343 "I do not know yet"   Ibid.

344 "I had hoped before this"   Andrew Donelson to Stockley Donelson, late June 1832, Mrs. John Lawrence Merritt Collection.

344 trouble had begun in Quebec   Parton, **Life**, III, 418–20. This was the cholera that had so decimated General Scott's mission in the Black Hawk War.

345 On June 27, 1832, Henry Clay proposed   **PHC**, VIII, 545–46.

345 could see Clay's initiative   A woman styling herself as "A Daughter of Massachusetts" wrote him "to offer you my sincere acknowledgement for your recent noble and spirited avowal of your belief of the Christian religion, and your reverence for its precepts; and I can assure you, Sir, that a large majority of the daughters of the descendants of the Pilgrims unite with me in the same sentiment" (**PHC**, VIII, 549).

345 he, too, believed in "the efficacy"   **Correspondence**, IV, 447.

345 "I could not do otherwise"   Ibid.

345 "It is the province"   Ibid. Jackson's reluctance to carry the presidency into the religious realm was shared by believers who thought that the church, broadly defined, risked corruption by contact with the government—that believers should, in the words of Roger Williams, the dissenter who left the Massachusetts Bay Colony to found Rhode Island, cherish a "hedge or wall of separation between the Garden of the Church and the wilderness of the world"—in order to protect religion from politics, not politics from religion (see my **American Gospel: God, the Founding Fathers, and the Making of a Nation** [New York, 2006], 54).

346 "I am no **sectarian**"   Ibid., 256.

346 was prepared to veto   Remini, **Jackson**, II, 361.

346 a veto message written by Louis McLane   Draft of Veto Message, Van Buren Papers, LOC.

346 "In the spirit"   Ibid.

Chapter 15: The Fury of a Chained Panther

348 Biddle thought he had Jackson where he wanted him   Swisher, ed., "Roger Taney's 'Bank War Manuscript,'" September 1958, 220.

348 "He was offended"   Ibid.

348 The Senate passed the bill   Remini, **Andrew Jackson and the Bank War**, 80.

348 One story sheds light   Swisher, ed., "Roger Taney's 'Bank War Manuscript,'" September 1958, 221–23.

349 "Now I do not mean"   Ibid., 222.

350 "is becoming desperate"   Andrew Donelson to Stockley Donelson, February 18, 1832, Donelson Family Private Collection, Cleveland Hall, Nashville.

350 Jackson sent Taney   Swisher, ed., "Roger B. Taney's 'Bank War Manuscript,'" September 1958, 226–28. I am indebted to Taney's description of the writing of the veto.

350 Taney joined Donelson . . . "even hearing"   Ibid., 227.

350 in the northern light   Earl's room faced north. Author tour of the White House.

351 "It is to be regretted"   **Messages**, II, 1153. Feller, **Jacksonian Promise**, 169–75, is interesting on the veto and its implications, as is Howe, **What Hath God Wrought**, 373–86, and Wilentz, **Rise of American Democracy**, 367–74.

352 "The Congress, the Executive"   Ibid., 1145.

353 "Sir, no President"   Remini, **Life of Andrew Jackson**, 231.

353 "I have now done my duty"   **Messages**, II, 1154.

353 Whose vision would prevail   Jackson's veto—indeed, his whole presidency—raises questions about the nature of power in American life. Gerard N. Magliocca, **Andrew Jackson and the Constitution: The Rise and Fall of Generational Regimes** (Lawrence, Kans., 2007), 48–60, is especially good on these issues (as are his source notes). Magliocca wrote: "The rise of the executive branch as the driving force for constitutional reform, which was contrary to the expectation of the Framers, is one of the most important institutional developments during the last two centuries. Jefferson was the first to experiment with using his office as a focal point of the popular will, which explains why leaders in the 1830s often invoked his acts as a precedent

for Jackson's decisions. But Jefferson always publicly proclaimed his deference to Congress. What makes Jackson unique is that he was the first president to declare that he was the tribune of the people and could assert an independent constitutional vision on their behalf" (ibid., 56). Magliocca noted that Lincoln defied **Dred Scott** and that Franklin Roosevelt threatened to defy the Supreme Court over abandoning the gold standard during the New Deal (ibid.).

354 Jackson believed that "the intelligence and wisdom"   **Messages**, II, 1154.

355 banking and finance and the American economy   Peter Temin, **The Jacksonian Economy** (New York, 1969), is a strong account and an interesting argument. Temin is responding in part to Schlesinger's classic work on the Jacksonian period, **The Age of Jackson**, which was written in the New Deal era.

355 The veto message "has all the fury"   **PHC**, VIII, 556.

355 "profound calculation"   Wilentz, **Rise of American Democracy**, 248.

356 a lucrative pepper trade   Belohlavek, **"Let the Eagle Soar!"** 151–53.

356 There was also a good deal of specie   Naval Affairs, 22nd Congress, 1st Session, No. 485, 155.

356 as well as opium   Ibid.

356 was ashore attending to the weighing of the pepper   Ibid., 154.

356 "rendered desperate by their habits"   Ibid.

356 stabbed Charles Knight, the first officer   Ibid., 155.

356 in his side and in his back   Ibid.

356 two seamen, John Davis and George Chester   Ibid., 153.

356 other crew members dove overboard   Ibid., 155.

356 plundered the ship   Ibid., 154.

356 tried to return   Ibid., 154–55, details Endicott's escape from the port.

357 A local rajah, Chute Dulah, accepted   Ibid., 155.

357 Endicott, with help, retook his ship   Ibid.

357 "Who great man now"   Ibid.

357 "May the mistake"   Ibid.

357 the president of the United States believed that "the flag of the Union"   Ibid., 153. The orders were signed by Navy Secretary Levi Woodbury.

357 "demand of the rajah"   Ibid.

357 If talks failed   Ibid.

358 "other ships-of-war"   Ibid.

358 Arriving at Quallah Battoo   Ibid., 157.

358 "No demand of satisfaction"   Ibid., 156.

358 An invading force of 250 sailors and marines   Belohlavek, "**Let the Eagle Soar!**" 155.

358 used javelins and darts   Naval Affairs, 22nd Congress, 1st Session, No. 485, 157.

358 and killing more than 100 natives   Belohlavek, "**Let the Eagle Soar!**" 156.

358 the ship's medicine chest   Naval Affairs, 22nd Congress, 1st Session, No. 485, 156.

359 assault on "a settlement filled"   **National Intelligencer**, July 13, 1832. The original attack on Jackson was published on July 10, 1832, the same day the Bank veto went to Congress (Belohlavek, "**Let the Eagle Soar!**" 157).

359 "from an impulse of national pride"   **National Intelligencer**, July 13, 1832.

359 asked for copies of the relevant papers on Thursday, July 12, 1832   Belohlavek, "**Let the Eagle Soar!**" 159.

360 Edward Everett of Massachusetts, a committed National Republican   Ibid., 161.

360 "From the papers communicated"   Ibid.

360 To avoid embarrassing Downes   Ibid., 159–61.

360 the episode . . . faded away   Ibid., 162.

360 jotting a note to Kendall   **Correspondence**, IV, 465. The emphasis is Jackson's.

360 "I have been most kindly received"   Irving, **Letters**, II, 705. The letter was written to Peter Irving on June 16, 1832.

361 "The campaign is over"   **PHC**, VIII, 555.

361 Emily took a trip to Baltimore   Emily Donelson to Mary Donelson, [September 1832,] Mrs. John Lawrence Merritt Collection.

361 "I regret the continuance"   **Correspondence**, IV, 475.

361 a letter to her mother   Emily Donelson to Mary Donelson, [September 1832,] Mrs. John Lawrence Merritt Collection. After mentioning her own health, Emily added: "As soon as I got well Andrew was taken with the same and when we arrived

at the springs looked like a ghost, but we had not been there more than a day before he began to improve and continued to do so until we reached home. We were at the Springs 10 days, were very much pleased and I have been very sorry that I did not remain longer but as my husband was obliged to be in Washington I thought we had all better be together and we were not then so much alarmed about the cholera."

362 In the early hours of Monday, August 22, 1831 Freehling, **Road to Disunion**, 180.

362 entered the house of his master Ibid.

362 a broader spree Ibid., 180–81. See also Howe, **What Hath God Wrought**, 323–27.

362 killed about fifty-seven whites, a large majority of them women and children Howe, **What Hath God Wrought**, 325.

362 believed that "the Spirit" Ibid., 324.

362 A solar eclipse that year Ibid.

362 answered in kind by whites Ibid., 325.

363 a debate over partial and gradual emancipation Ibid., 325–27. See also Freehling, **Road to Disunion**, 181–96.

363 to "await a more definite" Ibid., 326.

363 "I heard" **Correspondence**, IV, 470. Calhoun, needless to say, would have disagreed. Ensconced at Fort Hill, Calhoun was thinking grandly, and unrealistically. Writing on the day of the state elections in South Carolina, Calhoun said: "The State rights party will triumph by a large majority. A convention of the State will certainly be called and the act nullified; but any movement will be made with the view of preserving the Union. The end arrived at will be a general Convention of all the States, in order to adjust all constitutional differences and thusly restore general harmony. We have run nearly fifty years on the first tack. It is a wonderful run; but it is time to bring up the reckoning in order to take a fresh departure" (**PJCC**, XI, 665). There was at least one obvious problem with Calhoun's musings: they took no account of Andrew Jackson. Calhoun's political judgment when it came to assessing Jackson was matched in its mediocrity only by Henry Clay's.

363 legislature was to meet on Monday, October 22, 1832 Freehling, **Prelude to Civil War**, 260.

363 plans for a possible mutiny **Correspondence**, IV, 475–76.
363 "The Presidential question" **PJCC**, XI, 665.

Chapter 16: Hurra for the Hickory Tree!

365 the first major personal presidential campaign tour For accounts of the 1832 campaign, see, for instance, Robert V. Remini, "Election of 1832," in **History of American Presidential Elections, 1789–2001**, ed. Arthur M. Schlesinger, Jr., and Fred L. Israel, vol. 2 (Philadelphia, 2002), 495–574; Cole, **Presidency of Andrew Jackson**, 137–52; Parton, **Life**, III, 417–32; Remini, **Jackson**, II, 374–92; and Wilentz, **Rise of American Democracy**, 372–74.

365 In Baltimore in late May 1832 Parton, **Life**, III, 421.

365 the 1826 disappearance and suspected murder of William Morgan Steven C. Bullock, **Revolutionary Brotherhood: Freemasonry and the Transformation of the American Social Order, 1730–1840** (Williamsburg, Va., 1996), 277–79.

366 A strong political force Ibid., 280–83.

366 the Anti-Masons nominated William Wirt Ibid., 282. See also Remini, "Election of 1832," 500–5. Charles Bankhead's assessment of the Anti-Mason movement is interesting. Writing Palmerston in October 1831, Bankhead said: "Delegates from thirteen states of the Union assembled last week at Baltimore for the purpose of nominating 'an Anti-Masonic President and Vice-President.' . . . It is necessary to premise that about four years ago a man named Morgan, in the State of New York, suddenly disappeared and no trace of him has since been discovered. It was suspected that he made some revelations relative to Free-Masonry, which, as a Mason, he was bound by oath to keep secret. Some short time afterward he was carried off and supposed to have been murdered by other Free Masons who thought themselves absolved by their Masonic oaths in pursuing to any extent any member of the Fraternity who should transgress the regulations. Out of this circumstance grew a party espousing Anti Masonic opinions, and they have not hesitated to propagate the idea that Free-Masonry in this country has assumed such an alarming importance that the very Courts of Jus-

tice are, in a degree, subservient to its regulations. On this belief gaining ground, many of its supporters conceived that the
Executive Officers of the Government should not belong to the
society of Free Masons. . . . General Jackson is a Free Mason
and under the pretence of objecting to his reelection upon **principle**, the Anti Masonic meeting (composed, in great measure,
of Northern and Eastern men) make use of that objection **politically** to defeat his prospects at the ensuing election" (Charles
Bankhead to Viscount Palmerston, October 4, 1831, National
Archives of the United Kingdom, Kew).

366 Clay, the National Republican nominee   Remini, **Henry Clay**,
403–11, is a good account of the campaign from Clay's perspective.

366 There were barbecues   Remini, "Election of 1832," 513. Here
is Remini on the barbecue factor: "In addition to parades, the
Democrats believed in barbecues as an important technique in
winning the voter's favor. Even when they lost local elections, as
they did in Kentucky, the Democrats seemed to think a barbecue was in order—or so the **Louisville Journal** reported. 'There
seems to be no way of convincing these fellows that they are
fairly beaten. They have one sort of answering for every thing.
If we show them that we have elected our Lieutenant Governor
by a majority of nearly 30,000, **they reply by swallowing a pig**.
If we show them that we have gained great strength in the Senate, and added to our superiority, **they reply by devouring a
turkey**. If we show them that we have obtained a majority of
two-thirds in the House of Representatives, **they reply by pour-
ing off a pint of whiskey or apple-toddy**. There is no with-
standing such arguments. We give it up'" (ibid.).

366 "The Jackson cause"   Ibid., 509.

366 "THE KING UPON THE THRONE"   Ibid., 511.

367 took in a mile-long Jackson parade   Parton, **Life**, III, 425.

367 Duff Green watched the rise   **PJCC**, XI, 667–68. Green added,
alluding to the Anti-Masons: "If I were permitted to make a
suggestion I would say that we must organize against their organization and the question to be considered is how is that organization to take place."

367 his autumn journey from Tennessee to Washington   Accord-

ing to Remini's account, Jackson denied that he was campaigning, at least in Tennessee (Remini, **Jackson**, II, 380).

367 at a Democratic barbecue in Lexington   Ibid., 384.

367 "This is certainly"   Ibid.

367 Blair helpfully published   Ibid.

368 saying he had promised that "whilst I continued"   **PHC**, VIII, 555.

368 "His opponents (and they are not few or unimportant)" Charles Bankhead to Viscount Palmerston, October 28, 1832, National Archives of the United Kingdom, Kew.

368 "belong to history"   Parton, **Life**, III, 425–26.

368 won overwhelmingly   Wilentz, **Rise of American Democracy**, 373–74.

369 The popular vote was closer   Remini, "Election of 1832," 515.

369 Jackson's popularity was "so unbounded"   Charles Bankhead to Viscount Palmerston, November 13, 1832, National Archives of the United Kingdom, Kew.

369 "The excitement during the last fortnight"   Ibid.

369 "The dark cloud"   **PHC**, VIII, 599.

369 the South Carolina convention nullified the Tariff of 1832 Freehling, ed., **Nullification Era**, 152.

370 a story making the rounds   "The Life and Times of James Hamilton of South Carolina by S. Hamilton," material owned by Herman P. Hamilton, Chester, S.C., James Hamilton Collection, Southern Historical Collection, Wilson Library, The University of North Carolina at Chapel Hill, microfilm.

370 John Randolph of Roanoke was supposed   Ibid.

370 "It is no longer to be doubted"   William Gaston, "Reply to invitation to dine in Montgomery 1832," October 3, 1832, William Gaston Papers, Southern Historical Collection, Wilson Library, The University of North Carolina at Chapel Hill.

Chapter 17: A Dreadful Crisis of Excitement and Violence

372 sat down by his fireside   Pierce M. Butler to James Henry Hammond, December 18, 1832, James Hammond Papers, LOC.

372 "bent on enforcing his mandate"   Ibid.

372 volunteered his military services Hayne, "Letters on the Nullification Movement in South Carolina," 751.

372 appointed a new military aide-de-camp Ibid., 752–53.

373 "this crisis in our affairs" Ibid., 753.

373 issued detailed secret orders Ibid., 753–55.

373 corps of "**Mounted Minute Men**" Ibid., 754.

373 "My plan is this" Ibid.

373 "a **short yellow crane Plume**" Ibid., 755. "Palmetto Buttons of a beautiful pattern" could be purchased, Hayne said, at Roche's in Charleston.

373 "Keep me constantly advised" **Correspondence**, V, 18.

373 "I have on every occasion" **Correspondence**, IV, 481.

374 thought Charleston more worried than exuberant Samuel Cram Jackson Diary, November 27, 1832, Southern Historical Collection, Wilson Library, The University of North Carolina Library at Chapel Hill.

374 "Anxiety and fear" Ibid.

374 "a dreadful crisis of excitement and violence" Samuel Cram Jackson Diary, November 28, 1832, Southern Historical Collection, Wilson Library, The University of North Carolina Library at Chapel Hill.

374 "the custom house where the battle will be fought" **Correspondence**, IV, 481.

374 "We are not disposed" Ibid.

375 recorded a near massacre Samuel Cram Jackson Diary, October 20, 1832, Southern Historical Collection, Wilson Library, The University of North Carolina Library at Chapel Hill.

375 "their blood was up" Ibid.

375 Hotheads in the Union ranks Ibid.

376 Jackson dispatched George Breathitt **Correspondence**, IV, 484–85.

376 "collect all the information" Ibid., 485.

376 Poinsett briefed Jackson Ibid., 486–88.

376 "Both parties [of the nullifiers]" Ibid., 487.

376 "a Southern man" Ibid., 487–88.

377 "We had rather die" Ibid., 492.

377 "I fully concur with you" Ibid., 493.

378 "calmness and firmness" Ibid., 494.

378 drafted in something of a conciliatory spirit   Ellis, **Union at Risk**, 81–83.

378 "This is all we want"   **Correspondence**, IV, 489.

378 created, he said, "discontent"   **Messages**, II, 1161.

378 "Limited to a general superintending power"   Ibid., 1169.

379 was "in substance a complete surrender"   **Memoirs of JQA**, VIII, 503.

379 Jackson's December strategy was threefold   For my narrative and analysis of Jackson and nullification, I am indebted to, among others: Freehling, **Prelude to Civil War**, 265–97; Ellis, **Union at Risk**, 74–177; Feller, **Jacksonian Promise**, 164–66; Howe, **What Hath God Wrought**, 395–410; and Wilentz, **Rise of American Democracy**, 374–89.

379 "The President has instructed me"   Lewis Cass to Joel Poinsett, December 7, 1832, Poinsett Papers, Historical Society of Pennsylvania.

Chapter 18: The Mad Project of Disunion

380 alone in his office   Parton, **Life**, III, 466.

380 standing at his desk   Jackson used a standup desk. Seale, **The White House**, 90.

380 a steel pen   Ibid.

380 "A gentleman who came in"   Ibid.

380 sent across Lafayette Square to Decatur House   Eberlein and Van Dyke Hubbard, **Historic Houses of George-Town and Washington City**, 269. Livingston lived at the Decatur House, on the northwest corner of Lafayette Park. Hunt, **Life of Edward Livingston**, 371–73, argues for Livingston's authorship of the proclamation; Parton, **Life**, III, 466, insists on Jackson's. The drafts show both men's work, though the spirit and logic are clearly Jackson's.

380 As the document went to press   Parton, **Life**, III, 466–67.

380 "Those are my views"   Ibid., 467.

381 **"incompatible with the existence of the Union"**   Messages, II, 1206.

381 an option "at an earlier day"   Ibid., 1205.

381 "The war into [which] we were forced"   Ibid.

381 "forms a **government**, not a league"   Ibid., 1211.

382 "Contemplate the condition of that country"   Ibid., 1217.

383 "Carolina is one of these proud states" Ibid.

383 "But the dictates of a high duty" Ibid., 1217–18.

384 "destined to bring about another reign of terror" Hayne, "Letters on the Nullification Movement in South Carolina," 751.

384 "wise, determined and firm" **Correspondence**, IV, 502.

384 "I pray God to preserve" Ibid., 499.

384 Marshall became one of Jackson's "warmest supporters" Smith, **John Marshall: Definer of a Nation**, 519–20. The characterization is from Joseph Story, who includes himself in it.

384 "One short week" **PHC, VIII**, 603.

384 "Who can have confidence" Ibid., 609.

386 the "mass of the people" Wiltse, **John C. Calhoun**, II, 172.

386 "The whole subject is discussed" Philip Hone, **The Diary of Philip Hone, 1828–1851** (Boston, 1889), 68–69.

387 "measures have been taken" Hayne, "Letters on the Nullification Movement in South Carolina," 753.

387 "These men are reckless" **Correspondence**, IV, 502.

387 "If I can judge" Ibid., 502–3.

387 Hayne ordered the preparation Hayne, "Letters on the Nullification Movement in South Carolina," 755.

388 "What have we to fear" **Correspondence**, IV, 504.

388 "I am lingering here" Irving, **Letters**, II, 742.

388 more than two thousand people there Samuel Cram Jackson Diary, November 29, 1832, Southern Historical Collection, Wilson Library, The University of North Carolina Library at Chapel Hill.

388 "I hope these southern Nullifiers". Rebecca Gratz, **Letters of Rebecca Gratz** (Philadelphia, 1929), 165–66.

388 resigned the vice presidency **PJCC, XI**, 685.

389 spent an entire Sunday William Gaston to Mrs. H. M. Manly, December 31, 1832, William Gaston Papers, Southern Historical Collection, Wilson Library, The University of North Carolina Library at Chapel Hill.

389 Virginia, North Carolina, Georgia, Alabama, and Mississippi Ellis, **Union at Risk**, 102–40; Freehling, **Prelude to Civil War**, 203–5.

390 In Alabama, the influential congressman Dixon Hall Lewis Freehling, **Prelude to Civil War**, 203.

390 In Mississippi, Senator George Poindexter Richard Aubrey McLemore, ed., **A History of Mississippi** (Jackson, Miss., 1973), I, 276–83, covers the state's role in nullification. "It is true that Senator Poindexter supported the theory of nullification in the Senate and opposed the president in the confrontation with South Carolina" (ibid.).

390 John A. Quitman, the chancellor of the state courts "Back on the home front the chief proponent of nullification was John A. Quitman. He joined Poindexter in predicting catastrophic consequences for the South on other basic issues, including slavery, if all Southerners did not stand together on state rights and nullification" (ibid., 277). For Quitman in particular, see Robert E. May, **John A. Quitman: Old South Crusader** (Baton Rouge, La., 1985), 29–75.

390 "the very existence" Cleo Hearon, "Nullification in Mississippi," **Publications of the Mississippi Historical Society** 12 (1912), 45.

390 Georgia stood by Jackson Ellis, **Union at Risk**, 102–22.

390 In North Carolina, officials Ibid., 159.

390 Virginia was perhaps the greatest threat Ibid., 123–40.

390 figures like the aged James Madison Ibid., 125–29.

390 the state's governor, John Floyd Ibid.

391 it was all "for the purpose" Ibid., 128.

391 not until Jackson's Nullification Proclamation Ibid., 129.

391 The vision of Jackson sweeping into the South Ibid., 129–30.

391 "He pursues enemies" Ibid., 130.

391 Floyd's confidence grew Ibid., 130–31.

391 the chief justice's post-proclamation euphoria John Marshall to William Gaston, December 20, 1832, William Gaston Papers, Southern Historical Collection, Wilson Library, The University of North Carolina Library at Chapel Hill.

391 "I look with anxious solicitude" Ibid.

391 Floyd was inclined Ellis, **Union at Risk**, 130. "If he uses force, I will oppose him with a military force," he wrote in his diary (ibid.).

392 "Separated from the East" Correspondence to John Branch, January 31, 1833, John Branch Papers, LOC.

392 "Insane as South Carolina unquestionably is" John Marshall

to William Gaston, December 20, 1832, William Gaston Papers, Southern Historical Collection, Wilson Library, The University of North Carolina Library at Chapel Hill.

392 "Were an open declaration"   Ibid.

393 "Old men are timid"   Ibid.

393 Jackson put on a brave face   **Correspondence**, V, 4.

393 "Virginia, except"   Ibid.

393 "the union **shall be** preserved"   Ibid.

393 "I will die with the Union"   **Correspondence**, IV, 500.

393 "Your account of Mr. Calhoun"   Leonidas Polk to Rufus Polk, February 28, 1833, Leonidas Polk Collection, The University of the South, University Archives and Special Collections, Sewanee.

394 New Year's Day 1833   **EDT**, II, 28–29.

394 skirmished a bit   Ibid., 27.

394 "was always of a tyrannical disposition"   Ibid.

394 "I am very glad that Uncle"   Ibid.

395 he had lost a Senate bid   **TPA**, 206–7.

395 "She has been quite ill"   **EDT**, II, 26.

395 "seem to enjoy themselves"   Ibid., 37.

395 "You must excuse this scrawl"   Ibid., 28.

396 when Washington Irving called   Irving, **Letters**, II, 743–44.

396 Irving "came away with a still warmer feeling"   Ibid.

396 introduced the administration's tariff reform bill   Remini, **Jackson**, III, 29. See also Cole, **Presidency of Andrew Jackson**, 164–65, and Freehling, **Road to Disunion**, 283.

396 Supreme Court justices gathered to dine   **EDT**, II, 33–35.

397 "If you were to see him"   Ibid., 35.

397 Justice Story, Mary said, "appears to be"   Ibid.

397 "what is more remarkable"   Ibid., 34.

398 Livingston had not bothered   **PJCC**, XII, 5.

398 "Our cause is doing well"   Ibid., 6.

Chapter 19: We Are Threatened to Have Our Throats Cut

399 did not yet know . . ."whether some of the eastern states"   **Correspondence**, V, 3.

399 "There is nothing certain"   **PHC**, VIII, 613.

400 "The people will never again"   **PJCC**, XII, 8–9.

400 a conversation he had at the White House   **Correspondence**, V, 4–5.

400 the state legislature had failed to condemn nullification   Ellis, **Union at Risk**, 141–57.

400 remained in New York in these tense weeks   **Correspondence**, V, 4. For example, on January 16, 1833, the day Jackson introduced the Force Bill to give him the power to put down South Carolina if it came to that, the president of the United States was reduced to adding this postscript to a letter to Van Buren: "I will be happy to hear from you often, and see you as early as a just sense of delicacy will permit" (ibid.).

400 worried that the proclamation   Ellis, **Union at Risk**, 145–57, details Van Buren's complex balancing act. See also Latner, **Presidency of Andrew Jackson**, 152–55.

400 For half an hour   **Correspondence**, V, 4.

400 "I learned from him"   Ibid.

400 were "holding regular drills"   Ibid.

400 had allowed the American flag to be flown upside down   Ibid.

400 It was a dark report   It was gloomy by design. Jackson needed to impress the New Yorker with the gravity of the moment. From the White House Wright went to see Cass at the War Department, who pressed the points Jackson had made, this time with particular reference to tariff reform. Jackson and his men knew what they were doing: New York and Van Buren needed to be convinced to go along with lowering the tariff in order to relieve the pressure for armed conflict, and Wright was being used as the messenger back to Albany. Jackson was playing the political game with shrewdness and skill. "The Secy. of War assures me that the reasons to apprehend force constantly increase and that he has little hope that any measures which can be taken will prevent it," Wright told Van Buren, "but that the South will remain firm if Mr. Verplanck's bill is passed, and without any bill there is reason to fear for the whole South, even for Tennessee." Wright also heard that General Scott was "saying that blood would be shed and that he did not believe any thing could prevent it" (ibid.).

401 the Force Bill   Latner, **Presidency of Andrew Jackson**, 150–51; and Ellis, **Union at Risk**, 94.

401 to move the collection of federal revenue   Ellis, **Union at Risk**, 94.

401 Felix Grundy of Tennessee   Ibid., 160.

401 Calhoun was not yet in the chamber   **PJCC**, XII, 15.

401 had joined the Union   Ibid., 14.

402 "No—I go too far"   Ibid.

402 the prospect of an armed Jacksonian dictatorship   Ibid.

402 "warmth"   Ibid., 15.

402 he knew was "unbecoming"   Ibid.

402 had "great effect"   Ibid.

402 rushed to reassure Jackson   **Correspondence**, V, 5.

403 more hopeful than realistic   Calhoun understood that the Force Bill message was problematic for Jackson, and possibly providential for South Carolina's cause. "I have no doubt the message will do more for us than the Proclamation," Calhoun wrote James Hamilton, Jr. "It has roused the Southern members more than any event which has yet occurred. The excitement extends even to the administration men of that quarter. I do not doubt that our cause gains daily and that in less than six months the South will be united if we but act prudently." It was a sound reading of a fluid political moment (**PJCC**, XII, 16).

403 Late that night   **Correspondence**, V, 5.   "I write in great haste, late at night, and much fatigued, and indisposed by a bad cold," Jackson wrote. "You will excuse this scrawl, it is intended for your own eye."

403 "Give me the earliest intelligence"   Ibid., 5–6.

403 "The Nullifiers are extremely active"   Ibid., 8.

404 to prepare for "protracted warfare"   Hayne, "Letters on the Nullification Movement in South Carolina," 760.

404 "revolutionists in North Carolina"   **Correspondence**, V, 8.

404 "I expect the next move will be secession"   Ibid., 9.

404 "The nullifiers in your state"   Ibid., 14.

404 "He has marked out"   **PHC**, VIII, 617.

404 the Force Bill "arms the executive"   Ellis, **Union at Risk**, 161.

404 Even a senator friendly to Jackson   Ibid., 162.

404 disliked putting "the whole military"   Ibid.

405 Much of the Force Bill   I drew on Freehling, **Prelude to Civil War**, 284–86, for the details in this paragraph.

405 After flirting with Calhoun and the nullifiers, Georgia   Ellis, **Union at Risk**, 116.

406 Alabama, Mississippi, and North Carolina Ibid., 158–59.

406 "We detest the tariff" McLemore, **History of Mississippi**, I, 278.

406 Under Governor Floyd, Virginia weighed Ellis, **Union at Risk**, 136–37.

406 "Even if the Governor of Virginia" **Correspondence**, V, 12.

406 "It is very late" Ibid.

406 "I understand that Governor Hayne" Irving, **Letters**, II, 751.

406 held a day of fasting Samuel Cram Jackson Diary, January 31, 1833, Southern Historical Collection, Wilson Library, The University of North Carolina Library at Chapel Hill.

407 "All went to the Methodists" Ibid.

407 "We walked up to the Capitol" Fanny Kemble, **Fanny Kemble: The American Journals** (London, 1990), 84–85. The entry is dated Monday, January 14, 1833. "We went first into the Senate, or upper house, because Webster was speaking, whom I especially wished to hear," Kemble wrote. "The room itself is neither large nor lofty; the senators sit in two semi-circular rows, turned towards the President, in comfortable arm-chairs. On the same ground, and literally sitting among the senators, were a whole regiment of ladies, whispering, talking, laughing, and fidgeting. A gallery, level with the floor, and only divided by a low partition from the main room, ran around the apartment: this, too, was filled with pink, and blue, and yellow bonnets; and every now and then, while the business of the house was going on, and Webster speaking, a tremendous bustle, and waving of feathers, and rustling of silks, would be heard, and in came streaming a reinforcement of political beauties, and then would commence a jumping up, a sitting down, a squeezing through, and a how-d'ye-doing, and a shaking of hands."

407 the narrow steps Author observation. I am grateful to Donald A. Ritchie, associate historian of the U.S. Senate, for giving me a tour of the Capitol as it was in Jackson's day.

407 GENTLEMEN WILL BE PLEASED Ibid.

407 The women, Coffee said, "fill" EDT, II, 37.

407 "I can give you no definitive opinion" PHC, VIII, 607–8.

408 "**To take issue now**" PJCC, XII, 38–39.

408 The nullifiers agreed Freehling, **Prelude to Civil War**, 288.

408   "The **famous day** fixed"   Samuel Cram Jackson Diary, February 1, 1833, Southern Historical Collection, Wilson Library, The University of North Carolina Library at Chapel Hill.

408   at work on a compromise tariff   PHC, VIII, 604–5.

408   spoke in the Senate   Ibid., 621–22.

408   Praising "that great principle"   Remini, **Henry Clay**, 426.

409   "If there be any"   Ibid.

409   "Notwithstanding all their tyranny"   **Correspondence**, V, 14–16.

410   Jackson was another Macbeth   Wiltse, **John C. Calhoun**, II, 178.

410   "a question of self-preservation"   PJCC, XII, 69.

410   "it will be resisted"   Ibid.

411   "Mr. Calhoun is **not** a fine looking man"   EDT, II, 32.

411   Calhoun, Clay said, seemed "careworn"   Freehling, **Road to Disunion**, 266. See also Peterson, **Great Triumvirate**, 222–23.

411   Webster, who favored the Force Bill, rose   Remini, **Daniel Webster**, 378.

411   "The people of the United States"   Ibid., 379.

411   "The bill granting the powers"   **Correspondence**, V, 18.

412   "Well, Clay, these are fine fellows"   Remini, **Henry Clay**, 429.

412   the Compromise of 1833   Peterson, **Great Triumvirate**, 222–33. Freehling, **Road to Disunion**, 283–85, details the Calhoun-Clay negotiations over tariff rates—negotiations Clay dominated. On the ground in South Carolina, Poinsett worried about compromise. To him, facing the nullifiers close at hand, cutting the tariff was giving the potential rebels at least part of what they wanted. In essence, Poinsett believed that a compromise in Washington amounted to surrendering to blackmail. "With regard to the tariff bill, I am disposed to believe that it will be better for the country that it should not pass during the present session," he told Jackson on February 28. "It is doubtless just and politic that the tariff should be modified; but to do it now would have the appearance of yielding to threats and might affect the character and diminish the strength of the government." Fortunately Jackson thought differently (**Correspondence**, V, 23–24).

412   tariff reform   Freehling, **Road to Disunion**, 284–85.

412   the olive branch to the sword   Merrill D. Peterson, **Olive**

Branch and Sword: The Compromise of 1833 (Baton Rouge, La., 1982), 79.

412 John Randolph of Roanoke   Remini, **Henry Clay**, 433.

412 "Help me up"   Ibid.

413 the Verplanck bill came from Treasury Secretary McLane   Remini, **Henry Clay**, 415–16. Jackson recalled the bill as a "tariff bill prepared by McLain [sic] under my view."

413 Operating on two levels   Freehling put this well. "In every confrontation, the tempestuous Westerner [Jackson] had been the iciest plotter," Freehling wrote. "For all his image as a hothead, Jackson usually fired the second shot. He allowed the enemy to spend initial fury. He then cut aggressors down. He won the Battle of New Orleans that way, and the Bank War, and his most famous duel. The counterpunching warrior now plotted to turn the brainy Calhoun into the provocative assaulter" (Freehling, **Road to Disunion**, 278).

413 "I beg of you"   **Correspondence**, V, 3.

414 "We have beat the Nullifiers"   Joel Poinsett to F. Tyrell, March 25, 1833, Poinsett Papers, Historical Society of Pennsylvania, Philadelphia.

414 "the most violent cold I ever had"   PHC, VIII, 633.

414 "Keep me constantly advised"   **Correspondence**, V, 29.

414 "the tariff was only"   **Correspondence**, V, 72.

414 named a postmaster for New Salem   David Herbert Donald, **Lincoln** (New York, 1995), 50.

Chapter 20: Great Is the Stake Placed in Our Hands

415 ceremonies moved indoors   EDT, II, 41. The **Globe** said: "In consequence of the inclemency of the weather the ceremonies of the Inauguration of the President and Vice President of the United States will take place in the Hall of the House of Representatives." See also Remini, **Jackson**, III, 45–46.

415 Flanked by Andrew Donelson   Ibid., 41. The **Globe**, again: "The President took the seat of the Speaker of the House, with Mr. Van Buren on his left, and his Private Secretary, Mr. Donelson, on his right. . . ."

415 a much more substantive speech   **Messages**, II, 1222–24.

415 "My experience"   Ibid., 1223.

416 "Solemnly impressed" Ibid.

416 "Without union our independence" Ibid.

418 he said he longed to "foster with our brethren" Ibid., 1224.

419 "a united and happy people" Ibid.

419 once called "the prudence" Ibid., 1219.

419 Jackson's "most fervent prayer" Ibid., 1224.

419 wore his great cloak . . . showed no signs of strain Remini, **Jackson**, III, 48.

420 took the oath again from John Marshall Smith, **John Marshall: Definer of a Nation**, 520.

420 the last of the chief justice's nine inaugurations Ibid.

420 One guest, Philip Hone Remini, **Jackson**, III, 48.

420 sent him to bed **EDT**, II, 42.

420 Emily and Andrew led the White House circle Ibid.

420 as Calhoun traveled south, fast Freehling, **Prelude to Civil War**, 295.

420 wrote, the Clay rates Ibid., 288.

420 even James Henry Hammond "confessed that he thought" Ibid.

420 the South Carolina convention met Ibid., 296.

421 George McDuffie "very eloquently" Samuel Cram Jackson Diary, March 15, 1833, Southern Historical Collection, Wilson Library, The University of North Carolina Library at Chapel Hill.

421 the convention nullified the Force Bill Ellis, **Union at Risk**, 176–77.

421 a test oath for officeholders Freehling, **Prelude to Civil War**, 309–22.

421 to pledge, according to one proposal Ibid., 310.

421 "We must not think of secession" Freehling, ed., **The Nullification Era**, 182.

421 Frustrated by Jackson's apparent victory Freehling, **Prelude to Civil War**, 297.

422 "A people, owning slaves" Ibid.

422 "Let Gentlemen not be deceived" Ibid.

422 Jackson even indulged in philosophy **Correspondence**, V, 29.

422 Welcome family news **EDT**, II, 43–44.

422 born just before the presidential election Remini, **Jackson**, II, 380.

422 "You know I have always been" **EDT**, II, 43.

422 had been sick   Ibid., 44.

423 "Washington will be very dull"   Emily Donelson to Mary Donelson, April 22, 1833, Mrs. John Lawrence Merritt Collection.

Chapter 21: My Mind Is Made Up

424 a steamboat excursion   Andrew Donelson to Stockley Donelson, May 9, 1833, Donelson Family Private Collection, Cleveland Hall, Nashville. My account of the episode is drawn from this previously unpublished letter of Andrew Donelson's. See also Parton, **Life**, III, 486–89, and Remini, **Jackson**, III, 60–62. Jackson described the incident in a letter to Van Buren (**Correspondence**, V, 74).

424 a disturbed former navy officer, Robert B. Randolph   Cole, **A Jackson Man**, 135–37; 181.

424 as though to assault him   Andrew Donelson to Stockley Donelson, May 9, 1833, Donelson Family Private Collection, Cleveland Hall, Nashville. Donelson called it a "brutal attempt by Randolph to insult the President."

424 Andrew Donelson lunged to protect Jackson   Ibid.

424 who was not armed   Ibid.

424 Randolph bloodied Jackson's face   Parton, **Life**, III, 487, and Remini, **Jackson**, III, 61.

424 the president's stare stopped the assailant   Andrew Donelson to Stockley Donelson, May 9, 1833, Donelson Family Private Collection, Cleveland Hall, Nashville.

425 "The object of the attack"   Ibid.

425 Washington Irving happened to be in Fredericksburg   Irving, **Letters**, II, 762.

425 "It is a brutal transaction"   Ibid.

425 An admirer of the president's from Alexandria   Parton, **Life**, III, 487–88.

425 "No, sir, I cannot do that"   Ibid., 488.

425 He told Van Buren   **Correspondence**, V, 74.

425 "a military guard around the President"   Remini, **Jackson**, III, 61.

425 Randolph was a figure   Cole, **A Jackson Man**, 135–37; 181.

426 the seas were rough   Parton, **Life**, III, 492–93.

427 deposits remained in the Bank   Remini, **Jackson**, III, 52–54.

427 "The hydra of corruption"   Ibid., 52.

427 The vote came after the House   Ibid., 53.

427 "Biddle is actually using"   Parton, **Life**, III, 500.

427 "the damned bank ought to be put down"   Ibid., 503.

427 Jackson agreed with his editor   Ibid., 500.

428 Blair then canvassed   Ibid.

428 "that the withdrawal"   Ibid.

428 Kendall and Van Buren had a tense conversation   **AAK**, 376.

428 "the parties separated"   Ibid.

428 "Oh, my mind is made up"   Parton, **Life**, III, 500.

429 "Let the removal"   **AAK**, 376.

429 Hearing that Kendall was to "take charge"   Samuel D. Ingham to Samuel McKean, May 27, 1831, Samuel D. Ingham Papers, Rare Books and Manuscripts Library, University of Pennsylvania.

429 William J. Duane   Remini, **Jackson**, III, 57–59. Jackson told Van Buren that the idea of appointing Duane had "flashed into [his] mind." Remini remarked that it was a "great misfortune that he did not suppress it on the spot" (ibid., 57–58). See also Parton, **Life**, III, 508–12.

430 A Philadelphian, the son   Ibid., 58.

430 Jackson apparently never asked him   This is the clear implication of Duane's own narrative of events (Parton, **Life**, III, 512–13).

430 By law the Treasury secretary   David P. Currie, **The Constitution in Congress: Democrats and Whigs, 1829–1861** (Chicago, 2005), 67–68.

430 visited at his lodgings by Reuben Whitney   Parton, **Life**, III, 512–13.

430 a merchant and former Bank official   Cole, **Presidency of Andrew Jackson**, 190. Whitney, Cole wrote, "had worked for the Bank but had deserted to the Jackson administration early in the Bank War."

430 Whitney undertook to explain   Parton, **Life**, III, 512–13.

430 "He stated that"   Ibid., 512.

431 Duane complained to Louis McLanc   Ibid.

431 Duane was correct and cool   Ibid., 513.

431 Duane went to the White House   Ibid.

432 "I had heard rumors"   Parton, **Life**, III, 513–14.

432 more thoughts from the road   Ibid., 513.

432 "reflect with a view to the public good"   Ibid.

Chapter 22: He Appeared to Feel as a Father

433 "Uncle's health is as usual"   Emily Donelson to Mary Donelson, April 22, 1833, Mrs. John Lawrence Merritt Collection.

433 Rising early   **Correspondence**, V, 106.

433 "I want relaxation"   Ibid. On the question of the deposits, Jackson wrote: "This is the only difficulty I see now in our way. I must meet it fearlessly as soon as I can digest [**sic**] a system that will insure a solvent currency and a sure system for the fiscal operations of the government" (ibid., 106–7).

434 parents in the Northeast sometimes invoked   Josiah Quincy, **Figures of the Past from the Leaves of Old Journals** (Boston, 1883), 363. Jackson may have been a popular bogyman, but Quincy admitted admiration for the general. "The name of Andrew Jackson was, indeed, one to frighten naughty children with," he wrote, "but the person who went by it wrought a mysterious charm upon old and young."

434 a New England Sunday school teacher   EDT, II, 46.

434 he sat in candlelight after dinner   **Correspondence**, V, 109. The letter was written from Philadelphia on June 10, 1833.

434 returned to his lodgings   Ibid. This account came from New York, dated June 14, 1833.

434 "I have witnessed"   Ibid.

434 In Boston thousands of children   **EDT**, II, 50.

434 the only sounds were "shouts"   Ibid. Donelson also wrote from Boston: "One of the most striking differences in the character of this population compared with ours in the South and West is its order and habitual respect for those in authority."

435 The sun was so hot   **Correspondence**, V, 109.

435 wadding from a cannon nearly singed his hair   Parton, **Life**, III, 490.

435 a low-lying bridge   **EDT**, II, 47.

435 "The smile—the grace"   Remini, **Jackson**, III, 74.

435 a steamboat trip to Staten Island   Parton, **Life**, III, 490–91.

436 There was some confusion   Ibid., 491.

437 On Wednesday, June 26, 1833 "Visit of the President to Harvard University," **Boston Courier,** June 27, 1833.

437 standing on Bunker Hill Remini, **Jackson,** III, 79–80.

437 "It is with great difficulty" **EDT,** II, 50.

437 sardonically called "this magnificent tour" Remini, **Jackson,** III, 83.

437 "Now, Doctor" Parton, **Life,** III, 489.

438 some feared for his life **EDT,** II, 51. John Quincy Adams was less generous about the news of Jackson's poor health. "I believe much of his debility is politic. . . . He is so ravenous of notoriety that he craves the sympathy for sickness as a portion of his glory" (**Memoirs of JQA,** IX, 5).

438 laurels of the journey "proved the increase" Sir Charles Vaughan to Viscount Palmerston, July 4, 1833, National Archives of the United Kingdom, Kew.

438 "The friends of the President" Ibid.

438 "were more like the homage" Remini, **Jackson,** III, 83.

439 a long paper **Correspondence,** V, 113–28.

439 accompanied by a letter Ibid., 111–13.

439 "the gamblers" Nicholas Biddle to Robert Lenox, July 30, 1833, Nicholas Biddle Papers, LOC. During Jackson's trip, men including Blair and Kendall, Duane recalled, "called on me, and made many of the identical observations in the identical language used by [Jackson] himself. They represented Congress as corruptible, and the new members as in need of especial guidance." They spoke in tactical political terms. "They pointed out the importance of a test question, at the opening of the new Congress, for party purposes," Duane said. "They argued that the exercise of the veto power must be secured; that it could be in no other way so effectually attained as by at once removing the deposits; and that, unless they were removed, the President would be thwarted by Congress" (Parton, **Life,** III, 514).

439 Duane replied to Jackson on Wednesday, July 10 Parton, **Life,** III, 520.

439 "Legislators alone" Ibid., 519.

440 Jackson asked Duane to call Ibid., 518.

440 "we did not understand each other" Ibid.

440 "My object, sir, is to save the country" Ibid.

440 "I wish to wait a little while" Nicholas Biddle to Robert Lenox, July 30, 1833, Nicholas Biddle Papers, LOC.

440 Kendall and Donelson were dispatched Cheathem, **Old Hickory's Nephew**, 97.

440 "They tell me the state banks" **AAK**, 378.

440 "Send me to ask them" Ibid.

441 a long debate with Duane Parton, **Life**, III, 520–23.

441 said that he would resign Ibid., 522.

441 whiled away the hours with Blair **FPB**, 81–82.

441 "My dear Mary" **Correspondence**, V, 158.

441 Jackson said that he was struck as David Ibid., 143.

441 from Psalm Sixty-eight The lines read: "A father of the fatherless, and a judge of the widows, is God in his holy habitation" (Psalm 68:5, King James Version).

442 "Mr. Blair," Jackson told his editor **FPB**, 82.

Chapter 23: The People, Sir, Are with *Me*

443 The Cabinet gathered at the White House Parton, **Life**, III, 524.

443 Kendall had returned Cole, **A Jackson Man**, 187. Of forty-seven banks, Kendall recommended seven: one in Maryland, one in Philadelphia, three in New York, and two in Boston. "The selections were a triumph for party patronage," Cole wrote. "Five of the banks were 'friendly' Democratic banks, and the other two . . . 'liberal' opposition banks. All seven had important party connections. . . ."

443 as though he feared Parton, **Life**, III, 524–25.

443 "How shall we answer to God" Ibid.

444 the **Globe** singled Duane out Ibid., 526.

444 denied any involvement Ibid.

444 "It is impossible to describe" Ibid.

444 the mission to Russia Ibid., 530.

444 Duane chose not to take it Ibid. Jackson was gloomy. "Would to God I could return from here to private life," he wrote Mary Coffee on September 15, 1833. But he would not bend in the meantime (**Correspondence**, V, 188).

444 "It is known" **Correspondence**, V, 189.

444 The Cabinet met again Parton, **Life**, III, 527.

444 a manuscript in Andrew Donelson's hand **Correspondence**, V, 192.

445 "The divine right of kings" Ibid., 193–94.

445 the paper was revised (by Taney) and read aloud (by Donelson) Ibid., 192.

445 it was drier For the full final text, see **Messages**, II, 1224–38.

445 "the object avowed" Ibid., 1225–26.

446 As the session broke up Parton, **Life**, III, 528.

446 he needed one more day Ibid.

446 news of Jackson's decision to remove the deposits Ibid.

447 "Then I suppose" Ibid., 529.

447 Duane would not resign Ibid., 530–31.

447 Jackson fired him **Correspondence**, V, 206.

447 Writing to Van Buren Ibid., 206–7.

447 "conduct has been such" Ibid., 206.

447 was to begin in a week's time Cole, **A Jackson Man**, 189.

447 Biddle held a board meeting in Philadelphia Remini, **Andrew Jackson and the Bank War**, 126–28.

447 call in loans and restrict credit Remini, **Jackson**, III, 108. See also Parton, **Life**, III, 533–34; Cole, **Presidency of Andrew Jackson**, 198–99.

448 "The ties of party allegiance" Remini, **Andrew Jackson and the Bank War**, 126–27.

448 New York business was "really" Remini, **Jackson**, III, 111.

449 (and would be) Cole, **Presidency of Andrew Jackson**, 209.

449 raised objection after objection Parton, **Life**, III, 505–6.

450 Lewis broke the silence Ibid., 506–7.

451 As lawmakers traveled Ibid., 537–61. See also Remini, **Jackson**, III, 111–15.

451 petition after petition Parton, **Life**, III, 545.

451 One day Jackson was seated at a table Ibid., 549–50.

451 "Excuse me a moment" Ibid.

452 "Well, sir" Ibid.

452 "Didn't I manage them well?" Ibid., 550.

453 "Go home, gentlemen, and tell the Bank" James, **TLOAJ**, 661–62.

453 "may as well send at once" **Correspondence of Nicholas Biddle**, 222.

453 took to referring to himself in the third person Parton, **Life**, III, 551–52.

453 "Well, what do you want?" James, **TLOAJ**, 661–62. All of the details of the proceedings in the following paragraphs come from this source.

454 wrote of "the violent withdrawal of public funds" Louis Sérurier to Paris, June 18, 1834, Correspondence politique: Etats-Unis: vol. 1834, 174–75, Archives de la Ministère des Affaires Étrangères.

454 that the army was protecting Jackson **FPB**, 86–87.

454 took up the issue in the **Globe** Ibid.

454 a delegation of Jacksonian congressmen Ibid., 87.

455 Donelson took Jackson's annual message Andrew Donelson to Stockley Donelson, December 4, 1833, Donelson Family Private Collection, Cleveland Hall, Nashville.

455 "the unquestionable proof" **Messages**, II, 1249.

455 "whether the people of the United States" Ibid.

455 "Violent opposition may be expected" Andrew Donelson to Stockley Donelson, December 4, 1833, Donelson Family Private Collection, Cleveland Hall, Nashville. Donelson also noted one of the political factors of the moment: "The grand object will be . . . the creation of resources to start a new candidate, or rather **a no administration candidate** for the Presidency. . . ." The thrust of Donelson's point: that the anti-Van Buren forces might attempt to use the Bank battle to field a rival to the vice president.

455 Henry Clay, fresh from Lexington **PHC**, VIII, 669. Clay arrived in Washington on the evening of November 30.

456 "Depend upon it" Ibid., 679.

456 "I mean myself to open and push" Ibid.

Chapter 24: We Are in the Midst of a Revolution

457 arrived in the city four days before Christmas R. K. Polk to James Polk, December 23, 1833, Polk and Yeatman Family Papers, Southern Historical Collection, Wilson Library, University of North Carolina at Chapel Hill.

457 what he called "a burning fever" Ibid.

457 Clay was to speak   Schurz, **Henry Clay**, II, 32.

457 consumed by callers and business   Emily Donelson to her sister, December 25, 1833, Mrs. John Lawrence Merritt Collection.

457 "I suppose you all are at my Dear Mother's"   Ibid.

458 "We are in the midst of a revolution"   Remini, **Henry Clay**, 449–50. See also **PHC**, VIII, 684.

458 "The eyes and hopes"   **AAK**, 396.

458 Van Buren was forced   **PHC**, VIII, 685.

459 "You would be surprised to see the General"   Andrew Jackson Donelson to Edward Livingston, March 7, 1834, Andrew Jackson Donelson Papers, LOC.

459 "was clearly and manifestly"   **PJCC**, XII, 207–8.

459 "There are but two channels"   Ibid.

460 "What, then, is the real question"   Ibid., 218.

460 "artful, cunning, and corrupt"   Ibid., 221.

460 removal of the deposits and the prospect of a national Democratic nominating convention   Ibid.

460 "dictate the **succession**"   Ibid., 221–22.

461 "We have arrived at a fearful crisis"   Ibid., 225.

461 a weak moment with Kendall   **AAK**, 416.

461 "The distress so much complained of"   Andrew Donelson to Stockley Donelson, March 1, 1834, Donelson Family Private Collection, Cleveland Hall, Nashville.

462 had brought about "indiscriminate ruin"   Remini, **Jackson**, III, 164.

462 "We are gaining strength politically"   Andrew Donelson to Stockley Donelson, March 1, 1834, Donelson Family Private Collection, Cleveland Hall, Nashville.

462 Benton would come down to the White House   Benton, **Thirty Years' View**, I, 424.

462 never seemed "more truly heroic"   Ibid.

462 "We shall whip them yet"   Ibid.

463 the Bank "ought not to be rechartered"   Remini, **Jackson**, III, 166–67.

463 "I have obtained a glorious triumph"   **Correspondence**, V, 260.

463 had at last "put to death"   Ibid., 259.

463 a resolution of Clay's   **PHC**, VIII, 685.

463 referred to Jackson as "Caesar"   Ibid., 686.

463 "The whole community of the United States" Sir Charles Vaughan to Viscount Palmerston, April 20, 1834, FO 5–290.

463 The tally in the Senate was 26 to 20 **PHC, VIII, 685.**

464 Resolved, That the President Ibid.

464 the Chamber of Deputies in France Duc de Broglie to Sérurier, April 8, 1834, Correspondence politique: Etats-Unis: vol. 1834, 95–96, Archives de la Ministère des Affaires Étrangères. In this letter, de Broglie writes Sérurier: "This bill was rejected by the legislature by a majority of 8 votes. I will not try to explain to you what is incomprehensible here for everyone—that is, how such powerful reasons for passing the bill were swept away, when we had every reason to believe that the law would be approved. Be that as it may, Monsieur, what is important for you to know, and what you will have to in-form the Cabinet in Washington, is that the king's government has formally resolved to call for a vote on the issue in the next session of the legislature. . . . **The king's government expects that this legislative decision will be received in the U.S. first with bitterness and** irritation." And de Broglie sounds a warn-ing: "**Any hasty measure, any behavior contrary to the good relations and friendship which the interests of our two na-tions ardently desire, would only decrease the king's govern-ment's chances of success.**"

464 by a margin of eight Ibid.

Chapter 25: So You Want War

467 in the form of dispatches from Edward Livingston Sérurier to Paris, May 11, 1834, Correspondence politique: Etats-Unis: vol. 1834, 127–37, Archives de la Ministère des Affaires Étrangères.

467 struggled to figure out what to do Ibid. "Since I have no in-structions from you," Sérurier wrote home, "I must just wait. Immobility and self-respect have often succeeded for me here. Will that be enough now?"

467 Thinking of "the President's fiery character" Ibid.

467 Sérurier called on McLane Ibid., 131. "Mr. McLane replied calmly and said that he appreciated the reasons for my visit and that he would inform the President."

467 "I was informed" Ibid., 129.

467 "It would no longer" Ibid.

468 Jackson's reaction "is what I feared the most" Ibid.

468 came to see the Frenchman Sérurier to Paris, May 20, 1834, Correspondence politique: Etats-Unis: vol. 1834, 140, Archives de la Ministère des Affaires Étrangères.

468 "He told me that" Ibid.

468 "had hit the President like a thunderbolt" Sérurier to Paris, May 11, 1834, Correspondence politique: Etats-Unis: vol. 1834, 131, Archives de la Ministère des Affaires Étrangères.

469 It was Henry Clay, in a fury Sérurier to Paris, May 11, 1834, Correspondence politique: Etats-Unis: vol. 1834, 133, Archives de la Ministère des Affaires Étrangères.

469 "Well, he said to me, so you want war" Ibid.

469 The two continued their conversation Ibid.

470 made his first visit to the White House Sérurier to Paris, May 20, 1834, Correspondence politique: Etats-Unis: vol. 1834, 143, Archives de la Ministère des Affaires Étrangères.

470 "The President was very cold" Ibid.

470 "take the political temperature" Sérurier to Paris, June 20, 1834, Correspondence politique: Etats-Unis: vol. 1834, 380, Archives de la Ministère des Affaires Étrangères.

470 "I have always loved France" Ibid.

Chapter 26: A Dark, Lawless, and Insatiable Ambition!

471 document entitled "Protest" **Messages**, II, 1288–1312. In his memoirs, John Quincy Adams writes that Jackson sent his "Protest" to the Senate on April 17, 1834.

471 "Having had the honor" Ibid., 1288.

471 "The judgment of **guilty**" Ibid., 1294.

472 "If the censures of the Senate" Ibid., 1310.

472 "the President is the direct representative" Ibid., 1309.

473 "In vain do I bear" Ibid., 1311–12.

474 seeking to "concentrate" Ibid.

474 "The domineering tone" **Memoirs of JQA**, IX, 51.

474 to Webster the protest amounted Peterson, **Great Triumvirate**, 244.

474 Calhoun was even angrier **PJCC**, XII, 310.

474 "Infatuated man!" Ibid.

475 recounted an interview John C. Hamilton to William Gaston, September 27, 1834, William Gaston Papers, Southern Historical Collection, Wilson Library, University of North Carolina at Chapel Hill.

475 saying the "charge" Ibid.

476 Clay referred to Jackson's foes as Whigs **PHC**, VIII, 714–15.

476 "a denomination which, according to the analogy of all history" Ibid., 714.

476 rescue the nation from "a Chief Magistrate" Ibid., 715.

476 Claiming to have heard a rumor Ibid., 717.

476 Sérurier wrote that "Mr. Forsyth" Sérurier to Paris, July 2, 1834, Correspondence politique: Etats-Unis: vol. 1834, 206–7, Archives de la Ministère des Affaires Étrangères.

477 because of "intolerable heat" Sérurier to Paris, July 8, 1834, Correspondence politique: Etats-Unis: vol. 1834, 216–18, Archives de la Ministère des Affaires Étrangères.

477 Sérurier marveled at the old man's enduring vitality Ibid.

477 Sérurier came across Nicholas Biddle Sérurier to Paris, August 18, 1834, Correspondence politique: Etats-Unis: vol. 1834, 248, Archives de la Ministère des Affaires Étrangères.

477 "One of the first people" Ibid.

477 "The South seems to be asleep" Frederick W. Moore, ed., "Calhoun as Seen by His Political Friends: Letters of Duff Green, Dixon H. Lewis, Richard K. Crallé During the Period from 1831 to 1848," **Publications of the Southern History Association** 7 (July 1903), 287.

478 Emily had given birth to her fourth child **EDT**, II, 68. Hearing the news, Sarah Jackson quickly dispatched congratulations from Nashville in a letter that was also filled with concern for the head of the family. Sending her regards to Emily, Sarah then took on a wifely tone with Jackson. "I have not been able to read the papers for some time, but heard of your triumph over your and our country's enemies," Sarah wrote Jackson. "I congratulate you, my dear Father, and pray that your health may be restored and your life prolonged, and that your strength increase" (Sarah Yorke Jackson to Andrew Jackson, May 2, 1834, Andrew Jackson Papers, LOC).

478 in the White House **FPB**, 88.

478 he gave her Rachel's wedding ring   **FPB,** 175–76.

478 he and Lewis had drunk "Ice sangree"   Ibid.

478 bought the house   Ibid., 92.

478 would bring the president a pail   Ibid.

478 "We are very much pleased"   **EDT,** II, 68.

479 Her niece Elizabeth Martin   Ibid., 66–68.

479 being courted by Lewis Randolph   Ibid.

479 Emily had entertained   Hunt, ed., **First Forty Years of Washington Society,** 307.

479 "I am well except [for] weakness"   **EDT,** II, 69.

Chapter 27: There Is a Rank Due
to the United States Among Nations

480 the construction of the first home of their own   **EDT,** II, 70.

480 Emily managed the details   Ibid.

480 kept a crate of her china   **Correspondence,** V, 302.

480 fire broke out at the Hermitage   Remini, **Jackson,** III, 179–91. The house burned on the afternoon of Monday, October 13, 1834.

481 "Oh, had I been there"   Ibid., 185.

481 the slaves who were on hand   Ibid.

481 Sarah "acted with firmness"   **Correspondence,** V, 296.

481 had given him "the means to build it"   Ibid., 302.

481 "Was it not on the site selected"   Ibid.

481 He gave orders about   Ibid.

481 "I suppose all the wines"   Ibid.

482 The French remained a problem   In an August 9, 1834, letter, Edward Livingston insisted that Sérurier had led Jackson to believe that the Chamber would resolve the problem before the American Congress met in December 1834 (Livingston to de Rigny, August 9, 1834, Correspondence politique: Etats-Unis: vol. 1834, 240–42, Archives de la Ministère des Affaires Étrangères). De Rigny denied that the government had made any such promise (ibid., 243–44). Still, Jackson held his temper, further perplexing the French. On October 2, 1834, Sérurier called on Jackson, expecting an unpleasant visit. Instead, Sérurier was "happily surprised. The President received me with his usual politeness and kindness without any visible change in his attitude."

Jackson avoided the subject altogether (Sérurier to Paris, October 8, 1834, Correspondence politique: Etats Unis: vol. 1834, 291, Archives de la Ministère des Affaires Étrangères).

482 met with Sérurier   Sérurier to Paris, October 22, 1834, Correspondence politique: Etats-Unis: vol. 1834, 302–7, Archives de la Ministère des Affaires Étrangères.

482 "The President was deeply hurt"   Ibid.

482 "No, gentlemen"   Parton, **Life**, III, 569–70.

482 in the eighteenth   **Messages**, II, 1319.

482 "the whole civilized world"   Ibid., 1325.

483 a law approving "reprisals upon French property"   Ibid.

483 "inflexible determination"   Ibid., 1326.

483 France "would but add violence to injustice"   Ibid.

483 "Threats are far from being avoided"   Sérurier to Paris, December 2, 1834, Correspondence politique: Etats-Unis: vol. 1834, 338, Archives de la Ministère des Affaires Étrangères.

483 fell back on the caricature of Jackson   Sérurier to Paris, December 5, 1834, Correspondence politique: Etats-Unis: vol. 1834, 342, Archives de la Ministère des Affaires Étrangères.

483 "It is generally agreed"   Ibid.

483 "iron will subdued all resistance"   Ibid.

483 "very cold and disagreeable"   Emily Donelson to Mary Donelson, December 25, 1834, Mrs. John Lawrence Merritt Collection.

483 Emily dined alone with Mrs. Forsyth   Ibid.

483 composing a coded message   Sérurier to Paris, December 25, 1834, Correspondence politique: Etats-Unis: vol. 1834, 360, Archives de la Ministère des Affaires Étrangères.

484 "If we have war with the U.S."   Ibid. Henry Clay also clearly thought things were heading in a warlike direction, and the situation brought out his instinct for compromise and conciliation. Clay came to see Sérurier and spoke as though he too believed war was not far off. "He told me that he was distressed by the Message, by its threats and the effect it would have on both sides of the Atlantic," Sérurier wrote Paris on December 28, 1834. "He added that the wisest men in Congress, all while blaming the rash step taken by the head of the republic, could not wish to abandon him when he was fighting for their own interests against a foreign power. However, he continued, every-

one was loath to be associated with the defiant tone, the threats, and even more, the reprisals . . . in this unfortunate document. He said that they would do what could be done to bring about reconciliation in the best interests of all" (Sérurier to Paris, December 28, 1834, Correspondence politique: Etats-Unis: vol. 1834, 362–69, Archives de la Ministère des Affaires Étrangères).

484 "Never since Washington's death" Sérurier to Paris, July 2, 1834, Correspondence politique: Etats-Unis: vol. 1834, 210, Archives de la Ministère des Affaires Étrangères.

484 On New Year's Eve, Adams rose in the House John Quincy Adams, **Oration on the Life and Character of Gilbert M. de Lafayette: Delivered at the Request of Both Houses of the Congress of the United States, Before Them, in the House of Representatives at Washington. December 31, 1834** (Trenton, N.J., 1835).

485 the king of France recalled Sérurier home to Paris De Rigny to Sérurier, January 14, 1835, Correspondence politique: Etats-Unis: vol. 1835, 389, Archives de la Ministère des Affaires Étrangères (Letter published by Courier des Etats-Unis, New York, January 30, 1836).

485 "The impression that President Jackson's message produced here" Ibid.

485 had summoned Edward Livingston Ibid.

485 "passports will be at his disposal" Ibid.

485 presented to the Chamber on Thursday, January 15, 1835 Ibid.

485 A new clause said that "all or part" Ibid.

485 an additional requirement Duc de Broglie to Alphonse Pageot, June 17, 1835, Correspondence politique: Etats-Unis: vol. 1836, 52, Archives de la Ministère des Affaires Étrangères.

486 "the true meaning and real purport" Ibid.

486 had to offer "new testimony to the good faith" Ibid.

486 John Quincy Adams rallied to his foe's side Parton, **Life**, III, 577.

486 "Sir, this treaty has been ratified" Ibid., 577–78.

487 "The President told me" Sir Charles Vaughan to Viscount Palmerston, Washington, November 5, 1835, National Archives of the United Kingdom, Kew.

487 the suggestion that he would apologize **Messages**, II, 1407–

8. The French chargé, Jackson reported to Congress on January 15, 1836, had asserted that "We will pay the money, says [the chargé], when 'the Government of the United States is ready on its part to declare to us, by addressing its claim to us officially in writing, that it regrets the misunderstanding which has arisen between the two countries; that this misunderstanding is founded on a mistake; that it never entered into its intention to call in question the good faith of the French Government nor to take a menacing attitude toward France.' And [the chargé] adds: 'If the Government of the United States does not give this assurance we shall be obliged to think that this misunderstanding is not the result of an error.'" And finally: "'the Government of the United States knows that upon itself depends henceforward the execution of the treaty of July 4, 1831'" (italics in the original).

487   "of naval preparations"   Ibid., 1411.

487   "large and speedy appropriations"   Ibid. Two days after this communication, Alphonse Pageot followed Sérurier in returning to France. It was January 17, 1836 (Correspondence politique: Etats-Unis: vol. 1836, 64, Archives de la Ministère des Affaires Étrangères).

487   "The conception that it was my intention"   I am indebted to Belohlavek, "Let the Eagle Soar!" 122, for the insight about the annual message. The full passage of Jackson's is a mouthful: "The conception that it was my intention to menace or insult the Government of France is as unfounded as the attempt to extort from the fears of that nation what her sense of justice may deny would be vain and ridiculous. But the Constitution of the United States imposes on the President the duty of laying before Congress the condition of the country in its foreign and domestic relations, and of recommending such measures as may in his opinion be required by its interests. From the performance of this duty he cannot be deterred by the fear of wounding the sensibilities of the people or government of whom it may become necessary to speak . . ." (Messages, II, 1376–77).

487   Britain, fearing that a war   London could see no good coming of a Franco-American war. "The British ambassador in France, Lord Granville, and Foreign Secretary Lord Palmerston had

carefully followed the seriousness of the situation, Great Britain growing steadily more troubled as her valuable continental ally seemed to be slipping into an unnecessary conflict with the United States," writes John M. Belohlavek. "Such an event would disrupt the French economy and enact untold havoc upon the French merchant marine and navy. While Louis Philippe probably possessed the maritime might to defeat the Americans, a war would drain limited resources and sidetrack him from the more vital arena of the European balance of power with the autocratic eastern monarchies. A Franco-American War would also mean a blockade of United States ports and the disruption of valuable cotton exports to English textile mills" (Belohlavek, **"Let the Eagle Soar!"** 122–23).

488 both sides accepted the offer **Messages**, II, 1432–33.

488 Jackson suspended his call Ibid., 1433.

488 Thomas P. Barton, Livingston's aide in France Parton, **Life**, III, 574–77.

488 "Tell me, sir" Ibid., 575.

488 Jackson jumped up Ibid., 576.

489 helped soothe "the irritation" Ibid.

489 The British resolved Belohlavek, **"Let the Eagle Soar!"** 122–25.

489 chose to take the conciliatory line of Jackson's from December as apology enough Ibid., 124–25.

490 "There is a rank due" **Messages**, II, 1436.

Chapter 28: The Wretched Victim of a Dreadful Delusion

491 a dinner in Washington Parton, **Life**, III, 580–81.

491 "The national debt is paid!" Ibid., 581.

491 Jackson was walking out of the House chamber Ibid., 582.

492 when the president's eyes met those **Washington Globe**, January 31, 1835.

492 "handsome . . . well-dressed" young man Ibid.

492 Armed with two pistols Ibid. For accounts of the assassination attempt and its aftermath, see also Benton, **Thirty Years' View**, 521–24; Richard C. Rohrs, "Partisan Politics and the Attempted Assassination of Andrew Jackson," **Journal of the Early Republic** 1 (Summer 1981), 149–63; and Remini, **Jackson**, III, 229.

492 less than ten feet   Ibid. The **Globe** of January 31 thought the distance had been "within two and a half yards" (**Washington Globe**, January 31, 1835).

492 raised the first gun and fired   Ibid.

492 charged his assailant   Ibid. According to Isaac Bassett, "The President instantly rushed upon him with uplifted cane . . ." (Papers of Isaac Bassett, U.S. Senate Commission on Art, Washington).

492 "The explosion of the cap"   Benton, **Thirty Years' View**, 521.

492 Lawrence dropped the gun   Papers of Isaac Bassett, U.S. Senate Commission on Art, Washington.

492 it too failed to fire   Parton, **Life**, III, 582.

492 had thought the assassin "firm and resolved"   **Washington Globe**, January 31, 1835.

492 "seemed to shrink"   Ibid.

492 a nearby navy lieutenant   Parton, **Life**, III, 582.

492 "The President pressed"   **Washington Globe**, January 31, 1835.

492 put into a carriage   Parton, **Life**, III, 582.

492 by George Washington and by the weather   I am indebted to Donald A. Ritchie, associate historian of the U.S. Senate, for the Washington tomb theory, which he laid out for me during a tour of the Capitol in which we recreated, as best we could, the path Jackson would have taken from the services for Davis in the old chamber through the Rotunda to the East Portico. Lawrence himself attributed the weapons' failure to the damp weather (Rohrs, "Partisan Politics and the Attempted Assassination of Andrew Jackson," 162–63).

493 "The pistols were examined"   Benton, **Thirty Years' View**, 521.

493 125,000 to one   **FPB**, 99. In the emotion of the moment, the **Globe** attributed the failures to fire to divine intervention. "How the caps could have exploded without firing the powder is miraculous," the paper wrote in the edition reporting the attack. "Providence has ever guarded the life of the man who has been destined to preserve and raise his country's glory, and maintain the cause of the People. In the multitude of instances in which he has hazarded his person for his country, it was never in more imminent danger than on yesterday . . ." (**Washington Globe**, January 31, 1835). One suspects the moisture had more to do with it than the miraculous.

493 Van Buren found him   **EDT**, II, 78.

493 claiming to be the king of England   Rohrs, "Partisan Politics and the Attempted Assassination of Andrew Jackson," 151.

493 believed Lawrence was an agent   Ibid., 152–54.

493 Harriet Martineau visited the White House   Parton, **Life**, III, 584.

493 the "insane attempt"   Ibid.

493 "He protested"   Ibid.

494 "taciturn and unwilling to talk"   **Washington Globe**, January 31, 1835.

494 "Whether Lawrence has caught"   Ibid.

494 "Someone told me"   Nathaniel Niles to William Cabell Rives, January 30, 1835, William Cabell Rives Papers, LOC.

494 "Yes, sir"   Ibid.

494 "This man has been hired"   Edwin A. Miles, "Andrew Jackson and Senator George Poindexter," **Journal of Southern History** 24 (February 1958), 62.

495 for the president "to name any person"   Nathaniel Niles to William Cabell Rives, January 30, 1835, William Cabell Rives Papers, LOC.

495 Poindexter demanded an investigation   **Report on Communication of Senator G. Poindexter**, S. Doc. 148, 23rd Congress, 2nd session, March 2, 1835, 1–50. The document includes the conclusions of the investigation and a series of transcripts of original documents.

495 two affidavits alleging that Lawrence had been seen   Rohrs, "Partisan Politics and the Attempted Assassination of Andrew Jackson," 155–57. See also **Report on Communication of Senator G. Poindexter**, S. Doc. 148, March 2, 1835, 11–12.

495 a blacksmith who did work for the White House   Ibid., 156. The blacksmith was named Mordecai Foy.

495 a man who had loaned money to Poindexter   Ibid. His name was David Stewart.

495 to have some hopes of being given work   Ibid., 157.

495 "has become of late years idle and intemperate"   **Report on Communication of Senator G. Poindexter**, S. Doc. 148, March 2, 1835, 3. Did Jackson play a role in ginning up allegations against Poindexter? Stewart said yes, claiming that "if

he had put into his affidavit all, and some say only part of what the General desired him to put in, it would have filled a newspaper" (ibid.). The committee exonerated Jackson of this (Rohrs, "Partisan Politics and the Attempted Assassination of Andrew Jackson," 158).

The committee did find that Charles Coltman, a government contractor, had played a role in shaping the affidavits. In the fullest scholarly treatment of the politics of the assassination attempt, Richard Rohrs wrote: "When several of the committee members conferred with the president, Jackson told them that approximately fifty people had seen Lawrence enter Poindexter's home. Yet the president stressed that he had only accepted those reports of individuals who were willing to file affidavits. He further explained that he had done nothing to secure the two existing ones. In testimony before the entire Senate committee, Foy and Stewart reaffirmed the statements in their earlier depositions. Foy, who occasionally worked as a blacksmith for the White House, testified that although a Mr. Coltman and another man, whose name he did not know, encouraged him to report what he had observed, he received no 'reward, bribery, or corruption' as compensation for presenting his affidavit. Stewart admitted that Poindexter owed him money, but denied that was the reason he came forward with the information. Like Foy, Stewart related that Mr. Coltman had urged him to report his observations.

"As the proceedings continued, it became evident that neither Foy nor Stewart were credible witnesses. Foy, for example, was unable to identify Poindexter's home. It seemed ironic to the committee that Foy remembered the exact date and time of day of the alleged meetings, but the wrong house. A shopkeeper testified that Stewart had been in his shop, which was more than a mile from the senator's home, at the same time he reportedly saw Lawrence and Poindexter together. Stewart's inability to describe Lawrence's stature or the color of his hair further diminished his reliability as a witness. . . .

"After challenging the credibility of Stewart and Foy, the committee concentrated on determining if anyone had committed improprieties in obtaining the affidavits. Although several witnesses testified that Stewart told them that Jackson asked him to include more information in his deposition than he knew to be true, the committee apparently considered this to be a lie. Foy, in a supplementary memorandum, admitted that Charles Coltman, a contractor for government buildings, had intimated that blacksmith work on the fence of the new Treasury Department building would be forthcoming if he filed a deposition. In response to this accusation, Coltman denied promising work to Foy or being actively engaged in gathering evidence to implicate Poindexter. He admitted only that he had encouraged both Foy and Stewart to notify the proper authorities, after learning of their observations. . . . The committee reproached Stewart and Coltman, but absolved the president, apparently rejecting Stewart's attempt to implicate him. While simply dismissing Foy as a man affected by 'his habits of inebriation,' the committee determined that Stewart, motivated by Poindexter's indebtedness, committed 'an offense of the deepest dye against the public morals.' According to the committee, Coltman then arranged for Foy to substantiate Stewart's lies by promising him work on the Treasury Department building. The committee members expressed hope that those involved would 'be held up to public odium and scorn'" (Rohrs, "Partisan Politics and the Attempted Assassination of Andrew Jackson," 156–58).

495   dismissed the allegations   Ibid., 7. Their conclusion: "That not a shade of suspicion rests upon the character of the Hon. George Poindexter" in the matter of the assassination attempt.

496   Questioned afterward by two physicians   Benton, **Thirty Years' View**, 521–23. Politics seemed less of a factor than madness. Asked by the examining doctors who would make a good president, Lawrence answered "Mr. Clay, Mr. Webster, [and] Mr. Calhoun," but also said that "Col. Benton, Mr. Van Buren, or Judge White" would also do well.

496   "Hallucination of mind was evident"   Ibid., 524.

496   settled for blaming anti-Jackson Senate speeches   **Washington Globe**, February 4, 1835.

496   "sullen and deep-brooding fanatic"   Ibid.

496   "violent in his expressions"   Ibid.

496   "Is it . . . a strained inference"   Ibid.

Chapter 29: How Would You Like to Be a Slave?

497 in the market for new slaves   Andrew Donelson to Stockley Donelson, July 4, 1835, Donelson Family Private Collection, Cleveland Hall, Nashville.

497 "waiting for an inspection"   Ibid.

497 "One of the boys I took"   Ibid.

497 his new wife's "trunk and guitar"   Andrew Jackson, Jr., to Samuel Hays, May 8, 1832, The Hermitage.

497 "Late on yesterday evening your kind favor"   Ibid. Andrew junior added: "If you do propose to take her I can immediately send her to you—she can be taught perhaps. You can take her for what she cost me [to bring] her on here, which is not much—her cost was $250, the expense in bringing her about 50, or 55—I shall however in a day or two either send you her or Charlotte, perhaps tomorrow—nothing will give me more pleasure than to accommodate you in every respect."

498 "Andrew has not yet bought me a girl"   Emily Donelson to Mary Donelson, May 10, 1829, Mrs. John Lawrence Merritt Collection.

498 "Advertisement for Runaway Slave"   Burstein, **The Passions of Andrew Jackson**, 24; **Papers**, II, 40–41.

498 owned about one hundred fifty slaves   Frederick M. Binder, **The Color Problem in Early National America As Viewed By John Adams, Jefferson and Jackson** (Paris, 1968), 124–25.

498 the nation's thinking on slavery   Wilentz, **Rise of American Democracy**, 330–47. See also Feller, **Jacksonian Promise**, 60–65; Howe, **What Hath God Wrought**, 423–29; Henry Mayer, **All on Fire: William Lloyd Garrison and the Abolition of Slavery** (New York, 1998), 97–239; James Brewer Stewart, **Holy Warriors: The Abolitionists and American Slavery** (New York, 1976), 35–74; William J. Cooper, Jr., **The South and the Politics of Slavery, 1828–1856** (Baton Rouge, La., 1978), 58–66.

498 he was not interested in reform   "Jackson's position on the question, and the position of the other leaders of the Democratic Party, was quite clear and unambiguous," wrote Remini. "He held that the Constitution expressly recognized slavery in the South and made provisions about representation in Congress to accommodate that fact of life. . . . 'There is no debat-

able ground left upon the subject,' editorialized the **Globe**" (Remini, **Legacy of Andrew Jackson**, 88).

499 a revealing exchange with Roeliff Brinkerhoff   Roeliff Brinkerhoff, **Recollections of a Lifetime** (Cincinnati, 1900), 61.

500 the battle was joined again in South Carolina   Freehling, **Prelude to Civil War**, 340–60.

500 its headquarters on Nassau Street   William Lee Miller, **Arguing About Slavery: The Great Battle in the United States Congress** (New York, 1996), 97.

500 arrived aboard the steamboat **Columbia**   Freehling, **Prelude to Civil War**, 340.

500 fell to Alfred Huger   Ibid.

500 wanted guidance from above   Ibid.

500 Local newspapers   Ibid., 340–41.

500 A mob came to the post office   Ibid.

500 along with effigies   Ibid.

501 exchanging notes with Kendall   **Correspondence**, V, 359–61.

501 as a "wicked plan"   Ibid., 361.

501 John W. Jones   Miller, **Arguing About Slavery**, 93.

502 Northern opinion was hardly enthusiastic   Freehling, **Prelude to Civil War**, 343.

502 "unconstitutional and wicked"   **Messages**, II, 1394.

502 asked Congress for a law   Ibid., 1394–95.

502 The states, Calhoun said, "possessed"   Miller, **Arguing About Slavery**, 100.

503 "virtually . . . clothe"   Freehling, **Prelude to Civil War**, 347.

503 "If you refuse"   Parton, **Life**, III, 589.

503 "This spirit of mob-law"   **Correspondence**, V, 360.

503 they tacitly allowed   Freehling, **Prelude to Civil War**, 346–48.

503 The episode affirmed   Miller, **Arguing About Slavery**, 100–5. See also Freehling, **Prelude to Civil War**, 343–48, and Stewart, **Holy Warriors**, 70–74.

504 "So the pamphlet controversy"   Ibid., 104.

504 "On principle, slavery has no advocates"   Latner, **Presidency of Andrew Jackson**, 212. Latner wrote: "However menacing the slavery issue began to appear in the mid-1830s, it had very little effect on the perceptions of men like Jackson, Kendall, and Blair. Reflecting their Jeffersonian heritage, they considered slav-

ery not as a permanent fixture, but as a blight that, somehow, Time and Providence would eradicate" (ibid.).

504 complained of the expense   Andrew Donelson to Stockley Donelson, October 15, 1835, Donelson Family Private Collection, Cleveland Hall, Nashville.

504 "I had to employ a man"   Ibid.

Chapter 30: The Strife About the Next Presidency

505 The politics of 1836   Wilentz, **Rise of American Democracy**, 446–54. See also Holt, **Rise and Fall of the American Whig Party**, 38–59, and Niven, **Martin Van Buren**, 386–403.

505 had nominated one of their own   Powell Moore, "The Revolt Against Jackson in Tennessee, 1835–1836," **Journal of Southern History** 2 (August 1936), 335–59. See also Joshua W. Caldwell, "John Bell of Tennessee: A Chapter of Political History," **American Historical Review** 4 (July 1899), 652–64; William G. Shade, "'The Most Delicate and Exciting Topics': Martin Van Buren, Slavery, and the Election of 1836," **Journal of the Early Republic** 18 (Autumn 1998), 459–84; Burton W. Folsom II, "The Politics of Elites: Prominence and Party in Davidson County, Tennessee, 1835–1861," **Journal of Southern History** 39 (August 1973), 359–78; Thomas Brown, "From Old Hickory to Sly Fox: The Routinization of Charisma in the Early Democratic Party," **Journal of the Early Republic** 11 (Autumn 1991), 339–69.

505 a former Democrat   Howe, **What Hath God Wrought**, 390.

505 The Whigs in the North   Wilentz, **Rise of American Democracy**, 448–49.

505 "He is not of the race"   Widmer, **Martin Van Buren**, 88.

506 was "a crawling reptile"   Ibid., 89.

506 could not help Van Buren too overtly   Jackson's opponents struck at the heart of Jackson's creed by arguing that the champion of democracy was betraying his own faith in the people by working for the election of a successor—any successor. To the Illinois Whigs, "the convention system . . . forced upon the American people by the Van Buren party" was "destructive of the freedom of the elective franchise, opposed to republican in-

stitutions, and dangerous to the liberties of the people" (Holt, **Rise and Fall of the American Whig Party**, 31).

506 "All my friends know" **Nashville Republican**, July 28, 1835.

507 "Permit me here to say" **Papers**, VII, 656.

507 In the autumn of 1834 Nancy N. Scott, ed., **A Memoir of Hugh Lawson White** (Philadelphia, 1856), 301–4. See 302–4 for Orville Bradley's complete letter on the Jackson episode.

507 "the subject of succession" Ibid., 302.

507 "General Jackson entered warmly" Ibid., 303.

507 The solution Ibid., 304.

507 wrote that "much as the people of Tennessee" **Nashville Republican**, July 25, 1835.

508 Blair . . . backed Richard M. Johnson Niven, **Martin Van Buren**, 395. See also Remini, **Jackson**, III, 256.

508 widely believed that Blair was doing Jackson's bidding **Nashville Republican**, July 28, 1835.

508 a series of attacks on Andrew and on Blair **Nashville Republican**, July 7, 14, 18, 25, 28, August 8, 18, 20; September 1, 8, 12, 15, 1835.

509 "For President HUGH WHITE" **Nashville Republican**, July 7, 1835.

509 affirmed by a "packed jury" Ibid.

509 carried "the grossest" Ibid.

510 "You must keep me advised" Andrew Donelson to Stockley Donelson, July 15, 1835, Donelson Family Private Collection, Cleveland Hall, Nashville.

510 "My inclinations as well as my duty" Ibid.

510 the day he returned to the White House Andrew Donelson to Stockley Donelson, July 21, 1835, Donelson Family Private Collection, Cleveland Hall, Nashville. Andrew wrote: "I came back last evening from the Rip Raps where I left Uncle and all our family in good health."

510 "I see that the **Republican**" Ibid.

510 "It would be just as reasonable" Ibid.

511 "But I have no time" Ibid.

511 "I have noticed" Andrew Donelson to Stockley Donelson, July 24, 1835, Donelson Family Private Collection, Cleveland Hall, Nashville.

511 In July, the paper kept raising the stakes   **Nashville Republican**, July 14, 1835.

511 "It has been the professed object"   **Nashville Republican**, July 18, 1835.

512 Jackson was behind the frank   Ibid. On the same day, the paper also asked: "Is it not exhibiting him as the anxious and active friend of Mr. Van Buren? Is it not degrading the Chief Magistrate of a great nation into a warm and reckless partisan—the mere tool of his supple but wily inferior?"

512 The **Republican**'s true agenda   **Nashville Republican**, July 28, 1835. Donelson was one proxy target, Blair another.

512 "That the Editor of the **Globe**"   Ibid.

512 "Always supposing"   Ibid.

513 denouncing the charges as "a vile calumny"   September 1, 1835. The **Republican** was responding to the **Globe**'s coverage of the events.

513 "Does he know"   Ibid.

513 The letter he wrote to rebut   Andrew Donelson to Stockley Donelson, August 18, 1835, Donelson Family Private Collection, Cleveland Hall, Nashville.

514 "drawn up in most haste"   Ibid.

514 "It is painful to me"   Ibid.

514 "not so much because my course"   Ibid.

514 "The Major, like all weak persons"   **Nashville Republican**, September 8, 1835.

515 "But we cannot afford"   Ibid.

515 Blair tried his hand   **Nashville Republican**, July 25, 1835.

515 Donelson began to read aloud   Ibid.

515 "It must be apparent"   Ibid.

515 "In the progress"   Ibid.

515 "a charge of **dictation**"   Ibid.

516 "The indelicacy, presumption"   Ibid.

516 "It is evident"   Ibid.

516 a "worthy pair"   Ibid.

517 "You may rest assured"   Andrew Donelson to Stockley Donelson, September 21, 1835, Donelson Family Private Collection, Cleveland Hall, Nashville.

517 "violence of party strife"   Ibid.

517 "It will be among"   Ibid.

517 "The Calhoun, the Eaton, and the ancient opposition"   Andrew Donelson to Stockley Donelson, August 18, 1835, Donelson Family Private Collection, Cleveland Hall, Nashville.

517 One night at the shore   Parton, **Life**, III, 601–2.

Chapter 31: Not One Would Have Ever Got Out Alive

518 Sunday, August 16, 1835   **EDT**, II, 88.

518 First mapped by the Spanish in 1519   Harry Hansen, ed., **Texas: A Guide to the Lone Star State** (New York, 1969), 30–47, is a straightforward telling of Texas history originally written in 1940 as part of the Federal Writers' Program of the WPA. For overviews of the history of Texas and Jackson's interest in it, see, for instance: Richard Bruce Winders, **Crisis in the Southwest: The United States, Mexico, and the Struggle over Texas** (Wilmington, De., 2002); Remini, **Jackson**, III, 352–68; and Howe, **What Hath God Wrought**, 658–73.

518 had long tantalized Americans   Hansen, ed., **Texas**, 37.

518 "a most delicious country"   Ibid., 39.

518 Stephen Austin   Ibid., 38.

518 An 1826 rebellion   Ibid., 39–40.

519 the Texas Revolution had begun   Ibid., 40–43.

519 "I cannot remember"   Ibid., 41.

519 maneuvered to win Texas, dispatching an envoy   Remini, **Jackson**, III, 352–53. See also Winders, **Crisis in the Southwest**, 76–77.

519 A land speculator in Texas   Quinton Curtis Lamar, "A Diplomatic Disaster: The Mexican Mission of Anthony Butler, 1829–1834," **The Americas** 45 (July 1988), 5.

519 Jackson regarded Butler's time   Remini, **Jackson**, III, 218–19.

520 ("A. Butler: What a scamp")   Ibid., 220.

520 Butler was simply   Remini makes this point clearly: "It would seem that the President was inviting his minister to gain the cession of Texas by encouraging Mexican greed" (ibid., 220).

520 "This must be an honest transaction"   Ibid., and **Papers**, VII, 489.

520 sent Mexico into "a perfect tempest"   **Correspondence**, V, 381.

520 Santa Anna, the powerful leader of Mexico   Winders, **Crisis in the Southwest**, xxviii, 10–11.

520 "perfectly furious" **Correspondence**, V, 381.

520 was convinced the Americans had fomented Ibid.

520 "would in due season" Ibid.

520 Sam Houston was advertising Hansen, ed., **Texas**, 41.

521 "Volunteers from the United States" Ibid.

521 Osceola led the Seminole war party John K. Mahon, **History of the Second Seminole War, 1835–1842** (Gainesville, Fla., 1985), 91–92; John Missall and Mary Lou Missall, **The Seminole Wars: America's Longest Indian Conflict** (Gainesville, Fla., 2004), 89–92. Prucha, **Great Father**, 229–33, is a good overview. See also, for instance, Milton Meltzer, **Hunted like a Wolf: The Story of the Seminole War** (Sarasota, Fla., 2004), 78–79; Herbert J. Doherty, **Richard Keith Call: Southern Unionist** (Gainesville, Fla., 1961), 93–108; Remini, **Andrew Jackson and His Indian Wars**, 272–77.

521 (murdered a rival) Missall and Missall, **Seminole Wars**, 92.

521 escaped slaves were finding sanctuary Mahon, **History of the Second Seminole War**, 93–94.

521 a Florida militia wagon train at Kanapaha Remini, **Andrew Jackson and His Indian Wars**, 274; see also Mahon, **History of the Second Seminole War**, 101.

521 180 Seminoles routed Missall and Missall, **Seminole Wars**, 96–97.

521 "I have been confined" Remini, **Jackson**, III, 310–11.

522 "Let the damned cowards" Ibid., 311–12.

522 completing the work of Cherokee removal Prucha, **Great Father**, 233–42. See also Heidler and Heidler, **Indian Removal**, 39–41, and Satz, **American Indian Policy in the Jacksonian Era**, 99–101.

522 the Treaty of New Echota Heidler and Heidler, **Indian Removal**, 68–76. See also Anderson, ed., **Cherokee Removal: Before and After**, 55–72, and Wilentz, **Andrew Jackson**, 142.

522 Ross, who represented Satz, **American Indian Policy in the Jacksonian Era**, 100.

523 an estimated 4,000 of the 16,000 Cherokees Anderson, ed., **Cherokee Removal: Before and After**, 75–95, contains a fascinating account of the origin of the 4,000 figure. The essay, by Russell Thornton, examined the demography of the Trail of Tears and found that, as he put it, "A total mortality figure of

8,000 for the Trail of Tears period, twice the supposed 4,000, may not be at all unreasonable" (ibid., 93).

523 "I fought through the Civil War"   Satz, **American Indian Policy in the Jacksonian Era**, 101.

523 "the philanthropist will rejoice"   Prucha, **Great Father**, 242.

524 a large party for Christmas Day   Mary Donelson Wilcox, **Christmas Under Three Flags** (Washington, D.C., 1900), 17–45. See also EDT, II, 90–97. My account of the Christmas festivities is heavily indebted to Wilcox's rendering, and to Burke's rerendering. It is worth noting that Wilcox was writing nearly seven decades after the event, during the Victorian era, when the colorful pageantry of Christmas took on a more central role in American culture; this may have influenced her memory of that Christmas morning.

524 Emily dispatched the invitations   Ibid., 18.

525 a warm, sunny winter day   Ibid., 25.

525 they were to meet him   EDT, II, 91.

525 were "always granting"   Wilcox, **Christmas Under Three Flags**, 23.

525 "To the Orphan Asylum"   Ibid.

525 (The petition to incorporate)   Holly C. Shulman, ed., "The Dolley Madison Digital Edition: Dolley Madison and the Founding of the Washington Orphan Asylum," University of Virginia Press, http://rotunda.upress.virginia.edu:8080/dmde/editorialnote.xqy?note=all#n3.

525 the children quizzed "Uncle"   Ibid., 24.

526 Arriving at the Asylum   Ibid., 25.

526 still-green parks   Ibid.

526 "a hand-painted"   Ibid., 25–26.

526 the president was up early   Ibid., 28.

526 "Spare the rod and spoil the child"   Ibid., 35.

527 At four that afternoon   Ibid., 38–40.

527 supper began   Ibid., 43.

527 filled with flakes of snow   Ibid., 44.

Chapter 32: I Fear Emily Will Not Recover

529 a Philadelphia merchant named George W. South   **Correspondence**, V, 382.

529   a shipment of furnishings for the rebuilt Hermitage   Ibid., 382–83.

529   three sets of wallpaper   Ibid., 383.

529   a favorite of Jackson's   Jackson had purchased a copy of the book during his White House years. **Papers**, VII, 403.

529   Written in 1699, the book   François de Fénelon, **Telemachus** (Cambridge, England, 1994).

529   "The whole world"   Ibid., 158. Fénelon also writes: "Both his understanding and virtue must be limited and imperfect. He must have passions, humors, habits which he cannot always control. He is surrounded by artful, mercenary men, and cannot find the assistance which he seeks after. Every day he is led into some error, either by his own passions or those of his ministers. Scarcely has he repaired one fault when he falls into another. Such is the condition of kings who are the most enlightened and the most virtuous."

530   "'True it is'"   Ibid., 324.

530   "Mentor replied to him patiently"   Ibid.

531   "You are assembled"   **Messages**, II, 1367.

531   "There is doubtless"   Ibid.

532   "Our happiness"   Ibid.

532   "The moral power of the world"   Howe, **What Hath God Wrought**, 512.

532   Angelina Grimké, a native South Carolinian   Mayer, **All on Fire**, 231.

532   Calhoun acknowledged the high price   Miller, **Arguing About Slavery**, 127.

532   petition the Congress in favor   Freehling, **Prelude to Civil War**, 348–57.

533   Congress employed what was called   Ibid., 353. See also Wilentz, **Rise of American Democracy**, 451–52, for Van Buren's maneuvering in the debate, and 470–73 for John Quincy Adams's strong objections to the gag rule.

533   devised by South Carolina congressman   Ibid., 351.

533   (The Senate did the same)   Ibid., 353.

533   John Quincy Adams saw the inherent tensions   Miller, **Arguing About Slavery**, 207–8.

534   An appeal for help from Stephen Austin   **Correspondence**, V, 397–98.

534 Texas declared its independence   Hansen, ed., **Texas**, 43.
534 stormed the Alamo   Ibid., 42–43.
534 at Goliad   Ibid., 43.
534 Sam Houston rallied his men   Ibid., 43–44.
534 the appearance of neutrality   **Correspondence**, V, 398.
534 "a war of barbarism"   Ibid., 397.
534 "The writer does not reflect"   Ibid., 398.
535 his true feelings on the subject   **EDT**, II, 97.
535 the spring racing season began   Ibid., 98.
535 lost a sister in April   Ibid., 102–3.
536 "I have intended to write to you"   Ibid.
536 was to take three of the four children   Ibid., 104–5.
537 he would "have nothing to do"   Ibid., 105.
537 reached Nashville on Sunday, June 26   Ibid., 107.
537 at work at Poplar Grove   Ibid., 105–6.
537 awaiting her husband and her eldest son   Ibid., 105.
537 slowed by terrible rains   **Correspondence**, V, 414.
537 "torn to the quick"   Ibid., 418.
537 (Jackson usually spelled it "Salum")   Ibid., 414.
537 "We reached here today"   **EDT**, II, 107.
537 "Jackson is in fine health"   Ibid., 108.
537 brought word that Mrs. Mary Ann McLemore   Ibid.
537 "not so well"   Ibid., 110.
538 "shaking hands," he said, "with at least 4,000"   Ibid., 111.
538 now demonstrably sick   Ibid.
538 it would turn out, tuberculosis   Cheathem, **Old Hickory's Nephew**, 121.
538 "I will be uneasy until I hear from you"   **EDT**, II, 112.
538 Jackson found himself without word from Nashville   Ibid.
538 "My mind is sorely oppressed"   Ibid.
539 "I pity the Major's situation"   **Correspondence**, V, 428.
540 "I find much business"   Ibid., 429.
540 signs, he wrote, of lung disease   Ibid., 428.
540 in "a kind of stupor"   Ibid.
540 Jackson spent the evening   Ibid., 427.
540 It was "with painful sensations"   Ibid.
540 "I trust in the mercy"   Ibid.
540 "But my dear Andrew"   Ibid.
541 "Still I have a hope"   Ibid.

541   could not stay away from politics   Ibid.

541   "I can say to you"   Ibid., 428.

541   decided to leave her . . . ten days later   **EDT**, II, 114–15.

541   he asked Roger Taney for help   **Correspondence**, V, 429–30.

542   already trying to assuage his own guilt   **EDT**, II, 114–15.

542   Emily approved   Ibid:, 114. "It was a call to the colors," Burke wrote. (Ibid.)

542   "in tears" at the thought   Ibid., 117.

542   "I would judge it would be best"   Ibid.

542   about eleven o'clock   Ibid., 116.

543   knew what she would want to hear   Ibid.

543   earned a salary signing public land warrants   Cheathem, **Old Hickory's Nephew**, 116.

543   "I trust, my dear Emily"   **EDT**, II, 117.

544   a list of clothes   **Correspondence**, V, 433.

544   "The Major is working night and day"   Ibid.

544   "I am constantly filled"   **EDT**, II, 120.

545   Writing to Andrew on Friday, November 11   Ibid., 122.

545   Jackson "has made but little"   Ibid., 123.

545   suffered his own hemorrhage attack   **Correspondence**, V, 439.

545   "Under the circumstances"   **EDT**, II, 123.

546   "You are young"   **Correspondence**, V, 439.

546   linking his own illness with hers   Ibid., 439–40.

547   "Your dear papa"   **EDT**, II, 126.

547   "I wish you to attend to your education"   Ibid.

547   a few lines jotted to Emily   Ibid.

547   had already begun to fail   Ibid., 127.

548   a small bird flew into Emily's room   Ibid.

548   came to Jackson in a dream   Ibid., 128.

549   is virtually breathless with his fright   Ibid.

549   Emily Donelson died   Ibid., 129.

549   Her mother delayed the burial   Ibid., 130–31.

549   on the morning of Wednesday, December 21   Cheathem, **Old Hickory's Nephew**, 123. Burke puts the date of Andrew's arrival as December 22, according to a letter Andrew sent dated December 23rd (**EDT**, II, 130), but, as Cheathem points out, this letter is most likely misdated (Cheathem, **Old Hickory's Nephew**, 123).

549   "Let me hear from you often"   Ibid., 131.

549 "Would to God I had been there" **Correspondence**, V, 442.

550 taking charge of the now motherless brood EDT, II, 133.

Chapter 33: The President Will Go Out Triumphantly

551 as the returns trickled in Niven, **Martin Van Buren**, 401.

551 If the vote was sent to the House Ibid., 401–2.

551 by the beginning of December Ibid.

551 Emily's death had touched EDT, II, 134–35.

552 Jackson had it boxed Ibid., 132.

552 asked Jackson to put it aside Ibid., 137.

553 ordered a supply of cold ham Papers of Isaac Bassett, U.S. Senate Commission on Art, Washington.

553 "the great part of the Senate" Ibid.

553 "The decree has gone forth" Daniel Mallory, ed., **Life and Speeches of Henry Clay** (New York, 1844), I, 278.

554 "No one, not blinded by party zeal" PJCC, XIII, 361–63.

554 (Bank men) Poore, **Perley's Reminiscences of Sixty Years in the National Metropolis**, 142. See also Papers of Isaac Bassett, U.S. Senate Commission on Art, Washington.

554 to send for guns Benton, **Thirty Years' View**, 731. See also Papers of Isaac Bassett, U.S. Senate Commission on Art, Washington.

554 "History has been ransacked" Benton, **Thirty Years' View**, 721–22.

555 "He came into office" Ibid., 725.

555 "Great has been the opposition" Ibid., 726.

556 "Great is the confidence" Ibid.

556 The motion to expunge carried Parton, **Life**, III, 619–20.

556 "a storm of hisses and groans" Papers of Isaac Bassett, U.S. Senate Commission on Art, Washington.

556 (the sergeant at arms) Ibid.

557 Jackson invited the senators Parton, **Life**, III, 620.

557 "head-expunger" Ibid.

557 "All going well here" Andrew Jackson, Jr., to Stockley Donelson, January 31, 1837, Donelson Family Private Collection, Cleveland Hall, Nashville.

557 what Benton called the "crowning mercy" Parton, **Life**, III, 620.

557 Benton sent Jackson the pen   Correspondence, V, 450–51.
According to Isaac Bassett, it "was a new pen that had never
been used for any other purpose. The President received it with
pleasure and informed Mr. Benton that he should preserve it
while he lived and at his death bequeath it to him as a mark of
his regard" (Papers of Isaac Bassett, U.S. Senate Commission
on Art, Washington).

557 "It has been my fortune"   Messages, II, 1511–12.

558 "My public life has been a long one"   Ibid., 1512.

558 cloudless and warm   Parton, Life, III, 628.

558 found the crowd "profoundly silent"   Benton, Thirty Years'
View, 735.

558 "In receiving from the people"   Messages, II, 1537.

559 on which "the rising was eclipsed"   Benton, Thirty Years' View,
735.

559 "My own race is nearly run"   Messages, II, 1527. The Farewell
Address was one of the presidential documents he cherished
most. In his retirement, a copy of it, framed in gold, hung in the
Hermitage, along with his First Annual Message, the Nullification Proclamation, and the Bank Veto Message (author observation; the Office of the Hermitage's Chief Curator / Director
of Museum Services confirmed that the framed documents were
in the house in Jackson's day).

Chapter 34: The Shock Is Great, and Grief Universal

560 a contemporary observer noted   J. Cunningham to Reuben
Lewis, April 9, 1837, Virginia Historical Society, Richmond. Jackson, Cunningham wrote, was greeted "with flags flying . . . amid
the roar of artillery." The former president arrived in Louisville at
seven-thirty in the morning on March 20, about two and a half
hours ahead of schedule. "Such however was the extreme anxiety
to see him that the bridges, wharves, roofs of the houses and the
boats at the landing were crowded with spectators," Cunningham
wrote. Led to a "splendid open barouch drawn by four beautiful
grey horses," Jackson made a hero's progress through the city, accompanied by forty carriages and a thousand people. As evening
came, Jackson departed. The crowds, Cunningham said, "cheered
the general as long as he was in sight."

Jackson seemed exhausted, but as on his northern tour four years before, he refused to disappoint the public. "The General is very much debilitated, indeed he was so feeble in appearance that his friends urged him strongly not to expose himself to the fatigue of shaking hands with the crowds that pressed to see him," Cunningham wrote, "but he withstood every solicitude utterly regardless of his own comfort and [was] only anxious to afford others gratification. And this has ever been one of the leading traits of his character. He has always been ready to do and suffer everything for his country regardless of self.

"As I gazed upon his toilworn face and shrunken cheek," Cunningham continued, "I thought of the language of Cardinal Wolsey: 'An old man, broken with the storms of life has come to lay his bones among you.'" [sic]

560 "I thought it was one of the most sublime" Ibid. Cunningham closed: "Did it not almost seem during the raging of the panic that money alone could move the pulse of this nation! Were you not then almost afraid that the virtuous days of the republic had departed!—that gold had eaten into and corrupted the vitals of the people and that they were ready to sell their liberties for a mess of pottage! It is not so. The Americans delight in great and gracious actions, they know how to appreciate and reward public virtue—and as long as they know that, liberty is safe!"

561 "The Major is so much engaged" **EDT**, II, 139.

561 a cold autumn Friday in 1838 **AAK**, 367–68.

561 advising Donelson in 1840 to "seek out" **Correspondence**, VI, 53.

561 Donelson married Elizabeth Martin Randolph Cheathem, **Old Hickory's Nephew**, 144.

562 (About this time the name) Robbie D. Jones, Landmarks of American History Teacher Workshop, "Architecture in Jacksonian America," **The Hermitage, Andrew Jackson and America, 1801–1861**, 7.

562 Tyler appointed him chargé d'affaires Cheathem, **Old Hickory's Nephew**, 170.

562 letter to the Danbury Baptist Association Thomas Jefferson, **Writings** (New York, 1984), 510.

562 sitting in his pew in the Hermitage church Parton, **Life**, III, 644.

562 "the interposition of Providence"   Ibid.

562 Jackson listening intently   Ibid., 645.

562 speak of "the career of a man"   Ibid.

563 Jackson insisted   Ibid.

563 appears to have had a kind of conversion   Ibid., 645–46.

563 "As the day was breaking"   Ibid., 646.

563 Jackson stood, leaning on a cane   Ibid., 647–48. For a more detailed account of the backstory of Jackson's joining the Church—one that involves Sarah Yorke Jackson and her attempts to have one of her children baptized—see Remini, **Jackson**, III, 444–47.

563 A financial panic, followed by depression   Howe, **What Hath God Wrought**, 501–8; Wilentz, **Rise of American Democracy**, 456–65; Temin, **Jacksonian Economy**, 113–77; and Feller, **Public Lands in Jacksonian Politics**, 182–88.

563 This Deposit Bill   Wilentz, **Rise of American Democracy**, 443–46. See also Remini, **Jackson**, III, 320–29.

563 an order called the Specie Circular   Remini, **Jackson**, III, 328–29. Wilentz, **Andrew Jackson**, 114–20, is a strong summary of the economic and political factors at work late in Jackson's administration.

564 the circular was aimed at speculators   Feller, **Public Lands in Jacksonian Politics**, 184. Wilentz wrote: "The federal land office turned into a gigantic government-sponsored confidence scheme, whereby speculators borrowed large amounts of paper money, used it to buy federal land, then used the land as collateral on further lands—all of which ensnared the federal government, as Benton observed, in 'the ups and downs of the whole paper system'" (Wilentz, **Rise of American Democracy**, 444).

564 plenty of blame   Temin, **The Jacksonian Economy**, offers a detailed defense of Jackson. "Despite its universal acceptance, this story [of Jackson's being responsible for the ensuing economic distress] will not stand close scrutiny; it is negated by extant data of the 1830s," Temin wrote. "Jackson's economic policies were not the most enlightened the country has ever seen, but they were by no means disastrous. The inflation and crises of the 1830's had their origin in events largely beyond Jackson's control and probably would have taken place whether or not he had acted as he did. The economy was not the victim of Jack-

sonian politics; Jackson's politics were the victims of economic fluctuations" (ibid., 16–17). Wilentz wrote: "Jackson's Specie Circular, by slamming the brakes on the western land mania and halting the shift of specie from eastern banks to the West, has traditionally received the blame for causing economic disaster. That interpretation now appears simplistic at best" (Wilentz, **Rise of American Democracy**, 444).

564 "It was reported that" Mrs. C. M. Stephens to Phila Ann Donelson, January 8, 1840, Mrs. John Lawrence Merritt Collection.

564 "I was in Nashville the other day" Leonidas Polk to his mother, June 4, 1840. Leonidas Polk Collection, The University of the South, University Archives and Special Collections, Sewanee.

564 George P. A. Healy James, **TLOAJ**, 782.

565 "I see that you" Ibid.

565 "our poor old grey headed" Letter to Stockley Donelson, July 25, 1841, Mrs. John Lawrence Merritt Collection.

565 "He is swollen all over" Sarah Yorke Jackson to Emma Donelson, April 30, 1845, Gilder Lehrman Collection, RGJ 496.36, The Hermitage.

565 a postscript dictated by Jackson Ibid.

565 Jackson "still continues about the same" Sarah Yorke Jackson to Emma Donelson, May 17, 1845, Gilder Lehrman Collection, RGJ 496.34, The Hermitage.

565 "that it was not far distant" Andrew Jackson, Jr., to A.O.P. Nicholson, June 17, 1845, The Hermitage.

565 "When I have suffered" Ibid.

566 "I cannot be long with you all" Ibid.

566 "I wish to be buried" Ibid.

566 Texas remained a question Ibid. Jackson explicitly mentioned Andrew Donelson, "our minister there."

566 tensions between London and Washington Ibid.

566 "He conversed generally" Andrew Jackson, Jr., to A.O.P. Nicholson, June 17, 1845, The Hermitage.

566 "let war come" Ibid. "He spoke of our Oregon difficulty and . . . expressed a hope and prayer that it would be amicably arranged by the two governments and if not let war come said he."

566 **"My dear Andrew"** Correspondence, VI, 408–9. The letter was dated May 24, 1845.

567 "This may be the last" Ibid., 397–98.

567 "On the subject of my papers" Ibid., 406–7.

567 On Friday, June 6, he wrote President Polk Ibid., 413–14.

567 a note to Thomas F. Marshall Thomas F. Marshall to Andrew Jackson, Jr., June 20, 1845, Scott Ward Collection. The letter was written from Versailles, Kentucky.

567 "cold, clammy perspiration" Andrew Jackson, Jr., to A.O.P. Nicholson, June 17, 1845, The Hermitage.

567 the attending doctor thought Jackson was gone Here is Andrew Jackson, Jr., on the incident: "On . . . Saturday [June 7, 1845] he felt tolerably comfortable the first part of the day. He was then seized with a cold clammy perspiration, an evidence of death approaching. He talked but little that day. . . . Late in the evening Doctor Esselman came and he tried to check his bowels but to no purpose. The General rested pretty well that night. The next morning early I called the Doctor in. Soon after the Doctor coming in, nature seemed to give away and the general fainted. When the Doctor remarked he is gone, we laid him in bed, where he immediately recovered" (Andrew Jackson, Jr., to A.O.P. Nicholson, June 17, 1845, The Hermitage).

567 after ten minutes Elizabeth Martin Donelson to Andrew Jackson Donelson, June 9, 1845, Stanley Horn Collection, The Hermitage. In describing Jackson's last moments, I have relied on the recollections and reports of Elizabeth Martin Donelson, Andrew Jackson, Jr., and Hannah, each of whom was in the room, and on the reconstruction found in Parton, **Life**, III, 678–79.

567 Lewis arrived Parton, **Life**, III, 678.

567 "Major, I am glad to see you" Ibid.

567 to defy expectations Hannah recalled: "About an hour before he died he [came] to—we had all thought he was dead before that" (**Correspondence**, VI, 415). These remarks are recorded in what is called "'Old Hannah's' Narrative of Jackson's Last Days." It is worth noting that Hannah's reminiscences were recorded when she was eighty-nine, in 1880—during an era in which there was much mythologizing about the relationship between

slaveholders and slaves. See David W. Blight, **Race and Re-union: The Civil War in American Memory** (Cambridge, Mass., 2001). Still, Hannah's memories have much in common with letters written close to the date of Jackson's death.

567 looked up at her and asked how everyone was at home   Elizabeth Martin Donelson to Andrew Jackson Donelson, June 9, 1845, Stanley Horn Collection, The Hermitage.

568 "Johnny went and kissed him"   Ibid.

568 Jackson asked for his spectacles   **Correspondence**, VI, 415.

568 licked the lenses, dried them on his sheet   Ibid.

568 "God will take care"   Andrew Jackson, Jr., to A.O.P. Nicholson, June 17, 1845, The Hermitage.

568 "Do not cry"   Elizabeth Martin Donelson to Andrew Jackson Donelson, June 9, 1845, Stanley Horn Collection, The Hermitage.

568 "My conversation is for you all"   **Correspondence**, VI, 415.

568 "Christ has no respect to color"   Ibid.

568 "What is the matter" Andrew Jackson, Jr., to A.O.P. Nicholson, June 17, 1845, The Hermitage.

568 asked one of the slaves   **Correspondence**, VI, 415.

568 "Just then"   Ibid.

569 It was six o'clock   Andrew Jackson, Jr., to A.O.P. Nicholson, June 17, 1845, The Hermitage.

569 what Elizabeth Donelson called "spasms"   Elizabeth Martin Donelson to Andrew Jackson Donelson, June 9, 1845, Stanley Horn Collection, The Hermitage.

569 fainted . . . bathed in camphor   **Correspondence**, VI, 415.

569 Andrew junior "seemed bewildered"   Elizabeth Martin Donelson to Andrew Jackson Donelson, June 9, 1845, Stanley Horn Collection, The Hermitage.

569 Hannah, in grief, would not leave   **Correspondence**, VI, 415.

569 "Although it was looked for"   Elizabeth Martin Donelson to Andrew Donelson, June 9, 1845, Stanley Horn Collection, The Hermitage.

569 "Yours to the Genl I will keep"   Ibid. The day after Jackson died, she wrote, "I have **just** received your letter."

569 Sam Houston, who had just left Donelson, arrived   James, **TLOAJ**, 786.

570 a reported three thousand people   Parton, **Life**, III, 679.

570   conducted the service from the front portico   Ibid.

570   "These are they which came"   In Parton, **Life,** III, 679, the verse appears as "These are they which came out of the great tribulation, and washed their robes white in the blood of the Lamb."

570   The Ninetieth psalm was read   Andrew Jackson, Jr., to A.O.P. Nicholson, June 17, 1845, The Hermitage.

570   "How Firm a Foundation"   Ibid.

570   Fear not, I am   "How Firm a Foundation, Ye Saints of the Lord," in **The Hymnal,** by the Presbyterian Church in the U.S.A., ed. Louis F. Benson, rev. ed. (Philadelphia, 1911), 505.

570   Thomas Marshall returned home   Thomas F. Marshall to Andrew Jackson, Jr., June 20, 1845, Scott Ward Collection.

570   to see "the last characters"   Ibid.

570   promised to visit the grave   Ibid.

570   "He knew"   Ibid.

571   "Before the nation, before the world"   B. M. Dusenbery, **Monument to the Memory of General Andrew Jackson** (Philadelphia, 1848), 50.

571   "Sleep sweetly, aged soldier"   Ibid., 69. In Pennsylvania, the governor, Francis R. Shunk, acknowledged the late hero's divisiveness, but spoke of the same feelings that had been evident in Louisville when Jackson was coming home from Washington eight years before. "Whatever differences may exist among his countrymen in regard to some measures of his administration, it must be admitted by all that the same courageous assumption of responsibility—the same patriotism—the same energy and decision—the same honesty of purpose—and the same devotion to the constitution and the Union which distinguished him as a general, he displayed as a statesman. During his administration, questions arose which agitated the whole community. Even the Union itself was threatened, and gave occasion for an exhibition of devotion to its preservation which commanded universal applause" (ibid.,149). Shunk had also heard of the closing hours of Jackson's life on the first floor of the Hermitage, and from afar the governor sensed the nature and strength of the bonds between Jackson and his broad family: "Childless, the pains of his last illness were assuaged, and its tedious hours beguiled by affection more than filial, and bursts

of grief from hearts in which not a drop of his blood was mingled, paid the holiest tribute to his memory when he died,"
Shunk said. "With paternal admonitions, tender adieus to
those to whom not blood, but affection, made him father, in
the confident hope of a blissful immortality, his spirit, released
from its frail and decaying tenement, has gone to receive its reward" (ibid., 153–54).

571 according to legend, a visitor   Oral tradition, The Hermitage.
571 Blair gave up the **Globe**   **FPB**, 163–67.
572 Blair had loaned . . . the Jacksonian tome   Ibid., 175–77.
572 Blair became a great Unionist   Ibid., 150–77, tells the story of
Blair's important role in antebellum politics.
572 Blair helped engineer   Ibid., 192–97.
572 Blair supported Lincoln   Ibid., 262–64.
572 he urged the new president   Ibid., 315–17.
572 On Lincoln's authority   Ibid., 283.
572 one of his sons, Montgomery Blair   Ibid., 271.
572 Francis Bicknell Carpenter's painting   "First Reading of the
Emancipation Proclamation of President Lincoln," http://
www.senate.gov/artandhistory/art/artifact/Painting_33_00005.
htm.
573 In the last days of 1864   **FPB**, 363–64.
573 "the cause of all our woes"   Ibid., 364–67.
573 a Friday, February 3, 1865   Ibid., 368.
573 Blair and his daughter Lizzie   Ibid., 371.
573 Blair asked to be baptized   Ibid., 434.
574 Blair died four years later   Ibid., 437.
574 retiring to Lindenwald   Niven, **Martin Van Buren**, 485.
574 candidate for the Free Soil Party   Ibid., 590.
574 He supported President Lincoln's fight   Ibid., 610–11.
574 died after a long illness   Ibid., 611. See also **New York Times**,
October 20, 1876.
574 "The grief of his patriotic friends"   Ibid., 612.
574 leaving office in 1840   **AAK**, 436.
575 published a biography of the general   Ibid., 505.
575 Kendall went to work for Samuel F. B. Morse   Ibid., 527.
575 supported President Lincoln   Ibid., 621. Kendall published
many articles denouncing secession, some of which are
reprinted in his **Autobiography**, 580–619.

575 a generous donor to Calvary Baptist Church   Ibid., 663–64.

575 a founder of Gallaudet University   Ibid., 555. The school was originally named the Columbia Institution for the Instruction of the Deaf and Dumb and the Blind.

575 He died on Friday, November 12, 1869   Ibid., 690–91.

575 After losing the Senate election   Remini, **Jackson,** II, 318.

575 president of the Chesapeake and Ohio Canal Company Howe, **What Hath God Wrought,** 544.

575 governor of the Florida territory   Remini, **Jackson,** II, 321.

575 "Our friend John Eaton is harassed"   TPA, 207.

575 Eaton was dispatched as the minister   Ratner, **Andrew Jackson and His Tennessee Lieutenants,** 89.

575 writing that "he and **she**"   TPA, 220.

576 campaigning for Van Buren's 1840 opponent   Ibid., 223.

576 "My friend Maj. Eaton comes home"   **Correspondence,** VI, 59.

576 the couple lived with Margaret's mother   TPA, 223.

576 Eaton practiced law   Ibid., 223–24.

576 "Never did I so much regret"   **Correspondence,** VI, 112–13.

576 "I have thought ever since"   TPA, 223.

576 In the summer of 1844   Ibid., 225.

576 Eaton died on Monday, November 17, 1856   Ibid., 227.

576 "We had been honored"   Eaton, **Autobiography of Peggy Eaton,** 205.

577 Italian dancing master named Antonio Buchignani   TPA, 229.

577 moved to New York City   Ibid., 230–33.

577 "a carriage with four horses"   Ibid., 224.

577 sent flowers to the funeral . . . unmarked grave   Ibid., 235–36.

577 "She belonged to the women"   Pollack, **Peggy Eaton,** 282.

577 secretary of state in John Tyler's Cabinet   PJCC, XXI, 395.

578 He died in Washington   Coit, **John C. Calhoun,** 509–10.

578 Floride was en route   Ibid., 512.

578 Clay saluted Calhoun's oratorical gifts   Ibid.

578 buried in the churchyard of St. Philip's   Ibid., 516.

578 served in the Senate until 1842   Remini, **Henry Clay,** 600.

578 seeking the presidency   Ibid., 610.

578 (Theodore Frelinghuysen of New Jersey)   Ibid., 645.

578 hailed as "Young Hickory"   Ibid., 654.

578 Clay asked after Jackson's health   Remini, **Jackson,** III, 481.

578 "The glorious result of the presidential election"   **Correspondence**, VI, 334.

579 Compromise of 1850   Remini, **Henry Clay**, 730–61.

579 "Tell Clay for me"   Ibid., 738.

579 Clay died on Tuesday, June 29, 1852 . . . lie in state   Ibid., 781–86

579 "the acutest, the astutest, the archest enemy"   Howe, **What Hath God Wrought**, 514.

579 rebellion aboard the **Amistad**   Nagel, **John Quincy Adams**, 379–81.

579 collapsed on the floor of the House   Ibid., 414.

579 His casket was taken . . . interred beside Abigail and John Adams   Ibid., 415–16.

579 "preside over the destinies"   **Papers**, V, 188.

579 considered for Van Buren's Cabinet   Cheathem, **Old Hickory's Nephew**, 189.

579 accepted President Tyler's appointment   Ibid., 171.

579 "**All** is safe"   Ibid., 207.

580 American envoy to Prussia   Ibid., 208.

580 edited the **Washington Union**   Ibid., 262–78.

580 vice president on the Know Nothing ticket   Ibid., 297.

580 "A great change"   Laura Donelson to John Donelson, February 22, 18[?], Mrs. John Lawrence Merritt Collection. The events described in the letter take place in 1856 (Cheathem, **Old Hickory's Nephew**, 301).

580 Andrew junior killed himself in a hunting accident   Remini, **Jackson**, III, 145, and supporting note.

581 "Uncle Andrew [Donelson] was up here"   William Donelson, Jr., to John Donelson, April 29, 1859, Mrs. John Lawrence Merritt Collection.

581 he moved from support for the Union   Cheathem, **Old Hickory's Nephew**, 316–19.

581 died on Monday, June 26, 1871   Ibid., 328.

Epilogue: He Still Lives

582 streets of mud and ice   I am indebted to Curtis Mann, the city historian of Springfield, Illinois, for describing the layout and conditions of the city during the winter of 1861.

582 his brother-in-law's brick general store   Emanuel Hertz, ed., **The Hidden Lincoln: From the Letters and Papers of William H. Herndon** (New York, 1940), 118.

582 need some "works" to consult   William H. Herndon and Jesse W. Weik, **Abraham Lincoln: The True Story of a Great Life** (New York, 1917), II, 188.

582 "I looked for a long list"   Ibid.

582 small, sparsely furnished   Interview with Curtis Mann, the city historian of Springfield, Illinois.

583 Lincoln looked to Jackson   With the admittedly large exception of the integrity of the Union, Lincoln had long been a Henry Clay Whig who opposed Jackson on most issues. In the crisis of the Civil War, however, the sixteenth president saw virtue in the seventh. A portrait of Jackson hung in Lincoln's White House office, and there are some echoes of Jackson's proclamation in Lincoln's first inaugural. The Constitution, Jackson had said, was "the perpetual bond of our Union." Scribbling across a sheet of paper, Lincoln wrote, "I hold that in contemplation of universal law and of the Constitution the Union of these states is perpetual." Speaking more in sorrow than in anger, Jackson had said: "I call upon you in the language of truth, and with the feelings of a Father, to retrace your steps." In the winter's light, Lincoln urged care and caution. "Do not rush to arms," Lincoln said, "in hot haste." Jackson had said: "Fellow citizens! The momentous case is before you." Lincoln wrote: "In **your** hands, my dissatisfied fellow countrymen, and not in **mine**, is the momentous issue of civil war." For Jackson's proclamation, see **Messages**, II, 1203–19; for Lincoln's first inaugural, see Lincoln, **Speeches and Writings**, 215–24.

583 "The right of a state to secede"   John G. Nicolay and John Hay, **Abraham Lincoln: A History** (New York, 1886), III, 248.

583 "A majority held in restraint"   Lincoln, **Speeches and Writings**, 220.

584 "Jackson had many faults"   Alfred Bushnell Hart and Herbert Ronald Ferleger, eds., **Theodore Roosevelt Cyclopedia** (New York, 1941), 272.

584 approved of Jackson's "instinct"   Theodore Roosevelt, **Letters and Speeches** (New York, 2004), 109.

585 "The course I followed"   Theodore Roosevelt, **The Rough Riders: An Autobiography** (New York, 2004), 620.

585 a visit to the Hermitage   Mary French Caldwell, "Another Breakfast at the Hermitage: Part II: 1934," **Tennessee Historical Quarterly** 26 (Fall 1967), 249–50.

585 "bowed gallantly"   Ibid.

585 ramps had been installed   Ibid.

586 he chose to stay on his feet   Ibid.

586 some occasions were so important to him   A similar one occurred when he met with Winston Churchill at sea off Newfoundland in August 1941; for a church parade aboard the **Prince of Wales**, Roosevelt walked to his seat on deck. See my **Franklin and Winston: An Intimate Portrait of an Epic Friendship** (New York, 2003), 107–8, for an account of the moment.

586 "Responsibility lay heavily"   Radio Address from the USS **Potomac** for Jackson Day Dinners, March 29, 1941. See John T. Woolley and Gerhard Peters, **The American Presidency Project** [online]. Santa Barbara, Calif.: University of California (hosted), Gerhard Peters (database). http://www.presidency.ucsb.edu/ws/?pid=16095.

586 with a "rugged, courageous spirit"   Ibid.

586 Eddie Jacobson, Truman's partner   Truman, **Where the Buck Stops**, 372–73. Sheepishly recalling Jacobson's complaint in retirement, Truman said: "I'll admit that I've probably read more about Jackson than anyone else in the country. It took us a long time to pay off our creditors, too. It was 1935 before they were all settled and taken care of " (ibid.).

586 spent his childhood soaking up   David McCullough, **Truman** (New York, 1992), 43. Jackson and Robert E. Lee were Truman's longtime heroes. To Merle Miller, Truman also claimed that his father, John Anderson Truman, was "an Andrew Jackson descendant, you understand, and those people are all fighters" (Merle Miller, **Plain Speaking: An Oral Biography of Harry S. Truman** [New York, 1973], 67–68).

586 commissioned a statue   McCullough, **Truman**, 180. Also see Miller, **Plain Speaking**, 135, and Robert H. Ferrell, **Harry S. Truman: A Life** (Columbia, Mo., 1994), 112.

586 traveled to the Hermitage   McCullough, **Truman**, 180. Also see Miller, **Plain Speaking**, 135.

587 put a small bronze   McCullough, **Truman,** 606

587 "He wanted sincerely"   Truman, **Where the Buck Stops,** 295. Truman did acknowledge Jackson's greatest failing, which was that his desire to help people did not extend to the original inhabitants of the land. "That's the only thing I hold against old Jackson . . . the fact that he didn't do anything to help the Indians when he was president. The Seminoles and the Choctaws were terribly mistreated when Jackson was president, and I do hold that against him" (ibid., 280).

587 "helped once again to make it clear"   Ibid., 303.

587 When Truman lit the National Community Christmas Tree **The New York Times,** December 25, 1945.

587 "It is well"   John T. Woolley and Gerhard Peters, **The American Presidency Project** [online]. Santa Barbara, Calif.: University of California (hosted), Gerhard Peters (database). http://www.presidency.ucsb.edu/ws/?pid=12250. The speech was broadcast nationally beginning at 5:15 P.M. on Christmas Eve.

588 His tombstone reads only   Author observation, The Hermitage.

588 slave quarters are near Jackson's tomb   Ibid.

588 "The victor **in a hundred battles**"   Dusenbery, ed., **Monument to Jackson,** 70.

588 whose bust   Author observation, The Hermitage.

589 "The moral of the great events"   Dusenbery, ed., **Monument to Jackson,** 46.

590 a sparkling, unusually warm   **Washington Union,** January 9, 1853.

590 Clark Mills's equestrian statue   Ibid.

590 A vast procession   Ibid.

590 Blair had drafted Douglas's remarks   **FPB,** 176.

590 "Nobly did the widowed mother"   **AJETH,** III, 566.

591 often sat in Pew 54   For the history of, and details about, Saint John's Church, see www.stjohns-dc.org/article.php?id=48. I am grateful to the rector, the Reverend Luis Leon, and to the parish's executive director of operations, Hayden G. Bryan, for their assistance.

592 "He still lives"   **AJETH,** III, 573.

BIBLIOGRAPHY

MANUSCRIPT COLLECTIONS

The Adams Papers, Massachusetts Historical Society, Boston, Massachusetts

George Bancroft Papers, Massachusetts Historical Society, Boston, Massachusetts

Papers of Isaac Bassett, U.S. Senate Commission on Art, Washington, D.C.

Edward Bates Papers, Virginia Historical Society, Richmond, Virginia

Nicholas Biddle Papers, Library of Congress, Washington, D.C.

Blair Family Papers, Library of Congress, Washington, D.C.

Blair and Lee Family Papers, Manuscripts Division, Department of Rare Books and Special Collections, Princeton University Library, Princeton, New Jersey

John Branch Papers, Library of Congress, Washington, D.C.

Branch Family Papers, Southern Historical Collection, Wilson Library, The University of North Carolina at Chapel Hill, Chapel Hill, North Carolina

Gertrude and Benjamin Caldwell Collection, Nashville, Tennessee

John C. Calhoun Papers, Library of Congress, Washington, D.C.

"Memoirs of Mrs. Eliza Williams Chotard Gould," Maria B. Campbell Private Collection, Birmingham, Alabama

Carter and Wellford Family Papers of Sabine Hall, 1650–1918, University of Virginia Library, Special Collections, Charlottesville, Virginia

Conner Family Papers, South Carolina Historical Society, Charleston, South Carolina

Dillon and Polk Papers, Southern Historical Collection, Wilson Library, The University of North Carolina at Chapel Hill, Chapel Hill, North Carolina

Dyas Collection–John Coffee Papers, 1770–1917, Tennessee Historical Society, War Memorial Building, Nashville, Tennessee. Papers housed at the Tennessee State Library and Archives, Nashville, Tennessee

Correspondance Politique, Etats Unis, volumes 1827–1829, 1830, 1831, 1832, 1833, 1834, 1835, 1836, Archives de la Ministère des Affaires Etrangères, Paris, France

Andrew Jackson Donelson Papers, Library of Congress, Washington, D.C.

Mrs. John Donelson IV (Angie Merritt) Scrapbook, Nashville, Tennessee

Donelson Family Private Collection, Cleveland Hall, Nashville, Tennessee

John H. Eaton Papers, Library of Congress, Washington, D.C.

Margaret O'Neale Eaton Papers, Library of Congress, Washington, D.C.

Margaret Eaton Papers, New-York Historical Society, New York, New York

Evarts Family Papers, Beinecke Library, Yale University, New Haven, Connecticut

Albert Gallatin Papers, New-York Historical Society, New York, New York

William Gaston Papers, Southern Historical Collection, Wilson Library, The University of North Carolina at Chapel Hill, Chapel Hill, North Carolina

Duff Green Papers, Library of Congress, Washington, D.C.

Halford Manuscripts, Record Office for Leicestershire, Leicester and Rutland, the United Kingdom

James A. Hamilton Papers, material owned by Herman P. Hamilton, Chester, S.C., James Hamilton Collection, Southern Historical Collection, Wilson Library, The University of North Carolina at Chapel Hill, Chapel Hill, North Carolina, microfilm

James H. Hammond Papers, Library of Congress, Washington, D.C.

Samuel D. Ingham Papers, Rare Books and Manuscripts Library, University of Pennsylvania, Philadelphia, Pennsylvania

"Andrew Jackson," Archive File, Harvard University Archives, Cambridge, Massachusetts

Andrew Jackson Papers, Library of Congress, Washington, D.C.

Andrew Jackson Papers, New York Public Library, New York, New York

Andrew Jackson, Scholarly Resources (microfilm)

Samuel C. Jackson Diary, Southern Historical Collection, Wilson Library, The University of North Carolina at Chapel Hill, Chapel Hill, North Carolina

Cave Johnson Papers, New-York Historical Society, New York, New York

Rufus King Papers, New-York Historical Society, New York, New York

Abraham Lincoln Papers, Library of Congress, Washington, D.C.

Edward Livingston Papers, Manuscripts Division, Department of Rare Books and Special Collections, Princeton University Library, Princeton, New Jersey

Edward McCrady Papers, Manuscripts Division, South Caroliniana Library, University of South Carolina, Columbia, South Carolina

Mrs. John Lawrence Merritt Collection, Winter Park, Florida

Ministerie van Buitenlandse Zaken 1813–1896, Nationaal Archief, Den Haag, Netherlands

Miscellaneous Manuscript Collections, New-York Historical Society, New York, New York

Miscellaneous Manuscript Collections, Manuscripts Division, South Caroliniana Library, University of South Carolina, Columbia, South Carolina

James Monroe Papers, New York Public Library, New York, New York

Moore Family Papers, Kroch Library, Cornell University, Ithaca, New York

National Archives of the United Kingdom, Kew, Richmond, Surrey, the United Kingdom

James Parton Papers, Harvard University, Cambridge, Massachusetts

Joel Roberts Poinsett Papers, the Historical Society of Pennsylvania, Philadelphia, Pennsylvania

George Washington Polk Papers, The University of the South, Sewanee, Tennessee

Leonidas Polk Collection, The University of the South, University Archives and Special Collections, Sewanee, Tennessee

Polk and Yeatman Papers, Southern Historical Collection, Wilson Library, The University of North Carolina at Chapel Hill, Chapel Hill, North Carolina

William Cabell Rives Papers, Library of Congress, Washington, D.C.

Margaret Bayard Smith Papers, Library of Congress, Washington, D.C.

John W. Taylor Papers, New-York Historical Society, New York, New York

Martin Van Buren Papers, Library of Congress, Washington, D.C.

Martin Van Buren Papers, New York Public Library, New York, New York

C. Scott Ward Papers (Private Collection), Atlanta, Georgia

BOOKS AND ARTICLES CONSULTED

Abernethy, Thomas Perkins. **From Frontier to Plantation in Tennessee: A Study in Frontier Democracy**. Chapel Hill: University of North Carolina Press, 1932. Reprint, University, Ala.: University of Alabama Press, 1967.

Adams, Henry. **History of the United States of America During** the Administrations of Thomas Jefferson. The Library of America. New York: Library of America, 1986.

Adams, John Quincy. Memoirs of John Quincy Adams, Comprising Portions of His Diary from 1795 to 1848. Edited by Charles Francis Adams. 12 vols. Philadelphia: J. B. Lippincott and Co., 1874–77.

————. Oration on the Life and Character of Gilbert M. de Lafayette: Delivered at the Request of Both Houses of the Congress of the United States, Before Them, in the House of Representatives at Washington. December 31, 1834. Trenton, N.J.: D. Fenton; Princeton, N.J.: Moore Baker, 1835.

Allen, William C. History of the United States Capitol: A Chronicle of Design, Construction, and Politics. Washington, D.C.: United States Government Printing Office, 2001.

Allgor, Catherine. Parlor Politics: In Which the Ladies of Washington Help Build a City and a Government. Charlottesville: University Press of Virginia, 2000.

Ammon, Harry. James Monroe: The Quest for National Identity. New York: McGraw-Hill, 1971. Reprint, Charlottesville: University Press of Virginia, 1990.

Anderson, William L., ed. Cherokee Removal: Before and After. Athens: University of Georgia Press, 1991.

Andrew, John A. From Revivals to Removal: Jeremiah Evarts, the Cherokee Nation, and the Search for the Soul of America. Athens: University of Georgia Press, 1992.

Appleby, Joyce. Inheriting the Revolution: The First Generation of Americans. Cambridge, Mass.: Belknap Press of Harvard University Press, 2000.

Austen, Jane. Pride and Prejudice. New York: Modern Library, 1995.

Bailey, Thomas A. "The Mythmakers of American History." Journal of American History 55 (June 1968): 5–21.

Bailyn, Bernard. The Origins of American Politics. The Charles K. Colver Lectures, Brown University. New York: Vintage Books, 1968.

————. To Begin the World Anew: The Genius and Ambiguities of the American Founders. New York: Alfred A. Knopf, 2003.

————, comp. The Debate on the Constitution: Federalist and Antifederalist Speeches, Articles, and Letters During the Struggle over Ratification. Vol. 1. The Library of America. New York: Library of America, 1993.

Baird, W. David, Robert A. Trennert, and James Wright. "Western History Association Prize Recipient, 1987: Francis Paul Prucha." Western Historical Quarterly 19 (May 1988): 133–40.

Bancroft, Frederic. Calhoun and the South Carolina Nullification Movement. Baltimore: Johns Hopkins Press, 1928. Reprint, Gloucester, Mass.: Peter Smith, 1966.

Banner, Stuart. How the Indians Lost Their Land: Law and Power on the Frontier. Cambridge, Mass.: Belknap Press of Harvard University Press, 2005.

Barbee, David Rankin. "Andrew Jackson and Peggy O'Neale." Tennessee Historical Quarterly 15 (March 1956): 37–52.

Barber, James G. Andrew Jackson: A Portrait Study. Washington, D.C.: National Portrait Gallery, Smithsonian Institution, 1991.

Bassett, John Spencer. The Life of Andrew Jackson. New York: Macmillan, 1925.

Belohlavek, John M. "Let the Eagle Soar!": The Foreign Policy of Andrew Jackson. Lincoln: University of Nebraska Press, 1985.

Belz, Herman. The Webster-Hayne Debate on the Nature of the Union: Selected Documents. Indianapolis, Ind.: Liberty Fund, 2000.

Berlin, Ira. Many Thousands Gone: The First Two Centuries of Slavery in North America. Cambridge, Mass.: Belknap Press of Harvard University Press, 1998.

Biddle, Nicholas. The Correspondence of Nicholas Biddle. Dealing with National Affairs, 1807–1844. Edited by Reginald C. McGrane. Boston: Houghton Mifflin, 1919.

Binder, Frederick M. **The Color Problem in Early National America as Viewed by John Adams, Jefferson and Jackson**. Studies in American History, no. 7. The Hague and Paris: Mouton Publishers, 1969.

Blackhawk, Ned. "Look How Far We've Come: How American Indian History Changed the Study of American History in the 1990s." **Magazine of History** 19 (November 2005): 13–17.

Blight, David W. **Race and Reunion: The Civil War in American Memory**. Cambridge, Mass.: Belknap Press of Harvard University Press, 2001.

Bobrick, Benson. **Angel in the Whirlwind: The Triumph of the American Revolution**. New York: Simon and Schuster, 1997.

Boller, Paul F., Jr. "Rachel Jackson, 1767–1828." In **Presidential Wives**, 65–72. 2nd, rev. ed. New York: Oxford University Press, 1998.

The Book of Common Prayer, and Administration of the Sacraments, and Other Rites and Ceremonies of the Church, According to the Use of the Protestant Episcopal Church in the United States of America. Together with the Psalter, or Psalms of David. New York: Protestant Episcopal Society for the Promotion of Evangelical Knowledge, 1828.

Booraem, Hendrik. **Young Hickory: The Making of Andrew Jackson**. Dallas: Taylor Trade Publishing, 2001.

Boorstin, Daniel J. **The Americans: The National Experience**. New York: Random House, 1965.

Boucher, Chauncey Samuel. **The Nullification Controversy in South Carolina**. Chicago: University of Chicago Press, 1916.

Bowers, Claude G. **The Party Battles of the Jackson Period**. Boston: Houghton Mifflin, 1922.

Bradley, Chester D. **Fort Wool**. Fort Monroe, Va.: Fort Monroe Casemate Museum, 196[?].

Brands, H. W. **Andrew Jackson: His Life and Times**. New York: Doubleday, 2005.

Breen, T. H. **The Marketplace of Revolution: How Consumer Politics Shaped American Independence**. New York: Oxford University Press, 2004.

Brewer, William M. "The Historiography of Frederick Jackson Turner." **Journal of Negro History** 44 (July 1959): 240–59.

Brinkerhoff, Roeliff. **Recollections of a Lifetime**. Cincinnati: Robert Clarke Co., 1900.

Brogan, Hugh. **The Penguin History of the United States of America**. London: Penguin Books, 2001.

Brookhiser, Richard. **America's First Dynasty: The Adamses, 1735–1918**. New York: Free Press, 2002.

Brownlow, Louis. **The President and the Presidency**. Chicago: Public Administration Service, 1949.

Bryan, Charles Faulkner, Jr. "The Prodigal Nephew: Andrew Jackson Donelson and the Eaton Affair." **East Tennessee Historical Society Publications** 50 (1978): 92–112.

Buchanan, John. **Jackson's Way: Andrew Jackson and the People of the Western Waters**. New York: John Wiley and Sons, 2001.

Bullock, Steven C. **Revolutionary Brotherhood: Freemasonry and the Transformation of the American Social Order, 1730–1840**. Chapel Hill: University of North Carolina Press, 1996.

Burke, Pauline Wilcox. **Emily Donelson of Tennessee**. 2 vols. Richmond, Va.: Garrett and Massie, 1941.

Burns, James MacGregor. **Presidential Government: The Crucible of Leadership**. Boston: Houghton Mifflin, 1965.

———. **The Vineyard of Liberty**. The American Experiment. New York: Alfred A. Knopf, 1982.

Burstein, Andrew. **The Passions of Andrew Jackson**. New York: Alfred A. Knopf, 2003.

Bushman, Richard Lyman. **Believing History: Latter-day Saint Essays**. Edited by Reid L. Neilson and Jed Woodworth. New York: Columbia University Press, 2004.

———. **Joseph Smith: Rough Stone Rolling**. New York: Alfred A. Knopf, 2005.

Bynum, William B. "'The Genuine Presbyterian Whine': Presbyterian Worship in the Eighteenth Century." **American Presbyterians: Journal of Presbyterian History** 74 (Fall 1996): 157–70.

Caldwell, Mary French. **Andrew Jackson's Hermitage: The Story of a Home in the Tennessee Blue-Grass Region.** Nashville: Ladies' Hermitage Association, 1949.

————. **General Jackson's Lady: A Story of the Life and Times of Rachel Donelson Jackson.** Nashville: Ladies' Hermitage Association, 1936.

Calhoun, John C. **The Papers of John C. Calhoun.** Edited by Robert L. Meriwether. 28 vols. to date. Columbia: Published by the University of South Carolina Press for the South Caroliniana Society, 1959–.

————. **Union and Liberty: The Political Philosophy of John C. Calhoun.** Edited by Ross M. Lence. Indianapolis: Liberty Fund, 1992.

Capers, Gerald Mortimer. **John C. Calhoun, Opportunist: A Reappraisal.** Gainesville: University of Florida Press, 1960.

Carroll, John. **The John Carroll Papers.** Edited by Thomas O'Brien Hanley. 3 vols. Notre Dame: University of Notre Dame Press, 1976.

"Carusi, Lewis" (obituary). **Historic Congressional Cemetery.** http://www.congressionalcemetery.org/ (accessed April 26, 2008).

Cash, W. J. **The Mind of the South.** New York: Alfred A. Knopf, 1941. Reprint, New York: Vintage Books, 1991.

Cave, Alfred A. "Abuse of Power: Andrew Jackson and the Indian Removal Act of 1830." **Historian** 65 (December 2003): 1330–53.

Chace, James, and Caleb Carr. **America Invulnerable: The Quest for Absolute Security from 1812 to Star Wars.** New York: Summit Books, 1988.

Cheathem, Mark R. **Old Hickory's Nephew: The Political and Private Struggles of Andrew Jackson Donelson.** Southern Biography Series. Baton Rouge: Louisiana State University Press, 2007.

Chesterfield, Philip Dormer Stanhope, Earl of. **Lord Chesterfield's Letters.** Edited by David Roberts. The World's Classics. New York: Oxford University Press, 1992.

————. Principles of Politeness, and of Knowing the World. Portsmouth, New-Hampshire: Printed by Melcher and Osborne, 1786.

Clark, Allen C. "Margaret Eaton (Peggy O'Neale)." **Records of the Columbia Historical Society** 44–45 (1942–1943): 1–33.

Clay, Henry. **The Papers of Henry Clay**. Edited by James F. Hopkins and Mary W. M. Hargreaves. 11 vols. Lexington: University of Kentucky Press, 1959–92.

Clay, Thomas H. "Two Years with Old Hickory." **Atlantic Monthly** 60 (August 1887): 187–99.

Clinton, Catherine. **Fanny Kemble's Civil Wars**. New York: Simon & Schuster, 2000.

Coit, Margaret L. **John C. Calhoun: American Portrait**. Boston: Houghton Mifflin, 1950.

Cole, Donald B. "**The Age of Jackson**: After Forty Years." Review of **The Age of Jackson**, by Arthur M. Schlesinger, Jr. **Reviews in American History** 14 (March 1986): 149–59.

————. **A Jackson Man: Amos Kendall and the Rise of American Democracy**. Southern Biography Series. Baton Rouge: Louisiana State University Press, 2004.

————. **The Presidency of Andrew Jackson**. American Presidency Series. Lawrence: University Press of Kansas, 1993.

Cooper, James Fenimore. **The American Democrat and Other Political Writings**. Edited by Bradley J. Birzer and John Willson. Conservative Leadership Series, no. 8. Washington, D.C.: Regnery Publishing, 2000.

Cooper, William J., Jr. **The South and the Politics of Slavery, 1828–1856**. Baton Rouge: Louisiana State University Press, 1978.

Corwin, Edward S., Randall W. Bland, Theodore T. Hindson, and J. W. Peltason. **The President: Office and Powers, 1787–1984; History and Analysis of Practice and Opinion**. 5th rev. ed. New York: New York University Press, 1984.

Crawford, Charles W., ed. "'The Subject Is a Painful One to Me.'" **Tennessee Historical Quarterly** 26 (Spring 1967): 59–63.

Cronon, William. "Revisiting the Vanishing Frontier: The Legacy of Frederick Jackson Turner." **Western Historical Quarterly** 18 (April 1987): 157–76.

Cumfer, Cynthia. "Local Origins of National Indian Policy: Cherokee and Tennessean Ideas about Sovereignty and Nationhood, 1790–1811." **Journal of the Early Republic** 23 (Spring 2003): 21–46.

Cunliffe, Marcus. "The Widening and Weakening of Republicanism in Nineteenth-Century America." Paper presented at the annual meeting of the American Historical Association, Washington, D.C., December 1982.

Curtis, James C. "Andrew Jackson and His Cabinet—Some New Evidence." **Tennessee Historical Quarterly** 27 (Summer 1968): 157–64.

————. **Andrew Jackson and the Search for Vindication.** The Library of American Biography. Boston: Little, Brown, 1976.

————. "Andrew Jackson: Symbol for What Age?" Review of **The Presidency of Andrew Jackson: White House Politics, 1829–1837**, by Richard B. Latner. **Reviews in American History** 8 (June 1980): 194–99.

Dahlgren, Madeleine Vinton. **Etiquette of Social Life in Washington**. Washington, D.C.: [J. A. Wineberger], 1873.

Dangerfield, George. **The Awakening of American Nationalism, 1815–1828**. The New American Nation Series. New York: Harper and Row, 1965.

Davis, Deering, Stephen P. Dorsey, and Ralph Cole Hall. **Georgetown Houses of the Federal Period, Washington, D.C., 1780–1830**. New York: Architectural Book Publishing Co., 1944.

Dodd, William E. "Andrew Jackson and His Enemies, and the Great Noise They Made in the World." **Century Magazine** 111 (April 1926): 734–45.

Doherty, Herbert J. **Richard Keith Call: Southern Unionist**. Gainesville: University of Florida Press, 1961.

————. "The Making of Andrew Jackson: All Things Worked Together for Good to Old Hickory." **Century Magazine** 111 (March 1926): 531–38.

Donald, David Herbert. **Lincoln.** New York: Simon & Schuster, 1995.

Dorris, Mary C. **Preservation of the Hermitage, 1889–1915: Annals, History, and Stories.** [Nashville: Smith and Lamar], 1915.

Durham, Walter T. **Balie Peyton of Tennessee: Nineteenth Century Politics and Thoroughbreds.** Franklin, Tenn.: Hillsboro Press, 2004.

———. **Daniel Smith: Frontier Statesman.** Gallatin, Tenn.: Sumner County Library Board, 1976.

Dusenbery, B. M., comp. **Monument to the Memory of General Andrew Jackson: Containing Twenty-five Eulogies and Sermons Delivered on Occasion of His Death.** Philadelphia: James A. Bill, 1848.

Earle, Jonathan H. **Jacksonian Antislavery and the Politics of Free Soil, 1824–1854.** Chapel Hill: University of North Carolina Press, 2004.

Earle, W. H. "Niles' Register, 1811–1849: Window on the World." **Journal of the War of 1812 and the Era 1800 to 1840 1** (Fall 1996). http://www.nisc.com/factsheets/NR_Window.htm.

Eaton, Clement. **Henry Clay and the Art of American Politics.** The Library of American Biography. Boston: Little, Brown, 1957.

———, ed. **The Leaven of Democracy: The Growth of the Democratic Spirit in the Time of Jackson.** New York: George Braziller, 1963.

Eaton, Margaret. **The Autobiography of Peggy Eaton.** With a preface by Charles F. Deems. New York: Charles Scribner's Sons, 1932. Reprint, New York: Arno Press, 1980.

Eberlein, Harold Donaldson, and Cortlandt Van Dyke Hubbard. **Historic Houses of George-Town and Washington City.** Richmond, Va.: Dietz Press, 1958.

Elkins, Stanley, and Eric McKitrick. **The Age of Federalism.** New York: Oxford University Press, 1993.

Ellet, E. F. **The Court Circles of the Republic; or, The Beauties** and Celebrities of the Nation. Hartford, Conn.: Hartford Publishing Co., 1870.

Elliot, Jonathan. **Historical Sketches of the Ten Miles Square Forming the District of Columbia**. Washington, D.C.: Printed by J. Elliot, Jr., 1830.

————, ed. **The Debates in the Several State Conventions on the Adoption of the Federal Constitution, as Recommended by the General Convention at Philadelphia in 1787**. 2d ed., with considerable additions. 5 vols. Washington, D.C.: Printed for the editor, 1836–45.

Ellis, Richard E. **The Union at Risk: Jacksonian Democracy, States' Rights, and the Nullification Crisis**. New York: Oxford University Press, 1987.

Ely, James W., Jr., and Theodore Brown, Jr., eds. **Legal Papers of Andrew Jackson**. Knoxville: University of Tennessee Press, 1987.

Emerson, Ralph Waldo. **The Essential Writings of Ralph Waldo Emerson**. Edited by Brooks Atkinson. Modern Library Classics. New York: Modern Library, 2000.

Eriksson, Erik M. "President Jackson's Propaganda Agencies." **Pacific Historical Review** 6 (March 1937): 47–57.

Farb, Peter. **Man's Rise to Civilization as Shown by the Indians of North America from Primeval Times to the Coming of the Industrial State**. New York: Dutton, 1968.

Faust, Drew Gilpin. **James Henry Hammond and the Old South: A Design for Mastery**. Southern Biography Series. Baton Rouge: Louisiana State University Press, 1985.

Fehrenbacher, Don E. **The Slaveholding Republic: An Account of the United States Government's Relations to Slavery**. Completed and edited by Ward M. McAfee. New York: Oxford University Press, 2001.

Feller, Daniel. **The Jacksonian Promise: America, 1815–1840**. The American Moment. Baltimore: Johns Hopkins University Press, 1995.

————. **The Public Lands in Jacksonian Politics**. Madison: University of Wisconsin Press, 1984.

———. "Rediscovering Jacksonian America." In **The State of U.S. History**, edited by Melvyn Stokes, 69–82. New York: Berg, 2002.

Ferling, John. **Almost a Miracle: The American Victory in the War of Independence**. New York: Oxford University Press, 2007.

Foner, Eric. **The Story of American Freedom**. New York: W. W. Norton, 1998.

———, ed. **The New American History**. Rev. and expanded ed. Critical Perspectives on the Past. Philadelphia: Temple University Press, 1997.

Foote, Henry S. **Casket of Reminiscences**. Washington, D.C.: Chronicle Publishing Co., 1874.

Ford, Henry Jones. **The Rise and Growth of American Politics: A Sketch of Constitutional Development**. New York: Macmillan, 1898.

Foreman, Grant. **Indian Removal: The Emigration of the Five Civilized Tribes of Indians**. Civilization of the American Indian Series. Norman: University of Oklahoma Press, 1972.

Formisano, Ronald P. "Toward a Reorientation of Jacksonian Politics: A Review of the Literature, 1959–1975." **Journal of American History** 63 (June 1976): 42–65.

Foster, Charles I. **An Errand of Mercy: The Evangelical United Front, 1790–1837**. Chapel Hill: University of North Carolina Press, 1960.

Frank Leslie's Popular Monthly, July and October 1898.

Freehling, William W. **The Nullification Era: A Documentary Record**. New York: Harper and Row, 1967.

———. **Prelude to Civil War: The Nullification Controversy in South Carolina, 1816–1836**. New York: Harper and Row, 1966.

———. **The Road to Disunion**. Vol. 1, **Secessionists at Bay, 1776–1854**. New York: Oxford University Press, 1990.

Freidel, Frank, and William Pencak, eds. **The White House: The First Two Hundred Years**. Boston: Northeastern University Press, 1994.

Frelinghuysen, Theodore. **Speech of Mr. Frelinghuysen, of New Jersey, Delivered in the Senate of the United States, April 6, 1830, on the Bill for an Exchange of Lands with the Indians Residing in Any of the States or Territories, and for Their Removal West of the Mississippi.** Washington, D.C.: Printed and published at the Office of the **National Journal** [by George Watterston], 1830.

Frémont, Jessie Benton. **The Letters of Jessie Benton Frémont.** Edited by Pamela Herr and Mary Lee Spence. Urbana: University of Illinois Press, 1993.

———. **Souvenirs of My Time.** Boston: D. Lothrop and Co., 1887.

Gagnon, Joshua A. "The 'Great American Desert': The Congressional Debate on the Indian Removal Act of 1830." **UMF Historian** 3, no. 2 (Spring 2006). http://studentorgs.umf.maine.edu/~aio/historian/vol3iss2/indianremoval_article.pdf (accessed April 27, 2008).

Genovese, Michael A. **The Power of the American Presidency, 1789–2000.** New York: Oxford University Press, 2001.

Goff, Reda C. "A Physical Profile of Andrew Jackson." **Tennessee Historical Quarterly** 28 (Fall 1969): 297–309.

Goldsmith, Oliver. **The Vicar of Wakefield.** New York: New American Library, 1982.

Goldsmith, William M. **The Growth of Presidential Power: A Documented History.** Vol. 1, **The Formative Years.** Vol. 2, **Decline and Resurgence.** New York: Chelsea House, 1974.

Good, Carter V. "Some Problems of Historical Criticism and Historical Writing." **Journal of Negro Education** 11 (April 1942): 135–49.

Govan, Thomas P. **Nicholas Biddle: Nationalist and Public Banker, 1786–1844.** Chicago: University of Chicago Press, 1959.

Gragg, Larry. "The Reign of King Mob, 1829." **History Today** 28 (April 1978): 236–41.

"Graham, George" (obituary). **Historic Congressional Cemetery.** http://www.congressionalcemetery.org/ (accessed April 26, 2008).

Gratz, Rebecca. **Letters of Rebecca Gratz**. Edited by David Philipson. Philadelphia: Jewish Publication Society of America, 1929.

Grayson, William J. **Witness to Sorrow: The Antebellum Autobiography of William J. Grayson**. Edited by Richard J. Calhoun. Columbia: University of South Carolina Press, 1990.

Green, Michael D. **The Politics of Indian Removal: Creek Government and Society in Crisis**. Lincoln: University of Nebraska Press, 1982.

Gressley, Gene M. "The Turner Thesis: A Problem in Historiography." **Agricultural History** 32 (October 1958): 227–49.

Gulliford, Andrew. Exhibition review. "The West as America: Reinterpreting Images of the Frontier, 1820–1920." **Journal of American History** 79 (June 1992): 199–208.

Haley, J. J. **Debates That Made History: The Story of Alexander Campbell's Debates with Rev. John Walker, Rev. W. L. McCalla, Mr. Robert Owen, Bishop Purcell and Rev. Nathan L. Rice**. St. Louis: Christian Board of Publication, 1920.

Hall, A. Oakey. "Andrew Jackson: His Life, Times and Compatriots. First Paper—Andrew Jackson's Private Life." **Frank Leslie's Popular Monthly** 44 (November 1897).

Hamilton, James A. **Reminiscences of James A. Hamilton; or, Men and Events, at Home and Abroad, During Three Quarters of a Century**. New York: Charles Scribner and Co., 1869.

Hamilton, Thomas. **Men and Manners in America**. Reprints of Economic Classics. Reprint of the 1833 ed., with additions from the edition of 1843. New York: A. M. Kelley, 1968.

Hammond, Bray. "Jackson's Fight with the 'Money Power.'" **American Heritage** 7 (June 1956): 8–11, 100–3.

Hammond, James Henry. **Secret and Sacred: The Diaries of James Henry Hammond, a Southern Slaveholder**. Edited by Carol Bleser. New York: Oxford University Press, 1988.

Harlan, Louis R. "Public Career of William Berkeley Lewis." Part 1. **Tennessee Historical Quarterly** 7 (March 1948): 3–37.

Harris, Cicero Willis. **The Sectional Struggle: An Account of the Troubles Between the North and the South, from the Earliest Times to the Close of the Civil War.** Philadelphia: J. B. Lippincott, 1902.

Hay, Robert P. "The Case for Andrew Jackson in 1824: Eaton's 'Wyoming Letters'." **Tennessee Historical Quarterly** 29 (Summer 1970): 139–51.

Hayne, Rob. Y. "Letters on the Nullification Movement in South Carolina, 1830–1834." **American Historical Review** 6 (July 1901): 736–65.

Healy, Gene. **The Cult of the Presidency: America's Dangerous Devotion to Executive Power.** Washington, D.C.: Cato Institute, 2008.

Hearon, Cleo. "Nullification in Mississippi." **Publications of the Mississippi Historical Society** 12 (1912): 37–71.

Heiskell, S. G. **Andrew Jackson and Early Tennessee History.** 2d ed. 3 vols. Nashville: Ambrose Printing Co., 1920–21.

Hellman, George S. **Washington Irving Esquire: Ambassador at Large from the New World to the Old.** New York: Alfred A. Knopf, 1925.

Hemphill, C. Dallett. **Bowing to Necessities: A History of Manners in America, 1620–1860.** New York: Oxford University Press, 1999.

Herndon, William H., and Jesse W. Weik. **Abraham Lincoln: The True Story of a Great Life.** Springfield, Ill.: Herndon's Lincoln Publishing Co. Reprint, New York: D. Appleton and Co., 1917.

Hofstadter, Richard. **The American Political Tradition and the Men Who Made It.** New York: Alfred A. Knopf, 1948.

———. **The Idea of a Party System: The Rise of Legitimate Opposition in the United States, 1780–1840.** Jefferson Memorial Lectures. Berkeley: University of California Press, 1970.

Hone, Philip. **The Diary of Philip Hone, 1828–1851.** Boston: Dodd, Mead, 1889.

———. **The Diary of Philip Hone, 1828–1851.** Edited by Allan Nevins. 2 vols. New York: Dodd, Mead, 1927.

Hoogenboom, Ari, and Herbert Ershkowitz. "Levi Woodbury's 'Intimate Memoranda' of the Jackson Administration." **Pennsylvania Magazine of History and Biography** 92 (October 1968): 507–15.

Hopkins, James F. "Election of 1824." In **History of American Presidential Elections, 1789–2001**, edited by Arthur M. Schlesinger, Jr., and Fred L. Israel, 347–409. Vol. 1. Philadelphia: Chelsea House, 2002.

Horsman, Reginald. "Well-Trodden Paths and Fresh Byways: Recent Writing on Native American History." **Reviews in American History** 10 (December 1982): 234–44.

Horwitz, Robert H., ed. **The Moral Foundations of the American Republic.** 3d ed. Charlottesville: University Press of Virginia, 1986.

Houston, David Franklin. **A Critical Study of Nullification in South Carolina.** New York: Longmans, Green, 1896. Reprint, Gloucester, Mass.: Peter Smith, 1968.

Howe, Daniel Walker. **What Hath God Wrought: The Transformation of America, 1815–1848.** New York: Oxford University Press, 2007.

Howe, M. A. Dewolfe. **The Life and Letters of George Bancroft.** 2 vols. New York: Charles Scribner's Sons, 1908.

Hughes, Emmet John. **The Living Presidency: The Resources and Dilemmas of the American Presidential Office.** New York: Coward, McCann and Geoghegan, 1973.

Hunt, Louise Livingston. **Memoir of Mrs. Edward Livingston, with Letters Hitherto Unpublished.** New York: Harper and Brothers, 1886.

Irving, Washington. **Letters.** Edited by Ralph M. Aderman, Herbert L. Kleinfield, and Jenifer S. Banks. 4 vols. Boston: Twayne Publishers, 1978–82.

Jackson, Andrew. **Correspondence of Andrew Jackson.** Edited by John Spencer Bassett. 7 vols. Washington, D.C.: Carnegie Institution of Washington, 1926–35.

———. **The Papers of Andrew Jackson.** Edited by Sam B. Smith and Harriet Chappell Owsley. Vols. 1–6. Knoxville:

University of Tennessee Press, 1980, 1984, 1991, 1994, 1996, 2002.

James, Marquis. **Andrew Jackson: Portrait of a President**. Indianapolis: Bobbs-Merrill, 1937.

———. **The Life of Andrew Jackson, Complete in One Volume**. Indianapolis: Bobbs-Merrill, 1938.

———. **The Raven: A Biography of Sam Houston**. Indianapolis: Bobbs-Merrill, 1929.

Jefferson, Thomas. **Writings**. Selected by Merrill D. Peterson. The Library of America. New York: Literary Classics of the U.S., 1984.

Jervey, Theodore D. **Robert Y. Hayne and His Times**. New York: Macmillan Co., 1909.

Johnson, Charles, and Patricia Smith. **Africans in America: America's Journey Through Slavery**. New York: Harcourt Brace, 1998.

Johnson, Paul. **The Birth of the Modern: World Society, 1815–1830**. New York: HarperCollins, 1991.

Johnson, Thomas H. **The Oxford Companion to American History**. New York: Oxford University Press, 1966.

Jung, Patrick J. **The Black Hawk War of 1832**. Campaigns and Commanders, vol. 10. Norman: University of Oklahoma Press, 2007.

Kaplan, Edward S. **The Bank of the United States and the American Economy**. Contributions in Economics and Economic History, no. 214. Westport, Conn.: Greenwood Press, 1999.

Kemble, Fanny. **Fanny Kemble: The American Journals**. Compiled and edited by Elizabeth Mavor. London: Weidenfeld and Nicolson, 1990.

Kendall, Amos. "Anecdotes of General Jackson." **United States Magazine and Democratic Review** 11 (September 1842): 272–74.

———. **Autobiography of Amos Kendall**. Edited by William Stickney. Boston: Lee and Shepard, 1872.

Kiple, Kenneth F., ed. **The Cambridge Historical Dictionary of Disease**. New York: Cambridge University Press, 2003.

Knupfer, Peter. Review of **The Presidency of Andrew Jackson**, by Donald B. Cole. **Reviews in American History** 22 (September 1994): 424–27.

Koenig, Louis W. **The Chief Executive**. New York: Harcourt, Brace and World, 1964.

Lamar, Quinton Curtis. "A Diplomatic Disaster: The Mexican Mission of Anthony Butler, 1829–1834." **The Americas** 45 (July 1988): 1–17.

Lancaster, Bruce. **The American Heritage Book of the Revolution**. Edited by Richard M. Ketchum. New York: American Heritage, 1958.

Laski, Harold J. **The American Presidency: An Interpretation**. New York: Harper and Brothers, 1940.

Latner, Richard. "The Eaton Affair Reconsidered." **Tennessee Historical Quarterly** 36 (Fall 1977): 330–51.

———. "The Kitchen Cabinet and Andrew Jackson's Advisory System." **Journal of American History** 65 (September 1978): 367–88.

———. **The Presidency of Andrew Jackson: White House Politics, 1829–1837**. Athens: University of Georgia Press, 1979.

Lavisse, Ernest, ed. **Histoire de France Contemporaine Depuis la Révolution Jusqu'à la Paix de 1919**. Vol. 5, **La Monarchie de Juillet (1830–1848)**, by S. Charléty. [Paris]: Librairie Hachette, 1921.

Lee, Henry. **A Biography of Andrew Jackson: Late Major-General of the Army of the United States**. Edited by Mark A. Mastromarino. Occasional Pamphlet, no. 3. Knoxville: Tennessee Presidents Trust, 1992.

"Letters from Andrew Jackson to R. K. Call," **Virginia Magazine of History and Biography** 29 (April 1921): 191.

Lincoln, Abraham. **Abraham Lincoln: Speeches and Writings**. Library of America. 2 vols. Vol. 1, **1832–1858**. Vol. 2, **1859–1865**. New York: Library of America, 1989.

———. **The Language of Liberty: The Political Speeches and Writings of Abraham Lincoln**. Edited by Joseph R. Fornieri.

Conservative Leadership Series, no. 13. Washington, D.C.: Regnery, 2003.

Lippmann, Walter. **A Preface to Politics**. New York: Macmillan, 1933.

Livermore, Shaw, Jr. **The Twilight of Federalism: The Disintegration of the Federalist Party, 1815–1830**. Princeton, N.J.: Princeton University Press, 1962.

Longaker, Richard P. "Was Jackson's Kitchen Cabinet a Cabinet?" **Mississippi Valley Historical Review** 44 (June 1957): 94–108.

Lowe, Gabriel L., Jr. "John H. Eaton, Jackson's Campaign Manager." **Tennessee Historical Quarterly** 11 (June 1952): 99–147.

Lutz, Regan A. "West of Eden: The Historiography of the Trail of Tears." Ph.D. diss., University of Toledo, 1995.

MacCulloch, Diarmaid. **The Reformation: A History**. New York: Viking, 2004.

Madison, James. **Letters and Other Writings of James Madison: Fourth President of the United States**. Vol. 3, 1816–1828. Philadelphia: J. B. Lippincott & Co., 1865.

Magliocca, Gerard N. **Andrew Jackson and the Constitution: The Rise and Fall of Generational Regimes**. Lawrence: University Press of Kansas, 2007.

Marszalek, John F. **The Petticoat Affair: Manners, Mutiny, and Sex in Andrew Jackson's White House**. New York: Free Press, 1997.

Martineau, Harriet. **Retrospect of Western Travel**. London: Saunders and Otley, 1838. Reprint, Armonk, N.Y.: M. E. Sharpe, 2000.

Mayer, Henry. **All on Fire: William Lloyd Garrison and the Abolition of Slavery**. New York: St. Martin's Press, 1998.

Mayo, Bernard, ed. "Henry Clay, Patron and Idol of White Sulphur Springs: His Letters to James Caldwell." **Virginia Magazine of History and Biography** 55 (October 1947): 301–17.

McCollin, Alice Graham. "The Sunshine of the White House." **Ladies' Home Journal** 11 (January 1894): 7.

McCrary, Royce C., Jr. "'The Long Agony Is Nearly Over': Samuel D. Ingham Reports on the Dissolution of Andrew Jackson's First Cabinet." **Pennsylvania Magazine of History and Biography** 100 (April 1976): 231–42.

McCullough, David. **John Adams**. New York: Simon & Schuster, 2001.

————. **1776**. New York: Simon & Schuster, 2005.

————. **Truman**. New York: Simon & Schuster, 1992.

McCutcheon, Marc. **Everyday Life in the 1800s**. Cincinnati: Writer's Digest Books, 1993.

McKenney, Thomas Loraine. **Memoirs, Official and Personal**. 2 vols. in 1. New York: Paine and Burgess, 1846. Reprint of vol. 1, Lincoln: University of Nebraska Press, 1973.

McKivigan, John R., and Mitchell Snay, eds. **Religion and the Antebellum Debate over Slavery**. Athens: University of Georgia Press, 1998.

McLoughlin, William G. **Cherokee Renascence in the New Republic**. Princeton, N.J.: Princeton University Press, 1992.

————, with Walter H. Conser, Jr., and Virginia Duffy McLoughlin. **The Cherokee Ghost Dance: Essays on the Southeastern Indians, 1789–1861**. [Macon, Ga.]: Mercer, 1984.

Meiden, G. W. van der. "The Letters of the Dutch Envoy C.D.E.J. Bangeman Huijgens (1772–1857) from Washington, 1825–1832." Master's thesis, Leiden University, 1968.

Meyers, Marvin. **The Jacksonian Persuasion: Politics and Belief**. Stanford: Stanford University Press, 1957.

Miles, Edwin A. "After John Marshall's Decision: **Worcester v. Georgia** and the Nullification Crisis," **The Journal of Southern History** 39 (November 1973): 519–44.

————. "Andrew Jackson and Senator George Poindexter." **Journal of Southern History** 24 (February 1958): 51–66.

Miller, Douglas T. **The Birth of Modern America, 1820–1850**. New York: Pegasus, 1970.

————, ed. **The Nature of Jacksonian America**. The Wiley Problems in American History Series. New York: John Wiley and Sons, 1972.

Miller, Edwin A. "The First People's Inaugural—1829." Tennessee Historical Quarterly 37 (Fall 1978): 293–307.

Miller, Merle. Plain Speaking: An Oral Biography of Harry S. Truman. New York: Berkley, 1974.

Monkman, Betty C. The White House: Its Historic Furnishings and First Families. Washington, D.C.: White House Historical Association; New York: Abbeville Press, 2000.

Morgan, George. The Life of James Monroe. Boston: Small, Maynard, 1921.

Morgan, William G. "John Quincy Adams versus Andrew Jackson: Their Biographers and the 'Corrupt Bargain' Charge." Tennessee Historical Quarterly 26 (Spring 1967): 43–58.

Moulton, Gary E. John Ross, Cherokee Chief. Brown Thrasher Books. Athens: University of Georgia Press, 1982.

Murphree, Daniel S. Review of American Indian Policy in the Jacksonian Era, by Ronald N. Satz. H-Tennessee, H-Net Reviews (July 2004). http://www.h-net.org/reviews/showrev.cgi?path=99551095078443 (accessed April 27, 2008).

Nagel, Paul C. John Quincy Adams: A Public Life, a Private Life. New York: Alfred A. Knopf, 1997.

Neustadt, Richard E. Presidential Power: The Politics of Leadership. New York: John Wiley and Sons, 1960.

Niven, John. John C. Calhoun and the Price of Union: A Biography. Southern Biography Series. Baton Rouge: Louisiana State University Press, 1988.

———. Martin Van Buren: The Romantic Age of American Politics. New York: Oxford University Press, 1983.

Norgren, Jill. The Cherokee Cases: Two Landmark Federal Decisions in the Fight for Sovereignty. Norman: University of Oklahoma Press, 2004.

Oakes, James. The Ruling Race: A History of American Slaveholders. New York: Alfred A. Knopf, 1982. Reprint, New York: W. W. Norton, 1998.

"Origin of the Democratic National Convention." American Historical Magazine and Tennessee Historical Society Quarterly 7 (July 1902): 267.

Otis, Laura, ed. **Literature and Science in the Nineteenth Century: An Anthology**. Oxford World's Classics. New York: Oxford University Press, 2002.

Owsley, Harriet Chappell. "Andrew Jackson and His Ward, Andrew Jackson Donelson." **Tennessee Historical Quarterly** 41 (Summer 1982): 124–39.

Paine, Thomas. **Collected Writings**. The Library of America. New York: Library of America, 1995.

Parton, James. **Life of Andrew Jackson**. 3 vols. Boston: Ticknor and Fields, 1866.

Pasley, Jeffrey L. **"The Tyranny of Printers": Newspaper Politics in the Early American Republic**. Charlottesville: University Press of Virginia, 2001.

Patterson, C. Perry. **Presidential Government in the United States: The Unwritten Constitution**. Chapel Hill: University of North Carolina Press, 1947.

Patterson, James T. "The Rise of Presidential Power Before World War II." **Law and Contemporary Problems** 40 (Spring 1976): 39–57.

Peacock, Virginia Tatnall. **Famous American Belles of the Nineteenth Century**. Philadelphia: J. B. Lippincott, 1901.

Pessen, Edward. **Jacksonian America: Society, Personality, and Politics**. Rev. ed. Homewood, Ill.: Dorsey Press, 1978. Reprint, Urbana: University of Illinois Press, 1985.

———, ed. **Jacksonian Panorama**. The American Heritage Series. Indianapolis: Bobbs-Merrill, 1976.

Peterson, Merrill D. **The Great Triumvirate: Webster, Clay, and Calhoun**. New York: Oxford University Press, 1987.

———. **Olive Branch and Sword: The Compromise of 1833**. The Walter Lynwood Fleming Lectures in Southern History. Baton Rouge: Louisiana State University Press, 1982.

Pettus, Louise. **The Waxhaws**. Rock Hill, S.C.: Regal Graphics, 1993.

Pierson, George Wilson. **Tocqueville and Beaumont in America**. New York: Oxford University Press, 1938.

Polk, William M. **Leonidas Polk: Bishop and General**. 2 vols. New York: Longmans, Green, 1893.

Poore, Benjamin Perley. **Perley's Reminiscences of Sixty Years in the National Metropolis.** 2 vols. Philadelphia: Hubbard Brothers; New York: W. A. Houghton, 1886.

Porter, Jane. **The Scottish Chiefs.** Edited by Kate Douglas Wiggin and Nora A. Smith. New York: Charles Scribner's Sons, 1921.

Powell, Edward Payson. **Nullification and Secession in the United States: A History of the Six Attempts During the First Century of the Republic.** New York: G. P. Putnam's Sons, 1898.

Presbyterian Church in the U.S.A. **The Hymnal.** Edited by Louis F. Benson. Rev. ed. Philadelphia: Presbyterian Board of Publication and Sabbath-School Work, 1911.

Prucha, Francis Paul. "Andrew Jackson's Indian Policy: A Reassessment." **Journal of American History** 56 (December 1969): 527–39.

———. "Books on American Indian Policy: A Half-Decade of Important Work, 1970–1975." **Journal of American History** 63 (December 1976): 658–69.

———. **The Great Father: The United States Government and the American Indians.** 2 vols. in 1. Lincoln: University of Nebraska Press, 1995.

———. **The Indians in American Society: From the Revolutionary War to the Present.** Berkeley: University of California Press, 1985.

Quincy, Josiah. **Figures of the Past from the Leaves of Old Journals, Illustrated from Old Prints and Photographs.** Boston: Little, Brown, 1926.

Ratcliffe, Donald J. "My Dinner with Andrew." **Timeline** (October–November 1987).

Ratner, Lorman A. **Andrew Jackson and His Tennessee Lieutenants.** Westport, Conn.: Greenwood Co., 1997.

Read, Allen W. "Could Andrew Jackson Spell?" **American Speech** 38 (October 1963): 188–95.

Remini, Robert V. **Andrew Jackson and His Indian Wars.** New York: Viking, 2001.

————. *Andrew Jackson and the Course of American Democracy, 1833–1845*. New York: Harper and Row, 1984. Volume 3 of the author's biography of Andrew Jackson.

————. *Andrew Jackson and the Course of American Empire, 1767–1821*. New York: Harper and Row, 1977. Volume 1 of the author's biography of Andrew Jackson.

————. *Andrew Jackson and the Course of American Freedom, 1822–1832*. New York: Harper and Row, 1981. Volume 2 of the author's biography of Andrew Jackson.

————. "Election of 1832." In *History of American Presidential Elections, 1789–2001*, edited by Arthur M. Schlesinger, Jr., and Fred L. Israel, 493–574. Vol. 2. Philadelphia: Chelsea House Publishers, 2002.

————. *Henry Clay: Statesman for the Union*. New York: W. W. Norton, 1991.

————. *John Quincy Adams*. The American Presidents Series. New York: Times Books, 2002.

————. *The Legacy of Andrew Jackson: Essays on Democracy, Indian Removal, and Slavery*. The Walter Lynwood Fleming Lectures in Southern History. Baton Rouge: Louisiana State University Press, 1988.

————. *The Life of Andrew Jackson*. New York: Harper and Row, 1988.

Rémond, René. *Les Etats-Unis Devant L'Opinion Française, 1815–1852*. Vol. 2. Cahiers de la Fondation Nationale des Sciences Politiques, no. 117. Paris: Librairie Armand Colin, 1962.

Richardson, James D., comp. *A Compilation of the Messages and Papers of the Presidents*. Vols. 2 and 3. New York: Bureau of National Literature, 1897.

Richter, Daniel K. *Facing East from Indian Country: A Native History of Early America*. Cambridge, Mass.: Harvard University Press, 2001.

Robbins, Peggy. "Andrew and Rachel Jackson." *American History Illustrated* 12 (August 1977): 22–28.

Robertson, Lindsay G. **Conquest by Law: How the Discovery of America Dispossessed Indigenous Peoples of Their Lands**. New York: Oxford University Press, 2005.

Rogers, Donald W., ed. **Voting and the Spirit of American Democracy: Essays on the History of Voting and Voting Rights in America**. Urbana: University of Illinois Press, 1992.

Rohrs, Richard C. "Partisan Politics and the Attempted Assassination of Andrew Jackson." **Journal of the Early Republic** 1 (Summer 1981): 149–63.

Roosevelt, Theodore. **Episodes from "The Winning of the West," 1769–1807**. Edited by Frank Lincoln Olmstead. The Knickerbocker Literature Series. New York: G. P. Putnam's Sons, 1900.

———. **Letters and Speeches**. The Library of America. New York: Library of America, 2004.

———. **The Rough Riders: An Autobiography**. The Library of America. New York: Library of America, 2004.

———. **Theodore Roosevelt Cyclopedia**. Edited by Albert Bushnell Hart and Herbert Ronald Ferleger. New York: Roosevelt Memorial Association, 1941.

———, and Edmund Heller. **Life-Histories of African Game Animals**. 2 vols. New York: Charles Scribner's Sons, 1914.

Ross, John. **The Papers of Chief John Ross**. Edited by Gary E. Moulton. Vol. 1, **1807–1839**. Norman: University of Oklahoma Press, 1985.

Rossiter, Clinton. **The American Presidency**. New York: Harcourt, Brace, 1956.

Russo, David J. "The Major Political Issues of the Jacksonian Period and the Development of Party Loyalty in Congress, 1830–1840." **Transactions of the American Philosophical Society**, n.s., 62, pt. 5 (1972): 3–49.

Sage, Agnes Carr. **Boys and Girls of the White House**. New York: Frederick A. Stokes Co., 1909.

Sanderson, John. **The American in Paris**. Vol. 2. Philadelphia: Carey, 1839.

Sandoz, Ellis. **Republicanism, Religion, and the Soul of America.** Eric Voegelin Institute Series in Political Philosophy. Columbia, Mo.: University of Missouri, 2006.

Sargent, Nathan. **Public Men and Events from the Commencement of Mr. Monroe's Administration, in 1817, to the Close of Mr. Fillmore's Administration, in 1853.** 2 vols. Philadelphia: J. B. Lippincott, 1875.

Satterfield, Robert Beeler. **Andrew Jackson Donelson: Jackson's Confidant and Political Heir.** Bowling Green, Ky.: Hickory Tales, 2000.

Satz, Ronald N. **American Indian Policy in the Jacksonian Era.** Lincoln: University of Nebraska Press, 1974.

———. Review of **Andrew Jackson and His Indian Wars,** by Robert V. Remini. **Journal of American History** 90 (December 2003): 1013–14.

Sayers, Dorothy L. **The Nine Tailors: Changes Rung on an Old Theme in Two Short Touches and Two Full Peals.** New York: Harcourt, Brace and World, 1934.

Scheer, George F., and Hugh F. Rankin. **Rebels and Redcoats.** New York: World Publishing, 1957.

Schlesinger, Arthur M., Jr. **The Age of Jackson.** Boston: Little, Brown, 1945.

———. **A Life in the Twentieth Century: Innocent Beginnings, 1917–1950.** Boston: Houghton Mifflin, 2000.

———. **A Thousand Days: John F. Kennedy in the White House.** Boston: Houghton Mifflin, 2002.

———, ed. **The Election of 1828 and the Administration of Andrew Jackson.** Major Presidential Elections and the Administrations That Followed. Philadelphia: Mason Crest Publishers, 2003.

Shade, William G. "'The Most Delicate and Exciting Topics': Martin Van Buren, Slavery, and the Election of 1836." **Journal of the Early Republic** 18 (Autumn 1998): 459–84.

Shakespeare, William. **The Tragedy of Hamlet, Prince of Denmark.** Edited by Sylvan Barnet. 2nd rev. ed. The Signet Classic Shakespeare. New York: Penguin Group, 1998.

Shulman, Holly C., ed. "The Dolley Madison Digital Edition: Dolley Madison and the Founding of the Washington Orphan Asylum." University of Virginia Press. http://rotunda. upress.virginia.edu:8080/dmde/editorialnote.xqy?note=all#n3

Schultz, George A. **An Indian Canaan: Isaac McCoy and the Vision of an Indian State**. The Civilization of the American Indian Series. Norman: University of Oklahoma Press, 1972.

Schurz, Carl. **Henry Clay**. American Classics. 2 vols. New York: Frederick Ungar, 1968. Reprint of the 1915 edition, titled **The Life of Henry Clay**.

Scott, Nancy N., ed. **A Memoir of Hugh Lawson White: Judge of the Supreme Court of Tennessee, Member of the Senate of the United States**. Library of American Civilization. Philadelphia: J. B. Lippincott, 1856.

Scott, Winfield. **Memoirs of Lieut.-General Scott, LL.D.** 2 vols. New York: Sheldon and Co., 1864. Reprint, Freeport, N.Y.: Books for Libraries Press, 1970.

Seale, William. **The President's House: A History**. 2 vols. Washington, D.C.: White House Historical Association with the cooperation of the National Geographic Society, 1986.

———. **The White House: The History of an American Idea**. Washington, D.C.: American Institute of Architects Press, in association with the White House Historical Association, 1992.

Sellers, Charles. **James K. Polk**. Vol. 1, **Jacksonian, 1795–1843**. Princeton, N.J.: Princeton University Press, 1957.

———. **The Market Revolution: Jacksonian America, 1815– 1846**. New York: Oxford University Press, 1991.

Shalhope, Robert E. "Toward a Republican Synthesis: The Emergence of an Understanding of Republicanism in American Historiography." **William and Mary Quarterly**, 3d ser., 29 (January 1972): 49–80.

Shapiro, Edward S. "Jackson and the 'Savages' of America." Review of **Andrew Jackson and His Indian Wars**, by Robert V. Remini. **World and I** 16 (December 2001): 244–49.

Sheehan, Bernard W. **Seeds of Extinction: Jeffersonian Philan-**

thropy and the American Indian. The Norton Library. New York: W. W. Norton, 1974.

Silbey, Joel H. Martin Van Buren and the Emergence of American Popular Politics. American Profiles. Lanham, Md.: Rowman and Littlefield, 2002.

Smith, Elbert B. Francis Preston Blair. New York: Free Press, 1980.

————. Magnificent Missourian: The Life of Thomas Hart Benton. Philadelphia: J. B. Lippincott, 1958.

————. "'Now Defend Yourself, You Damned Rascal!'" American Heritage 9 (February 1958): 44–47, 106.

Smith, Jane F., and Robert M. Kvasnicka, eds. Indian-White Relations: A Persistent Paradox. National Archives Conference on Research in the History of Indian-White Relations. National Archives Conferences, vol. 10. Washington, D.C.: Howard University Press, 1976.

Smith, Margaret Bayard. The First Forty Years of Washington Society in the Family Letters of Margaret Bayard Smith. Edited by Gaillard Hunt. American Classics. New York: Frederick Ungar, 1965. Reprint of the 1906 edition, titled The First Forty Years of Washington Society, Portrayed by the Family Letters of Mrs. Samuel Harrison Smith (Margaret Bayard) from the Collection of Her Grandson, J. Henley Smith.

Smith, William E. "Francis P. Blair, Pen-Executive of Andrew Jackson." Mississippi Valley Historical Review 17 (March 1931): 543–56.

————. The Francis Preston Blair Family in Politics. 2 vols. New York: Macmillan, 1933.

Smollett, Tobias George. The History of England: From the Revolution in 1688, to the Death of George II. 6 vols. London: Printed for R. Scholey, 1810–11.

Smucker, Samuel M. The Life, Speeches and Memorials of Daniel Webster: Containing His Most Celebrated Orations, a Selection from the Eulogies Delivered on the Occasion of His Death, and His Life and Times. Chicago: Belford, Clarke, 1859.

Snay, Mitchell. **Gospel of Disunion: Religion and Separatism in the Antebellum South**. New York: Cambridge University Press, 1993.

Somit, Albert. "New Papers: Some Sidelights upon Jacksonian Administration." **Mississippi Valley Historical Review** 35 (June 1948): 91–98.

Sparks, W. H. **The Memories of Fifty Years: Containing Brief Biographical Notices of Distinguished Americans, and Anecdotes of Remarkable Men**. Philadelphia: E. Claxton, 1882.

Stampp, Kenneth M. **The Peculiar Institution: Slavery in the Ante-Bellum South**. New York: Alfred A. Knopf, 1956. Reprint, New York: Vintage Books, 1989.

Steiner, Bernard, ed. "The South Atlantic States in 1833, as Seen by a New Englander, Being a Narrative of a Tour Taken by Henry Barnard." Parts 1 and 2. **Maryland Historical Magazine** 13 (September, December 1918): 267–94, 295–386.

Stenberg, Richard R. "The Jefferson Birthday Dinner, 1830." **Journal of Southern History** 4 (August 1938): 334–45.

Stewart, James Brewer. **Holy Warriors: The Abolitionists and American Slavery**. New York: Hill and Wang, 1976.

Story, William W., ed. **Life and Letters of Joseph Story, Associate Justice of the Supreme Court of the United States, and Dane Professor of Law at Harvard University**. 2 vols. Boston: C. C. Little and J. Brown, 1851.

Sumner, William Graham. **Andrew Jackson**. American Statesmen Series, vol. 17. Boston: Houghton Mifflin, 1899.

Swisher, Carl Brent. **Roger B. Taney**. New York: Macmillan, 1935. Reprint, Hamden, Conn.: Archon Books, 1961.

————, ed. "Roger B. Taney's 'Bank War Manuscript.'" Parts 1 and 2. **Maryland Historical Magazine** 53 (June, September 1958): 103–30, 215–37.

Sydnor, Charles S. **The Development of Southern Sectionalism, 1819–1848**. A History of the South, vol. 5. Baton Rouge: Louisiana State University Press, 1948.

Takaki, Ronald T. **Iron Cages: Race and Culture in 19th-Century America**. New York: Oxford University Press, 1990.

Taylor, George Rogers. **The Transportation Revolution, 1815–1860**. The Economic History of the United States, vol. 4. New York: Harper and Row, 1951.

Tocqueville, Alexis de. **Democracy in America**. Translated and edited by Harvey C. Mansfield and Delba Winthrop. Chicago: University of Chicago Press, 2000.

Tracy, E. C. **Memoir of the Life of Jeremiah Evarts**. Boston: Crocker and Brewster, 1845. Reprint, Whitefish, Mont.: Kessinger Publishing, 2007.

Truman, Harry S. **Public Papers of the Presidents of the United States—Harry S. Truman: Containing the Public Messages, Speeches, and Statements of the President, April 12 to December 31, 1945**. Washington, D.C.: U.S. Government Printing Office, 1961.

————. **Where the Buck Stops: The Personal and Private Writings of Harry S. Truman**. Edited by Margaret Truman. New York: Warner Books, 1989.

Turnbull, Robert J. [Brutus, pseud.] **The Crisis; or, Essays on the Usurpations of the Federal Government**. Charleston: Printed by A. E. Miller, 1827.

Upton, Harriet Taylor. **Our Early Presidents: Their Wives and Children; From Washington to Jackson**. Boston: D. Lothrop, 1891.

Van Buren, Martin. **The Autobiography of Martin Van Buren**. Edited by John C. Fitzpatrick. Washington, D.C.: U.S. Government Printing Office, 1920. Reprint, New York: A. M. Kelley, 1969.

Viola, Herman J. Review of **American Indian Policy in the Jacksonian Era**, by Ronald N. Satz. **Ethnohistory** 21 (Fall 1974): 380–81.

————. **Thomas L. McKenney: Architect of America's Early Indian Policy, 1816–1830**. Chicago: Sage Books, 1974.

Walker, Arda. "The Educational Training and Views of Andrew Jackson." **East Tennessee Historical Society's Publications** 16 (1944): 22–29.

Walker, Arda S. "John Henry Eaton, Apostate." **East Tennessee Historical Society's Publications** 24 (1952): 26–43.

Wallace, Anthony F. C. **Jefferson and the Indians: The Tragic Fate of the First Americans**. Cambridge, Mass.: Belknap Press of Harvard University Press, 1999.

————. **The Long, Bitter Trail: Andrew Jackson and the Indians**. A Critical Issue. New York: Hill and Wang, 1993.

Wallace, Sarah Agnes, ed. "Opening Days of Jackson's Presidency As Seen in Private Letters." **Journal of Southern History** 17 (May 1951): 285–96.

Walton, Emily Donelson. **Autobiography of Emily Donelson Walton**. [N.p., n.d.]

Walton, John, Paul B. Beeson, and Ronald Bodley Scott, eds. **The Oxford Companion to Medicine**. New York: Oxford University Press, 1986.

Ward, John William. **Andrew Jackson, Symbol for an Age**. New York: Oxford University Press, 1953.

————. "Jacksonian Democratic Thought: 'A Natural Charter of Privilege.'" In **The Development of an American Culture**, edited by Stanley Coben and Lorman Ratner, 58–79. 2d ed. New York: St. Martin's Press, 1983.

Warner, Henry Whiting [Frelinghuysen, Theodore, supposed author]. **An Inquiry into the Moral and Religious Character of the American Government**. New York: Wiley and Putnam, 1838.

Warshauer, Matthew. **Andrew Jackson and the Politics of Martial Law: Nationalism, Civil Liberties, and Partisanship**. Knoxville, Tenn.: University of Tennessee Press, 2006.

————. "Contested Mourning: The New York Battle over Andrew Jackson's Death." **New York History** 87 (Winter 2006), 29–65.

————. "A Review Essay on Burstein, **The Passions of Andrew Jackson**." **Tennessee Historical Quarterly** 62 (Winter 2003): 366–73.

Washburn, Wilcomb E. Review of **Indian-White Relations: A Persistent Paradox**, edited by Jane F. Smith and Robert M. Kvasnicka. **Pacific Historical Review** 46 (November 1977): 649–50.

Washington, George. **Writings**. Selected by John H. Rhode-hamel. The Library of America. New York: Library of America, 1997.

Watson, Harry L. "Old Hickory's Democracy." **Wilson Quarterly** 9 (Autumn 1985): 101–33.

Watts, Isaac. **The Psalms of David, Imitated in the Language of the New Testament and Applied to the Christian State and Worship in the United States of America**. Philadelphia: McCarty and Davis, 1828.

Waugh, Elizabeth Dey Jenkinson. **West Point: The Story of the United States Military Academy Which, Rising from the Revolutionary Forces, Has Taught American Soldiers the Art of Victory**. New York: Macmillan, 1944.

Wayland, Francis Fry. **Andrew Stevenson: Democrat and Diplomat, 1785–1857**. Philadelphia: University of Pennsylvania Press, 1949.

Webster, Daniel. **The Papers of Daniel Webster. Series One: Correspondence**. Edited by Charles M. Wiltse and Harold D. Moser. Vols. 1–5. Hanover, N.H.: University Press of New England for Dartmouth College, 1974, 1976, 1977, 1980, 1982.

Weed, Thurlow. **Life of Thurlow Weed**. 2 vols. Boston: Houghton Mifflin, 1883–84. Reprint, New York: Da Capo Press, 1970.

Weston, Florence. **The Presidential Election of 1828**. Perspectives in American History, no. 22. Philadelphia: Porcupine Press, 1974.

Wharton, Anne Hollingsworth. **Social Life in the Early Republic**. Philadelphia: J. B. Lippincott, 1902. Reprint, Williamstown, Mass.: Corner House Publishers, 1970.

White, Leonard D. **The Jacksonians: A Study in Administrative History, 1829–1861**. New York: Macmillan Co., 1954.

Widmer, Ted. **Martin Van Buren**. The American Presidents Series. New York: Times Books, 2005.

Wilcox, Mary Emily Donelson. **Christmas Under Three Flags**. Washington, D.C.: Neale, 1900.

Wilentz, Sean. **Andrew Jackson**. The American Presidents. New York: Times Books, 2005.

————. **Chants Democratic: New York City and the Rise of the American Working Class, 1788–1850**. New York: Oxford University Press, 1984.

————. **The Rise of American Democracy: Jefferson to Lincoln**. New York: W. W. Norton, 2005.

Wilkins, Thurman. **Cherokee Tragedy: The Ridge Family and the Decimation of a People**. 2d ed., rev. The Civilization of the American Indian Series. Norman: University of Oklahoma Press, 1986.

Williams, Stanley T. **The Life of Washington Irving**. 2 vols. New York: Oxford University Press, 1935.

Williamson, Chilton. **American Suffrage: From Property to Democracy, 1760–1860**. Princeton, N.J.: Princeton University Press, 1960.

Wills, Garry. **James Madison**. The American Presidents Series. New York: Times Books, 2002.

————. **A Necessary Evil: A History of American Distrust of Government**. New York: Simon & Schuster, 1999.

Wilson, Major L. "Andrew Jackson: The Great Compromiser." **Tennessee Historical Quarterly** 26 (Spring 1967): 64–78.

————. **Space, Time, and Freedom: The Quest for Nationality and the Irrepressible Conflict, 1815–1861**. Contributions in American History, no. 35. Westport, Conn.: Greenwood Press, 1974.

Wilson, Woodrow. **Congressional Government: A Study in American Politics**. Boston: Houghton Mifflin, 1913.

————. **Constitutional Government in the United States**. Columbia University Lectures. New York: Columbia University Press, 1908.

————. **Division and Reunion, 1829–1889**. New York: Longmans, Green, 1893. Reprint, New York: Collier Books, 1961.

Wiltse, Charles M. **John C. Calhoun**. Vol. 1, **Nationalist, 1782–1828**. Vol. 2, **Nullifier, 1829–1839**. Indianapolis: Bobbs-Merrill, 1944, 1949.

Winders, Richard Bruce. **Crisis in the Southwest: The United States, Mexico, and the Struggle over Texas**. The American Crisis Series, no. 6. Wilmington, Del.: SR Books, 2002.

Wise, Henry A. **Seven Decades of the Union: The Humanities and Materialism**. Philadelphia: J. B. Lippincott, 1872. Reprint, Freeport, N.Y.: Books for Libraries Press, 1971.

Wood, Gordon S. **The Creation of the American Republic, 1776–1787**. Chapel Hill: University of North Carolina Press for the Institute of Early American History and Culture at Williamsburg, Virginia, 1969.

———. **The Purpose of the Past: Reflections on the Uses of History**. New York: Penguin Press, 2008.

Wood, Kirsten E. "'One Woman So Dangerous to Public Morals': Gender and Power in the Eaton Affair." **Journal of the Early Republic** 17 (Summer 1997): 237–75.

Woodson, Thomas, ed. **Nathaniel Hawthorne: The French and Italian Notebooks**. Columbus, Ohio: Ohio State University, 1980.

Woodward, C. Vann. "The Age of Reinterpretation." **American Historical Review** 66 (October 1960): 1–19.

Writers' Program of the Work Projects Administration in the State of Texas. **Texas: A Guide to the Lone Star State**. Edited by Harry Hansen. New rev. ed., American Guide Series. New York: Hastings House, 1969[?].

Wyatt-Brown, Bertram. **Southern Honor: Ethics and Behavior in the Old South**. New York: Oxford University Press, 1982.

Young, James Sterling. **The Washington Community, 1800–1828**. New York: Columbia University Press, 1966.

Young, Mary E. "Indian Removal and Land Allotment: The Civilized Tribes and Jacksonian Justice." **American Historical Review** 64 (October 1958): 31–45.

PERIODICALS CONSULTED

American Heritage
American Historical Review
The Atlantic Monthly
The Charleston (S.C.) Mercury
The East Tennessee Historical Society's Publications
Frank Leslie's Illustrated Monthly
Journal of American History
The Journal of the Early Republic
Journal of Presbyterian History
The Journal of Southern History
The Ladies' Home Journal
Maryland Historical Magazine
Nashville (Tenn.) Banner
Nashville (Tenn.) Republican and State Gazette

The New York Times
Niles' Weekly Register
The Pennsylvania Magazine of History and Biography
The Review of Religion
The South Atlantic Quarterly
South Carolina Historical Magazine
Tennessee Historical Quarterly
Virginia Cavalcade
Washington (D.C.) Courier
(Washington, D.C.) Daily National Intelligencer
Washington (D.C.) Globe
(Washington, D.C.) National Journal
(Washington, D.C.) United States' Telegraph
The William and Mary Quarterly

ILLUSTRATION CREDITS

John Quincy Adams: Brown Brothers, Sterling, Pa.

Louisa Catherine Adams: Smithsonian American Art Museum, Washington, D.C., U.S.A./Art Resource, N.Y.

Bill of atrocities: The Granger Collection, New York

View of the city of Washington: White House Historical Association (White House Collection)

Jackson's inauguration: Ceiling mural by Allyn Cox, part of The Hall of Capitols of the Cox Corridors in the House wing of the U.S. Capitol. Photo courtesy of the Architect of the Capitol / Library of Congress.

The White House: Brown Brothers, Sterling, Pa.

View from outside of the "storming of the White House": Brown Brothers, Sterling, Pa.

Inaugural festivities and chaos inside the White House: White House Historical Association (White House Collection). Painting by Louis S. Glanzman.

Martin Van Buren: Brown Brothers, Sterling, Pa.

John C. Calhoun: Brown Brothers, Sterling, Pa.

Amos Kendall: Print Collection, Miriam and Ira D. Wallach Division of Art, Prints and Photographs, The New York Public Library, Astor, Lenox and Tilden Foundations

Francis Preston Blair: Culver Pictures

Margaret Bayard Smith: After the portrait by Charles Bird King, in the possession of her grandson, J. Henley Smith, Washington, from **The First Forty Years of Washington Society** by Gaillard Hunt (ed.)

Ezra Stiles Ely: Print Collection, Miriam and Ira D. Wallach Division of Art, Prints and Photographs, The New York Public Library, Astor, Lenox and Tilden Foundations

Joel R. Poinsett: The Granger Collection, New York

Theodore Frelinghuysen: Print Collection, Miriam and Ira D. Wallach Division of Art, Prints and Photographs, The New York Public Library, Astor, Lenox and Tilden Foundations

Daniel Webster: Brown Brothers, Sterling, Pa.

Henry Clay: Brown Brothers, Sterling, Pa.

Cartoon of Clay sewing Jackson's lips: Bettmann/Corbis

Struggle in Charleston Harbor: Painting by Robert Lavin, from the U.S. Coast Guard Art Collection. Permission to reprint courtesy of John Lavine and Susan Foregger.

Portrait of Margaret Eaton: Bettmann/Corbis

Cartoon of Jackson abandoned by "rats": Bettmann/Corbis

Second Bank of the United States: Hulton Archive, photo by Kean Collection/Getty Images

Nicholas Biddle: National Portrait Gallery, Smithsonian Institution, Washington, D.C., U.S.A./Art Resource, N.Y.

Portrait of John Henry Eaton: Culver Pictures

Portrait of Edward Livingston: Stapleton Collection/Corbis

First assassination attempt: Brown Brothers, Sterling, Pa.

Portrait of Roger B. Taney: Brown Brothers, Sterling, Pa.

Cartoon of "King" Jackson: Culver Pictures

Quallah Battoo: Colonel Charles Waterhouse and the Waterhouse Museum

Second assassination attempt: Culver Pictures

Portrait of Hugh Lawson White: Culver Pictures

Portrait of Thomas Hart Benton: The Granger Collection, New York

Jeremiah Evarts: Print Collection, Miriam and Ira D. Wallach Division of Art, Prints and Photographs, The New York Public Library, Astor, Lenox and Tilden Foundations

Battle of Bad Axe: The Granger Collection, New York

Supreme Court ruling on the Cherokees: Private Collection/Peter Newark American Pictures/The Bridgeman Art Library

The Trail of Tears: The Granger Collection, New York

Jackson in old age: Tennessee Historical Society Collections, Tennessee State Library and Archives

Jackson on his deathbed: The Granger Collection, New York

Jackson's tomb: The Hermitage, Home of President Andrew Jackson, Nashville, Tenn.

Lincoln's inauguration: The Granger Collection, New York

Index

Note: AJ refers to Andrew Jackson.

and Compromise of
1833, 412
and Force Bill, 404–5
and nullification, 372,
377–78, 379, 384, 387,
400, 403–4, 409, 414
as source of information
for AJ, 296, 373,
376–77, 403–4, 414
and use of federal troops,
405
political parties, 79–80,
315. **See also specific
party**
politics
Adams (JQ) views about,
293
AJ's views about, 99, 280,
293, 582
and Bank debate, 461
and church-state
relations, 128, 146
fluidity of, 353–54
impact of Eaton matter
on, 116, 129–30, 169,
181, 197, 207, 329
in Jackson era, 79–80
as matter of faith, 101
poetry of, 475
and religion, 92–93, 127
and sunshine patriots,
315

as theater, 66, 177
Van Buren's views about,
374
See also specific person
Polk, James K., 321,
337–38, 427, 479, 567,
571–72, 578, 580
Polk, Leonidas, 87, 393,
564
Polk, Lucius, 338
Polk, Mary Eastin. **See**
Eastin, Mary
Polk, R. K., 457
Polk, Rufus, 393
Polk, Sarah Rachel,
422–23
Polk, William, 84
Poore, Benjamin, 141
Poplar Grove (Donelson
home), 480, 537, 538,
561, 562
popular will
and Adams (JQ) election
to congress, 275
AJ as representative of,
331
and AJ as success, 385
AJ's views about, 77,
81–82, 143, 200, 201,
203, 204, 225, 310,
354, 428–29, 582,
583